The Essential Chomsky

NOAM CHOMSKY

Edited by ANTHONY ARNOVE

By the same author

Linguistics:

Syntactic Structures (1957)

Aspects of the Theory of Syntax (1965)

The Sound Pattern of English (1968)

The Logical Structure of Linguistic Theory (1975)

Rules and Representations (1980)

Lectures on Government and Binding (1981)

Knowledge of Language: Its Nature, Origin and Use (1986)

The Minimalist Program (1995)

Language and Mind (2006, third edition)

Politics:

The Responsibility of Intellectuals (1967)

American Power and the New Mandarins (1969)

Manufacturing Consent: The Political Economy of the Mass Media (1988)

Necessary Illusions (1989)

Deterring Democracy (1992)

Class Warfare (1996)

Media Control: the Spectacular Achievements of Propaganda (2002)

Hegemony or Survival: America's Quest for Global Dominance (2003)

Objectivity and Liberal Scholarship (2003)

Failed States: The Abuse of Power and the Assault on Democracy (2006)

Interventions (2008)

The Essential Chomsky

NOAM CHOMSKY

Edited by ANTHONY ARNOVE

THE BODLEY HEAD
LONDON

Published by The Bodley Head 2008

3

First published in Great Britain in 2008 by
The Bodley Head
Random House, 20 Vauxhall Bridge Road,
London SW1V 2SA

www.randomhouse.co.uk

Addresses for companies within The Random House Group Limited can be found at:
www.randomhouse.co.uk/offices.htm

The Random House Group Limited Reg. No. 954009

A CIP catalogue record for this book
is available from the British Library

ISBN 9781847925213

Penguin Random House is committed to a sustainable future for our business, our readers and our planet. This book is made from Forest Stewardship Council® certified paper.

FSC www.fsc.org MIX Paper from responsible sources FSC® C018179

Printed and bound in Great Britain by Clays Ltd, Elcograf S.p.A.

Contents

Foreword vii

1. A Review of B. F. Skinner's *Verbal Behavior* 1
2. Preface to *Aspects of the Theory of Syntax* 31
3. Methodological Preliminaries 33
4. The Responsibility of Intellectuals 39
5. On Resistance 63
6. Language and Freedom 75
7. Notes on Anarchism 92
8. The Rule of Force in International Affairs 105
9. Watergate: A Skeptical View 134
10. The Remaking of History 141
11. Foreign Policy and the Intelligentsia 160
12. The United States and East Timor 187
13. The Origins of the "Special Relationship" 198
14. Planning for Global Hegemony 223
15. The View Beyond: Prospects for the Study of Mind 232
16. Containing the Enemy 257
17. Introduction to *The Minimalist Program* 277
18. New Horizons in the Study of Language and Mind 285
19. Intentional Ignorance and Its Uses 300
20. A World Without War 325
21. Reflections on 9-11 341
22. Language and the Brain 347

23. United States—Israel—Palestine 368
24. Imperial Grand Strategy 373
25. Afterword to *Failed States* 403

Acknowledgments 415
Permissions 417
Notes 421
Select Bibliography of Works by Noam Chomsky 485
Index 491

Foreword

From his early essays in the liberal intellectual journal the *New York Review of Books* to his most recent books *Hegemony or Survival, Failed States*, and *Interventions*, Noam Chomsky has produced a singular body of political criticism.[1] *American Power and the New Mandarins* (1969), his first published collection of political writing (dedicated "To the brave young men who refuse to serve in a criminal war"), contains essays that still stand out for their insight and biting wit nearly four decades later. "It is easy to be carried away by the sheer horror of what the daily press reveals and to lose sight of the fact that this is merely the brutal exterior of a deeper crime, of commitment to a social order that guarantees endless suffering and humiliation and denial of elementary human rights," Chomsky wrote in that book, setting himself apart from the vast majority of the war's critics who saw it as a "tragic mistake," rather than as part of a long history of U.S. imperialism.[2]

Since 1969, Chomsky has produced a series of books on U.S. foreign policy in Asia, Latin America, and the Middle East, all while maintaining his commitments to linguistics research, philosophy, and to teaching. And throughout, he has consistently lent his support to movements and organizations involved in efforts for social change, continuing a tradition of intellectual and active social engagement he developed early in his youth.

Avram Noam Chomsky was born in Philadelphia on December 7, 1928, and raised among Jewish immigrants from Eastern Europe. His father, William Chomsky, fled from Russia in 1913 to escape conscription into the Tsarist army. His mother, Elsie Simonofsky, left Eastern Europe when she was one. Chomsky grew up during the Depression and the international rise of the fascist threat. As he later recalled, "Some of my earliest memories, which are very vivid, are of people selling rags at our door, of violent police strikebreaking, and other Depression scenes."[3] Chomsky was imbued at an early age with a sense of class solidarity and struggle. While his parents were, as he puts it, "normal Roosevelt Democrats," he had aunts and uncles who were garment workers in the International Ladies' Garment Workers' Union, communists, Trotskyists, and anarchists. As a child, Chomsky was influenced by the radical Jewish intellectual culture in New York City, where he regularly visited newsstands and bookstores with anarchist literature. According to Chomsky, this was a "working class culture with working class values, solidarity, socialist values."[4]

After having almost dropped out of the University of Pennsylvania, where he had enrolled as an undergraduate when he was sixteen, Chomsky found intellectual and political stimulation from linguist Zellig Harris. Chomsky gravitated toward the unusual intellectual milieu around Harris. Harris taught seminars on linguistics that involved philosophical debates, reading, and independent research outside the standard constraints of the university structure. Chomsky began graduate work with Harris and, in 1951, joined Harvard's Society of Fellows, where he continued his research into linguistics. By 1953, Chomsky had broken "almost entirely from the field as it existed," and set down a path that would lead him to reexamine the rich insights of the seventeenth-century linguistics of the Port-Royal school and the French philosopher René Descartes, and the later work of the Prussian philosopher Wilhelm von Humboldt, on the "creative aspect of language use."[5] Though Chomsky would at times downplay or deny the connection, his political and linguistic work have both built on the philosophical tradition that he has traced back from contemporary strains of anarchism through "classical liberalism" to the Enlightenment and the early rationalists of the seventeenth century.

While Chomsky, who joined the faculty of the Massachusetts Institute of Technology in 1955 at the age of twenty-six, received tremendous early recognition for his linguistic work, he began to make a wider political mark when he started writing long, detailed essays denouncing the war and the role of mainstream intellectuals who supported it for the *New York Review of Books* and then for left journals such as *Liberation*, *Ramparts*, *New Politics*, and *Socialist Revolution* (later *Socialist Review*). These essays brilliantly documented and condemned the actions of the U.S. government in Indochina and connected the war effort to the history of U.S. imperialism more generally. Chomsky became one of the most important and respected critics of the U.S. war effort, earning a place on President Nixon's infamous "enemies list." From this point on, he was the subject of intense vilification by various apologists for the system, much as he would later be subjected to repeated attacks for his critical writings on Israel. In these early essays, we see Chomsky developing the basic themes of his best work: rigorously detailed analyses of U.S. planning documents, declassified records, official statements, and hard-to-find sources; merciless critique of liberals, establishment intellectuals, and media commentators who provided a cover for U.S. imperialism; and an analysis that showed that the war in Vietnam was not the result of "mistakes," "honest misunderstanding," "attempts to do good gone awry," or of incompetent officials who could just be replaced by better ones. Rather, the war against Indochina was a product of systematic, deeply rooted features of the capitalist state.

Not just an intellectual critic of the war against the people of Indochina, he participated in direct action to back up his beliefs. Chomsky took part in early tax resistance efforts in early 1965 and one of the first public protests against the war, in Boston in October 1965, at which protesters were outnumbered by counterdemonstrators and police, and became an important day-to-day organizer in the movement. These commitments extended well beyond Vietnam to involvement in the Central American solidarity movement, protest against the 1991 and 2003 U.S. interventions in Iraq, and much more. Chomsky has continued to speak out, write, give interviews, sign petitions, and reach out individually wherever he has felt he might be able to make a difference. And yet, he has also maintained his passionate engagement with his students and others in the field of linguistics, an area where he has continued to challenge and revise his own theories and work.[6]

People around the world take inspiration from Chomsky's example, and rightly so. He reminds a world that sees the United States through the lens of Fox News or that primarily knows the United States through its blunt instruments of foreign control that the people of the country have far different values and ideals than its political elite. He speaks within a vital but often neglected tradition of dissent and from a standpoint of solidarity with people around the world who are engaged in struggles for justice and social change. On his trips to countries such as Colombia and Nicaragua, usually with his lifetime partner Carol Chomsky, he travels more to learn from the struggles of others than to teach or instruct, but his words still carry the immense power that criticism and analysis at its best can exemplify: the power of people to understand the world in order to better understand how to change it.

Anthony Arnove

THE ESSENTIAL CHOMSKY

1.

A Review of B. F. Skinner's *Verbal Behavior*

Verbal Behavior. By B. F. SKINNER. (The Century Psychology Series.) Pp. viii, 478. New York: Appleton-Century-Crofts, Inc., 1957.

1. A great many linguists and philosophers concerned with language have expressed the hope that their studies might ultimately be embedded in a framework provided by behaviorist psychology, and that refractory areas of investigation, particularly those in which meaning is involved, will in this way be opened up to fruitful exploration. Since this volume is the first large-scale attempt to incorporate the major aspects of linguistic behavior within a behaviorist framework, it merits and will undoubtedly receive careful attention. Skinner is noted for his contributions to the study of animal behavior. The book under review is the product of study of linguistic behavior extending over more than twenty years. Earlier versions of it have been fairly widely circulated, and there are quite a few references in the psychological literature to its major ideas.

The problem to which this book is addressed is that of giving a "functional analysis" of verbal behavior. By functional analysis, Skinner means identification of the variables that control this behavior and specification of how they interact to determine a particular verbal response. Furthermore, the controlling variables are to be described completely in terms of such notions as stimulus, reinforcement, deprivation, which have been given a reasonably clear

This chapter first appeared in the journal *Language* 35, no. 1 (January–March 1959), 26–58.

meaning in animal experimentation. In other words, the goal of the book is to provide a way to predict and control verbal behavior by observing and manipulating the physical environment of the speaker.

Skinner feels that recent advances in the laboratory study of animal behavior permit us to approach this problem with a certain optimism, since "the basic processes and relations which give verbal behavior its special characteristics are now fairly well understood . . . the results [of this experimental work] have been surprisingly free of species restrictions. Recent work has shown that the methods can be extended to human behavior without serious modification" (3).[1]

It is important to see clearly just what it is in Skinner's program and claims that makes them appear so bold and remarkable. It is not primarily the fact that he has set functional analysis as his problem, or that he limits himself to study of "observables," i.e., input-output relations. What is so surprising is the particular limitations he has imposed on the way in which the observables of behavior are to be studied, and, above all, the particularly simple nature of the "function" which, he claims, describes the causation of behavior. One would naturally expect that prediction of the behavior of a complex organism (or machine) would require, in addition to information about external stimulation, knowledge of the internal structure of the organism, the ways in which it processes input information and organizes its own behavior. These characteristics of the organism are in general a complicated product of inborn structure, the genetically determined course of maturation, and past experience. Insofar as independent neurophysiological evidence is not available, it is obvious that inferences concerning the structure of the organism are based on observation of behavior and outside events. Nevertheless, one's estimate of the relative importance of external factors and internal structure in the determination of behavior will have an important effect on the direction of research on linguistic (or any other) behavior, and on the kinds of analogies from animal behavior studies that will be considered relevant or suggestive.

Putting it differently, anyone who sets himself the problem of analyzing the causation of behavior will (in the absence of independent neurophysiological evidence) concern himself with the only data available, namely the record of inputs to the organism and the organism's present response, and will try to describe the function specifying the response in terms of the history of inputs. This is nothing more than the definition of his problem. There are no possible grounds for argument here, if one accepts the problem as legitimate, though Skinner has often advanced and defended this definition of a problem as if it were a thesis which other investigators reject. The differences that arise between those who affirm and those who deny the importance of the specific "contribution of the organism" to learning and performance concern the particular character and complexity of this function, and the kinds of observations and research necessary for arriving at a precise specification of it. If the contribution of the organism is complex, the only hope of predicting behavior even in a gross way will be through a very indirect program of research that begins by studying the detailed character of the behavior itself and the particular capacities of the organism involved.

Skinner's thesis is that external factors consisting of present stimulation and the history of reinforcement (in particular the frequency, arrangement, and withholding of reinforcing stimuli) are of overwhelming importance, and that the general principles revealed in laboratory studies of these phenomena provide the basis for understanding the complexities of verbal behavior. He confidently and repeatedly voices his claim to have demonstrated that the contribution of the speaker is quite trivial and elementary, and that precise prediction of verbal behavior involves only specification of the few external factors that he has isolated experimentally with lower organisms.

Careful study of this book (and of the research on which it draws) reveals, however, that these astonishing claims are far from justified. It indicates, furthermore, that the insights that have been achieved in the laboratories of the reinforcement theorist, though quite genuine, can be applied to complex human behavior only in the most gross and superficial way, and that speculative attempts to discuss linguistic behavior in these terms alone omit from consideration factors of fundamental importance that are, no doubt, amenable to scientific study, although their specific character cannot at present be precisely formulated. Since Skinner's work is the most extensive attempt to accommodate human behavior involving higher mental faculties within a strict behaviorist schema of the type that has attracted many linguists and philosophers, as well as psychologists, a detailed documentation is of independent interest. The magnitude of the failure of this attempt to account for verbal behavior serves as a kind of measure of the importance of the factors omitted from consideration, and an indication of how little is really known about this remarkably complex phenomenon.

The force of Skinner's argument lies in the enormous wealth and range of examples for which he proposes a functional analysis. The only way to evaluate the success of his program and the correctness of his basic assumptions about verbal behavior is to review these examples in detail and to determine the precise character of the concepts in terms of which the functional analysis is presented. §2 of this review describes the experimental context with respect to which these concepts are originally defined, §§3–4 deal with the basic concepts "stimulus," "response," and "reinforcement," §§6–10 with the new descriptive machinery developed specifically for the description of verbal behavior. In §5 we consider the status of the fundamental claim, drawn from the laboratory, which serves as the basis for the analogic guesses about human behavior that have been proposed by many psychologists. The final section (§11) will consider some ways in which further linguistic work may play a part in clarifying some of these problems.

2. Although this book makes no direct reference to experimental work, it can be understood only in terms of the general framework that Skinner has developed for the description of behavior. Skinner divides the responses of the animal into two main categories. *Respondents* are purely reflex responses elicited by particular stimuli. *Operants* are emitted responses, for which no obvious stimulus can be discovered. Skinner has been concerned primarily with operant behavior. The experimental arrangement that he introduced consists basically of a box with a bar attached to one wall in such a way that when the bar is pressed, a food pellet is dropped into a tray (and the bar press is recorded). A rat placed in the box will soon press the bar, releasing a pellet into the tray. This state of affairs, resulting from the bar press, increases the *strength* of the bar pressing operant. The food pellet is called a *reinforcer*; the event, a reinforcing event. The strength of an operant is defined by Skinner in terms of the rate of response during extinction (i.e., after the last reinforcement and before return to the preconditioning rate).

Suppose that release of the pellet is conditional on the flashing of a light. Then the rat will come to press the bar only when the light flashes. This is called *stimulus discrimination*. The response is called a *discriminated operant* and the light is called the *occasion* for its emission; this is to be distinguished from elicitation of a response by a stimulus in the case of the respondent.[2] Suppose that the apparatus is so arranged that bar-pressing of only a certain character (e.g., duration) will release the pellet. The rat will then come to press the bar in the required way. This process is called *response differentiation*. By successive slight changes in the conditions under which the response will be reinforced it is possible to shape the response of a rat or a pigeon in very surprising ways in a very short time, so that rather complex behavior can be produced by a process of successive approximation.

A stimulus can become reinforcing by repeated association with an already reinforcing stimulus. Such a stimulus is called a *secondary reinforcer*. Like many contemporary behaviorists, Skinner considers money, approval, and the like to be secondary reinforcers which have become reinforcing because of their association with food etc.[3] Secondary reinforces can be *generalized* by associating them with a variety of different primary reinforcers.

Another variable that can affect the rate of the bar-pressing operant is drive, which Skinner defines operationally in terms of hours of deprivation. His major scientific book, *Behavior of organisms*, is a study of the effects of food-deprivation and conditioning on the strength of the bar-pressing response of healthy mature rats. Probably Skinner's most original contribution to animal behavior studies has been his investigation of the effects of intermittent reinforcement, arranged in various different ways, presented in *Behavior of organisms* and extended (with pecking of pigeons as the operant under investigation) in the recent *Schedules of Reinforcement* by Ferster and Skinner (1957). It is apparently these studies that Skinner has in mind when he refers to the recent advances in the study of animal behavior.[4]

The notions "stimulus," "response," "reinforcement" are relatively well defined with respect to the bar-pressing experiments and others similarly restricted. Before we can extend them to real-life behavior, however, certain difficulties must be faced. We must decide, first of all, whether any physical event to which the organism is capable of reacting is to be called a stimulus on a given occasion, or only one to which the organism in fact reacts; and correspondingly, we must decide whether any part of behavior is to be called a response, or only one connected with stimuli in lawful ways. Questions of this sort pose something of a dilemma for the experimental psychologist. If he accepts the broad definitions, characterising any physical event impinging on the organism as a stimulus and any part of the organism's behavior as a response, he must conclude that behavior has not been demonstrated to be lawful. In the present state of our knowledge, we must attribute an overwhelming influence on actual behavior to ill-defined factors of attention, set, volition, and caprice. If we accept the narrower definitions, then behavior is lawful by definition (if it consists of responses); but this fact is of limited significance, since most of what the animal does will simply not be considered behavior. Hence the psychologist either must admit that behavior is not lawful (or that he cannot at present show that it is—not at all a damaging admission for a developing science), or must restrict his attention to those highly limited areas in which it is lawful (e.g., with adequate controls, bar-pressing in rats; lawfulness of the observed behavior provides, for Skinner, an implicit definition of a good experiment).

Skinner does not consistently adopt either course. He utilizes the experimental results as evidence for the scientific character of his system of behavior, and analogic guesses (formulated in terms of a metaphoric extension of the technical vocabulary of the laboratory) as evidence for its scope. This creates the illusion of a rigorous scientific theory with a very broad scope, although in fact the terms used in the description of real-life and of laboratory behavior may be mere homonyms, with at most a vague similarity of meaning. To substantiate this evaluation, a critical account of his book must show that with a literal reading (where the terms of the descriptive system have something like the technical meanings given in Skinner's definitions) the book covers almost no aspect of linguistic behavior, and that with a metaphoric reading, it is no more scientific than the traditional approaches to this subject matter, and rarely as clear and careful.[5]

3. Consider first Skinner's use of the notions "stimulus" and "response." In *Behavior of organisms* (9) he commits himself to the narrow definitions for these terms. A part of the environment and a part of behavior are called stimulus (eliciting, discriminated, or reinforcing) and response, respectively, only if they are lawfully related; that is, if the "dynamic laws" relating them show smooth and reproducible curves. Evidently stimuli and responses, so defined, have not been shown to figure very widely in ordinary human behavior.[6] We can, in the face of presently available evidence, continue to maintain the lawfulness of the relation between stimulus and response only by depriving them of their objective character. A typical example of "stimulus control" for Skinner would be the response to a piece of music with the utterance *Mozart* or to a painting with the response *Dutch*. These responses are asserted to be "under the control of extremely subtle properties" of the physical object or event (108). Suppose instead of saying *Dutch* we had said *Clashes with the wallpaper, I thought you liked abstract work, Never saw it before, Tilted, Hanging too low, Beautiful, Hideous, Remember our camping trip last summer?*, or whatever else might come into our minds when looking at a picture (in Skinnerian translation, whatever other responses exist in sufficient strength). Skinner could only say that each of these responses is under the control of some other stimulus property of the physical object. If we look at a red chair and say *red*, the response is under the control of the stimulus "redness," if we say *chair*, it is under the control of the collection of properties (for Skinner, the object) "chairness" (110), and similarly for any other response. This device is as simple as it is empty. Since properties are free for the asking (we have as many of them as we have nonsynonymous descriptive expressions in our language, whatever this means exactly), we can account for a wide class of responses in terms of Skinnerian functional analysis by identifying the "controlling stimuli." But the word "stimulus" has lost all objectivity in this usage. Stimuli are no longer part of the outside physical world; they are driven back into the organism. We identify the stimulus when we hear the response. It is clear from such examples, which abound, that the talk of "stimulus control" simply disguises a complete retreat to mentalistic psychology. We cannot predict verbal behavior in terms of the stimuli in the speaker's environment, since we do not know what the current stimuli are until he responds. Furthermore, since we cannot control the property of a physical object to which an individual will respond, except in highly artificial cases, Skinner's claim that his system, as opposed to the traditional one, permits the practical control of verbal behavior[7] is quite false.

Other examples of "stimulus control" merely add to the general mystification. Thus a proper noun is held to be a response "under the control of a specific person or thing" (as controlling stimulus, 113). I have often used the words *Eisenhower* and *Moscow*, which I presume are proper nouns if anything is, but have never been "stimulated" by the corresponding objects. How can this fact be made compatible with this definition? Suppose that I use the name of a friend who is not present. Is this an instance of a proper noun under the control of the friend as stimulus? Elsewhere it is asserted that a stimulus controls a response in the sense that presence of the stimulus increases the probability of the response. But it is obviously untrue that the probability that a speaker will produce a full name is increased when its bearer faces the speaker. Furthermore, how can one's own name be a proper noun in this sense? A multitude of similar questions arise immediately. It appears that the word "control" here is merely a misleading paraphrase for the traditional "denote" or "refer." The assertion (115) that so far as the speaker is concerned, the relation of reference is "simply the probability that the speaker will emit a response of a given form in the presence of a stimulus having specified properties" is surely incorrect if we take the words "presence," "stimulus," and "probability" in their literal sense. That they are not intended to be taken literally is indicated by many examples, as when a response is said to be "controlled" by a situation or state of affairs as "stimulus." Thus, the expression *a needle in a haystack* "may be controlled as a unit by a particular type of situation" (116); the words in a single part of speech, e.g., all adjectives, are under the control of a single set of subtle properties of stimuli (121); "the sentence *The boy runs a store* is under the control of an extremely complex stimulus situation" (335); "*He is not at all well* may function as a standard response under the control of a state of affairs which might also control *He is ailing*" (325); when an envoy observes events in a foreign country and reports upon his return, his report is under "remote stimulus control" (416); the statement *This is war* may be a response to a "confusing international situation" (441); the suffix *-ed* is controlled by that "subtle property of stimuli which we speak of as action-in-the-past" (121) just as the *-s* in *The boy runs* is under the control of such specific features of the situation as its "currency" (332). No characterization of the notion "stimulus control" that is remotely related to the bar-pressing experiment (or that preserves the faintest objectivity) can be made to cover a set of examples like these, in which, for example, the "controlling stimulus" need not even impinge on the responding organism.

Consider now Skinner's use of the notion "response." The problem of identifying units in verbal behavior has of course been a primary concern of linguists, and it seems very likely that experimental psychologists should be able to provide much-needed assistance in clearing up the many remaining difficulties in systematic identification. Skinner recognizes (20) the fundamental character of the problem of identification of a unit of verbal behavior, but is satisfied with an answer so vague and subjective that it does not really contribute to its solution. The unit of verbal behavior—the verbal operant—is defined as a class of responses of identifiable form functionally related to one or more controlling variables. No method is suggested for determining in a particular instance what are the controlling variables, how many such units have occurred, or where their boundaries are in the total response. Nor is any attempt made to specify how much or what kind of similarity in form or "control" is required for two physical events to be considered instances of the same operant. In short, no answers are suggested for the most elementary questions that must be asked of anyone proposing a method for description of behavior. Skinner is content with what he calls an "extrapolation" of the concept of operant developed in the laboratory to the verbal field. In the typical Skinnerian experiment, the problem of identifying the unit of behavior is not too crucial. It is defined, by fiat, as a recorded peck or bar-press, and systematic variations in the rate of this operant and its resistance to extinction are studied as a function of deprivation and scheduling of reinforcement (pellets). The operant is thus defined with respect to a particular experimental procedure. This is perfectly reasonable, and has led to many interesting results. It is, however, completely meaningless to speak of extrapolating this concept of operant to ordinary verbal behavior. Such "extrapolation" leaves us with no way of justifying one or another decision about the units in the "verbal repertoire."

Skinner specifies "response strength" as the basic datum, the basic dependent variable in his functional analysis. In the bar-pressing experiment, response strength is defined in terms of rate of emission during extinction. Skinner has argued[8] that this is "the only datum that varies significantly and in the expected direction under conditions which are relevant to the "learning process." In the book under review, response strength is defined as "probability of emission" (22). This definition provides a comforting impression of objectivity, which, however, is quickly dispelled when we look into the matter more closely. The term "probability" has some rather obscure meaning for Skinner in this book.[9] We are told, on the one hand, that "our evidence for the contribution of each variable [to response strength] is based on observation of frequencies alone" (28). At the same time, it appears that frequency is a very misleading measure of strength, since, for example, the frequency of a response may be "primarily attributable to the frequency of occurrence of controlling variables" (27). It is not clear how the frequency of a response can be attributable to anything BUT the frequency of occurrence of its controlling variables if we accept Skinner's view that the behavior occurring in a given situation is "fully determined" by the relevant controlling variables (175, 228). Furthermore, although the evidence for the contribution of each variable to response strength is based on observation of frequencies alone, it turns out that "we base the notion of strength upon several kinds of evidence" (22), in particular (22–8): emission of the response (particularly in unusual circumstances), energy level (stress), pitch level, speed and delay of emission, size of letters, etc, in writing, immediate repetition, and—a final factor, relevant but misleading—overall frequency.

Of course, Skinner recognizes that these measures do not co-vary, because (among other reasons) pitch, stress, quantity, and reduplication may have internal linguistic functions.[10] However, he does not hold these conflicts to be very important, since the proposed factors indicative of strength are "fully understood by everyone" in the culture (27). For example, "if we are shown a prized work of art and exclaim *Beautiful!*, the speed and energy of the response will not be lost on the owner." It does not appear totally obvious that in this case the way to impress the owner is to shriek *Beautiful* in a loud, high-pitched voice, repeatedly, and with no delay (high response strength). It may be equally effective to look at the picture silently (long delay), and then to murmur *Beautiful* in a soft, low-pitched voice (by definition, very low response strength).

It is not unfair, I believe, to conclude from Skinner's discussion of response strength, the "basic datum" in functional analysis, that his "extrapolation" of the notion of probability can best be interpreted as, in effect, nothing more than a decision to use the word "probability," with its favorable connotations of objectivity, as a cover term to paraphrase such low-status words as "interest," "intention," "belief," and the like. This interpretation is fully justified by the way in which Skinner uses the terms "probability" and "strength." To cite just one example, Skinner defines the process of confirming an assertion in science as one of "generating additional variables to increase its probability" (425), and more generally, its strength (425–9). If we take this suggestion quite literally, the degree of confirmation of a scientific assertion can be measured as a simple function of the loudness, pitch, and frequency with which it is proclaimed, and a general procedure for increasing its degree of confirmation would be, for instance, to train machine guns on large crowds of people who have been instructed to shout it. A better indication of what Skinner probably has in mind here is given by his description of how the theory of evolution, as an example, is confirmed. This "single set of verbal responses . . . is made more plausible—is strengthened—by several types of construction based upon verbal responses in geology, paleontology, genetics, and so on" (427). We are no doubt to interpret the terms "strength" and "probability" in this context as paraphrases of more familiar locutions such as "justified belief" or "warranted assertability," or something of the sort. Similar latitude of interpretation is presumably expected when we read that "frequency of effective action accounts in turn for what we may call the listener's 'belief' " (88) or that "our belief in what someone tells us is similarly a function of, or identical with, our tendency to act upon the verbal stimuli which he provides" (160).[11]

I think it is evident, then, that Skinner's use of the terms "stimulus," "control," "response," and "strength," justify the general conclusion stated in the last paragraph of 12 above. The way in which these terms are brought to bear on the actual data indicates that we must interpret them as mere paraphrases for the popular vocabulary commonly used to describe behavior, and as having no particular connection with the homonymous expressions used in the description of laboratory experiments. Naturally, this terminological revision adds no objectivity to the familiar "mentalistic" mode of description.

4. The other fundamental notion borrowed from the description of bar-pressing experiments is "reinforcement." It raises problems which are similar, and even more serious. In *Behavior of organisms*, "the operation of reinforcement is defined as the presentation of a certain kind of stimulus in a temporal relation with either a stimulus or response. A reinforcing stimulus is defined as such by its power to produce the resulting change [in strength]. There is no circularity about this: some stimuli are found to produce the change, others not, and they are classified as reinforcing and non-reinforcing accordingly" (62). This is a perfectly appropriate definition[12] for the study of schedules of reinforcement. It is perfectly useless, however, in the discussion of real-life behavior, unless we can somehow characterize the stimuli which are reinforcing (and the situations and conditions under which they are reinforcing). Consider first of all the status of the basic principle that Skinner calls the "law of conditioning" (law of effect). It reads: "if the occurrence of an operant is followed by presence of a reinforcing stimulus, the strength is increased" (*Behavior of organisms* 21). As "reinforcement" was defined, this law becomes a tautology.[13] For Skinner, learning is just change in response strength.[14] Although the statement that presence of reinforcement is a sufficient condition for learning and maintenance of behavior is vacuous, the claim that it is a necessary condition may have some content, depending on how the class of reinforcers (and appropriate situations) is characterized. Skinner does make it very clear that in his view reinforcement is a necessary condition for language learning and for the continued availability of linguistic responses in the adult.[15] However, the looseness of the term "reinforcement" as Skinner uses it in the book under review makes it entirely pointless to inquire into the truth or falsity of this claim. Examining the instances of what Skinner calls "reinforcement," we find that not even the requirement that a reinforcer be an identifi-

able stimulus is taken seriously. In fact, the term is used in such a way that the assertion that reinforcement is necessary for learning and continued availability of behavior is likewise empty.

To show this, we consider some examples of "reinforcement." First of all, we find a heavy appeal to automatic self-reinforcement. Thus, "a man talks to himself . . . because of the reinforcement he receives" (163); "the child is reinforced automatically when he duplicates the sounds of airplanes, streetcars . . ." (164); "the young child alone in the nursery may automatically reinforce his own exploratory verbal behavior when he produces sounds which he has heard "in the speech of others" (58); "the speaker who is also an accomplished listener 'knows when he has correctly echoed a response' and is reinforced thereby" (68); thinking is "behaving which automatically affects the behaver and is reinforcing because it does so" (438; cutting one's finger should thus be reinforcing, and an example of thinking); "the verbal fantasy whether overt or covert, is automatically reinforcing to the speaker as listener. Just as the musician plays or composes what he is reinforced by hearing, or as the artist paints what reinforces him visually, so the speaker engaged in verbal fantasy says what he is reinforced by hearing or writes what he is reinforced by reading" (439); similarly, care in problem solving, and rationalization, are automatically self-reinforcing (442–3). We can also reinforce someone by emitting verbal behavior as such (since this rules out a class of aversive stimulations, 167), by not emitting verbal behavior (keeping silent and paying attention, 199), or by acting appropriately on some future occasion (152: "the strength of [the speaker's] behavior is determined mainly by the behavior which the listener will exhibit with respect to a given state of affairs"; this Skinner considers the general case of "communication" or "letting the listener know"). In most such cases, of course, the speaker is not present at the time when the reinforcement takes place, as when "the artist . . . is reinforced by the effects his works have upon . . . others" (224), or when the writer is reinforced by the fact that his "verbal behavior may reach over centuries or to thousands of listeners or readers at the same time. The writer may not be reinforced often or immediately, but his net reinforcement may be great" (206; this accounts for the great "strength" of his behavior). An individual may also find it reinforcing to injure someone by criticism or by bringing bad news, or to publish an experimental result which upsets the theory of a rival (154), to describe circumstances which would be reinforcing if they were to occur (165), to avoid repetition (222), to "hear" his own name though in fact it was not mentioned or to hear nonexistent words in his child's babbling (259), to clarify or otherwise intensify the effect of a stimulus which serves an important discriminative function (416), etc.

From this sample, it can be seen that the notion of reinforcement has totally lost whatever objective meaning it may ever have had. Running through these examples, we see that a person can be reinforced though he emits no response at all, and that the reinforcing "stimulus" need not impinge on the "reinforced person" or need not even exist (it is sufficient that it be imagined or hoped for). When we read that a person plays what music he likes (165), says what he likes (165), thinks what he likes (438–9), reads what books he likes (163), etc., BECAUSE he finds it reinforcing to do so, or that we write books or inform others of facts BECAUSE we are reinforced by what we hope will be the ultimate behavior of reader or listener, we can only conclude that the term "reinforcement" has a purely ritual function. The phrase "X is reinforced by Y (stimulus, state of affairs, event, etc.)" is being used as a cover term for "X wants Y," "X likes Y," "X wishes that Y were the case," etc. Invoking the term "reinforcement" has no explanatory force, and any idea that this paraphrase introduces any new clarity or objectivity into the description of wishing, liking, etc., is a serious delusion. The only effect is to obscure the important differences among the notions being paraphrased. Once we recognize the latitude with which the term "reinforcement" is being used, many rather startling comments lose their initial effect—for instance, that the behavior of the creative artist is "controlled entirely by the contingencies of reinforcement" (150). What has been hoped for from the psychologist is some indication how the casual and informal description of everyday behavior in the popular vocabulary can be explained or clarified in terms of the notions developed in careful experiment and observation, or perhaps replaced in terms of a better scheme. A mere terminological revision, in which a term borrowed from the laboratory is used with the full vagueness of the ordinary vocabulary, is of no conceivable interest.

It seems that Skinner's claim that all verbal behavior is acquired and maintained in "strength" through reinforcement is quite empty, because his notion of reinforcement has no clear content, functioning only as a cover term for any factor, detectable or not, related to acquisition or maintenance of verbal behavior.[16] Skinner's use of the term "conditioning" suffers from a similar difficulty. Pavlovian and operant conditioning are processes about which psychologists have developed real understanding. Instruction of human beings is not. The claim that instruction and imparting of information are simply matters of conditioning (357–66) is pointless. The claim is true, if we extend the term "conditioning" to cover these processes, but we know no more about them after having revised this term in such a way as to deprive it of its relatively clear and objective character. It is, as far as we know, quite false, if we use "conditioning" in its literal sense. Similarly, when we say that "it is the function of predication to facilitate the transfer of response from one term to another or from one object to another" (361), we have said nothing of any significance. In what sense is this true of the predication *Whales are mammals?* Or, to take Skinner's example, what point is there in saying that the effect of *The telephone is out of order* on the listener is to bring behavior formerly controlled by the stimulus *out of order* under control of the stimulus *telephone* (or the telephone itself) by a process of simple conditioning (362)? What laws of conditioning hold in this case? Furthermore, what behavior is "controlled" by the stimulus *out of order*, in the abstract? Depending on the object of which this is predicated, the present state of motivation of the listener, etc., the behavior may vary from rage to pleasure, from fixing the object to throwing it out, from simply not using it to trying to use it in the normal way (e.g., to see if it is really out of order), and so on. To speak of "conditioning" or "bringing previously available behavior under control of a new stimulus" in such a case is just a kind of play-acting at science. Cf. also note 43.

5. The claim that careful arrangement of contingencies of reinforcement by the verbal community is a necessary condition for language learning has appeared, in one form or another, in many places.[17] Since it is based not on actual observation, but on analogies to laboratory study of lower organisms, it is important to determine the status of the underlying assertion within experimental psychology proper. The most common characterization of reinforcement (one which Skinner explicitly rejects, incidentally) is in terms of drive reduction. This characterization can be given substance by defining drives in some way independently of what in fact is learned. If a drive is postulated on the basis of the fact that learning takes place, the claim that reinforcement is necessary for learning will again become as empty as it is in the Skinnerian framework. There is an extensive literature on the question of whether there can be learning without drive-reduction (latent learning). The "classical" experiment of Blodgett indicated that rats who had explored a maze without reward showed a marked drop in number of errors (as compared to a control group which had not explored the maze) upon introduction of a food reward, indicating that the rat had learned the structure of the maze without reduction of the hunger drive. Drive-reduction theorists' countered with an exploratory drive which was reduced during the prereward learning, and claimed that a slight decrement in errors could be noted before food reward. A wide variety of experiments, with somewhat conflicting results, have been carried out with a similar design.[18] Few investigators still doubt the existence of the phenomenon. Hilgard, in his general review of learning theory,[19] concludes that "there is no longer any doubt but that, under appropriate circumstances, latent learning is demonstrable."

More recent work has shown that novelty and variety of stimulus are sufficient to arouse curiosity in the rat and to motivate it to explore (visually), and in fact, to learn (since on a presentation of two stimuli, one novel, one repeated, the rat will attend to the novel one);[20] that rats will learn to choose the arm of a single-choice maze that leads to a complex maze, running through this being their only "reward";[21] that monkeys can learn object discriminations and maintain their performance at a high level of efficiency with visual exploration (looking out of a window for 30 seconds) as the only reward;[22] and, perhaps most strikingly of all, that monkeys and apes will solve rather complex manipulation problems that are simply placed in their cages, and will solve discrimination problems with only exploration and manipulation as incentives.[23] In these cases, solving the problem is apparently its own 'reward'. Results of this kind can be handled by reinforcement theorists only if they are willing to set up curiosity, exploration, and manipulation drives, or to speculate somehow about acquired drives[24] for which there is no evidence outside of the fact that learning takes place in these cases.

There is a variety of other kinds of evidence that has been offered to challenge the view that drive-reduction is necessary for learning. Results on sensory-sensory conditioning have been interpreted as demonstrating learning without drive-reduction.[25] Olds has reported reinforcement by direct stimulation of the brain, from which he concludes that reward need not satisfy a physiological need or withdraw a drive stimulus.[26] The phenomenon of imprinting, long observed by zoologists, is of particular interest in this connection. Some of the most complex patterns of behavior of birds, in particular, are directed towards objects and animals of the type to which they have been exposed at certain critical early periods of life.[27] Imprinting is the most striking evidence for the innate disposition of the animal to learn in a certain direction, and to react appropriately to patterns and objects of certain restricted types, often only long after the original learning has taken place. It is, consequently, unrewarded learning, though the resulting patterns of behavior may be refined through reinforcement. Acquisition of the typical songs of song birds is, in some cases, a type of imprinting. Thorpe reports studies that show "that some characteristics of the normal song have been learnt in the earliest youth, before the bird itself is able to produce any kind of full song."[28] The phenomenon of imprinting has recently been investigated under laboratory conditions and controls with positive results.[29]

Phenomena of this general type are certainly familiar from everyday experience. We recognize people and places to which we have given no particular attention. We can look up something in a book and learn it perfectly well with no other motive than to confute reinforcement theory, or out of boredom, or idle curiosity. Everyone engaged in research must have had the experience of working with feverish and prolonged intensity to write a paper which no one else will read or to solve a problem which no one else thinks important and which will bring no conceivable reward—which may only confirm a general opinion that the researcher is wasting his time on irrelevancies. The fact that rats and monkeys do likewise is interesting, and important to show in careful experiment. In fact, studies of behavior of the type mentioned above have an independent and positive significance that far outweighs their incidental importance in bringing into question the claim that learning is impossible without drive-reduction. It is not at all unlikely that insights arising from animal behavior studies with this broadened scope may have the kind of relevance to such complex activities as verbal behavior that reinforcement theory has, so far, failed to exhibit. In any event, in the light of presently available evidence, it is difficult to see how anyone can be willing to claim that reinforcement is necessary for learning, if reinforcement is taken seriously as something identifiable independently of the resulting change in behavior.

Similarly, it seems quite beyond question that children acquire a good deal of their verbal and nonverbal behavior by casual observation and imitation of adults and other children.[30] It is simply not true that children can learn language only through "meticulous care" on the part of adults who shape their verbal repertoire through careful differential reinforcement, though it may be that such care is often the custom in academic families. It is a common observation that a young child of immigrant parents may learn a second language in the streets, from other children, with amazing rapidity, and that his speech may be completely fluent and correct to the last allophone, while the subtleties that become second nature to the child may elude his parents despite high motivation and continued practice. A child may pick up a large part of his vocabulary and "feel" for sentence structure from television, from reading, from listening to adults, etc. Even a very young child who has not yet acquired a minimal repertoire from which to form new utterances may imitate a word quite well on an early try, with no attempt on the part of his parents to teach it to him. It is also perfectly obvious that, at a later stage, a child will be able to construct and understand utterances which are quite new, and are, at the same time, acceptable sentences in his language. Every time an adult reads a newspaper, he undoubtedly comes upon countless new sentences which are not at all similar, in a simple, physical sense, to any that he has heard before, and which he will recognize as sentences and understand; he will also be able to detect slight distortions or misprints. Talk of "stimulus generalization" in such a case simply perpetuates the mystery under a new title. These abilities indicate that there must be fundamental processes at work quite independently of "feedback" from the environment. I have been able to find no support whatsoever for the doctrine of Skinner and others that slow and careful shaping of verbal behavior through differential reinforcement is an absolute necessity. If reinforcement theory really requires the assumption that there be such meticulous care, it seems best to regard this simply as a reductio ad absurdum argument against this approach. It is also not easy to find any basis (or, for that matter, to attach very much content) to the claim that reinforcing contingencies set up by the verbal community are the single factor responsible for maintaining the strength of verbal behavior. The sources of the "strength" of this behavior are almost a total mystery at present. Reinforcement undoubtedly plays a significant role, but so do a variety of motivational factors about which nothing serious is known in the case of human beings.

As far as acquisition of language is concerned, it seems clear that reinforcement, casual observation, and natural inquisitiveness (coupled with a strong tendency to imitate) are important factors, as is the remarkable capacity of the child to generalize, hypothesize, and "process information" in a variety of very special and apparently highly complex ways which we cannot yet describe or begin to understand, and which may be largely innate, or may develop through some sort of learning or through maturation of the nervous system. The manner in which such factors operate and interact in language acquisition is completely unknown. It is clear that what is necessary in such a case is research, not dogmatic and perfectly arbitrary claims, based on analogies to that small part of the experimental literature in which one happens to be interested.

The pointlessness of these claims becomes clear when we consider the well-known difficulties in determining to what extent inborn structure, maturation, and learning are responsible for the particular form of a skilled or complex performance.[31] To take just one example,[32] the gaping response of a nestling thrush is at first released by jarring of the nest, and at a later stage, by a moving object of specific size, shape, and position relative to the nestling. At this later stage the response is directed towards the part of the stimulus object corresponding to the parent's head, and characterized by a complex configuration of stimuli that can be precisely described. Knowing just this, it would be possible to construct a speculative, learning-theoretic account of how this sequence of behavior patterns might have developed through a process of differential reinforcement, and it would no doubt be possible to train rats to do something similar. However, there appears to be good evidence that these responses to fairly complex "sign stimuli" are genetically determined and mature without learning. Clearly, the possibility cannot be discounted. Consider now the comparable case of a child imitating new words. At an early stage we may find rather gross correspondences. At a later stage, we find that repetition is of course far from exact (i.e., it is not mimicry, a fact which itself is interesting), but that it reproduces the highly complex configuration of sound features that constitute the phonological structure of the language in question. Again, we can propose a speculative account of how this result might have been obtained through elaborate arrangement of reinforcing contingencies. Here too, however, it is possible that ability to select out of the complex auditory input those features that are phonologically relevant may develop largely independently of reinforcement, through genetically determined maturation. To the extent that this is true, an account of the development and causation of behavior that fails to consider the structure of the organism will provide no understanding of the real processes involved.

It is often argued that experience, rather than innate capacity to handle information in certain specific ways, must be the factor of overwhelming dominance in determining the specific character of language acquisition, since a child speaks the language of the group in which he lives. But this is a superficial argument. As long as we are speculating, we may consider the possibility that the brain has evolved to the point where, given an input of observed Chinese sentences, it produces (by an "induction" of apparently fantastic complexity and suddenness) the "rules" of Chinese grammar, and given an input of observed English sentences, it produces (by, perhaps, exactly the same process of induction) the rules of English grammar; or that given an observed application of a term to certain instances it automatically predicts the extension to a class of complexly related instances. If clearly recognized as such, this speculation is neither unreasonable nor fantastic; nor, for that matter, is it beyond the bounds of possible study. There is of course no known neural structure capable of performing this task in the specific ways that observation of the resulting behavior might lead us to postulate; but for that matter, the structures capable of accounting for even the simplest kinds of learning have similarly defied detection.[33]

Summarizing this brief discussion, it seems that there is neither empirical evidence nor any known argument to support any SPECIFIC claim about the relative importance of "feedback" from the environment and the "independent contribution of the organism" in the process of language acquisition.

6. We now turn to the system that Skinner develops specifically for the description of verbal behavior. Since this system is based on the notions "stimulus," "response," and "reinforcement," we can conclude from the preceding sections that it will be vague and arbitrary. For reasons noted in §1, however, I think it is important to see in detail how far from the mark any analysis phrased solely in these terms must be and how completely this system fails to account for the facts of verbal behavior.

Consider first the term "verbal behavior" itself. This is defined as "behavior reinforced through the mediation of other persons" (2). The definition is clearly much too broad. It would include as "verbal behavior," for example, a rat pressing the bar in a Skinner-box, a child brushing his teeth, a boxer retreating before an opponent, and a mechanic repairing an automobile. Exactly how much of ordinary linguistic behavior is "verbal" in this sense, however, is something of a question: perhaps, as I have pointed out above, a fairly small fraction of it, if any substantive meaning is assigned to the term "reinforced." This definition is subsequently refined by the additional provision that the mediating response of the reinforcing person (the "listener") must itself "have been conditioned *precisely in order to reinforce* the behavior of the speaker" (225, italics his). This still covers the examples given above, if we can assume that the "reinforcing" behavior of the psychologist, the parent, the opposing boxer, and the paying customer are the result of appropriate training, which is perhaps not unreasonable. A significant part of the fragment of linguistic behavior covered by the earlier definition will no doubt be excluded by the refinement, however. Suppose, for example, that while crossing the street I hear someone about *Watch out for the car* and jump out of the way. It can hardly be proposed that my jumping (the mediating, reinforcing response in Skinner's usage) was conditioned (that is, I was trained to jump) precisely in order to reinforce the behavior of the speaker. Similarly for a wide class of cases. Skinner's assertion that with this refined definition "we narrow our subject to what is traditionally recognized as the verbal field" (225) appears to be grossly in error.

7. Verbal operants are classified by Skinner in terms of their "functional" relation to discriminated stimulus, reinforcement, and other verbal responses. A *mand* is defined as "a verbal operant in which the response is reinforced by a characteristic consequence and is therefore under the functional control of relevant conditions of deprivation or aversive stimulation" (35). This is meant to include questions, commands, etc. Each of the terms in this definition raises a host of problems. A mand such as *Pass the salt* is a class of responses. We cannot tell by observing the form of a response whether it belongs to this class (Skinner is very clear about this), but only by identifying the controlling variables. This is generally impossible. Deprivation is defined in the bar-pressing experiment in terms of length of time that the animal has not been fed or permitted to drink. In the present context, however, it is quite a mysterious notion. No attempt is made here to describe a method for determining "relevant conditions of deprivation" independently of the "controlled" response. It is of no help at all to be told (32) that it can be characterized in terms of the operations of the experimenter. If we define deprivation in terms of elapsed time, then at any moment a person is in countless states of deprivation.[34] It appears that we must decide that the relevant condition of deprivation was (say) salt-deprivation, on the basis of the fact that the speaker asked for salt (the reinforcing community which "sets up" the mand is in a similar predicament). In this case, the assertion that a mand is under the control of relevant deprivation is empty, and we are (contrary to Skinner's inten-

tion) identifying the response as a mand completely in terms of form. The word "relevant" in the definition above conceals some rather serious complications.

In the case of the mand *Pass the salt*, the word "deprivation" is not out of place, though it appears to be of little use for functional analysis. Suppose however that the speaker says *Give me the book*, *Take me for a ride*, or *Let me fix it*. What kinds of deprivation can be associated with these mands? How do we determine or measure the relevant deprivation? I think we must conclude in this case, as before, either that the notion "deprivation" is relevant at most to a minute fragment of verbal behavior, or else that the statement "X is under Y-deprivation" is just an odd paraphrase for "X wants Y," bearing a misleading and unjustifiable connotation of objectivity.

The notion "aversive control" is just as confused. This is intended to cover threats, beating, and the like (33). The manner in which aversive stimulation functions is simply described. If a speaker has had a history of appropriate reinforcement (e.g., if a certain response was followed by "cessation of the threat of such injury—of events which have previously been followed by such injury and which are therefore conditioned aversive stimuli"), then he will tend to give the proper response when the threat which had previously been followed by the injury is presented. It would appear to follow from this description that a speaker will not respond properly to the mand *Your money or your life* (38) unless he has a past history of being killed. But even if the difficulties in describing the mechanism of aversive control are somehow removed by a more careful analysis, it will be of little use for identifying operants for reasons similar to those mentioned in the case of deprivation.

It seems, then, that in Skinner's terms there is in most cases no way to decide whether a given response is an instance of a particular mand. Hence it is meaningless, within the terms of his system, to speak of the *characteristic* consequences of a mand, as in the definition above. Furthermore, even if we extend the system so that mands can somehow be identified, we will have to face the obvious fact that most of us are not fortunate enough to have our requests, commands, advice, and so on characteristically reinforced (they may nevertheless exist in considerable "strength"). These responses could therefore not be considered mands by Skinner. In fact, Skinner sets up a category of "magical mands" (48–9) to cover the case of "mands which cannot be accounted for by showing that they have ever had the effect specified or any similar effect upon similar occasions" (the word "ever" in this statement should be replaced by "characteristically"). In these pseudo mands, "the speaker simply describes the reinforcement appropriate to a given state of deprivation or aversive stimulation." In other words, given the meaning that we have been led to assign to "reinforcement" and "deprivation," the speaker asks for what he wants. The remark that "a speaker appears to create new mands on the analogy of old ones" is also not very helpful.

Skinner's claim that his new descriptive system is superior to the traditional one "because its terms can be defined with respect to experimental operations" (45) is, we see once again, an illusion. The statement "X wants Y" is not clarified by pointing out a relation between rate of bar-pressing and hours of food-deprivation; replacing "X wants Y" by "X is deprived of Y" adds no new objectivity to the description of behavior. His further claim for the superiority of the new analysis of mands is that it provides an objective basis for the traditional classification into requests, commands, etc. (38–41). The traditional classification is in terms of the intention of the speaker. But intention, Skinner holds, can be reduced to contingencies of reinforcement, and, correspondingly, we can explain the traditional classification in terms of the reinforcing behavior of the listener. Thus a question is a mand which "specifies verbal action, and the behavior of the listener permits us to classify it as a request, a command, or a prayer" (39). It is a request if "the listener is independently motivated to reinforce the speaker," a command if "the listener's behavior is reinforced by reducing a threat," a prayer if the mand "promotes reinforcement by generating an emotional disposition." The mand is advice if the listener is positively reinforced by the consequences of mediating the reinforcement of the speaker; it is a warning if "by carrying out the behavior specified by the speaker the listener escapes from aversive stimulation," and so on. All this is obviously wrong if Skinner is using the words "request," "command," etc., in anything like the sense of the corresponding English words. The word "question" does not cover commands. *Please pass the salt* is a request (but not a question), whether or not the listener happens to be motivated to fulfill it; not everyone to whom a request is addressed is favorably disposed. A response does not cease to be a command if it is not followed; nor does a question become a command if the speaker answers it because of an implied or imagined threat. Not all advice is good advice, and a response does not cease to be advice if it is not followed. Similarly, a warning may be misguided; heeding it, may cause aversive stimulation, and ignoring it might be positively reinforcing. In short, the entire classification is beside the point. A moment's thought is sufficient to demonstrate the impossibility of distinguishing between requests, commands, advice, etc., on the basis of the behavior or disposition of the particular listener. Nor can we do this on the basis of the typical behavior of all listeners. Some advice is never taken, is always bad, etc., and similarly with other kinds of mands. Skinner's evident satisfaction with this analysis of the traditional classification is extremely puzzling.

8. Mands are operants with no specified relation to a prior stimulus. A *tact*, on the other hand, is defined as "a verbal operant in which a response of given

form is evoked (or at least strengthened) by a particular object or event or property of an object or event" (81). The examples quoted in the discussion of stimulus control (§3) are all tacts. The obscurity of the notion "stimulus control" makes the concept of the tact rather mystical. Since, however, the tact is "the most important of verbal operants," it is important to investigate the development of this concept in more detail.

We first ask why the verbal community "sets up" tacts in the child—that is how the parent is reinforced by setting up the tact. The basic explanation for this behavior of the parent (85–6) is the reinforcement he obtains by the fact that, his contact with the environment is extended; to use Skinner's example, the child may later be able to call him to the telephone. (It is difficult to see, then, how first children acquire tacts, since the parent does not have the appropriate history of reinforcement.) Reasoning in the same way, we may conclude that the parent induces the child to walk so that he can make some money delivering newspapers. Similarly, the parent sets up an "echoic repertoire" (e.g., a phonemic system) in the child because this makes it easier to teach him new vocabulary, and extending the child's vocabulary is ultimately useful to the parent. "In all these cases we explain the behavior of the reinforcing listener by pointing to an improvement in the possibility of controlling the speaker whom he reinforces" (56). Perhaps this provides the explanation for the behavior of the parent in inducing the child to walk: the parent is reinforced by the improvement in his control of the child when the child's mobility increases. Underlying these modes of explanation is a curious view that it is somehow more scientific to attribute to a parent a desire to control the child or enhance his own possibilities for action than a desire to see the child develop and extend his capacities. Needless to say, no evidence is offered to support this contention.

Consider now the problem of explaining the response of the listener to a tact. Suppose, for example, that B hears A say *fox* and reacts appropriately, looks around, runs away, aims his rifle, etc. How can we explain B's behavior? Skinner rightly rejects analyses of this offered by Watson and Bertrand Russell. His own equally inadequate analysis proceeds as follows (87–8). We assume (1) "that in the history of [B] the stimulus *fox* has been an occasion upon which looking around has been followed by seeing a fox" and (2) "that the listener has some current 'interest in seeing foxes'—that behavior which depends upon a seen fox for its execution is strong, and that the stimulus supplied by a fox is therefore reinforcing." B carries out the appropriate behavior, then, because "the heard stimulus *fox* is the occasion upon which turning and looking about is frequently followed by the reinforcement of seeing a fox," i.e., his behavior is a discriminated operant. This explanation is unconvincing. B may never have seen a fox and may have no current interest in seeing one, and yet may react appropriately to the stimulus *fox*.[35] Since exactly the same behavior may take place when neither of the assumptions is fulfilled, some other mechanism must be operative here.

Skinner remarks several times that his analysis of the tact in terms of stimulus control is an improvement over the traditional formulations in terms of reference and meaning. This is simply not true. His analysis is fundamentally the same as the traditional one, though much less carefully phrased. In particular, it differs only by indiscriminate paraphrase—of such notions as denotation (reference) and connotation (meaning), which have been kept clearly apart in traditional formulations, in terms of the vague concept "stimulus control." In one traditional formulation a descriptive term is said to denote a set of entities and to connote or designate a certain property or condition that an entity must possess or fulfil if the term is to apply to it.[36] Thus the term *vertebrate* refers to (denotes, is true of) vertebrates and connotes the property "having a spine" or something of the sort. This connoted defining property is called the meaning of the term. Two terms may have the same reference but different meanings. Thus it is apparently true that the creatures with hearts are all and only the vertebrates. If so, then the term *creature with a heart* refers to vertebrates and designates the property "having a heart." This is presumably a different property (a different general condition) from having a spine; hence the terms *vertebrate* and *creature with a heart* are said to have different meanings. This analysis is not incorrect (for at least one sense of meaning), but its many limitations have frequently been pointed out.[37] The major problem is that there is no good way to decide whether two descriptive terms designate the same property.[38] As we have just seen, it is not sufficient that they refer to the same objects. *Vertebrate* and *creature with a spine* would be said to designate the same property (distinct from that designated by *creature with a heart*). If we ask why this is so, the only answer appears to be that the terms are synonymous. The notion "property" thus seems somehow language-bound, and appeal to "defining properties" sheds little light on questions of meaning and synonymy.

Skinner accepts the traditional account in toto, as can be seen from his definition of a tact as a response under control of a property (stimulus) of some physical object or event. We have found that the notion "control" has no real substance, and is perhaps best understood as a paraphrase of "denote" or "connote" or, ambiguously, both. The only consequence of adopting the new term "stimulus control" is that the important differences between reference and meaning are obscured. It provides no new objectivity. The stimulus controlling the response is determined by the response itself; there is no independent and objective method of identification (see §3 above). Consequently, when Skinner defines "synonymy" as the case in which "the same stimulus leads to quite different responses" (118), we can have no objection. The responses *chair* and *red* made alternatively to the same object are not synonymous, because the stimuli are called different. The responses *vertebrate* and *creature with a spine* would be considered synonymous because they are controlled by the same property of the object under investigation; in more traditional and no less scientific terms, they evoke the same concept. Similarly, when metaphorical extension is explained as due to "the control exercised by properties of the stimulus which, though present at reinforcement, do not enter into the contingency respected by the verbal community" (92; traditionally, accidental properties), no objection can be raised which has not already been levelled against the traditional account. Just as we could "explain" the response *Mozart* to a piece of music in terms of subtle properties of the controlling stimuli, we can, with equal facility, explain the appearance of the response *sun* when no sun is present, as in *Juliet is* [*like*] *the sun*. "We do so by noting that Juliet and the sun have common properties, at least in their effect on the speaker" (93). Since any two objects have indefinitely many properties in common, we can be certain that we will never be at a loss to explain a response of the form *A is like B*, for arbitrary A and B. It is clear, however, that Skinner's recurrent claim that his formulation is simpler and more scientific than the traditional account has no basis in fact.

Tacts under the control of private stimuli (Bloomfield's "displaced speech") form a large and important class (130–46), including not only such responses as *familiar* and *beautiful*, but also verbal responses referring to past, potential, or future events or behavior. For example, the response *There was an elephant at the zoo* "must be understood as a response to current stimuli, including events within the speaker himself" (143).[39] If we now ask ourselves what proportion of the tacts in actual life are responses to (descriptions of) actual current outside stimulation, we can see just how large a role must be attributed to private stimuli. A minute amount of verbal behavior, outside the nursery, consists of such remarks as *This is red* and *There is a man*. The fact that "functional analysis" must make such a heavy appeal to obscure internal stimuli is again a measure of its actual advance over traditional formulations.

9. Responses under the control of prior verbal stimuli are considered under a different heading from the tact. An *echoic operant* is a response which "generates a sound pattern similar to that of the stimulus" (55). It covers only cases of immediate imitation.[40] No attempt is made to define the sense in which a child's echoic response is "similar" to the stimulus spoken in the father's bass voice; it seems, though there are no clear statements about this, that Skinner would not accept the account of the phonologist in this respect, but nothing else is offered. The development of an echoic repertoire is attributed completely to differential reinforcement. Since the speaker will do no more, ac-

cording to Skinner, than what is demanded of him by the verbal community, the degree of accuracy insisted on by this community will determine the elements of the repertoire, whatever these may be (not necessarily phonemes). "In a verbal community which does not insist on a precise correspondence, an echoic repertoire may remain slack and will be less successfully applied to novel patterns." There is no discussion of such familiar phenomena as the accuracy with which a child will pick up a second language or a local dialect in the course of playing with other children, which seem sharply in conflict with these assertions. No anthropological evidence is cited to support the claim that an effective phonemic system does not develop (this is the substance of the quoted remark) in communities that do not insist on precise correspondence.

A verbal response to a written stimulus (reading) is called "textual behavior."

Other verbal responses to verbal stimuli are called 'intraverbal operants.' Paradigm instances are the response *four* to the stimulus *two plus two* or the response *Paris* to the stimulus *capital of France*. Simple conditioning may be sufficient to account for the response *four* to *two plus two*,[41] but the notion of intraverbal response loses all meaning when we find it extended to cover most of the facts of history and many of the facts of science (72, 129); all word association and "flight of ideas" (73–6); all translations and paraphrase (77); reports of things seen, heard, or remembered (315); and, in general, large segments of scientific, mathematical, and literary discourse. Obviously the kind of explanation that might be proposed for a student's ability to respond with *Paris* to *capital of France*, after suitable practice, can hardly be seriously offered to account for his ability to make a judicious guess in answering the questions (to him new) *What is the seat of the French government?*, . . . *the source of the literary dialect?*, . . . *the chief target of the German blitzkrieg?*, etc., or his ability to prove a new theorem, translate a new passage, or paraphrase a remark for the first time or in a new way.

The process of "getting someone to see a point," to see something your way, or to understand a complex state of affairs (e.g., a difficult political situation or a mathematical proof) is, for Skinner, simply a matter of increasing the strength of the listener's already available behavior.[42] Since "the process is often exemplified by relatively intellectual scientific or philosophical discourse," Skinner considers it "all the more surprising that it may be reduced to echoic, textual, or intraverbal supplementation" (269). Again, it is only the vagueness and latitude with which the notions "strength" and "intraverbal response" are used that save this from absurdity. If we use these terms in their literal sense, it is clear that understanding a statement cannot be equated to shouting it frequently in a high-pitched voice (high response strength), and a clever and convincing argument cannot be accounted for on the basis of a history of pairings of verbal responses.[43]

10. A final class of operants, called *autoclitics*, includes those that are involved in assertion, negation, quantification, qualification of responses, construction of sentences, and the "highly complex manipulations of verbal thinking." All these acts are to be explained "in terms of behavior which is evoked by or acts upon other behavior of the speaker" (313). Autoclitics are, then, responses to already given responses, or rather, as we find in reading through this section, they are responses to covert or incipient or potential verbal behavior. Among the autoclitics are listed such expressions as *I recall, I imagine, for example, assume, let X equal* . . . , the terms of negation, the *is* of predication and assertion, *all, some, if, then*, and, in general, all morphemes other than nouns, verbs, and adjectives, as well as grammatical processes of ordering and arrangement. Hardly a remark in this section can be accepted without serious qualification. To take just one example, consider Skinner's account of the autoclitic *all* in *All swans are white* (329). Obviously we cannot assume that this is a tact to all swans as stimulus. It is suggested, therefore, that we take *all* to be an autoclitic modifying the whole sentence *Swans are white. All* can then be taken as equivalent to *always*, or *always it is possible to say.* Notice, however, that the modified sentence *Swans are white* is just as general as *All swans are white.* Furthermore, the proposed translation of *all* is incorrect if taken literally. It is just as possible to say *Swans are green* as to say *Swans are white.* It is not always possible to say either (e.g., while you are saying something else or sleeping). Probably what Skinner means is that the sentence can be paraphrased "*X is white* is true, for each swan X." But this paraphrase cannot be given within his system, which has no place for *true*.

Skinner's account of grammar and syntax as autoclitic processes (Chapter 13) differs from a familiar traditional account mainly in the use of the pseudo-scientific terms "control" or "evoke" in place of the traditional "refer." Thus in *The boy runs*, the final *s* of *runs* is a tact under control of such "subtle properties of a situation" as "the nature of running as an *activity* rather than an object or property of an object."[44] (Presumably, then, in *The attempt fails, The difficulty remains, His anxiety increases*, etc., we must also say that the *s* indicates that the object described as the attempt is carrying out the activity of failing, etc.) In *the boy's gun*, however, the *s* denotes possession (as, presumably, in *the boy's arrival, . . . story, . . . age*, etc.) and is under the control of this "relational aspect of the situation" (336). The "relational autoclitic of order" (whatever it may mean to call the order of a set of responses a response to them) in *The boy runs the store* is under the control of an "extremely complex stimulus situation," "namely, that the boy is running the store (335). *And* in *the hat and the shoe* is under the control of the property "pair." *Through in the dog went through the hedge* is under the control of the "relation between the going dog and the hedge" (342). In general, nouns are evoked by objects, verbs by actions, and so on.

Skinner considers a sentence to be a set of key responses (nouns, verbs, adjectives) on a skeletal frame (346). If we are concerned with the fact that Sam rented a leaky boat, the raw responses to the situation are *rent*, *boat*, *leak*, and *Sam*. Autoclitics (including order) which qualify these responses, express relations between them, and the like, are then added by a process called "composition" and the result is a grammatical sentence, one of many alternatives among which selection is rather arbitrary. The idea that sentences consist of lexical items placed in a grammatical frame is of course a traditional one, within both philosophy and linguistics. Skinner adds to it only the very implausible speculation that in the internal process of composition, the nouns, verbs, and adjectives are chosen first and then are arranged, qualified, etc., by autoclitic responses to these internal activities.[45]

This view of sentence structure, whether phrased in terms of autoclitics, syncategorematic expressions, or grammatical and lexical morphemes, is inadequate. *Sheep provide wool* has no (physical) frame at all, but no other arrangement of these words is an English sentence. The sequences *furiously sleep ideas green colorless* and *friendly young dogs seem harmless* have the same frames, but only one is a sentence of English (similarly, only one of the sequences formed by reading these from back to front). *Struggling artists can be a nuisance* has the same frame as *marking papers can be a nuisance*, but is quite different in sentence structure, as can be seen by replacing *can be* by *is* or *are* in both cases. There are many other similar and equally simple examples. It is evident that more is involved in sentence structure than insertion of lexical items in grammatical frames; no approach to language that fails to take these deeper processes into account can possibly achieve much success in accounting for actual linguistic behavior.

11. The preceding discussion covers all the major notions that Skinner introduces in his descriptive system. My purpose in discussing the concepts one by one was to show that in each case, if we take his terms in their literal meaning, the description covers almost no aspect of verbal behavior, and if we take them metaphorically, the description offers no improvement over various traditional formulations. The terms borrowed from experimental psychology simply lose their objective meaning with this extension, and take over the full vagueness of ordinary language. Since Skinner limits himself to such a small set of terms for paraphrase, many important distinctions are obscured. I think that this analysis supports the view expressed in §1 above, that elimination of the independent contribution of the speaker and learner (a result which Skinner considers of great importance, cf. 311–2) can be achieved only at the cost

of eliminating all significance from the descriptive system, which then operates at a level so gross and crude that no answers are suggested to the most elementary questions.[46] The questions to which Skinner has addressed his speculations are hopelessly premature. It is futile to inquire into the causation of verbal behavior until much more is known about the specific character of this behavior; and there is little point in speculating about the process of acquisition without much better understanding of what is acquired.

Anyone who seriously approaches the study of linguistic behavior, whether linguist, psychologist, or philosopher, must quickly become aware of the enormous difficulty of stating a problem which will define the area of his investigations, and which will not be either completely trivial or hopelessly beyond the range of present-day understanding and technique. In selecting functional analysis as his problem, Skinner has set himself a task of the latter type. In an extremely interesting and insightful paper,[47] K. S. Lashley has implicitly delimited a class of problems which can be approached in a fruitful way by the linguist and psychologist, and which are clearly preliminary to those with which Skinner is concerned. Lashley recognizes, as anyone must who seriously considers the data, that the composition and production of an utterance is not simply a matter of stringing together a sequence of responses under the control of outside stimulation and intraverbal association, and that the syntactic organization of an utterance is not something directly represented in any simple way in the physical structure of the utterance itself. A variety of observations lead him to conclude that syntactic structure is "a generalized pattern imposed on the specific acts as they occur," and that "a consideration of the structure of the sentence and other motor sequences will show . . . that there are, behind the overtly expressed sequences, a multiplicity of integrative processes which can only be inferred from the final results of their activity." He also comments on the great difficulty of determining the "selective mechanisms" used in the actual construction of a particular utterance.

Although present-day linguistics cannot provide a precise account of these integrative processes, imposed patterns, and selective mechanisms, it can at least set itself the problem of characterizing these completely. It is reasonable to regard the grammar of a language *L* ideally as a mechanism that provides an enumeration of the sentences of *L* in something like the way in which a deductive theory gives an enumeration of a set of theorems. ("Grammar," in this sense of the word, includes phonology.) Furthermore, the theory of language can be regarded as a study of the formal properties of such grammars, and, with a precise enough formulation, this general theory can provide a uniform method for determining, from the process of generation of a given sentence, a structural description which can give a good deal of insight into how this sentence is used and understood. In short, it should be possible to derive from a properly formulated grammar a statement of the integrative processes and generalized patterns imposed on the specific acts that constitute an utterance. The rules of a grammar of the appropriate form can be subdivided into the two types, optional and obligatory; only the latter must be applied in generating an utterance. The optional rules of the grammar can be viewed, then, as the selective mechanisms involved in the production of a particular utterance. The problem of specifying these integrative processes and selective mechanisms is nontrivial and not beyond the range of possible investigation. The results of such a study might, as Lashley suggests, be of independent interest for psychology and neurology (and conversely). Although such a study, even if successful, would by no means answer the major problems involved in the investigation of meaning and the causation of behavior, it surely will not be unrelated to these. It is at least possible, furthermore, that such notions as "semantic generalization," to which such heavy appeal is made in all approaches to language in use, conceal complexities and specific structure of inference not far different from those that can be studied and exhibited in the case of syntax, and that consequently the general character of the results of syntactic investigations may be a corrective to oversimplified approaches to the theory of meaning.

The behavior of the speaker, listener, and learner of language constitutes, of course, the actual data for any study of language. The construction of a grammar which enumerates sentences in such a way that a meaningful structural description can be determined for each sentence does not in itself provide an account of this actual behavior. It merely characterizes abstractly the ability of one who has mastered the language to distinguish sentences from nonsentences, to understand new sentences (in part), to note certain ambiguities, etc. These are very remarkable abilities. We constantly read and hear new sequences of words, recognize them as sentences, and understand them. It is easy to show that the new events that we accept and understand as sentences are not related to those with which we are familiar by any simple notion of formal (or semantic or statistical) similarity or identity of grammatical frame. Talk of generalization in this case is entirely pointless and empty. It appears that we recognize a new item as a sentence not because it matches some familiar item in any simple way, but because it is generated by the grammar that each individual has somehow and in some form internalized. And we understand a new sentence, in part, because we are somehow capable of determining the process by which this sentence is derived in this grammar.

Suppose that we manage to construct grammars having the properties outlined above. We can then attempt to describe and study the achievement of the speaker, listener, and learner. The speaker and the listener, we must assume, have already acquired the capacities characterized abstractly by the grammar. The speaker's task is to select a particular compatible set of optional rules. If we know, from grammatical study, what choices are available to him and what conditions of compatibility the choices must meet, we can proceed meaningfully to investigate the factors that lead him to make one or another choice. The listener (or reader) must determine, from an exhibited utterance, what optional rules were chosen in the construction of the utterance. It must be admitted that the ability of a human being to do this far surpasses our present understanding. The child who learns a language has in some sense constructed the grammar for himself on the basis of his observation of sentences and nonsentences (i.e., corrections by the verbal community). Study of the actual observed ability of a speaker to distinguish sentences from nonsentences, detect ambiguities, etc., apparently forces us to the conclusion that this grammar is of an extremely complex and abstract character, and that the young child has succeeded in carrying out what from the formal point of view, at least, seems to be a remarkable type of theory construction. Furthermore, this task is accomplished in an astonishingly short time, to a large extent independently of intelligence, and in a comparable way by all children. Any theory of learning must cope with these facts.

It is not easy to accept the view that a child is capable of constructing an extremely complex mechanism for generating a set of sentences, some of which he has heard, or that an adult can instantaneously determine whether (and if so, how) a particular item is generated by this mechanism, which has many of the properties of an abstract deductive theory. Yet this appears to be a fair description of the performance of the speaker, listener, and learner. If this is correct, we can predict that a direct attempt to account for the actual behavior of speaker, listener, and learner, not based on a prior understanding of the structure of grammars, will achieve very limited success. The grammar must be regarded as a component in the behavior of the speaker and listener which can only be inferred, as Lashley has put it, from the resulting physical acts. The fact that all normal children acquire essentially comparable grammars of great complexity with remarkable rapidity suggests that human beings are somehow specially designed to do this, with data-handling or "hypothesis-formulating" ability of unknown character and complexity.[48] The study of linguistic structure may ultimately lead to some significant insights into this matter. At the moment the question cannot be seriously posed, but in principle it may be possible to study the problem of determining what the built-in structure of an information-processing (hypothesis-forming) system must be to enable it to arrive at the grammar of a language from the available data in the available time. At any rate, just as the attempt to eliminate the contribution of the speaker leads to a "mentalistic" descriptive system that succeeds only in blurring important traditional distinctions, a refusal to study the contribution of the child to language learning permits only a superficial account of language acquisition, with a vast and unanalyzed contribution attributed to a step called "generalization" which in fact includes just about everything of interest in this process. If the study of language is limited in these ways, it seems inevitable that major aspects of verbal behavior will remain a mystery.

2.

Preface to *Aspects of the Theory of Syntax*

The idea that a language is based on a system of rules determining the interpretation of its infinitely many sentences is by no means novel. Well over a century ago, it was expressed with reasonable clarity by Wilhelm von Humboldt, in his famous but rarely studied introduction to general linguistics (Humboldt, 1836). His view that a language "makes infinite use of finite means" and that its grammar must describe the processes that make this possible is, furthermore, an outgrowth of a persistent concern, within rationalistic philosophy of language and mind, with this "creative" aspect of language use (for discussion, see Chomsky, 1964, *Cartesian Linguistics*). What is more, it seems that even Panini's grammar can be interpreted as a fragment of such a "generative grammar," in essentially the contemporary sense of this term.

Nevertheless, within modern linguistics, it is chiefly within the last few years that fairly substantial attempts have been made to construct explicit generative grammars for particular languages and to explore their consequences. No great surprise should be occasioned by the extensive discussion and debate concerning the proper formulation of the theory of generative grammar and the correct description of the languages that have been most intensively studied. The tentative character of any conclusions that can now be advanced concerning linguistic theory, or, for that matter, English grammar, should certainly be obvious to anyone working in this area. (It is sufficient to consider the vast range of linguistic phenomena that have resisted insightful formula-

This chapter first appeared in *Aspects of the Theory of Syntax* (Cambridge, MA: MIT Press, 1965), v–vii.

tion in any terms.) Still, it seems that certain fairly substantial conclusions are emerging and receiving continually increased support. In particular, the central role of grammatical transformations in any empirically adequate generative grammar seems to me to be established quite firmly, though there remain many questions as to the proper form of the theory of transformational grammar.

This monograph is an exploratory study of various problems that have arisen in the course of work on transformational grammar, which is presupposed throughout as a general framework for the discussion. What is at issue here is precisely how this theory should be formulated. This study deals, then, with questions that are at the border of research in transformational grammar. For some, definite answers will be proposed; but more often the discussion will merely raise issues and consider possible approaches to them without reaching any definite conclusion.

3.

Methodological Preliminaries

§1. GENERATIVE GRAMMARS AS THEORIES OF LINGUISTIC COMPETENCE

This study will touch on a variety of topics in syntactic theory and English syntax, a few in some detail, several quite superficially, and none exhaustively. It will be concerned with the syntactic component of a generative grammar, that is, with the rules that specify the well-formed strings of minimal syntactically functioning units (*formatives*) and assign structural information of various kinds both to these strings and to strings that deviate from well-formedness in certain respects.

The general framework within which this investigation will proceed has been presented in many places, and some familiarity with the theoretical and descriptive studies listed in the bibliography is presupposed. In this chapter, I shall survey briefly some of the main background assumptions, making no serious attempt here to justify them but only to sketch them clearly.

Linguistic theory is concerned primarily with an ideal speaker-listener, in a completely homogeneous speech-community, who knows its language perfectly and is unaffected by such grammatically irrelevant conditions as memory limitations, distractions, shifts of attention and interest, and errors (random or characteristic) in applying his knowledge of the language in actual performance. This seems to me to have been the position of the founders

---

This chapter first appeared as part 1 of "Methodological Preliminaries," in *Aspects of the Theory of Syntax* (Cambridge, MA: MIT Press, 1965), 3–9.

of modern general linguistics, and no cogent reason for modifying it has been offered. To study actual linguistic performance, we must consider the interaction of a variety of factors, of which the underlying competence of the speaker-hearer is only one. In this respect, study of language is no different from empirical investigation of other complex phenomena.

We thus make a fundamental distinction between *competence* (the speaker-hearer's knowledge of his language) and *performance* (the actual use of language in concrete situations). Only under the idealization set forth in the preceding paragraph is performance a direct reflection of competence. In actual fact, it obviously could not directly reflect competence. A record of natural speech will show numerous false starts, deviations from rules, changes of plan in mid-course, and so on. The problem for the linguist, as well as for the child learning the language, is to determine from the data of performance the underlying system of rules that has been mastered by the speaker-hearer and that he puts to use in actual performance. Hence, in the technical sense, linguistic theory is mentalistic, since it is concerned with discovering a mental reality underlying actual behavior.[1] Observed use of language or hypothesized dispositions to respond, habits, and so on, may provide evidence as to the nature of this mental reality, but surely cannot constitute the actual subject matter of linguistics, if this is to be a serious discipline. The distinction I am noting here is related to the *langue-parole* distinction of Saussure; but it is necessary to reject his concept of *langue* as merely a systematic inventory of items and to return rather to the Humboldtian conception of underlying competence as a system of generative processes.[2]

A grammar of a language purports to be a description of the ideal speaker-hearer's intrinsic competence. If the grammar is, furthermore, perfectly explicit—in other words, if it does not rely on the intelligence of the understanding reader but rather provides an explicit analysis of his contribution—we may (somewhat redundantly) call it a *generative grammar*.

A fully adequate grammar must assign to each of an infinite range of sentences a structural description indicating how this sentence is understood by the ideal speaker-hearer. This is the traditional problem of descriptive linguistics, and traditional grammars give a wealth of information concerning structural descriptions of sentences. However, valuable as they obviously are, traditional grammars are deficient in that they leave unexpressed many of the basic regularities of the language with which they are concerned. This fact is particularly clear on the level of syntax, where no traditional or structuralist grammar goes beyond classification of particular examples to the stage of formulation of generative rules on any significant scale. An analysis of the best existing grammars will quickly reveal that this is a defect of principle, not just a matter of empirical detail or logical preciseness.

Nevertheless, it seems obvious that the attempt to explore this largely uncharted territory can most profitably begin with a study of the kind of structural information presented by traditional grammars and the kind of linguistic processes that have been exhibited, however informally, in these grammars.[3]

The limitations of traditional and structuralist grammars should be clearly appreciated. Although such grammars may contain full and explicit lists of exceptions and irregularities, they provide only examples and hints concerning the regular and productive syntactic processes. Traditional linguistic theory was not unaware of this fact. For example, James Beattie remarks that

> Languages, therefore, resemble men in this respect, that, though each has peculiarities, whereby it is distinguished from every other, yet all have certain qualities in common. The peculiarities of individual tongues are explained in their respective grammars and dictionaries. Those things, that all languages have in common, or that are necessary to every language, are treated of in a science, which some have called *Universal* or *Philosophical* grammar.[4]

Somewhat earlier, Du Marsais defines universal and particular grammar in the following way:

> Il y a dans la grammaire des observations qui conviènnent à toutes les langues; ces observations forment ce qu'on appelle la grammaire générale: telles sont les remarques que l'on a faites sur les sons articulés, sur les lettres qui sont les signes de ces sons; sur la nature des mots, et sur les différentes manières dont ils doivent être ou arrangés ou terminés pour faire un sens. Outre ces observations générales, il y en a qui ne sont propres qu'à une langue particulière; et c'est ce qui forme les grammaires particulières de chaque langue.[5]

Within traditional linguistic theory, furthermore, it was clearly understood that one of the qualities that all languages have in common is their "creative" aspect. Thus an essential property of language is that it provides the means for expressing indefinitely many thoughts and for reacting appropriately in an indefinite range of new situations.[6] The grammar of a particular language, then, is to be supplemented by a universal grammar that accommodates the creative aspect of language use and expresses the deep-seated regularities which, being universal, are omitted from the grammar itself. Therefore it is quite proper for a grammar to discuss only exceptions and irregularities in any detail. It is only when supplemented by a universal grammar that the grammar of a language provides a full account of the speaker-hearer's competence.

Modern linguistics, however, has not explicitly recognized the necessity for supplementing a "particular grammar" of a language by a universal grammar if it is to achieve descriptive adequacy. It has, in fact, characteristically rejected the study of universal grammar as misguided; and, as noted before, it has not attempted to deal with the creative aspect of language use. It thus suggests no way to overcome the fundamental descriptive inadequacy of structuralist grammars.

Another reason for the failure of traditional grammars, particular or universal, to attempt a precise statement of regular processes of sentence formation and sentence interpretation lay in the widely held belief that there is a "natural order of thoughts" that is mirrored by the order of words. Hence, the rules of sentence formation do not really belong to grammar but to some other subject in which the "order of thoughts" is studied. Thus in the *Grammaire générale et raisonnée* it is asserted that, aside from figurative speech, the sequence of words follows an "ordre naturel," which conforms "à l'expression naturelle de nos pensées."[7] Consequently, few grammatical rules need be formulated beyond the rules of ellipsis, inversion, and so on, which determine the figurative use of language. The same view appears in many forms and variants. To mention just one additional example, in an interesting essay devoted largely to the question of how the simultaneous and sequential array of ideas is reflected in the order of words, Diderot concludes that French is unique among languages in the degree to which the order of words corresponds to the natural order of thoughts and ideas.[8] Thus "quel que soit l'ordre des termes dans une langue ancienne ou moderne, l'esprit de l'écrivain a suivi l'ordre didactique de la syntaxe française"[9]; "Nous disons les choses en français, comme l'esprit est forcé de les considérer en quelque langue qu'on écrive."[10] With admirable consistency he goes on to conclude that "notre langue *pédestre* a sur les autres l'avantage de l'utile sur l'agréable"[11]; thus French is appropriate for the sciences, whereas Greek, Latin, Italian, and English "sont plus avantageuses pour les lettres." Moreover,

> le bons sens choisirait la langue française; mais . . . l'imagination et les passions donneront la préférence aux langues anciennes et à celles de nos voisins . . . il faut parler français dans la société et dans les écoles de philosophie; et grec, latin, anglais, dans les chaires et sur les théâtres; . . . notre langue sera celle de la vérité, si jamais elle revient sur la terre; et . . . la grecque, la latine et les autres seront les langues de la fable et du mensonge. Le français est fait pour instruire, éclairer et convaincre; le grec, le latin, l'italien, l'anglais, pour persuader, émouvoir et tromper: parlez grec, latin, italien au peuple; mais parlez français au sage.[12]

In any event, insofar as the order of words is determined by factors independent of language, it is not necessary to describe it in a particular or universal grammar, and we therefore have principled grounds for excluding an explicit formulation of syntactic processes from grammar. It is worth noting that this naïve view of language structure persists to modern times in various forms, for example, in Saussure's image of a sequence of expressions corresponding to an amorphous sequence of concepts or in the common characterization of language use as merely a matter of use of words and phrases.[13]

But the fundamental reason for this inadequacy of traditional grammars is a more technical one. Although it was well understood that linguistic processes are in some sense "creative," the technical devices for expressing a system of recursive processes were simply not available until much more recently. In fact, a real understanding of how a language can (in Humboldt's words) "make infinite use of finite means" has developed only within the last thirty years, in the course of studies in the foundations of mathematics. Now that these insights are readily available it is possible to return to the problems that were raised, but not solved, in traditional linguistic theory, and to attempt an explicit formulation of the "creative" processes of language. There is, in short, no longer a technical barrier to the full-scale study of generative grammars.

Returning to the main theme, by a generative grammar I mean simply a system of rules that in some explicit and well-defined way assigns structural descriptions to sentences. Obviously, every speaker of a language has mastered and internalized a generative grammar that expresses his knowledge of his language. This is not to say that he is aware of the rules of the grammar or even that he can become aware of them, or that his statements about his intuitive knowledge of the language are necessarily accurate. Any interesting generative grammar will be dealing, for the most part, with mental processes that are far beyond the level of actual or even potential consciousness; furthermore, it is quite apparent that a speaker's reports and-viewpoints about his behavior and his competence may be in error. Thus a generative grammar attempts to specify what the speaker actually knows, not what he may report about his knowledge. Similarly, a theory of visual perception would attempt to account for what a person actually sees and the mechanisms that determine this rather than his statements about what he sees and why, though these statements may provide useful, in fact, compelling evidence for such a theory.

To avoid what has been a continuing misunderstanding, it is perhaps worthwhile to reiterate that a generative grammar is not a model for a speaker or a hearer. It attempts to characterize in the most neutral possible terms the knowledge of the language that provides the basis for actual use of language by a speaker-hearer. When we speak of a grammar as generating a sentence with a certain structural description, we mean simply that the grammar assigns this structural description to the sentence. When we say that a sentence has a certain derivation with respect to a particular generative grammar, we say nothing about how the speaker or hearer might proceed, in some practical or efficient way, to construct such a derivation. These questions belong to the theory of language use—the theory of performance. No doubt, a reasonable model of language use will incorporate, as a basic component, the generative grammar that expresses the speaker-hearer's knowledge of the language; but this generative grammar does not, in itself, prescribe the character or functioning of a perceptual model or a model of speech production.[14]

Confusion over this matter has been sufficiently persistent to suggest that a terminological change might be in order. Nevertheless, I think that the term "generative grammar" is completely appropriate, and have therefore continued to use it. The term "generate" is familiar in the sense intended here in logic, particularly in Post's theory of combinatorial systems. Furthermore, "generate" seems to be the most appropriate translation for Humboldt's term *erzeugen*, which he frequently uses, it seems, in essentially the sense here intended. Since this use of the term "generate" is well established both in logic and in the tradition of linguistic theory, I can see no reason for a revision of terminology.

4.

The Responsibility of Intellectuals

Twenty years ago, Dwight Macdonald published a series of articles in *Politics* on the responsibilities of peoples, and specifically, the responsibility of intellectuals. I read them as an undergraduate, in the years just after the war, and had occasion to read them again a few months ago. They seem to me to have lost none of their power or persuasiveness. Macdonald is concerned with the question of war guilt. He asks the question: To what extent were the German or Japanese people responsible for the atrocities committed by their governments? And, quite properly, he turns the question back to us: To what extent are the British or American people responsible for the vicious terror bombings of civilians, perfected as a technique of warfare by the Western democracies and reaching their culmination in Hiroshima and Nagasaki, surely among the most unspeakable crimes in history? To an undergraduate in 1945–1946—to anyone whose political and moral consciousness had been formed by the horrors of the 1930s, by the war in Ethiopia, the Russian purge, the "China incident," the Spanish Civil War, the Nazi atrocities, the Western reaction to these events and, in part, complicity in them—these questions had particular significance and poignancy.

With respect to the responsibility of intellectuals, there are still other, equally disturbing questions. Intellectuals are in a position to expose the lies of

---

This is a revised version of a talk given at Harvard and published in *Mosaic*, June 1966. It appeared in substantially this form in the *New York Review of Books*, February 23, 1967. The present version is reprinted from Theodore Roszak, ed., *The Dissenting Academy* (New York: Pantheon Books, 1968), reprinted in *American Power and the New Mandarins* (New York: Pantheon Books, 1969; New York: The New Press, 2002), 323–366.

governments, to analyze actions according to their causes and motives and often hidden intentions. In the Western world at least, they have the power that comes from political liberty, from access to information and freedom of expression. For a privileged minority, Western democracy provides the leisure, the facilities, and the training to seek the truth lying hidden behind the veil of distortion and misrepresentation, ideology, and class interest through which the events of current history are presented to us. The responsibilities of intellectuals, then, are much deeper than what Macdonald calls the "responsibility of peoples," given the unique privileges that intellectuals enjoy.

The issues that Macdonald raised are as pertinent today as they were twenty years ago. We can hardly avoid asking ourselves to what extent the American people bear responsibility for the savage American assault on a largely helpless rural population in Vietnam, still another atrocity in what Asians see as the "Vasco da Gama era" of world history. As for those of us who stood by in silence and apathy as this catastrophe slowly took shape over the past dozen years, on what page of history do we find our proper place? Only the most insensible can escape these questions. I want to return to them, later on, after a few scattered remarks about the responsibility of intellectuals and how, in practice, they go about meeting this responsibility in the mid-1960s.

It is the responsibility of intellectuals to speak the truth and to expose lies. This, at least, may seem enough of a truism to pass without comment. Not so, however. For the modern intellectual, it is not at all obvious. Thus we have Martin Heidegger writing, in a pro-Hitler declaration of 1933, that "truth is the revelation of that which makes a people certain, clear, and strong in its action and knowledge"; it is only this kind of "truth" that one has a responsibility to speak. Americans tend to be more forthright. When Arthur Schlesinger was asked by the *New York Times*, in November 1965, to explain the contradiction between his published account of the Bay of Pigs incident and the story he had given the press at the time of the attack, he simply remarked that he had lied; and a few days later, he went on to compliment the *Times* for also having suppressed information on the planned invasion, in "the national interest," as this was defined by the group of arrogant and deluded men of whom Schlesinger gives such a flattering portrait in his recent account of the Kennedy administration. It is of no particular interest that one man is quite happy to lie in behalf of a cause which he knows to be unjust; but it is significant that such events provoke so little response in the intellectual community—no feeling, for example, that there is something strange in the offer of a major chair in humanities to a historian who feels it to be his duty to persuade the world that an American-sponsored invasion of a nearby country is nothing of the sort. And what of the incredible sequence of lies on the part of our government and its spokesmen concerning such matters as negotiations in Vietnam? The facts are known to all who care to know. The press, foreign and domestic, has presented documentation to refute each falsehood as it appears. But the power of the government propaganda apparatus is such that the citizen who does not undertake a research project on the subject can hardly hope to confront government pronouncements with fact.[1]

The deceit and distortion surrounding the American invasion of Vietnam are by now so familiar that they have lost their power to shock. It is therefore well to recall that although new levels of cynicism are constantly being reached, their clear antecedents were accepted at home with quiet toleration. It is a useful exercise to compare government statements at the time of the invasion of Guatemala in 1954 with Eisenhower's admission—to be more accurate, his boast—a decade later that American planes were sent "to help the invaders."[2] Nor is it only in moments of crisis that duplicity is considered perfectly in order. "New Frontiersmen," for example, have scarcely distinguished themselves by a passionate concern for historical accuracy, even when they are not being called upon to provide a "propaganda cover" for ongoing actions. For example, Arthur Schlesinger describes the bombing of North Vietnam and the massive escalation of military commitment in early 1965 as based on a "perfectly rational argument": ". . . so long as the Vietcong thought they were going to win the war, they obviously would not be interested in any kind of negotiated settlement."[3] The date is important. Had the statement been made six months earlier, one could attribute it to ignorance. But this statement appeared after months of front-page news reports detailing the United Nations, North Vietnamese, and Soviet initiatives that preceded the February 1965 escalation and that, in fact, continued for several weeks after the bombing began, after months of soulsearching by Washington correspondents who were trying desperately to find some mitigating circumstances for the startling deception that had been revealed. (Chalmers Roberts, for example, wrote with unconscious irony that late February 1965 "hardly seemed to Washington to be a propitious moment for negotiations [since] Mr. Johnson . . . had just ordered the first bombing of North Vietnam in an effort to bring Hanoi to a conference table where bargaining chips on both sides would be more closely matched."[4]) Coming at this moment, Schlesinger's statement is less an example of deceit than of contempt—contempt for an audience that can be expected to tolerate such behavior with silence, if not approval.[5]

To turn to someone closer to the actual formation and implementation of policy, consider some of the reflections of Walt Rostow, a man who, according to Schlesinger, brought a "spacious historical view" to the conduct of foreign affairs in the Kennedy administration.[6] According to his analysis, the guerrilla warfare in Indochina in 1946 was launched by Stalin,[7] and Hanoi initiated the guerrilla war against South Vietnam in 1958 (*The View from the Seventh Floor*, pp. 39 and 152). Similarly, the Communist planners probed the "free world spectrum of defense" in Northern Azerbaijan and Greece (where Stalin "supported substantial guerrilla warfare"—ibid., pp. 36 and 148), operating from plans carefully laid in 1945. And in Central Europe, the Soviet Union was not "prepared to accept a solution which would remove the dangerous tensions from Central Europe at the risk of even slowly staged corrosion of communism in East Germany" (ibid., p. 156).

It is interesting to compare these observations with studies by scholars actually concerned with historical events. The remark about Stalin's initiating the first Vietnamese war in 1946 does not even merit refutation. As to Hanoi's purported initiative of 1958, the situation is more clouded. But even government sources[8] concede that in 1959 Hanoi received the first direct reports of what Diem referred to[9] as his own Algerian war, and that only after this did they lay their plans to involve themselves in this struggle. In fact, in December 1958 Hanoi made another of its many attempts—rebuffed once again by Saigon and the United States—to establish diplomatic and commercial relations with the Saigon government on the basis of the status quo.[10] Rostow offers no evidence of Stalin's support for the Greek guerrillas: in fact, though the historical record is far from clear, it seems that Stalin was by no means pleased with the adventurism of the Greek guerrillas, who, from his point of view, were upsetting the satisfactory postwar imperialist settlement.[11]

Rostow's remarks about Germany are more interesting still. He does not see fit to mention, for example, the Russian notes of March–April 1952, which proposed unification of Germany under internationally supervised elections, with withdrawal of all troops within a year, *if* there was a guarantee that a reunified Germany would not be permitted to join a Western military alliance.[12] And he has also momentarily forgotten his own characterization of the strategy of the Truman and Eisenhower administrations: "to avoid any serious negotiation with the Soviet Union until the West could confront Moscow with German rearmament within an organized European framework, as a *fait accompli*"[13]—to be sure, in defiance of the Potsdam agreements.

But most interesting of all is Rostow's reference to Iran. The facts are that there was a Russian attempt to impose by force a pro-Soviet government in Northern Azerbaijan that would grant the Soviet Union access to Iranian oil. This was rebuffed by superior Anglo-American force in 1946, at which point the more powerful imperialism obtained full rights to Iranian oil for itself, with the installation of a pro-Western government. We recall what happened when, for a brief period in the early 1950s, the only Iranian government with something of a popular base experimented with the curious idea that Iranian oil should belong to the Iranians. What is interesting, however, is the description of Northern Azerbaijan as part of "the free world spectrum of defense." It is pointless, by now, to comment on the debasement of the phrase "free world." But by what law of nature does Iran, with its resources, fall within Western dominion? The bland assumption that it does is most revealing of deep-seated attitudes towards the conduct of foreign affairs.

In addition to this growing lack of concern for truth, we find, in recent statements, a real or feigned naiveté with regard to American actions that reaches startling proportions. For example, Arthur Schlesinger has recently characterized our Vietnamese policies of 1954 as "part of our general program of international goodwill."[14] Unless intended as irony, this remark shows either a colossal cynicism or an inability, on a scale that defies comment, to comprehend elementary phenomena of contemporary history. Similarly, what is one to make of the testimony of Thomas Schelling before the House Foreign Affairs Committee, January 27, 1966, in which he discusses the two great dangers if all Asia "goes Communist"?[15] First, this would exclude "the United States and what we call Western civilization from a large part of the world that is poor and colored and potentially hostile." Second, "a country like the United States probably cannot maintain self-confidence if just about the greatest thing it ever attempted, namely to create the basis for decency and prosperity and democratic government in the underdeveloped world, had to be acknowledged as a failure or as an attempt that we wouldn't try again." It surpasses belief that a person with even minimal acquaintance with the record of American foreign policy could produce such statements.

It surpasses belief, that is, unless we look at the matter from a more historical point of view, and place such statements in the context of the hypocritical moralism of the past; for example, of Woodrow Wilson, who was going to teach the Latin Americans the art of good government, and who wrote (1902) that it is "our peculiar duty" to teach colonial peoples "order and self-control . . . [and] . . . the drill and habit of law and obedience." Or of the missionaries of the 1840s, who described the hideous and degrading opium wars as "the result of a great design of Providence to make the wickedness of men subserve his purposes of mercy toward China, in breaking through her wall of exclusion, and bringing the empire into more immediate contact with western and Christian nations." Or, to approach the present, of A. A. Berle, who, in commenting on the Dominican intervention, has the impertinence to attribute the problems of the Caribbean countries to imperialism—*Russian* imperialism.[16]

As a final example of this failure of skepticism, consider the remarks of Henry Kissinger in concluding his presentation in a Harvard-Oxford television debate on American Vietnam policies. He observed, rather sadly, that what disturbs him most is that others question not our judgment but our motives—a remarkable comment on the part of one whose professional concern is political analysis, that is, analysis of the actions of governments in terms of motives that are unexpressed in official propaganda and perhaps only dimly perceived by those whose acts they govern. No one would be disturbed by an analysis of the political behavior of Russians, French, or Tanzanians, questioning their motives and interpreting their actions in terms of long-range interests, perhaps well concealed behind official rhetoric. But it is an article of faith that American motives are pure and not subject to analysis (see note 1). Although it is nothing new in American intellectual history—or, for that matter, in the general history of imperialist apologia—this innocence becomes increasingly distasteful as the power it serves grows more dominant in world affairs and more capable, therefore, of the unconstrained viciousness that the mass media present to us each day. We are hardly the first power in history to combine material interests, great technological capacity, and an utter disregard for the suffering and misery of the lower orders. The long tradition of naiveté and self-righteousness that disfigures our intellectual history, however, must serve as a warning to the Third World, if such a warning is needed, as to how our protestations of sincerity and benign intent are to be interpreted.

The basic assumptions of the "New Frontiersmen" should be pondered carefully by those who look forward to the involvement of academic intellectuals in politics. For example, I have referred to Arthur Schlesinger's objections to the Bay of Pigs invasion, but the reference was imprecise. True, he felt that it was a "terrible idea," but "not because the notion of sponsoring an exile attempt to overthrow Castro seemed intolerable in itself." Such a reaction would be the merest sentimentality, unthinkable to a tough-minded realist. The difficulty, rather, was that it seemed unlikely that the deception could succeed. The operation, in his view, was ill-conceived but not otherwise objectionable.[17] In a similar vein, Schlesinger quotes with approval Kennedy's "realistic" assessment of the situation resulting from Trujillo's assassination: "There are three possibilities in descending order of preference: a decent democratic regime, a continuation of the Trujillo regime or a Castro regime. We ought to aim at the first, but we really can't renounce the second until we are sure that we can avoid the third." [18] The reason why the third possibility is so intolerable is explained a few pages later: "Communist success in Latin America would deal a much harder blow to the power and influence of the United States." Of course, we can never really be sure of avoiding the third possibility; therefore, in practice, we will always settle for the second, as we are now doing in Brazil and Argentina, for example.[19]

Or consider Walt Rostow's views on American policy in Asia.[20] The basis on which we must build this policy is that "we are openly threatened and we feel menaced by Communist China." To prove that we are menaced is of course unnecessary, and the matter receives no attention; it is enough that we feel menaced. Our policy must be based on our national heritage and our national interests. Our national heritage is briefly outlined in the following terms: "Throughout the nineteenth century, in good conscience Americans could devote themselves to the extension of both their principles and their power on this continent," making use of "the somewhat elastic concept of the Monroe doctrine" and, of course, extending "the American interest to Alaska and the mid-Pacific islands. . . . Both our insistence on unconditional surrender and the idea of postwar occupation . . . represented the formulation of American security interests in Europe and Asia." So much for our heritage. As to our interests, the matter is equally simple. Fundamental is our "profound interest that societies abroad develop and strengthen those elements in their respective cultures that elevate and protect the dignity of the individual against the state." At the same time, we must counter the "ideological threat," namely "the possibility that the Chinese Communists can prove to Asians by progress in China that Communist methods are better and faster than democratic methods." Nothing is said about those people in Asian cultures to whom our "conception of the proper relation of the individual to the state" may not be the uniquely important value, people who might, for example, be concerned with preserving the "dignity of the individual" against concentrations of foreign or domestic capital, or against semifeudal structures (such as Trujillo-type dictatorships) introduced or kept in power by American arms. All of this is flavored with allusions to "our religious and ethical value systems" and to our "diffuse and complex concepts," which are to the Asian mind "so much more difficult to grasp" than Marxist dogma, and are so "disturbing to some Asians" because of "their very lack of dogmatism."

Such intellectual contributions as these suggest the need for a correction to De Gaulle's remark, in his memoirs, about the American "will to power, cloaking itself in idealism." By now, this will to power is not so much cloaked in idealism as it is drowned in fatuity. And academic intellectuals have made their unique contribution to this sorry picture.

Let us, however, return to the war in Vietnam and the response that it has aroused among American intellectuals. A striking feature of the recent debate on Southeast Asian policy has been the distinction that is commonly drawn between "responsible criticism," on the one hand, and "sentimental" or "emotional" or "hysterical" criticism, on the other. There is much to be learned from a careful study of the terms in which this distinction is drawn. The "hysterical critics" are to be identified, apparently, by their irrational refusal to accept one fundamental political axiom, namely, that the United States has the right to extend its power and control without limit, insofar as is feasible. Responsible criticism does not challenge this assumption, but argues, rather, that we probably can't "get away with it" at this particular time and place.

A distinction of this sort seems to be what Irving Kristol has in mind, for example, in his analysis of the protest over Vietnam policy, in *Encounter*, August 1965. He contrasts the responsible critics, such as Walter Lippmann, the *New York Times*, and Senator Fulbright, with the "teach-in movement." "Unlike the university protesters," he maintains, "Mr. Lippmann engages in no presumptuous suppositions as to 'what the Vietnamese people really want'—he obviously doesn't much care—or in legalistic exegesis as to whether, or to what extent, there is 'aggression' or 'revolution' in South Vietnam. His is a *realpolitik* point of view; and he will apparently even contemplate the possibility of a *nuclear* war against China in extreme circumstances." This is commendable, and contrasts favorably, for Kristol, with the talk of the "unreasonable, ideological types" in the teach-in movement, who often seem to be motivated by such absurdities as "simple, virtuous 'anti-imperialism,' " who deliver "harangues on 'the power structure,' " and who even sometimes stoop so low as to read "articles and reports from the foreign press on the American presence in Vietnam." Furthermore, these nasty types are often psychologists, mathematicians, chemists, or philosophers (just as, incidentally, those most vocal in protest in the Soviet Union are generally physicists, literary intellectuals, and others remote from the exercise of power), rather than people with Washington contacts, who of course realize that "had they a new, good idea about Vietnam, they would get a prompt and respectful hearing" in Washington.

I am not interested here in whether Kristol's characterization of protest and dissent is accurate, but rather in the assumptions that it expresses with respect to such questions as these: Is the purity of American motives a matter that is beyond discussion, or that is irrelevant to discussion? Should decisions be left to "experts" with Washington contacts—that is, even if we assume that they command the necessary knowledge and principles to make the "best" decision, will they invariably do so? And, a logically prior question, is "expertise" applicable—that is, is there a body of theory and of relevant information, not in the public domain, that can be applied to the analysis of foreign policy or that demonstrates the correctness of present actions in some way that the psychologists, mathematicians, chemists, and philosophers are incapable of comprehending? Although Kristol does not examine these questions directly, his attitudes presuppose answers, answers which are wrong in all cases. American aggressiveness, however it may be masked in pious rhetoric, is a dominant force in world affairs and must be analyzed in terms of its causes and motives. There is no body of theory or significant body of relevant information, beyond the comprehension of the layman, which makes policy immune from criticism. To the extent that "expert knowledge" is applied to world affairs, it is surely appropriate—for a person of any integrity, quite necessary—to question its quality and the goals that it serves. These facts seem too obvious to require extended discussion.

A corrective to Kristol's curious belief in the administration's openness to new thinking about Vietnam is provided by McGeorge Bundy in a recent article.[21] As Bundy correctly observes, "on the main stage . . . the argument on Viet Nam turns on tactics, not fundamentals," although, he adds, "there are wild men in the wings." On stage center are, of course, the President (who in his recent trip to Asia had just "magisterially reaffirmed" our interest "in the progress of the people across the Pacific") and his advisers, who deserve "the understanding support of those who want restraint." It is these men who deserve the credit for the fact that "the bombing of the North has been the most accurate and the most restrained in modern warfare."—a solicitude which will be appreciated by the inhabitants, or former inhabitants, of Nam Dinh and Phu Ly and Vinh. It is these men, too, who deserve the credit for what was reported by Malcolm Browne as long ago as May 1965: "In the South, huge sectors of the nation have been declared 'free bombing zones,' in which anything that moves is a legitimate target. Tens of thousands of tons of bombs, rockets, napalm and cannon fire are poured into these vast areas each week. If only by the laws of chance, bloodshed is believed to be heavy in these raids."

Fortunately for the developing countries, Bundy assures us, "American democracy has no enduring taste for imperialism," and "taken as a whole, the stock of American experience, understanding, sympathy and simple knowledge is now much the most impressive in the world." It is true that "four-fifths of all the foreign investing in the world is now done by Americans" and that "the most admired plans and policies . . . are no better than their demonstrable relation to the American interest"—just as it is true, so we read in the same issue of *Foreign Affairs*, that the plans for armed action against Cuba were put into motion a few weeks after Mikoyan visited Havana, "invading what had so long been an almost exclusively American sphere of influence." Unfortunately, such facts as these are often taken by unsophisticated Asian intellectuals as indicating a "taste for imperialism." For example, a number of Indians have expressed their "near exasperation" at the fact that "we have done everything we can to attract foreign capital for fertilizer plants, but the American and the other Western private companies know we are over a barrel, so they demand stringent terms which we just cannot meet,"[22] while "Washington . . . doggedly insists that deals be made in the private sector with private enterprise."[23] But this reaction, no doubt, simply reveals once again how the

Asian mind fails to comprehend the "diffuse and complex concepts" of Western thought.

It may be useful to study carefully the "new, good ideas about Vietnam" that are receiving a "prompt and respectful hearing" in Washington these days. The United States Government Printing Office is an endless source of insight into the moral and intellectual level of this expert advice. In its publications one can read, for example, the testimony of Professor David N. Rowe, director of graduate studies in international relations at Yale University, before the House Committee on Foreign Affairs (see note 15). Professor Rowe proposes (p. 266) that the United States buy all surplus Canadian and Australian wheat, so that there will be mass starvation in China. These are his words: "Mind you, I am not talking about this as a weapon against the Chinese people. It will be. But that is only incidental. The weapon will be a weapon against the Government because the internal stability of that country cannot be sustained by an unfriendly Government in the face of general starvation." Professor Rowe will have none of the sentimental moralism that might lead one to compare this suggestion with, say, the *Ostpolitik* of Hitler's Germany.[24] Nor does he fear the impact of such policies on other Asian nations, for example Japan. He assures us, from his "very long acquaintance with Japanese questions," that "the Japanese above all are people who respect power and determination." Hence "they will not be so much alarmed by American policy in Vietnam that takes off from a position of power and intends to seek a solution based upon the imposition of our power upon local people that we are in opposition to." What would disturb the Japanese is "a policy of indecision, a policy of refusal to face up to the problems [in China and Vietnam] and to meet our responsibilities there in a positive way," such as the way just cited. A conviction that we were "unwilling to use the power that they know we have" might "alarm the Japanese people very intensely and shake the degree of their friendly relations with us." In fact, a full use of American power would be particularly reassuring to the Japanese, because they have had a demonstration "of the tremendous power in action of the United States . . . because they have felt our power directly." This is surely a prime example of the healthy "*realpolitik* point of view" that Irving Kristol so much admires.

But, one may ask, why restrict ourselves to such indirect means as mass starvation? Why not bombing? No doubt this message is implicit in the remarks to the same committee of the Reverend R. J. de Jaegher, regent of the Institute of Far Eastern Studies, Seton Hall University, who explains that like all people who have lived under Communism, the North Vietnamese "would be perfectly happy to be bombed to be free" (p. 345).

Of course, there must be those who support the Communists. But this is really a matter of small concern, as the Honorable Walter Robertson, Assistant Secretary of State for Far Eastern Affairs from 1953 to 1959, points out in his testimony before the same committee. He assures us that "The Peiping regime . . . represents something less than 3 percent of the population" (p. 402).

Consider, then, how fortunate the Chinese Communist leaders are, compared to the leaders of the Vietcong, who, according to Arthur Goldberg, represent about "one-half of one percent of the population of South Vietnam," that is, about one half the number of new Southern recruits for the Vietcong during 1965, if we can credit Pentagon statistics.[25]

In the face of such experts as these, the scientists and philosophers of whom Kristol speaks would clearly do well to continue to draw their circles in the sand.

Having settled the issue of the political irrelevance of the protest movement, Kristol turns to the question of what motivates it—more generally, what has made students and junior faculty "go left," as he sees it, amid general prosperity and under liberal, welfare state administrations. This, he notes, "is a riddle to which no sociologist has as yet come up with an answer." Since these young people are well off, have good futures, etc., their protest must be irrational. It must be the result of boredom, of too much security, or something of this sort.

Other possibilities come to mind. It might be, for example, that as honest men the students and junior faculty are attempting to find out the truth for themselves rather than ceding the responsibility to "experts" or to government; and it might be that they react with indignation to what they discover. These possibilities Kristol does not reject. They are simply unthinkable, unworthy of consideration. More accurately, these possibilities are inexpressible; the categories in which they are formulated (honesty, indignation) simply do not exist for the tough-minded social scientist.

In this implicit disparagement of traditional intellectual values, Kristol reflects attitudes that are fairly widespread in academic circles. I do not doubt that these attitudes are in part a consequence of the desperate attempt of the social and behavioral sciences to imitate the surface features of sciences that really have significant intellectual content. But they have other sources as well. Anyone can be a moral individual, concerned with human rights and problems; but only a college professor, a trained expert, can solve technical problems by "sophisticated" methods. Ergo, it is only problems of the latter sort that are important or real. Responsible, nonideological experts will give advice on tactical questions; irresponsible "ideological types" will "harangue" about principle and trouble themselves over moral issues and human rights, or over the traditional problems of man and society, concerning which "social and behavioral science" have nothing to offer beyond trivialities. Obviously, these emotional, ideological types are irrational, since, being well off and having power in their grasp, they shouldn't worry about such matters.

At times this pseudoscientific posing reaches levels that are almost pathological. Consider the phenomenon of Herman Kahn, for example. Kahn has been both denounced as immoral and lauded for his courage. By people who should know better, his *On Thermonuclear War* has been described "without qualification . . . [as] . . . one of the great works of our time" (Stuart Hughes). The fact of the matter is that this is surely one of the emptiest works of our time, as can be seen by applying to it the intellectual standards of any existing discipline, by tracing some of its "well-documented conclusions" to the "objective studies" from which they derive, and by following the line of argument, where detectable. Kahn proposes no theories, no explanations, no empirical assumptions that can be tested against their consequences, as do the sciences he is attempting to mimic. He simply suggests a terminology and provides a façade of rationality. When particular policy conclusions are drawn, they are supported only by *ex cathedra* remarks for which no support is even suggested (e.g., "The civil defense line probably should be drawn somewhere below $5 billion annually" to keep from provoking the Russians—why not $50 billion, or $5?). What is more, Kahn is quite aware of this vacuity; in his more judicious moments he claims only that "there is no reason to believe that relatively sophisticated models are more likely to be misleading than the simpler models and analogies frequently used as an aid to judgment." For those whose humor tends towards the macabre, it is easy to play the game of "strategic thinking" à la Kahn, and to prove what one wishes. For example, one of Kahn's basic assumptions is that "an all-out surprise attack in which all resources are devoted to counter-value targets would be so irrational that, barring an incredible lack of sophistication or actual insanity among Soviet decision makers, such an attack is highly unlikely." A simple argument proves the opposite. Premise 1: American decision makers think along the lines outlined by Herman Kahn. Premise 2: Kahn thinks it would be better for everyone to be red than for everyone to be dead. Premise 3: If the Americans were to respond to an all-out counter-value attack, then everyone would be dead. Conclusion: The Americans will not respond to an all-out counter-value attack, and therefore it should be launched without delay. Of course, one can carry the argument a step further. Fact: The Russians have not carried out an all-out counter-value attack. It follows that they are not rational. If they are not rational, there is no point in "strategic thinking." Therefore . . .

Of course this is all nonsense, but nonsense that differs from Kahn's only in the respect that the argument is of slightly greater complexity than anything to be discovered in his work. What is remarkable is that serious people actually pay attention to these absurdities, no doubt because of the façade of tough-mindedness and pseudoscience.

It is a curious and depressing fact that the "antiwar movement" falls prey all too often to similar confusions. In the fall of 1965, for example, there was an International Conference on Alternative Perspectives on Vietnam, which circulated a pamphlet to potential participants stating its assumptions. The plan was to set up study groups in which three "types of intellectual tradition" will be represented: (1) area specialists; (2) "social theory, with special emphasis on theories of the international system, of social change and development, of conflict and conflict resolution, or of revolution"; (3) "the analysis of public policy in terms of basic human values, rooted in various theological, philosophical and humanist traditions." The second intellectual tradition will provide "general propositions, derived from social theory and tested against historical, comparative, or experimental data"; the third "will provide the framework out of which fundamental value questions can be raised and in terms of which the moral implications of societal actions can be analyzed." The hope was that "by approaching the questions [of Vietnam policy] from the moral perspectives of all great religions and philosophical systems, we may find solutions that are more consistent with fundamental human values than current American policy in Vietnam has turned out to be."

In short, the experts on values (i.e., spokesmen for the great religions and philosophical systems) will provide fundamental insights on moral perspectives, and the experts on social theory will provide general empirically validated propositions and "general models of conflict." From this interplay, new policies will emerge, presumably from application of the canons of scientific method. The only debatable issue, it seems to me, is whether it is more ridiculous to turn to experts in social theory for general well-confirmed propositions, or to the specialists in the great religions and philosophical systems for insights into fundamental human values.

There is much more that can be said about this topic, but without continuing, I would simply like to emphasize that, as is no doubt obvious, the cult of the expert is both self-serving, for those who propound it, and fraudulent. Obviously, one must learn from social and behavioral science whatever one can; obviously, these fields should be pursued in as serious a way as is possible. But it will be quite unfortunate, and highly dangerous, if they are not accepted and judged on their merits and according to their actual, not pretended, accomplishments. In particular, if there is a body of theory, well tested and verified, that applies to the conduct of foreign affairs or the resolution of domestic or international conflict, its existence has been kept a well-guarded secret. In the case of Vietnam, if those who feel themselves to be experts have access to principles or information that would justify what the American government is doing in that unfortunate country, they have been singularly ineffective in making this fact known. To anyone who has any familiarity with the social and behavioral sciences (or the "policy sciences"), the claim that there are certain considerations and principles too deep for the outsider to comprehend is simply an absurdity, unworthy of comment.

When we consider the responsibility of intellectuals, our basic concern must be their role in the creation and analysis of ideology. And in fact, Kristol's contrast between the unreasonable ideological types and the responsible experts is formulated in terms that immediately bring to mind Daniel Bell's interesting and influential essay on the "end of ideology,"[26] an essay which is as important for what it leaves unsaid as for its actual content. Bell presents and discusses the Marxist analysis of ideology as a mask for class interest, in particular quoting Marx's well-known description of the belief of the bourgeoisie "that the *special* conditions of its emancipation are the *general* conditions through which alone modern society can be saved and the class struggle avoided." He then argues that the age of ideology is ended, supplanted, at least in the West, by a general agreement that each issue must be settled on its own individual terms, within the framework of a welfare state in which, presumably, experts in the conduct of public affairs will have a prominent role. Bell is quite careful, however, to characterize the precise sense of "ideology" in which "ideologies are exhausted." He is referring only to ideology as "the conversion of ideas into social levers," to ideology as "a set of beliefs, infused with passion, . . . [which] . . . seeks to transform the whole of a way of life." The crucial words are "transform" and "convert into social levers." Intellectuals in the West, he argues, have lost interest in converting ideas into social levers for the radical transformation of society. Now that we have achieved the pluralistic society of the welfare state, they see no further need for a radical transformation of society; we may tinker with our way of life here and there, but it would be wrong to try to modify it in any significant way. With this consensus of intellectuals, ideology is dead.

There are several striking facts about Bell's essay. First, he does not point out the extent to which this consensus of the intellectuals is self-serving. He does not relate his observation that, by and large, intellectuals have lost interest in "transforming the whole way of life" to the fact that they play an increasingly prominent role in running the welfare state; he does not relate their general satisfaction with the welfare state to the fact that, as he observes elsewhere, "America has become an affluent society, offering place . . . and prestige . . . to the onetime radicals." Second, he offers no serious argument to show that intellectuals are somehow "right" or "objectively justified" in reaching the consensus to which he alludes, with its rejection of the notion that society should be transformed. Indeed, although Bell is fairly sharp about the empty rhetoric of the "New Left," he seems to have a quite utopian faith that technical experts will be able to come to grips with the few problems that still remain; for example, the fact that labor is treated as a commodity, and the problems of "alienation."

It seems fairly obvious that the classical problems are very much with us; one might plausibly argue that they have even been enhanced in severity and scale. For example, the classical paradox of poverty in the midst of plenty is now an ever increasing problem on an international scale. Whereas one might conceive, at least in principle, of a solution within national boundaries, a sensible idea as to how to transform international society in such a way as to cope with the vast and perhaps increasing human misery is hardly likely to develop within the framework of the intellectual consensus that Bell describes.

Thus it would seem natural to describe the consensus of Bell's intellectuals in somewhat different terms than his. Using the terminology of the first part of his essay, we might say that the welfare state technician finds justification for his special and prominent social status in his "science," specifically, in the claim that social science can support a technology of social tinkering on a domestic or international scale. He then takes a further step, proceeding, in a familiar way, to claim universal validity for what is in fact a class interest: he argues that the special conditions on which his claims to power and authority are based are, in fact, the general conditions through which alone modern society can be saved; that social tinkering within a welfare state framework must replace the commitment to the "total ideologies" of the past, ideologies which were concerned with a transformation of society. Having found his position of power, having achieved security and affluence, he has no further need for ideologies that look to radical change. The scholar-expert replaces the "free-floating intellectual" who "felt that the wrong values were being honored, and rejected the society," and who has now lost his political role (now, that is, that the right values are being honored).

Conceivably, it is correct that the technical experts who will (or hope to) manage the "postindustrial society" will be able to cope with the classic problems without a radical transformation of society. Just so, it is conceivably true that the bourgeoisie was right in regarding the special conditions of its emancipation as the general conditions through which alone modern society would be saved. In either case, an argument is in order, and skepticism is justified where none appears.

Within the same framework of general utopianism, Bell goes on to pose the issue between welfare state scholar-experts and Third World ideologists in a rather curious way. He points out, quite correctly, that there is no issue of Communism, the content of that doctrine having been "long forgotten by friends and foes alike." Rather, he says, "the question is an older one: whether new societies can grow by building democratic institutions and allowing people to make choices—and sacrifices—voluntarily, or whether the new elites, heady with power, will impose totalitarian means to transform their countries." The question is an interesting one; it is odd, however, to see it referred to as "an older one." Surely he cannot be suggesting that the West chose the democratic way—for example, that in England during the industrial revolution, the farmers voluntarily made the choice of leaving the land, giving up cottage industry, becoming an industrial proletariat, and voluntarily decided, within the framework of the existing democratic institutions, to make the sacrifices that are graphically described in the classic literature on nineteenth-century industrial society. One may debate the question whether authoritarian control is necessary to permit capital accumulation in the underdeveloped world, but the Western model of development is hardly one that we can point to with any pride. It is perhaps not surprising to find a Walt Rostow referring to "the more humane processes [of industrialization] that Western values would suggest."[27] Those who have a serious concern for the problems that face backward countries and for the role that advanced industrial societies might, in principle, play in development and modernization must use somewhat more care in interpreting the significance of the Western experience.

Returning to the quite appropriate question, whether "new societies can grow by building democratic institutions" or only by totalitarian means, I think that honesty requires us to recognize that this question must be directed more to American intellectuals than to Third World ideologists. The backward countries have incredible, perhaps insurmountable problems, and few available options; the United States has a wide range of options, and has the economic and technological resources, though evidently neither the intellectual nor the moral resources, to confront at least some of these problems. It is easy for an American intellectual to deliver homilies on the virtues of freedom and liberty, but if he is really concerned about, say, Chinese totalitarianism or the burdens imposed on the Chinese peasantry in forced industrialization, then he should face a task that is infinitely more significant and challenging—the task of creating, in the United States, the intellectual and moral climate, as well as the social and economic conditions, that would permit this country to participate in modernization and development in a way commensurate with its material wealth and technical capacity. Massive capital gifts to Cuba and China might not succeed in alleviating the authoritarianism and terror that tend to accompany early stages of capital accumulation, but they are far more likely to have this effect than lectures on democratic values. It is possible that even without "capitalist encirclement" in its varying manifestations, the truly democratic elements in revolutionary movements—in some instances soviets and collectives, for example—might be undermined by an "elite" of bureaucrats and technical intelligentsia; but it is a near certainty that the fact of capitalist encirclement, which all revolutionary movements now have to face, will guarantee this result. The lesson, for those who are concerned to strengthen the democratic, spontaneous, and popular elements in developing societies, is quite clear. Lectures on the two-party system, or even the really substantial democratic values that have been in part realized in Western society, are a monstrous irrelevance in the face of the effort that is required to raise the level of culture in Western society to the point where it can provide a "social lever" for both economic development and the development of true democratic institutions in the Third World—and for that matter, at home as well.

A good case can be made for the conclusion that there is indeed something of a consensus among intellectuals who have already achieved power and affluence, or who sense that they can achieve them by "accepting society" as it is and promoting the values that are "being honored" in this society. And it is also true that this consensus is most noticeable among the scholar-experts who are replacing the free-floating intellectuals of the past. In the university, these scholar-experts construct a "value-free technology" for the solution of technical problems that arise in contemporary society,[28] taking a "responsible stance" towards these problems, in the sense noted earlier. This consensus among the responsible scholar-experts is the domestic analogue to that proposed, in the international arena, by those who justify the application of American power in Asia, whatever the human cost, on the grounds that it is necessary to contain the "expansion of China" (an "expansion" which is, to be sure, hypothetical for the time being)[29]—to translate from State Department Newspeak, on the grounds that it is essential to reverse the Asian nationalist revolutions, or at least to prevent them from spreading. The analogy becomes clear when we look carefully at the ways in which this proposal is formulated. With his usual lucidity, Churchill outlined the general position in a remark to his colleague of the moment, Joseph Stalin, at Teheran in 1943: ". . . the government of the world must be entrusted to satisfied nations, who wished nothing more for themselves than what they had. If the world-government were in the hand of hungry nations, there would always be danger. But none of us had any reason to seek for anything more. The peace would be kept by peoples who lived in their own way and were not ambitious. Our power placed us above the rest. We were like rich men dwelling at peace within their habitations."[30]

For a translation of Churchill's biblical rhetoric into the jargon of contemporary social science, one may turn to the testimony of Charles Wolf, senior economist of the RAND Corporation, at the congressional committee hearings cited earlier:

> I am dubious that China's fears of encirclement are going to be abated, eased, relaxed in the long-term future. But I would hope that what we do in Southeast Asia would help to develop within the Chinese body politic more of a realism and willingness to live with this fear than to indulge it by support for liberation movements, which admittedly depend on a great deal more than external support . . . the operational question for American foreign policy is not whether that fear can be eliminated or substantially alleviated, but whether China can be faced with a structure of incentives, of penalties and rewards, of inducements that will make it willing to live with this fear.[31]

The point is further clarified by Thomas Schelling: "There is growing experience which the Chinese can profit from, that although the United States may be interested in encircling them, may be interested in defending nearby areas from them, it is, nevertheless, prepared to behave peaceably if they are."[32]

In short, we are prepared to live peaceably within our—to be sure, rather extensive—habitations. And, quite naturally, we are offended by the undignified noises from the servants' quarters. If, let us say, a peasant-based revolutionary movement tries to achieve independence from foreign domination or to overthrow semifeudal structures supported by foreign powers, or if the Chinese irrationally refuse to respond properly to the schedule of reinforcement that we have prepared for them, if they object to being encircled by the benign and peace-loving "rich men" who control the territories on their borders as a natural right, then, evidently, we must respond to this belligerence with appropriate force.

It is this mentality that explains the frankness with which the U.S. government and its academic apologists defend the American refusal to permit a political settlement in Vietnam at a local level, a settlement based on the actual distribution of political forces. Even government experts freely admit that the National Liberation Front is the only "truly mass-based political party in South Vietnam";[33] that the NLF had "made a conscious and massive effort to extend political participation, even if it was manipulated, on the local level so as to involve the people in a self-contained, self-supporting revolution" (p. 374); and that this effort had been so successful that no political groups, "with the possible exception of the Buddhists, thought themselves equal in size and power to risk entering into a coalition, fearing that if they did the whale would swallow the minnow" (p. 362). Moreover, they concede that until the introduction of overwhelming American force, the NLF had insisted that the struggle "should be fought out at the political level and that the use of massed military might was in itself illegitimate. . . . The battleground was to be the minds and loyalties of the rural Vietnamese, the weapons were to be ideas" (pp. 91–92; cf. also pp. 93, 99–108, 155 f.); and correspondingly, that until mid-1964, aid from Hanoi "was largely confined to two areas—doctrinal know-how and leadership personnel" (p. 321). Captured NLF documents contrast the enemy's "military superiority" with their own "political superiority" (p. 106), thus fully confirming the analysis of American military spokesmen who define our problem as how, "with considerable armed force but little political power, [to] contain an adversary who has enormous political force but only modest military power."[34]

Similarly, the most striking outcome of both the Honolulu conference in February and the Manila conference in October was the frank admission by high officials of the Saigon government that "they could not survive a 'peaceful settlement' that left the Vietcong *political* structure in place even if the Vietcong guerrilla units were disbanded," that "they are not able to compete *politically* with the Vietnamese Communists."[35] Thus, Mohr continues, the Vietnamese demand a "pacification program" which will have as "its core . . . the destruction of the clandestine Vietcong political structure and the creation of an iron-like system of government political control over the population." And from Manila, the same correspondent, on October 23, quotes a high South Vietnamese official as saying: "Frankly, we are not strong enough now to compete with the Communists on a purely political basis. They are organized and disciplined. The non-Communist nationalists are not—we do not have any large, well-organized political parties and we do not yet have unity. We cannot leave the Vietcong in existence." Officials in Washington understand the situation very well. Thus Secretary Rusk has pointed out that "if the Vietcong come to the conference table as full partners they will, in a sense, have been victorious in the very aims that South Vietnam and the United States are pledged to prevent" (January 28, 1966). Similarly, Max Frankel reported from Washington: "Compromise has had no appeal here because the Administration concluded long ago that the non-Communist forces of South Vietnam could not long survive in a Saigon coalition with Communists. It is for that reason—and not because of an excessively rigid sense of protocol—that Washington has steadfastly refused to deal with the Vietcong or recognize them as an independent political force."[36]

In short, we will—magnanimously—permit Vietcong representatives to attend negotiations, but only if they will agree to identify themselves as agents of a foreign power and thus forfeit the right to participate in a coalition government, a right which they have now been demanding for a half-dozen years. We know well that in any representative coalition, our chosen delegates could not last a day without the support of American arms. Therefore, we must increase American force and resist meaningful negotiations, until the day when a client government can exert both military and political control over its own population—a day which may never dawn, for as William Bundy has pointed out, we could never be sure of the security of a Southeast Asia "from which the Western presence was effectively withdrawn." Thus if we were to "negotiate in the direction of solutions that are put under the label of neutralization," this would amount to capitulation to the Communists.[37] According to this reasoning, then, South Vietnam must remain, permanently, an American military base.

All of this is of course reasonable, so long as we accept the fundamental political axiom that the United States, with its traditional concern for the rights of the weak and downtrodden, and with its unique insight into the proper mode of development for backward countries, must have the courage and the persistence to impose its will by force until such time as other nations are prepared to accept these truths—or simply to abandon hope.

If it is the responsibility of the intellectual to insist upon the truth, it is also his duty to see events in their historical perspective. Thus one must applaud the insistence of the Secretary of State on the importance of historical analogies, the Munich analogy, for example. As Munich showed, a powerful and agressive nation with a fanatic belief in its manifest destiny will regard each victory, each extension of its power and authority, as a prelude to the next step. The matter was very well put by Adlai Stevenson, when he spoke of "the old, old route whereby expansive powers push at more and more doors, believing they will open, until, at the ultimate door, resistance is unavoidable and major war breaks out." Herein lies the danger of appeasement, as the Chinese tirelessly point out to the Soviet Union, which they claim is playing Chamberlain to our Hitler in Vietnam. Of course, the aggressiveness of liberal imperialism is not that of Nazi Germany, though the distinction may seem rather academic to a Vietnamese peasant who is being gassed or incinerated. We do not want to occupy Asia; we merely wish, to return to Mr. Wolf, "to help the Asian countries progress toward economic modernization, as relatively 'open' and stable societies, to which our access, as a country and as individual citizens, is free and comfortable."[38] The formulation is appropriate. Recent history shows that it makes little difference to us what form of government a country has as long as it remains an "open society," in our peculiar sense of this term—a society, that is, which remains open to American economic penetration or political control. If it is necessary to approach genocide in Vietnam to achieve this objective, then this is the price we must pay in defense of freedom and the rights of man.

It is, no doubt, superfluous to discuss at length the ways in which we assist other countries to progress towards open societies "to which our access is free and comfortable." One enlightening example is discussed in the recent congressional hearings from which I have now quoted several times, in the testimony of Willem Holst and Robert Meagher, representing the Standing

Committee on India of the Business Council for International Understanding.[39] As Mr. Meagher points out: "If it was possible, India would probably prefer to import technicians and know-how rather than foreign corporations. Such is not possible; therefore India accepts foreign capital as a necessary evil." Of course, "the question of private capital investment in India . . . would be no more than a theoretical exercise" had the groundwork for such investment not been laid by foreign aid, and were it not that "necessity has forced a modification in India's approach to private foreign capital." But now, "India's attitude toward private foreign investment is undergoing a substantial change. From a position of resentment and ambivalence, it is evolving toward an acceptance of its necessity. As the necessity becomes more and more evident, the ambivalence will probably be replaced by a more accommodating attitude." Mr. Holst contributes what is "perhaps a typical case history," namely, "the plan under which it was proposed that the Indian Government in partnership with a United States private consortium was to have increased fertilizer production by a million tons per year, which is just double presently installed capacity in all of India. The unfortunate demise of this ambitious plan may be attributed in large part to the failure of both Government and business to find a workable and mutually acceptable solution within the framework of the well-publicized 10 business incentives." The difficulty here was in connection with the percentage of equity ownership. Obviously, "fertilizers are desperately needed in India." Equally obviously, the consortium "insisted that to get the proper kind of control majority ownership was in fact needed." But "the Indian Government officially insisted that they shall have majority ownership," and "in something so complex it was felt that it would be a self-defeating thing."

Fortunately, this particular story has a happy ending. The remarks just quoted were made in February 1966, and within a few weeks, the Indian government had seen the light, as we read in a series of reports in the *New York Times*. The criticism, inside India, that "the American Government and the World Bank would like to arrogate to themselves the right to lay down the framework in which our economy must function," was stilled (April 24); and the Indian government accepted the conditions for resumed economic aid, namely, "that India provide easier terms for foreign private investment in fertilizer plants" and that the American investors "have substantial management rights" (May 14). The development is summarized in a dispatch datelined April 28, from New Delhi, in these terms:

> There are signs of change. The Government has granted easy terms to private foreign investors in the fertilizer industry, is thinking about decontrolling several more industries and is ready to liberalize import policy if it gets sufficient foreign

> aid. . . . Much of what is happening now is a result of steady pressure from the United States and the International Bank for Reconstruction and Development, which for the last year have been urging a substantial freeing of the Indian economy and a greater scope for private enterprise. The United States pressure, in particular, has been highly effective here because the United States provides by far the largest part of the foreign exchange needed to finance India's development and keep the wheels of industry turning. Call them "strings," call them "conditions" or whatever one likes, India has little choice now but to agree to many of the terms that the United States, through the World Bank, is putting on its aid. For India simply has nowhere else to turn.

The heading of the article refers to this development as India's "drift from socialism to pragmatism."

Even this was not enough, however. Thus we read a few months later, in the *Christian Science Monitor* (December 5), that American entrepreneurs insist "on importing all equipment and machinery when India has a tested capacity to meet some of their requirements. They have insisted on importing liquid ammonia, a basic raw material, rather than using indigenous naphtha which is abundantly available. They have laid down restrictions about pricing, distribution, profits, and management control." The Indian reaction, I have already cited (see page 47).

In such ways as these, we help India develop towards an open society, one which, in Walt Rostow's words, has a proper understanding of "the core of the American ideology," namely, "the sanctity of the individual in relation to the state." And in this way, too, we refute the simpleminded view of those Asians who, to continue with Rostow's phrasing, "believe or half-believe that the West has been driven to create and then to cling to its imperial holdings by the inevitable workings of capitalist economies." [40]

In fact, a major postwar scandal is developing in India as the United States, cynically capitalizing on India's current torture, applies its economic power to implement India's "drift from socialism to pragmatism."

In pursuing the aim of helping other countries to progress towards open societies, with no thought of territorial aggrandizement, we are breaking no new ground. Hans Morgenthau has aptly described our traditional policy towards China as one of favoring "what you might call freedom of competition with regard to the exploitation of China." [41] In fact, few imperialist powers have had explicit territorial ambitions. Thus in 1784, the British Parliament announced that "to pursue schemes of conquest and extension of dominion in India are measures repugnant to the wish, honor, and policy of this nation." Shortly after, the conquest of India was in full swing. A century later, Britain announced its intentions in Egypt under the slogan "Intervention, Reform, Withdrawal." It is unnecessary to comment on which parts of this promise were fulfilled, within the next half century. In 1936, on the eve of hostilities in North China, the Japanese stated their Basic Principles of National Policy. These included the use of moderate and peaceful means to extend her strength, to promote social and economic development, to eradicate the menace of Communism, to correct the aggressive policies of the great powers, and to secure her position as the stabilizing power in East Asia. Even in 1937, the Japanese government had "no territorial designs upon China." In short, we follow a well-trodden path.

It is useful to remember, incidentally, that the United States was apparently quite willing, as late as 1939, to negotiate a commercial treaty with Japan and arrive at a *modus vivendi* if Japan would "change her attitude and practice towards our rights and interests in China," as Secretary Hull put it. The bombing of Chungking and the rape of Nanking were rather unpleasant, it is true, but what was really important was our rights and interests in China, as the responsible, unhysterical men of the day saw quite clearly. It was the closing of the Open Door by Japan that led inevitably to the Pacific war, just as it is the closing of the Open Door by "Communist" China itself that may very well lead to the next, and no doubt last, Pacific war.

Quite often, the statements of sincere and devoted technical experts give surprising insight into the intellectual attitudes that lie in the background of the latest savagery. Consider, for example, the following comment by economist Richard Lindholm, in 1959, expressing his frustration over the failure of economic development in "free Vietnam": ". . . the use of American aid is determined by how the Vietnamese use their incomes and their savings. The fact that a large portion of the Vietnamese imports financed with American aid are either consumer goods or raw materials used rather directly to meet consumer demands is an indication that the Vietnamese people desire these goods, for they have shown their desire by their willingness to use their piasters to purchase them."[42]

In short, the Vietnamese *people* desire Buicks and air conditioners, rather than sugar-refining equipment or road-building machinery, as they have shown by their behavior in a free market. And however much we may deplore their free choice, we must allow the people to have their way. Of course, there are also those two-legged beasts of burden that one stumbles on in the countryside, but as any graduate student of political science can explain, they are not part of a responsible modernizing elite, and therefore have only a superficial biological resemblance to the human race.

In no small measure, it is attitudes like this that lie behind the butchery in

Vietnam, and we had better face up to them with candor, or we will find our government leading us towards a "final solution" in Vietnam, and in the many Vietnams that inevitably lie ahead.

Let me finally return to Macdonald and the responsibility of intellectuals. Macdonald quotes an interview with a death-camp paymaster who bursts into tears when told that the Russians would hang him. "Why should they? What have I done?" he asked. Macdonald concludes: "Only those who are willing to resist authority themselves when it conflicts too intolerably with their personal moral code, only they have the right to condemn the death-camp paymaster." The question "What have I done?" is one that we may well ask ourselves, as we read, each day, of fresh atrocities in Vietnam—as we create, or mouth, or tolerate the deceptions that will be used to justify the next defense of freedom.

5.

On Resistance

Several weeks after the demonstrations in Washington, I am still trying to sort out my impressions of a week whose quality is difficult to capture or express. Perhaps some personal reflections may be useful to others who share my instinctive distaste for activism, but who find themselves edging towards an unwanted but almost inevitable crisis.

For many of the participants, the Washington demonstrations symbolized the transition "from dissent to resistance." I will return to this slogan and its meaning, but I want to make clear at the outset that I do feel it to be not only accurate with respect to the mood of the demonstrations but, properly interpreted, appropriate to the present state of protest against the war. There is an irresistible dynamics to such protest. One may begin by writing articles and

---

This article first appeared in the *New York Review of Books*, December 7, 1967. It is reprinted with a few revisions. The demonstrations referred to took place at the Justice Department and the Pentagon, on the weekend of October 19–21, 1967. The draft card turn-in at the Justice Department was one of the events that led to the sentencing of Dr. Benjamin Spock, Rev. William Sloane Coffin, Mitchell Goodman, and Michael Ferber to two-year prison sentences for "conspiracy." For details, see Noam Chomsky, Paul Lauter, and Florence Howe, "Reflections on a Political Trial," *New York Review of Books*, August 22, 1968, 23–30. The Pentagon demonstration, which by some estimates involved several hundred thousand people, was a remarkable, unforgettable manifestation of opposition to the war. The spirit and character of the demonstrations are captured, with marvelous accuracy and perception, in Norman Mailer's *The Armies of the Night* (New York: New American Library, 1968). This chapter is reprinted from *American Power and the New Mandarins* (New York: Pantheon Books, 1969; New York: The New Press, 2002), 367–85.

giving speeches about the war, by helping in many ways to create an atmosphere of concern and outrage. A courageous few will turn to direct action, refusing to take their place alongside the "good Germans" we have all learned to despise. Some will be forced to this decision when they are called up for military service. The dissenting senators, writers, and professors will watch as young men refuse to serve in the armed forces, in a war that they detest. What then? Can those who write and speak against the war take refuge in the fact that they have not urged or encouraged draft resistance, but have merely helped to develop a climate of opinion in which any decent person will want to refuse to take part in a miserable war? It is a very thin line. Nor is it very easy to watch from a position of safety while others are forced to take a grim and painful step. The fact is that most of the one thousand draft cards and other documents turned in to the Justice Department on October 20 came from men who can escape military service but who insisted on sharing the fate of those who are less privileged. In such ways the circle of resistance widens. Quite apart from this, no one can fail to see that to the extent that he restricts his protest, to the extent that he rejects actions that are open to him, he accepts complicity in what the government does. Some will act on this realization, posing sharply a moral issue that no person of conscience can evade.

On Monday, October 16, on the Boston Common I listened as Howard Zinn explained why he felt ashamed to be an American. I watched as several hundred young men, some of them my students, made a terrible decision which no young person should have to face: to sever their connection with the Selective Service System. The week ended, the following Monday, with a quiet discussion in Cambridge in which I heard estimates, by an academic consultant to the Department of Defense, of the nuclear megatonnage that would be necessary to "take out" North Vietnam ("Some will find this shocking, but . . ."; "No civilian in the government is suggesting this, to my knowledge . . ."; "Let's not use emotional words like 'destruction' "; etc.), and listened to a leading expert on Soviet affairs who explained how the men in the Kremlin are watching very carefully to determine whether wars of national liberation can succeed—if so, they will support them all over the world. (Try pointing out to such an expert that on these assumptions, if the men in the Kremlin are rational, they will surely support dozens of such wars right now, since at a small cost they can confound the American military and tear our society to shreds—you will be told that you don't understand the Russian soul.)

The weekend of the peace demonstrations in Washington left impressions that are vivid and intense, but unclear to me in their implications. The dominant memory is of the scene itself, of tens of thousands of young people surrounding what they believe to be—I must add that I agree—the most hideous institution on this earth and demanding that it stop imposing misery and destruction. Tens of thousands of *young* people. This I find hard to comprehend. It is pitiful but true that by an overwhelming margin it is the young who are crying out in horror at what we all see happening, the young who are being beaten when they stand their ground, and the young who have to decide whether to accept jail or exile, or to fight in a hideous war. They have to face this decision alone, or almost alone. We should ask ourselves why this is so.

Why, for example, does Senator Mansfield feel "ashamed for the image they have portrayed of this country," and not feel ashamed for the image of this country portrayed by the institution these young people were confronting, an institution directed by a sane and mild and eminently reasonable man who can testify calmly before Congress that the amount of ordnance expended in Vietnam has surpassed the total expended in Germany and Italy in World War II? Why is it that Senator Mansfield can speak in ringing phrases about those who are not living up to our commitment to "a government of laws"—referring to a small group of demonstrators, not to the ninety-odd responsible men on the Senate floor who are watching, with full knowledge, as the state they serve clearly, flagrantly violates the explicit provisions of the United Nations Charter, the supreme law of the land? He knows quite well that prior to our invasion of Vietnam there was no armed attack against any state. It was Senator Mansfield, after all, who informed us that "when the sharp increase in the American military effort began in early 1965, it was estimated that only about 400 North Vietnamese soldiers were among the enemy forces in the South which totaled 140,000 at that time"; and it is the Mansfield Report from which we learn that at that time there were 34,000 American soldiers already in South Vietnam, in violation of our "solemn commitment" at Geneva in 1954.

The point should be pursued. After the first International Days of Protest in October 1965, Senator Mansfield criticized the "sense of utter irresponsibility" shown by the demonstrators. He had nothing to say then, nor has he since, about the "sense of utter irresponsibility" shown by Senator Mansfield and others who stand by quietly and vote appropriations as the cities and villages of North Vietnam are demolished, as millions of refugees in the South are driven from their homes by American bombardment. He has nothing to say about the moral standards or the respect for law of those who have permitted this tragedy.

I speak of Senator Mansfield precisely because he is not a breast-beating superpatriot who wants America to rule the world, but is rather an American intellectual in the best sense, a scholarly and reasonable man—the kind of man who is the terror of our age. Perhaps this is merely a personal reaction, but when I look at what is happening to our country, what I find most terrifying is not Curtis LeMay, with his cheerful suggestion that we bomb our "enemies" back into the Stone Age, but rather the calm disquisitions of the political scientists on just how much force will be necessary to achieve our ends, or just what form of government will be acceptable to us in Vietnam. What I find terrifying is the detachment and equanimity with which we view and discuss an unbearable tragedy. We all know that if Russia or China were guilty of what we have done in Vietnam, we would be exploding with moral indignation at these monstrous crimes.

There was, I think, a serious miscalculation in the planning of the Washington demonstrations. It was expected that the march to the Pentagon would be followed by a number of speeches, and that those who were committed to civil disobedience would then separate themselves from the crowd and go to the Pentagon, a few hundred yards away across an open field. I had decided not to take part in civil disobedience, and I do not know in detail what had been planned. As everyone must realize, it is very hard to distinguish rationalization from rationality in such matters. I felt, however, that the first large-scale acts of civil disobedience should be more specifically defined, more clearly in support of those who are refusing to serve in Vietnam, on whom the real burden of dissent must inevitably fall. While appreciating the point of view of those who wished to express their hatred of the war in a more explicit way, I was not convinced that civil disobedience at the Pentagon would be either meaningful or effective.

In any event, what actually happened was rather different from what anyone had anticipated. A few thousand people gathered for the speeches, but the mass of marchers went straight on to the Pentagon, some because they were committed to direct action, many because they were simply swept along. From the speakers' platform where I stood it was difficult to determine just what was taking place at the Pentagon. All we could see was the surging of the crowd. From secondhand reports, I understand that the marchers passed through and around the front line of troops and took up a position, which they maintained, on the steps of the Pentagon. It soon became obvious that it was wrong for the few organizers of the march and the mostly middle-aged group that had gathered near them to remain at the speakers' platform while the demonstrators themselves, most of them quite young, were at the Pentagon. (I recall seeing near the platform Robert Lowell, Dwight Macdonald, Monsignor Rice, Sidney Lens, Benjamin Spock and his wife, Dagmar Wilson, Donald Kalish.) Dave Dellinger suggested that we try to approach the Pentagon. We found a place not yet blocked by the demonstrators, and walked up to the line of troops standing a few feet from the building. Dellinger suggested that those of us who had not yet spoken at the rally talk directly to the soldiers through a small portable sound system. From this point on, my impressions are rather fragmentary. Monsignor Rice spoke, and I followed. As I was speaking, the line of soldiers advanced, moving past me—a rather odd experience. I don't recall just what I was saying. The gist was, I suppose, that we were there because we didn't want the soldiers to kill and be killed, but I do remember feeling that the way I was putting it seemed silly and irrelevant.

The advancing line of soldiers had partially scattered the small group that had come with Dellinger. Those of us who had been left behind the line of soldiers regrouped, and Dr. Spock began to speak. Almost at once, another line of soldiers emerged from somewhere, this time in a tightly massed formation, rifles in hand, and moved slowly forward. We sat down. As I mentioned earlier, I had no intention of taking part in any act of civil disobedience, until that moment. But when that grotesque organism began slowly advancing—more grotesque because its cells were recognizable human beings—it became obvious that one could not permit that thing to dictate what one was going to do. I was arrested at that point by a federal marshal, presumably for obstructing the soldiers (the technical term for this behavior is "disorderly conduct"). I should add that the soldiers, so far as I could see (which was not very far), seemed rather unhappy about the whole matter, and were being about as gentle as one can be when ordered (I presume this was the order) to kick and club passive, quiet people who refuse to move. The federal marshals, predictably, were very different. They reminded me of the police officers I had seen in a Jackson, Mississippi, jail several summers ago, who had laughed when an old man showed us a bloody homemade bandage on his leg and tried to describe to us how he had been beaten by the police. In Washington, the ones who got the worst of it at the hands of the marshals were the young boys and girls, particularly boys with long hair. Nothing seemed to bring out the marshals' sadism more than the sight of a boy with long hair. Yet, although I witnessed some acts of violence by the marshals, their behavior largely seemed to range from indifference to petty nastiness. For example, we were kept in a police van for an hour or two with the doors closed and only a few airholes for ventilation—one can't be too careful with such ferocious criminal types.

In the prison dormitory and after my release I heard many stories, which I feel sure are authentic, of the courage of the young people, many of whom were quite frightened by the terrorism that began late at night after the TV cameramen and most of the press had left. They sat quietly hour after hour through the cold night; many were kicked and beaten and dragged across police lines (more "disorderly conduct"). I also heard stories, distressing ones, of provocation of the troops by the demonstrators—usually, it seems, those who were not in the front rows. Surely this was indefensible. Soldiers are unwitting instruments of terror; one does not blame or attack the club that is used to bludgeon someone to death. They are also human beings, with sensibilities to which one can perhaps appeal. There is in fact strong evidence that one soldier, perhaps three or four, refused to obey orders and was placed under arrest. The soldiers, after all, are in much the same position as the draft resisters. If they obey orders, they become brutalized by what they do; if they do not, the personal consequences are severe. It is a situation that deserves compassion, not abuse. But we should retain a sense of proportion in the matter. Everything that I saw or heard indicates that the demonstrators played only a small role in initiating the considerable violence that occurred.

The argument that resistance to the war should remain strictly nonviolent seems to me overwhelming. As a tactic, violence is absurd. No one can compete with the government in this arena, and the resort to violence, which will surely fail, will simply frighten and alienate some who can be reached, and will further encourage the ideologists and administrators of forceful repression. What is more, one hopes that participants in nonviolent resistance will themselves become human beings of a more admirable sort. No one can fail to be impressed by the personal qualities of those who have grown to maturity in the civil rights movement. Whatever else it may have accomplished, the civil rights movement has made an inestimable contribution to American society in transforming the lives and characters of those who took part in it. Perhaps a program of principled, nonviolent resistance can do the same for many others, in the particular circumstances that we face today. It is not impossible that this may save the country from a terrible future, from yet another generation of men who think it clever to discuss the bombing of North Vietnam as a question of tactics and cost-effectiveness, or who support our attempt to conquer South Vietnam, with the human cost that they well know, blandly asserting that "our primary motivation is self-interest—the self-interest of our own country in this shrinking world" (Citizens Committee for Peace with Freedom, *New York Times*, October 26, 1967).

Returning to the demonstrations, I must admit that I was relieved to find people whom I had respected for years in the prison dormitory—Norman Mailer, Jim Peck, Dave Dellinger, and a number of others. I think it was reassuring to many of the kids who were there to be able to feel that they were not totally disconnected from a world that they knew and from people whom they admired. It was moving to see that defenseless young people who had a great deal to lose were willing to be jailed for what they believed—young instructors from state universities, college kids who have a very bright future if they are willing to toe the line, many others whom I could not identify.

What comes next? Obviously, that is the question on everyone's mind. The slogan "From Dissent to Resistance" makes sense, I think, but I hope it is not taken to imply that dissent should cease. Dissent and resistance are not alternatives but activities that should reinforce each other. There is no reason why those who take part in tax refusal, draft resistance, and other forms of resistance should not also speak to church groups or town forums, or become involved in electoral politics to support peace candidates or referenda on the war. In my experience, it has often been those committed to resistance who have been most deeply involved in such attempts at persuasion. Putting aside the matter of resistance for a moment, I think it should be emphasized that the days of "patiently explain" are far from over. As the coffins come home and the taxes go up, many people who were previously willing to accept government propaganda will become increasingly concerned to try to think for themselves. The reasons for their change are unfortunate; the opportunities for educational activity are nevertheless very good.

Furthermore, the recent shift in the government's propaganda line offers important opportunities for critical analysis of the war. There is a note of shrill desperation in the recent defense of the American war in Vietnam. We hear less about "bringing freedom and democracy" to the South Vietnamese and more about the "national interest." Secretary Rusk broods about the dangers posed to us by a billion Chinese; the vice president tells us that we are fighting "millitant Asian Communism" with "its headquarters in Peking" and adds that a Vietcong victory would directly threaten the United States; Eugene Rostow argues that "it is no good building model cities if they are to be bombed in twenty years time," and so on (all of this "a frivolous insult to the United States Navy," as Walter Lippmann rightly commented).

This shift in propaganda makes it much easier for critical analysis to attack the problem of Vietnam at its core, which is in Washington and Boston, not in Saigon and Hanoi. There is something ludicrous, after all, in the close attention that opponents of the war give to the political and social problems of Vietnam. Those who were opposed to the Japanese conquest of Manchuria a generation ago did not place emphasis on the political and social and economic problems of Manchuria, but on those of Japan. They did not engage in farcical debate over the exact degree of support for the puppet emperor, but looked to the sources of Japanese imperialism. Now opponents of the war can much more easily shift attention to the source of the aggression, to our own country, its ideology and institutions. We can ask whose "interest" is served by 100,000 casualties and 100 billion dollars expended in the attempt to subjugate a small country halfway around the world. We can point to the absurdity of the idea that we are "containing China" by destroying popular and independent forces on its borders, and to the cynicism of the claim that we are in Vietnam because "to Americans, peace and freedom are inseparable" and because "suppression of freedom" must not "go unchallenged" (the Citizens Committee again). We can ask why it is that those who make this claim do not suggest that an American expeditionary force be sent to Taiwan, to Rhodesia, to Greece, or to Mississippi, but only to Vietnam, where, they want us to believe, the master aggressor Mao Tse-tung is following a Hitlerian course in his cunning way, committing aggression without troops and announcing world conquest by insisting, through the medium of Lin Piao, that indigenous wars of national liberation can expect little from China beyond applause. We can ask why Secretary McNamara reads such statements as a new *Mein Kampf*—or why those who admit that "a Vietnamese communist regime would probably be . . . anti-Chinese" (Ithiel de Sola Pool, *Asian Survey*, August 1967) nevertheless sign statements which pretend that in Vietnam we are facing the expansionist aggressors from Peking. We can ask what factors in American ideology make it so easy for intelligent and well-informed men to say that we "insist upon nothing for South Vietnam except that it be free to chart its own future" (Citizens Committee) although they know quite well that the regime we imposed excluded all those who took part in the struggle against French colonialism, "and properly so" (Secretary Rusk, 1963); that we have since been attempting to suppress a "civil insurrection" (General Stilwell) led by the only "truly mass-based political party in South Vietnam" (Douglas Pike); that we supervised the destruction of the Buddhist opposition; that we offered the peasants a "free choice" between the Saigon government and the National Liberation Front by herding them into strategic hamlets from which NLF cadres and sympathizers were eliminated by the police (Roger Hilsman); and so on. The story is familiar. And we can emphasize what must be obvious to a person with a grain of political intelligence: that the present world problem is not "containing China" but containing the United States.

More important, we can ask the really fundamental question. Suppose that it were in the American "national interest" to pound into rubble a small nation that refuses to submit to our will. Would it then be legitimate and proper for us to act "in this national interest"? The Rusks and the Humphreys and the Citizens Committee say yes. Nothing could show more clearly how we are taking the road of the fascist aggressors of a generation ago.

We are, of course, in a domestic political environment very different from that of the citizens of Germany or Japan. Here, it takes no heroism to protest. We have many avenues open to us to drive home the lesson that there is not one law for the United States and one for the rest of mankind, that no one has appointed us judge and executioner for Vietnam or anywhere else. Many avenues of political education, on and off the campus, have been explored in the past two years. There can be no question that this effort should continue and grow to whatever limit the degree of commitment permits.

Some seem to feel that resistance will "blacken" the peace movement and make it difficult to reach potential sympathizers through more familiar channels. I don't agree with this objection, but I feel that it should not be lightly disregarded. Resisters who hope to save the people of Vietnam from destruction must select the issues they confront and the means they employ in such a way as to attract as much popular support as possible for their efforts. There is no lack of clear issues and honorable means, surely, hence no reason why one should be impelled to ugly actions on ambiguous issues. In particular, it seems to me that draft resistance, properly conducted (as it has been so far), is not only a highly principled and courageous act, but one that might receive broad support and become politically effective. It might, furthermore, succeed in raising the issues of passive complicity in the war which are now much too easily evaded. Those who face these issues may even go on to free themselves from the mind-destroying ideological pressures of American life, and to ask some serious questions about Amerca's role in the world, and the sources, in American society, for this criminal behavior.

Moreover, I feel that this objection to resistance is not properly formulated. The "peace movement" exists only in the fantasies of the paranoid right. Those who find some of the means employed or ends pursued objectionable can oppose the war in other ways. They will not be read out of a movement that does not exist; they have only themselves to blame if they do not make use of the other forms of protest that are available.

I have left to the end of the most important question, the one about which I have least to say. This is the question of the forms resistance should take. We all take part in the war to a greater or lesser extent, if only by paying taxes and permitting domestic society to function smoothly. A person has to choose for himself the point at which he will simply refuse to take part any longer. Reaching that point, he will be drawn into resistance. I believe that the reasons for resistance I have already mentioned are cogent ones: they have an irreducible moral element that admits of little discussion. The issue is posed in its starkest form for the boy who faces induction, and in a form that is somewhat more complex for the boy who must decide whether to participate in a system of selective service that may pass the burden from him to others less fortunate and less privileged. It is difficult for me to see how anyone can refuse to engage himself, in some way, in the plight of these young men. There are many ways to do so: legal aid and financial support; participation in support demonstrations; draft counseling, organization of draft-resistance unions or community-based resistance organizations; assisting those who wish to escape the country; the steps proposed by the clergymen who recently announced that they are ready to share the fate of those who will be sent to prison. About this aspect of the program of resistance I have nothing to say that will not be obvious to anyone who is willing to think the matter through.

Considered as a political tactic, resistance requires careful thought, and I do not pretend to have very clear ideas about it. Much depends on how events unfold in the coming months. Westmoreland's war of attrition may simply continue with no foreseeable end, but the domestic political situation makes this unlikely. If the Republicans do not decide to throw the election again, they could have a winning strategy: they can claim that they will end the war, and remain vague about the means. Under such circumstances, it is unlikely that Johnson will permit the present military stalemate to persist. There are, then, several options. The first is American withdrawal, in whatever terms it would be couched. It might be disguised as a retreat to "enclaves," from which the troops could then be removed. It might be arranged by an international conference, or by permitting a government in Saigon that would seek peace among contending South Vietnamese and then ask us to leave. This policy might be politically feasible; the same public relations firm that invented terms like "revolutionary development" can depict withdrawal as victory. Whether there is anyone in the executive branch with the courage or imagination to urge this course, I do not know. A number of senators are proposing, in essence, that this is the course we should pursue, as are such critics of the war as Walter Lippmann and Hans Morgenthau, if I understand them correctly. A detailed and quite sensible plan for arranging withdrawal along with new, more meaningful elections in the South is outlined by Philippe Devillers in *Le Monde hebdomadaire* of October 26, 1967. Variants can easily be imagined. What is central is the decision to accept the principle of Geneva that the problems of Vietnam be settled by the Vietnamese.

A second possibility would be annihilation. No one doubts that we have the technological capacity for this, and only the sentimental doubt that we have the moral capacity as well. Bernard Fall predicted this outcome in an interview shortly before his death. "The Americans can destroy," he said, "but they cannot pacify. They may win the war, but it will be the victory of the graveyard. Vietnam will be destroyed."

A third option would be an invasion of North Vietnam. This would saddle us with two unwinnable guerrilla wars instead of one, but if the timing is right, it might be used as a device to rally the citizenry around the flag.

A fourth possibility is an attack on China. We could then abandon Vietnam and turn to a winnable war directed against Chinese industrial capacity. Such a move should win the election. No doubt this prospect also appeals to that insane rationality called "strategic thinking." If we intend to keep armies of occupation or even strong military bases on the Asian mainland, we would do well to make sure that the Chinese do not have the means to threaten them. Of course, there is the danger of a nuclear holocaust, but it is difficult to see why this should trouble those whom John McDermott calls the "crisis managers," the same men who were willing, in 1962, to accept a high probability of nuclear war to establish the principle that we, and we alone, have the right to keep missiles on the borders of a potential enemy.

There are many who regard "negotiations" as a realistic alternative, but I do not understand the logic or even the content of this proposal. If we stop bombing North Vietnam we might well enter into negotiations with Hanoi, but there would then be very little to discuss. As to South Vietnam, the only negotiable issue is the withdrawal of foreign troops; other matters can only be settled among whatever Vietnamese groups have survived the American onslaught. The call for "negotiations" seems to me not only empty, but actually a trap for those who oppose the war. If we do not agree to withdraw our troops, the negotiations will be deadlocked, the fighting will continue, American troops will be fired on and killed, the military will have a persuasive argument to escalate, to save American lives. In short, the Symington solution: we offer them peace on our terms, and if they refuse—the victory of the graveyard.

Of the realistic options, only withdrawal (however disguised) seems to me at all tolerable, and resistance, as a tactic of protest, must be designed so as to increase the likelihood that this option will be selected. Furthermore, the time in which to take such action may be very short. The logic of resorting to resistance as a tactic for ending the war is fairly clear. There is no basis for supposing that those who will make the major policy decisions are open to reason on the fundamental issues, in particular the issue of whether we, alone among the nations of the world, have the authority and the competence to determine the social and political institutions of Vietnam. What is more, there is little likelihood that the electoral process will bear on the major decisions. As I have pointed out, the issue may be settled before the next election. Even if it is not, it is hardly likely that a serious choice will be offered at the polls. And if by a miracle such a choice is offered, how seriously can we take the campaign promises of a "peace candidate" after the experience of 1964? Given the enormous dangers of escalation and its hateful character, it makes sense, in such a situation, to search for ways to raise the domestic cost of American aggression, to raise it to a point where it cannot be overlooked by those who have to calculate such costs. One must then consider in what ways it is possible to pose a serious threat. Many possibilities come to mind: a general strike, university strikes, attempts to hamper war production and supply, and so on.

Personally, I feel that disruptive acts of this sort would be justified were they likely to be effective in averting an imminent tragedy. I am skeptical, however, about their possible effectiveness. At the moment, I cannot imagine a broad base for such action, in the white community at least, outside the universities. Forcible repression would not, therefore, prove very difficult. My guess is that such actions would, furthermore, primarily involve students and younger faculty from the humanities and the theological schools, with a scattering of scientists. The professional schools, engineers, specialists in the technology of manipulation and control (much of the social sciences), would probably remain relatively uninvolved. Therefore the long-range threat, such as it is, would be to American humanistic and scientific culture. I doubt that this would seem important to those in decision-making positions. Rusk and Rostow and their accomplices in the academic world seem unaware of the serious threat that their policies already pose in these spheres. I doubt that they appreciate the extent, or the importance, of the dissipation of creative energies and the growing disaffection among young people who are sickened by the violence and deceit that they see in the exercise of American power. Further disruption in these areas might, then, seem to them a negligible cost.

Resistance is in part a moral responsibility, in part a tactic to affect government policy. In particular, with respect to support for draft resistance, I feel that it is a moral responsibility that cannot be shirked. On the other hand, as a tactic, it seems to me of doubtful effectiveness, as matters now stand. I say this with diffidence and considerable uncertainty.

Whatever happens in Vietnam, there are bound to be significant domestic repercussions. It is axiomatic that no army ever loses a war; its brave soldiers and all-knowing generals are stabbed in the back by treacherous civilians. American withdrawal is likely, then, to bring to the surface the worst features of American culture, and perhaps to lead to a serious internal repression. On the other hand, an American "victory" might well have dangerous consequences both at home and abroad. It might give added prestige to an already far too powerful executive. There is, moreover, the problem emphasized by A. J. Muste: ". . . the problem after a war is with the victor. He thinks he has just proved that war and violence pay. Who will now teach him a lesson?" For the most powerful and most aggressive nation in the world, this is indeed a danger. If we can rid ourselves of the naive belief that we are somehow different and more pure—a belief held by the British, the French, the Japanese, in their moments of imperial glory—then we will be able honestly to face the truth in this observation. One can only hope that we will face this truth before too many innocents, on all sides, suffer and die.

Finally, there are certain principles that I think must be stressed as we try to build effective opposition to this and future wars. We must not, I believe, thoughtlessly urge others to commit civil disobedience, and we must be careful not to construct situations in which young people will find themselves induced, perhaps in violation of their basic convictions, to commit civil disobedience. Resistance must be freely undertaken. I also hope, more sincerely than I know how to say, that it will create bonds of friendship and mutual trust that will support and strengthen those who are sure to suffer.

6.

Language and Freedom

When I was invited to speak on the topic "language and freedom," I was puzzled and intrigued. Most of my professional life has been devoted to the study of language. There would be no great difficulty in finding a topic to discuss in that domain. And there is much to say about the problems of freedom and liberation as they pose themselves to us and to others in the mid-twentieth century. What is troublesome in the title of this lecture is the conjunction. In what way are language and freedom to be interconnected?

As a preliminary, let me say just a word about the contemporary study of language, as I see it. There are many aspects of language and language use that raise intriguing questions, but—in my judgment—only a few have so far led to productive theoretical work. In particular, our deepest insights are in the area of formal grammatical structure. A person who knows a language has acquired a system of rules and principles—a "generative grammar," in technical terms—that associates sound and meaning in some specific fashion. There are many reasonably well-founded and, I think, rather enlightening hypotheses as to the character of such grammars, for quite a number of languages. Furthermore, there has been a renewal of interest in "universal gram-

---

This essay was presented as a lecture at the University Freedom and Human Sciences Symposium, Loyola University, Chicago, January 8–9, 1970. It appeared in the Proceedings of the Symposium, edited by Thomas R. Gorman. It also was published in *Abraxas* 1, no. 1 (1970), and in *TriQuarterly*, no. 23–24 (1972). A number of the topics mentioned here are discussed further in my *Problems of Knowledge and Freedom* (New York: Pantheon Books, 1971; New York: The New Press, 2003). This chapter was reprinted in *For Reasons of State* (New York: Pantheon Books, 1970; New York: The New Press, 2003), 387–408.

mar," interpreted now as the theory that tries to specify the general properties of these languages that can be learned in the normal way by humans. Here too, significant progress has been achieved. The subject is of particular importance. It is appropriate to regard universal grammar as the study of one of the essential faculties of mind. It is, therefore, extremely interesting to discover, as I believe we do, that the principles of universal grammar are rich, abstract, and restrictive, and can be used to construct principled explanations for a variety of phenomena. At the present stage of our understanding, if language is to provide a springboard for the investigation of other problems of man, it is these aspects of language to which we will have to turn our attention, for the simple reason that it is only these aspects that are reasonably well understood. In another sense, the study of formal properties of language reveals something of the nature of man in a negative way: it underscores, with great clarity, the limits of our understanding of those qualities of mind that are apparently unique to man and that must enter into his cultural achievements in an intimate, if still quite obscure, manner.

In searching for a point of departure, one turns naturally to a period in the history of Western thought when it was possible to believe that "the thought of making freedom the sum and substance of philosophy has emancipated the human spirit in all its relationships, and . . . has given to science in all its parts a more powerful reorientation than any earlier revolution."[1] The word "revolution" bears multiple associations in this passage, for Schelling also proclaims that "man is born to act and not to speculate"; and when he writes that "the time has come to proclaim to a nobler humanity the freedom of the spirit, and no longer to have patience with men's tearful regrets for their lost chains," we hear the echoes of the libertarian thought and revolutionary acts of the late eighteenth century. Schelling writes that "the beginning and end of all philosophy is—Freedom." These words are invested with meaning and urgency at a time when men are struggling to cast off their chains, to resist authority that has lost its claim to legitimacy, to construct more humane and more democratic social institutions. It is at such a time that the philosopher may be driven to inquire into the nature of human freedom and its limits, and perhaps to conclude, with Schelling, that with respect to the human ego, "its essence is freedom"; and with respect to philosophy, "the highest dignity of Philosophy consists precisely therein, that it stakes all on human freedom."

We are living, once again, at such a time. A revolutionary ferment is sweeping the so-called Third World, awakening enormous masses from torpor and acquiescence in traditional authority. There are those who feel that the industrial societies as well are ripe for revolutionary change—and I do not refer only to representatives of the New Left.[2]

The threat of revolutionary change brings forth repression and reaction. Its signs are evident in varying forms, in France, in the Soviet Union, in the United States—not least, in the city where we are meeting. It is natural, then, that we should consider, abstractly, the problems of human freedom, and turn with interest and serious attention to the thinking of an earlier period when archaic social institutions were subjected to critical analysis and sustained attack. It is natural and appropriate, so long as we bear in mind Schelling's admonition, that man is born not merely to speculate but also to act.

One of the earliest and most remarkable of the eighteenth-century investigations of freedom and servitude is Rousseau's *Discourse on Inequality* (1755), in many ways a revolutionary tract. In it, he seeks to "set forth the origin and progress of inequality, the establishment and abuse of political societies, insofar as these things can be deduced from the nature of man by the light of reason alone." His conclusions were sufficiently shocking that the judges of the prize competition of the Academy of Dijon, to whom the work was originally submitted, refused to hear the manuscript through.[3] In it, Rousseau challenges the legitimacy of virtually every social institution, as well as individual control of property and wealth. These are "usurpations . . . established only on a precarious and abusive right . . . having been acquired only by force, force could take them away without [the rich] having grounds for complaint." Not even property acquired by personal industry is held "upon better titles." Against such a claim, one might object: "Do you not know that a multitude of your brethren die or suffer from need of what you have in excess, and that you needed express and unanimous consent of the human race to appropriate for yourself anything from common subsistence that exceeded your own?" It is contrary to the law of nature that "a handful of men be glutted with superfluities while the starving multitude lacks necessities."

Rousseau argues that civil society is hardly more than a conspiracy by the rich to guarantee their plunder. Hypocritically, the rich call upon their neighbors to "institute regulations of justice and peace to which all are obliged to conform, which make an exception of no one, and which compensate in some way for the caprices of fortune by equally subjecting the powerful and the weak to mutual duties"—those laws which, as Anatole France was to say, in their majesty deny to the rich and the poor equally the right to sleep under the bridge at night. By such arguments, the poor and weak were seduced: "All ran to meet their chains thinking they secured their freedom. . . ." Thus society and laws "gave new fetters to the weak and new forces to the rich, destroyed natural freedom for all time, established forever the law of property and inequality, changed a clever usurpation into an irrevocable right, and for the profit of a few ambitious men henceforth subjected the whole human race to work, servitude and misery." Governments inevitably tend toward arbitrary power, as "their corruption and extreme limit." This power is "by its nature illegitimate," and new revolutions must

> dissolve the government altogether or bring it closer to its legitimate institution. . . . The uprising that ends by strangling or dethroning a sultan is as lawful an act as those by which he disposed, the day before, of the lives and goods of his subjects. Force alone maintained him, force alone overthrows him.

What is interesting, in the present connection, is the path that Rousseau follows to reach these conclusions "by the light of reason alone," beginning with his ideas about the nature of man. He wants to see man "as nature formed him." It is from the nature of man that the principles of natural right and the foundations of social existence must be deduced.

> This same study of original man, of his true needs, and of the principles underlying his duties, is also the only good means one could use to remove those crowds of difficulties which present themselves concerning the origin of moral inequality, the true foundation of the body politic, the reciprocal rights of its members, and a thousand similar questions as important as they are ill explained.

To determine the nature of man, Rousseau proceeds to compare man and animal. Man is "intelligent, free . . . the sole animal endowed with reason." Animals are "devoid of intellect and freedom."

> In every animal I see only an ingenious machine to which nature has given senses in order to revitalize itself and guarantee itself, to a certain point, from all that tends to destroy or upset it. I perceive precisely the same things in the human machine, with the difference that nature alone does everything in the operations of a beast, whereas man contributes to his operations by being a free agent. The former chooses or rejects by instinct and the latter by an act of freedom, so that a beast cannot deviate from the rule that is prescribed to it even when it would be advantageous for it to do so, and a man deviates from it often to his detriment. . . . [I]t is not so much understanding which constitutes the distinction of man among the animals as it is his being a free agent. Nature commands every animal, and the beast obeys. Man feels the same impetus, but he realizes that he is free to acquiesce or resist; and it is above all in the consciousness of this freedom that the spirituality of his soul is shown. For physics explains in some way the mechanism of the senses and the formation of ideas; but in the power of willing, or rather of choosing, and in the sentiment of this power are found only purely spiritual acts about which the laws of mechanics explain nothing.

Thus the essence of human nature is man's freedom and his consciousness of his freedom. So Rousseau can say that "the jurists, who have gravely pronounced that the child of a slave would be born a slave, have decided in other terms that a man would not be born a man."[4]

Sophistic politicians and intellectuals search for ways to obscure the fact that the essential and defining property of man is his freedom: "they attribute to men a natural inclination to servitude, without thinking that it is the same for freedom as for innocence and virtue—their value is felt only as long as one enjoys them oneself and the taste for them is lost as soon as one has lost them." In contrast, Rousseau asks rhetorically "whether, freedom being the most noble of man's faculties, it is not degrading one's nature, putting oneself on the level of beasts enslaved by instinct, even offending the author of one's being, to renounce without reservation the most precious of all his gifts and subject ourselves to committing all the crimes he forbids us in order to please a ferocious or insane master"—a question that has been asked, in similar terms, by many an American draft resister in the last few years, and by many others who are beginning to recover from the catastrophe of twentieth-century Western civilization, which has so tragically confirmed Rousseau's judgment:

> Hence arose the national wars, battles, murders, and reprisals which make nature tremble and shock reason, and all those horrible prejudices which rank the honor of shedding human blood among the virtues. The most decent men learned to consider it one of their duties to murder their fellowmen; at length men were seen to massacre each other by the thousands without knowing why; more murders were committed on a single day of fighting and more horrors in the capture of a single city than were committed in the state of nature during whole centuries over the entire face of the earth.

The proof of his doctrine that the struggle for freedom is an essential human attribute, that the value of freedom is felt only as long as one enjoys it, Rousseau sees in "the marvels done by all free peoples to guard themselves from oppression." True, those who have abandoned the life of a free man

> do nothing but boast incessantly of the peace and repose they enjoy in their chains. . . . But when I see the others sacrifice pleasures, repose, wealth, power, and life itself for the preservation of this sole good which is so disdained by those who have lost it; when I see animals born free and despising captivity break their heads against the bars of their prison; when I see multitudes of entirely naked

> savages scorn European voluptuousness and endure hunger, fire, the sword, and death to preserve only their independence, I feel that it does not behoove slaves to reason about freedom.

Rather similar thoughts were expressed by Kant, forty years later. He cannot, he says, accept the proposition that certain people "are not ripe for freedom," for example, the serfs of some landlord.

> If one accepts this assumption, freedom will never be achieved; for one can not arrive at the maturity for freedom without having already acquired it; one must be free to learn how to make use of one's powers freely and usefully. The first attempts will surely be brutal and will lead to a state of affairs more painful and dangerous than the former condition under the dominance but also the protection of an external authority. However, one can achieve reason only through one's own experiences and one must be free to be able to undertake them. . . . To accept the principle that freedom is worthless for those under one's control and that one has the right to refuse it to them forever, is an infringement on the rights of God himself, who has created man to be free.[5]

The remark is particularly interesting because of its context. Kant was defending the French Revolution, during the Terror, against those who claimed that it showed the masses to be unready for the privilege of freedom. Kant's remarks have contemporary relevance. No rational person will approve of violence and terror. In particular, the terror of the postrevolutionary state, fallen into the hands of a grim autocracy, has more than once reached indescribable levels of savagery. Yet no person of understanding or humanity will too quickly condemn the violence that often occurs when long-subdued masses rise against their oppressors, or take their first steps towards liberty and social reconstruction.

Let me return now to Rousseau's argument against the legitimacy of established authority, whether that of political power or of wealth. It is striking that his argument, up to this point, follows a familiar Cartesian model. Man is uniquely beyond the bounds of physical explanation; the beast, on the other hand, is merely an ingenious machine, commanded by natural law. Man's freedom and his consciousness of this freedom distinguish him from the beast-machine. The principles of mechanical explanation are incapable of accounting for these human properties, though they can account for sensation and even the combination of ideas, in which regard "man differs from a beast only in degree."

To Descartes and his followers, such as Cordemoy, the only sure sign that another organism has a mind, and hence also lies beyond the bounds of mechanical explanation, is its use of language in the normal, creative human fashion, free from control by identifiable stimuli, novel and innovative, appropriate to situations, coherent, and engendering in our minds new thoughts and ideas.[6] To the Cartesians, it is obvious by introspection that each man possesses a mind, a substance whose essence is thought; his creative use of language reflects this freedom of thought and conception. When we have evidence that another organism too uses language in this free and creative fashion, we are led to attribute to it as well a mind like ours. From similar assumptions regarding the intrinsic limits of mechanical explanation, its inability to account for man's freedom and consciousness of his freedom, Rousseau proceeds to develop his critique of authoritarian institutions, which deny to man his essential attribute of freedom, in varying degree.

Were we to combine these speculations, we might develop an interesting connection between language and freedom. Language, in its essential properties and the manner of its use, provides the basic criterion for determining that another organism is a being with a human mind and the human capacity for free thought and self-expression, and with the essential human need for freedom from the external constraints of repressive authority. Furthermore, we might try to proceed from the detailed investigation of language and its use to a deeper and more specific understanding of the human mind. Proceeding on this model, we might further attempt to study other aspects of that human nature which, as Rousseau rightly observes, must be correctly conceived if we are to be able to develop, in theory, the foundations for a rational social order.

I will return to this problem, but first I would like to trace further Rousseau's thinking about the matter. Rousseau diverges from the Cartesian tradition in several respects. He defines the "specific characteristic of the human species" as man's "faculty of self-perfection," which, "with the aid of circumstances, successively develops all the others, and resides among us as much in the species as in the individual." The faculty of self-perfection and of perfection of the human species through cultural transmission is not, to my knowledge, discussed in any similar terms by the Cartesians. However, I think that Rousseau's remarks might be interpreted as a development of the Cartesian tradition in an unexplored direction, rather than as a denial and rejection of it. There is no inconsistency in the notion that the restrictive attributes of mind underlie a historically evolving human nature that develops within the limits that they set; or that these attributes of mind provide the possibility for self-perfection; or that, by providing the consciousness of freedom, these essential attributes of human nature give man the opportunity to create social conditions and social forms to maximize the possibilities for freedom, diversity, and individual self-realization. To use an arithmetical analogy, the integers do not fail to be an infinite set merely because they do not exhaust the rational numbers. Analogously, it is no denial of man's capacity for infinite "self-perfection" to hold that there are intrinsic properties of mind that constrain his development. I would like to argue that in a sense the opposite is true, that without a system of formal constraints there are no creative acts; specifically, in the absence of intrinsic and restrictive properties of mind, there can be only "shaping of behavior" but no creative acts of self-perfection. Furthermore, Rousseau's concern for the evolutionary character of self-perfection brings us back, from another point of view, to a concern for human language, which would appear to be a prerequisite for such evolution of society and culture, for Rousseau's perfection of the species, beyond the most rudimentary forms.

Rousseau holds that "although the organ of speech is natural to man, speech itself is nonetheless not natural to him." Again, I see no inconsistency between this observation and the typical Cartesian view that innate abilities are "dispositional," faculties that lead us to produce ideas (specifically, innate ideas) in a particular manner under given conditions of external stimulation, but that also provide us with the ability to proceed in our thinking without such external factors. Language too, then, is natural to man only in a specific way. This is an important and, I believe, quite fundamental insight of the rationalist linguists that was disregarded, very largely, under the impact of empiricist psychology in the eighteenth century and since.[7]

Rousseau discusses the origin of language at some length, though he confesses himself to be unable to come to grips with the problem in a satisfactory way. Thus

> if men needed speech in order to learn to think, they had even greater need of knowing how to think in order to discover the art of speech. . . . So that one can hardly form tenable conjectures about this art of communicating thoughts and establishing intercourse between minds; a sublime art which is now very far from its origin. . . .

He holds that "general ideas can come into the mind only with the aid of words, and the understanding grasps them only through propositions"—a fact that prevents animals, devoid of reason, from formulating such ideas or ever acquiring "the perfectibility which depends upon them." Thus he cannot conceive of the means by which "our new grammarians began to extend their ideas and to generalize their words," or to develop the means "to express all the thoughts of men": "numbers, abstract words, aorists, and all the tenses of verbs, particles, syntax, the linking of propositions, reasoning, and the forming of all the logic of discourse." He does speculate about later stages of the perfection of the species, "when the ideas of men began to spread and multiply, and when closer communication was established among them, [and] they sought more numerous signs and a more extensive language." But he must, unhappily, abandon "the following difficult problem: which was most necessary, previously formed society for the institution of languages, or previously invented languages for the establishment of society?"

The Cartesians cut the Gordian knot by postulating the existence of a species-specific characteristic, a second substance that serves as what we might call a "creative principle" alongside the "mechanical principle" that determines totally the behavior of animals. There was, for them, no need to explain the origin of language in the course of historical evolution. Rather, man's nature is qualitatively distinct: there is no passage from body to mind. We might reinterpret this idea in more current terms by speculating that rather sudden and dramatic mutations might have led to qualities of intelligence that are, so far as we know, unique to man, possession of language in the human sense being the most distinctive index of these qualities.[8] If this is correct, as at least a first approximation to the facts, the study of language might be expected to offer an entering wedge, or perhaps a model, for an investigation of human nature that would provide the grounding for a much broader theory of human nature.

To conclude these historical remarks, I would like to turn, as I have elsewhere,[9] to Wilhelm von Humboldt, one of the most stimulating and intriguing thinkers of the period. Humboldt was, on the one hand, one of the most profound theorists of general linguistics, and on the other, an early and forceful advocate of libertarian values. The basic concept of his philosophy is *Bildung*, by which, as J. W. Burrow expresses it, "he meant the fullest, richest and most harmonious development of the potentialities of the individual, the community or the human race."[10] His own thought might serve as an exemplary case. Though he does not, to my knowledge, explicitly relate his ideas about language to his libertarian social thought, there is quite clearly a common ground from which they develop, a concept of human nature that inspires each. Mill's essay *On Liberty* takes as its epigraph Humboldt's formulation of the "leading principle" of his thought: "the absolute and essential importance of human development in its richest diversity." Humboldt concludes his critique of the authoritarian state by saying: "I have felt myself animated throughout with a sense of the deepest respect for the inherent dignity of human nature, and for freedom, which alone befits that dignity." Briefly put, his concept of human nature is this:

> The true end of Man, or that which is prescribed by the eternal and immutable dictates of reason, and not suggested by vague and transient desires, is the highest and most harmonious development of his powers to a complete and consistent whole.

> Freedom is the first and indispensable condition which the possibility of such a development presupposes; but there is besides another essential—intimately connected with freedom, it is true—a variety of situations.[11]

Like Rousseau and Kant, he holds that

> nothing promotes this ripeness for freedom so much as freedom itself. This truth, perhaps, may not be acknowledged by those who have so often used this unripeness as an excuse for continuing repression. But it seems to me to follow unquestionably from the very nature of man. The incapacity for freedom can only arise from a want of moral and intellectual power; to heighten this power is the only way to supply this want; but to do this presupposes the exercise of the power, and this exercise presupposes the freedom which awakens spontaneous activity. Only it is clear we cannot call it giving freedom, when bonds are relaxed which are not felt as such by him who wears them. But of no man on earth—however neglected by nature, and however degraded by circumstances—is this true of all the bonds which oppress him. Let us undo them one by one, as the feeling of freedom awakens in men's hearts, and we shall hasten progress at every step.

Those who do not comprehend this "may justly be suspected of misunderstanding human nature, and of wishing to make men into machines."

Man is fundamentally a creative, searching, self-perfecting being: "to inquire and to create—these are the centres around which all human pursuits more or less directly revolve." But freedom of thought and enlightenment are not only for the elite. Once again echoing Rousseau, Humboldt states: "There is something degrading to human nature in the idea of refusing to any man the right to be a man." He is, then, optimistic about the effects on all of "the diffusion of scientific knowledge by freedom and enlightenment." But "all moral culture springs solely and immediately from the inner life of the soul, and can only be stimulated in human nature, and never produced by external and artificial contrivances. . . . The cultivation of the understanding, as of any of man's other faculties, is generally achieved by his own activity, his own ingenuity, or his own methods of using the discoveries of others. . . ." Education, then, must provide the opportunities for self-fulfillment; it can at best provide a rich and challenging environment for the individual to explore, in his own way. Even a language cannot, strictly speaking, be taught, but only "awakened in the mind: one can only provide the thread along which it will develop of itself." I think that Humboldt would have found congenial much of Dewey's thinking about education. And he might also have appreciated the recent revolutionary extension of such ideas, for example, by the radical Catholics of Latin America who are concerned with the "awakening of consciousness," referring to "the transformation of the passive exploited lower classes into conscious and critical masters of their own destinies"[12] much in the manner of Third World revolutionaries elsewhere. He would, I am sure, have approved of their criticism of schools that are

> more preoccupied with the transmission of knowledge than with the creation, among other values, of a critical spirit. From the social point of view, the educational systems are oriented to maintaining the existing social and economic structures instead of transforming them.[13]

But Humboldt's concern for spontaneity goes well beyond educational practice in the narrow sense. It touches also the question of labor and exploitation. The remarks, just quoted, about the cultivation of understanding through spontaneous action continue as follows:

> . . . man never regards what he possesses as so much his own, as what he does; and the labourer who tends a garden is perhaps in a truer sense its owner, than the listless voluptuary who enjoys its fruits . . . In view of this consideration,[14] it seems as if all peasants and craftsmen might be elevated into artists; that is, men who love their labour for its own sake, improve it by their own plastic genius and inventive skill, and thereby cultivate their intellect, ennoble their character, and exalt and refine their pleasures. And so humanity would be ennobled by the very things which now, though beautiful in themselves, so often serve to degrade it. . . . But, still, freedom is undoubtedly the indispensable condition, without which even the pursuits most congenial to individual human nature, can never succeed in producing such salutary influences. Whatever does not spring from a man's free choice, or is only the result of instruction and guidance, does not enter into his very being, but remains alien to his true nature; he does not perform it with truly human energies, but merely with mechanical exactness.

If a man acts in a purely mechanical way, reacting to external demands or instruction rather than in ways determined by his own interests and energies and power, "we may admire what he does, but we despise what he is."[15]

On such conceptions Humboldt grounds his ideas concerning the role of the state, which tends to "make man an instrument to serve its arbitrary ends, overlooking his individual purposes." His doctrine is classical liberal, strongly opposed to all but the most minimal forms of state intervention in personal or social life.

Writing in the 1790s, Humboldt had no conception of the forms that industrial capitalism would take. Hence he is not overly concerned with the dangers of private power.

> But when we reflect (still keeping theory distinct from practice) that the influence of a private person is liable to diminution and decay, from competition, dissipation of fortune, even death; and that clearly none of these contingencies can be applied to the State; we are still left with the principle that the latter is not to meddle in anything which does not refer exclusively to security. . . .

He speaks of the essential equality of the condition of private citizens, and of course has no idea of the ways in which the notion "private person" would come to be reinterpreted in the era of corporate capitalism. He did not foresee that "Democracy with its motto of *equality of all citizens before the law* and Liberalism with its *right of man over his own person* both [would be] wrecked on realities of capitalist economy."[16] He did not foresee that in a predatory capitalist economy, state intervention would be an absolute necessity to preserve human existence and to prevent the destruction of the physical environment—I speak optimistically. As Karl Polanyi, for one, has pointed out, the self-adjusting market "could not exist for any length of time without annihilating the human and natural substance of society; it would have physically destroyed man and transformed his surroundings into a wilderness."[17] Humboldt did not foresee the consequences of the commodity character of labor, the doctrine (in Polanyi's words) that "it is not for the commodity to decide where it should be offered for sale, to what purpose it should be used, at what price it should be allowed to change hands, and in what manner it should be consumed or destroyed." But the commodity, in this case, is a human life, and social protection was therefore a minimal necessity to constrain the irrational and destructive workings of the classical free market. Nor did Humboldt understand that capitalist economic relations perpetuated a form of bondage which, as early as 1767, Simon Linguet had declared to be even worse than slavery.

> It is the impossibility of living by any other means that compels our farm laborers to till the soil whose fruits they will not eat, and our masons to construct buildings in which they will not live. It is want that drags them to those markets where they await masters who will do them the kindness of buying them. It is want that compels them to go down on their knees to the rich man in order to get from him permission to enrich him. . . . What effective gain has the suppression of slavery brought him? . . . He is free, you say. Ah! That is his misfortune. The slave was precious to his master because of the money he had cost him. But the handicraftsman costs nothing to the rich voluptuary who employs him. . . . These men, it is said, have no master—they have one, and the most terrible, the most imperious of masters, that is *need*. It is this that reduces them to the most cruel dependence.[18]

If there is something degrading to human nature in the idea of bondage, then a new emancipation must be awaited, Fourier's "third and last emancipatory phase of history," which will transform the proletariat to free men by eliminating the commodity character of labor, ending wage slavery, and bringing the commercial, industrial, and financial institutions under democratic control.[19]

Perhaps Humboldt might have accepted these conclusions. He does agree that state intervention in social life is legitimate if "freedom would destroy the very conditions without which not only freedom but even existence itself would be inconceivable"—precisely the circumstances that arise in an unconstrained capitalist economy. In any event, his criticism of bureaucracy and the autocratic state stands as an eloquent forewarning of some of the most dismal aspects of modern history, and the basis of his critique is applicable to a broader range of coercive institutions than he imagined.

Though expressing a classical liberal doctrine, Humboldt is no primitive individualist in the style of Rousseau. Rousseau extols the savage who "lives within himself"; he has little use for "the sociable man, always outside of himself, [who] knows how to live only in the opinion of others . . . from [whose] judgment alone . . . he draws the sentiment of his own existence."[20] Humboldt's vision is quite different:

> . . . the whole tenor of the ideas and arguments unfolded in this essay might fairly be reduced to this, that while they would break all fetters in human society, they would attempt to find as many new social bonds as possible. The isolated man is no more able to develop than the one who is fettered.

Thus he looks forward to a community of free association without coercion by the state or other authoritarian institutions, in which free men can create and inquire, and achieve the highest development of their powers—far ahead of his time, he presents an anarchist vision that is appropriate, perhaps, to the next stage of industrial society. We can perhaps look forward to a day when these various strands will be brought together within the framework of libertarian socialism, a social form that barely exists today though its elements can be perceived: in the guarantee of individual rights that has achieved its highest form—though still tragically flawed—in the Western democracies; in the Israeli *kibbutzim*; in the experiments with workers' councils in Yugoslavia; in the effort to awaken popular consciousness and create a new involvement in the social process which is a fundamental element in the Third World revolutions, coexisting uneasily with indefensible authoritarian practice.

A similar concept of human nature underlies Humboldt's work on language. Language is a process of free creation; its laws and principles are fixed, but the manner in which the principles of generation are used is free and infinitely varied. Even the interpretation and use of words involves a process of free creation. The normal use of language and the acquisition of language depend on what Humboldt calls the fixed form of language, a system of generative processes that is rooted in the nature of the human mind and constrains but does not determine the free creations of normal intelligence or, at a higher and more original level, of the great writer or thinker. Humboldt is, on the one hand, a Platonist who insists that learning is a kind of reminiscence, in which the mind, stimulated by experience, draws from its own internal resources and follows a path that it itself determines; and he is also a romantic, attuned to cultural variety, and the endless possibilities for the spiritual contributions of the creative genius. There is no contradiction in this, any more than there is a contradiction in the insistence of aesthetic theory that individual works of genius are constrained by principle and rule. The normal, creative use of language, which to the Cartesian rationalist is the best index of the existence of another mind, presupposes a system or rules and generative principles of a sort that the rationalist grammarians attempted, with some success, to determine and make explicit.

The many modern critics who sense an inconsistency in the belief that free creation takes place within—presupposes, in fact—a system of constraints and governing principles are quite mistaken; unless, of course, they speak of "contradiction" in the loose and metaphoric sense of Schelling, when he writes that "without the contradiction of necessity and freedom not only philosophy but every nobler ambition of the spirit would sink to that death which is peculiar to those sciences in which that contradiction serves no function." Without this tension between necessity and freedom, rule and choice, there can be no creativity, no communication, no meaningful acts at all.

I have discussed these traditional ideas at some length, not out of antiquarian interest, but because I think that they are valuable and essentially correct, and that they project a course we can follow with profit. Social action must be animated by a vision of a future society, and by explicit judgments of value concerning the character of this future society. These judgments must derive from some concept of the nature of man, and one may seek empirical foundations by investigating man's nature as it is revealed by his behavior and his creations, material, intellectual, and social. We have, perhaps, reached a point in history when it is possible to think seriously about a society in which freely constituted social bonds replace the fetters of autocratic institutions, rather in the sense conveyed by the remarks of Humboldt that I quoted, and elaborated more fully in the tradition of libertarian socialism in the years that followed.[21]

Predatory capitalism created a complex industrial system and an advanced technology; it permitted a considerable extension of democratic practice and fostered certain liberal values, but within limits that are now being pressed and must be overcome. It is not a fit system for the mid-twentieth century. It is incapable of meeting human needs that can be expressed only in collective terms, and its concept of competitive man who seeks only to maximize wealth and power, who subjects himself to market relationships, to exploitation and external authority, is antihuman and intolerable in the deepest sense. An autocratic state is no acceptable substitute; nor can the militarized state capitalism evolving in the United States or the bureaucratized, centralized welfare state be accepted as the goal of human existence. The only justification for repressive institutions is material and cultural deficit. But such institutions, at certain stages of history, perpetuate and produce such a deficit, and even threaten human survival. Modern science and technology can relieve men of the necessity for specialized, imbecile labor. They may, in principle, provide the basis for a rational social order based on free association and democratic control, if we have the will to create it.

A vision of a future social order is in turn based on a concept of human nature. If in fact man is an indefinitely malleable, completely plastic being, with no innate structures of mind and no intrinsic needs of a cultural or social character, then he is a fit subject for the "shaping of behavior" by the state authority, the corporate manager, the technocrat, or the central committee. Those with some confidence in the human species will hope this is not so and will try to determine the intrinsic human characteristics that provide the framework for intellectual development, the growth of moral consciousness, cultural achievement, and participation in a free community. In a partly analogous way, a classical tradition spoke of artistic genius acting within and in some ways challenging a framework of rule. Here we touch on matters that are little understood. It seems to me that we must break away, sharply and radically, from much of modern social and behavioral science if we are to move towards a deeper understanding of these matters.[22]

Here, too, I think that the tradition I have briefly reviewed has a contribution to offer. As I have already observed, those who were concerned with human distinctiveness and potential repeatedly were led to a consideration of the properties of language. I think that the study of language can provide some glimmerings of understanding of rule-governed behavior and the possibilities for free and creative action within the framework of a system of rules that in part, at least, reflect intrinsic properties of human mental organization. It seems to me fair to regard the contemporary study of language as in some ways a return to the Humboldtian concept of the form of language: a system of generative processes rooted in innate properties of mind but permitting, in

Humboldt's phrase, an infinite use of finite means. Language cannot be described as a system of organization of behavior. Rather, to understand how language is used, we must discover the abstract Humboldtian form of language—its generative grammar, in modern terms. To learn a language is to construct for oneself this abstract system, of course unconsciously. The linguist and psychologist can proceed to study the use and acquisition of language only insofar as he has some grasp of the properties of the system that has been mastered by the person who knows the language. Furthermore, it seems to me that a good case can be made in support of the empirical claim that such a system can be acquired, under the given conditions of time and access, only by a mind that is endowed with certain specific properties that we can now tentatively describe in some detail. As long as we restrict ourselves, conceptually, to the investigation of behavior, its organization, its development through interaction with the environment, we are bound to miss these characteristics of language and mind. Other aspects of human psychology and culture might, in principle, be studied in a similar way.

Conceivably, we might in this way develop a social science based on empirically well-founded propositions concerning human nature. Just as we study the range of humanly attainable languages, with some success, we might also try to study the forms of artistic expression or, for that matter, scientific knowledge that humans can conceive, and perhaps even the range of ethical systems and social structures in which humans can live and function, given their intrinsic capacities and needs. Perhaps one might go on to project a concept of social organization that would—under given conditions of material and spiritual culture—best encourage and accommodate the fundamental human need—if such it is—for spontaneous initiative, creative work, solidarity, pursuit of social justice.

I do not want to exaggerate, as I no doubt have, the role of investigation of language. Language is the product of human intelligence that is, for the moment, most accessible to study. A rich tradition held language to be a mirror of mind. To some extent, there is surely truth and useful insight in this idea.

I am no less puzzled by the topic "language and freedom" than when I began—and no less intrigued. In these speculative and sketchy remarks there are gaps so vast that one might question what would remain, when metaphor and unsubstantiated guess are removed. It is sobering to realize—as I believe we must—how little we have progressed in our knowledge of man and society, or even in formulating clearly the problems that might be seriously studied. But there are, I think, a few footholds that seem fairly firm. I like to believe that the intensive study of one aspect of human psychology—human language—may contribute to a humanistic social science that will serve, as well, as an instrument for social action. It must, needless to say, be stressed that social action cannot await a firmly established theory of man and society, nor can the validity of the latter be determined by our hopes and moral judgments. The two—speculation and action—must progress as best they can, looking forward to the day when theoretical inquiry will provide a firm guide to the unending, often grim, but never hopeless struggle for freedom and social justice.

7.

Notes on Anarchism

A French writer, sympathetic to anarchism, wrote in the 1890s that "anarchism has a broad back, like paper it endures anything"—including, he noted, those whose acts are such that "a mortal enemy of anarchism could not have done better."[1] There have been many styles of thought and action that have been referred to as "anarchist." It would be hopeless to try to encompass all of these conflicting tendencies in some general theory or ideology. And even if we proceed to extract from the history of libertarian thought a living, evolving tradition, as Daniel Guérin does in *Anarchism*, it remains difficult to formulate its doctrines as a specific and determinate theory of society and social change. The anarchist historian Rudolf Rocker, who presents a systematic conception of the development of anarchist thought toward anarchosyndicalism, along lines that bear comparison to Guérin's work, puts the matter well when he writes that anarchism is not

> a fixed, self-enclosed social system but rather a definite trend in the historic development of mankind, which, in contrast with the intellectual guardianship of all clerical and governmental institutions, strives for the free unhindered unfolding of all the individual and social forces in life. Even freedom is only a relative, not an absolute concept, since it tends constantly to become broader and to affect wider cir-

This essay is a revised version of the introduction to Daniel Guérin's *Anarchism: From Theory to Practice* (New York: Monthly Review Press, 1970). In a slightly different version, it appeared in the *New York Review of Books,* May 21, 1970, reprinted in *For Reasons of State* (New York: Pantheon Books, 1973; New York: The New Press, 2003), 370–86.

> cles in more manifold ways. For the anarchist, freedom is not an abstract philosophical concept, but the vital concrete possibility for every human being to bring to full development all the powers, capacities, and talents with which nature has endowed him, and turn them to social account. The less this natural development of man is influenced by ecclesiastical or political guardianship, the more efficient and harmonious will human personality become, the more will it become the measure of the intellectual culture of the society in which it has grown.[2]

One might ask what value there is in studying a "definite trend in the historic development of mankind" that does not articulate a specific and detailed social theory. Indeed, many commentators dismiss anarchism as utopian, formless, primitive, or otherwise incompatible with the realities of a complex society. One might, however, argue rather differently: that at every stage of history our concern must be to dismantle those forms of authority and oppression that survive from an era when they might have been justified in terms of the need for security or survival or economic development, but that now contribute to—rather than alleviate—material and cultural deficit. If so, there will be no doctrine of social change fixed for the present and future, nor even, necessarily, a specific and unchanging concept of the goals towards which social change should tend. Surely our understanding of the nature of man or of the range of viable social forms is so rudimentary that any far-reaching doctrine must be treated with great skepticism, just as skepticism is in order when we hear that "human nature" or "the demands of efficiency" or "the complexity of modern life" requires this or that form of oppression and autocratic rule.

Nevertheless, at a particular time there is every reason to develop, insofar as our understanding permits, a specific realization of this definite trend in the historic development of mankind, appropriate to the tasks of the moment. For Rocker, "the problem that is set for our time is that of freeing man from the curse of economic exploitation and political and social enslavement"; and the method is not the conquest and exercise of state power, nor stultifying parliamentarianism, but rather "to reconstruct the economic life of the peoples from the ground up and build it up in the spirit of Socialism."

> But only the producers themselves are fitted for this task, since they are the only value-creating element in society out of which a new future can arise. Theirs must be the task of freeing labor from all the fetters which economic exploitation has fastened on it, of freeing society from all the institutions and procedure of political power, and of opening the way to an alliance of free groups of men and women based on co-operative labor and a planned administration of things in the interest of the community. To prepare the toiling masses in city and country for

> this great goal and to bind them together as a militant force is the objective of modern Anarcho-syndicalism, and in this its whole purpose is exhausted. [p. 108]

As a socialist, Rocker would take for granted "that the serious, final, complete liberation of the workers is possible only upon one condition: that of the appropriation of capital, that is, of raw material and all the tools of labor, including land, by the whole body of the workers."[3] As an anarchosyndicalist, he insists, further, that the workers' organizations create "not only the ideas, but also the facts of the future itself" in the prerevolutionary period, that they embody in themselves the structure of the future society—and he looks forward to a social revolution that will dismantle the state apparatus as well as expropriate the expropriators. "What we put in place of the government is industrial organization."

> Anarcho-syndicalists are convinced that a Socialist economic order cannot be created by the decrees and statutes of a government, but only by the solidaric collaboration of the workers with hand and brain in each special branch of production; that is, through the taking over of the management of all plants by the producers themselves under such form that the separate groups, plants, and branches of industry are independent members of the general economic organism and systematically carry on production and the distribution of the products in the interest of the community on the basis of free mutual agreements. [p. 94]

Rocker was writing at a moment when such ideas had been put into practice in a dramatic way in the Spanish Revolution. Just prior to the outbreak of the revolution, the anarchosyndicalist economist Diego Abad de Santillan had written:

> . . . in facing the problem of social transformation, the Revolution cannot consider the state as a medium, but must depend on the organization of producers.
>
> We have followed this norm and we find no need for the hypothesis of a superior power to organized labor, in order to establish a new order of things. We would thank anyone to point out to us what function, if any, the State can have in an economic organization, where private property has been abolished and in which parasitism and special privilege have no place. The suppression of the State cannot be a languid affair; it must be the task of the Revolution to finish with the State. Either the Revolution gives social wealth to the producers in which case the producers organize themselves for due collective distribution and the State has nothing to do; or the Revolution does not give social wealth to the producers, in which case the Revolution has been a lie and the State would continue.
>
> Our federal council of economy is not a political power but an economic and

> administrative regulating power. It receives its orientation from below and operates in accordance with the resolutions of the regional and national assemblies. It is a liaison corps and nothing else.[4]

Engels, in a letter of 1883, expressed his disagreement with this conception as follows:

> The anarchists put the thing upside down. They declare that the proletarian revolution must *begin* by doing away with the political organization of the state. . . . But to destroy it as such a moment would be to destroy the only organism by means of which the victorious proletariat can assert its newly-conquered power, hold down its capitalist adversaries, and carry out that economic revolution of society without which the whole victory must end in a new defeat and in a mass slaughter of the workers similar to those after the Paris commune.[5]

In contrast, the anarchists—most eloquently Bakunin—warned of the dangers of the "red bureaucracy," which would prove to be "the most vile and terrible lie that our century has created."[6] The anarchosyndicalist Fernand Pelloutier asked: "Must even the transitory state to which we have to submit necessarily and fatally be the collectivist jail? Can't it consist in a free organization limited exclusively by the needs of production and consumption, all political institutions having disappeared?"[7]

I do not pretend to know the answer to this question. But it seems clear that unless there is, in some form, a positive answer, the chances for a truly democratic revolution that will achieve the humanistic ideals of the left are not great. Martin Buber put the problem succinctly when he wrote: "One cannot in the nature of things expect a little tree that has been turned into a club to put forth leaves."[8] The question of conquest or destruction of state power is what Bakunin regarded as the primary issue dividing him from Marx.[9] In one form or another, the problem has arisen repeatedly in the century since, dividing "libertarian" from "authoritarian" socialists.

Despite Bakunin's warnings about the red bureaucracy, and their fulfillment under Stalin's dictatorship, it would obviously be a gross error in interpreting the debates of a century ago to rely on the claims of contemporary social movements as to their historical origins. In particular, it is perverse to regard Bolshevism as "Marxism in practice." Rather, the left-wing critique of Bolshevism, taking account of the historical circumstances of the Russian Revolution, is far more to the point.[10]

> The anti-Bolshevik, left-wing labor movement opposed the Leninists because they did not go far enough in exploiting the Russian upheavals for strictly proletarian

ends. They became prisoners of their environment and used the international radical movement to satisfy specifically Russian needs, which soon became synonymous with the needs of the Bolshevik Party-State. The "bourgeois" aspects of the Russian Revolution were now discovered in Bolshevism itself: Leninism was adjudged a part of international social-democracy, differing from the latter only on tactical issues.[11]

If one were to seek a single leading idea within the anarchist tradition, it should, I believe, be that expressed by Bakunin when, in writing on the Paris Commune, he identified himself as follows:

> I am a fanatic lover of liberty, considering it as the unique condition under which intelligence, dignity and human happiness can develop and grow; not the purely formal liberty conceded, measured out and regulated by the State, an eternal lie which in reality represents nothing more than the privilege of some founded on the slavery of the rest; not the individualistic, egoistic, shabby, and fictitious liberty extolled by the School of J.-J. Rousseau and the other schools of bourgeois liberalism, which considers the would-be rights of all men, represented by the State which limits the rights of each—an idea that leads inevitably to the reduction of the rights of each to zero. No, I mean the only kind of liberty that is worthy of the name, liberty that consists in the full development of all of the material, intellectual and moral powers that are latent in each person; liberty that recognizes no restrictions other than those determined by the laws of our own individual nature, which cannot properly be regarded as restrictions since these laws are not imposed by any outside legislator beside or above us, but are immanent and inherent, forming the very basis of our material, intellectual and moral being—they do not limit us but are the real and immediate conditions of our freedom.[12]

These ideas grow out of the Enlightenment; their roots are in Rousseau's *Discourse on Inequality*, Humboldt's *Limits of State Action*, Kant's insistence, in his defense of the French Revolution, that freedom is the precondition for acquiring the maturity for freedom, not a gift to be granted when such maturity is achieved (see chapter 6, pp. 79–80). With the development of industrial capitalism, a new and unanticipated system of injustice, it is libertarian socialism that has preserved and extended the radical humanist message of the Enlightenment and the classical liberal ideals that were perverted into an ideology to sustain the emerging social order. In fact, on the very same assumptions that led classical liberalism to oppose the intervention of the state in social life, capitalist social relations are also intolerable. This is clear, for example, from the classic work of Humboldt, *The Limits of State Action*, which anticipated and perhaps inspired Mill and to which we return below (chapter

6, pp. 83–88). This classic of liberal thought, completed in 1792, is in its essence profoundly, though prematurely, anticapitalist. Its ideas must be attenuated beyond recognition to be transmuted into an ideology of industrial capitalism.

Humboldt's vision of a society in which social fetters are replaced by social bonds and labor is freely undertaken suggests the early Marx (see chapter 6, note 16), with his discussion of the "alienation of labor when work is external to the worker . . . not part of his nature . . . [so that] he does not fulfill himself in his work but denies himself . . . [and is] physically exhausted and mentally debased," alienated labor that "casts some of the workers back into a barbarous kind of work and turns others into machines," thus depriving man of his "species character" of "free conscious activity" and "productive life." Similarly, Marx conceives of "a new type of human being who *needs* his fellow-men. . . . [The workers' association becomes] the real constructive effort to create the social texture of future human relations."[13] It is true that classical libertarian thought is opposed to state intervention in social life, as a consequence of deeper assumptions about the human need for liberty, diversity, and free association. On the same assumptions, capitalist relations of production, wage labor, competitiveness, the ideology of "possessive individualism"—all must be regarded as fundamentally antihuman. Libertarian socialism is properly to be regarded as the inheritor of the liberal ideals of the Enlightenment.

Rudolf Rocker describes modern anarchism as "the confluence of the two great currents which during and since the French revolution have found such characteristic expression in the intellectual life of Europe: Socialism and Liberalism." The classical liberal ideals, he argues, were wrecked on the realities of capitalist economic forms. Anarchism is necessarily anti-capitalist in that it "opposes the exploitation of man by man." But anarchism also opposes "the dominion of man over man." It insists that "*socialism will be free or it will not be at all*. In its recognition of this lies the genuine and profound justification for the existence of anarchism."[14] From this point of view, anarchism may be regarded as the libertarian wing of socialism. It is in this spirit that Daniel Guérin has approached the study of anarchism in *Anarchism* and other works.[15]

Guérin quotes Adolph Fischer, who said that "every anarchist is a socialist but not every socialist is necessarily an anarchist." Similarly Bakunin, in his "anarchist manifesto" of 1865, the program of his projected international revolutionary fraternity, laid down the principle that each member must be, to begin with, a socialist.

A consistent anarchist must oppose private ownership of the means of production and the wage slavery that is a component of this system, as incompatible with the principle that labor must be freely undertaken and under the control of the producer. As Marx put it, socialists look forward to a society in which labor will "become not only a means of life, but also the highest want in life,"[16] an impossibility when the worker is driven by external authority or need rather than inner impulse: "no form of wage-labor, even though one may be less obnoxious than another, can do away with the misery of wage-labor itself."[17] A consistent anarchist must oppose not only alienated labor but also the stupefying specialization of labor that takes place when the means for developing production

> mutilate the worker into a fragment of a human being, degrade him to become a mere appurtenance of the machine, make his work such a torment that its essential meaning is destroyed; estrange from him the intellectual potentialities of the labor process in very proportion to the extent to which science is incorporated into it as an independent power. . . .[18]

Marx saw this not as an inevitable concomitant of industrialization, but rather as a feature of capitalist relations of production. The society of the future must be concerned to "replace the detail-worker of today . . . reduced to a mere fragment of a man, by the fully developed individual, fit for a variety of labours . . . to whom the different social functions . . . are but so many modes of giving free scope to his own natural powers."[19] The prerequisite is the abolition of capital and wage labor as social categories (not to speak of the industrial armies of the "labor state" or the various modern forms of totalitarianism or state capitalism). The reduction of man to an appurtenance of the machine, a specialized tool of production, might in principle be overcome, rather than enhanced, with the proper development and use of technology, but not under the conditions of autocratic control of production by those who make man an instrument to serve their ends, overlooking his individual purposes, in Humboldt's phrase.

Anarchosyndicalists sought, even under capitalism, to create "free associations of free producers" that would engage in militant struggle and prepare to take over the organization of production on a democratic basis. These associations would serve as "a practical school of anarchism."[20] If private ownership of the means of production is, in Proudhon's often quoted phrase, merely a form of "theft"—"the exploitation of the weak by the strong"[21]—control of production by a state bureaucracy, no matter how benevolent its intentions, also does not create the conditions under which labor, manual and intellectual, can become the highest want in life. Both, then, must be overcome.

In his attack on the right of private or bureaucratic control over the means of production, the anarchist takes his stand with those who struggle to bring about "the third and last emancipatory phase of history," the first having made serfs out of slaves, the second having made wage earners out of serfs, and the third which abolishes the proletariat in a final act of liberation that places control over the economy in the hands of free and voluntary associations of producers (Fourier, 1848).[22] The imminent danger to "civilization" was noted by de Tocqueville, also in 1848:

> As long as the right of property was the origin and groundwork of many other rights, it was easily defended—or rather it was not attacked; it was then the citadel of society while all the other rights were its outworks; it did not bear the brunt of attack and, indeed, there was no serious attempt to assail it. But today, when the right of property is regarded as the last undestroyed remnant of the aristocratic world, when it alone is left standing, the sole privilege in an equalized society, it is a different matter. Consider what is happening in the hearts of the working-classes, although I admit they are quiet as yet. It is true that they are less inflamed than formerly by political passions properly speaking; but do you not see that their passions, far from being political, have become social? Do you not see that, little by little, ideas and opinions are spreading amongst them which aim not merely at removing such and such laws, such a ministry or such a government, but at breaking up the very foundations of society itself?[23]

The workers of Paris, in 1871, broke the silence, and proceeded

> to abolish property, the basis of all civilization! Yes, gentlemen, the Commune intended to abolish that class property which makes the labor of the many the wealth of the few. It aimed at the expropriation of the expropriators. It wanted to make individual property a truth by transforming the means of production, land and capital, now chiefly the means of enslaving and exploiting labor, into mere instruments of free and associated labor.[24]

The Commune, of course, was drowned in blood. The nature of the "civilization" that the workers of Paris sought to overcome in their attack on "the very foundations of society itself" was revealed, once again, when the troops of the Versailles government reconquered Paris from its population. As Marx wrote, bitterly but accurately:

> The civilization and justice of bourgeois order comes out in its lurid light whenever the slaves and drudges of that order rise against their masters. Then this civilization and justice stand forth as undisguised savagery and lawless revenge . . . the infernal deeds of the soldiery reflect the innate spirit of that civilization of which

> they are the mercenary vindicators. . . . The bourgeoisie of the whole world, which looks complacently upon the wholesale massacre after the battle, is convulsed by horror at the desecration of brick and mortar. [Ibid., pp. 74, 77]

Despite the violent destruction of the Commune, Bakunin wrote that Paris opens a new era, "that of the definitive and complete emancipation of the popular masses and their future true solidarity, across and despite state boundaries . . . the next revolution of man, international and in solidarity, will be the resurrection of Paris"—a revolution that the world still awaits.

The consistent anarchist, then, should be a socialist, but a socialist of a particular sort. He will not only oppose alienated and specialized labor and look forward to the appropriation of capital by the whole body of workers, but he will also insist that this appropriation be direct, not exercised by some elite force acting in the name of the proletariat. He will, in short, oppose

> the organization of production by the Government. It means State-socialism, the command of the State officials over production and the command of managers, scientists, shop-officials in the shop. . . . The goal of the working class is liberation from exploitation. This goal is not reached and cannot be reached by a new directing and governing class substituting itself for the bourgeoisie. It is only realized by the workers themselves being master over production.

These remarks are taken from "Five Theses on the Class Struggle" by the left-wing Marxist Anton Pannekoek, one of the outstanding theorists of the council communist movement. And in fact, radical Marxism merges with anarchist currents.

As a further illustration, consider the following characterization of "revolutionary Socialism":

> The revolutionary Socialist denies that State ownership can end in anything other than a bureaucratic despotism. We have seen why the State cannot democratically control industry. Industry can only be democratically owned and controlled by the workers electing directly from their own ranks industrial administrative committees. Socialism will be fundamentally an industrial system; its constituencies will be of an industrial character. Thus those carrying on the social activities and industries of society will be directly represented in the local and central councils of social administration. In this way the powers of such delegates will flow upwards from those carrying on the work and conversant with the needs of the community. When the central administrative industrial committee meets it will represent every phase of social activity. Hence the capitalist political or geographical state will be replaced by the industrial administrative committee of Socialism. The transition

> from the one social system to the other will be the *social revolution*. The political State throughout history has meant the government *of men* by ruling classes; the Republic of Socialism will be the government of *industry* administered on behalf of the whole community. The former meant the economic and political subjection of the many; the latter will mean the economic freedom of all—it will be, therefore, a true democracy.

This programmatic statement appears in William Paul's *The State, its Origins and Function*, written in early 1917—shortly before Lenin's *State and Revolution*, perhaps his most libertarian work (see note 9). Paul was a member of the Marxist-De Leonist Socialist Labor Party and later one of the founders of the British Communist Party.[25] His critique of state socialism resembles the libertarian doctrine of the anarchists in its principle that since state ownership and management will lead to bureaucratic despotism, the social revolution must replace it by the industrial organization of society with direct workers' control. Many similar statements can be cited.

What is far more important is that these ideas have been realized in spontaneous revolutionary action, for example in Germany and Italy after World War I and in Spain (not only in the agricultural countryside, but also in industrial Barcelona) in 1936. One might argue that some form of council communism is the natural form of revolutionary socialism in an industrial society. It reflects the intuitive understanding that democracy is severely limited when the industrial system is controlled by any form of autocratic elite, whether of owners, managers, and technocrats, a "vanguard" party, or a state bureaucracy. Under these conditions of authoritarian domination the classical libertarian ideals developed further by Marx and Bakunin and all true revolutionaries cannot be realized; man will not be free to develop his own potentialities to their fullest, and the producer will remain "a fragment of a human being," degraded, a tool in the productive process directed from above.

The phrase "spontaneous revolutionary action" can be misleading. The anarchosyndicalists, at least, took very seriously Bakunin's remark that the workers' organizations must create "not only the ideas but also the facts of the future itself" in the prerevolutionary period. The accomplishments of the popular revolution in Spain, in particular, were based on the patient work of many years of organization and education, one component of a long tradition of commitment and militancy. The resolutions of the Madrid Congress of June 1931 and the Saragossa Congress in May 1936 foreshadowed in many ways the acts of the revolution, as did the somewhat different ideas sketched by Santillan (see note 4) in his fairly specific account of the social and economic organization to be instituted by the revolution. Guérin writes: "The Spanish revolution was relatively mature in the minds of the libertarian thinkers, as in the popular consciousness." And workers' organizations existed with the structure, the experience, and the understanding to undertake the task of social reconstruction when, with the Franco coup, the turmoil of early 1936 exploded into social revolution. In his introduction to a collection of documents on collectivization in Spain, the anarchist Augustin Souchy writes:

> For many years, the anarchists and syndicalists of Spain considered their supreme task to be the social transformation of the society. In their assemblies of Syndicates and groups, in their journals, their brochures and books, the problem of the social revolution was discussed incessantly and in a systematic fashion.[26]

All of this lies behind the spontaneous achievements, the constructive work of the Spanish Revolution.

The ideas of libertarian socialism, in the sense described, have been submerged in the industrial societies of the past half century. The dominant ideologies have been those of state socialism or state capitalism (of an increasingly militarized character in the United States, for reasons that are not obscure).[27] But there has been a rekindling of interest in the past few years. The theses I quoted by Anton Pannekoek were taken from a recent pamphlet of a radical French workers' group (*Informations Correspondance Ouvrière*). The remarks by William Paul on revolutionary socialism are cited in a paper by Walter Kendall given at the National Conference on Workers' Control in Sheffield, England, in March 1969. The workers' control movement has become a significant force in England in the past few years. It has organized several conferences and has produced a substantial pamphlet literature, and counts among its active adherents representatives of some of the most important trade unions. The Amalgamated Engineering and Foundryworkers' Union, for example, has adopted, as official policy, the program of nationalization of basic industries under "workers' control at all levels."[28] On the Continent, there are similar developments. May 1968 of course accelerated the growing interest in council communism and related ideas in France and Germany, as it did in England.

Given the general conservative cast of our highly ideological society, it is not too surprising that the United States has been relatively untouched by these developments. But that too may change. The erosion of the cold-war mythology at least makes it possible to raise these questions in fairly broad circles. If the present wave of repression can be beaten back, if the left can overcome its more suicidal tendencies and build upon what has been accomplished in the past decade, then the problem of how to organize industrial society on truly democratic lines, with democratic control in the workplace and in the community, should become a dominant intellectual issue for those who are alive to the problems of contemporary society, and, as a mass movement for libertarian socialism develops, speculation should proceed to action.

In his manifesto of 1865, Bakunin predicted that one element in the social revolution will be "that intelligent and truly noble part of the youth which, though belonging by birth to the privileged classes, in its generous convictions and ardent aspirations, adopts the cause of the people." Perhaps in the rise of the student movement of the 1960s one sees steps towards a fulfillment of this prophecy.

Daniel Guérin has undertaken what he has described as a "process of rehabilitation" of anarchism. He argues, convincingly I believe, that "the constructive ideas of anarchism retain their vitality, that they may, when reexamined and sifted, assist contemporary socialist thought to undertake a new departure . . . [and] contribute to enriching Marxism."[29] From the "broad back" of anarchism he has selected for more intensive scrutiny those ideas and actions that can be described as libertarian socialist. This is natural and proper. This framework accommodates the major anarchist spokesmen as well as the mass actions that have been animated by anarchist sentiments and ideals. Guérin is concerned not only with anarchist thought but also with the spontaneous actions of popular forces that actually create new social forms in the course of revolutionary struggle. He is concerned with social as well as intellectual creativity. Furthermore, he attempts to draw from the constructive achievements of the past lessons that will enrich the theory of social liberation. For those who wish not only to understand the world, but also to change it, this is the proper way to study the history of anarchism.

Guérin describes the anarchism of the nineteenth century as essentially doctrinal, while the twentieth century, for the anarchists, has been a time of "revolutionary practice."[30] *Anarchism* reflects that judgment. His interpretation of anarchism consciously points towards the future. Arthur Rosenberg once pointed out that popular revolutions characteristically seek to replace "a feudal or centralized authority ruling by force" with some form of communal system which "implies the destruction and disappearance of the old form of State." Such a system will be either socialist or an "extreme form of democracy . . . [which is] the preliminary condition for Socialism inasmuch as Socialism can only be realized in a world enjoying the highest possible measure of individual freedom." This ideal, he notes, was common to Marx and the anarchists.[31] This natural struggle for liberation runs counter to the prevailing tendency towards centralization in economic and political life.

A century ago Marx wrote that the bourgeosie of Paris "felt there was but one alternative—the Commune, or the empire—under whatever name it might reappear."

> The empire had ruined them economically by the havoc it made of public wealth, by the wholesale financial swindling it fostered, by the props it lent to the artificially accelerated centralization of capital, and the concomitant expropriation of their own ranks. It had suppressed them politically, it had shocked them morally by its orgies, it had insulted their Voltairianism by handing over the education of their children to the *frères Ignorantins*, it had revolted their national feeling as Frenchmen by precipitating them headlong into a war which left only one equivalent for the ruins it made—the disappearance of the empire.[32]

The miserable Second Empire "was the only form of government possible at a time when the bourgeoisie had already lost, and the working class had not yet acquired, the faculty of ruling the nation."

It is not very difficult to rephrase these remarks so that they become appropriate to the imperial systems of 1970. The problem of "freeing man from the curse of economic exploitation and political and social enslavement" remains the problem of our time. As long as this is so, the doctrines and the revolutionary practice of libertarian socialism will serve as an inspiration and a guide.

8.

The Rule of Force in International Affairs

Two different issues arise when the American experience in Vietnam is considered in the context of the Nuremberg trials and related international conventions: the issue of "legality" and the issue of justice. The first is a technical question of law and history—by the standards of international law as formally accepted by the great powers, how is the American war in Indochina to be judged? The second question is more elusive. It is the question of proper standards. Are the principles of Nuremberg and related international law satisfactory and appropriate in the case of great-power intervention, as in Vietnam and Czechoslovakia, for example? The recent study of Nuremberg and Vietnam by Telford Taylor—the chief counsel for the prosecution at Nuremberg, a historian, professor of law, and retired brigadier general—is devoted to the first of these topics, but occasional remarks bear on the second as well. It is possible that Taylor's brief but informative study will set the framework for much of the subsequent debate over war crimes and broader questions of proper international conduct. Though conservative in assumptions and narrow in compass—overly so, in my opinion—Taylor's investigation leads to strong conclusions. He comes close to suggesting that the military and civilian leadership of the United States from 1965 to the present are liable to prosecution as war criminals under the standards of Nuremberg. No less controver-

---

This essay is a revised version of a contribution to a symposium on war crimes, based on Telford Taylor, *Nuremberg and Vietnam: An American Tragedy.* The original version was published in the *Yale Law Journal* 80, no. 7 (June 1971), reprinted in *For Reasons of State* (New York: Pantheon Books, 1973; New York: The New Press, 2003), 212–58.

sial are the self-imposed limitations of his study. In many respects, Taylor's book offers a convenient point of departure for an investigation of the issues of legality and justice.

I. "WAR CRIMES" AND "JUSTICE"

The issue of justice is not to be discounted. International law is in effect a body of moral principles accepted as valid by those who ratify treaties and other agreements. Furthermore, as Taylor emphasizes, treaties and manuals "are only partial embodiments of the laws of war." The preamble of the 1907 Hague Convention, for example, states that questions not covered should be resolved by "the principles of the law of nations, as they result from the usages established among civilized peoples, from the laws of humanity, and from the dictates of the public conscience."[1] It therefore makes sense to inquire into the *acceptability* as well as the political and social *content* of such principles as have been codified and generally adopted, and to consider them in the light of the dictates of public conscience and the laws of humanity, unclear as these may be. As to "usages established among civilized peoples," Justice Jackson, in an interim report to the president in 1945, wrote that "we are put under a heavy responsibility to see that our behavior during this unsettled period will direct the world's thought toward a firmer enforcement of the laws of international conduct, so as to make war less attractive to those who have governments and the destinies of peoples in their power" (p. 77). How have we met this responsibility in the postwar era? The question touches not only on the legality of American conduct in the light of Nuremberg and related principles, but also on the character of these principles themselves.

Taylor's discussion of the Nuremberg judgments reveals a fundamental moral flaw in the principles that emerged from those trials. Rejecting the argument that the bombing of North Vietnam constitutes a war crime, Taylor observes that "whatever the laws of war in this field *ought* to be, certainly Nuremberg furnishes no basis for these accusations" (p. 142). Yet this bombing has laid waste most of North Vietnam, including large cities with the exceptions of Hanoi and Haiphong.[2] The reason the law of war crimes does not reach American bombing is straightforward:

> Since both sides [in World War II] had played the terrible game of urban destruction—the Allies far more successfully—there was no basis for criminal charges against Germans or Japanese, and in fact no such charges were brought. [pp. 140–1]

> Aerial bombardment had been used so extensively and ruthlessly on the Allied side as well as the Axis side that neither at Nuremberg nor Tokyo was the issue made a part of the trials. [p. 89]

Similarly, charges against German admirals for violating the London Naval Treaty of 1930 were dismissed after testimony by Admiral Nimitz, which "established that in this regard the Germans had done nothing that the British and Americans had not also done" (p. 37). The Nuremberg Tribunal ruled that the German admirals should be subjected to no criminal penalties for their violation of international law, because the laws in question "had been abrogated by the practice of the belligerents on both sides under the stress of military necessity" (p. 38). Taylor concludes that "to punish the foe—especially the vanquished foe—for conduct in which the enforcing nation has engaged, would be so grossly inequitable as to discredit the laws themselves" (p. 39).

From such comments we can derive the operational definition of "crime of war" as conceived at Nuremberg. Criminal acts were to be treated as crimes only if the defeated enemy, but not the victors, had engaged in them. No doubt it would be "grossly inequitable" to punish the vanquished foe for conduct in which the enforcing nation had engaged. It would, however, be just and equitable to punish both victor and vanquished for their criminal acts. This option, which Taylor does not mention, was not adopted by the postwar tribunals. They chose instead "to discredit the laws themselves" by restricting their definition of criminal conduct so as to exclude punishment of the victors.[3]

The conclusion that Nuremberg is to be understood as the judgment of victors, rather than as the achievement of a new level of international morality, is reinforced by Taylor's discussion of aggressive war. The distinctive contribution of Nuremberg, he points out, was to establish the category of crimes against peace: "Planning, preparation, initiation or waging of a war of aggression or a war in violation of international treaties, agreements or assurances," or "participation in a common plan or conspiracy" to this end.[4] "In terms of substantive international law," Taylor writes, "and in the mind of the general public, the salient feature of the Nuremberg trials was the decision that individuals could be held guilty for participation in the planning and waging of 'a war of aggression' " (p. 84). "Indisputably it was a cardinal part of the postwar policy of the United States Government to establish the criminality under international law of aggressive warfare . . ." (p. 76).

But, Taylor argues, a court could hardly decide the question of whether the United States has violated the antiaggression provisions of the Nuremberg or United Nations charters.[5] For one reason, "the evidentiary problems would be well-nigh insuperable." At Nuremberg and Tokyo, the Allies had access to secret diplomatic and military document files, which would not be made available by the United States and South Vietnamese governments. "Total military victories such as those that ended the Second World War are comparatively rare in modern history, and it is difficult to envisage other circumstances that would unlock the secret files" (pp. 118–19). But if only access to the secret files can provide proof that aggressive war has been waged, then it follows that the "salient feature of the Nuremberg trials" will normally be relevant only to the case of an enemy that has suffered total military defeat.

Actually, Taylor vacillates somewhat on the matter of proof of aggression, in that he seems to trust the executive branch to make unilateral judgments regarding aggression by other states, despite the "insuperable" evidentiary problems. He writes that "until 1965 [he] supported American intervention in Vietnam as an aggression-checking undertaking in the spirit of the United Nations Charter" (p. 206).[6] It was permissible in Taylor's opinion for the American executive to determine unilaterally that North Vietnam was engaged in aggressive war prior to 1965, and to join South Vietnam in collective self-defense against the armed attack from the North, under article 51 of the United Nations Charter. So uniquely competent is the United States to exercise this judgment, he seems to believe, that it was unnecessary even to adhere to the provision in article 51 that measures taken in the exercise of the right of self-defense be immediately reported to the Security Council,[7] or to the provision in article 39 that "the Security Council shall determine the existence of any threat to the peace, breach of the peace, or act of aggression" and shall determine what measures shall be taken.

In fact, I think that Taylor exaggerates the "evidentiary problems" of determining whether the United States is engaged in aggression in Southeast Asia, just as he underestimates the difficulty of establishing that it was engaged in collective self-defense against armed attack. His discussion of aggressive war seems to me inadequate in other respects as well.

There is still a more serious issue at stake when we consider the acceptability of the principles of international law as codified in the Charter of Nuremberg and elsewhere. These principles were formulated by representatives of established governments, without the participation of representatives of mass-based popular movements that seek to overthrow recognized governments or that establish revolutionary governments. Richard Falk holds that "from the perspective of international order the capacity to govern is certainly an element in claiming political legitimacy,"[8] and Thomas J. Farer speaks of "the dangerous ambiguity of just when the insurgency has achieved sufficient status to require equal treatment."[9] This point is crucial in assessing Taylor's belief that the United States was engaged in an "aggression-checking" undertaking in Vietnam in, say, 1962. In that year American officials in Saigon estimated that half the population supported the National Liberation Front.[10] Furthermore, there was no evidence of North Vietnamese participation in any combat, and ten thousand American troops were in South Vietnam, many directly engaged in military actions.[11] Bernard Fall noted that "since 1961 Americans die in Viet-Nam, and in American uniforms. And they die fighting."[12] In March 1962, United States officials admitted that American pilots were flying combat missions (bombing and strafing). By October, it was reported that 30 percent of all air missions in South Vietnam had American Air Force pilots at their controls.[13] By late 1962, the United States was directly involved in large military actions in the Mekong Delta and the Camau Peninsula.[14] In a book published in 1963, Richard Tregaskis reported interviews with American helicopter pilots who describe how the "wild men" of the 362nd Squadron used to shoot civilians for sport in "solid VC areas."[15] It has also been reported that in 1962, air commandos of the Special Operations Force, "wearing civilian clothes and flying planes with the markings of the South Vietnamese Air Force . . . attacked Vietcong concentrations in the jungles."[16]

There is, in short, a good case that the United States was involved in direct military attacks against indigenous popular forces in South Vietnam as early as 1962. It would be fair to call this "aggressive war" if, indeed, the capacity to govern is an element in claiming political legitimacy. Suppose that one were to hold, on the contrary, that governments recognized by the major powers are legally permitted to call in outside force to put down a domestic insurgency, while insurgents are not entitled to seek outside help. Suppose further that this rule applies even where the insurgents constitute the only effective government in large areas and the only mass-based political organization,[17] and where these insurgents are asking support from a state from which they have been arbitrarily separated by great-power intervention and subversion.[18] If this hypothesized rule is an accurate interpretation of the currently prevailing system of international law, then the only appropriate conclusion is that this system of law is to be disregarded as without moral force. Or, to be more precise, the conclusion must be that this system of law is simply a device for ratifying imperial practice.

These questions do not arise in any direct way in Taylor's discussion, in part because he scarcely touches on the pre-1965 period to which they are directly relevant. Similar problems, however, are implicit in his discussion of the legality of various modes of warfare. As already noted, Taylor argues that aerial warfare is not intrinsically unlawful, although the "silence of Nuremberg" on this matter raises questions "especially relevant to American bombing policies . . . in South Vietnam" (p. 142). The routine destruction of villages by American firepower and ground sweeps and the forced evacuation of population are, he argues, of doubtful legality, and reprisal attacks against villages harboring Vietcong—official policy, as he notes—are a "flagrant violation" of the Geneva Conventions (p. 145). What is more, Taylor believes the establishment of free-fire zones to be illegal (p. 147). But he emphasizes the great problems in determining how legal principles should apply under the circumstances of Vietnam, where a superpower is using its technological resources to destroy guerrilla forces that conceal themselves among the population. The basic problem is this:

> The enemy does not respect those laws, the terrain lends itself to clandestine operations in which women and children frequently participate, the hostile and the friendly do not label themselves as such, and individuals of the yellow race are hard for our soldiers to identify. As in the Philippines 65 years ago, our troops are thousands of miles from home in uncomfortable, dangerous and unfamiliar surroundings. No one not utterly blind to the realities can fail to acknowledge and make allowance for the difficulties and uncertainties they face in distinguishing inoffensive noncombatants from hostile partisians. [p. 152]

The enemy "is undeniably in violation of the traditional laws of war and the Geneva Conventions, based as they are on the distinction between combatants and noncombatants" in two specific respects: the enemy does not wear "a fixed distinctive emblem recognizable at a distance" or "carry arms openly," as American soldiers do. The law, as reaffirmed at Nuremberg, states that "a civilian who aids, abets, or participates in the fighting is liable to punishment as a war criminal." This may seem harsh, Taylor writes, but "it is certainly the law" (pp. 136–7),[19] just as the law may not apply to aerial bombardment of towns and villages in an effort to break the enemy's will or to deny him material or human resources.

These observations come very close to branding "people's war" illegal, while permitting the use of the technology of the industrial powers to suppress it. An essential feature of revolutionary people's war, Vietnamese style, is that it combines political and military action, thus blurring the distinction between combatants and noncombatants. The Vietnamese revolutionaries in general attempted to follow the Maoist injunction that "a bloodless transition is what we would like and we should strive for it."[20] Even Douglas Pike concedes that the National Liberation Front (NLF) "maintained that its contest with the Government of the Republic of Vietnam (GVN) and the United States should be fought out at the political level and that the use of massed military might was in itself illegitimate," until forced by the United States and the GVN "to use counterforce to survive."[21] When the NLF resorted to counterforce to survive, it exploited its natural advantage, the ability of the guerrillas to blend into the sympathetic local population, just as the United States exploited its natural advantage in the technology of surveillance and destruction.

These characteristics of people's war were outlined years ago by the leading Vietnamese Communist ideologist Truong Chinh:

> [There are] those who have a tendency only to rely on military action. . . . They tend to believe that everything can be settled by armed force; they do not apply political mobilization, are unwilling to give explanations and to convince people; . . . fighting spiritedly, they neglect political work; they do not . . . act in such a way that the army and the people can wholeheartedly help one another.[22]

Citing this passage, Bernard Fall noted that "once more, the enemy has been kind enough to give us the recipe of his victory."[23] The recipe is to gain political support among the people and to engage the population as a whole in the struggle against the central government backed—in this case imposed—by foreign military force. The participation of civilians in the revolutionary war reflects its political and social character, just as saturation bombing by B-52s based in sanctuaries in Guam and Thailand reveals the essential political and social character of American "counterinsurgency." The laws of war rule the former illegal, while the silence of Nuremberg falls over American practice. These laws, Taylor maintains, condemn as war criminals the civilians who take up arms against a foreign enemy or its local protégés; such civilians are "undeniably in violation" of the laws of war. But with regard to the American pilots who have destroyed towns and villages and devastated farmland and forest, driving millions from their homes and killing unknown numbers throughout Indochina, or to those who planned this policy, the laws of war have little to say. At most "the silence of Nuremberg . . . asks [questions] . . . relevant to American bombing policies . . . in South Vietnam" (p. 142), and presumably in Laos and Cambodia as well (but see above, p. 110).

These laws, so understood, are the weapon of the strong, and are of no moral force or validity. It is a political decision to accept an interpretation of the law that holds that a government installed and maintained by a foreign power (as in South Vietnam or Hungary) has the right to call upon this foreign power to suppress an insurgency that has gained such extensive political support that insurgents are indistinguishable from the population, and holds that civilian participants in the insurgency are war criminals. It is a political decision to accept as valid the law that combatants must identify themselves as such to the soldiers of the foreign army, while that same law raises no objection to the dispatch of soldiers "thousands of miles from home" to "unlovely circumstances" in which they cannot distinguish noncombatants from partisans.

Though Taylor is quite right to insist on the difficulties and uncertainties faced by these troops, there is no reason to withhold condemnation from the political leaders who sent them there, or to grant any validity to the legal system that permits this while condemning the enemy's recipe for victory: winning popular support and using this support in the only way a popular movement can to overthrow the local representatives of a foreign superpower. No reason, that is, apart from the political judgment that a great power has the right to impose a regime of its choice, by force, in some foreign land. The system of law, so interpreted, is merely a ratification of imperialist practice.

Though Taylor is not entirely explicit, it seems that he accepts the political judgment that the United States has the right to impose the regime of its choice in South Vietnam. In his discussion of war aims, he refers to "our stated policy," namely, "to gain and hold the political allegiance of the South Vietnamese to a non-communist government, while giving them defensive assistance against any military means used by the North" (p. 189). His only stated objection to this policy is that it was unlikely to work, under the circumstances of Vietnam. As to the "defensive assistance" against the North, surely he is aware that the main NLF fighting units were indigenous from the start, and remained so until the United States internationalized the war. He apparently believes that it was legitimate for the United States to introduce its military forces, as it did in the early 1960s, to gain and hold the political allegiance of the South Vietnamese to the noncommunist government installed by the United States in 1954. Taylor refers to the "deeply idealistic strain in the American interventionist tradition" (p. 186), as when McKinley justified the war against Spain in 1898. This is a very superficial historical judgment. Virtually every imperial power has justified its actions on "idealistic" grounds. This was true of the British and French empires, the Japanese in East Asia,[24] and the Russians in Eastern Europe. That the leaders and populations of the imperial powers may even succumb to these delusions is hardly significant. It is remarkable that the standards by which we would judge other cases of imperial intervention seem so difficult to comprehend when applied to our own actions.[25]

Taylor asks whether the American conduct of the war, with forced resettlement, complicity in the torture of prisoners, enthusiasm for body counts, devastation of large areas to expose the insurgents, free-fire zones, and the Son My massacre, was merely "a terrible, mad aberration" (p. 152). He answers correctly that in part it was a consequence of the specific features of the Vietnam war cited above, which make the laws of war so difficult to apply. In fact, the policy of forced resettlement and devastation of large areas of the country was a rational, perhaps even a necessary, response to the specific circumstances of the Vietnam war. Bernard Fall, bitterly anticommunist and a strong supporter of the American war before it reached its full fury, explained this fact very well in the early 1960s.

> Why is it that we must use top-notch elite forces, the cream of the crop of American, British, French, or Australian commando and special warfare schools; armed with the very best that advanced technology can provide; to defeat Viet-Minh, Algerians, or Malay "CT's" [Chinese terrorists], almost none of whom can lay claim to similar expert training and only in the rarest of cases to equality in fire power?
>
> The answer is very simple: It takes all the technical proficiency our system can provide to make up for the woeful lack of popular support and political savvy of most of the regimes that the West has thus far sought to prop up. The Americans who are now fighting in South Viet-Nam have come to appreciate this fact out of first-hand experience.[26]

Today, there is vastly more evidence to support Fall's conclusion. "The element of real popular support is vital," he wrote.[27] And it was exactly this "real popular support" that led Washington to adopt the policy of forced population removal that has reduced the peasantry from about 85 percent to about half of the population, while laying waste the countryside. If international law has nothing to say about this except that civilians aiding the resistance are war criminals, then its moral bankruptcy is revealed with stark clarity.

II. "WAR CRIMES" IN VIETNAM

The major topic that Taylor considers, however, is the more narrow question of the legality of American actions in Vietnam when measured against the framework of Nuremberg and related conventions. In his analysis of the American intervention after 1965, Taylor concludes that there is definite evidence that war crimes have been committed and that culpability for these crimes extends to high levels of military command and civilian leadership. The evidence in this regard is extensive.

The primary example that Taylor considers is the My Lai massacre. Dr. Alje Vennema, director of a Canadian hospital near the site of the massacre, reports that he knew of it at once but did nothing because it was not at all out of the ordinary. His patients were constantly reporting such incidents to him. The province of Quang Ngai, in which My Lai is located, had been virtually destroyed. Half the population had been forced into refugee camps, and children were starving and wounded.[28] Colonel Oran Henderson, the highest ranking officer to have faced court-martial charges for the My Lai massacre, states that "every unit of brigade size has its Mylai hidden some place," though "every unit doesn't have a Ridenhour."[29]

This observation is borne out by direct testimony of veterans throughout the country. To cite just a few random examples, a highly decorated helicopter gunner testified in El Paso, Texas, on May 5, 1971, that of the thirty-nine Vietnamese he had killed, one was an old man riding a bicycle and ten were a group of unarmed civilians. In each case, he claims to have acted on direct order from his commanding officer. A former member of the Coast Guard testified that his orders were to pilot a small motorboat through delta canals shooting randomly into every village to see if there were inhabitants. In hearings conducted by the Citizens' Commission of Inquiry on United States War Crimes, in Washington, D.C., December 1–3, 1970, a medic in the 101st Airborne Division testified that approximately twenty-seven civilians in a peaceful meeting were killed in an unprovoked attack by American tanks firing a barrage of tiny arrowlike nails. A marine forward observer testified that he counted twenty dead civilians after an unprovoked artillery strike on two villages. Another marine corporal testified that his unit was ordered to fire on starving civilians scavenging in a garbage dump after their food supplies had been destroyed in 1966 (rice fields had been napalmed to destroy food in this free-fire zone). A former army sergeant testified before an unofficial House committee headed by Representative Ronald Dellums that he took part in killing about thirty unresisting Vietnamese civilians in the village of Truong Khanh, near My Lai, in April 1969. This testimony was confirmed to reporters by Vietnamese women in a refugee camp.[30] The Winter Soldier Investigation in Detroit produced voluminous testimony on atrocities,[31] as have other inquiries.

A former helicopter gunner with 176 confirmed "kills" told reporter Joseph Lelyveld that his gunship was ordered to halt a flight of peasants. When the pilot reported that he had no way to do so, he received orders to "shoot them." Thirty or forty unarmed villagers were then killed by the gunship. Trainees said that their instructor had written President Nixon after the Calley verdict about his own involvement in an incident in which six gunships attacked a village, killing 350 villagers,[32] after a helicopter crew member had been shot.

Refugees, reporters, and other observers have presented voluminous substantiating evidence. What is particularly important is that these episodes appear to be quite routine.

> I have personally accompanied a routine operation in which U.S. Cobra helicopters fired 20mm. cannons into the houses of a typical village in territory controlled by the National Liberation Front. They also shot the villagers who ran out of the

> houses. This was termed "prepping the area" by the American lieutenant colonel who directed the operation. "We sort of shoot it up to see if anything moves," he explained, and he added by way of reassurance that this treatment was perfectly routine.[33]

An official map of the 25th Infantry Division delineates large areas subjected to artillery and air bombardment prior to the ground sweeps of Operation Junction City in 1967. Within these areas there were over twenty identifiable villages with populations of 5,000, according to earlier census figures.

New York Times correspondent R. W. Apple writes that he heard the "mere gook rule," according to which "anything that moves and has a yellow skin is an enemy, unless there is incontrovertible evidence to the contrary," repeated "100 times by majors and sergeants and privates." This, he writes, is "official policy, a part of everyday life." He goes on:

> Not so evident to the average rifleman, but clear enough to those of us who have had an opportunity to travel about the country, is a deliberate policy of creating refugees wherever possible. An Army general . . . explained the idea to me as follows: "You've got to dry up the sea the guerrillas swim in—that's the peasants—and the best way to do that is blast the hell out of their villages so they'll come into our refugee camps. No villages, no guerrillas: simple.[34]

He adds further that Generals Westmoreland and Abrams, as well as Presidents Johnson and Nixon, surely knew this.[35]

It is this policy of "no villages, no guerrillas"—the policy of destroying the rural society—that is referred to as "forced-draft urbanization and modernization" by some of the more cynical academic technocrats who deal with Vietnam; "a euphemism to end all euphemisms" (p. 202), as Taylor appropriately comments. Apple's account indicates that this policy was not inadvertent, something that the United States command "stumbled upon" in an "absent-minded way,"[36] but rather was planned and understood in advance.

Neil Sheehan's widely discussed article on war crimes[37] makes the same point. Sheehan claims that "classified military documents specifically talk about bombing villages in communist-held areas 'to deprive the enemy of the population resource.' " He refers to a secret study in the summer of 1966 which proposed reconsideration of the policy of unrestricted bombing and shelling which was "urbanizing" the population.[38] This proposal was vetoed at the highest level of American authority in Saigon, he writes. It was decided instead to continue to employ "air and artillery to terrorize the peasantry and raze the countryside." One of the basic American tactics was "unrestricted air and artillery bombardments of peasant hamlets"—"devastation had become a fundamental element in [the American] strategy to win the war." The rural civilian population was the target of the American attack "because it was believed that their existence was important to the enemy." The idea was to defeat the Vietnamese Communists "by obliterating their strategic base, the rural population." [39]

The United States authorities have a point when they argue that My Lai is not the typical incident of the Vietnam war. More typical, almost the war in microcosm, is the story of the village of Phuqui on the Batangan Peninsula, 130 miles southeast of Hue. In January 1969, twelve thousand peasants in this region were forced from their homes in an American ground sweep, loaded on helicopters, and shipped to interrogation centers and a waterless camp near Quang Ngai over which floated a banner saying, "We thank you for liberating us from communist terror." According to official military statistics, there were 158 NVA and Vietcong dead and 268 wounded in the six-month campaign of which this was a part. These refugees (who incidentally seem to have included the remnants of My Lai) had lived in caves and bunkers for months before the forced evacuation because of the heavy American bombing and artillery and naval shelling. A dike was "blasted by American jets to deprive the North Vietnamese of a food supply." [40]

As of April 1971, the dike had not been repaired: "As a result, the salt water of the South China Sea continues to submerge the fields where rice once grew." About four thousand refugees, including one thousand five hundred in Phuqui, have since returned. Phuqui is now surrounded by ten-foot rows of bamboo. It is under guard, and no one may enter or leave between 6:00 P.M. and 5:00 A.M. "The hills that overlook the flooded paddies, once scattered with huts, are 'ironed'—a word used by the peasants to mean filled with bomb fragments, mines and unexploded artillery shells. B-52 bomb craters nearly 20 feet deep pock the hills." One reason why the dike has not been rebuilt may be that—in the words of an American official—"two years ago the people on the peninsula were written off as communists. It would not be surprising if the attitudes still linger among the Vietnamese today." Most of the population go without basic food. "Province officials neither affirm nor deny police action to limit the peasant's rice. . . . It has long been a practice to control the supply of South Vietnam's food, however, to insure that the Vietcong cannot eat excess peasant food." An American working in the province said, "You might say that Phuqui has been forgotten."

Forgotten it has been, along with hundreds of other villages like it.

The American war in Indochina is a record of war crimes and crimes against humanity, a record of mounting horror. For the reasons noted by Bernard Fall in the early stages of the war,[41] there may well have been no alternative.[42] The war has been directed against the rural population and the land that sustains them. Since 1961–1962, American forces have been directly involved in bombing, strafing, forced population removal of millions of peasants, crop destruction and defoliation, and destruction of agricultural lands and the irrigation system. The land is pockmarked with millions of bomb craters. Lumber operations are impossible in forests where trees are riddled with shell fragments. Some six and a half million acres have been defoliated with chemical poisons, often applied at tremendous concentrations. Included are perhaps a half-million acres of crop-growing land. South Vietnam, once a major rice exporter, is now importing enormous quantities of food, according to Vietnamese sources.[43] About one acre in six has been sprayed by defoliants. In many areas, there are no signs of recovery. Crop destruction is done largely with an arsenical compound which may remain in the soil for years and is not cleared for use on crops in the United States. A contaminant in the herbicides, dioxin, is known to be a highly potent agent causing birth defects in mammals. Through 1969, a half-million acres of forest had been destroyed by giant tractors with Rome plow blades, widely used in other areas as well. These areas are scraped bare. Nothing may grow again. Arthur Westing, a biologist, former marine officer, and director of the Herbicide Assessment Commission of the American Association for the Advancement of Science, writes that "we may well be altering drastically and detrimentally the ecology of vast acreages of South Vietnam."[44] "These vegetational wastelands will remain one of the legacies of our presence for decades to come"[45]—perhaps permanently.

The effects of these policies on the population can be easily imagined. Hunger and starvation from crop destruction and forced population removal have been noted since 1961.[46] Millions of people had been removed—often by force—into controlled areas, by the early 1960s. After 1965, air and artillery bombardment and ground sweeps accounted for the overwhelming majority of the refugees.

In South Vietnam, perhaps half the population has been killed, maimed, or driven from their homes. In Laos, perhaps a quarter of the population of about three million are refugees. Another third live under some of the most intense bombardment in history. Refugees report that they lived in caves and tunnels, under bombing so intensive that not even a dog could cross a path without being attacked by an American jet. Whole villages were moved repeatedly into tunnels deeper and deeper in the forest as the scope of the bombing was extended. The fertile Plain of Jars in northern Laos was finally cleared and turned into a free-fire zone. These refugees, incidentally, report that they rarely saw NVA troops and that Pathet Lao soldiers were rarely to be found in the villages. The areas in question are far from South Vietnam or the "Ho Chi Minh Trail." In Cambodia, the Kennedy subcommittee estimated that by September 1970—after four months of regular bombardment—there were about a million refugees out of a population of about six million. The intensive bombardment also has been reported by captured correspondents. According to Richard Dudman's direct observations in captivity, "the bombing and shooting was radicalizing the people of rural Cambodia and was turning the countryside into a massive, dedicated, and effective revolutionary base."[47] As elsewhere in Indochina, this is both a consequence and a cause of the American bombardment.

On April 21, 1971, Representative Paul McCloskey, just returned from Indochina, testified before the Kennedy subcommittee that an air force lieutenant colonel at Udorn Air Force Base in Thailand said that "there just aren't any villages in Northern Laos anymore, or in southern North Viet Nam either, for that matter." Government reports, secret until unearthed with great effort by McCloskey, confirm the overwhelming evidence of refugee reports concerning the virtual destruction of large areas of rural Laos controlled by the Pathet Lao.[48]

Much the same is true in Vietnam. McCloskey quotes a top Civil Operations and Revolutionary Development Support (CORDS) official who informed him, in Vietnam a year ago, "that in a single province, Quang Nam, American and allied forces had destroyed and razed 307 of the original 555 hamlets of the province." He adds, "I was flown over square mile after square mile where every village, home, and treeline had been burned to the ground; this was part of a rice denial and search and destroy program admittedly based on the need to deny the Vietcong the ability to obtain food, hospitalization, cover and concealment which the villages would otherwise afford."[49]

The *United States Army Field Manual* permits measures to "destroy, through chemical or bacterial agents harmless to man, crops intended solely for consumption by the armed forces (if that fact can be determined)."[50] Yet the descriptions of crop destruction cited above, and those of the AAAS Herbicide Assessment Commission, suggest that nearly all the food destroyed would have been consumed by civilians. It should be remembered that Goering was convicted at Nuremberg for crimes against humanity in part because of orders requiring diversion of food from occupied territories to German needs, and that the United States in Tokyo also supported prosecution of Japanese military officials for crop destruction in China.[51]

The province that McCloskey described, Quang Nam, is the subject of a book by the former senior AID official there, William Nighswonger.[52] He explains that "the battle for Quang Nam was lost by the government to Viet-Cong forces recruited for the most part from within the province." A major reason for their success was "the progressive social and economic results" shown by their programs. As elsewhere in Indochina, it was the success of the

Communist-led forces in gaining popular support through successful programs[53] that led to the American effort to destroy the rural society in which the revolution was rooted.

Robert Shaplen concludes that "the war's overall effects on the Vietnamese have been cataclysmically destructive, not only in physical terms but psychologically and socially."[54] Furthermore, these effects are overwhelmingly attributable to American firepower and tactics. Unless one assumes a high degree of idiocy on the part of the American command and the civilian leadership in Washington, it is necessary to suppose that something of the sort was anticipated when these tactics were designed. Furthermore, there is mounting evidence, some of it just cited, that the probable effects were understood in advance, and were even intended. Finally, it is important to bear in mind that these tactics, though sharply intensified in 1965 and again in 1968, can be traced back to the early 1960s. In fact the Diem regime, installed and kept in power by the United States, initiated a virtual war on peasant supporters of the Viet Minh in the mid-1950s.[55]

In the face of such evidence, which has by now been recorded at great length in many easily accessible sources, it requires a real act of faith to doubt that the American command and the civilian authorities are responsible for war crimes and crimes against humanity in the sense of Nuremberg. In fact, it is difficult to understand the surprise or concern over My Lai, considering the relative triviality of this incident in the context of the overall American policies in Indochina.

Taylor observes, correctly and appropriately, that "the war, in the massive, lethal dimensions it acquired after 1964, was the work of highly educated academics and administrators"—the Kennedy advisers, Rusk, McNamara, Bundy, Rostow, who stayed on with President Johnson and "who must bear major responsibility for the war and the course it took" (p. 205). The same is true of the war in the years 1961–1964, with its lethal effects—small, to be sure, compared with what was to come, but nonetheless hardly acceptable by civilized standards.

Discussion of American war crimes in Vietnam is often sharply criticized as dishonest, or even as a form of self-hatred, if not "balanced" by an account of the crimes of the "enemy." Such criticism is at best thoughtless and at worst hypocritical. Not only has the criminal violence of the United States in Vietnam (and throughout Indochina) been far greater in scale than anything attributable to any Indochinese forces, but it is also in an entirely different category from a moral as well as legal point of view for the obvious reason that it is foreign in origin. How would we respond to the claim that discussion of the acts of the fascist aggressors in World War II must be "balanced" by an account of the terrorism of the resistance in occupied countries?[56] Furthermore, such critics rarely note that if the crimes of all participants are to be discussed in a balanced manner, then it is also necessary to detail the crimes of the Korean and other Asian mercenaries employed by the United States and, more important still, the criminal violence of the regime instituted and protected by United States force. Its terroristic attack on the people of South Vietnam long preceded and also always outweighed by a considerable margin the terrorism of its Vietnamese antagonists.[57] Equally thoughtless, or hypocritical, is the opinion commonly expressed by critics of the U.S. intervention who say that the American command has descended to the level of the Communists. There can be no doubt that the savagery and barbarism of the American attack on the population of South Vietnam is entirely without parallel in this miserable conflict.[58]

The one example that is repeatedly cited in an effort to prove the contrary is the massacre that took place in Hue during the Tet offensive of February 1968. Let us put aside the fact that it occurred in a region that had already been devastated by U.S. military force, from early 1965, and consider the massacre itself, which in the United States and England has become notorious as the classic example of a Communist bloodbath. Don Oberdorfer describes this as "the most extensive political slaughter of the war."[59] Estimates of the scale of the Communist massacre range from 200 (police chief of Hue) to 2,800 (Oberdorfer, based on data from Douglas Pike whom he regards, surprisingly, as a reliable source). Len Ackland, an IVS worker in Hue in 1967 who returned in April 1968 to investigate, was informed by American and Vietnamese officials that about 700 Vietnamese were killed by the Vietcong, an estimate generally supported by his detailed investigations, which also indicate that the killings were by local NLF forces and primarily during the last days of the bloody month-long battle as these forces were retreating.[60] Whatever the exact numbers may be, there is no doubt that a brutal massacre took place.

There was also another slaughter in Hue at the same time, scarcely mentioned by Oberdorfer[61] and forgotten or passed over in silence by most others. The same officials who reported 700 killed by the Vietcong estimated that 3,000 to 4,000 civilians had been killed in the United States–GVN bombing and shelling. Undersecretary of the Air Force Townsend Hoopes reports that 2,000 civilians were buried in the rubble of the bombardment. The NLF reported that 2,000 victims of the bombardment were buried in mass graves. (Oberdorfer reports that "2800 victims of the occupation" were discovered in mass graves—it may, perhaps, be doubted that when these graves were discovered many months later it was determined by careful autopsy that these were victims of the Communist "political slaughter.") The marines, according to Oberdorfer, list "Communist losses" at more than 5,000, while Hoopes states that a "sizable part" of the Communist force of 1,000 men who had captured the city escaped. A French priest from Hue estimates that about 1,100, mostly students, teachers, and priests, were killed by the GVN after U.S. Marines had recaptured the city.[62] Richard West, who was in Hue shortly after the battle, estimates "several hundred Vietnamese and a handful of foreigners" killed by Communists and suggests that victims of My Lai–style massacres may be among those buried in the mass graves.[63] British photographer-journalist Philip Jones Griffiths concludes that most of the victims "were killed by the most hysterical use of American firepower ever seen," and then designated "as the victims of a Communist massacre."[64]

Even if the U.S. government propaganda that is widely accepted as fact in the English-speaking countries were true and told the whole story, the Communist massacre at Hue would be a minor event in the context of the American slaughter of the people of South Vietnam. When the full range of facts is considered, however, it appears that the Hue massacre is attributable in large part, and perhaps predominantly, to the American military. This is not surprising, in view of the relative scale of the means of violence available to the contending forces.

It remains to discuss two essential points: first, the argument that the American actions were permitted by "military necessity," and second, the claim that U.S. intervention was justified in collective self-defense against armed attack, under article 51 of the United Nations Charter. Taylor discusses both of these matters, but in what seems to me an unsatisfactory way.

III. MILITARY NECESSITY

In a sense, it is correct that the American policy of "no villages, no guerrillas" was based on military necessity. American planners were well aware of the enormous popular support for the Communist-led resistance forces, the so-called "Viet Cong," and the lack of any significant popular base for the government (see pp. 108–09 above). Furthermore, there is no great secret as to why the Vietcong were so successful in gaining popular support.[65]

The field operations coordinator of the United States Operations Mission, John Paul Vann, circulated a report[66] in 1965 on how the war should be fought. His premises were that a social revolution was in process in South Vietnam, "primarily identified with the National Liberation Front," and that "a popular political base for the Government of South Vietnam does not now exist." "The dissatisfaction of the agrarian population . . . today is largely expressed through alliance with the NLF," he wrote. "The existing government is oriented toward the exploitation of the rural and lower class urban populations." Since it is "naive," he explained, to expect that "an unsophisticated, relatively illiterate, rural population [will] recognize and oppose the evils of Communism," the United States must institute "effective political indoctrination of the population" under an American-maintained "autocratic government." The document opposes mere reliance on gadgetry, air power, and artillery, and rejects the expressed view of a U.S. officer who stated that "if these people want to stay there and support the Communists, then they can expect to be bombed." The report is based on the further assumption that the social revolution is "not incompatible" with U.S. aims, but that "the aspirations of the majority" can only be realized "through a non-Communist government." According to Vann, the United States should be the judge of what would be "best" for the unsophisticated peasants of Vietnam. The United States, he argued, must impose "a benevolently inclined autocracy or dictatorship . . . while laying the foundation for a democratically oriented [government]." Vann's report expresses the benevolent face of imperialism. It is outspoken in its colonialist assumptions. From Taylor's few remarks on the subject, one might surmise that he would agree with Vann's proposals and leading assumptions.

As already noted, Taylor accepts the legitimacy of the effort to "gain and hold the political allegiance of the South Vietnamese to a non-Communist government" (p. 189), while doubting the possibility of doing so. He regards faulty judgment and overreliance on military means as the primary defects of American policy (pp. 188–9). He accuses U.S. authorities of "undermaintenance": too much bombing and not enough concentration on the "civil half" (pp. 196–202). He raises no objection to the direct use of force in the early 1960s or to the support of large-scale terror in the late 1950s in the interest of maintaining the regime that the United States had installed.[67] Nowhere does he raise the fundamental question: Is it legitimate for the United States to use its power to impose a particular social and political order on some foreign land, supposing that it can do so within the limits of "proportionality" of force applied?

Failure to raise this question makes Taylor's discussion of "causation" quite unsatisfactory. He rejects the view, attributed to unnamed critics, that "things [went] so wrong . . . because our leaders were war criminals." This "is an unsatisfactory answer in terms of causation, for it assumes that the leaders wanted things to turn out as they have, whereas in fact it is plain that those responsible are exceedingly dissatisfied with the present consequences of their policies." Both the criticism and Taylor's rejection of it are intelligible only on the assumption that questions of legitimacy of intent do not arise in the case of the American leadership. If we regard the intentions of the American leadership as criminal, then it would be correct—indeed, virtually tautological—to say that things went wrong (that is, criminal acts were undertaken) because our leaders were war criminals. On this assumption, it would be irrelevant to remark that things did not turn out as they hoped. Thus no one would argue that the defendants at Nuremberg should have been acquitted merely because they too were "dissatisfied with the consequences of their policies."

In referring to "things go[ing] so wrong," Taylor seems to have in mind "the avalanche of death and destruction" that destroyed the credibility of "whatever peace-keeping and protective intentions may have governed our initial involvement in Vietnam." In Taylor's view, the evidence "strongly indicate[s] that there was a misfit between ends and means; that the military leaders never grasped the essentially political aims of intervention, and the political leaders neglected or were unable to police the means that the military adopted to fulfill what they conceived to be their mission." Instead of pursuing "our stated policy," namely, "to gain and hold the political allegiance of the South Vietnamese to a non-Communist government, while giving them defensive assistance against any military means used by the North," our leaders chose to "ignore the South Vietnamese people, treat South Vietnam as a battlefield, and kill all the North Vietnamese or Vietcong found on or moving toward the battlefield"—and in fact, to treat the rural population of South Vietnam in much the same way. "The sad story of America's venture in Vietnam is that the military means rapidly submerged the political ends. . . ." We were "prone to shatter what we try to save" (pp. 188–9, 207).

Whether "our stated policy" could have been successfully followed "is and will remain an unanswered question," Taylor observes. Whether "our stated policy" was legitimate in the first place and should have been undertaken at all is a question that is not only unanswered but unasked. But surely this is the fundamental question.

Taylor expresses a very common view when he criticizes American policy because we destroyed the country in order to save it, in the phrase of the unhappy American air force major who was responsible for the destruction of Ben Tre during the Tet offensive. The true "American tragedy"—a potential tragedy for many others, in a far more real sense—is, in my opinion, our continued inability to apply to ourselves the standards that we properly use in evaluating the behavior of other powers. If Americans had the moral courage to do so, they would ask themselves for whom they were "saving" Vietnam, and whether they had a right to intervene to "save" it. They would perceive that the American intervention should be described as a war against the rural society of South Vietnam, not an effort to save it for anyone except collaborationist leaders and such marginal political forces as they could rally. Ultimately, the American leadership was saving Vietnam for its own global interests. The interests of the Vietnamese people amounted to 10 percent of the American objective, in the calculation of Assistant Secretary of Defense

John McNaughton, as revealed in the Pentagon Papers (the other 90 percent is an amalgam of fantasy and self-delusion, as he expresses American aims—cf. chapter 1, note 195 in *For Reasons of State*). What American aims really were is a matter of legitimate debate (for my views, see chapter 1, section V in *For Reasons of State*). But it is hardly a matter of debate that the needs and interests of the Vietnamese people counted for as little as the legal prohibition against the threat or use of force in international affairs.

Had the American political leadership been concerned with the needs and interests of the people of South Vietnam or with the solemn treaty obligations of the United States, they would not have undertaken the "stated policy" of imposing a noncommunist government and defending it from its own population through 1964, and invading South Vietnam to destroy the indigenous resistance in later years. The Pentagon Papers make it quite clear that the American political leadership undertook its attack on the rural society of South Vietnam with eyes open. The Vann memorandum cited above, and much other evidence, reveals that the same was true of those who were implementing the policy laid down in Washington.

Taylor believes that some of the American failures in Vietnam can be traced to the fact that "the armed services no longer possess leaders of stature and influence comparable to the heroes of the Second World War" (p. 201). This is an unfair criticism. The difference between World War II and Vietnam has to do with the character of the wars, not the character of the military commanders. The military in both wars was entrusted with implementation of the policies laid down by the civilian leadership. In the case of Vietnam, this was the policy of "gain[ing] and hold[ing] the political allegiance of the South Vietnamese to a non-Communist government." To implement this policy effectively, the military command was compelled to abandon the benevolent imperialist pose and to destroy the rural society, the social base of the revolution. The civilian leadership was well aware of what was taking place and made no effort to change policy.

Ambassador Robert W. Komer, chief pacification adviser to the GVN in 1967–1968, explains that "U.S. military intervention had averted final collapse of the coup-ridden GVN and had created a favorable military environment in which the largely political competition for control and support of the key rural population could begin again."[68] The United States escalation overcame the difficulty that there was "little GVN administration . . . outside Saigon," and made it possible ultimately to initiate the "comprehensive" and "massive" 1967–1970 pacification program in an effort to cope with what was clearly "a revolutionary, largely political conflict."[69] Despite the qualms of the benevolent imperialists such as Vann, it is difficult to see how this aim could have been achieved except through the means employed, namely, what Komer describes as "massive U.S. military intervention at horrendous cost." [70]

In this sense, it can be argued that the horrendous cost of the American military intervention—including defoliation, forced population removal, bombing, harassment and interdiction, free-fire zones, antipersonnel weapons, the Phoenix program of assassination and terror,[71] the torture of prisoners to gain information—was a military necessity, and thus no crime if military necessity justifies departure from the language of international agreements. All of this is arguable given the essential premise that the United States was justified in intervening by force in this "revolutionary, largely political conflict" to guarantee the rule of the regime it had originally imposed in 1954 and its successors—the rule of the landholding and urban elite, the military officers, and the Northern Catholics who provided the social base for a regime that was clearly incapable of holding out on its own against a domestic insurgency.

The question whether this premise is valid arises in its sharpest form in the pre-1965 period with which Taylor does not concern himself. By 1965, as Vann noted,[72] these questions of principle were largely irrelevant. After the "large scale participation by U.S. ground forces," he wrote, "it is almost inconceivable that the United States will withdraw from Vietnam short of a military victory or a negotiated settlement that assures the autonomy of South Vietnam." [73] The same view was held by civilians close to the administration, including some who were later to become outspoken doves. Thus Richard Goodwin wrote in 1966 that continued American combat was justified by "the bedrock vital interest of the United States" which must serve as the "single standard" for policy formation, namely, "to establish that American military power, once committed to defend another nation,[74] cannot be driven from the field." [75]

Even today, it is well understood by the American command that military force must be used to destroy the political movement that the Saigon regime has never been able to defeat politically. A special intelligence survey ordered by General John H. Cushman, the top American official in the Mekong Delta, warns that the enemy is expanding his political network and "reverting to a political-struggle phase." [76] William Colby adds that "we need to prevent the enemy from putting in this network, because that will permit the Communists to revive later on." [77] Once again, given the premise that the United States has the right to intervene to impose the regime of its choice, "military necessity" could justify the continued use of overwhelming military force against the Vietnamese, the Laotians, and the rural Cambodians as well.

It should be added that the premise that American military intervention in other nations' affairs is justified is solidly enshrined in American history. Taylor refers to the American conquest of the Philippines at the turn of the century. Whatever "idealistic" motives McKinley may have professed, the fact is that the United States overcame a domestic popular movement by force and terror, at tremendous cost to the native inhabitants. Seventy years later, the peasantry—three-quarters of the population—still lives under material conditions not very different from those of the Spanish occupation.[78] In Thailand, a postwar effort at parliamentary democracy led by the liberal democrat Pridi Phanomyong was overthrown by a military coup that reinstituted the Japanese collaborator who had declared war on the United States. Substantial and continuing American assistance has supported a terroristic regime that has willingly integrated itself into the American-Japanese Pacific system. Pridi, who had fought with the American OSS against the Japanese during World War II, found his way to China. In Korea in 1945, the United States overthrew an already established popular regime, making use of Japanese troops and collaborators. By 1949, the American command had succeeded in destroying the existing unions, the popular local councils, and all popular indigenous groups, and had instituted a right-wing dictatorship of the wealthy elite and military-police forces—employing ample terror in the process.

Vietnam is exceptional only because these familiar objectives have been so difficult to achieve. The goal in Vietnam remains: to concentrate and control the population, separating it from main force guerrilla units, and to create a dependent economy that adapts itself to the needs and capacities of the industrialized societies of the West (and Japan), under the rule of wealthy collaborators, with a mere pretense of democracy. As to the peasants, one can recall the words of a South Vietnamese writer speaking of the period of French domination: "the peasants [can] grit their teeth and nurse their hatred amidst the paddy fields."[79] And the residents of the miserable urban slums can do the same.

This is in fact the model of national and social development that the benevolent imperialists such as Vann offer to underdeveloped societies, whether they are aware of it or not. It is to achieve such magnificent results as these that they are willing to subject the population of Indochina, allegedly for their own good, to the benefits of American technology, as has been done in Vietnam for the past decade.

IV. AGGRESSION AND COLLECTIVE SELF-DEFENSE

The final matter to be considered is what Taylor describes as the "salient feature" of Nuremberg, namely, the issue of crimes against peace. As Taylor observes, the justification for the American intervention in Vietnam can only be article 51 of the United Nations Charter. Invocation of this article assumes that the United States is engaged in collective self-defense against an armed attack from North Vietnam. There has been extensive discussion of this matter. It is curious that Taylor barely alludes to it and makes no effort to deal with arguments that have been presented repeatedly in legal and historical literature.[80] The fundamental problem in establishing the United States' case is that American military intervention preceded and has always been far more extensive than North Vietnamese involvement. (There is, in addition, a question as to the relative rights of North Vietnamese and Americans to be fighting in South Vietnam, after the unification provisions of the Geneva Agreements were subverted.) To cite one crucial moment, consider early 1965, the point at which Taylor begins to have doubts about the legitimacy of the American involvement. Chester Cooper, who had been directly involved in Southeast Asian affairs since 1954 and was in charge of Asian affairs for the White House under the Johnson administration, wrote:

> Communist strength had increased substantially during the first few months of 1965. By the end of April it was believed that 100,000 Viet Cong irregulars and between 38,000 and 46,000 main-force enemy troops, including *a full battalion of regular North Vietnamese troops*, were in South Vietnam. Meanwhile American combat forces were moving into South Vietnam at a rapid rate; in late April more than 35,000 American troops had been deployed and by early May the number had increased to 45,000.[81]

The single North Vietnamese battalion of 400 to 500 men was tentatively identified in late April.[82]

In February 1965, the Johnson administration attempted to justify the new escalation with a White Paper, which, Cooper notes, "proved to be a dismal disappointment." The problem was that "the actual findings [regarding North Vietnamese involvement] seemed pretty frail." No regular troops could be identified. As for infiltrators, even if allegedly "known" and "probable" infiltrators were combined, the average southward movement beginning in 1959, when the insurrection was already solidly in progress, was "little more than 9000 per year," which did not "loom very large" as compared with the half-million-man Saigon army and the 23,000 regular American troops deployed. "The information on enemy weapons," he observed, "was even less earth-shaking." The three 75-millimeter recoilless rifles of Chinese Communist origin, forty-six Soviet-made rifles, forty submachine guns, and one automatic pistol of Czech origin that had been captured (and that might have been bought on the open market) did not seem too impressive as compared with over $860 million in military assistance given by the United States to the

Saigon government since 1961.[83] In fact, the weapons of Communist origin constituted less than 2½ percent of the captured weapons, as I.F. Stone noted at the time.[84]

As to the infiltrators, the figures seem even less impressive when we recall that so far as is known, these were overwhelming South Vietnamese returning to their homes. It is difficult to see why this should be impermissible, after the subversion of the Geneva Agreements and the American and Saigon violations of the Geneva Accords,[85] the Diemist repression, and the renewal of guerrilla war in the South in 1957. Furthermore, Cooper makes no mention of the "infiltration" by the United States into South Vietnam of South Vietnamese trained at American military bases; nor, for that matter, of the saboteur groups and guerrilla teams of South Vietnamese infiltrated to the North since 1956, according to Bernard Fall.[86] Nor, finally, does Cooper mention that American troops had been directly involved in military operations since 1961–1962.

All in all, the case that the United States was merely exercising the inherent right of collective self-defense against an armed attack from North Vietnam is frail indeed. Yet one who defends the legitimacy of the American involvement must go beyond even this and claim that the United States had the right to determine unilaterally that there had been "aggression from the North" and to escalate its already substantial military involvement in South Vietnam, bypassing the stipulations in the U.N. Charter concerning the role of the Security Council in determining the existence of a threat to peace. Unless all of this is accepted, one must conclude that the American military actions are illegal, and themselves constitute aggression—that there was aggression, not from the north, but from the east.

Unfortunately, Taylor has virtually nothing to say about these frequently debated questions. His treatment of the matter of aggression is, in general, unsatisfying. In discussing the allegation that North Vietnam is guilty of aggression in South Vietnam, Taylor points to "strong evidence." "Indisputably, the ground fighting has all taken place in South Vietnam," not in North Vietnam. But, he argues, the case is not clear, since the Geneva Agreements merely established two "zones" and explicitly declared the military demarcation line to be "provisional" and not "a political or territorial boundary" (pp. 101–2). Furthermore, South Vietnam, with U.S. support, declined to proceed with the scheduled elections. Of course, if it is unclear whether North Vietnam is guilty of aggression, it is correspondingly unclear whether American military action is justified by article 51, which in fact speaks not of "aggression," but of "armed attack," a narrower category.[87]

Furthermore, the "strong evidence" that Taylor cites and questions cuts other ways as well. Thus, for example, ground fighting has taken place in

South Vietnam, not the United States. By Taylor's standards, there is thus "strong evidence" that the United States is guilty of aggression in South Vietnam, particularly since American authorities have admitted that the GVN had little administrative authority outside of Saigon by 1965 (see pp. 121, 124 above). Taylor never considers this question in his discussion of aggressive war.[88] Rather, he states the case for possible American aggression as follows:

> . . . the case . . . is based on the conclusions that both South Vietnam and the United States violated the Geneva Declaration of 1954 by hostile acts against the North, unlawful rearmament, and refusal to carry out the 1956 national elections provided for in the Declaration, and that the United States likewise violated the United Nations Charter by bombing North Vietnam. [pp. 96–7]

But these charges constitute only part of the case. A much more serious charge is that the United States has engaged in aggressive warfare in South Vietnam in violation of the provisions of the United Nations Charter concerning the use of force. These charges are based on military actions taken against an insurgency that the United States recognized to be popular and successful—far more popular than the government it had installed and maintained, which had lost the war by 1965, despite the absence of any regular North Vietnamese troops. Taylor does not mention these matters, I presume, because of his tacit assumption that the United States had the right to intervene with its ground, helicopter, and air forces in what some American authorities have recognized to be a "revolutionary, largely political conflict" (see p. 124 above).

It might be argued that the stipulations of the United Nations Charter regarding the threat or use of force (specifically, article 2[4]) have been so eroded as to be effectively inoperative. The issue is discussed by Thomas M. Franck in a recent study.[89] He discusses "the changed realities of the postwar quarter-century" that have so shattered the precepts of article 2(4) that "only the words remain." Franck is surely right in arguing that "both super-Powers have succeeded in establishing norms of conduct within their regional organizations which have effectively undermined Article 2(4)," beginning with the insistence by the United States "that a state's sovereignty is subject to the overriding right of a region to demand conformity to regional standards." An example is the United States condemnation of "not intervention by foreign troops but of a 'foreign' ideology," as in the Guatemalan affair of 1954. This was the direct precursor of the Brezhnev doctrine. Franck is also correct in observing that "national self-interest, particularly the national self-interest of the super-Powers, has usually won out over treaty obligations." It might be added that the United States has developed a concept of "regional organization" that incorporates large parts of Southeast Asia in a "regional organization" where it assumes the right to operate freely, and that the violations of article 2(4) can arguably be traced back to the immediate postwar activities of the great powers in securing their spheres of influence. The British and then American interventions in Greece, beginning in 1944, would be particularly significant examples.

Despite his important observations on the behavior of the great powers, Franck's discussion seems to me to be flawed, in several instances, by an implicit bias in favor of these powers. In discussing the "changing nature of warfare" he cites two categories: "wars of agitation, infiltration, and subversion carried on by proxy through national liberation movements," and nuclear wars. With respect to direct violations of article 2(4), it is of course the first category that is of primary concern, notwithstanding the great powers' attempts to disguise their interventions on grounds of a presumed relation to great-power conflict. But Franck's discussion of this category begs the basic question. As he points out later in the same article, "One man's war of national liberation is another's aggression or subversion, and vice versa." A bias is revealed in that he generally takes the position of the second man: the new kinds of warfare which, he argues, have led to the erosion of article 2(4) are characterized as wars of infiltration and subversion carried on by proxy. If, taking the contrary view, these should be characterized as imperial interventions to repress movements of national liberation, then it follows that the erosion of article 2(4) has not been caused by the "changing realities of the postwar quarter-century," but primarily by the postwar forms of the traditional behavior of great powers. By begging the question in the particular way he does, Franck seems to take his stand, without argument or even explicit assertion, on the side of the great powers. This bias is only partially mitigated by his later references to a third factor in the erosion of article 2(4), namely, "the increased authoritarianism of regional systems dominated by a super-Power," and by his extensive discussion of the role of the great powers in undermining article 2(4) by continual intervention within their respective "regional organizations."

A similar bias appears when Franck refers to the "significant support" given to indigenous Communist insurgents by China in Laos and South Vietnam, for example. As his further comments indicate, the available evidence suggests that Chinese aid has always been small as compared with that given by the United States and its allies to the right-wing forces. Franck's reference to propaganda as a form of intervention hardly applies in this case. China's position has generally been that wars of national liberation must be indigenous and cannot rely on China for substantive material support. Incidentally, so far as is known, the only Chinese troops fighting in the Indochina war are the Chinese Nationalist troops employed by the United States, particularly in clandestine operations in Laos.

The same questions are begged when Franck asserts that "the small-scale and diffuse but significant and frequent new wars of insurgency have, by their nature, made clearcut distinctions between aggression and self-defense . . . exceedingly difficult." Thus he points out that it strains credulity "to be told that Poland had attacked Germany or South Korea the North," but in the case of wars of national liberation, "it is often difficult even to establish convincingly" who is the aggressor. He might have used a different analogy. It would strain credulity to be told that Hungary attacked the Soviet Union in 1956, or that the Philippines attacked the United States at the turn of the century, or that the American colonies attacked England in 1776. If one takes the view that wars of national liberation and great-power interventions constitute a continuation of the classic pattern, to be sure with certain modifications, then these are more appropriate analogies, and there is nothing strikingly new about the postwar period.

As to the outside support for wars of national liberation, recall the vast support given by the French to the American colonies in the Revolutionary War.

> There is no question but that the American Revolutionary War, when considered as a "normal" insurgency, entirely fits the bill of the many revolutionary wars which afflict the middle of the twentieth century. Shorn of almost two centuries of 4th-of-July oratory, it was a military operation fought by a very small armed minority—at almost no time did Washington's forces exceed 8,000 men in a country which had at least 300,000 able-bodied males—and backed by a force of 31,897 French ground troops, and 12,660 sailors and Marines manning sixty-one major vessels.[90]

Even compensating for the effect of Fourth-of-July oratory, we would have no difficulty in evaluating the bias of a contemporary British writer who referred to the American Revolution, in Franck's terms, as a war of agitation, infiltration, and subversion carried on by proxy through a national liberation movement. Taking Fall's point of view, which I believe to be much closer to accuracy than the position implicit in the parts of Franck's discussion cited here, we must conclude that there is no strikingly new factor in the postwar era that led to the erosion of article 2(4). Rather, one must agree with U Thant, I believe, when he says, in words that Franck quotes: "In the final analysis there can be no solid foundation for peace in the world so long as the super-Powers insist on taking unilateral military action whenever they claim to see a threat to their security"[91]—or, we may add, a threat to the perceived self-interest of dominant social groups.

While it is beyond question that what remains of article 2(4) is "only the words," there seems no reason to suppose that this is any change from earlier norms or that it is a consequence of changes in world affairs that could not have been foreseen by the framers of the U.N. Charter. There is, furthermore, no reason to conclude that the precepts of article 2(4) should not be considered applicable. Of course, these precepts suffer from the absence of an enforcing authority, which is a general defect of international law.

The question of the right of intervention and the threat or use of force by the great powers to impose social and political arrangements in developing countries should be at the forefront of any investigation of Vietnam, whether in the light of Nuremberg or in a broader historical context. By failing even to raise such questions, Taylor considerably reduces the significance of his discussion, it seems to me. For future policy decisions, these are surely the major issues. In a dozen places in the world the United States is providing military support to regimes that are attempting to suppress internal insurgency, in ways that might lead to direct military intervention.[92] It can be plausibly argued that in Greece it is the American military support for the colonels that prevents a popular insurgency. In much of Latin America, the same is true.

> Almost all Latin American regimes can now suppress rural insurrections of willful foes. Because of a number of factors, none is as weak as Fulgencio Batista's government of the 1950s. U.S. AID's Public Safety Division has trained police as a first line of defense against terrorism in at least 14 republics; armies are better equipped as $1.75 billion in U.S. military aid has poured into the Americas; upward of 20,000 latino officers and enlisted men have trained at Ft. Gulick in the Canal Zone, and now available are new antiguerrilla weapons developed in Vietnam, which run the gamut from specially designed helicopters to body smellers.[93]

These remarks recall the observation of General Maxwell Taylor in 1963 that in Vietnam "we have a going laboratory where we see subversive insurgency . . . being applied in all its forms." The Pentagon, recognizing "the importance of the area as a laboratory," had already sent "teams out there looking at the equipment requirements of this kind of guerrilla warfare."[94] There is considerable evidence, in fact, that the United States has exploited Vietnam as a laboratory for counterinsurgency, testing weapons and tactics for the wars it anticipates in much the same way that other powers used Spain in 1936–1939.[95]

Among the Latin American regimes that are using the technology designed in the Vietnam laboratory for countering insurgency, there are several that owe their existence to interference from the United States. In Guatemala, a promising reform-minded regime was overthrown by U.S. subversion in 1954. For the past several years, in the course of an anticommunist extermination campaign, there has been a virtual bloodbath, as some four thousand peasants were killed indiscriminately with weapons supplied by the American military aid program.[96] Donald Robinson reports that he observed a Special Operations Force team training Guatemalan Air Force men to use newly designed Bell helicopters to pursue guerrillas.[97] It is even possible that there was still more direct U.S. military involvement. Vice President Marroquin Rojas claimed several years ago that American planes based in Panama were conducting raids in Guatemala, using napalm in areas suspected of harboring guerrillas,[98] and returning to their Panamanian bases. Missionaries working in Guatemala report that they have seen the results of napalm raids.

The extent of American involvement in counterrevolutionary warfare in the postwar period cannot be realistically estimated. There is enough information available to indicate that it is very great. While the United States is surely not alone in undertaking forceful intervention in the internal affairs of other nations, no other power in the postwar period has employed even a fraction of the military force used by the United States in its efforts to destroy indigenous forces to which it has been opposed in other lands.

It is this general policy of counterrevolutionary intervention, raised almost to the level of a national ideology during the Kennedy administration and inherent in Henry Kissinger's doctrine of "limited wars,"[99] which must be reconsidered if we are to be serious about an inquiry into national policy or into the general issues of legality and justice raised and sometimes skirted at Nuremberg, approached but rarely faced directly in treaties and international agreements, and forced upon the consciousness of any civilized person by the tragedy of Vietnam.

9.

Watergate: A Skeptical View

Even the most cynical can hardly be surprised by the antics of Nixon and his accomplices as they are gradually revealed. It matters little, at this point, where the exact truth lies in the maze of perjury, evasion, and of contempt for the normal—hardly inspiring—standards of political conduct. It is plain that Nixon's pleasant crew succeeded in stealing the 1972 election, which probably could have been theirs legally, given the power of the presidency, in spite of Muskie's strength at the polls when the affair was set in motion. The rules of the political game were violated in other respects as well. As a number of commentators have pointed out, Nixon attempted a small-scale coup. The political center was subjected to an attack with techniques that are usually reserved for those who depart from the norms of acceptable political belief. Powerful groups that normally share in setting public policy were excluded, irrespective of party, and the counterattack thus crosses party lines.

The Dean-Colson list of enemies, a minor feature of the whole affair, is a revealing index of the miscalculations of Nixon's mafia and raises obvious questions about the general response. The list elicited varied reactions, ranging from flippancy to indignation. But suppose that there had been no Thomas Watson or James Reston or McGeorge Bundy on the White House hate list. Suppose that the list had been limited to political dissidents, antiwar activists, and radicals. Then, it is safe to assume, there would have

This chapter first appeared in the *New York Review of Books*, September 20, 1973, 3–8.

been no front-page story in the *New York Times* and little attention on the part of responsible political commentators. Rather the incident, if noted at all, would have been recognized as merely another step, inelegant perhaps, in the legitimate defense of order and responsible belief.

The general reaction to the Watergate affair exhibits the same moral flaw. We read lofty sermons on Nixon's move to undermine the two-party system, the foundations of American democracy. But plainly what the Committee to Re-elect the President (CREEP) was doing to the Democrats is insignificant in comparison with the bipartisan attack on the Communist Party in the postwar period or, to take a less familiar case, the campaign against the Socialist Workers Party, which in the post-Watergate climate has filed suit to restrain government agencies from their perpetual harassment, intimidation, surveillance, and worse. Serious civil rights or antiwar groups have regularly discovered government provocateurs among their most militant members. Judicial and other harassment of dissidents and their organizations has been common practice, whoever happens to be in office. So deeply ingrained are the habits of the state agencies of repression that even in the glare of Watergate the government could not refrain from infiltrating an informer into the defense team in the Gainesville VVAW trial; while the special prosecutor swore under oath that the informer, since revealed, was not a government agent.[1]

Watergate is, indeed, a deviation from past practice, not so much in scale or in principle as in the choice of targets. The targets now include the rich and respectable, spokesmen for official ideology, men who are expected to share power, to design social policy, and to mold popular opinion. Such people are not fair game for persecution at the hands of the state.

A hypocrite might argue that the state attack on political dissidence has often been within the bounds of the law—at least as the courts have interpreted the Constitution—whereas Watergate and the other White House horrors were plainly illegal. But surely it is clear that those who have the power to impose their interpretation of legitimacy will so construct and construe the legal system as to permit them to root out their enemies. In periods when political indoctrination is ineffective and dissent and unrest are widespread, juries may refuse to convict. In fact, in case after case they have done so, inspiring tributes to our political system on the part of commentators who overlook a crucial point. Judicial persecution serves quite well to immobilize people who are a nuisance to the state, and to destroy organizations with limited resources or to condemn them to ineffectiveness. The hours and dollars devoted to legal defense are not spent in education, organization, and positive action. The government rarely loses a political trial, whatever the verdict of the courts, as specialists in thought control are no doubt well aware.

In the president's "longer perspective," stated in his April 16 speech, we are to recall the "rising spiral of violence and fear, of riots and arson and bombing, all in the name of peace and justice." He reminds us that "free speech was brutally suppressed as hecklers shouted down or even physically assaulted those with whom they disagreed." True enough. In 1965 and 1966, peaceful public meetings protesting the war were broken up and demonstrators physically assaulted (for example, in Boston, later the center of antiwar activity). Liberal senators and the mass media, meanwhile, denounced the demonstrators for daring to question the legitimacy of the America war in Indochina. Peace movement and radical political centers were bombed and burned with no audible protest on the part of those who later bewailed the decline of civility and the "totalitarianism of the left"—those "serious people" (in Nixon's phrase) who "raised serious questions about whether we could survive as free democracy." Surely nothing was heard from Richard Nixon, who was then warning that freedom of speech would be destroyed for all time if the United States were not to prevail in Vietnam—though when awards are given out for hypocrisy in this regard, Nixon will not even be a contender.

There is nothing new in any of this. Recall the reaction of defenders of free speech when Senator Joseph McCarthy attacked the *New York Times* and, by contrast, the *National Guardian*.[2] Recall the pleas that McCarthy was impeding the legitimate struggle against domestic subversion and Russian aggression, or the reaction to the judicial murder of the Rosenbergs. In fact, the mistake of the Watergate conspirators is that they failed to heed the lesson of the McCarthy hearings twenty years ago. It is one thing to attack the left, or the remnants of the Communist Party, or a collapsing liberal opposition that had capitulated in advance by accepting—in fact, creating—the instruments of postwar repression, or those in the bureaucracy who might impede the evolving state policy of counterrevolutionary intervention. It is something else again to turn the same weapons against the U.S. Army. Having missed this subtle distinction, McCarthy was quickly destroyed. Nixon's cohorts, as recent events have amply demonstrated, committed a similar error of judgment.

The immediate consequence of this deviation is that Nixon's wings have been clipped and power is being more broadly shared among traditional ruling groups, Congress has imposed constraints on executive actions, and, in the changed political climate, the courts have refused to permit executive encroachment on the legislative function through impoundment.

Most important of all, Nixon and Kissinger were unable to kill as many Cambodians as they would have liked, and were thus denied such limited successes in Cambodia as they achieved in South Vietnam, where all authentic popular forces were severely weakened by the murderous assault on the civilian society. Although the failure of the terror bombing of Christmas 1972 may have compelled Nixon and Kissinger to accept the DRV/PRG offer of a negotiated settlement (formally at least),[3] they nevertheless continued to support the openly announced efforts of the Thieu regime to undermine the Paris Agreements of January 1973. At the same time, they simply shifted the bombing to Cambodia in the hope of decimating the indigenous guerrilla movement. As recently as April 1973, Senate doves feared that the "political mood is not right" for a challenge to Nixon's war policy, though they recognized that compliance might be the "final act of surrender" to presidential power.[4] But as Nixon's domestic position eroded, it became possible to enact the legislation urged by opponents of the American war and by politically more significant groups who have come to realize, since the Tet offensive of 1968, that the war was a dubious bargain for American capitalism.

To John Connally, it is "an impressive fact, and a depressing fact, that the persistent underlying balance-of-payments deficit which causes such concern, is more than covered, year in and year out, by our net military expenditures abroad, over and above amounts received from foreign military purchases in the United States."[5] Rational imperialists who find this fact impressive were, no doubt, less than impressed by the fact that Nixon and Kissinger were able to "wind down the war" over a period equal to that of American participation in World War II, and were still intent on pouring resources into an attempt to crush revolutionary nationalism in Indochina. Though the attempt will surely continue,[6] the scale—temporarily at least—will be reduced. This is surely the most significant outcome of Watergate.

Nixon's personal authority has suffered from Watergate, and power will return to men who better understand the nature of American politics. But it is likely that the major long-term consequence of the present confrontation between Congress and the president will be to establish executive power still more firmly. Nixon's legal strategy is probably a winning one, if not for him (for he has violated the rules), then for the position that the presidency is beyond the reach of the law. Richard Kleindienst, John Ehrlichman, and Nixon's lawyers have laid the issue out squarely. In spite of their occasional disclaimers, the import of their position is that the president is subject to no legal constraints. The executive alone determines when and whom to prosecute, and is thus immune. When issues of national security are invoked, all bars are down.

It takes little imagination for presidential aides to conjure up a possible foreign intelligence or national security issue to justify whatever acts they choose to initiate. And they do this with impunity. The low point of the Ervin committee hearings was the failure to press Ehrlichman on the alleged "national security issue" in the release of the Pentagon Papers, or his implication that Daniel Ellsberg was suspected of providing these documents to the Russian embassy. Mary McGrory has suggested plausibly that the factor that led the White House to such excesses in the Ellsberg affair was the fear that it might inspire further exposures, in particular of the secret military attack on Cambodia.

More generally, the president's position is that if there is some objection to what he does, he can be impeached. But reverence for the presidency is far too potent an opiate for the masses to be diminished by a credible threat of impeachment. Such an effective device for stifling dissent, class consciousness, or even critical thought will not be lightly abandoned. Furthermore, Congress has neither the will nor the capacity to manage the domestic economy or the global system. These related enterprises take on new scope with the increasing internationalization of production and economic affairs and with the Nixon-Kissinger diplomacy, which accepts the USSR as a junior partner in managing what Kissinger likes to call "the over-all framework of order,"[7] much as Stalin seems to have intended in the early postwar years. It is fitting, in more ways than one, that Nixon's most loyal constituency should prove to be the POWs and the politburo.

If the choice is between impeachment and the principle that the president has absolute power (subject only to the need to invoke national security), then the latter principle will prevail. Thus the precedent will probably be established, more firmly and clearly than heretofore, that the president is above the law, a natural corollary to the doctrine[8] that no law prevents a superpower from enforcing ideological conformity within its domains.

The Watergate affair and the sordid story that has unfolded since are not without significance. They indicate, once again, how frail are the barriers to some form of fascism in a state capitalist system in crisis. There is little prospect for a meaningful reaction to the Watergate disclosures, given the narrow conservatism of American political ideology and the absence of any mass political parties or organized social forces that offer an alternative to the centralization of economic and political power in the major corporations, the law firms that cater to their interests, and the technical intelligentsia who do their bidding, both in the private sector and in state institutions. With no real alternative in view, opposition is immobilized and there is a natural fear, even among the liberal opposition, that the power of the presidency will be eroded and the ship of state will drift aimlessly. The likely result will therefore be a continuation of the process of centralization of power in the executive, which will continue to be staffed by representatives of those who rule the economy and which will be responsive to their conception of domestic and global order.

It is true, as critics allege, that Nixon's tactics threatened to subvert the two-party system. The illusion that the people rule rests on the regular opportunity to choose between two political organizations dominated by similar interests and restricted to the narrow range of doctrine that receives expression in the corporate media and, with rare exceptions, the educational institutions of American society. Nixon's tactics thus tend to undermine the conventional basis for stability and obedience, while falling far short of supplying some form of totalitarian doctrine as an ideological alternative.

But the conditions that permitted the rise of McCarthy and Nixon endure. Fortunately for us and for the world, McCarthy was a mere thug and Nixon's mafia overstepped the bounds of acceptable trickery and deceit with such obtuseness and blundering vulgarity that they were called to account by powerful forces that had not been demolished or absorbed. But sooner or later, under the threat of political or economic crisis, some comparable figure may succeed in creating a mass political base, bringing together socioeconomic forces with the power and the finesse to carry out plans such as those that were conceived in the Oval Office. Only perhaps he will choose his domestic enemies more judiciously and prepare the ground more thoroughly.

Nixon's front men now plead that in 1969–1970 the country was on the verge of insurrection and that it was therefore necessary to stretch the constitutional limits. The turmoil of those years was largely a reaction to the American invasion of Indochina. The conditions, domestic and international, that have led successive administrations to guide "Third World development" in the particular channels that suit the needs of industrial capitalism have not changed. There is every reason to suppose that similar circumstances will impel their successors to implement similar policies. Furthermore, the basic premises of the war policy in Indochina have not been seriously challenged though its failures led to retrenchment. These premises are shared by most of the enemies on the Dean-Colson list and by others within the consensus of respectable opinion.

The reaction to recent disclosures illustrates the dangers well enough. While public attention was captivated by Watergate, Ambassador Godley testified before Congress that between fifteen thousand and twenty thousand Thai mercenaries had been employed by the United States in Laos, in direct and explicit violation of congressional legislation.[9] This confirmation of Pathet Lao charges, which had been largely ignored or ridiculed in the West, evoked little editorial comment or public indignation, though it is a more serious matter than anything revealed in the Ervin committee hearings.

The revelation of secret bombings in Cambodia and northern Laos from the earliest days of the Nixon administration is by far the most important disclosure of the past several months.[10] It would be difficult to imagine more persuasive ground for impeachment were this a feasible political prospect. But in this case, too, the reaction is largely misplaced. It seems that congressional leaders and commentators in the press are disturbed more by the cover-up and the deceit than by the events themselves. Congress was deprived of its right to ratify—no one who has studied the Symington committee hearings of the fall of 1969 can have much doubt that Congress would have ratified the bombings and incursions had the opportunity been given.

As for the press, it showed as much interest in the bombings at the time as it devotes to the evidence that Thai mercenaries in Laos are being shipped to Cambodia and that casualties of fighting in Cambodia have already arrived in Bangkok hospitals.[11] The press is much too concerned with past deception to investigate these critical ongoing events, which may well have long-term implications for southeast Asia.[12] Similarly, when Jacques Decornoy reported in *Le Monde* on the intense bombing of towns and villages in northern Laos in the spring of 1968, the American press not only failed to investigate, but even failed to cite his eyewitness reports. A Cambodian government White Book of January 1970, giving details of American and ARVN attacks, evoked no greater interest or concern. Nor did the reports of large-scale defoliation of Cambodian rubber plantations in early 1969 or the occasional incidents of "bombing errors" that were conceded by the American government since 1966 when American observers happened to be present.[13] The complaints over government deception ring hollow, whether in the halls of Congress or on the editorial pages.

Still more cynical is the current enthusiasm over the health of the American political system, as shown by the curbing of Nixon and his subordinates, or by the civilized compromise that permitted Nixon and Kissinger to kill Cambodians and destroy their land only until August 15, truly a model of how a democracy should function, with no disorder or ugly disruption.

Liberal political commentators sigh with relief that Kissinger has barely been tainted—a bit of questionable wiretapping, but no close involvement in the Watergate shenanigans. Yet by any objective standards, the man is one of the great mass murderers of the modern period. He presided over the expansion of the war in Cambodia, with consequences that are now well-known, and the vicious escalation of the bombing of rural Laos, not to speak of the atrocities committed in Vietnam, as he sought to achieve a victory of some sort for imperial power in Indochina. But he wasn't implicated in the burglary at the Watergate or in the undermining of Senator Ed Muskie, so his hands are clean.

If we try to keep a sense of balance, the exposures of the past several months are analogous to the discovery that the directors of Murder Inc. were also cheating on their income taxes. Reprehensible, to be sure, but hardly the main point.

10.

The Remaking of History

American imperialism has suffered a stunning defeat in Indochina. But the same forces are engaged in another war against a much less resilient enemy, the American people. Here, the prospects for success are much greater. The battleground is ideological, not military. At stake are the lessons to be drawn from the American war in Indochina; the outcome will determine the course and character of new imperial ventures.

As the American-imposed regime in Saigon finally collapsed, Japan's leading newspaper, *Asahi Shimbun*, made the following editorial comment:

> The war in Vietnam has been in every way a war of national emancipation. The age in which any great power can suppress indefinitely the rise of nationalism has come to an end.

The comment on the war in Vietnam is fairly accurate. The projection for the future, far too optimistic.

The question is a critical one. The great powers surely do not take the American failure in Vietnam as an indication that they can no longer use force to "suppress the rise of nationalism." In fact, during the period of its Vietnam debacle, the United States achieved some notable successes elsewhere, for example in Indonesia, Brazil, Chile, and the Dominican Republic. And the lessons of Vietnam surely do not teach our partners in détente that they must relax their brutal grip on their imperial domains.

This chapter first appeared in *Towards a New Cold War: U.S. Foreign Policy from Vietnam to Reagan* (New York: Pantheon Books, 1982; New York: The New Press, 2003), 144–64.

Apologists for state violence understand very well that the general public has no real stake in imperial conquest and domination. The public costs of empire may run high, whatever the gains to dominant social and economic groups. Therefore the public must be aroused by jingoist appeals, or at least kept disciplined and submissive, if American force is to be readily available for global management.

Here lies the task for the intelligentsia. If it is determined that we must, say, invade the Persian Gulf for the benefit of mankind, then there must be no emotional or moral objections from the unsophisticated masses, and surely no vulgar display of protest. The ideologists must guarantee that no "wrong lessons" are learned from the experience of the Indochina war and the resistance to it.

During the Vietnam war a vast gap opened between the nation's ideologists and a substantial body of public opinion. This gap must be closed if the world system is to be managed properly in coming years. Thus we are enjoined to "avoid recriminations," and serious efforts will be made to restrict attention to questions that have no significance or long-term implications. It will be necessary to pursue the propaganda battle with vigor and enterprise to reestablish the basic principle that the use of force by the United States is legitimate, if only it can succeed.

If America's Vietnam "intervention" is understood, as it properly must be, as a major crime against peace, then an ideological barrier will be erected against the future use of U.S. force for global management. Hence those who are committed to the founding principles of American imperialism must ensure that such questions are never raised. They may concede the stupidity of American policy, and even its savagery, but not the illegitimacy inherent in the entire enterprise, the fact that this was a war of aggression waged by the United States, first against South Vietnam, and then the rest of Indochina. These issues must be excluded from current and future debate over the "lessons of the debacle," because they go directly to the crucial matter of the resort to force and violence to guarantee a certain vision of global order.

Pursuit of the forbidden questions leads to examination of the origins and causes of the American war. Elaborate documentation is now available, and the conclusions indicated seem to me fairly clear. It was feared—under the plausible assumptions of the more rational versions of the "domino theory"—that Communist social and economic success in Indochina might cause "the rot to spread" to the rest of mainland Southeast Asia and perhaps beyond, to Indonesia and South Asia as well. In internal policy documents, the war planners wasted little time on the lurid variants of the domino theory served up to terrorize the public. What concerned them primarily was the demonstration effect, what was sometimes characterized as "ideological successes."

An egalitarian, modernizing revolutionary movement in one area might serve as a model elsewhere. The long-term effects, it was feared, might go so far as an accommodation between Japan, the major industrial power of the East, and Asian countries that had extricated themselves from the U.S.-dominated global system. The end effect would be as if the United States had lost the Pacific war, which had been fought, in part, to prevent Japan from creating a "new order" from which the United States would be effectively excluded. Certainly the issues are more complex; I have examined them elsewhere in more detail.[1] But this, I think, is the heart of the matter.

It is possible to condemn American imperialism and yet remain within the framework of official ideology. This can be achieved by explaining imperialism in terms of some abstract "will to power and dominion," again, a neutral category that does not relate to the actual structure of our social and economic system. Thus, an opponent of the Vietnam war can write that "American involvement in Vietnam represented, more than anything else, the triumph of an expansionist and imperial interest"; "America's interventionist and counterrevolutionary policy is the expected response of an imperial power with a vital interest in maintaining an order that, apart from the material benefits this order confers, has become synonymous with the nation's vision of its role in history." But his criticism is not labeled "irresponsible" by mainstream scholarship and commentary, for he adds that "in the manner of all imperial visions, the vision of a preponderant America was solidly rooted in the will to exercise dominion over others, however benign the intent of those who entertained the vision." The criticism is responsible because it presupposes benign intent and does not explore the nature of this "dominion," which may therefore be understood as some socially neutral trait.[2] A threat to dominant ideology arises only when this "will to exercise dominion" is analyzed in terms of its specific social and economic components and is related to the actual structure of power and control over institutions in American society.[3] One who raises these further questions must be excluded from polite discourse, as a "radical" or "Marxist" or "economic determinist" or "conspiracy theorist," not a sober commentator on serious issues.

In short, there are ideologically permissible forms of opposition to imperial aggression. One may criticize the intellectual failures of planners, their moral failures, and even the generalized and abstract "will to exercise dominion" to which they have regrettably, but so understandably succumbed. But the principle that the United States may exercise force to guarantee a certain global order that will be "open" to the penetration and control of transnational corporations—that is beyond the bounds of polite discourse.

Accordingly, the American intelligentsia now face several major tasks. They must rewrite the history of the war to disguise the fact that it was, in essence, an American war against South Vietnam, a war of annihilation that spilled over to the rest of Indochina. And they must obscure the fact that this aggression was constrained and hampered by a mass movement of protest and resistance, which engaged in effective direct action outside the bounds of "propriety," long before established political spokesman proclaimed themselves to be its leaders. In sum, they must ensure that all issues of principle are excluded from debate, so that no significant lessons will be drawn from the war.

What conclusions then, are to be drawn from the horrendous experience of Vietnam as the war draws to an end? There are those who regard the question as premature. The editors of the *New York Times* tell us that:

> Clio, the goddess of history, is cool and slow and elusive in her ways. . . . Only later, much later, can history begin to make an assessment of the mixture of good and evil, of wisdom and folly, of ideals and illusions in the long Vietnam story.

We must not "try to pre-empt history's role." Rather, "this is a time for humility and for silence and for prayer" (April 5, 1975).

There is at least one lesson that the Vietnam war should have taught even the most obtuse: It is a good idea to watch the performance of the free press with a cautious and skeptical eye. The editorial just cited is a case in point. The editors call for reason and restraint. Who can object? But let us look a little further. They go on:

> There are those Americans who believe that the war to preserve a non-Communist, independent South Vietnam could have been waged differently. There are other Americans who believe that a viable, non-Communist South Vietnam was always a myth and that its present military defeats confirm the validity of their political analysis. A decade of fierce polemics has failed to resolve this ongoing quarrel.

We must be silent and pray as we await the verdict of history on this "complex disagreement."

The *New York Times* editors, in their humility, do not presume to deliver Clio's verdict. But they are careful to define the issues properly. The hawks allege that we could have won, while the doves reply that victory was always beyond our grasp. As for the merits of these opposing views, which mark the limits of responsible thinking, we must await the judgment of history.

There is, to be sure, a third logically possible position: Regardless of Clio's final judgment on the controversy between hawks and the doves, the United States simply had no legal or moral right to intervene in the internal affairs of Vietnam in the first place. It had no right to support the French effort to reconquer Indochina, or to attempt—successfully or not—to establish "a viable, non-Communist South Vietnam" in violation of the 1954 Geneva Accords, or to use force and violence to "preserve" the regime it had imposed.

The only judgment that Clio is permitted to hand down is a judgment of tactics: Could we have won? Other questions might be imagined. Should we have won? Did we have the right to try? Were we engaged in criminal aggression? But these questions are excluded from the debate, as the *New York Times* sets the ground rules.

There is method in the call for humility, silence, and prayer. Its manifest purpose is to restrict such controversy as may persist to questions of tactics, so that the basic principle of official ideology will stand: Alone among the states of the world, the United States has the authority to impose its rule by force. Correspondingly, the authentic peace movement, which challenged this basic doctrine, must be excluded from all future debate. Its position does not even enter into the "complex disagreement" that so troubles the editors of the *New York Times*.

It is interesting that not a single letter was published challenging the remarkable editorial stand of the *Times* in these terms. I say "published." At least one was sent; probably many more. The *Times* saw fit to publish quite a range of opinion in response to the editorial, including advocacy of nuclear bombardment (May 4, 1975). But there must, after all, be some limits in a civilized journal.

The *Times* is not alone in trying to restrict discussion to the narrow and trivial issues formulated in its editorial. The *Christian Science Monitor* gives this assessment:

> Many voices, including this newspaper, regard the communist victory as a tragedy, believing the U.S. involvement in Vietnam to have been honorable, although the conduct of the war in both its political and military phases was fraught with mistakes and misjudgments. Others will argue, with equal cogency, that America should long ago have realized its mistakes and moved rapidly to extricate itself and permit the South Vietnamese to work things out for themselves. But surely there can be a unifying consensus . . . (April 22)

Note that the opposing view is assumed to share the *Monitor*'s basic premises, while differing on a question of timing. In fact, this is the standard position put forth in the national media, with a few honorable exceptions. Criticism of state policy is always welcome, but it must remain within civilized bounds. An Arthur Schlesinger may express his skepticism with regard to Joseph Alsop's prediction that the American war will succeed, for he goes on to stress that "we all pray that Mr. Alsop will be right." It is obvious, without discussion, than any right-thinking person must pray for the victory of American arms. As Schlesinger explained in 1967, American policy may yet succeed, in which event "we may all be saluting the wisdom and statesmanship of the American government" in conducting a war that was turning Vietnam into "a land of ruin and wreck."[4] But he thought success to be unlikely. Had he gone on to urge that the United States abandon its failed enterprise, the *Monitor* would concede, in retrospect, that this extreme proposal had cogency equal to its own.

The *Washington Post* has perhaps been the most consistent critic of the war among the national media. Consider, then, its editorial response to the termination of the war. In an April 30 editorial entitled "Deliverance," the *Post* insists that we can "afford the luxury of a debate" over the meaning of this "particular agony." Americans should develop "a larger judgment of the war as a whole," but it must be a balanced judgment, including both the positive and negative elements:

> For if much of the actual conduct of Vietnam policy over the years was wrong and misguided—even tragic—it cannot be denied that some part of the purpose of that policy was right and defensible. Specifically, it was right to hope that the people of South Vietnam would be able to decide on their own form of government and social order. The American public is entitled, indeed obligated, to explore how good impulses came to be transmuted into bad policy, but we cannot afford to cast out all remembrance of that earlier impulse. For the fundamental "lesson" of Vietnam surely is not that we as a people are intrinsically bad, but rather that we are capable of error—and on a gigantic scale. That is the spirit in which the post-mortems on Vietnam ought now to go forward. Not just the absence of recrimination, but also the presence of insight and honesty is required to bind up the nation's wounds.

Note again the crucial words "wrong," "misguided," "tragic," "error." That is as far as "insight and honesty" can carry us in reaching our judgment.

The *Post* encourages us to recall that "some part of the purpose" of our policy in Vietnam was "right and defensible," namely, our early effort to help the people of South Vietnam "to decide on their own form of government and social order." Surely we must agree that it is right and defensible to help people to achieve this end. But exactly when was this "early impulse" revealed in action? Let us try to date it more precisely, recalling on the way some of the crucial facts about the war.

Was it in the pre-1954 period that we were trying to help the people of

South Vietnam in this way? That can hardly be what the *Post* editors have in mind. At that time, the United States was backing the French in their effort to reconquer Indochina.[5] As Truman's Secretary of State, Dean Acheson, noted, success in this effort "depends, in the end, on overcoming opposition of indigenous population." The Vietnamese resistance forces were led by Ho Chi Minh, whose appeals for American assistance had been rebuffed. No one had the slightest doubt that he had immense popular support as the leader of Vietnamese national forces. But, Acheson explained, "Question whether Ho is as much nationalist as Commie is irrelevant." He is an "outright Commie." We must therefore help the French who are determined, in Acheson's phrase, "to protect IC [Indochina] from further COMMIE encroachments." Nothing here about helping the people of South Vietnam to determine their own fate.

Perhaps it was after the Geneva Accords that our "early impulse" flourished. Hardly a plausible contention. The ink was barely dry on the agreements when the National Security Council adopted a general program of subversion to undermine the political settlement, explicitly reserving the right (subject to congressional approval) to use military force "to defeat local Communist subversion or rebellion not constituting armed attack"—that is, in direct violation of the "supreme law of the land." Such force might be used "either locally or against the external source of such subversion or rebellion (including Communist China if determined to be the source)." The U.S.-backed Diem regime launched a violent and bloody repression, in defiance of the accords that we had pledged to uphold, in an effort to destroy the southern forces that had participated in defeating French colonialism. This slaughter appeared to be fairly successful, but by 1959 the former Viet Minh forces, abandoning their hope that the Geneva Accords would be implemented, returned to armed struggle, evoking the predictable wail of protest in Washington. Surely, then, this was not the period when the United States showed its deep concern for the right of the South Vietnamese people to self-determination.

Perhaps the *Post* is referring to the early 1960s, when U.S. officials estimated that about half the population of South Vietnam supported the National Liberation Front (NLF) and, in the words of the Pentagon Papers historian, "Only the Viet Cong had any real support and influence on a broad base in the countryside," where 80 percent of the population lived. President Kennedy dispatched U.S. forces to suppress the "subversion or rebellion" that was bringing about the collapse of the Diem regime, which was described in the Pentagon Papers as "essentially the creation of the United States." By 1962, U.S. pilots were flying 30 percent of the combat missions, attacking "Viet Cong" guerrillas and the population that supported them. The local forces organized, trained, advised, and supplied by the United States undertook to remove more than one-third of the population by force to "strategic hamlets," where, in the phrase of the Administration's leading dove, Roger Hilsman, they would have a "free choice" between the Government and the Vietcong. This magnanimous effort failed, Hilsman explains, because of inefficient police work. It was never possible to eradicate the Vietcong political agents from the hamlets where the population was concentrated. How could a person exercise a "free choice" between the Government and the Vietcong when the Vietcong agents—his brothers or cousins—had not been eliminated?[6]

Plainly, we may dismiss the possibility that this was the period in question.

After the coup that overthrew Diem in November 1963, South Vietnam was finally on its way to democracy, according to official propaganda. But this period, unfortunately is not a likely candidate for the *Post*'s award for good behavior.[7] Through 1964 the NLF was offering a settlement on the Laotian model, with a coalition government and a neutralist program. Meanwhile the United States was maneuvering desperately to avoid what internal documents refer to as "premature negotiations." The reason, as explained by U.S. government scholar Douglas Pike, was that the non-Communists in South Vietnam, with the possible exception of the Buddhists, could not risk entering a coalition, "fearing that if they did the whale would swallow the minnow." As for the "Buddhists" (i.e., the politically organized Buddhist groups), General Westmoreland explained in September of that year they were not acting "in the interests of the Nation." As Ambassador Henry Cabot Lodge later saw it, according to the Pentagon historian, the Buddhists were "equivalent to card-carrying Communists." The United States' position was that the two substantial political forces in the south, the southern whale and the Buddhists, must be prevented from deciding on their own form of government and social order. Only the United States understood "the interests of the Nation." Thus the United States tried to nourish its minnow, which at that point was General Khanh and the Armed Forces Council. As Ambassador Lodge explained, the generals are "all we have got." "The armed forces," Ambassador Maxwell Taylor elaborated, "were the only component of Vietnamese society which could serve as a stabilizing force."

By January 1965, even the minnow was slipping from the American grasp. According to Ambassador Taylor's memoirs,[8] "The U.S. government had lost confidence in Khanh" by late January 1965. Khanh, he writes, "was a great disappointment." He might have been "the George Washington of his country," but he lacked "character and integrity," and was therefore told to get lost a few weeks later. Khanh's lack of character and integrity was clearly revealed that fateful January. He was moving then towards "a dangerous Khanh-

Buddhist alliance which might eventually lead to an unfriendly government with which we could not work," Taylor explained.

Actually there was more to it than that. Khanh apparently was also close to a political settlement with the NLF. Speaking in Paris on "South Vietnam Day" (January 26, 1975), General Khanh stated, as he had before, that "foreign interference" had aborted his "hopes for national reconciliation and concord between the belligerent parties in South Vietnam" ten years earlier. In support of this contention, he released the text of a letter sent to him on January 28, 1965, by Huynh Tan Phat, then vice president of the Central Committee of the NLF, in reply to an earlier letter of Khanh's. Phat affirmed his support for Khanh's express demand that "the U.S. must let South Vietnam settle the problems of South Vietnam" and his stand "against foreign intervention in South Vietnam's domestic affairs." He expressed the willingness of the NLF to join Khanh in "combat for national sovereignty and independence, and against foreign intervention." These negotiations would have led to unity against the United States and an end to the war, Khanh stated. But within a month of this interchange, "I was forced to leave my country, as a result of foreign pressure."

In late January, according to the Pentagon Papers, General Westmoreland "obtained his first authority to use U.S. forces for combat within South Vietnam," including "authority to use U.S. jet aircraft in a strike role in emergencies" (three years after U.S. pilots began to participate in the bombing of South Vietnam). The timing was not accidental. To avert a political settlement among South Vietnamese, the United States undertook the regular, systematic bombing of South Vietnam in February (at more than triple the level of the more publicized bombing of the North), and not long after, an American expeditionary force invaded South Vietnam.

In short, the period from the Diem coup to the outright U.S. invasion of early 1965 can hardly be described as a time when the United States acted on its early impulse to help the people of South Vietnam to decide their own future.

What about the period after February 1965? Here, the question is merely obscene.

In January 1973, Nixon and Kissinger were compelled to accept the peace proposals that they had sought to modify the preceding November, after the presidential elections. Perhaps this marks the beginning of the period to which the *Post* editors are referring. Again, the facts demonstrate clearly that this cannot be the period in question.[9]

It must be, then, that the last days of the war mark the period when the United States sought to contribute to self-determination in South Vietnam. In fact, the editors of the *Post* tell us that "the last stage of an era-long American involvement in Vietnam was distinctive . . . because during that brief stage the United States acted with notable responsibility and care," removing Americans and thousands of Vietnamese. "The United States also, in the last days, made what seems to us an entirely genuine and selfless attempt to facilitate a political solution that would spare the Vietnamese further suffering."

Very touching. Granting, for the sake of discussion, the sincerity of this genuine and selfless attempt, this certainly proves that our involvement in Vietnam was a mixture of good and evil, and that "some part of the purpose of [U.S.] policy was right and defensible," specifically, our "early impulse" to help the people of South Vietnam "to decide on their own form of government and social order." Let the debate go forward, then, without recriminations and with insight and honesty, as we proceed to bind up the nation's wounds, recognizing that we are capable of tragic error, but insisting on our "good impulses" which "came to be transmuted into bad policy" by some incomprehensible irony of history.

The U.S. government was (partially) defeated in Vietnam, but only bruised at home. Its intellectual elite is therefore free to interpret recent history without any need for self-examination.

In the current flood of essays on "the lessons of Vietnam," one finds very little honest self-appraisal. James Reston explains "the truth" about the recent disaster in the following terms:

> The truth is that the United States Government, in addition to its own mistakes, was deceived by both the North Vietnamese, who broke the Paris agreements, and by the South Vietnamese, who broke the Paris agreements, and then gave up most of their country without advance notice. (*New York Times*, April 4, 1975)

The United States commits mistakes, but the Vietnamese—North and South—are guilty of crimes, breaking agreements that they had undertaken to uphold. The facts are a little different. As the Paris Agreements were signed, the White House announced that it would reject every major principle expressed in the scrap of paper the the United States was forced to sign in Paris.[10]

The United States proceeded to support the Thieu regime in its announced efforts to violate the agreements by massive repression within its domains and military action to conquer the remainder of South Vietnam. In the summer of 1974, U.S. officials expressed their great pleasure at the success of these efforts, noting that the Thieu regime had succeeded in conquering some 15 percent of the territory administered by the PRG, making effective use of the enormous advantage in firepower it enjoyed thanks to the bounty of the United States. They looked forward with enthusiasm to still further successes.[11]

But none of this counts as an American violation of the Paris Agreements. It is only the evil Vietnamese, North and South, who are guilty of such crimes. This is a matter of doctrine. Facts are irrelevant.

Furthermore, "our Vietnamese" not only broke the Paris Agreements, but also gave up most of their country without giving us advance notice. Reston complains that "the Thieu Government didn't even give Mr. Ford a chance to be fair at the end. It just ordered the retreat, called in the television cameras, and blamed America for the human wreckage of its own failures." How ungrateful and unworthy are these Vietnamese. Ford in his innocence, was again deceived; he "was almost unfair to his own country. For he left the impression that somehow the United States was responsible for the carnage in Southeast Asia." That we should be so falsely accused . . .

After many years, one expects nothing different from this worthy pundit. Let us turn, then, to the *Times*'s most outspoken dove, Anthony Lewis, a serious and effective critic of the war in the 1970s. Summing up the history of the war, he concludes:

> The early American decision on Indochina can be regarded as blundering efforts to do good. But by 1969 it was clear to most of the world—and most Americans—that the intervention had been a disastrous mistake.

Congress and most of the American people "know now that intervention in Southeast Asia was a mistake from the beginning," "that the idea of building a nation on the American model in South Vietnam was a delusion," "that it did not work and that no amount of arms or dollars or blood could ever make it work." Only Ford and Kissinger have failed to learn "the lessons of folly." The lesson of Vietnam is that "deceit does not pay; it may have worked in some other century or some other country, but in the United States at the end of the twentieth century it cannot." Thus "a crucial element at the end was the same one that caused disaster all along: deception by American officials—deception of others and ourselves." This should "afford insight into what went wrong in general." He quotes with approval the judgment of the London *Sunday Times:* "The massive lies involved in the Asian policy have done as much to damage American society and America's reputation as the failure of the policy itself."[12]

The lesson, then, is that we should avoid mistakes and lies, and keep to policies that succeed and are honestly portrayed. If only our early efforts to do good had not been so "blundering," they would have been legitimate.

This includes, one must assume, such efforts to do good as our support for the Diemist repression after 1954, or the combat operations of the early 1960s by U.S. forces and the troops they trained and controlled, or the strategic hamlet program, or the bombing of more than a hundred thousand montagnards into "safe areas" in 1962, and on, and on. Recall Bernard Fall's estimate that by April 1965, before the first North Vietnamese battalion was detected in the South, more than 160,000 "Viet Cong" had fallen "under the crushing weight of American armor, napalm, jet bombers and, finally, vomiting gases." [13] But all of these were "blundering efforts to do good," though *by 1969* we should have seen that the "intervention" was a "disastrous mistake."

Finally, consider the thoughts of TRB (Richard Strout), the regular commentator of the *New Republic* (April 25). He writes from Paris, where he has been visiting monuments that record Hitler's crimes. The emotional impact is overwhelming: "I hated the maniac Hitler crew; I could never forgive the Germans." But, he continues, "other nations have lost their senses too; was this not the land of the guillotine? And then, of course, I thought of Vietnam."

At last, someone is willing to contemplate the *criminal* nature of the American war. But not for long. The next sentence reads: "It was not wickedness; it was stupidity." It was "one of the greatest blunders of our history." There is a message: "Watching the long tragedy in living color has been a chastening experience but the act of bravery is to face up to it." If we can do so, perhaps there will be "the dawn of a new maturity—a coming of age."

Our "bravery," however, can go only so far. Our "new maturity" cannot tolerate the questioning of our fundamental decency.

Since TRB recalls "the maniac Hitler crew," perhaps we may go on to recall the self-judgment of the Nazi criminals whom he so passionately detests. We might recall the words of Heinrich Himmler, speaking of the massacre of the Jews:

> To have gone through this and—except for instances of human weakness—to have remained decent, that has made us tough. This is an unwritten, never to be written, glorious page of our history.[14]

By Himmler's standards, the toughness of the American government must be exalted indeed. We have gone through this, and yet remained decent. Blundering perhaps, but fundamentally decent. And if anyone doubts our toughness, let them ask the Cambodians.

We did, of course, have our instances of human weakness. By our standards, My Lai was such an instance; the criminals were dealt with properly in a demonstration of our system of justice. It is true that we did not apply exactly the same standards that were brought to bear in the case of General Yamashita, hanged for crimes committed by troops over whom he had no control in the last months of the Philippine campaign. But at least Lieutenant Calley spent some time under house arrest. The long arm of justice, however, does not reach as far as those responsible, say, for Operation SPEEDY EXPRESS in the Delta province of Kien Hoa in early 1969, which succeeded in massacring eleven thousand of those South Vietnamese whose right to self-determination we were so vigorously defending, capturing 750 weapons and destroying the political and social structure established by the NLF. This operation was more than merely decent: "The performance of this division has been magnificent," General Abrams rhapsodized, in promoting its commander.[15] We can be sure that the custodians of history will place these glorious pages in our history in the proper light.

Our own respectable doves share some fundamental assumptions with the hawks. The U.S. government is honorable. It may make mistakes, but it does not commit crimes. It is continually deceived and often foolish (we are so "naive and idealistic" in our dealings with our allies and dependencies, Chester Cooper remarks), but it is never wicked. Crucially, it does not act on the basis of the perceived self-interest of dominant social groups, as other states do. "One of the difficulties of explaining [American] policy," Ambassador Charles Bohlen explained at Columbia University in 1969, is that "our policy is not rooted in any national material interest of the United States, as most foreign policies of other countries in the past have been."[16] Only those who are "radical" or "irresponsible" or "emotional"—and thus quite beyond the pale—will insist on applying to the United States the intellectual and moral standards that are taken for granted when we analyze and evaluate the behavior of officially designated enemies or, for that matter, any other power.

It is a highly important fact that the majority of the American people strayed beyond the bounds of legitimate criticism, regarding the war as immoral, not merely a tactical error. The intellectuals, however, generally remained more submissive to official ideology, consistent with their social role. This is evident from commentary in the press and academic scholarship. The polls revealed a negative correlation between educational level and opposition to the war—specifically, principled opposition, that is, advocacy of withdrawal of American forces. The correlation has been obscured by the fact that visible and articulate opposition to the war, not surprisingly, disproportionately involved more privileged social strata. The greater subservience of the intelligentsia to state ideology is also demonstrated in a recent study of the "American intellectual elite"[17]—if one is willing to tolerate this absurd concept for the sake of discussion. The study reveals, as should have been anticipated, that these more subtle thinkers generally opposed the war on "pragmatic" grounds. Translating to more honest terms, the intellectual elite generally felt that we couldn't get away with it (at least after the Tet offensive), or that the cost was too high (for some, the cost to the victims).

The essential features of U.S. policy in Indochina were clearly illustrated in the final incident of the American war, the *Mayagüez* incident. On May 12, 1975, the U.S. merchant ship *Mayagüez* was intercepted by Cambodian patrol boats within three miles of a Cambodian island, according to Cambodia—within seven miles, according to the ship's captain. Shortly after midnight (U.S. Eastern Daylight Time) on May 14, U.S. planes sank three Cambodian gunboats. That afternoon, the secretary-general of the United Nations requested the parties to refrain from acts of force. At 7:07 P.M., Cambodian radio announced that the ship would be released. A few minutes later, Marines attacked Tang Island and boarded the deserted ship nearby. At 10:45 P.M., a boat approached the U.S. destroyer *Wilson* with the crew of the *Mayagüez* aboard. Shortly after, U.S. planes attacked the mainland. A second strike against civilian targets took place forty-three minutes after the captain of the *Wilson* reported to the White House that the crew of the *Mayagüez* was safe. U.S. Marines were withdrawn after heavy fighting. The Pentagon announced that its largest bomb, fifteen thousand pounds, had been used. The operation cost the lives of forty-one Americans, according to the Pentagon (fifty wounded), along with an unknown number of Cambodians.

A few days later, in an incident barely noted in the press, the U.S. Coast Guard boarded the Polish trawler *Kalmar* and forced it to shore in San Francisco. The ship was allegedly fishing two miles within the twelve-mile limit established by the United States. The crew was confined to the ship under armed guard as a court pondered the penalty, which might include sale of the ship and its cargo. There have been many similar incidents. In one week of January 1975, Ecuador reportedly seized seven American tuna boats, some up to one hundred miles at sea, imposing heavy fines.

President Ford stated in a May 19 interview that the United States was aware that Cambodian gunboats had intercepted a Panamanian and a South Korean ship a few days before the *Mayagüez* incident, then releasing the ships and crews unharmed. Kissinger alleged that the United States had informed insurance companies that Cambodia was defending its coastal waters, but the president of the American Institute of Marine Underwriters was unable to verify any such "forewarning."

Evidently, the *Kalmar* and *Mayagüez* incidents are not comparable. Cambodia had just emerged from a brutal war, for which the United States bears direct responsibility. For twenty years, Cambodia had been the victim of U.S. subversion, harassment, devastating air attacks, and direct invasion. Cambodia announced that hostile U.S. actions were still continuing, including espionage flights and "subversive, sabotage and destructive activities" and penetration of coastal waters by U.S. spy ships "engaged in espionage activities there almost daily." Thai and Cambodian nationals had been landed, Cambodia alleged, to contact espionage agents, and had confessed that they were in the employ of the CIA. Whether these charges were true or not, there can be no doubt that Cambodia had ample reason, based on history and perhaps current actions, to be wary of U.S. subversion and intervention. In contrast, Poland poses no threat to the security or territorial integrity of the United States.

According to Kissinger, the United States decided to use military force to avoid "a humiliating discussion," failing to add that the supreme law of the land obliges the United States to limit itself to "humiliating discussion" and other peaceful means if it perceives a threat to peace and security. Aware of its legal obligations, the United States informed the United Nations Security Council that it was exercising the inherent right of self-defense against armed attack, though evidently it is ludicrous to describe the Cambodian action as an "armed attack" against the United States in the sense of international law.

Despite official denials, the American military actions were clearly punitive in intent. The *Washington Post* reported (May 17) that U.S. sources privately conceded "that they were gratified to see the Khmer Rouge government hit hard." Cambodia had to be punished for its insolence in withstanding the armed might of the United States. The domestic response indicated that the illegal resort to violence will continue to enjoy liberal support, if only it can succeed (assuming that we regard the loss of forty-one marines to save thirty-nine crewmen who were about to be released as "success"). Senator Kennedy stated that "the President's firm and successful action gave an undeniable and needed lift to the nation's spirit, and he deserves our genuine support."[18] That everyone's spirits were lifted by still another blow at Cambodia may be doubted. Still, this reaction, from the senator who had been most closely concerned with the human impact of the American war, is important and revealing. Senator Mansfield explained that Ford's political triumph weakens antimilitarist forces in Congress. Supporting his conclusion, on May 20 the House voted overwhelmingly against reducing American troop commitments overseas. House Majority leader Thomas p. O'Neill reversed his earlier support for troop reductions.

There were a few honorable voices of protest. Anthony Lewis observed that "for all the bluster and righteous talk of principle, it is impossible to imagine the United States behaving that way toward anyone other than a weak, ruined country of little yellow people who have frustrated us."

On the liberal wing of the mainstream, John Osborne chided Lewis in the *New Republic* (June 7) for his failure to see "some good and gain" in the

Mayagüez incident. Osborne himself felt that the president acted "properly, legally, courageously, and as necessity required." There were, to be sure, some "flaws." One of these flaws, "disturbing, avoidable, and to be deplored," was the tentative plan to use B-52s. But our honor was saved, according to Osborne, when the plan was rejected "partly because of predictable domestic and world reaction and partly because heavy bombing would almost certainly have worsened rather than bettered the lot of the *Mayagüez* crewmen."

Another possible consideration comes to mind: Bombing of defenseless Cambodia with B-52s, once again, would have constituted another major massacre of the Cambodian people. But no such thoughts trouble the mind or conscience of this austere tribune of the people, who sternly rebuked those "journalistic thumb-suckers" who raised questions in the wrong "manner and tone" in "a disgrace to journalism."

Top Administration officials informed the press that it was Henry Kissinger who "advocated bombing the Cambodian mainland with B-52s during the recent crisis over the captured ship *Mayagüez*."[19] Thankfully, he was overruled by others more humane, who felt that carrier-based bombers would be punishment enough.

The incident reveals the basic elements in U.S. policy toward Indochina: lawlessness, savagery, and stupidity—but not complete stupidity, as one can see from the success in arousing jingoist sentiments at home. The crucial matter is lawlessness, in the specific sense of violating the principle that force may not be used for any purpose except for genuine self-defense against armed attack. The significance of this matter is obvious if only from the fact that it is so generally excluded from discussion of the "lessons of Vietnam" in the mass media, the journals of opinion, and—we may safely predict—academic scholarship.

Within the ideological institutions—the mass media, the schools, and the universities—there is every reason to expect that the task of excluding these issues will be carried out with a fair measure of success. Whether these efforts will succeed in restoring the conformism and submissiveness of earlier years remains to be seen.

The *Post* editorial was certainly correct in denying that "we as a people are intrinsically bad." In fact, "we as a people" recognized that the war was something more than a mistake. In 1965, teach-ins, demonstrations, town forums, extensive lobbying, and other forms of protest reached substantial proportions, and by 1967 there were enormous mass demonstrations, large-scale draft resistance, and other forms of nonviolent civil disobedience. Not long after, the American political leadership came to understand why imperial powers have generally relied on mercenaries to fight brutal colonial wars, as the conscript army, much to its credit, began to disintegrate in the field. By 1971, to judge by the polls, two-thirds of the population regarded the war as immoral and called for the withdrawal of American troops. Thus "we as a people" were, by then, neither doves nor hawks in the sense of responsible editorial opinion and the overwhelming majority of the political commentators.

It has become a matter of critical importance to reverse the ideological defeats of the past decade and to reestablish the doctrine that the United States is entitled to use force and violence to impose order as it sees fit. Some propagandists are willing to put the matter quite crudely. Thus Kissinger, in his academic days, wrote of the great risks if there is "no penalty for intransigence." But there are more subtle and effective means. The best, no doubt, is to reconstruct somehow the shattered image of the United States as a public benefactor. Hence the emphasis on our naiveté, our blunders, our early impulses to do good, our moralism and lack of concern for the material interests that dominate the policy of other powers.

Where this doctrine is not blandly asserted in foreign policy debate, it is insinuated. Consider, as a crucial case in point, the current debate over the use of military force to ensure American control over the world's major energy resources in the Middle East, and thus to maintain our capacity to control and organize the "free world." For the moment, the debate over such intervention is the pastime of intellectuals.

But the situation is unstable. No one can predict what the future may bring. Within the narrow spectrum of responsible opinion there is room for disagreement over the tactical question of how American hegemony is to be established, in the Middle East or elsewhere. Some feel that force is necessary to guarantee. "American interests."[20] Others conclude that economic power and normal business procedures will suffice. No serious question may be raised, however, concerning our right to intervene, or the benevolent purposes that will guide such moves, if we are forced to counteract "the aggression of the oil-producing countries against the economies of the developing and developed worlds."[21]

It comes as no surprise, then, to discover that in the current debate over U.S. intervention in the Arabian peninsula it is generally accepted on all sides that after having successfully established its rule, the United States will guarantee a fair and equitable distribution of Middle East oil. The proposition that the United States will or might act in this way is rarely questioned. But consider now the basis for this tacit assumption. Is it an induction from the historical record? That is, can we found this belief on American conduct in the past with regard to its agricultural resources or raw materials or the products of its industrial plant? When the United States dominated world trade in oil, did it use its power to guarantee that its European allies, for example, would benefit from the low production cost of Middle Eastern petroleum? These questions are hardly worth discussing.

Of course, it might be argued that the leopard will, for some reason, change its spots. But then, we might speculate that the Arab oil producers are no less likely to use their control over petroleum to ensure a fair and equitable distribution. The Arab oil producers, for example, expend a far greater proportion of their GNP for foreign aid than the United States for other industrial powers have ever done, and a far larger proportion of their aid goes to poorer countries.[22] Thus, if history is a guide, perhaps we should encourage Saudi Arabia and Kuwait to conquer Texas, rather than debating the merits of an American invasion of the Middle East. In fact, the whole discussion suggests a dangerous case of advanced cretinism. What is remarkable about the recent debate is that it proceeds at all, given the absurdity of the hidden premise.

Nothing could indicate more clearly how wedded the intelligentsia remain to the doctrine of American benevolence, and the corollary principle that the United States is entitled to resort to force and violence to maintain "global order"—if only we can succeed, and, as the more sensitive will add, if only we are not too brutal about it.

The entire American record in Indochina can be captured in the three words "lawlessness," "savagery," and "stupidity"—in that order. From the outset, it was understood, and explicitly affirmed, at the highest level of policymaking, that the U.S. "intervention" in South Vietnam and elsewhere was to be pursued in defiance of any legal barrier to the use of force in international affairs. Given the indigenous strength and courage of the South Vietnamese resistance, the United States was compelled to undertake a war of annihilation to destroy the society in which it gained its support—the society "controlled by the Viet Cong," in the terminology of the propagandists. The United States partially succeeded in this aim, but was never able to construct a viable client regime out of the wreckage. When Washington was no longer able to call out the B-52s, the whole rotten structure collapsed from within. In the end, the interests of American ruling groups were damaged, in Southeast Asia, in the United States itself, and throughout the world. Lawlessness led to savagery in the face of resistance to aggression. And in retrospect, the failure of the project may be attributed, in part, to stupidity.

Intellectual apologists for state violence, including those who describe themselves as doves, will naturally focus on the stupidity, alleging that the war was a tragic error, a case of worthy impulse transmuted into bad policy, perhaps because of the personal failings of a generation of political leaders and incompetent advisers. Stupidity is a politically neutral category. If American policy was stupid, as in retrospect all can see it was, then the remedy is to find smarter policymakers; presumably, the critics.

Some opponents of the war were appalled by the savagery of the American attack. Even such a prominent hawk as Bernard Fall turned against the war in the belief that Vietnam was unlikely to survive as a cultural and historic entity under the American model of counterrevolutionary violence. It is true that the Nazi-like barbarity of U.S. war policy was the most salient and unforgettable feature of the war, in South Vietnam and elsewhere in Indochina. But savagery too is a politically neutral category. If the American leadership was sadistic, as it surely was, the remedy—it will be argued—is to find people who will pursue the same policies in a more humane fashion.

The more critical matter is the lawlessness, specifically the resort to force to maintain a "stable world order" primarily in the interests of those who claim the right to manage the global economy.

Suppose that the system of thought control reestablishes the doctrine that the United States remains exempt from the principles we correctly but hypocritically invoke in condemning the resort to force and terror on the part of others. Then the basis is laid for the next stage of imperial violence and aggression. As long as these doctrines hold sway, there is every reason to expect a reenactment of the tragedy of Vietnam.

11.

Foreign Policy and the Intelligentsia

So it would seem that our repeated interventions, covert and overt, in Latin America and elsewhere, our brutal assault on the Vietnamese people, not to mention our benign inattentiveness to the abolition of democracy in Greece by a few crummy colonels wholly dependent on American arms and loans, are all mere accidents or mistakes perhaps.

—Philip Rahv, *New York Review of Books*, October 12, 1967

If we hope to understand anything about the foreign policy of any state, it is a good idea to begin by investigating the domestic social structure: Who sets foreign policy? What interests do these people represent? What is the domestic source of their power? It is a reasonable surmise that the policy that evolves will reflect the special interests of those who design it. An honest study of history will reveal that this natural expectation is quite generally fulfilled. The evidence is overwhelming, in my opinion, that the United States is no exception to the general rule—a thesis that is often characterized as a "radical critique," in a curious intellectual move to which I will return.

Some attention to the historical record, as well as common sense, leads to a second reasonable expectation: In every society there will emerge a caste of

---

This chapter first appeared in *"Human Rights" and American Foreign Policy* (Nottingham: Spokesman, 1978) and reprinted in *Towards a New Cold War: U.S. Foreign Policy from Vietnam to Reagan* (New York: Pantheon Books, 1982; New York: The New Press, 2003), 86–114.

propagandists who labor to disguise the obvious, to conceal the actual workings of power, and to spin a web of mythical goals and purposes, utterly benign, that allegedly guide national policy. A typical thesis of the propaganda system is that *the nation* is an agent in international affairs, not special groups within it, and that *the nation* is guided by certain ideals and principles, all of them noble. Sometimes the ideals miscarry, because of error or bad leadership or the complexities and ironies of history. But any horror, any atrocity will be explained away as an unfortunate—or sometimes tragic—deviation from the national purpose. A subsidiary thesis is that the nation is not an active agent, but rather responds to threats posed to its security, or to order and stability, by awesome and evil outside forces.

Again, the United States is no exception to the general rule. If it is exceptional at all, its uniqueness lies in the fact that intellectuals tend to be so eager to promulgate the state religion and to explain away whatever happens as "tragic error" or inexplicable deviation from our most deeply held ideals. In this respect the United States is perhaps unusual, at least among the industrial democracies. In the midst of the worst horrors of the American war in Vietnam, there was always a Sidney Hook to dismiss "the unfortunate accidental loss of life" or the "unintended consequences of military action"[1] as B-52s carried out systematic carpet bombing in the densely populated Mekong Delta in South Vietnam, or other similar exercises of what Arthur Schlesinger once described as "our general program of international good will" (referring to United States Vietnam policy in 1954).[2] There are many similar examples.

Here is one case, not untypical. William V. Shannon, liberal commentator for the *New York Times*, explains how "in trying to do good, we have been living beyond our moral resources and have fallen into hypocrisy and self-righteousness."[3] A few passages convey the flavor:

> For a quarter century, the United States has been trying to do good, encourage political liberty, and promote social justice in the Third World. But in Latin America where we have traditionally been a friend and protector and in Asia where we have made the most painful sacrifices of our young men and our wealth, our relationships have mostly proved to be a recurring source of sorrow, waste and tragedy. . . . Thus through economic assistance and the training of anti-guerrilla army teams we have been intervening with the best of motives [in Latin America]. But benevolence, intelligence and hard work have proved not to be enough. Chile demonstrates the problem [where with the best of motives] by intervening in this complicated situation, the C.I.A. implicated the United States in the unexpected sequel of a grim military dictatorship that employs torture and has destroyed the very freedom and liberal institutions we were trying to protect.

And so on. He concludes that we must observe Reinhold Niebuhr's warning that "no nation or individual, even the most righteous, is good enough to fulfill God's purposes in history"—not even the United States, that paragon of righteousness and selfless benevolence, which has been a friend and protector for so long in Nicaragua and Guatemala, and had made such painful sacrifices for the peasants of Indochina in the preceding twenty-five years. We must therefore be more constrained in our efforts to "advance our moral ideals," or we will be trapped in "ironic paradoxes" as our efforts to fulfill God's purposes lead to unexpected sequels.

Had these words been written twenty years earlier, they would have been disgraceful enough. That they should appear in September 1974 surpasses belief, or would do so were it not that such depraved submissiveness to the state propaganda system is so typical of substantial segments of the liberal intelligentsia as virtually to go unnoticed.

It is commonly believed that an adversary relationship developed between the government and the intelligentsia during the Vietnam war. We read, for example, that "most American intellectuals have since Vietnam come to believe that the exercise of American power is immoral" and that a new "convergence is emerging now around [a new] objective: the dismantling of American power throughout the world."[4] This is sheer myth, akin to the belief that the media have become a "notable new source of national power," opposed to the state.[5] In fact, through the war and since, the national media remained properly subservient to the basic principles of the state propaganda system, with a few exceptions,[6] as one would expect from major corporations. They raised a critical voice when rational imperialists determined that the Vietnam enterprise should be limited or liquidated, or when powerful interests were threatened, as in the Watergate episode.[7]

As for the intellectuals, while it is true that an articulate and principled opposition to the war developed, primarily among students, it never passed quite limited bounds. Illusions to the contrary are common, and are fostered often by those who are so frightened by any sign of weakening of ideological controls that they respond with hysteria and vast exaggeration. Critics of new initiatives in strategic weapons development are commonly denounced for their "call for unilateral disarmament." Correspondingly, the call for a "pragmatic" retreat from the exuberant interventionism of earlier years is transmuted into a demand for "the dismantling of American power throughout the world."[8]

A typical version of the dominant "pragmatic" position is presented by columnist Joseph Kraft, commenting on Kissinger's diplomacy and the reaction to it:

> The balance-of-power approach was acceptable as long as it worked. More specifically, while the Vietnam war lasted, particularly while chances of an indecisive or happy end seemed open, the Kissinger diplomacy commanded general approval. But the debacle in Vietnam showed that the United States has broken with its traditional policy of selflessly supporting the good guys. It demonstrated that American policymakers had used all the dirty tricks in the game on behalf of the baddies.[9]

Note the curious reasoning: Our clients become "baddies" when they lose, and our tricks become "dirty" when they fail. Kraft's comment is characteristic in its reference to our alleged "traditional policy" and is accurate in noting that Kissinger's attempt to maintain an American client regime in South Vietnam in explicit violation of the 1973 Paris Agreements did command substantial support until events revealed that it could not succeed.[10]

In a revealing study of public attitudes toward the Vietnam war, Bruce Andrews discusses the well-documented fact that "lower-status groups" tended to be less willing than others to support government policy.[11] One reason, he suggests, is that "with less formal education, political attentiveness, and media involvement, they were saved from the full brunt of Cold War appeals during the 1950s and were, as a result, inadequately socialized into the anticommunist world view." His observation is apt. There are only two avenues of escape from the awesome American propaganda machine. One way is to escape "formal education" and "media involvement," with their commitment to the state propaganda system. The second is to struggle to extract the facts that are scattered in the flood of propaganda, while searching for "exotic" sources not considered fit for the general public—needless to say, a method available to very few.

In discussing the intellectuals, we may invoke a distinction sometimes drawn between the "technocratic and policy-oriented intellectuals" and the "value-oriented intellectuals," in the terminology of the study of the Trilateral Commission cited above.[12] The technocratic and policy-oriented intellectuals at home are the good guys, who make the system work and raise no annoying questions. If they oppose government policy, they do so on "pragmatic" grounds, like the bulk of the "American intellectual elite." Their occasional technical objections are "hard political analysis" in contrast to the "moralism" or "dreamy utopianism" of people who raise objections of principle to the course of policy.[13] As for the value-oriented intellectuals, who "devote themselves to the derogation of leadership, the challenging of authority, and the unmasking and delegitimation of established institutions," they constitute "a challenge to democratic government which is, potentially at least, as serious as those posed in the past by the aristocratic cliques, fascist movements, and communist parties," in the judgment of the trilateral scholars. Much of the current writing on "the time of troubles" in the 1960s is a variation on the same theme, and a fantastic "history" of the period is in the process of creation, to be exposed, perhaps, by the "revisionist historians" of a future generation.

A variant of the trilateral argument, not uncommon, is that the "American commitment to democracy is being undermined by analyses—generally from the liberal and left part of the political spectrum—which assert that concern for democracy has played no role in American foreign policy."[14] In fact, a strong case can be made—and often is made, by no means from the left—that "it is only when her own concept of democracy, closely identified with private, capitalistic enterprise, is threatened by communism [or, we may add, by mild reform, as in Guatemala, for example] that [the United States] has felt impelled to demand collective action to defend it," or to intervene outright: "There has been no serious question of her intervening in the case of the many right-wing coups, from which, of course, this [anti-Communist] policy generally has benefited."[15] Is it such analyses, or the facts which they accurately describe, that "undermine the American commitment to democracy," or, better, reveal how shallow is the commitment? For the statist intelligentsia, it does not matter that such analyses may be correct; they are dangerous, because they "challenge the existing structures of authority" and the effectiveness of "those institutions which have played the major role in the indoctrination of the young," in the terminology of the trilateral theorists, for whom such categories as "truth" and "honesty" are simply beside the point.[16]

We can distinguish two categories among the "secular priesthood"[17] who serve the state. There are, in the first place, the outright propagandists; and alongside them are the technocratic and policy-oriented intellectuals who simply dismiss any question of ends and interests served by policy and do the work laid out for them, priding themselves on their "pragmatism" and freedom from contamination by "ideology," a term generally reserved for deviation from the doctrines of the state religion. Of the two categories, the latter are probably far more effective in inculcating attitudes of obedience and in "socializing" the public.

A personal experience may be relevant at this point. Like many others who have been involved in writing and actions opposed to state policy, I am frequently asked for comments on current affairs or social and political issues by press, radio, and television in Canada, Western Europe, Japan, Latin America, and Australia—but almost never in the United States. Here, commentary is reserved for professional experts, who rarely depart from a rather narrow ideological range; as Henry Kissinger has accurately commented, in our "age of the expert" the "expert has his constituency—those who have a vested interest in commonly held opinions; elaborating and defining its consensus at a high level has, after all, made him an expert."[18] The academic profession has numerous devices to ensure that professional expertise remains "responsible," though it is true that this system of control was partially threatened in the 1960s. Since the media in the United States, in part perhaps from naiveté, conform virtually without question to the cult of expertise, there is little danger that dissident analyses will be voiced, and if they are, they are clearly labeled "dissident opinion" rather than dispassionate, hard, political analysis. This is another example of "American exceptionalism" within the world of industrial democracies.

To return to the main theme: The United States, in fact, is no more engaged in programs of international good will than any other state has been. Furthermore, it is just mystification to speak of the nation, with its national purpose, as an agent in world affairs. In the United States, as elsewhere, foreign policy is designed and implemented by narrow groups who derive their power from domestic sources—in our form of state capitalism, from their control over the domestic economy, including the militarized state sector. Study after study reveals the obvious: Top advisory and decision-making positions relating to international affairs are heavily concentrated in the hands of representatives of major corporations, banks, investment firms, the few law firms that cater to corporate interests,[19] and the technocratic and policy-oriented intellectuals who do the bidding of those who own and manage the basic institutions of the domestic society, the private empires that govern most aspects of our lives with little pretense of public accountability and not even a gesture to democratic control.

Within the nation-state, the effective "national purpose" will be articulated, by and large, by those who control the central economic institutions, while the rhetoric to disguise it is the province of the intelligentsia. An Arthur Schlesinger can write, presumably without irony, that under the Carter Administration, "human rights is replacing self-determination as the guiding value in American foreign policy."[20] In such pronouncements we see very clearly the contribution of the technocratic and policy-oriented intellectual to what we properly call "thought control" in the totalitarian states, where obedience is secured by force rather than by density of impact. Ours is surely a more effective system, one that would be used by dictators if they were smarter. It combines highly effective indoctrination with the impression that the society really is "open," so that pronouncements conforming to the state religion are not to be dismissed out of hand as propaganda.

It should be noted that the United States *is* in certain important respects an "open society," not only in that dissident opinion is not crushed by state violence (generally; see, however, note 7), but also in the freedom of inquiry and expression, which is in many respects unusual even in comparison with other industrial democracies such as Great Britain. The United States has no Official Secrets Act, nor the heavily constraining libel laws to be found elsewhere. And in the past few years it has had an important Freedom of Information Act. But this relatively high degree of internal freedom merely highlights the treachery of the intellectuals, who cannot plead that their subordination to the state religion is compelled by force or by constraints on access to information.

Much of the writing on the "national interest" serves to obscure the basic social facts. Consider, for example, the work of Hans Morgenthau, who has written extensively and often perceptively on this topic. In a recent presentation of his views, he states that the national interest underlying a rational foreign policy "is not defined by the whim of a man or the partisanship of party but imposes itself as an objective datum upon all men applying their rational faculties to the conduct of foreign policy." He then cites in illustration such commitments as support for South Korea, containment of China, and upholding of the Monroe Doctrine. He further observes that "the concentrations of private power which have actually governed America since the Civil War have withstood all attempts to control, let alone dissolve them [and] have preserved their hold upon the levers of political decision" (*New Republic*, January 22, 1977). True, no doubt. Under such circumstances, do we expect the "national interest" as actually articulated and pursued to be simply the outcome of the application of rational faculties to objective data, or to be an expression of specific class interests? Obviously the latter, and a serious investigation of the cases Morgenthau cites will demonstrate that the expectation is amply fulfilled. The real interests of Americans were in no way advanced by "containing China" (where was it expanding?) or crushing popular forces in South Korea in the late 1940s and supporting a series of dictatorial regimes since, or ensuring that Latin America remains subordinated to the needs of U.S.-based transnational corporations—the real meaning of our upholding of the Monroe Doctrine in the modern period, or of the (Theodore) Roosevelt Corollary to the Monroe Doctrine, which made it the duty of the United States, as a "civilized nation," to exercise its "international police power" in the case of "chronic wrongdoing, or an impotence which results in a general loosening of the ties of civilized society" (cf. Connell-Smith, note 15 above). But it can be argued that the interests of the "concentrations of private power" in the United States that largely dominated the world capitalist system have been advanced by this pursuit of the "national interest." The same holds generally. The idea that foreign policy is derived in the manner of physics, as an objective datum immune to class interest, is hardly credible.

Or, consider a recent analysis by Walter Dean Burnham in the journal of the Trilateral Commission.[21] He notes that the "basic functions" of the state are "the promotion externally and internally of the basic interests of the dominant mode of production and the need to maintain social harmony." The formulation is misleading. These basic functions are not a matter of metaphysical necessity but arise from specific social causes. Furthermore, the "dominant mode of production" does not have interests; rather, individuals or groups who participate in it have interests, often conflicting ones, a distinction that is no mere quibble. And since those who manage this system are also in effective control of the state apparatus, the "basic interests" pursued will tend to be theirs. There are no grounds in history or logic to suppose that these interests will coincide to any significant extent with the interests of those who participate in the dominant mode of production by renting themselves to its owners and managers.

A standard and effective device for obscuring social reality is the argument that the facts are more complex than as represented in the "simplistic theories" of the "value-oriented" critics. Note first that the charge is of course correct: The facts are always more complex than any description we may give. Faced with this contingency of empirical inquiry, we may adopt several courses: (1) We may abandon the effort; (2) we may try to record many facts in enormous detail, a course that reduces in effect to the first, for all the understanding it provides; (3) we may proceed in the manner of rational inquiry in the sciences and elsewhere to try to extract some principles that have explanatory force over a fair range, thus hoping to account for at least the major effects. Pursuing the third—i.e., the rational—approach, we will always be subject to the criticism that the facts are more complex, and if rational, we dismiss the charge as correct but irrelevant. It is instructive that we have no difficulty in adopting a rational stance when considering the behavior of official enemies. The Russian invasion of Afghanistan, for example, surely involves complexities beyond those introduced even in fairly careful analyses of contemporary Soviet international behavior, and surely beyond the standard media accounts. For example, it appears that the major guerrilla groups have been engaged in disruptive operations in Afghanistan since 1973, backed by Pakistan in an effort to destabilize the Afghan regime and bring it to accept Pakistani border claims ("international terrorism," from one point of view; cf. Lawrence Lifschultz, *Far Eastern Economic Review*, January 30, 1981). Nevertheless, such facts as these do not prevent us from focusing on the main point—the Russian invasion—though some commissar might complain that we are ignoring the complexities of history and the difficulties faced by a great power attempting to maintain order with the noblest of intentions.

Another device is the pretense—virtually a reflex reaction—that those who pursue the rational approach are invoking a "conspiracy theory," as they proceed to document the fact that elite groups with an interest in foreign policy (e.g., transnational corporations) attempt to use their power to influence it or direct it, to assume major roles in the state executive, to produce geopolitical analyses and specific programs to guarantee a favorable climate for business operations, etc. With equal logic, one could argue that an analyst of General Motors who concludes that its managers try to maximize profits (instead of selflessly laboring to satisfy the needs of the public) is adopting a conspiracy theory—perhaps business propagandists actually take this stance. Once some analysis is labeled "a conspiracy theory" it can be relegated to the domain of flat-earth enthusiasts and other cranks, and the actual system of power, decision-making, and global planning is safely protected from scrutiny.

A related claim is that critical analysis of the ideological system is a form of paranoia.[22] As noted, it would not be surprising to find in any society a pervasive and systematic bias in the treatment of foreign affairs: Crimes of the state (which can be stopped) are ignored or downplayed, while the spotlight is focused on crimes of official enemies (about which little can be done). In the former category, standards of evidence must match those of physics; in the latter, any fanciful construction will do. In the extreme case, the Soviet press effaces state crimes completely while trumpeting such "facts" as U.S. germ warfare in Korea. Suppose that one documents the expected pattern in the case of the United States. This obviously reveals an extreme form of paranoia. With regard to the first category, it is unfair, ridiculous, to expect the media to be able to discover an eyewitness account of U.S. bombing in northern Laos in *Le Monde* (even when it is brought to their attention), or a Sihanouk press conference calling on the international press to condemn the bombing of Khmer peasants in March 1969 (besides, he didn't specifically say "B-52s" so suppression was legitimate) or a subsequent White Paper of the Sihanouk government on U.S. and U.S.-backed attacks on neutral Cambodia, or Timorese refugees in Lisbon; or to explore the relation between U.S. policies and state terror, starvation and slavery in Latin America, etc. With regard to the second category, the standard line is still more intriguing. Someone who suggests normal standards of adherence to evidence thereby falls into the category of "apologist for atrocities," "defender of the honor of Hanoi," etc. The suggestion that facts matter is easily transmuted into another service for the propagandist. It is not gratifying to the ego merely to march in a parade; therefore those who join in ritual condemnation of an official enemy must show that they are engaged in a courageous struggle against powerful forces that defend it. Since these rarely exist, even on a meager scale, they must be concocted; if nothing else is at hand, those who propose a minimal concern for fact will do. The system that has been constructed enables one to lie freely with regard to the crimes, real or alleged, of an official enemy, while suppressing the systematic involvement of one's own state in atrocities, repression, or aggression on the grounds that the facts are more complex than the emotional and naive critics believe (an exception is tolerated if some evil or misguided individual can be identified as responsible for policy, so that institutional critique is deflected). Given that those who do not accept standard doctrine—e.g., that of the "American intellectual elite" discussed above—have virtually no access to a general audience and that little is required in the way of argument or credible evidence from those of a higher degree of doctrinal purity, the farce plays quite well. It is a system of no small degree of elegance, and effectiveness.

Attempting to pursue a rational course, let us consider American foreign policy since World War II. We are faced at once with some striking features of the world that emerged from the wreckage of the war. Primary among them is the enormous preponderance of American power with respect to the other industrial societies, and *a fortiori*, the rest of the world. During the war, most of the industrial world was destroyed or severely damaged, while industrial production rose dramatically in the United States. Furthermore, long before, the United States had become the leading industrial society, with unparalleled internal resources, natural advantages and scale, and a reasonably high degree of social cohesion. It was natural to expect, under these circumstances, that the United States would use its enormous power in an effort to organize a global system, and it is uncontroversial that this is exactly what happened, though the question "What were the guiding principles?" is indeed controversial. Let us consider these principles.

Where should we look to discover some formulation of them? In a totalitarian society this would pose problems, but the United States really is open in this respect, and there is considerable documentary evidence concerning the vision of the postwar world developed by the very people who were to play the major part in constructing it.

One obvious documentary source is the series of memoranda of the War and Peace Studies Project of the Council on Foreign Relations (CFR) during the war. Participants included top government planners and a fair sample of the "foreign policy elite," with close links to government, major corporations, and private foundations.[23] These memoranda deal with the "requirement[s] of the United States in a world in which it proposes to hold unquestioned power," foremost among them being "the rapid fulfillment of a program of complete re-armament" (1940). In the early years of the war it was assumed that part of the world might be controlled by Germany. Therefore, the major task was to develop "an integrated policy to achieve military and economic supremacy for the United States within the non-German world," including plans "to secure the limitation of any exercise of sovereignty by foreign nations that constitutes a threat to the world area essential for the security and economic prosperity of the United States and the Western Hemisphere."

(The concern for the "prosperity of the Western Hemisphere" is adequately revealed by United States policies, say, in Central America and the Caribbean, before and since; this opposition to imperial prerogatives that constrain U.S. capital and access to resources is often adduced by scholarship as evidence that U.S. foreign policy is guided by "anti-imperialist" commitments). These areas, which are to serve the prosperity of the United States, include the Western Hemisphere, the British Empire, and the Far East, described as a natural integrated economic unity in the geopolitical analysis of the planners.

The major threat to United States hegemony in the non-German world was posed by the aspirations of Britain. The contingencies of the war served to restrict these, and the American government exploited Britain's travail to help the process along. Lend-Lease aid was kept within strict bounds: enough to keep Britain in the war but not enough to permit it to maintain its privileged imperial position.[24] There was a mini-war between the United States and Great Britain within the context of the common struggle against Germany, where, of course, Britain was on the front line—more accurately, the overwhelming burden of fighting Nazi Germany fell to the Russians,[25] but let us keep now to the Anglo-American alliance. In this conflict within the alliance, American interests succeeded in taking over traditional British markets in Latin America and in partially displacing Britain in the Middle East, particularly in Saudi Arabia, which was understood to be "a stupendous source of strategic power, and one of the greatest material prizes in world history," in the words of the State Department.[26] I will return to this matter, but let us continue to explore the CFR planning documents.

The U.S.-led non-German bloc was entitled the "Grand Area" in the CFR discussions. Actually, a U.S.-dominated Grand Area was only a second-best alternative. It was explained in June 1941 that "the Grand Area is not regarded by the Group as more desirable than a world economy, nor as an entirely satisfactory substitute." The Grand Area was seen as a nucleus or model that could be extended, optimally, to a global economy. It was soon recognized that with the coming defeat of Nazi Germany, at least Western Europe could be integrated into the Grand Area. Participants in the CFR discussions recognized that "the British Empire as it existed in the past will never reappear and . . . the United States may have to take its place." One stated frankly that the United States "must cultivate a mental view toward world settlement after this war which will enable us to impose our own terms, amounting perhaps to a pax-Americana." Another argued that the concept of United States security interests must be enlarged to incorporate areas "strategically necessary for world control." It is a pervasive theme that international trade and investment are closely related to the economic health of the United States, as is access to the resources of the Grand Area, which must be so organized as to guarantee the health and structure of the American economy, its internal structure unmodified.

The notion of "access to resources" is marvelously expressed in a State Department memorandum of April 1944 called "Petroleum Policy of the United States," dealing with the primary resource.[27] There must be equal access for American companies everywhere, but no equal access for others, the document explained. The United States dominated Western Hemisphere production,[28] and this position must be maintained while United States holdings are diversified elsewhere. The policy "would involve the preservation of the absolute position presently obtaining, and therefore vigilant protection of existing concessions in United States hands coupled with insistence upon the Open Door principle of equal opportunity for United States companies in new areas." That is a fair characterization of the principle of the "Open Door."[29]

All of this is in accord with the concepts of Grand Area planning, and it also corresponded to the evolving historical process. The United States retained its dominance of Western Hemisphere petroleum resources while the American share of Middle East oil rapidly increased.[30] The British maintained their control of Iranian oil until 1954, when the United States government imposed an international consortium after the CIA-backed coup that restored the Shah, with American companies granted a 40 percent share.[31] Similarly, in the Far East "occupied Japan was not permitted to reconstruct the oil-refining facilities that had been destroyed by Allied bombings, a policy widely attributed in the oil industry of Japan to the fact that the oil bureau of General MacArthur's headquarters was heavily staffed with American personnel on temporary leave from Jersey Standard and Mobil." Later, American-based companies were able to take over a dominant position in controlling Japan's energy resources. "Under the Allied occupation the Japanese government was powerless to block such business links."[32]

Much the same was true elsewhere. For example, the United States succeeded in expelling French interests from Saudi Arabia in 1947 by some legal legerdemain, alleging that French companies were "enemies" as a result of Hitler's occupation of France, so that the 1928 Red Line agreement on sharing oil in the former Ottoman Empire was abrogated (see *Towards a New Cold War*; note 29 of this chapter). British interests in Saudi Arabia were excluded by a different device—namely, when American companies expressed their fear that "the British may be able to lead either Ibn Saud or his successors to diddle them out of the concession and the British into it" (Navy Under Secretary William Bullitt), and "told the Roosevelt Administration that direct U.S. Lend-Lease assistance for King Saud was the only way to keep their Arabian concession from falling into British hands," the president obligingly issued the following directive to the Lend Lease administrator: "In order to enable you to arrange Lend Lease aid to the Government of Saudi Arabia, I hereby find that the defense of Saudi Arabia is vital to the defense of the United States"—its defense from whom, he did not stipulate, though a cynic might remark that the tacit identification of the United States with the Aramco concession is consistent with the actual usage of the phrase "national interest." Lend Lease had been authorized by Congress for "democratic allies" fighting the Nazis. In other ways as well, the Roosevelt Administration acted to support the American companies against their British rivals, through aid (Saudi Arabia received almost $100 million under Lend Lease, including scarce construction materials) or direct government intervention (*MNOC*, pp. 36f.).

As an aside, recall what happened when Iranians experimented with the curious idea of taking control of their own oil in the early 1950s. After an oil company boycott, a successful CIA-backed coup put an end to that, installing the regime of the Shah, which became a powerful United States client state purchasing vast quantities of American arms, conducting counterinsurgency in the Arabian peninsula, and, of course, subjecting the Iranian people to the Shah's pleasant whims.

The coup had other useful consequences. Exxon (i.e., its predecessor corporation) feared that the USSR might gain some share of Iranian oil unless "the problem was solved," in which case it might dump Iranian oil on the world market, depressing prices (*MNOC*, p. 67). But that threat to the free enterprise system was eliminated with the coup.

We should bear in mind that the CIA-backed coup that ended the experiment in Iranian democracy and led to a further displacement of British power was welcomed as a great triumph here. When the agreement was signed between Iran and the new oil consortium organized by the United States government, the *New York Times* commented editorially (August 6, 1954) that this was "good news indeed": "Costly as the dispute over Iranian oil has been to all concerned, the affair may yet be proved worthwhile if lessons are learned from it." The crucial lessons are then spelled out as follows:

> Underdeveloped countries with rich resources now have an object lesson in the heavy cost that must be paid by one of their number which goes berserk with fanatical nationalism. It is perhaps too much to hope that Iran's experience will prevent the rise of Mossadeghs in other countries, but that experience may at least strengthen the hands of more reasonable and more far-seeing leaders.

Like the Shah. With typical ruling-class cynicism, the *Times* then goes on to say that "the West, too, must study the lessons of Iran" and must draw the conclusion that "partnership, even more in the future than the past, must be the relationship between the industrialized Western nations and some other countries, less industrialized, but rich in raw materials, outside Europe and North America," a statement that must have been most inspiring for the underdeveloped countries that had enjoyed the great privilege of partnership with the West in the past.

The "costs" incurred in this affair, according to the *Times*, do not include the suffering of the people of Iran but rather the propaganda opportunities offered to the Communists, who will denounce the whole affair in their wicked fashion, and the fact that "in some circles in Great Britain the charge will be pushed that American 'imperialism'—in the shape of the American oil firms in the consortium—has once again elbowed Britain from a historic stronghold." The implication is that this charge, or even the concept of American "imperialism," is too obviously absurd to deserve comment, a conclusion based as always on the doctrines of the state religion rather than an analysis of the facts. The exuberance over the "demonstration effect" of the CIA achievement is also typical, though the vulgarity of the *Times* account perhaps goes beyond the ordinary. The theme became familiar with reference to Vietnam in subsequent years.

But let us return to the CFR global planning, which laid out a program for organizing the Grand Area, or if possible, the world, as an integrated economic system that would offer the American economy "the 'elbow room' . . . needed in order to survive without major readjustments"—that is, without any change in the distribution of power, wealth, ownership, and control.

The memoranda, which are explicit enough about Grand Area planning, are careful to distinguish between principle and propaganda. They observed in mid-1941 that "formulation of a statement of war aims for propaganda purposes is very different from formulation of one defining the true national interest." Here is a further recommendation:

> If war aims are stated, which seem to be concerned solely with Anglo-American imperialism, they will offer little to people in the rest of the world, and will be vulnerable to Nazi counter-promises. Such aims would also strengthen the most reactionary elements in the United States and the British Empire. The interests of other peoples should be stressed, not only those of Europe, but also of Asia, Africa and Latin America. This would have a better propaganda effect.

The participants must have been relieved when the Atlantic Charter, suitably vague and idealistic in tone, was announced a few months later.

The CFR studies were extended in subsequent years to include analyses of prospects and plans for most parts of the world. The sections on Southeast Asia are interesting in the light of developments there. The analyses that issued from CFR study groups closely resemble the National Security Council memoranda and other material now available in the Pentagon Papers, a remarkable documentary record of the design and execution of imperial planning.[33] The similarity is hardly accidental. The same interests and often the same people are involved. The basic theme is that Southeast Asia must be integrated within the U.S.-dominated global system to ensure that the needs of the American economy are satisfied, and also the specific needs of Japan, which might be tempted again to set its independent course or to flood Western markets unless granted access to Southeast Asian markets and resources, within the overarching framework of the Pax Americana—the Grand Area. These principles were firmly set by the 1950s and guided the course of the American intervention, then outright aggression, when the Vietnamese, like the Iranians, went "berserk with fanatical nationalism," failing to comprehend the sophisticated Grand Area concepts and the benefits of "partnership" with the industrialized West.

The material that I have been reviewing constitutes a primary documentary source for the study of formation of American foreign policy, compiled by those who carried out this policy. We might ask how this material is dealt with in academic scholarship. The answer is simple: It is ignored. The book by Shoup and Minter (see note 22) seems to be the first to examine these records. American scholars justly complain that the Russians refuse to release documentary materials, thus raising all sorts of barriers to the understanding of the evolution of their policies. Another just complaint is that American scholars avoid documentary materials that might yield much insight into the formation of American policy, a fact easily explained in this instance, I believe: The documentary record is no more consistent with the doctrines of the state religion, in this case, than is the historical record itself.

Parenthetically, it might be noted that the Pentagon Papers, which provide a record of high-level policy planning that is unusual in its richness, have suffered the same fate. This record too is ignored—indeed, often misrepresented. There is indeed a spate of scholarly work on United States Vietnam policy, some of which makes extensive use of material in the Pentagon Papers. Typically, however, attention is focused on the 1960s. Then we have a detailed microanalysis of bureaucratic infighting, political pressures, and the like, completely disregarding the general framework, set long before and never challenged by those who were simply applying imperial doctrine as carefully elaborated ten to twenty years earlier. This is a marvelous device for obscuring the social reality by diverting attention from the documentary record concerning the guiding principles of state policy, as clearly revealed in the basic documentation that is characteristically ignored.

Space prevents a detailed review here, but one example may suffice to illustrate. Consider a review of several books on Vietnam by William S. Turley, one of the more critical and independent American academic scholars with a professional involvement in Indochina.[34] He discusses two "prevailing images of American policy-making on Vietnam": the "quagmire hypothesis," which "held that involvement was the result of incremental decisions made without adequate understanding of probable consequences," and "the interpretation that American policy was stalemated by the need of successive administrations, for domestic political reasons, to do what was minimally necessary to avoid losing a war." The book he reviews, by Robert Galluci,[35] finds both of these images too simple and seeks a more complex interpretation through application of a bureaucratic process model. Turley points out that the Pentagon Papers provide important evidence bearing on the questions.

In fact, the Pentagon Papers provide extensive evidence for a different hypothesis, one that goes unmentioned, as it is passed over in silence in the scholarly literature—namely, that American policy in Vietnam was a conscious application of principles of imperial planning that formed part of a consensus established long before the specific period, the 1960s, to which attention is generally restricted. This hypothesis is extensively documented in the Pentagon Papers and elsewhere, but the documentary record is never so much as mentioned in the book under review, the review itself, or academic scholarship generally. The hypothesis in question is simply not fit for discussion in polite company, no matter what the documentation may be. It is not even a competitor, to be rejected.[36]

I do not suggest that in refusing to consider the hypothesis in question or the substantial documentation supporting it, scholars are being dishonest. It is simply that nothing in their training or in the literature generally available to them makes this hypothesis comprehensible. It is a reflection of the success of the educational system in "socialization," the success of what the trilateral analysts call the "institutions which have played the major role in the indoctrination of the young," that certain ideas, however natural and well-supported, do not even come to mind or, if noticed, can be dismissed with derision. People who break away from the consensus have dubious prospects in the media or the academy, in general. The resulting subversion of scholarship is systematic, not individual. Similar phenomena are familiar from the history of organized religion. Anyone who has spent some time in a university knows how it is done. Some young scholars are "hard to get along with" or are "too strident" or "show poor taste in their choice of topics" or "don't use the proper methodology," or in other ways do not meet the professional standards that not infrequently serve to insulate scholarship from uncomfortable challenge.[37] The ideological disciplines are particularly subject to these tendencies.

Primary documentary sources like the CFR studies and the Pentagon

Papers must be investigated with a critical eye and supplemented by much additional evidence if one wants to reach any serious understanding of the evolution of American policy. It might turn out to be the case that the analyses cited above, which are among the few even to concern themselves with the basic documentary record, are inadequate or even seriously in error in the interpretations they provide. What is remarkable and noteworthy, however, is how consistently American scholarship takes a different tack, simply ignoring the documentary record that does not accord with received opinion.

Consider one final example of how the central questions are evaded in academic scholarship. Let us return again to our hypothetical rational observer attempting to discern some of the major factors in foreign policy formation and consider some further facts that should immediately strike him as significant.

Since World War II, there has been a continuing process of centralization of decision making in the state executive, certainly with regard to foreign policy. Second, there has been a tendency through much of this period toward domestic economic concentration. Furthermore, these two processes are closely related, because of the enormous corporate influence over the state executive. And finally, there has been a vast increase in overseas investment, marketing, and resource extraction in the postwar period, greatly increasing the stake of the masters of the corporate economy in foreign affairs. To cite one indication, "It has been estimated that earnings from these foreign operations by 1970 contributed between 20 and 25 percent of total U.S. corporate profits after taxes, a very considerable magnitude indeed."[38] The basic facts are uncontroversial. They suggest, perhaps, a certain hypothesis for investigation: Corporations have some influence, perhaps considerable influence, in setting foreign policy. How does academic scholarship deal with this issue?

There is a (rare) discussion of the question by political scientist Dennis M. Ray in the volume on the multinational corporation just cited.[39] He observes that "we know virtually nothing about the role of corporations in American foreign relations." Scholarship has "clarified the influence of Congress, the press, scientists, and nonprofit organizations, such as RAND, on the foreign policy process. The influence of corporations on the foreign policy process, however, remains clouded in mystery."

Is this "mystery" somehow inherent in the difficulty of discerning the corporate role, as distinct from the massive impact of scientists and the press on foreign policy? Not at all. As Ray points out, the issue remains clouded in mystery because it is systematically evaded:

> My search through the respectable literature on international relations and U.S. foreign policy shows that less than 5 percent of some two hundred books granted

> even passing attention to the role of corporations in American foreign relations. From this literature, one might gather that American foreign policy is formulated in a social vacuum, where national interests are protected from external threats by the elaborate machinery of governmental policymaking. There is virtually no acknowledgement in standard works within the field of international relations and foreign policy of the existence and influence of corporations.

Note that Ray limits himself to the "respectable literature." He excludes what he calls the literature of "advocacy," which includes two streams: statements by corporate executives and business school professors, and "radical and often neo-Marxist analyses." In this literature, particularly the latter category, there is much discussion of the role of corporations in foreign policy formation. Furthermore, as Ray turns to the topic itself, he discovers that the conclusions reached seem to be correct. "Few if any interest groups, outside of business, have generalized influence on the broad range of foreign policy," he observes, citing one of the few works in the "respectable literature" that raises the question. Ray believes that scholars will discover these facts if they "begin to examine the question."

In short, if scholars begin to study the question, they will discover the truth of truisms that have been discussed and documented for years outside of the "respectable literature," exactly as one would expect in the light of such basic and fundamental facts about American society as those noted earlier.

It is interesting that Ray never inquires into the causes of this strange lapse in "respectable" scholarship. In fact, the answer does not seem obscure. If we are interested in careful investigation of the inner workings of the politburo, we do not turn to studies produced at Moscow and Leningrad Universities, and we know exactly why. There is no reason not to apply the same standards of rationality when we find something similar in the United States, though here the mechanisms are entirely different: willing subversion of scholarship rather than obedience to external force.

Moreover, consider Ray's attitude towards those who do study the major and dominant themes, providing the obvious answers that he himself repeats: They are not respectable scholars, in his view, but are engaged in "advocacy"—while the scholarly mainstream, which carefully skirts the major formative influence on foreign policy, does not lose its "respectability" for this curious oversight, and does not seem to him to be engaged in "advocacy."

An anthropologist observing the phenomenon I have been describing would have no hesitation in concluding that we are dealing here with a form of taboo, a deep-seated superstitious avoidance of some terrifying question: in this case, the question of how private economic power functions in American society. Among the secular priesthood of academic scholars, the issue can be mentioned only, if at all, in hushed tones. Those who do raise the question seriously are no longer "respectable." As diplomatic historian Gaddis Smith asserts in a review of recent work by William Appleman Williams and Gabriel Kolko, they are "essentially pamphleteers" rather than authentic historians.[40]

In a free society, we do not imprison those who violate profound cultural taboos or burn them at the stake. But they must be identified as dangerous radicals, not fit to be counted among the priesthood. The reaction is appropriate. To raise the dread question is to open the possibility that the institutions responsible "for the indoctrination of the young" and the other propaganda institutions may be infected by the most dangerous of plagues: insight and understanding. Awareness of the facts might threaten the social order, protected by a carefully spun web of pluralist mysticism, faith in the benevolence of our pure-hearted leadership, and general superstitious belief.

An ideological structure, to be useful for some ruling class, must conceal the exercise of power by this class either by denying the facts or more simply ignoring them—or by representing the special interests of this class as universal interests, so that it is seen as only natural that representatives of this class should determine social policy, in the general interest. As Ray notes, it is not unexpected that foreign policy decisionmakers should perceive the world from the same perspective as businessmen: "In this context, we are not dealing simply with phenomena of influence, for national goals may in fact by synonymous with business goals." Extricating the expression "national goals" from its typical mystical usage, the remark approaches tautology.

Outside the ranks of the priesthood the facts are clearly presented in the socially marginal literature of "advocacy" by "pamphleteers" who make extensive and often very insightful use of the relevant documentary sources. Here, it is recognized that the notion of "national goals" is merely a device of mystification, and that the often conflicting goals of various social groups can be conceived in terms other than those set by the masters of the private economy. But the universities, the scholarly professions, the mass media, and society at large are carefully insulated from these dangerous heresies in a highly indoctrinated society, which is commonly described—the ultimate irony—as "pragmatic" and "nonideological." All of this is the more interesting when we realize that the society really is free from ugly forms of totalitarian control and coercion that are prevalent elsewhere.

Carl Landauer, who participated in the short-lived revolutionary government in Bavaria after World War I, remarked that the censorship of the bourgeois press by the revolutionary government marked the "beginning of freedom of public opinion."[41] His point was that the organs of propaganda and opinion, firmly in the hands of ruling groups, destroyed freedom of opinion by their dominance of the means of expression.[42] Clearly, one cannot accept the view that state censorship is the answer to the distortion and deceit of intellectual servants of ruling groups. Just as surely, we cannot pretend that there is freedom of opinion in any serious sense when social and cultural taboos shield the formation of policy from public awareness and scrutiny.

It is, in fact, quite true that the business press sometimes tends to be more honest about social reality than academic scholarship. Consider, for example, this reaction to the American failure in Vietnam (and elsewhere) in *Business Week* (April 7, 1975). The editors fear that "the international economic structure, under which U.S. companies have flourished since the end of World War II, is in jeopardy." They go on to explain how,

> fueled initially by the dollars of the Marshall Plan, American business prospered and expanded on overseas orders despite the cold war, the end of colonialism, and the creation of militant and often anti-capitalistic new countries. No matter how negative a development, there was always the umbrella of American power to contain it. . . . The rise of the multinational corporation was the economic expression of this political framework.

But "this stable world order for business operations is falling apart" with the defeat of American power in Indochina. Nothing here about our unremitting campaign "to do good" and "advance our moral ideals." They explain further how congressional obstinacy is undermining our efforts to persuade our European allies to support our concept of "a floor price on oil," and the "debilitating impact on international economics" with the "the collapse of U.S. foreign policy around the globe," particularly "if Japan cannot continue to export a third of its products to Southeast Asia." Unless a new "bipartisan foreign policy" (i.e., one-party state) is reestablished, it may be "impossible to maintain a successful international economic framework."

A year later, however, things were looking up, and "it appears that the future of the West again lies in the hands of the U.S. and to a lesser extent, West Germany," American oil policies perhaps being one reason.[43] As the *Business Week* editors note, "Trends now at work in the world have greatly strengthened the competitive position of the U.S. economy" with the result that "Washington will have more freedom to maneuver in formulating foreign economic policies than it has had since the early 1960s."[44] In short, the Grand Area is being successfully reconstituted, though the optimism proved a bit premature, in this case.

Occasionally, the light breaks through in statements of public officials as well. Consider for example a Statement by Frank M. Coffin, Deputy Administrator, Agency for International Development (AID), outlining "Objectives of the AID Program":

> Our basic, broadest goal is a long-range political one. It is not development for the sake of sheer development. . . . An important objective is to open up the maximum opportunity for domestic private initiative and enterprise and to insure that foreign private investment, particularly from the United States, is welcomed and well treated. . . . The fostering of a vigorous and expanding private sector in the less developed countries is one of our most important responsibilities. Both domestic private initiative and management and outside investment are important. . . . Politically, a strong and progressive private business community provides a powerful force for stable, responsible Government and a built-in check against Communist dogma.[45]

Another "built-in check" is counterinsurgency, as Coffin goes on to explain, "And we in AID of course have a public safety program which, perhaps to oversimplify, seeks to equip countries to utilize the civilian police in preventive action so that they do not have to place excessive reliance on the military." Oversimplification indeed. Many thousands of people in Latin America and Asia have benefited from this particular element in their "partnership with the West" over the years.[46] Needless to say, all of this is spiced with rhetoric on how our aid program seeks "partnership"—in contrast to those of the Russians and the Chinese, which seek "domination"—and so on. Spectacularly lacking is a comparative analysis of the aid programs to support this claim.

While noting occasional flashes of honesty in the business press, I would not want to imply that businessmen are free from the cant of much academic scholarship. Here is a single example, which could easily be duplicated in years before and since, to the present:

> You will point an accusing finger and you will hurl the challenging question: "What about Hayti [sic] and San Domingo, what about Nicaragua, Honduras, and so forth?" It is true we did send military forces to these countries. There did, most regrettably, occur some bloodshed. In the execution of our program we did commit some errors in judgment and in manners. We did, in certain measures, proceed bunglingly and clumsily, as Governments and their agents not infrequently do, especially when, as in the cases under discussion, the task to be undertaken is an unusual and unexpected one, and there are neither traditions which afford guidance nor a trained personnel to attend to the execution. (Incidentally, the very absence of such personnel tends to prove how little the thoughts of our Government and people were on Imperialism.)
>
> But the test is in the answer to the question which in my turn I ask of you: "What was our purpose? Did we go to oppress and exploit, did we go to add these territories to our domain? Or did we go to end an inveterate rule of tyranny, malefactions and turmoil, to set up decent and orderly government and the rule of law,

> to foster progress, to establish stable conditions and with them the basis for prosperity to the population concerned?"
>
> I think there can be no doubt that it was these latter things we aimed to attain. And having measurably accomplished the task, we did withdraw, or shall withdraw. We left behind, or shall leave behind, a few persons charged with the collection and proper administration of certain revenues, but such arrangements . . . are no more in the nature of exploitation or oppression than the appointment of a person under deed of trust is in the nature of exploitation and oppression.[47]

It would be superfluous to discuss how the United States proceeded to foster progress, prosperity, and an end to tyranny and malefactions in Haiti, San Domingo, Nicaragua, Honduras, and the other parts of Latin America "where we have traditionally been a friend and protector" (see p. 161). The immunity of doctrine to mere fact, in such cases, easily compares with the so-called Communist countries. Such pronouncements closely resemble the blather produced by pundits of the press as the Vietnam war came to an end: The United States involvement was "honorable" though "fraught with mistakes and misjudgments"; "good impulses came to be transmuted into bad policy"; it would be unfair to leave "the impression somehow the United States was responsible for the carnage in Southeast Asia"; our "blundering efforts to do good" turned into a "disastrous mistake"; and so on.[48] Again, it is remarkable how impervious the state religion is to mere factual evidence, extended now over eighty years of imperial aggression, following upon the bloody conquest of the national territory.

I have been discussing one major persistent theme of United States foreign policy, and not a very surprising one—namely, the attempt to create a Grand Area, a global economy, adapted to the needs of those who design United States government policy and the corporate interests that they largely represent. One concomitant of this dominant commitment is the repeated reliance on military force. This is, of course, only the most visible and dramatic device—United States policy towards Chile under Allende or Brazil since the early 1960s illustrates more typical and preferred procedures. But military force is the ultimate weapon to preserve a Grand Area. It is not exactly something new in American history.

James Chace, editor of *Foreign Affairs*, comments on this matter in a recent article. He counts up 159 instances of United States armed intervention abroad prior to 1945. Since World War II, he adds, "We have used military forces in Korea, Indochina, Lebanon, the Dominican Republic and the Congo." He then cites various reasons why we should expect all of this to continue: fears of resource scarcity, concern for the United States sphere of influence in the Caribbean and "regional balances of power" elsewhere, and, finally, the American "concern for human rights and the espousal of liberal, pluralistic democracies."[49]

Recall the cases cited, or other examples of intervention not cited: Iran, Cuba, Guatemala, Chile. In which of these cases was American intervention motivated by concern for human rights and espousal of liberal, pluralistic democracies? It remains a matter of great interest and importance that such utter nonsense can be produced with a straight face and be taken seriously in journalism and academic scholarship.

Chace points out (in part, correctly) that the American people continue to support an activist, interventionist foreign policy. One of the contributing factors is the ideology of American benevolence and international good will, as illustrated in his own remarks. I have cited a number of examples to show how this doctrinal framework governs scholarship, as well as the mass media, journals of current affairs, and the like. Most of these examples illustrate how the facts are simply ignored in the interests of doctrinal purity. But it is interesting to see that even direct and overt self-contradiction poses no particular problem for the secular priesthood, which rarely achieves the sophistication of its theological counterparts. As an illustration, consider another article in which Chace returns to the same themes.[50] Here he discusses the "ironies and ambiguities" of "the American experience," referring to the "moral concern" that is "a typical expression of the American spirit" though "we have found that the pursuit of justice sometimes leads to consequences contrary to those we had intended [and] that, at times, our proclaimed ideals serve to hide—from ourselves even more than from others—motivations of a darker and more complex character." "Experience should have taught us," he concludes, "that we do not always completely understand our own motivations," though he does not discuss the elaborate system of deceit that has been constructed to prevent such understanding. What is remarkable, however, is his discussion of particular cases, for example the *Realpolitik* of the Nixon-Kissinger period. "We were determined to seek stability," Chace asserts, and as an illustration—literally—he offers "our efforts to destabilize a freely elected Marxist government in Chile." Even a direct self-contradiction in successive sentences[51] does not suffice to raise a question about "our own motivations." Rather, the example falls under the category of "irony."

This category serves in the most astonishing ways to disguise reality in the ideological disciplines. Here is a final example, particularly revealing, I think, because of the source. Norman Graebner is an excellent historian, a critic of Cold War idiocies, a "realist" of more or less the variety of George Kennan, to whom the study from which I will quote is dedicated.[52] Graebner accepts the conventional belief that American foreign policy has been guided by the "Wilsonian principles of peace and self-determination."

The United States is not "an aggressive, imperialist country" in the twentieth century, as is demonstrated by the many "references to principle" in "its diplomatic language," references notably lacking in the rhetoric of truly aggressive and imperial powers, of course. The "traditional American dilemma" lies in the delusion that, given "the energy or determination of its antagonists," nevertheless "the nation was always assured that it could anticipate the eventual collapse of its enemies and the creation of the illusive world of justice and freedom." He asserts without qualification that "certainly all fundamental American relations with the U.S.S.R. and mainland China after 1950 were anchored to that assumption." It is this "American idealism" that caused so many problems in the postwar period.

Having laid down these basic principles, Graebner proceeds to investigate some particular examples of foreign policy in action. He then makes the following observation: "It was ironic that this nation generally ignored the principles of self-determination in Asia and Africa where it had some chance of success and promoted it behind the Iron and Bamboo curtains where it had no chance of success at all."

Consider the logic. A general principle is proposed: The United States follows the Wilsonian principles of self-determination. Then specific examples are surveyed. We discover that where the principles could be applied, they were not applied; where they could not be applied, in enemy domains, they were advocated (and their advocacy demonstrates that we are not aggressive and imperialistic). Conclusion: It is ironic that the general thesis fails when tested. But the general principle remains in force. In fact, Graebner goes on to lament that "this nation's selfless search for order in world affairs could not sustain the gratitude of a troubled world."

By similar logic, a physicist might formulate a general hypothesis, put it to the test, discover that it is refuted in each specific instance, and conclude that it is ironic that the facts are the opposite of what the principle predicts—but the principle nevertheless stands. The example illustrates the difference between ideological disciplines such as academic history and political science, on the one hand, and subjects that are expected to meet rational intellectual standards, on the other.

This example is interesting precisely because the historian in question was an early critic of Cold War doctrine. He argues, on Kennanesque lines, that United States policy was in error. "Error," however, is a socially neutral category. To invoke it is to remain safely within the bounds of the primary dogma: that the United States simply responds to external challenges, and that its policy reflects no special material interests of dominant social groups.

This discussion has so far been fairly abstract. I have not tried to deal with the human consequences of the policy of military intervention against those too weak to strike back, or other measures undertaken to ensure the stability of the Grand Area—policies that it is only reasonable to assume will continue in the future, since there have been no significant institutional changes, and even the critique that developed in some circles during the Indochina war has been fairly well deflected and contained. We may recall how all of this looks from the wrong end of the guns. Eighty years ago a Filipino nationalist wrote that the Filipinos "have already accepted the arbitrament of war, and war is the worst condition conceivable, especially when waged by an Anglo-Saxon race which despises its opponent as an alien or inferior people. Yet the Filipinos accepted it with a full knowledge of its horror and of the sacrifices in life and property which they knew they would be called upon to make."[53] It will be recalled that on that occasion too, our selfless leadership was merely attempting "to fulfill God's purposes in history." Even James Chace concedes that in this case, though there were "moral purposes" alongside of self-interest, "We were hard put to find a moral defense for our behavior. The atrocities committed by American troops there were horrifying, as they resorted to a no-quarter war, taking no prisoners, burning villages and often shooting innocent men, women and children."[54]

One might think that after Vietnam it would be superfluous to go into this matter. Unfortunately, that supposition would be false. When President Carter, in the midst of one of his sermons on human rights, explains that we owe no debt and have no responsibility to Vietnam because "the destruction was mutual,"[55] there is not a comment nor a whisper of protest in the American press. And the history of that "tragic error" is now being rewritten to make the people of Indochina the villain of the piece. And when Ford and Kissinger sent their bombers over Cambodia in one final act of violence and murder in that land ravaged by American terror at the time of the *Mayagüez* incident in May 1975, even Senator Kennedy, one of the very few senators to have shown genuine concern over the human consequences of the American war, saw fit to state that "the President's firm and successful action gave an undeniable and needed lift to the nation's spirit, and he deserves our genuine support."[56] The world was put on notice—as if notice were needed—that the world's most violent power had not renounced its commitment to the use of force as a consequence of its defeat in Indochina, at least when the victims are defenseless.

The pattern has continued since. Consider what happened in the demilitarized zone between North and South Korea in August 1976, when two American soldiers were killed by North Korean troops as they attempted to trim a tree under circumstances that remain disputed. For the sake of discussion, let us assume the American account to be entirely accurate: The North Koreans simply murdered them in cold blood. The United States army then cut down the tree, with a considerable show of force, including a flight of B-52s. An important account of this incident was given by William Beecher, former Deputy Assistant Secretary of Defense for Public Affairs, now a diplomatic correspondent. He writes that the original plan was to have the B-52s drop "about 70,000 tons of bombs on a South Korean bombing range only about 10 miles from Panmunjom. . . . But well-placed sources say that at the eleventh hour it was decided that to drop the bombs would be too provocative and might trigger a military response from the truculent North Koreans."[57]

Let us assume that the figure of seventy thousand tons—more than three Hiroshima equivalents—is mistaken. But why should heavy bombing a few miles from Panmunjom appear "provocative" to the "truculent North Koreans"? Perhaps because they retain some memories of things that happened a quarter-century ago when the United States Air Force so thoroughly devastated their land that there were simply no remaining targets. In keeping with the principle of believing only the American side of the story, let us recall how these events were officially perceived in an Air Force study of "an object lesson in air power to all the Communist world and especially to the Communists in North Korea," a "lesson" delivered a month before the armistice:

> On 13 May 1953 twenty USAF F-84 fighter-bombers swooped down in three successive waves over Toksan irrigation dam in North Korea. From an altitude of 300 feet they skip-bombed their loads of high explosives into the hard-packed earthen walls of the dam. The subsequent flash flood scooped clean 27 miles of valley below, and the plunging flood waters wiped out large segments of a main north-south communication and supply route to the front lines. The Toksan strike and similar attacks on the Chasan, Kuwonga, Kusong, and Toksang dams accounted for five of the more than twenty irrigation dams targeted for possible attack—dams up-stream from all the important enemy supply routes and furnishing 75 percent of the controlled water supply for North Korea's rice production. These strikes, largely passed over by the press, the military observers, and news commentators in favor of attention-arresting but less meaningful operations events, constituted one of the most significant air operations of the Korean war. They sent the Communist military leaders and political commissars scurrying to their press and radio centers to blare to the world the most severe, hate-filled harangues to come from the Communist propaganda mill in the three years of warfare.
>
> In striking one target system, the USAF had hit hard at two sensitive links in the enemy's armor—his capability to supply his front-line troops and his capability to produce food for his armies. To the U.N. Command the breaking of the irrigation dams meant disruption of the enemy's lines of communication and supply. But to the Communists the smashing of the dams meant primarily the destruction of their chief sustenance—rice. The Westerner can little conceive the awesome meaning

> which the loss of this staple food commodity has for the Asian—starvation and slow death. "Rice famine," for centuries the chronic scourge of the Orient, is more feared than the deadliest plague. Hence the show of rage, the flare of violent tempers, and the avowed threats of reprisals when bombs fell on five irrigation dams.[58]

Recall that this is not quoted from Communist black propaganda but from an official USAF study.

The North Koreans, truculent as ever, could not see the beauty of this magnificent air operation, and might find heavy bombing "provocative" today as well, so the original plan was called off.

Only a few years after the USAF succeeded in bringing starvation and slow death to the Asians in Northeast Asia, they were at it again in Southeast Asia. As that war ended, after vast destruction and massacre, the United States insisted on a show of force against defenseless Cambodia during the *Mayagüez* incident. Sihanoukville was bombed, but a planned B-52 attack was called off—wisely, the *New Republic* commented, because of "predictable domestic and world reaction" and possible adverse effects on the *Mayagüez* crewmen—not because it would have constituted another major massacre of Cambodians.[59] A year later, U.S. planes almost carried out heavy bombing in Korea to impress the truculent North Koreans. The American people continue to support an activist foreign policy, so the polls indicate, and the articulate intelligentsia are as usual urging us to forget the "errors" and "miscalculations" of the past and to set forth again on our campaign to instill our moral ideals in an evil and ungrateful world. The institutional structures that lie behind the military episodes and other interventions of the postwar years and the ideological framework of Grand Area planning all remain intact, subjected to little public challenge, effectively removed from popular scrutiny or, in part, even scholarly analysis. It is only reasonable to conclude that the editor of *Foreign Affairs* is quite right when he predicts that military intervention will continue, as will other attempts to enforce "stability" through "destabilization" and to contain and destroy movements that threaten to secede from the Grand Area. It is this threat, whether called "Communist" or something else, that the U.S. government will bend every effort to contain and destroy, by force if need be, by more delicate means if they suffice, while the intelligentsia divert us with tales about our selfless devotion to principle and moral idealism.

12.

The United States and East Timor

Why should we devote attention to East Timor, a small and remote place that most Americans have never even heard of? There are two reasons, each more than sufficient. The first is that East Timor has been, and still is, the scene of enormous massacres and suffering. Many of the terrible things that happen in the world are out of our control. We may deplore them, but we cannot do very much about them. This case is quite different, hence far more important. What has happened and what lies ahead are very much under our control, so directly that the blood is on our hands. The second reason is that by considering what has happened in East Timor since 1975, we can learn some important things about ourselves, our society, and our institutions. If we do not like what we find when we look at the facts—and few will fail to be appalled if they take an honest look—we can work to bring about changes in the practices and structure of institutions that cause terrible suffering and slaughter. To the extent that we see ourselves as citizens in a democratic community, we have a responsibility to devote our energies to these ends. The recent history of Timor provides a revealing insight into the policies of the U.S. government, the factors that enter into determining them, and the ways in which our ideological system functions.

The bare facts are as follows.[1] East Timor was a Portuguese colony. The western half of the island of Timor, a Dutch colony, became part of Indone-

---

This chapter first appeared in *Towards a New Cold War: U.S. Foreign Policy from Vietnam to Reagan* (New York: Pantheon Books, 1982; New York: The New Press, 2003), 358–69.

sia when Indonesia gained its own independence. After the Portuguese revolution of 1974, several political parties emerged in East Timor, of which two, UDT and Fretilin, had significant popular support. In August 1975, an attempted coup by UDT, backed and perhaps inspired by Indonesia, led to a brief civil war in which two to three thousand people were killed. By early September, Fretilin had emerged victorious. The country was open to foreign observers, including representatives of the International Red Cross and Australian aid organizations, journalists, and others. Their reactions were quite positive. They were impressed by the level of popular support and the sensible measures of agricultural reform, literacy programs, and so on that were being undertaken. The outstanding Australian specialist on East Timor, James Dunn, describes Fretilin at the time as "populist Catholic." These facts are significant, in the light of subsequent allegations to which we turn below.

The territory was then at peace, apart from Indonesian military attacks at the border and naval bombardment. Indonesian military harassment began immediately after the Fretilin victory in September, including a commando attack that killed five Australian journalists, a clear and well-understood warning to foreigners that the Indonesian military wanted no one to observe what it was contemplating. Fretilin requested that Portugal take responsibility for the process of decolonization and called on other countries to send observers, but there was no response. Recognizing that international support would not be forthcoming, Fretilin declared independence on November 28, 1975. On December 7, Indonesia launched a full-scale invasion, capturing the capital city of Dili. The attack took place a few hours after the departure of President Gerald Ford and Henry Kissinger from Jakarta. There is no serious doubt that the United States knew of the impending invasion and specifically authorized it. Ford conceded as much in an interview with Jack Anderson, while claiming ignorance of the exact circumstances.[2]

The invading Indonesian army was 90 percent supplied with U.S. arms. In congressional hearings, government representatives testified that the United States had imposed a six-month arms ban in response to the invasion, but this was so secret that Indonesia was never informed about it. Arms continued to flow, and in fact new offers of arms were made, including counterinsurgency equipment, during the period of the "arms ban," as was conceded by Administration spokesmen when the facts were exposed by Cornell University Indonesian specialist Benedict Anderson. The invasion was bloody and brutal. Subsequently, Indonesia extended its aggression to other parts of the territory, and by 1977–78 was engaged in a program of wholesale destruction including massive bombardment, forced population removal, destruction of villages and crops, and all the familiar techniques used by modern armies to subjugate a resisting population. The precise scale of the atrocities is difficult to assess, in part because Indonesia refused to admit outside observers, for reasons that are readily understood. Even the International Red Cross was excluded until 1979, and then was allowed entry only on a limited basis. But there has been ample evidence from refugees, letters smuggled out, church sources, the occasional journalist granted a brief guided tour, and the Indonesian authorities themselves. If the facts were not known in the West, it was the result of the decision not to let them be known. It appears likely that of the prewar population of close to 700,000 perhaps one quarter have succumbed to outright slaughter or starvation caused by the Indonesian attack, and that the remaining population, much of which is herded into military-run concentration camps, may suffer a similar fate unless properly supervised international assistance is forthcoming on a substantial scale. Relief officials who were finally permitted limited access to the territory after almost four years described the prevailing situation as comparable to Cambodia in 1979. The world reaction has been somewhat different in the two cases.

The U.S. government continued throughout to provide the military and diplomatic support that was required for the slaughter to continue. By late 1977, Indonesian supplies had been depleted. The Human Rights Administration dramatically increased the flow of military equipment, enabling Indonesia to undertake the fierce offensives that reduced East Timor to the level of Cambodia.[3] U.S. allies have also joined in providing the needed military and diplomatic support.

The United Nations has repeatedly condemned the Indonesian aggression and called for the exercise of the right of self-determination in East Timor, as have the nonaligned nations. But the West has succeeded in blocking any significant measures. The U.N. General Assembly met immediately after the invasion, but was unable to react in a meaningful way. The reasons are explained by U.N. Ambassador Daniel P. Moynihan in his memoirs: "The United States wished things to turn out as they did, and worked to bring this about. The Department of State desired that the United Nations prove utterly ineffective in whatever measures it undertook. This task was given to me, and I carried it forward with no inconsiderable success."[4]

Ambassador Moynihan was presumably aware of the nature of his success. He cites a February 1976 estimate by the deputy chairman of the provisional government installed by Indonesian force "that some sixty thousand persons had been killed since the outbreak of civil war"—recall that two to three thousand had been killed during the civil war itself—"10 percent of the population, almost the proportion of casualties experienced by the Soviet Union during the Second World War." Thus, in effect, he is claiming credit for "success" in helping to cause a massacre that he compares to the consequences of

Nazi aggression, not to speak of the growing number of victims in the subsequent period.

Moynihan was much admired for the great courage that he displayed in the United Nations in confronting the mighty Third World enemies of the United States. Somehow, his self-congratulation in this case escaped notice.[5]

Ambassador Moynihan commented further that the Indonesian invasion must have been successful by March 1976, since "the subject disappeared from the press and from the United Nations after that time." It did virtually disappear from the press, though not from the United Nations, which has regularly condemned Indonesian aggression. The curtain of silence drawn by the press in the United States and much of the West for four years hardly demonstrates the success of Indonesian arms, though it does stand as a remarkable testimonial to the effectiveness of Western propaganda systems.[6]

Throughout, the U.S. government has pretended that it knew very little about events in East Timor, a transparent fabrication. Or else government representatives claimed at each stage that though there might have been some unfortunate excesses in the past, the situation is now calm and the sensible and humane course is to recognize Indonesian control. This was, for example, the stance taken by the government in 1977 congressional hearings, at exactly the time when Indonesia was preparing the murderous offensives of 1977–78 and the Human Rights Administration was accelerating the flow of arms for use in these military operations. The "Human Rights" reports of the State Department not only fail to consider the ample evidence of massive atrocities, but go so far as to pretend that the issue does not arise. A report prepared by the Congressional Research Service is typical of government pronouncements.[7] The report discusses the alleged improvement in Indonesia's human rights record—students of Orwell may be intrigued by the fact that in government "Human Rights" reports dealing with friendly states, the record is invariably one of "improvement," whatever unpleasant events may have occurred in the past. The November 1979 report informs us that

> Indonesia's takeover of East Timor, formerly Portuguese Timor, in December 1975 may have been an exception to this trend of improvement, but the conflicting claims and lack of access into Timor by non-Indonesians make it difficult if not impossible to ascertain the loss of life in the heavy fighting of December 1975–March 1976. Recently, reports from Timor indicate a partial return to normalcy there although genuine self-determination for the Timorese is a dim prospect.

The latter conclusion is certainly correct, as long as the U.S. government persists in its policy of supporting Indonesian terror while denying its existence, and as long as the media loyally refrain from exposing the facts. This report is typical not only in its claim that now things are finally improving (the constant plea throughout) but also in its failure to concede that questions even arise about the period after March 1976.

The picture is a bit different when we turn to eyewitness testimony, for example, that of Father Leoneto Vieira do Rego, a sixty-three-year-old Portuguese priest who spent three years in the mountains before surrendering to Indonesian forces in January 1979, suffering from malaria and starvation. After imprisonment and interrogation, he was permitted to return to Portugal in June. His accounts of what he had observed were then reported in the world press, outside of the United States. Shortly after the appearance of the government report cited above, Father Leoneto was interviewed by the *New York Times*.[8] The transcript of the interview was leaked to the *Boston Globe*.[9] Father Leoneto said that during 1976, things were normal in the mountains where he was living, and where most of the population was, including those who had fled from Dili:

> Apart from the main towns, people in the interior weren't aware of the war. People had food commodities aplenty. It was a normal life under not-normal circumstances. Problems started in early 1977. A full-scale bombardment of the whole island began. From that point there emerged death, illness, despair. The second phase of the bombing was late 1977 to early 1979, with modern aircraft. This was the firebombing phase of the bombing. Even up to this time, people could still live. The genocide and starvation was the result of the full-scale incendiary bombing. . . . We saw the end coming. People could not plant. I personally witnessed—while running to protected areas, going from tribe to tribe—the great massacre from bombardment and people dying from starvation. In 1979 people began surrendering because there was no other option. When people began dying, then others began to give up.

Father Leoneto estimated that 200,000 people had died during the four years of war.

Of all of this, what survived in the *Times* account was the following sentence:

> He said that bombardment and systematic destruction of croplands in 1978 were intended to starve the islanders into submission.[10]

Recall that the offensives of 1977–79 reported by Father Leoneto, as by many others during this period and since, coincided with the sharp increase in arms supplies from the Human Rights Administration.

Refugees continue to report large-scale atrocities. By 1979, some foreign aid was reaching the territory, but distribution was largely under Indonesian military control. A report from Lisbon in the London *Observer* notes that "all relief work in the former Portuguese colony is being supervised by only four foreign field workers" and states that "food and medical supplies for famine hit East Timor are being diverted to Indonesian troops and shopkeepers, according to refugees arriving in Portugal."[11] The report continues:

> "We appeal to anyone left in the world with a minimum sense of human rights to ensure that relief goes directly to our people," said a refugee who preferred to remain anonymous as his family is still in East Timor. . . . Refugees insisted that there was still starvation in East Timor and that, contrary to other reports, fighting between the Indonesians and the Timorese Liberation Movement was continuing in the mountains to the east of the island. They claimed Indonesian troops were terrorising the local population with arrests, torture, and summary executions. They described the methods by which the authorities manipulated tours by visiting journalists. The Timorese claim that troops and war material are removed to give the impression of calm. One woman said that she had seen crosses taken from the local military cemetery. The authorities kept a tight control, informing their "representatives" in relief camps and placing armed plain-clothed military officers among the crowds. The growing evidence of the corruption and violation of human rights in East Timor has begun to filter out and is threatening to put the issue at the centre of a diplomatic offensive. Portugal and the US are particularly involved.

Though, it must be added, they are involved in quite different ways. Portugal, particularly the new conservative government, is seeking to gain international support to save the Timorese from final destruction and to compel Indonesia to withdraw. The U.S. government is trying to stem the increasing flow of exposures and to guarantee Indonesian control over the miserable remnants of the U.S.-backed Indonesian assault.

In December 1979, David Watts of the London *Times* filed a report from Dili, East Timor, on "a tour supervised by the Indonesian military. He reports the success of the Red Cross relief operation in saving the lives of tens of thousands of people on "the brink of starvation." "Others will die, but at least help is coming to the innocent victims of the vicious starvation policy practised by the Indonesian armed forces against the Marxist militant and civilian alike in East Timor's little known war, which has been fought out of sight of the world since 1975." Watts's reference to the "Marxist" victims is as reliable as his statement that, on retreating to the mountains after the Indonesian invasion, Fretilin "[took] with them an estimated 100,000 lowland Timorese who were either relatives or people 'co-opted' into the movement to provide support by growing food," and presumably derives from the same source, namely, his tour guides.

Watts writes further that

> the Indonesian armed forces sealed off East Timor from the rest of the world with air and naval patrols to prevent outside assistance reaching the Fretilin fighters. The civilian population was constantly forced to flee from place to place. It was impossible for the lowlanders to return to the few fertile areas around river valleys and even the highlanders were unable to practise their own, crude slash and burn agriculture. The people were reduced to stealing what they could, and when they could not get supplies they lived on leaves, mice and dead dogs, according to an official of the Indonesian Red Cross. They ate the dogs after they had died because their animist beliefs prevented them from killing them.
>
> But the real crisis for the mountain people came in 1977–78 when the Indonesian military, tiring of the inconclusive campaign, launched a big sweep through the east of the island to eradicate the last of the Fretilin forces. Using paratroop drops and North American Rockwell Bronco counter-insurgency aircraft they fought through the island, denying the Fretilin forces sanctuaries and food supplies. . . . Here and there throughout the eastern half of the island there is evidence of what appear to have been napalm attacks by the Bronco aircraft. Made desperate by the situation in the mountains the people began to flock down to the lowlands in search of food and shelter.[12]

Like his American colleagues, Watts is silent on the role of the United States, apart from its contribution to aid for the remnants in 1979, and on the role of the press in ensuring that this would remain a "little known war" during the period when an aroused public opinion could have brought these atrocities to an end.

For four long and bloody years, the U.S. media, with very rare exceptions, kept close to the U.S. government propaganda line. During 1975, there was considerable coverage of East Timor, a reflection of the concern over decolonization in the former Portuguese empire. In late 1975, the *New York Times* was reporting Indonesia's "remarkable restraint" at the same time that Australian journalists were filing eyewitness reports of Indonesian naval bombardment of Timorese towns and military attacks along the border. An Australian journalist, the first to enter East Timor after the August–September civil war, wrote a lengthy report in the London *Times* in which he rejected allegations of Fretilin atrocities, which he attributed to Indonesian and other propaganda services. His report appeared in the *New York Times*, edited to make it appear that the charges were accurate, as *Newsweek* then reported, basing itself on the *New York Times* account. After the Indonesian invasion, reporting in the United States diminished rapidly, approaching zero (apart from occasional U.S. government and Indonesian propaganda handouts) as the U.S.-backed Indonesian assault expanded in scale and violence. Timorese refugees were scrupulously avoided, in dramatic contrast to refugees from Communist oppression. When Henry Kamm, the Pulitzer Prize–winning Southeast Asian correspondent of the *New York Times*, deigned to mention East Timor while the war raged in full fury, he did not rely on the reports of refugees, priests, or the numerous other sources available. Rather, he interviewed Indonesian generals, and on their authority presented the "fact" that Fretilin had "forced" the people to live under its "control," though now they were fleeing to Indonesian-held areas.[13] Reporting on a four-day visit to East Timor in 1980, Kamm now informs the reader that 300,000 Timorese were "displaced by persistent civil war and struggle against the invaders"—there had been no civil war, apart from U.S. and Indonesian propaganda handouts and the "news columns" of the Western press, since September 1975. He reports that "the Fretilin hold over the population" was broken by the 1978 Indonesian offensive and that Fretilin "controlled significant parts of the population at least until 1977." Nowhere is there any indication of even the possibility that Fretilin may have had popular support. These conclusions, along with reports of Fretilin savagery, are based on evidence derived from Indonesian authorities, Timorese collaborators, or Timorese who, as he notes, were so intimidated by the ever-present Indonesian military authorities that their statements were obviously meaningless.[14]

By late 1979, the truth was beginning to break through, even in the U.S. press, and a number of congressmen, notably Tom Harkin of Iowa, had become aware of the true nature of what had been concealed by the media. The *New York Times* ran an honest editorial on December 24, 1979 (see note 10), and James Markham filed the first report on the many Timorese refugees in Lisbon.[15] The press began to present some of the information that had been available for four years,[16] though much distortion persists and the crucial U.S. role is generally ignored or downplayed.

The importance of the behavior of the media and journals of opinion during these years cannot be overemphasized. The events described by Father Leoneto and many others, and the horrendous consequences that are now at last widely conceded, are the direct responsibility of the United States government, and to a lesser extent, its Western allies. Correspondingly, these monstrous acts could have been—and still can be—brought to an end by withdrawal of direct U.S. support for them.

The U.S. government has been backing the Indonesian military not because it takes pleasure in massacre and starvation, but because the fate of the

Timorese is simply a matter of no significance when measured against higher goals. Since 1965, when the Indonesian military took power in a coup that led to the slaughter of perhaps half a million to a million people, mostly landless peasants, Indonesia has been a valued ally.[17] The military rulers have opened the country to Western plunder, hindered only by the rapacity and corruption of our friends in Jakarta. In this potentially rich country, much of the population has suffered enormously—even apart from the huge massacres, which demonstrated proper anti-Communist credentials to an appreciative Western audience—as the country has been turned into a "paradise for investors."[18] Given these overriding considerations, it was only to be expected that the Human Rights Administration, like its predecessor, would pour arms into Indonesia to enable it to achieve its ends in East Timor, and would attempt in every way to conceal the truth.

The importance of the deception becomes clear when we observe what happens when the system of indoctrination begins to unravel. However institutions may function, individuals are not prepared to support actions that verge on genocide. As the truth has begun to break through, a number of members of Congress and increasing segments of the population are beginning to demand an end to these atrocious acts. One result was that some aid was sent, though without adequate international supervision it is questionable how much reached those who need it, given the corruption of the Indonesian military. There is, for the first time, a real possibility that pressure will be put on the U.S. government to stop providing the military supplies that Indonesia requires, and that international efforts may be organized to induce Indonesia to withdraw, so that what is left of the population may have the opportunity to realize their long-sought right to self-determination.

It is intriguing to see how some segments of the media are reacting to the fact that information about East Timor is now beginning to reach the public. In the *Nation*—the only U.S. journal to have published a serious article on Timor from 1975 through 1978[19]—A.J. Langguth dismissed the concern over Timor with the following remarkable comment: "If the world press were to converge suddenly on Timor, it would not improve the lot of a single Cambodian."[20] The irrationality of the comment is at first startling, but the sentiment becomes intelligible on the assumption that it is only the other fellow's crimes that deserve attention. In the *Washington Journalism Review*, Richard Valeriani of NBC and Asia specialist and former foreign correspondent Stanley Karnow discussed a report on East Timor that appeared in the *New York Times* in late January 1980.[21] Valeriani said that he had read it, though "I don't care about Timor." Karnow couldn't bring himself even to read the story: "I just didn't have time. . . . There was no connection; it didn't have anything to do with me." Their point was that the *Times* was giving *too much coverage* to the insignificant fact that massacres in Timor rival those of Cambodia and that the population has been reduced to the state of the miserable victims on the Thai-Cambodian border as a direct result of U.S. policies. The *Times* is failing its responsibilities by wasting space on such trivia—but not, for example, by devoting the entire front cover and twenty-five pages of the Sunday magazine section a few days earlier (January 20, 1980) to the horrendous experiences of Dith Pran in Cambodia, recapitulating stories that had received massive media attention.

Their reactions are not unique. The U.N. correspondent of the *New York Times*, Bernard Nossiter, refused an invitation to a press conference on East Timor in October 1979 on the grounds that the issue was "rather esoteric," and in fact reported not a word on the U.N. debate, which included testimony from Timorese refugees and others on the continuing atrocities and the U.S. responsibility for them.[22] A look at the stories he did publish during those days reveals that events must be insignificant indeed to fall below the threshold for the *Times*. Thus, Nossiter devoted a full-page column to the world-shaking fact that the government of Fiji had not been paid for its contingent in Southern Lebanon and, shortly after, reported a debate over a missing comma, of undeterminable import, in a U.N. document[23]—though in this case, his report is to be understood as part of the campaign of ridicule that has been directed against the United Nations, in particular its Third World membership, ever since the U.N. escaped from the control of the United States and fell under what is called here "the tyranny of the majority," or what others call "democracy." Hence the sarcastic report of the debate over the missing comma, coupled with total silence on the role of Third World nations in bringing to the United Nations the story of the U.S.-backed massacres in Timor.

Perhaps the most intriguing response to the recent breakdown of media suppression is that of the *Wall Street Journal*, which devoted an editorial to the topic.[24] The *Journal* takes note of "an interesting campaign" that "has been shaping up over the past few weeks on the issue of East Timor." It observes that a hundred thousand people may have died during the war, adding that "it sounds suspiciously like Cambodia, some people are saying. And this one is ours: Indonesia is our ally and oil supplier, it's American arms that the Indonesians used to perpetrate their atrocities." But this charge, the *Journal* continues, "tells less about Timor than it does about certain varieties of American political thinking." There are two factors that crucially distinguish Timor from Cambodia. The first is that the United States is sending some aid to Timor, and the Indonesian, "however grudgingly and imperfectly," are letting the food in, whereas "the Cambodians would be in considerably better shape if the Soviet Union undertook comparable behavior for itself and its ally"—the editors ignore the fact that the Soviet Union provided aid to starving Cambodians before the United States did, and, it appears, in substantial quantities, as well as the fact, reported by international aid workers, that their aid was let in not at all grudgingly. But the crucial distinction is this:

> But more important, it's self-deluding to talk as if the U.S. had the power any longer to determine the outcome of a situation like Timor. The violence that has cursed the place is the wholly unsurprising mark of a disintegrating world order; talk about the evils of U.S. power is likely to hasten that disintegration, not arrest it. Those worried about the human costs of such chaos might do well to start facing up to that connection.

The reasoning is remarkable. The editors are trying to tell us that when U.S.-supplied aircraft demolish villages, destroy crops, massacre mountain tribesmen, and drive them to concentration camps, we are to understand these facts as "the mark of a disintegrating world order," not the results of U.S. actions, consciously undertaken. And if the United States were to withhold the crucial military and diplomatic support that enables Indonesia to carry out these policies, the terror might be even worse. One wonders whether *Pravda* rises to such intellectual heights when it justifies Soviet support for the Ethiopian war in Eritrea.

It is easy enough to poke fun at the *Wall Street Journal*, but that would be to overlook the more significant point. The slight exposure of U.S.-backed Indonesian atrocities during the past several months has frightened the Indonesian military, the U.S. government, and the business circles represented by the *Wall Street Journal*, all of whom want to play their games with people's lives in secret. The message is clear. By significantly extending the pressure on the U.S. government to abandon its appalling policies, and continuing to work to bring the facts to a larger public, one can contribute materially to the survival of the people of East Timor. It is rare that an opportunity arises in which a relatively small amount of effort may save hundreds of thousands of lives, and it would be criminal to allow it to pass.

13.

The Origins of the "Special Relationship"

LEVELS OF SUPPORT: DIPLOMATIC, MATERIAL, IDEOLOGICAL

The relationship between the United States and Israel has been a curious one in world affairs and in American culture. Its unique character is symbolized by recent votes at the United Nations. For example, on June 26, 1982, the United States stood alone in vetoing a U.N. Security Council resolution calling for simultaneous withdrawal of Israeli and Palestinian armed forces from Beirut, on the grounds that this plan "was a transparent attempt to preserve the P.L.O. as a viable political force," evidently an intolerable prospect for the U.S. government.[1] A few hours later, the United States and Israel voted against a General Assembly resolution calling for an end to hostilities in Lebanon and on the Israel-Lebanon border, passed with two "nays" and no abstentions. Earlier, the U.S. had vetoed an otherwise unanimous Security Council resolution condemning Israel for ignoring the earlier demand for withdrawal of Israeli troops.[2] The pattern has, in fact, been a persistent one.

More concretely, the special relationship is expressed in the level of U.S. military and economic aid to Israel over many years. Its exact scale is unknown, since much is concealed in various ways. Prior to 1967, before the "special relationship" had matured, Israel received the highest per capita aid

---

This chapter first appeared in *Fateful Triangle: The United States, Israel, and the Palestinians* (Cambridge, MA: South End Press, 1983; expanded edition Cambridge, MA: South End Press, 1999), 9–37.

from the United States of any country. Commenting on the fact, Harvard Middle East specialist Nadav Safran also notes that this amounts to a substantial part of the unprecedented capital transfer to Israel from abroad that constitutes virtually the whole of Israel's investment—one reason why Israel's economic progress offers no meaningful model for underdeveloped countries.[3] It is possible that recent aid amounts to something like $1,000 per year for each citizen of Israel when all factors are taken into account. Even the public figures are astounding.* For fiscal years 1978 through 1982, Israel received 48 percent of all U.S. military aid and 35 percent of U.S. economic aid, worldwide. For FY 1983, the Reagan administration requested almost $2.5 billion for Israel out of a total aid budget of $8.1 billion, including $500 million in outright grants and $1.2 billion in low-interest loans.[4] In addition, there is a regular pattern of forgiving loans, offering weapons at special discount prices, and a variety of other devices, not to mention the tax-deductible "charitable" contributions (in effect, an imposed tax), used in ways to which we return.[5] Not content with this level of assistance from the American taxpayer, one of the Senate's most prominent liberal Democrats, Alan Cranston of California, "proposed an amendment to the foreign aid bill to establish the principle that American economic assistance to Israel would not be less than the amount of debt Israel repays to the United States," a commitment to cover "all Israeli debts and future debts," as Senator Charles Percy commented.[6]

This was before the Lebanon war. The actual vote on foreign aid came after the invasion of Lebanon, after the destruction of much of southern Lebanon, the merciless siege and bombardment of Beirut, the September massacres, and Israel's rapid expansion of settlement in the occupied territories in response to Reagan's plea to suspend settlement in accord with his peace proposals, which Israel rejected. In the light of these events, the only issue arising in Congress was whether to "punish" Israel by accepting the president's proposal for a substantial increase in the already phenomenal level of aid—what is called taking "a get-tough approach with Israel"[7]—or to take a softer line by adding even more to the increases that the president requested, as the Senate and most liberals demanded. Fortunately, the press was sufficiently disciplined so that the comic aspects of this characteristic performance were suppressed. The consequences of this message of approval to Israel for its recent actions on the part of the president and Congress are not at all comic, needless to say.

---

* The General Accounting Office (GAO) has informed Congress that the actual level of U.S. aid may be as much as 60 percent higher than the publicly available figures. This is the preliminary result of a detailed study of U.S. aid to Israel by the GAO. "A major issue could develop next year [1983] over how much of the GAO study may be made public." James McCartney, *Philadelphia Inquirer*, August 25, 1982.

It should be noted that in theory there are restrictions on the use of American aid (e.g., cluster bombs can be used only in self-defense; development funds cannot be spent beyond Israel's recognized—i.e., pre-June 1967—borders). But care has been taken to ensure that these restrictions will not be invoked, though the illegal use of weapons occasionally elicits a reprimand or temporary cutoff of shipments when the consequences receive too much publicity. As for the ban on use of U.S. funds for the settlement and development programs that the U.S. has officially regarded as illegal and as a barrier to peace (i.e., beyond the pre-June 1967 borders), this has never been enforced, and the aid program is designed so that it cannot be enforced: "in contrast to most other aid relationships, the projects we fund in Israel are not specified," Ian Lustick observes, and no official of the State Department or the aid program has "ever been assigned to supervise the use of our funds by the Israeli government."

For comparison, one may consider the U.S. aid program to Egypt (the largest recipient of non-military U.S. aid since Camp David), which is run by an office of 125 people who supervise it in meticulous detail. Many knowledgeable Egyptians have been highly critical of the aid program, alleging that it reflects American rather than Egyptian priorities, financing U.S. imports that must be brought on American ships and U.S. consultants, when trained personnel are available in Egypt for a fraction of the cost. They also note the emphasis on the private sector, "pay[ing] Mid-west farmers for wheat which could be grown at half the price in Egypt" (according to a former AID director), and in general the infiltration of Egyptian society to the extent that some perceive a threat to Egyptian national security.[8]

These examples illustrate the diplomatic and material support that the U.S. provides for Israel. A concomitant, at the ideological level, is the persistence of considerable illusion about the nature of Israeli society and the Arab-Israeli conflict. Since 1967, discussion of these issues has been difficult or impossible in the United States as a result of a remarkably effective campaign of vilification, abuse, and sometimes outright lying directed against those who dared to question received doctrine.* This fact has regularly been deplored by

---

* Israeli intelligence apparently contributes to these efforts. According to a CIA study, one of its functions is to acquire "data for use in silencing anti-Israel factions in the West," along with "sabotage, paramilitary and psychological warfare projects, such as character assassination and black propaganda." "Within Jewish communities in almost every country of the world, there are Zionists and other sympathizers, who render strong support to the Israeli intelligence effort. Such contracts are carefully nurtured and serve as channels for information, deception material, propaganda and other purposes." "They also attempt to penetrate anti-Zionist elements in order to neutralize the opposition."[9]

Israeli doves, who have been subjected to similar treatment here. They observe that their own position within Israel suffers because of lack of support within the U.S., where, as General (Res.) Mattityahu Peled observed, the "state of near hysteria" and the "blindly chauvinistic and narrow-minded" support for the most reactionary policies within Israel poses "the danger of prodding Israel once more toward a posture of calloused intransigence."[10] The well-known Israeli journalist and Zionist historian Simha Flapan describes "the prejudice of American Jewry" as now "the major obstacle to an American-Palestinian and Israeli-Palestinian dialogue, without which there is little chance to move forward in the difficult and involved peace process."[11] In concentrating on the role of American Jewry, these Israeli writers focus much too narrowly, I believe.

To cite one last example, an article in the American Jewish press quotes a staff writer for *Ha'aretz* (essentially, the Israeli *New York Times*) who says that "you American Jews, you liberals, you lovers of democracy are supporting its destruction here by not speaking out against the government's actions," referring to the wave of repression in the occupied territories under the "civilian administration" of Professor Menachem Milson and General Ariel Sharon introduced in November 1981.[12] He goes on to explain the plans of Begin and Sharon: to drive a large number of Arabs out of the West Bank, specifically, the leaders and those with a potential for leadership, "by every illegal means." How?

> You activate terrorists to plant bombs in the cars of their elected mayors, you arm the settlers and a few Arab quislings to run rampages through Arab towns, pogroms against property, not against people. A few Arabs have been killed by settlers. The murderers are known, but the police are virtually helpless. They have their orders. What's your excuse for not speaking out against these violations of Israeli law and Jewish morality?

The settlers, he adds, are "Religious Jews who follow a higher law and do whatever their rabbis tell them. At least one of the Gush Emunim rabbis has written that it is a mitzvah [religious duty] to destroy Amalek [meaning, the non-Jewish inhabitants], including women and children."[13] The *Ha'aretz* journalist adds that his journal has "a file of horror stories reported to us by soldiers returning from occupation duty in the West Bank. We can refer to them in general terms—we can rail against the occupation that destroys the moral fibre and self-respect of our youth—but we can't print the details because military censorship covers actions by soldiers on active duty."[14] One can imagine what the file contains, given what has been printed in the Israeli press. It should be noted, in this connection, that many crucial issues that are freely discussed in the Hebrew press in Israel and much that is documented there are virtually excluded from the American press, so that the people who are expected to pay the bills are kept largely in the dark about what they are financing or about the debates within Israel concerning these matters. Many examples will be given below.

The dangers posed to Israel by its American supporters have consistently been realized, leading to much suffering in the region and repeated threat of a larger, perhaps global war.

CAUSAL FACTORS

Domestic Pressure Groups and Their Interests

The "special relationship" is often attributed to domestic political pressures, in particular, the effectiveness of the American Jewish community in political life and in influencing opinion.[15] While there is some truth to this, it is far from the whole story, in two major respects: first, it underestimates the scope of the "support for Israel," and second, it overestimates the role of political pressure groups in decision-making. Let us consider these factors in turn.

In the first place, what Seth Tillman calls the "Israeli lobby" (see note 15) is far broader than the American Jewish community, embracing the major segments of liberal opinion, the leadership of the labor unions,* religious fundamentalists,[17] "conservatives" of the type who support a powerful state apparatus geared to state-induced production of high technology waste (i.e., military production) at home and military threats and adventurism abroad, and—cutting across these categories—fervent cold warriors of all stripes. These connections are appreciated in Israel, not only by the right wing. Thus Yitzhak Rabin, reputedly a dove and soon to become the Labor Prime Minis-

---

* Leon Hadar writes: "Along with the organized American-Jewish community, the labour movement has been a major source of support for Israel"; true with regard to the labor union bureaucracy, whatever the membership may think. Hadar quotes ILGWU president Sol Chaikin who condemns Reagan for his willingness "to 'sell' both Israel and the Solidarity movement in Poland . . . to appease his big business friends." Victor Gotbaum discusses the problems posed for Israel's supporters by the Begin government and its "antagonizing" foreign policy decisions: "We couldn't justify [the Golan annexation], so we preferred to remain silent"; many labor leaders find themselves "divorcing their love for Israel from their relations with Begin" (Gotbaum).[16] Such rhetoric has not been heard since the peak days of American Stalinism and Trotskyite "critical support." It is, however, rather common among Western intellectuals with regard to Israel. See *TNCW*, chapter 10, for some examples. More will appear below.

ter, argued against moves towards political settlement after the 1973 war. Israel should try to "gain time," he urged, in the hope that "we will later find ourselves in a better situation: the U.S. may adopt more aggressive positions vis-a-vis the USSR . . ."[18]

Many American Zionist leaders recognize these factors. In December 1980, several of them argued in the American Jewish press that "there is far greater potential commonality of interests among Jews and the Moral Majority than there is among Jews and the National Council of Churches" *(Jewish Week)*. Jacques Torczyner, former President of the Zionist Organization of America and an executive of the World Zionist Organization, wrote that "We have, first of all, to come to a conclusion that the right-wing reactionaries are the natural allies of Zionism and not the liberals"[19]—he is wrong about the latter, mistakenly assuming that they do not join in the cold war consensus whereas in fact they have consistently promoted and helped to maintain it. It should furthermore be noted that the American left and pacifist groups, apart from fringe elements, have quite generally been extremely supportive of Israel (contrary to many baseless allegations), some passionately so, and have turned a blind eye to practices that they would be quick to denounce elsewhere. Again, examples will appear below.

There is an interesting expression of views akin to Rabin's in a recent study of "the real anti-Semitism in America" by Nathan and Ruth Perlmutter, respectively, the National Director of the Anti-Defamation League of B'nai Brith and his wife, also an active Zionist leader. In the United States, the Anti-Defamation League is regarded as a civil libertarian organization, at one time, a deserved reputation. Now, it specializes in trying to prevent critical discussion of policies of Israel by such techniques as maligning critics, including Israelis who do not pass its test of loyalty, distributing alleged "information" that is often circulated in unsigned pamphlets, and so on.[20] In Israel, it is casually described as "one of the main pillars" of Israeli propaganda in the United States. Seth Tillman refers to it as part of "the Israeli lobby." We return to some of its public performance.[21] The well-known Israeli military historian Meir Pail, formerly head of the Officers Training School of the IDF and an Israeli dove, might well have had the League in mind when he described the ways in which "Golda Meir and the Labor Party destroyed pluralism and debate within the old Zionist framework," mimicking "Joseph Stalin's tendency towards communist parties all over the world," whose interests were to be "subjugated . . . to the power interests of the Soviet Union"; "And the Israeli regime's tendency has been similar" as it has "destroyed the very process of dissent and inquiry," beginning (he says) with the Golda Meir labor government.[22] The League has proven a more than willing instrument.

The Perlmutters cite studies showing that whereas anti-Semitism "was once virulent" in the U.S., today there is little support for discrimination against Jews; there may be dislike of Jews, anti-Jewish attitudes, etc., but then much the same is true with regard to ethnic and religious groups quite generally. What then is "the real anti-semitism," which is still rampant, in fact perhaps more dangerous than before? The *real* anti-Semitism, it turns out, lies in the actions of "peacemakers of Vietnam vintage, transmuters of swords into plowshares, championing the terrorist PLO . . ."* The Perlmutters fear that "nowadays war is getting a bad name and peace too favorable a press . . ." They are concerned by "the defamations by the Left of the promptings for our warring in Vietnam and latterly . . . their sniping at American defense budgets . . ." "Beyond oil it is the very ideology of the liberals in which peace, even if it is pockmarked by injustice, is preferable to the prospect of confrontation that today imperils Jews." Similarly, Jewish interests are threatened "by this decade's Leftists, here and abroad, as they demonstrate against and scold the United States for its involvement in Nicaragua and El Salvador." Jewish interests are threatened because the Central American dictators have been friends of Israel—friendship which has been and is being reciprocated with much enthusiasm, though the Perlmutters do not discuss these facts, which help explain why victims of Somoza and the Salvadoran and Guatemalan generals are not friends of Israel, not because of anti-Semitism, but for quite understandable reasons; peasants being massacred with Israeli arms or tortured by military forces who boast of their Israeli training and support are not likely to be friends of Israel. According to the Perlmutters, such groups as the National Council of Churches also threaten Jewish interests by calling on Israel "to include the PLO in its Middle East peace negotiations." "Apologists for the Left—like those for the Right—have frequently rationalized anti-Semitism or indifference to Jewish interests as being merely a transitory phase," but Jews should know better.

Throughout, the argument is that Israel's interests—understood implicitly as the interests of a rejectionist Greater Israel that denies Palestinian rights—are the "Jewish interests," so that anyone who recognizes Palestinian rights or in other ways advocates policies that threaten "Israel's interests" as the authors conceive them is, to paraphrase Stalinist rhetoric of earlier years, "objectively" anti-Semitic. Those who are "innocent of bigotry" are now placing Jews in "greater jeopardy" than traditional anti-Semites, with

* It is a common claim, perhaps believed by its proponents, that there are many "champions of the PLO" in the U.S., even that the press is "pro-PLO" (*Fateful Triangle*; see p. 1*). When examples are given, it regularly turns out that these "champions" are critics (often harsh critics) of the PLO who, however, believe that Palestinians have the same human and national rights as Jews.

their advocacy of peace, criticism of U.S. interventionism, opposition to bloodthirsty tyrants and torturers, etc. This is the "real anti-Semitism," and it is exceedingly dangerous. So the Anti-Defamation League has its work cut out for it.[23]

It might be noted that the resort to charges of "anti-Semitism" (or in the case of Jews, "Jewish self-hatred") to silence critics of Israel has been quite a general and often effective device. Even Abba Eban, the highly regarded Israeli diplomat of the Labor Party (considered a leading dove), is capable of writing that "One of the chief tasks of any dialogue with the Gentile world is to prove that the distinction between anti-Semitism and anti-Zionism [generally understood as criticism of policies of the Israeli state] is not a distinction at all," and that Jewish critics (I. F. Stone and I are specifically mentioned) have a "basic complex . . . of guilt about Jewish survival." Similarly, Irving Howe, typically without argument, simply attributes Israel's dangerous international isolation to "skillful manipulation of oil" and that "sour apothegm: *In the warmest of hearts there's a cold spot for the Jews*"—so that it is quite unnecessary to consider the impact of the policies of the Labor government that he supported, for example, the brutality of the occupation,* already fully apparent and sharply condemned in Israel when he wrote.[25]

The Perlmutters deride those who voice "criticism of Israel while fantasizing countercharges of anti-Semitism," but their comment is surely disingenuous. The tactic is standard. Christopher Sykes, in his excellent study of the pre-state period, traces the origins of this device ("a new phase in Zionist propaganda") to a "violent counterattack" by David Ben-Gurion against a British court that had implicated Zionist leaders in arms-trafficking in 1943: "henceforth to be anti-Zionist was to be anti-Semitic."[26] It is, however, primarily in the post-1967 period that the tactic has been honed to a high art, increasingly so, as the policies defended became less and less defensible.

Within the Jewish community, the unity in "support for Israel" that has been demanded, and generally achieved, is remarkable—as noted, to the chagrin of Israeli doves who plausibly argue that this kind of "support" has seriously weakened their efforts to modify harsh and ultimately self-destructive government policies. There is even a lively debate within the American Jewish community as to whether it is legitimate to criticize Israel's policies at all, and perhaps even more amazing, the existence of such a debate is not recog-

---

* It might be noted that to people concerned with the facts, "skillful manipulation of oil" also seems too easy an excuse (while the "sour apothegm" hardly merits comment). See, for example, the discussion by Zionist historian Jon Kimche of how the Labor government's apparent duplicity and rejection of possible peaceful settlement alienated friendly African countries well before the use of the "oil weapon."[24]

nized to be the amazing phenomenon it surely is. The position that criticism is illegitimate is defended, for example, by Elie Wiesel, who says:

> I support Israel—period. I identify with Israel—period. I never attack, never criticize Israel when I am not in Israel.

As for Israel's policies in the occupied territories, Wiesel is unable to offer a comment:

> What to do and how to do it, I really don't know because I lack the elements of information and knowledge . . . You must be in a position of power to possess all the information . . . I don't have that information, so I don't know . . . [27]

A similar stance of state-worship would be difficult to find, apart from the annals of Stalinism and fascism. Wiesel is regarded in the United States as a critic of fascism, and much revered as a secular saint.

The reason generally offered in defense of the doctrine that Israel may not be criticized outside its borders is that only those who face the dangers and problems have a right to express such criticism, not those who observe in safety from afar. By similar logic, it is illegitimate for Americans to criticize the PLO, or the Arab states, or the USSR. This argument actually extends a bit more broadly: it is legitimate—in fact, a duty—to provide Israel with massive subsidies and to praise it to the skies while vilifying its adversaries, particularly those it has conquered, but it is illegitimate to voice any critical comment concerning the use of the bounty we provide.

U.S. Strategic Interests

Returning to the main theme, reference to Jewish influence over politics and opinion seriously underestimates the scope of the so-called "support for Israel." Turning to the second point, the argument much overestimates the pluralism of American politics and ideology. No pressure group will dominate access to public opinion or maintain consistent influence over policy-making unless its aims are close to those of elite elements with real power. These elements are not uniform in interests or (in the case of shared interests) in tactical judgments; and on some issues, such as this one, they have often been divided. Nevertheless, a closer look will illustrate the correctness of the assessment that the evolution of America's relationship to Israel "has been determined primarily by the changing role that Israel occupied in the context of America's changing conceptions of its political-strategic interests in the Middle East." [28]

Let us consider some of the relevant historical background, in an attempt to clarify this issue.

Despite the remarkable level of U.S. support for Israel, it would be an error to assume that Israel represents the major U.S. interest in the Middle East. Rather, the major interest lies in the energy reserves of the region, primarily in the Arabian peninsula. A State Department analysis of 1945 described Saudi Arabia as ". . . a stupendous source of strategic power, and one of the greatest material prizes in world history."[29] The U.S. was committed to win and keep this prize. Since World War II, it has been virtually an axiom of U.S. foreign policy that these energy reserves should remain under U.S. control. A more recent variant of the same theme is that the flow of petrodollars should be largely funnelled to the United States through military purchases, construction projects, bank deposits, investment in Treasury securities, etc. It has been necessary to defend this primary interest against various threats.

Threats to U.S. Control of Middle East Oil

At the rhetorical level, the threat from which the Middle East must be "defended" is generally pictured to be the USSR. While it is true that the United States would not tolerate Soviet moves that threatened to provide the USSR with a significant role in Middle East oil production or distribution, this has rarely been a realistic concern—which is not to say that ideologists have not come to believe the fantasies they conjure up to serve other needs.[30] In fact, the USSR has been hesitant to intrude on what is recognized to be American turf.

The pattern was set early on in the Cold War, when the United States organized its first major postwar counterinsurgency campaign, in Greece in 1947. Entering Greece after the Nazis had withdrawn, Britain had imposed the rule of royalist elements and former Nazi collaborators, suppressing the anti-Nazi resistance—in Athens, under Churchill's order to British forces "to act as if you were in a conquered city where a local rebellion is in progress."[31] The repression and corruption of the British-imposed regime revived the resistance. Severely weakened by the war, Britain was unable to cope with the problem and the U.S. took over the task of destroying the Communist-led peasant and worker-based nationalist movement that had fought the Nazis, while maintaining in power its own favorites, such as King Paul and Queen Frederika, whose background was in the fascist youth movements, and Minister of the Interior Mavromichalis, described by U.S. intelligence as a former Nazi collaborator and given responsibility for internal security. Some Senators found all of this difficult to reconcile with Truman Doctrine rhetoric about supporting "free peoples who are resisting attempted subjugation by armed minorities or by outside pressures," under which the counterinsurgency campaign was mounted. To them, Senator Henry Cabot Lodge explained that "this fascist government through which we have to work is incidental." [32]

The counterinsurgency effort was no small enterprise: in the war that ensued, 160,000 Greeks were killed and 800,000 became refugees. The American Mission set itself the task of eliminating those to whom Ambassador Lincoln MacVeagh referred as "subversive social forces," rooted in the insidious "new growth of class-consciousness and proletarianism"—"an alien and subversive influence," as American chargé Karl Rankin described them, to which "no leniency" should be shown until "the state has successfully reasserted its dominance" and the "bandit uprising has been quelled" (the Ambassador's phrase, standard usage in U.S. documents as in Soviet documents concerning Afghanistan). It was the American Mission and its fascist clients (and, of course, the wealthy and, later, American corporations, who were the real beneficiaries) who represented the "native" element in Greece, as distinct from the "alien" influence of Greek peasants and workers subverted by class-consciousness.

The dedicated savagery with which the U.S. Mission set about the task of liquidating the class enemy was a bit too much even for the British, who are not known for their gentlemanly decorum in such procedures; they were also not too happy about being displaced from yet another outpost of British influence and power. With the enthusiastic approval and direct participation of the U.S. Mission, tens of thousands were exiled, tens of thousands more were sent to prison islands where many were tortured or executed (or if lucky, only "re-educated"), the unions were broken, and even mild anti-Communist socialists were suppressed, while the United States shamelessly manipulated the electoral process to ensure that the right men won. The social and economic consequences were grim. A decade later, "between 1959 and 1963, almost a third of the Greek labor force emigrated in search of satisfactory employment." [33] The fascist coup of 1967, again with apparent U.S. backing, had its roots in the same events.

A major motivation for this counterinsurgency campaign was concern over Middle East oil. In his March 12, 1947, speech announcing the Truman Doctrine, the president observed that "It is necessary only to glance at a map" to see that if Greece should fall to the rebels "confusion and disorder might well spread throughout the entire Middle East." A February 1948 CIA study warned that in the event of a rebel victory, the United States would face "the possible loss of the petroleum resources of the Middle East (comprising 40 percent of world reserves)." [34] A Russian threat was fabricated to justify U.S. intervention, but without factual basis; Stalin was trying to rein in the Greek guerrillas, knowing that the United States would not tolerate the loss of this Middle East outpost, as Greece was regarded, and not at all pleased at the prospect of a possible Balkan Communist confederation under Titoist influence. Again, it does not follow from the fact that the threat was fabricated that it was not believed in some planning circles; in public as in personal life, it is easy to come to believe what it is convenient to believe. The exaggeration of the Russian threat should be understood as an early example of the functioning of the Cold War system by which each superpower exploits the threat of the great enemy (its "Great Satan," to borrow Ayatollah Khomeini's term) to mobilize support for actions it intends to undertake in its own domains.

The success of the Greek counterinsurgency campaign, both at the military and ideological level, left its stamp on future U.S. policy-making. Since that time there has been recurrent talk about Russia's attempts to gain control of Middle East oil, the Soviet drive to the Gulf, etc. But no serious case has been made that the USSR would risk nuclear war—for that would be the likely consequence—by pursuing any such objective.

A more realistic threat to U.S. dominance of the region has been posed by Europe.* In the 1940s, the United States succeeded in displacing France, and to a large extent Britain, in part by design, in part simply as a reflection of the power balance.[35] One consequence of the CIA-backed coup that restored the Shah in Iran in 1953 was to transfer 40 percent of Iranian oil from British to American hands, a fact that led the *New York Times* editors to express concern that some misguided British circles might believe that "American 'imperialism' . . . has once again elbowed Britain from a historic stronghold." At the same time, the editors exulted that "underdeveloped countries with rich resources now have an object lesson in the heavy cost that must be paid by one of their number which goes berserk with fanatical nationalism."[36] The costs of the object lesson were indeed heavy, as events were to show, and are still being paid; and many others have been compelled to learn the same lesson since.

Concern over European involvement in the region persisted. The United States strongly opposed the attempt by Britain and France to reassert their influence in the area with the 1956 Suez invasion (in conjunction with Israel); the United States was instrumental in expelling all three powers from Egyptian territory, though Soviet threats may also have played their part. Henry Kissinger, in his 1973 "Year of Europe" address, warned of the dangers of a Europe-dominated trading bloc including the Middle East and North Africa from which the United States might be excluded. Later, he confided in a private meeting that one basic element in his post-1973 diplomacy was "to ensure that the Europeans and Japanese did not get involved in the diplomacy" concerning the Middle East.[37] Subsequent U.S. opposition to the "Euro-Arab dia-

* And more recently, Japan, which in 1982 replaced the U.S. as Saudi Arabia's number one trading partner and is also first or second as supplier for most other Gulf oil producers. Still, the Middle East is "the only U.S. foreign market that has experienced any significant growth in the past few years." William O. Beeman, *Christian Science Monitor*, March 30, 1983.

logue" stems from the same concerns. Today, competition among the state capitalist societies (including now some lesser powers such as South Korea) for a share in the wealth generated by oil production is a matter of growing significance.

The Indigenous Threat: Israel as a Strategic Asset

A third threat from which the region must be "defended" is the indigenous one: the threat of radical nationalism. It is in this context that the U.S.-Israel "special relationship" has matured. In the early 1950s, the U.S.-Israel relationship was decidedly uneasy, and it appeared for a time that Washington might cement closer relations with Egyptian President Nasser, who had some CIA support. These prospects appeared sufficiently worrisome so that Israel organized terrorist cells within Egypt to carry out attacks on U.S. installations (also on Egyptian public facilities) in an effort to drive a wedge between Egypt and the U.S., intending that these acts would be attributed to ultranationalist Egyptian fanatics.*

From the late 1950s, however, the U.S. government increasingly came to accept the Israeli thesis that a powerful Israel is a "strategic asset" for the United States, serving as a barrier against indigenous radical nationalist threats to American interests, which might gain support from the USSR. A recently declassified National Security Council memorandum of 1958 noted that a "logical corollary" of opposition to radical Arab nationalism "would be to support Israel as the only strong pro-West power left in the Near East."[39] Meanwhile, Israel concluded a secret pact with Turkey, Iran, and Ethiopia. According to David Ben-Gurion's biographer, this "periphery pact" was encouraged by Secretary of State John Foster Dulles, and was "long-lasting."[40] Through the 1960s, American intelligence regarded Israel as a barrier to Nasserite pressure on the Gulf oil-producing states, a serious matter at the time, and to Russian influence. This conclusion was reinforced by Israel's smashing victory in 1967, when Israel quickly conquered the Sinai, Gaza, the West Bank, and the Golan Heights; the last, after violating the cease-fire in an operation ordered by Defense Minister Moshe Dayan without notifying the Prime Minister or Chief of Staff.[41]

The Israeli thesis that Israel is a "strategic asset" was again confirmed by

---

* The official in charge of these operations, Defense Minister Pinhas Lavon, became Secretary-General of the Histadrut (the socialist labor union). According to the respected Israeli journalist Nahum Barnea, Lavon gave orders that were "much more severe" than those leading to the terrorist operations in Egypt, including an attempt "to poison the water sources in the Gaza Strip and the demilitarized zones" (*Davar*, January 26, 1979). He does not indicate whether these alleged orders were executed.[38]

Israel's moves to block Syrian efforts to support Palestinians being massacred by Jordan in September 1970, at a time when the U.S. was unable to intervene directly against what was perceived as a threat to U.S. clients in the Arab world. This contribution led to a substantial increase in U.S. aid. In the 1970s, U.S. analysts argued that Israel and Iran under the Shah served to protect U.S. control over the oil-producing regions of the Gulf. After the fall of the Shah, Israel's role as a Middle East Sparta in the service of American power has evoked increasing American support.

At the same time, Israel aided the U.S. in penetrating Black Africa with substantial secret CIA subsidies—supporting Haile Selassie in Ethiopia, Idi Amin in Uganda, Mobutu in Zaire, Bokassa in the Central African Republic, and others at various times[42]—as well as in circumventing the ban on aid to Rhodesia and South Africa* and, more recently, in providing military and technological aid, as well as many advisers, for U.S. clients in Central America. An increasingly visible alliance between Israel, South Africa, Taiwan, and the military dictatorships of the southern cone in South America has also proven an attractive prospect for major segments of American power.[44] Now, Israel is surely regarded as a crucial part of the elaborate U.S. base and backup system for the Rapid Deployment Force ringing the Middle East oil producing regions.[45] These are highly important matters that deserve much more attention than I can give them here.

Had it not been for Israel's perceived geopolitical role—primarily in the Middle East, but elsewhere as well—it is doubtful that the various pro-Israeli lobbies in the U.S. would have had much influence in policy formation, or that the climate of opinion deplored by Peled and other Israeli doves could have

---

* UPI, *Boston Globe*, May 16, 1982: the item reads, *in toto*, "American-made helicopters and spare parts went from Israel to Rhodesia—now Zimbabwe—despite a trade embargo during the bitter war against guerrillas, the Commerce Department has disclosed." The Labor Party journal quotes the head of South Africa's military industry as saying that Israeli "technological assistance permits South Africa to evade the arms embargo imposed upon it because of its racial policies" (*Davar*, December 17, 1982). *Yediot Ahronot*, citing the *London Times*, reports that "Israeli technicians are helping South Africa evade the French military embargo" by transferring and repairing French armaments in Israeli hands (October 29, 1981). Close relations with South Africa were established by the Rabin Labor government in the mid-1970s and remain warm, because, as Minister of Industry and Commerce Gidon Pat recently stated in Pretoria, "Israel and South Africa are two of the only 30 democracies in the world." Similarly, Gad Yaakovi of the Labor Party "praised the economic and 'other' [i.e., military] relations with South Africa in a television interview" in Israel, Yoav Karni reports, adding that if he had said similar things in Britain, Holland or Sweden he would have lost his membership in the Social Democratic party, though his remarks caused no distress in the Israeli Labor Party.[43]

been constructed and maintained. Correspondingly, it will very likely erode if Israel comes to be seen as a threat rather than a support to the primary U.S. interest in the Middle East region, which is to maintain control over its energy reserves and the flow of petrodollars.

Support for the concept of Israel as a "strategic asset" has, then, been considerable among those who exercise real power in the U.S., and this position has regularly won out in internal policy debate, assisted, to some extent, by domestic political pressures. But the position has not been unchallenged. There have also been powerful forces in favor of the kind of peaceful political settlement that has long been possible, a matter to which we turn in the next chapter.

Michael Klare has suggested that a useful distinction can be drawn between the "Prussians," who advocate the threat or use of violence to attain desired policy ends, and the "Traders," who share the same goals but believe that peaceful means will be more effective.[46] These are tactical assessments, and positions may therefore shift. It is, to first approximation, accurate to say that the "Prussians" have supported Israel as a "strategic asset," while the "Traders" have sought a political accommodation of some sort. The point is implicitly recognized in much pro-Israeli propaganda, for example, a full-page *New York Times* advertisement signed by many luminaries (including some who are doves in other contexts), which calls for establishment of a pro-Israel political pressure group (National PAC) under the heading "Faith in Israel strengthens America." To support their case, they write: ". . . if U.S. interests in the Middle East were threatened, it would take months to mount a significant presence there. With Israel as an ally, it would take only a few days." Similarly, Joseph Churba, director of the Center for International Security, complains that "the left in Israel" lacks appreciation of U.S. and Israeli interests and "many in their ranks, as in the ranks of the American left, are working for the same purpose, i.e., that neither country should function as an international policeman, be it in El Salvador or in Lebanon"—the left in Israel and the U.S., then, are contributing to anti-Semitism, "threatening the interests of Jews," according to the doctrine of "the *real* anti-Semitism" developed by the Anti-Defamation League, discussed above. Those who understand U.S. and Israeli interests believe, as Churba does, that "Western power" should be "effectively used to moderate Soviet and radical adventurism,"[47] and that the U.S. and Israel should function as international policemen in El Salvador, Lebanon and elsewhere.

The authentic voice of the "Prussians," in both cases.

The same distinction is implicit in the argument as to whether Israel's "Peace for Galilee" invasion of Lebanon strengthened the American position in the Middle East and, in general, served U.S. ends. The *New Republic* argues that this is so; hence the operation was justified. Others believe that American interests in the region have been harmed. Thus Thomas Friedman, after an extensive investigation of opinion in the Arab world, concludes that "not only did respect for many Arab leaders die in Lebanon [because they did not come to the defense of the victims of the Israeli attack, even when a besieged Arab capital was being defended by "a popular movement," as a Lebanese political scientist explained], but so too much of America's respect in the Middle East," because of the perception that "America cannot be trusted" (the director of the Kuwait Fund for Arab Economic Development) and that the U.S. supports Israel "as an instrument of its own policy." A senior Kuwaiti official, echoing widely expressed opinions, stated: "You have lost where it matters most—on the humanitarian level. Whatever respect there was in the Arab world for the United States as a moral authority has been lost."[48]

Who is right in this debate? Both sides are, in their own terms. Those who deride "the humanitarian level" and the concept of "moral authority" can argue, with some plausibility, that Israel's military might enhances the capacity of the United States to rule the region by force and violence, and that the invasion of Lebanon contributed to this end, at least in the short term. Those who have a different conception of what the U.S. role should be in world affairs will draw different conclusions from the same evidence.

Subsidiary Services

After the Lebanon invasion, Israel moved at once to underscore its status as a "strategic asset" and to reinforce its own position by improving relations with its allies (which, not by accident, are U.S. allies) in Africa and Latin America. Renewing relations established under CIA auspices in the 1960s (see above), Foreign Minister Yitzhak Shamir visited General Mobutu in Zaire, informing him that apart from direct military and technical support, "Israel will aid Zaire through its influence over Jewish organizations in the United States, which will help in improving [Zaire's] image."* This is a rather serious matter, since

* Mobutu is not the only brutal dictator to whom this idea occurred, or was suggested. In an interview with the left-wing journal *Al-Hamishmar* (Mapam), December 29, 1981, Imelda Marcos, acting as an "international advocate" for her husband, explained their intention of exploiting improved relations with Israel and the influence of American Jews "to improve the tainted image [of the Philippine dictatorship] in the American media, and to combat its unpopularity in the American Congress." Commenting, journalist Leon Hadar reports the opinion of Israeli officials that other third world dictatorships with a "negative image" are also interested in using this device to obtain greater political, economic and military aid from the U.S., and that strengthening of Israel's role in the Third World is one of the "advantages" that Israel will gain from strategic cooperation with the U.S.

the image of this corrupt and brutal dictatorship is not of the highest, and as Mobutu complained, "the main antagonists [of Zaire] in the U.S. are Jewish members of Congress." Shamir's comforting response was: "Jews criticize us too." He went on to explain that "with the cooperation of Israeli groups and with the money that American Jews will contribute, it will be possible to aid Zaire," militarily and materially and in improving its image. General Mobutu expressed his pleasure that Israeli officers are providing military training (specifically, for his Presidential Guard) along with French and Chinese advisers. In January 1983, Defense Minister Ariel Sharon visited Zaire and an agreement was reached that Israeli military advisers would restructure Zaire's armed forces. Sharon "defended Israel's new arms and military aid agreement with Zaire today as a step towards increasing Israeli influence in Africa," UPI reported. Sharon added that the program (which must be secret) would be "a contribution to Israeli exports in arms and equipment" and that it would lead other African countries to turn to Israel for military aid.[49]

A few weeks earlier, Sharon had visited Honduras "to cement relations with a friendly country which has shown interest in connection with our defense establishment." Israeli radio reported that Israel had helped Honduras acquire what is regarded as the strongest air force in Central America, and noted that "the Sharon trip raised the question of whether Israel might act as an American proxy in Honduras." "It has also been reported that Israeli advisers have assisted in training Honduran pilots."[50] A "top-level military source" in Honduras stated that the new Israel-Honduras agreement involved sophisticated jet fighters, tanks, Galil assault rifles (standard issue for state terrorists in Central America), training for officers, troops, and pilots, and perhaps missiles. Sharon's entourage included the head of the Israeli Air Force and the director-general of the Defense Ministry; they "were accorded the full measure of honors usually accorded to a visiting head of state." A government functionary stated that Sharon's visit was "more positive" than Reagan's shortly before, since Sharon "sold us arms" while "Reagan only uttered platitudes, explaining that Congress was preventing him from doing more." There is no significant domestic force to prevent Israel from "doing more," a fact deplored by Israeli doves. "The unannounced visit and military accord underline Israel's growing role as U.S. arms broker and proxy in crisis-ridden Central America." Meanwhile in Guatemala, Chief of Staff Mario Lopez Fuentes, who regards President Rios Montt as insufficiently violent, complained about U.S. meddling concerning human rights; "What we want is to be left at liberty," he said; "It would be preferable if the U.S. were to take an attitude similar to that of other allies such as Israel, he indicated."[51]

Israel's services in Central America have been considerable, including Nicaragua (under Somoza), Guatemala, El Salvador, and Honduras, and now apparently Costa Rica since it began to draw closer to U.S. policy in the region after the election of Luis Alberto Monge in February 1982. The Israeli contributions to Guatemalan and Honduran military forces are particularly significant: in the former case, because the military regimes placed in power through U.S. intervention were finding it difficult to resist a growing insurrection while congressional human rights restrictions were impeding direct U.S. military aid to these mass murderers; and in the case of Honduras, because of Reagan's increasingly visible efforts to foment disorder and strife by supporting the Somozist National Guard based in Honduras in their forays into Nicaragua, where they torture and destroy in the manner in which they were trained by the United States for many years.[52] Before the Falklands war, it had been hoped that Argentine neo-Nazis could be employed for this purpose, as well as for improving the efficiency of state terrorism in El Salvador and Guatemala. A more reliable client-ally may be needed to perform this proxy role, however.

Charles Maechling, who led counterinsurgency and internal-defense planning for Presidents Johnson and Kennedy from 1961–66 and is now an associate of the Carnegie Endowment for International Peace, described U.S. trainees in Latin America as "indistinguishable from the war criminals hanged at Nuremberg after World War II,"* adding that "for the United States, which led the crusade against the Nazi evil, to support the methods of Heinrich Himmler's extermination squads is an outrage."[53] Apart from being an outrage, it has become difficult, because of congressional legislation. Hence the importance of Israel's contributions through the 1970s and increasingly today, in support of those who employ the methods of Himmler's extermination squads.

The congressional human rights campaign (often misleadingly attributed to the American presidency) was a reflection of the "Vietnam syndrome," a dread malady that afflicted much of the population in the wake of the Vietnam war, with such terrifying symptoms as insight into the ways in which American power is used in the world and concern over torture, murder, aggression, and oppression. It had been hoped that the disease had been cured, but the popular reaction to Reagan's revival of Kennedy-style counterinsurgency showed that the optimism was premature, so Israel's contributions are per-

* The extensive direct U.S. involvement in state terrorism in Latin America, as Maechling notes, began under the Kennedy Administration, when the mission of the Latin American military was shifted from "hemispheric defense" to "internal security," i.e., war against their own populations. The effects were catastrophic, throughout Latin America. In terms of its impact, this 1961 decision of the Kennedy liberals was one of the most significant ones of recent history. It is little known here.

haps even more welcome than before. It has, incidentally, been alleged that the U.S. has been opposed to Israel's Latin American ventures (e.g., that Carter opposed Israel's aid to Somoza), but this is hardly likely. There is little doubt that the U.S. could have prevented any intervention of which it did not approve, and it sometimes did so, though not in Nicaragua, where the Human Rights Administration in fact supported Somoza to the end of his bloody rule, even after the natural allies of the U.S., the Nicaraguan business community, had turned against him.

Israel's services have extended beyond the Middle East, Africa, and Latin America, to Asia as well. Thus, on one occasion, Israel supplied American jets to Indonesia when its arms were depleted in the course of the massacre of Timorese, and the Human Rights Administration, while doing its best to provide the armaments required to consummate this mission, was still reluctant to do so too openly, perhaps fearing that the press might depart from its complicity in this slaughter.[54] Taiwan has been a particularly close ally. The Israeli press speaks of "the Fifth World"—Israel, South Africa, Taiwan—a new alliance of technologically advanced states that is engaged in advanced weapons development, including nuclear weapons, missiles, and so on.[55]

With Reagan's efforts to enflame the Nicaragua-Honduras border and Sharon's trip to Honduras, the Israeli connection became so visible as to call forth some official denials, duly reported as fact in the *New York Times*. Noting that Israel is "enlarging its military training missions and role as a principal supplier of arms to Central America," Leslie Gelb writes that "from every indication, the Israelis are not there, as are most of the others [Americans, PLO, Cubans, East Germans], as participants in a form of East-West confrontation or to engage in revolutionary or counterrevolutionary intrigue." These "indications" turn out to be statements to this effect by Israeli and American officials, none of whom "said that Israel was in Central America to do Washington's bidding or to help out in countries such as Guatemala where the Administration is barred from providing military aid because of civil rights abuses." Naturally, one would expect Israeli and American officials to proclaim any such arrangements openly, so their failure to do so suffices to prove that there is nothing to this canard. A State Department official comments that "we've indicated we're not unhappy they are helping out" in places like Guatemala and Honduras, "but I wouldn't say we and the Israelis have figured out together what to do."[56] Elaborate "figuring out" would seem to be superfluous, given the shared perceptions and interests, not to speak of the extremely close relations at all levels, including the military itself, military industry, intelligence, diplomatic, etc.

It is striking that Gelb assumes as a matter of course that while Israel might be pursuing its own interests (as it no doubt is, one of these being to render services to U.S. power), this could not be true of, say, Cuba, which surely has no reason to feel threatened and therefore could not be trying to break out of its "isolation" (as Israel is, he reports) by supporting friendly governments. One might have expected Gelb, perhaps, to be sensitive to this issue. He was the director of the Pentagon Papers study, which contained the astonishing revelation that U.S. intelligence, over the twenty-year period surveyed, was so completely indoctrinated by Cold War propaganda that it was unable to conceive of the possibility that the North Vietnamese might have been motivated by their own perceived interests, instead of simply acting as lackeys of the USSR or China.[57]

AMERICAN LIBERALISM AND IDEOLOGICAL SUPPORT FOR ISRAEL

As noted, the view of the "Prussians" has generally won out in internal policy debate. But the story is more complex. American liberalism has led the way in constructing the "blindly chauvinistic and narrow-minded" support for Israeli policy that General Peled deplores. On the same day that the U.S. and Israel stood alone against the world at the United Nations (see p. 198), the national conference of the Democratic Party "adopted a statement highly sympathetic to Israel's recent attacks in Lebanon, qualifying it only with an expression of regret over 'all loss of life on both sides in Lebanon.' " In contrast, the Foreign Ministers of the European Community "vigorously condemned the new Israeli invasion of Lebanon" as a "flagrant violation of international law as well as of the most elementary humanitarian principles," adding that this "unjustifiable action" posed the risk of "leading to a generalized war."[58] This is by no means an isolated case.

In fact, the front page of the *New York Times* on that day (June 27) encapsulates the U.S.-Israel "special relationship" rather neatly. There are three adjacent columns. One is a report by William Farrell from Beirut, describing the effects of Israel's latest bombardments: cemeteries jammed, people buried in mass graves, hospitals in desperate need of supplies, garbage heaped everywhere in stinking piles, bodies decomposing under tons of rubble, buildings little more than shattered hulks, morgue refrigerators full, bodies piled on the floors of hospitals, the few doctors desperately trying to treat victims of cluster and phosphorus bombs, Israel blocking Red Cross medical supplies, hospitals bombed, surgery interrupted by Israeli shelling, etc. The second is a report by Bernard Nossiter from New York, reporting how the U.S. blocked UN action to stop the slaughter on the grounds that the PLO might be preserved as "a viable political force." The third is a report by Adam Clymer from Philadelphia on the sympathetic support of the Democratic national conference for Israel's war in Lebanon. The three front-page reports, side-by-side, capture the nature of the "special relationship" with some accuracy—as does the lack of editorial comment.

American liberalism had always been highly sympathetic to Israel, but there was a noticeable positive shift in attitudes in 1967 with the demonstration of Israel's military might. Top Israeli military commanders made it clear not long after that Israel had faced no serious military threat and that a quick victory was anticipated with confidence—that the alleged threat to Israel's existence was "a bluff."[59] But this fact was suppressed here in favor of the image of an Israeli David confronting a brutal Arab Goliath,[60] enabling liberal humanitarians to offer their sympathy and support to the major military power of the region as it turned from crushing its enemies to suppressing those who fell under its control, while leading Generals explained that Israel could conquer everything from Khartoum to Baghdad to Algeria within a week, if necessary (Ariel Sharon).[61]

The rise in Israel's stock among liberal intellectuals with this demonstration of its military prowess is a fact of some interest. It is reasonable to attribute it in large part to domestic American concerns, in particular, to the inability of the U.S. to crush indigenous resistance in Indochina. That Israel's lightning victory should have been an inspiration to open advocates of the use of violence to attain national goals is not surprising, but there are many illusions about the stance of the liberal intelligentsia on this matter. It is now sometimes forgotten that in 1967 they overwhelmingly supported U.S. intervention (more accurately, aggression) in Indochina and continued to do so, though many came to oppose this venture for the reasons that impelled business circles to the same judgment: the costs became too high, out of proportion to the benefits that might be gained—a "pragmatic" rather than principled opposition, quite different from the stance adopted toward depredations of official enemies, the Soviet invasion of Czechoslovakia, for example. (In contrast, the central elements of the peace movement opposed aggression in both cases on principled grounds; these facts have been much obscured in the subsequent rewriting of history). Thus the appeal of Israel's efficient and successful use of force was, in fact, quite broad. It was only half jokingly that people spoke of sending Moshe Dayan to Vietnam to show how to do the job right.

At the same time, the challenge to authority at home was regarded with much distress. A dread image was conjured up of Vietcong, Maoist fanatics, bearded Cuban revolutionaries, rampaging students, Black Panthers, Arab terrorists, and other forces—perhaps on the Russian leash—conspiring to shake the foundations of our world of privilege and domination. Israel showed how to treat Third World upstarts properly, winning the allegiance of many frightened advocates of the virtues of knowing one's place. For some, the military might that Israel displayed induced open admiration and respect, while others disguised these feelings, appealing to the alleged vulnerability of Israel before the forces it had so decisively crushed, and still others were deluded by the effective " 'David and Goliath' legend" (see note 60).

Individuals have their own reasons, but tendencies of this nature are readily detectable and go a long way towards explaining the outpouring of "support for Israel" as it demonstrated its capacity to wield the mailed fist. It is since 1967 that questioning of Israel policies has largely been silenced, with effective use of the moral weapons of anti-Semitism and "Jewish self-hatred." Topics that were widely discussed and debated in Europe or in Israel itself were effectively removed from the agenda here, and a picture was established of Israel, its enemies and victims, and the U.S. role in the region, that bore only a limited resemblance to reality. The situation slowly began to change in the late 1970s, markedly so, after the increasingly visible repression under the Milson-Sharon regime in the occupied territories (only partially reported here) and the 1982 invasion of Lebanon, which offered a serious challenge to the talents of propagandists.

The immense popularity that Israel won by demonstrating its military efficiency also offered a weapon that could be usefully employed against domestic dissidents. Considerable effort was devoted to showing that the New Left supported Arab terrorism and the destruction of Israel, a task largely accomplished in defiance of the facts (the New Left, as the documentary record clearly shows, quite generally tended to support the position of Israeli doves).[62]

It is interesting that one of the devices currently used to meet the new challenge is to extend to the press in general the deceptive critique applied to the New Left in earlier years. Now, the insistent complaint is that the media are antagonistic to Israel and subject to the baleful influence of the PLO, motivated by their reflex sympathy for Third World revolutionary struggles against Western power. While this may appear ludicrous given the evident facts, neither the effort (*Fateful Triangle*; see p. 1*, and further examples below) nor its not insignificant success in containing deviations toward a minimal degree of even-handedness will come as any surprise to students of twentieth-century propaganda systems, just as there was no surprise in the earlier successes of those who were fabricating a picture of New Left support for PLO terrorism and contempt for Israel precisely because it is a democracy advancing towards socialism, one of Irving Howe's insights.[63] We are, after all, living in the age of Orwell.

One can, perhaps, offer a more sympathetic psychological interpretation. Those who are accustomed to near total dominance of articulate opinion may feel that the world is coming to an end if their control is threatened or weakened ever so slightly, reacting in the manner of an overindulged child who is chided for the first time. Hence the wailing about the reflex sympathy of the press for the PLO and its immutable hatred of Israel when, say, there is an occasional report of the bombing of hospitals or beating of defenseless prisoners. Or the phenomenon may simply be an expression of a totalitarian mentality: any deviation from the orthodox spectrum of "support for Israel" (which includes a variety of permissible "critical support") is an intolerable affront, and it is therefore barely an exaggeration to describe slight deviation as if it were near total.

As an illustration (there are many), consider a March 1983 newsletter of the American Professors for Peace in the Middle East—a well-funded organization that is concerned about peace in the Middle East in the same sense in which the Communist Party is concerned about peace in Afghanistan—sent to its fifteen Regional Chairmen and its many Campus Representatives. It warns of an "organized, centrally controlled, information plan" on the "Arab side" which is not matched by anything representing "the Israeli position." Their concern is aroused by "a list of speakers who are being toured through the university circuit . . . to present the Arab point of view," giving presentations that "smack more of propaganda than of education." "In order of frequency and virulence the speakers are: Hatem Hussaini, Edward Said, Noam Chomsky, Fawaz Turki, Stokely Carmichael, James Zogby, Hassan Rahman, Chris Giannou, M.D., Israel Shahak, and Gail Pressberg." As any observer of the American scene will be aware, these nefarious figures almost completely dominate discussion of the Middle East in the United States, and "the Israeli point of view" virtually never obtains a hearing, though, the newsletter adds, "there are doubtless many speakers who espouse the Israeli position" and would speak if only there were an opportunity for them to do so. Even if there were some truth to the paranoid concept of "an organized, centrally controlled, information plan," or the belief that these speakers are part of it, or that they "present the Arab point of view,"* it should be obvious that this

* Among them are people who have always been harsh critics of all the Arab states and the PLO, for example, the third in order of virulence and others as well, but it is true that no one on the list meets the approved standards of servility to the Israeli government propaganda system, so they might be considered "pro-Arab" by someone who takes this to be the criterion for distinguishing "education" from "propaganda." For the record, virtually every talk I have given on this topic has been arranged by some tiny student or faculty group, as any sane person familiar with the United States would of course know without being told.

would be a phenomenon of marginal significance in the United States and could not begin to compare with the massive pro-Israel propaganda system, of which this organization—which alone surely dwarfs anything on the "Arab side"—is a tiny element. But the frightened little men of the APPME probably believe all of this. Perhaps they are aware that this "information plan" and its agents have virtually no access to the mass media or journals of opinion, but they are right in noting that no way has yet been found to prevent them from responding to invitations at one or another college, a flaw in the American system that still remains to be addressed.

As the invasion of Lebanon proceeded, the list of those who were deliberately falsifying the facts to place Israel in a less than favorable light grew quite long, including the European press and much of the American press and television, the International Red Cross and other relief agencies, American diplomats, and in fact virtually everyone except spokesmen for the Israeli government and selected Americans returning from guided tours. The general tone is conveyed by Eliahu Ben-Elissar, chairman of the Knesset's Committee on Foreign Affairs, who received "the most applause" at the convention of B'nai Brith when he said: "We have been attacked, criticized, dirtied, besmirched . . . I wouldn't want to accuse the whole world of anti-Semitism, but how to explain this violent outburst."[64] A similar perception, widely shared, was expressed by Israeli Defense Minister Ariel Sharon:

> Today we are in the arena opposite the entire world. It is the people of Israel, a small and isolated people, against the entire world.[65]

This "horrible thing that is now taking place around us in the world" is "no doubt" the result of anti-Semitism, not the Lebanon war or the Beirut massacres a few days before. We return to some details of this intriguing story.

The truth of the matter is that Israel has been granted a unique immunity from criticism in mainstream journalism and scholarship, consistent with its unique role as a beneficiary of other forms of American support. We have already seen a number of examples and many more will appear below. Two examples noted earlier in this chapter offer a clear enough indication of this immunity: the Israeli terrorist attacks on U.S. facilities and other public places in Egypt (the Lavon affair), and the attack on the unmistakeably identified USS *Liberty* with rockets, aircraft cannon, napalm, torpedoes, and machine guns, clearly premeditated, leaving 34 crewmen dead and 75 wounded in "the Navy's bloodiest 'peacetime' international incident of the

20th century"* (see notes 38, 41). In both cases, the general reaction of the press and scholarship has been silence or misrepresentation. Neither has entered history as a deplorable act of terrorism and violence, either at the time or in retrospect. In the case of the bombings in Egypt, the Israeli novelist Amos Oz, writing in the *New York Times*, refers to the terrorist acts obliquely as "certain adventurist Israeli intelligence operations"—the standard formulation—in a highly regarded article on the "beautiful Israel" of pre-Begin days.[66] The nature of the attack on the *Liberty* was also evaded not only by the press fairly generally but by the government and by a U.S. Naval Board of Inquiry, though high-ranking figures had no doubt that the official report was a whitewash; former chairman of the Joint Chiefs of Staff Admiral Thomas H. Moorer, for example, states that the attack "could not possibly have been a case of mistaken identity," as officially claimed.[67]

Can one imagine that any other country could carry out terrorist bombings of U.S. installations or attack a U.S. ship killing or wounding 100 men with complete impunity, without even critical comment for many years? That is about as likely as that across the spectrum of mainstream opinion, some country (other than our own) should be depicted as guided by a "high moral purpose" through the years, while its enemies are dehumanized and despised, and history is reconstructed to preserve the desired illusions.

* Richard Smith (see note 41). He notes that the only comparable incident in recent years was the Japanese attack upon the U.S. gunboat *Panay* in 1937 in which 3 were killed, and contrasts the "strangely callous" Israeli attitude with the far more forthcoming Japanese reaction, both at the personal and governmental levels. His conclusion is that nations have no friends, only interests; but he overlooks the fact that Japan could not count upon the American intelligentsia to cover up the incident, a privilege that Israel correctly took for granted.

14.

Planning for Global Hegemony

As World War II came to an end, U.S. ideas concerning Latin America were clarified by Secretary of War Henry Stimson (May 1945), in a discussion of how we must eliminate and dismantle all regional systems dominated by any other power, particularly the British, while maintaining and extending our own. With regard to Latin America, he explained privately: "I think that it's not asking too much to have our little region over here [namely, Latin America] which never has bothered anybody."[1]

It should be noted that U.S. officials had a ready explanation for the distinction between control by the U.S. and by other powers. As Abe Fortas explained with regard to U.S. trusteeship plans in the Pacific, which Churchill regarded as a cover for annexation: "When we take over the Marianas and fortify them we are doing so not only on the basis of our own right to do so but as part of our obligation to the security of the world . . . These reservations were being made in the interest of world security rather than of our own security . . . what was good for us was good for the world."[2] On such assumptions, naturally regarded highly by U.S. officials and ideologists, quite a range of actions become legitimate.

In keeping with Stimson's conception, the Joint Chiefs of Staff, through 1945 and early 1946, insisted that non-American forces must be kept out of the Western Hemisphere, which "is a distinct military entity, the integrity of which is a fundamental postulate of our security in the event of another world war."[3] In January 1947, Secretary of War Patterson added that the resources

---

This chapter first appeared in *Turning the Tide: U.S. Intervention in Central America and the Struggle for Peace* (Cambridge, MA: South End Press, 1985), 62–73.

of Latin America were essential to the U.S. because "it is imperative that our war potential be enhanced . . . during any national emergency." Patterson gave an expansive interpretation of the Monroe Doctrine, consistent with the Wilson corollary: the Doctrine meant "that we not only refuse to tolerate foreign colonization, control, or the extension of a foreign political system to our hemisphere, but we take alarm from the appearance on the continent of foreign ideologies, commercial exploitation, cartel arrangements, or other symptoms of increased non-hemispheric influence." The U.S. must have "a stable, secure, and friendly flank to the South, not confused by enemy penetration, political, economic or military." The prime concern was not the USSR but rather Europe, including sales of arms by the British to Chile and Ecuador, by Sweden to Argentina, and by France to Argentina and Brazil.

From January 1945, military and civilian officials of the War and Navy departments argued for an extensive system of U.S. bases, curtailment of all foreign military aid and military sales, training of Latin American military officers and supply of arms to Latin America by the United States under a comprehensive military assistance program. While laying these plans for "our little region over here which never has bothered anybody," the United States was in no mood to allow others similar rights elswhere, certainly not the USSR. Secretary of State Byrnes in fact objected to these plans for Latin America because it might prejudice U.S. initiatives elsewhere that he regarded as more important, in particular, in Greece and Turkey, which "are our outposts"—on the borders of the USSR, which had far more serious security concerns than the United States. The "outposts" were also intended to buttress U.S. ambitions in the crucial Middle East region with its incomparable energy reserves, then passing into American hands.

Commenting on an array of material of this sort laying out U.S. plans, much of it classified and recently released, Leffler notes that these moves were made while U.S. officials were "paying lip service to the United Nations and worrying about the impact of regional agreements in the Western Hemisphere on Soviet actions and American influence in Europe." The problem was the one that concerned Stimson: how to extend our own regional systems while dismantling all others, particularly those of Britain and the USSR. The same problems were arising in Europe, where the USSR observed the unilateral United States and British takeover in Italy, Belgium, and elsewhere with equanimity, later using this as a model for its brutal takeover of Eastern Europe, to much outrage in the West—justified, but not lacking in hypocrisy.[4]

The geopolitical conception that underlies Kennan's nutshell presentation of U.S. foreign policy had been elaborated during the war by the War and Peace Studies project of the Council on Foreign Relations, whose thoughts on the suppression of war aims and on "elbow room" were cited earlier.

These high-level sessions took place from 1939–1945, producing extensive plans for the postwar period. Their concern was to elaborate the requirements of the United States "in a world in which it proposes to hold unquestioned power." It was clear by the early 1940s that the United States would emerge from the war in a position of unparalleled dominance, initiating a period in which it would be the "hegemonic power in a system of world order," in the words of an elite group thirty years later.[5] The group developed the concept of the "Grand Area," understood to be a region subordinated to the needs of the U.S. economy. As one participant put it, the Grand Area was a region "strategically necessary for world control." A geopolitical analysis concluded that the Grand Area must include the Western Hemisphere, the Far East, and the former British empire, then being dismantled and opened to U.S. penetration and control—an exercise referred to as "anti-imperialism" in much of the literature.

As the war proceeded, it became clear that Western Europe would join the Grand Area as well as the oil-producing regions of the Middle East, where U.S. control expanded at the expense of its major rivals, France and Britain, a process continued in the postwar period. Specific plans were outlined for particular regions, and institutional structures were proposed for the Grand Area, which was regarded as a nucleus or model that could be extended, optimally to a global system.[6] It is in this context that Kennan's proposals should be understood.

The memoranda of the National Security Council and other government documents in subsequent years often closely follow the recommendations of the wartime planners, not surprisingly, since the same interests were represented, often the same people. They also accord with Kennan's principles. For example, NSC 48/1 in December 1949 states that "While scrupulously avoiding assumption of responsibility for raising Asiatic living standards, it is to the U.S. interest to promote the ability of these countries to maintain . . . the economic conditions prerequisite to political stability." Thus in accordance with Kennan's precepts, we should not be "hampered by idealistic slogans" about "the raising of the living standards," though economic aid may be in order when we have something to gain by it.

It is not, of course, proposed that we should assist—or even permit—the nationalist movement of Vietnam to achieve economic health and political stability; on the contrary, a State Department Policy Statement of September 1948 had explained that it is "an unpleasant fact" that "Communist Ho Chi Minh is the strongest and perhaps the ablest figure in Indochina and that any suggested solution which excludes him is an expedient of uncertain outcome," a serious problem, since plainly we must seek to exclude him in pursuit of the Fifth Freedom.[7] Political stability under his leadership was not what was contemplated. Rather, "stability" is a code word for obedience. Those familiar with the peculiar terminology of U.S. ideological discourse will understand that it is no contradiction when James Chace, editor of *Foreign Affairs*, cites "our efforts to destabilize a freely elected Marxist government in Chile" as an illustration of the efforts of Nixon-Kissinger *Realpolitik* "to seek stability."[8] Destabilization in the interest of stability makes perfect sense in the age of Orwell. The problem, when noted, is placed under the rubric of "irony" in mainstream commentary, including much scholarship.[9]

NSC 48/1 proceeds to develop the conventional explanation found in secret documents of the period for U.S. participation in the French war against Indochina, then the U.S. takeover of that war. The reasoning, which extends directly to Latin America, merits attention. Despite references by Eisenhower and others to Vietnam's resources, Indochina was not of major concern in itself. Rather, its importance derived from the context of the domino theory. This theory has two versions. One, invoked when there is a need to frighten the public, warns that if we don't stop them there, they'll land in California and take all we have. As expressed by President Lyndon Johnson at the height of U.S. aggression in Vietnam:

> There are 3 billion people in the world and we have only 200 million of them. We are outnumbered 15 to one. If might did make right they would sweep over the United States and take what we have. We have what they want.

"If we are going to have visits from any aggressors or any enemies," Johnson said in a speech in Alaska, "I would rather have that aggression take place out 10,000 miles from here than take place here in Anchorage," referring to the aggression of the Vietnamese against U.S. forces in Vietnam. Therefore, as he had warned twenty years earlier, we must maintain our military strength, particularly air power: "without superior air power America is a bound and throttled giant; impotent and easy prey to any yellow dwarf with a pocket knife."[10]

The sense that we will be "a pitiful, helpless giant" unless we act forthrightly in defense against the overwhelming power of our Third World adversaries, in the terms used later by President Nixon in announcing the invasion of Cambodia, is a common refrain in U.S. political discourse, reminiscent of a rich and spoiled child who whines that he does not have *everything*—though to render the image more accurate, we should place a squadron of storm troopers at the child's command.

This version of the domino theory is undoubtedly believed at some level of consciousness, and expresses in a vulgar way the concerns over maintaining the "disparity" outlined in more sophisticated terms by Kennan at the time when Lyndon Johnson was voicing his fears about the "yellow dwarves." This crude domino theory is, however, regularly dismissed with scorn if things go sour and policy must be revised. But there is also a rational version of the domino theory, the operative version, which is rarely questioned and has considerable plausibility; adopting the terminology of the planners, we might call it the "rotten apple theory." The rotten apple theory was outlined by Dean Acheson when he concocted a remarkable series of fabrications concerning alleged Soviet pressure on Greece, Turkey, and Iran in February 1947 in a successful effort to convince reluctant congressional leaders to support the Truman Doctrine, an incident that he cites with much pride in his memoirs; "Like apples in a barrel infected by one rotten one, the corruption of Greece would infect Iran and all to the east" and would "carry infection" to Asia Minor, Egypt, and Africa, as well as Italy and France, which were "threatened" by Communist participation in democratic politics.[11] This adroit and cynical invocation of a fabricated "Russian threat" to prepare the way for measures to prevent "infection" from spreading has been imitated with great efficacy since.

The prime concern throughout is that if there is one rotten apple in the barrel, then "the rot will spread," namely, the "rot" of successful social and economic development of a form that would constrain the Fifth Freedom. This might have a demonstration effect. To cite another case, Kissinger's aides recall that he was far more concerned over Allende in Chile than over Castro because "Allende was a living example of democratic social reform in Latin America," and Allende's success within the democratic process might cause Latin America to become "unraveled" with effects as far as Europe, where Eurocommunism, operating within parliamentary democracy, "scared him" no less. Allende's success would send the wrong message to Italian voters, Kissinger feared. The "contagious example" of Chile would "infect" not only Latin America but also southern Europe, Kissinger stated, using the conventional imagery.[12] Soon, we might find that the Grand Area is beginning to erode.

These concerns are persistent. The CIA warned in 1964 that "Cuba's experiment with almost total state socialism is being watched closely by other nations in the hemisphere and any appearance of success there would have an extensive impact on the statist trend elsewhere in the area," to the detriment of the Fifth Freedom.[13] Hence the appearance of success must be aborted by a major terrorist war including repeated attempts to assassinate Castro, bombing of petrochemical and other installations, sinking of fishing boats, shelling of hotels, crop and livestock poisoning, destruction of civilian airlines in flight, etc.

We might observe that none of this counts as "terrorism," by definition, since the United States or its associates are the perpetrators. In fact, it is a staple of Western propaganda that the Communist bloc is immune to terrorist acts, sure proof that they are responsible for this scourge of the modern age. Walter Laqueur, for example, writes that Claire Sterling, who pioneered this concept to much acclaim, has provided "ample evidence" that terrorism occurs "almost exclusively in democratic or relatively democratic countries"; as examples of such "multinational terrorism" he cites Polisario in the western Sahara (its defense of its territory counts as terrorism, since it is fighting a takeover by Morocco, a U.S. ally), and also terrorism in "some Central American countries," referring, as the context makes clear, to the guerrilla forces, not the state terrorism of El Salvador and Guatemala, which are apparently "relatively democratic countries," like Morocco, and being U.S. clients, by definition cannot be engaged in terrorism. Similarly, the London *Economist* notes sagely in reviewing Sterling's *Terror Network* that "no terrorist has ever attempted anything against the Soviet-controlled regimes." Many others also chimed in, and the point is now a cliché of learned discourses on the topic.[14] In the real world, Cuba has been the major target of international terrorism, narrowly construed to exclude the U.S. proxy war against Nicaragua.

Returning to the rotten apple theory, the State Department warned in 1959 that "a fundamental source of danger we face in the Far East derives from Communist China's rate of economic growth," while the Joint Chiefs added that "the dramatic economic improvements realized by Communist China over the past ten years impress the nations of the region greatly and offer a serious challenge to the Free World." Similar fears were expressed concerning North Vietnam and North Korea. The conclusion drawn was that the United States must do what it can to retard the economic progress of the Communist Asian states.[15]

The larger concern was Japan—the "superdomino" as John Dower called it. Japan, it was recognized, would become again the "workshop of Asia," but requires access to raw materials and markets. We must therefore guarantee Japan such access, so that the entire region can be incorporated within the Grand Area instead of developing as part of a "new order" with Japan as its industrial center, from which the United States might be excluded; concern over this prospect was a factor in the complex interactions that led to the Japanese-American war. But, it was feared, social and economic development in Indochina in terms that might be meaningful to the Asian poor might cause the rot to spread through Southeast and South Asia, leading Japan to associate itself with a bloc of nations independent of the Grand Area, or even worse, to accommodate to the Soviet bloc. A 1949 report of the State Department Policy Planning Staff urged that Washington should "develop the economic interdependence between [Southeast Asia] as a supplier of raw materials, and Japan, Western Europe and India as suppliers of finished goods . . . ," so that "the region could begin to fulfill its major function as a source of raw materials and a market for Japan and Western Europe."[16] In this context, Vietnam gained a significance as a rotten apple that it did not have for American planners on its own.

Such thinking is not original to American planners; similar concerns had been evoked, for example, by the American revolution. A few days before the Monroe Doctrine was announced, the Czar of Russia warned:

> Too many examples demonstrate that the contagion of revolutionary principles is arrested by neither distance nor physical obstacles. It crosses the seas, and often appears with all the symptoms of destruction which characterize it, in places where not even any direct contact, any relation of proximity might give ground for apprehension. France knows with what facility and promptitude a revolution can be carried from America to Europe.

Metternich feared that the Monroe Doctrine would "lend new strength to the apostles of sedition, and reanimate the courage of every conspirator. If this flood of evil doctrines and pernicious examples should extend over the whole of America, what would become of our religious and political institutions, of the moral force of our governments, and of that conservative system which has saved Europe from complete dissolution?" One of the Czar's diplomats warned that "we must work to prevent or defer this terrible revolution, and above all to save and fortify the portion [of the Christian world] which may escape the contagion and the invasion of vicious principles," namely, "the pernicious doctrines of republicanism and popular self-rule."[17]

The contemporary heirs of Metternich and the Czar are animated by similar fears, and have even adopted similar rhetoric—in Kissinger's case, perhaps with full awareness—as the United States took over the role of the Czar in the nineteenth century as the defender of "civilization" against the yellow dwarves and others whose pretensions threaten the "disparity."

Note incidentally that the United States achieved its major objectives in Indochina: it is a mistake to describe the Vietnam war simply as a U.S. "defeat," as is commonly done, a fact that became evident as the war reached its peak of violence in the late 1960s. The devastation of Indochina by U.S. violence guarantees that it will not be a model for anyone for a long time to come, if ever. It will be lucky to survive. The harsh and cruel measures undertaken by the United States in the past decade are intended to ensure that this partial victory is maintained.[18] Meanwhile, behind the "shield" provided by the destruction of South Vietnam, then much of Indochina, the United States worked to buttress the second line of defense by supporting a military coup in Indonesia in 1965 that wiped out hundreds of thousands of landless peasants (a development much applauded by Western liberals as vindication of the war against

Vietnam), backing the imposition of a Latin American-style terror-and-torture state in the Philippines in 1972, etc.

A further useful consequence of the attack against South Vietnam, Laos, and Cambodia was to ensure North Vietnamese dominance. It was clear enough by 1970, if not before, that "by employing the vast resources of violence and terror at its command" the United States might be able to destroy the NLF in South Vietnam and independent forces in Laos and Cambodia, thus "creat[ing] a situation in which, indeed, North Vietnam will necessarily dominate Indochina, for no other viable society will remain."[19] This predictable consequence of U.S. savagery is regularly invoked in retrospective justification for it, another ideological victory that would have impressed Orwell. Note that this achievement is a special case of the device discussed earlier: when conquest fails, efforts are made to encourage assimilation to the Soviet bloc, to justify further hostile acts, and to limit the danger that independence and success will "infect" others.

Still another notable achievement of U.S. violence was to ensure control by the harshest elements, those capable of surviving an attack of extraordinary barbarism and destructiveness; people whose homes and families are destroyed by a cruel invader have a way of becoming angry, even brutal, a fact that Westerners profess not to comprehend, having effectively suppressed the memory of their own behavior under far less onerous circumstances.[20] Then their terrible acts can be invoked to justify the attack that helped to create this outcome. With a docile intelligentsia and well-behaved ideological institutions, Western Agitprop can achieve quite notable results.

The United States is intent on winning its war against Nicaragua in the same way. Nicaragua must first be driven to dependence on the USSR, to justify the attack that must be launched against it to punish it for its violation of the Fifth Freedom. If this attack does not succeed in restoring the country to the happy state of Haiti or the Dominican Republic, or of the Somoza years, then at least it must ensure that no successful social and economic development can take place there; the rotten apple must not be allowed to infect the barrel. It is very hard for a great power with the strength of the United States to be defeated in a conflict with such adversaries, and it rarely is, though a failure to achieve maximal objectives is naturally regarded as a great defeat by those of limitless ambition and aims, further proof that we are a pitiful, helpless giant at the mercy of yellow dwarves.

The same essentially invariant nexus of principles and assumptions, often internalized to the point of lack of conscious awareness, explains another curious feature of U.S. international behavior: the hysteria evoked by threats to "stability" in countries of no economic or strategic interest to the United States, such as Laos or Grenada. In the case of Grenada, U.S. hostility was immediate after the Bishop government took power in 1979. It was seriously maintained that this speck in the Caribbean posed a security threat to the United States. Distinguished military figures and commentators issued solemn pronouncements on the threat posed by Grenada to shipping lanes in the event of a Soviet attack on Western Europe; in fact, in this event, if a Russian toothpick were found on Grenada the island would be blown away, on the unlikely assumption that such a war would last long enough for anyone to care. Laos, halfway round the world, is perhaps a still more remarkable case. Laos actually had a relatively free election in 1958, despite massive U.S. efforts to subvert it. The election was won by a coalition dominated by the Pathet Lao, the Communist-led anti-French guerrillas. The government was immediately overthrown by U.S. subversion in favor of "pro-western neutralists," soon replaced by right-wing military elements so reactionary and corrupt that even the pro-American groups found themselves lined up with the Pathet Lao, and supported by the USSR and China. By 1961, a U.S.-organized army of highland tribesmen (utterly decimated, finally, as a result of their mobilization for U.S. subversion and aggression) was fighting under the leadership of former French collaborators under CIA control. Through the sixties, Pathet Lao-controlled areas were subjected to the fiercest bombing in history (soon to be exceeded in Cambodia), in an effort "to destroy the physical and social infrastructure" (in the words of a Senate subcommittee). The government conceded that this bombardment was not related to the war in South Vietnam or Cambodia. This was what is called in American Agitprop a "secret bombing"—a technical term referring to U.S. aggression that is well-known but concealed by the media, and later blamed on evil men in the government who have departed from the American Way—as also in the case of Cambodia, a fact that is suppressed until today. The purpose of this attack against a country of scattered villages, against people who may not have even known that Laos existed, was to abort a mild revolutionary-nationalist movement that was attempting to bring about some reforms and popular mobilization in northern Laos.[21]

Why should such great powers as Grenada and Laos evoke this hysteria? The security arguments are too ludicrous to consider, and it is surely not the case that their resources were too valuable to lose, under the doctrine of the Fifth Freedom. Rather, the concern was the domino effect. Under the rotten apple theory, it follows that the tinier and weaker the country, the less endowed it is with resources, the more dangerous it is. If even a marginal and impoverished country can begin to utilize its own limited human and material resources and can undertake programs of development geared to the needs of the domestic population, then others may ask: why not us? The contagion may spread, infecting others, and before long the Fifth Freedom may be threatened in places that matter.

15.

The View Beyond: Prospects for the Study of Mind

I began these lectures by posing four central questions that arise in the study of language:

1. What do we know when we are able to speak and understand a language?
2. How is this knowledge acquired?
3. How do we use this knowledge?
4. What are the physical mechanisms involved in the representation, acquisition, and use of this knowledge?

The first question is logically prior to the others. We can proceed with the investigation of questions 2, 3, and 4 to the extent that we have some understanding of the answer to question 1.

The task of answering question 1 is basically descriptive: In pursuing it, we attempt to construct a grammar, a theory of a particular language that describes how this language assigns specific mental representations to each linguistic expression, determining its form and meaning. The second and much harder task carries us beyond, to the level of genuine explanation. In pursuing it, we attempt to construct a theory of universal grammar, a theory of the fixed and invariant principles that constitute the human language faculty and

---

This chapter first appeared in *Language and Problems of Knowledge: The Managua Lectures* (Cambridge, MA: MIT Press, 1988), 133–70.

the parameters of variation associated with them. We can then, in effect, deduce particular languages by setting the parameters in one or another way. Furthermore, given the lexicon, which also satisfies the principles of universal grammar, and with the parameters set in a particular way, we can explain why the sentences of these languages have the form and meaning they do by deriving their structured representations from the principles of universal grammar.

Question 2 is the special case of Plato's problem that arises in the study of language. We can solve the problem to the extent that we succeed in constructing the theory of universal grammar, though other factors are also involved, for example, the mechanisms of parameter setting. Other special cases of Plato's problem, in other domains, will have to be addressed in much the same fashion.

Language learning, then, is the process of determining the values of the parameters left unspecified by universal grammar, of setting the switches that make the network function, to use the image I mentioned earlier. Beyond that, the language learner must discover the lexical items of the language and their properties. To a large extent this seems to be a problem of finding what labels are used for preexisting concepts, a conclusion that is so surprising as to seem outrageous but that appears to be essentially correct nevertheless.

Language learning is not really something that the child does; it is something that happens to the child placed in an appropriate environment, much as the child's body grows and matures in a predetermined way when provided with appropriate nutrition and environmental stimulation. This is not to say that the nature of the environment is irrelevant. The environment determines the way the parameters of universal grammar are set, yielding different languages. In a somewhat similar way the early visual environment determines the density of receptors for horizontal and vertical lines, as has been shown experimentally. Furthermore, the difference between a rich and stimulating environment and an impoverished environment may be substantial, in language acquisition as in physical growth or, more accurately, as in other aspects of physical growth, the acquisition of language being simply one of these aspects. Capacities that are part of our common human endowment can flourish or can be restricted and suppressed, depending on the conditions provided for their growth.

The point is probably more general. It is a traditional insight, which merits more attention than it receives, that teaching should not be compared to filling a bottle with water but rather to helping a flower to grow in its own way. As any good teacher knows, the methods of instruction and the range of material covered are matters of small importance as compared with the success in arousing the natural curiosity of the students and stimulating their interest in exploring on their own. What the student learns passively will be quickly forgotten. What students discover for themselves when their natural curiosity and creative impulses are aroused not only will be remembered but will be the basis for further exploration and inquiry and perhaps significant intellectual contributions. A truly democratic community is one in which the general public has the opportunity for meaningful and constructive participation in the formation of social policy: in their own immediate community, in the workplace, and in the society at large. A society that excludes large areas of crucial decision making from public control, or a system of governance that merely grants the general public the opportunity to ratify decisions taken by the elite groups that dominate the private society and the state, hardly merits the term "democracy."

Question 3 has two aspects: the perception aspect and the production aspect. Thus we would like to know how people who have acquired a language put their knowledge to use in understanding what they hear and in expressing their thoughts. I have touched on the perception aspect of the question in these lectures. But I have said nothing so far about the production aspect, what I called Descartes's problem, the problem posed by the creative aspect of language use, a normal and commonplace but quite remarkable phenomenon. For a person to understand a linguistic expression, the mind/brain must determine its phonetic form and its words and then use the principles of universal grammar and the values of the parameters to project a structured representation of this expression and determine how its parts are associated. I have given a number of examples to illustrate how this process might take place. Descartes's problem, however, raises other issues that lie beyond anything we have discussed.

As for question 4, I have said nothing. Inquiry into this problem is largely a task for the future. Part of the problem in undertaking such inquiry is that experiments with human subjects are excluded for ethical reasons. We do not tolerate experimental study of humans in the manner regarded as legitimate (rightly or wrongly) in the case of animal subjects. Thus children are not raised in controlled environments to see what kind of language would develop under various experimentally devised conditions. We do not permit researchers to implant electrodes in the human brain to investigate its internal operations or to remove parts of the brain surgically to determine what the effects would be, as is done routinely in the case of nonhuman subjects. Researchers are restricted to "nature's experiments": injury, disease, and so on. To attempt to discover brain mechanisms under these conditions is extremely difficult.

In the case of other systems of the mind/brain, the human visual system, for example, the experimental study of other organisms (cats, monkeys, etc.) is highly informative because the visual systems are apparently quite similar among these species. But as far as we know, the language faculty is a distinctive human possession. Study of the brain mechanisms of other animals tells us little if anything about this faculty of the mind/brain.

The answers to these four questions that we would be inclined to give today (or at least, that we *should* be inclined to give today, in my view) are quite different from those that were accepted with little controversy as recently as a generation ago. To the extent that these questions were even posed, the answers offered would then have been something like the following. Language is a habit system, a system of dispositions to behavior, acquired through training and conditioning. Any innovative aspects of this behavior are the result of "analogy." The physical mechanisms are essentially those involved in catching a ball and other skilled performances. Plato's problem was unrecognized or dismissed as trivial. It was generally believed that language is "overlearned"; the problem is to account for the fact that so much experience and training are needed to establish such simple skills. As for Descartes's problem, it too was unrecognized within academic circles, the applied disciplines, and the intellectual community at large.

Attention to the facts quickly demonstrates that these ideas are not simply in error but entirely beyond any hope of repair. They must be abandoned, as essentially worthless. One has to turn to the domain of ideology to find comparable instances of a collection of ideas accepted so widely and with so little question, and so utterly divorced from the real world. And, in fact, that is the direction in which we should turn if we are interested in finding out how and why these myths achieved the respectability accorded to them, how they came to dominate such a large part of intellectual life and discourse. That is an interesting topic, one well worth pursuing, but I will not undertake this project here, apart from a few comments later on.

Let us return to Descartes's problem, the problem of how language is used in the normal creative fashion, as I described earlier. Notice that I am not concerned here with use of language that has true aesthetic value, with what we call true creativity, as in the work of a fine poet or novelist or an exceptional stylist. Rather, what I have in mind is something more mundane: the ordinary use of language in everyday life, with its distinctive properties of novelty, freedom from control by external stimuli and inner states, coherence and appropriateness to situations, and its capacity to evoke appropriate thoughts in the listener. The history of this problem is of some interest.

The issue arose in the context of the mind-body problem or, more specifically, what was later called "the problem of other minds." Descartes developed a mechanical theory of the universe, a major contribution to the physical sciences of his day. He convinced himself that virtually everything that takes place in the universe of our experience can be explained in terms of his mechanical conceptions, in terms of bodies that interact through direct contact—a "contact mechanics" we might call it. In these terms he sought to explain everything from the motion of the heavenly bodies to the behavior of animals and much of the behavior and perception of humans as well. He apparently felt that he had largely succeeded in this task and that all that remained was to fill in the details in his overarching conceptions. But not all our experience could be accommodated within this framework. The most striking exception, he suggested, was what I called earlier the creative aspect of language use. This falls entirely beyond the conceptions of mechanics, so Descartes argued.

Through introspection, each person can perceive that he or she has a mind, which is quite distinct in its properties from the bodies that constitute the physical world. Suppose now that I want to determine whether another creature also has a mind. The Cartesians proposed that in this case, one should undertake a certain experimental program, designed to determine whether this organism exhibits distinctive features of human behavior, the creative aspect of language use being the most striking example and the one most readily investigated. If the organs of a parrot are placed in a certain configuration under given stimulus conditions, the Cartesians argued, what the parrot "says" is strictly determined (or it may be random). But this is not true of an organism with a mind like ours, and experiment should be able to reveal this fact. Many specific tests were proposed. If these tests convince us that the organism exhibits the creative aspect of language use, then it would be unreasonable to doubt that it has a mind like ours.

More generally, as I mentioned earlier, the problem is that a "machine" is compelled to act in a certain way under fixed environmental conditions and with its parts arranged in a certain way, while a human under these circumstances is only "incited and inclined" to behave in this fashion. The human may often, or even always, do what it is incited or inclined to do, but each of us knows from introspection that we have a choice in the matter over a large range. And we can determine by experiment that this is true of other humans as well. The difference between being *compelled*, and merely being *incited and inclined*, is a crucial one, the Cartesians concluded—and quite accurately. The distinction would remain crucial even if it were not manifested in actual behavior. If it were not, one could give an accurate description of human behavior in mechanical terms, but it would not be a true characterization of essential features of the human being and of the sources of human behavior.

To account for the facts about the world that surpass the possibilities of mechanical explanation, it is necessary to find some extramechanical principle, what we might call a creative principle. This principle, the Cartesians argued, belongs to mind, a "second substance" entirely separate from body, which is subject to mechanical explanation. Descartes himself wrote a lengthy treatise in which he laid out the principles of the mechanical world. It was to include a final volume devoted to the mind, but allegedly Descartes destroyed this part of his comprehensive work when he learned of the fate of Galileo before the Inquisition, which compelled him to renounce his beliefs about the physical world. In his preserved writings Descartes suggests that we may not "have intelligence enough" to discover the nature of mind, although "we are so conscious of the liberty and indifference [absence of strict determination] which exists in us that there is nothing that we comprehend more clearly and perfectly," and "it would be absurd to doubt that of which we inwardly experience and perceive as existing within ourselves just because we do not comprehend a matter which from its nature we know to be incomprehensible."

For the Cartesians, mind is a single substance, distinct from body. Much of the speculation and debate of the period dealt with the question of how these two substances interact—how the decisions of the mind might lead to actions of the body, for example. There is no such thing as an "animal mind" because animals are merely machines, subject to mechanical explanation. There is no possibility in this conception of a *human mind* as distinct from other kinds of mind, or of differently constituted human minds. A creature is either human or it is not; there are no "degrees of humanness," no essential variation among humans apart from superficial physical aspects. As the philosopher Harry Bracken has pointed out, racism or sexism is a logical impossibility under this dualist conception.

The mind, Descartes held, is a "universal instrument which can serve for all contingencies." Notice that this claim is not consistent with his belief that we may not have intelligence enough to discover the nature of mind. The conclusion that the mind has intrinsic limits is surely the correct one; the idea that it is a "universal instrument" might be regarded as one of the ancestors of the widely held belief that the human language faculty, and other cognitive systems, all fall within the bounds of "general learning mechanisms" that are applicable to every intellectual task.

The Cartesian tests for the existence of other minds have been resurrected in a new guise in recent years, most notably by the British mathematician Alan Turing, who devised what is now called the Turing test, to determine whether a machine (for example, a programmed computer) exhibits intelligent behavior. We apply the Turing test to a device by submitting to it a series of questions and asking whether its responses can deceive a human observer who will conclude that the responses are being offered by another human being. In Cartesian terms this would be a test of whether the device has a mind like ours.

How should we respond today to these ideas? Descartes's argument is far from absurd and cannot easily be discounted. If indeed the principles of mechanics do not suffice to explain certain phenomena, then we must appeal to something beyond these principles to explain them. So far, that is familiar science. We need not accept the Cartesian metaphysics, which required postulation of a "second substance," a "thinking substance" (*res cogitans*), undifferentiated, without components or interacting subparts, the seat of consciousness that accounts for the "unity of consciousness" and the immortality of the soul. All of this is entirely unsatisfying and provides no real answer to any of the problems raised. The problems themselves, however, are quite serious ones, and much as Descartes held, it would be absurd to deny the facts that are apparent to us merely because we can conceive of no way of solving them.

It is interesting to observe the fate of the Cartesian version of the mind-body problem and the problem of the existence of other minds. The mind-body problem can be posed sensibly only insofar as we have a definite conception of body. If we have no such definite and fixed conception, we cannot ask whether some phenomena fall beyond its range. The Cartesians offered a fairly definite conception of body in terms of their contact mechanics, which in many respects reflects commonsense understanding. Therefore they could sensibly formulate the mind-body problem and the problem of other minds. There was important work attempting to develop the concept of mind further, including studies by British Neoplatonists of the seventeenth century that explored the categories and principles of perception and cognition along lines that were later extended by Kant and that were rediscovered, independently, in twentieth-century gestalt psychology.

Another line of development was the "general and philosophical grammar" (in our terms, scientific grammar) of the seventeenth, eighteenth, and early nineteenth centuries, which was much influenced by Cartesian conceptions, particularly in the early period. These inquiries into universal grammar sought to lay bare the general principles of language. These were regarded as not essentially different from the general principles of thought, so that language is "a mirror of mind," in the conventional phrase. For various reasons—some good, some not—these inquiries were disparaged and abandoned for a century, to be resurrected, again independently, a generation ago, though in quite different terms and without recourse to any dualist assumptions.

It is also interesting to see how the Cartesian conception of body and mind entered social thought, most strikingly in the libertarian ideas of Jean-Jacques Rousseau, which were based on strictly Cartesian conceptions of body and mind. Because humans, possessing minds, are crucially distinct from machines (including animals), so Rousseau argued, and because the properties of mind crucially surpass mechanical determinacy, therefore any infringement on human freedom is illegitimate and must be confronted and overcome. Although the later development of such thinking abandoned the Cartesian framework, its origins lie in significant measure in these classical ideas.

The Cartesian conception of a second substance was generally abandoned in later years, but it is important to recognize that it was not the theory of mind that was refuted (one might argue that it was hardly clear enough to be confirmed or refuted). Rather, the Cartesian concept of *body* was refuted by seventeenth-century physics, particularly in the work of Isaac Newton, which laid the foundations for modern science. Newton demonstrated that the motions of the heavenly bodies could not be explained by the principles of Descartes's contact mechanics, so that the Cartesian concept of body must be abandoned. In the Newtonian framework there is a "force" that one body exerts on another, without contact between them, a kind of "action at a distance." Whatever this force may be, it does not fall within the Cartesian framework of contact mechanics. Newton himself found this conclusion unsatisfying. He sometimes referred to gravitational force as "occult" and suggested that his theory gave only a mathematical description of events in the physical world, not a true "philosophical" (in more modern terminology, "scientific") explanation of these events. Until the late nineteenth century it was still widely held that a true explanation must be framed somehow in mechanical or quasi-mechanical terms. Others, notably the chemist and philosopher Joseph Priestley, argued that bodies themselves possess capacities that go beyond the limits of contact mechanics, specifically the property of attracting other bodies, but perhaps far more. Without pursuing subsequent developments further, the general conclusion is that the Cartesian concept of body was found to be untenable.

What is the concept of body that finally emerged? The answer is that there is no clear and definite concept of body. If the best theory of the material world that we can construct includes a variety of forces, particles that have no mass, and other entities that would have been offensive to the "scientific common sense" of the Cartesians, then so be it: We conclude that these are properties of the physical world, the world of body. The conclusions are tentative, as befits empirical hypotheses, but are not subject to criticism because they transcend some a priori conception of body. There is no longer any definite conception of body. Rather, the material world is whatever we discover it to be, with whatever properties it must be assumed to have for the purposes of explanatory theory. Any intelligible theory that offers genuine explanations and that can be assimilated to the core notions of physics becomes part of the theory of the material world, part of our account of body. If we have such a theory in some domain, we seek to assimilate it to the core notions of physics, perhaps modifying these notions as we carry out this enterprise. In the study of human psychology, if we develop a theory of some cognitive faculty (the language faculty, for example) and find that this faculty has certain properties, we seek to discover the mechanisms of the brain that exhibit these properties and to account for them in the terms of the physical sciences—keeping open the possibility that the concepts of the physical sciences might have to be modified, just as the concepts of Cartesian contact mechanics had to be modified to account for the motion of the heavenly bodies, and as has happened repeatedly in the evolution of the natural sciences since Newton's day.

In short, there is no definite concept of body. Rather, there is a material world, the properties of which are to be discovered, with no a priori demarcation of what will count as "body." The mind-body problem can therefore not even be formulated. The problem cannot be solved, because there is no clear way to state it. Unless someone proposes a definite concept of body, we cannot ask whether some phenomena exceed its bounds. Similarly, we cannot pose the problem of other minds. We can, and I think should, continue to use mentalistic terminology, as I have done throughout in discussing mental representations and operations that form and modify them in mental computation. But we do not see ourselves as investigating the properties of some "second substance," something crucially distinct from body that interacts with body in some mysterious way, perhaps through divine intervention. Rather, we are studying the properties of the material world at a level of abstraction at which we believe, rightly or wrongly, that a genuine explanatory theory can be constructed, a theory that provides genuine insight into the nature of the phenomena that concern us. These phenomena, in fact, are of real intellectual interest not so much in themselves but in the avenue that they provide for us to penetrate into the deeper workings of the mind. Ultimately, we hope to assimilate this study to the mainstream of the natural sciences, much as the study of genes or of valence and the properties of the chemical elements was assimilated to more fundamental sciences. We recognize, however, that, as in the past, it may turn out that these fundamental sciences must be modified or extended to provide foundations for the abstract theories of complex systems, such as the human mind.

Our task, then, is to discover genuine explanatory theories and to use these discoveries to facilitate inquiry into physical mechanisms with the properties outlined in these theories. Wherever this inquiry leads, it will be within the domain of "body." Or more accurately, we simply abandon the whole conception of body as possibly distinct from something else and use the methods of rational inquiry to learn as much as we can about the world—what we call the material world, whatever exotic properties it turns out to have.

The mind-body problem remains the subject of much controversy, debate, and speculation, and in this regard the problem is still very much alive. But the discussion seems to me incoherent in fundamental respects. Unlike the Cartesians, we have no definite concept of body. It is therefore quite unclear how we can even ask whether some phenomena lie beyond the range of the study of body, falling within the separate study of mind.

Recall the logic of Descartes's argument for the existence of a second substance, *res cogitans*. Having defined "body" in terms of contact mechanics, he argued that certain phenomena lie beyond its domain, so that some new principle was required; given his metaphysics, a second substance must be postulated. The logic is essentially sound; it is, in fact, much like Newton's, when he demonstrated the inadequacy of Cartesian contact mechanics for the explanation of the motion of the heavenly bodies so that a new principle, the principle of gravitational attraction, had to be postulated. The crucial difference between the Cartesian and the Newtonian enterprises was that the latter offered a genuine explanatory theory of the behavior of bodies, whereas the Cartesian theory offered no satisfactory account of properties such the creative aspect of language use that lie beyond mechanical explanation in Descartes's view. Therefore Newton's conceptions came to be the "scientific common sense" of later generations of scientists, while Descartes's fell by the wayside.

Returning now to Descartes's problem, notice that it still stands, unresolved by these developments in the natural sciences. We still have no way to come to terms with what appears to be a fact, even an obvious fact: Our actions are free and undetermined, in that we need not do what we are "incited and inclined" to do; and if we do what we are incited and inclined to do, an element of free choice nevertheless enters. Despite much thought and often penetrating analysis, it seems to me that this problem still remains unsolved, much in the way Descartes formulated it. Why should this be so?

One possibility, of course, is that no one has yet thought of the right idea that will yield a solution to the problem. That is possible, but it is not the only possibility. Another possibility is the one suggested by Descartes: The problem escapes our intellectual grasp.

When we investigate other organisms, we discover that their capacities have a certain scope and certain limits. Thus a rat can do certain things very well. Suppose that we construct a radial maze, an experimental design consisting of a center with straight paths leading from it much like the spokes of a wheel. Suppose that at the end of each path there is a container with a single pellet of food. A rat placed in the center can quickly learn to obtain the food with maximal efficiency, running through each path only once. This remains true even if the device is rotated, leaving the food containers fixed, so that the rate has to traverse the same physical path more than once. This is no mean accomplishment; it requires rather sophisticated spatial concepts. On the other hand, rats apparently cannot learn to run mazes that involve sequential concepts (for example, turn right twice, then turn left twice). Surely, no rat could learn to run a maze that required turning right at every choice point corresponding to a prime number, left elsewhere: thus turn right at the second, third, fifth, seventh, eleventh, etc., choice point. A human could presumably solve this problem, though not without difficulty and not without conscious knowledge of arithmetic. Putting particular examples aside, it is obvious that the rat (pigeon, monkey, etc.) has fixed capacities, with a definite scope and definite limits.

The point is a logical one. If a creature has the capacity to perform certain tasks well, then these very capacities will lead to failure in some other tasks. If we can learn what these capacities are, we can design problems that the creature will be unable to solve, because they fall beyond its capacities. A creature is fortunate if there are problems that it cannot solve, because this means that it has the capacity to solve certain other problems well. The distinction may be one of ease or difficulty, or it may be one of possibility versus literal impossibility. But the distinction must exist, as a matter of logic. The nature of the distinction is a matter of fact; the existence of such distinctions cannot be in doubt.

Furthermore, a problem that is readily solved by one organism may be too difficult or impossible for another. We can, for example, easily design a device that will solve the "prime number maze" and do so instantaneously and without effort or trials, namely, by building the answer into the mechanisms themselves. But this device will not be able to solve what we regard as much simpler mazes. Organisms are not arrayed along a spectrum, with some "more intelligent" than others, simply capable of solving more complex problems. Rather, they differ in the array of problems that they are capable of addressing and solving. A certain species of wasp, or a pigeon, is designed to find its way home; a human is not designed in the same way and cannot perform similar tasks readily or at all. It is not that a wasp or pigeon is "more intelligent" than a human; rather, it is different in its biologically determined capacities. Furthermore, there is no clear "absolute sense" in which problems are simple or difficult. It may be possible to formulate an "absolute notion" of difficulty that is useful for certain purposes in terms of the mathematical theory of computation. But it is not clear that this notion would be of much interest for psychology or biology, at least in the present context, because what is important for the behavior of an organism is its special design and the array of "difficulty" of problems that is determined by this special design.

We suppose that humans are part of the natural world. They plainly have the capacity to solve certain problems. It follows that they lack the capacity to solve other problems, which will either be far too difficult for them to handle within existing limitations of time, memory, and so on or will literally be beyond the scope of their intelligence in principle. The human mind cannot be in Descartes's terms a "universal instrument which can serve for all contingencies." That is fortunate, for if it were such a universal instrument, it would serve equally badly for all contingencies. We could deal with no problems at all with any measure of success.

In the case of language, the language faculty, a physical mechanism in the sense already explained, has certain definite properties, not others. These are the properties that the theory of universal grammar seeks to formulate and describe. These properties permit the human mind to acquire a language of a specific type, with curious and surprising features, as we have seen. The same properties exclude other possible languages as "unlearnable" by the language faculty. Possibly a human could come to understand such a nonhuman language by using other faculties of the mind, much in the manner in which humans can come to understand many things about the nature of the physical world through an arduous process of controlled inquiry and experimentation extending over many generations and with the intervention of individual genius (whatever that may be). Other such languages would be beyond the bounds of possible human thought. To the extent that we can discover the properties of the language faculty, we can construct "unlearnable languages," languages that cannot be acquired by the language faculty because at every point it will make the wrong choices, the wrong guesses as to the nature of the language. To the extent that we can discover the properties of other faculties of the mind, we can construct languages that can be acquried only with great difficulty, in the manner of scientific inquiry, or, presumably, not at all, and we can design other tasks that are extremely difficult or insoluble (for human intelligence).

There is nothing particularly mysterious about all of this. Much of what I have just said is a matter of logic. The specific scope and limits of the various faculties of the human mind are matters of fact, matters in principle amenable to human inquiry, unless they transcend the limits of the human mind. We might, someday, even be able to discover that the human mind is so constructed that certain problems, which we can formulate, are beyond the possibility of solution by a human intelligence. Such problems might be quite "simple" for an intelligence differently constructed, just as the prime number maze would have an obvious solution for a device designed to solve this problem.

All of this is transparent in the study of physical growth. Humans are designed to grow arms and legs, not wings. Lacking appropriate nutrition or in an environment that is deficient in other ways, the embryo may fail to grow arms and legs properly, but no change in the environment will lead it to grow wings. If physical growth merely reflected properties of the environment, we would be shapeless, formless creatures, unlike one another, with extremely limited physical capacities. Since our biological endowment is intricate and highly specific, the way we grow does not reflect properties of the physical environment but rather our essential nature. We therefore grow to be complex organisms with quite specific physical properties, very similar to one another in our basic properties, adapted to certain tasks but not to others—walking but not flying, for example. The environment is not irrelevant to growth. Rather, growth is triggered by the environment in numerous ways, stimulated by environmental factors or retarded or distorted if the requisite factors are lacking. But it takes place largely in predetermined ways. We are lucky that we are incapable of becoming birds, because this follows from the fact that we are capable of becoming humans.

There is every reason to suppose that much the same is true of mental development. Indeed, this must be so if we are truly part of the physical world. It follows that we can readily deal with certain problems—learning of human language, for example—while others, which are neither "harder" nor "easier" in any useful absolute terms, are beyond our reach, some of them forever. We are fortunate that this is so.

Let us return again to Descartes's problem. One possible reason for the lack of success in solving it or even presenting sensible ideas about it is that it is not within the range of human intellectual capacities: It is either "too difficult," given the nature of our capacities, or beyond their limits altogether. There is some reason to suspect that this may be so, though we do not know enough about human intelligence or the properties of the problem to be sure. We are able to devise theories to deal with strict determinacy and with randomness. But these concepts do not seem appropriate to Descartes's problem, and it may be that the relevant concepts are not accessible to us. A Martian scientist, with a mind different from ours, might regard this problem as trivial, and wonder why humans never seem to hit on the obvious way of solving it. This observer might also be amazed at the ability of every human child to acquire language, something that seems to him incomprehensible, requiring divine intervention, because the elements of the language faculty lie beyond his conceptual range.

The same is true of the arts. Work of true aesthetic value follows canons and principles that are only in part subject to human choice; in part, they reflect our fundamental nature. The result is that we can experience deep emotion—pleasure, pain, excitement, and so on—from certain creative work, though how and why remains largely unknown. But the very capacities of mind that open these possibilities to us exclude other possibilities, some forever. The limits of artistic creativity should, again, be a matter of joy, not sorrow, because they follow from the fact that there is a rich domain of aesthetic experience to which we have access.

The same is true of moral judgment. What its basis may be we do not know, but we can hardly doubt that it is rooted in fundamental human nature. It cannot be merely a matter of convention that we find some things to be right, others wrong. Growing up in a particular society, a child acquires standards and principles of moral judgment. These are acquired on the basis of limited evidence, but they have broad and often quite precise applicability. It is often though not always true that people can discover or be convinced that their judgments about a particular case are wrong, in the sense that the judgments are inconsistent with the person's own internalized principles. Moral argument is not always pointless, merely a matter of "I assert this" and "you assert that." The acquisition of a specific moral and ethical system, wide ranging and often precise in its consequences, cannot simply be the result of "shaping" and "control" by the social environment. As in the case of language, the environment is far too impoverished and indeterminate to provide this system to the child, in its full richness and applicability. Knowing little about the matter, we are compelled to speculate; but it certainly seems reasonable to speculate that the moral and ethical system acquired by the child owes much to some innate human faculty. The environment is relevant, as in the case of language, vision, and so on; thus we can find individual and cultural divergence. But there is surely a common basis, rooted in our nature.

The course of our own civilization may offer some insight into the matter. Not long ago, slavery was considered legitimate, even estimable; slave owners did not characteristically regard what they were doing as wrong but rather saw it as a proof of their high moral values. Their arguments were, furthermore, not absurd, though we now regard them as morally grotesque. Thus, in the early days of industrial capitalism, slave owners could—and did—point out that if you own a piece of machinery, you are likely to treat it with more care than if you merely rent it. Similarly, the slave owner is likely to treat his possession with more care and solicitude than the capitalist who merely rents people for his temporary purposes. Slavery, then, reflects higher moral standards than "wage slavery." No sane person would now accept this argument, though it is not entirely absurd by any means. As civilization progressed, it came to be understood that slavery is an infringement on essential human rights. We may look forward to the day when wage slavery and the need to rent oneself to survive may be seen in a similar light, as we come to have better understanding of the moral values rooted in our inner nature.

Many of us have experienced something similar during our own lifetimes. Not many years ago the problems of sexism were barely on the agenda. They are far from overcome, but they are at least recognized, and it is widely understood that they must be addressed. This is a change of moral consciousness, probably irrevocable, like the realization that slavery is an intolerable affront to human dignity. It is not merely a change but an advance, an advance toward understanding of our own nature and the moral and ethical principles that derive from it.

There may be no end to such discoveries, if civilization survives. A truly decent and honest person will always seek to discover forms of oppression, hierarchy, domination, and authority that infringe fundamental human rights. As some are overcome, others will be revealed that previously were not part of our conscious awareness. We thus come to a better understanding of who and what we are in our inner nature, and who and what we should be in our actual lives.

This is an optimistic view, and it would not be difficult to bring forth historical evidence that apparently refutes it, but perhaps it is not unrealistic to adopt this perspective in thinking about our history and the prospects for what lies ahead. Moral thought and discourse may not end with such considerations as these. But such considerations should, nevertheless, inform and enrich it.

I mentioned that Rousseau derived libertarian conceptions from Cartesian principles of body and mind. These ideas were developed further in French and German Romanticism, still framed within assumptions about essential human nature. In the libertarian social theory of Wilhelm von Humboldt, who greatly influenced John Stuart Mill (and was also, incidentally, a major figure in linguistics whose ideas are only now coming to be appreciated), it is an essential human right, rooted in the "human essence," to be able to carry out productive and creative work under one's own control in solidarity with others. If a person creates some beautiful object under external direction and control, Humboldt argued, we may admire what he does, but we despise what he is—a machine, not a full human being. Marx's theory of alienated labor, the basis of his social thought, developed from these grounds, and in his early work he too formulated these conceptions in terms of a "species property" that determines certain fundamental human rights: crucially, the right of workers to control production, its nature and conditions. Bakunin argued that humans have "an instinct of freedom" and that infringement on this essential feature of human nature is illegitimate. The tradition of libertarian socialism developed in much these terms. Its conceptions have yet to be realized except in the most limited ways in existing societies, but in my view, at least, they are essentially correct and capture crucial features of essential human nature and the moral code that should be brought to conscious awareness, reflecting these properties.

We might observe that every form of engagement in social life is based on assumptions about human nature, usually only implicit. Adam Smith held that humans are born "to truck and barter" and, on the basis of this and similar assumptions, developed his justification for free market capitalism. The line of thought I have just briefly indicated was based on very different concepts of human nature. In ordinary everyday life the same is true. Suppose that a person decides to accept the status quo, or to try to change it, whether by reform or revolution. If not based simply on fear, greed, or other forms of abdication of moral responsibility, the decision is taken in a specific way on the basis of beliefs—explicit or implicit—about what is good and right for human beings, hence ultimately on assumptions about fundamental human nature. It could hardly be otherwise. There is, then, a truth about the matter to be discovered, and it is an intellectually challenging task, and in this case one with profound human implications, to discover the truth about the matter.

Still remaining within the realm of speculation, let us return to the study of human cognition in domains that may be more accessible to scientific inquiry. As intellectual history shows, scientists have been able over time to construct a theoretical edifice of remarkable depth in certain areas while other questions remain in much the state they were when raised millennia ago. Why should this be so? There might be some value in approaching this matter along the lines of our schematic account of language acquisition. Recalling the essentials, a child endowed with the human language faculty is presented with certain data and constructs a language, using the data to set the parameters of the language faculty. The language then provides specific interpretations for linguistic expressions over an unbounded range.

Suppose that we think of theory construction in similar terms. As part of the human biological endowment, the scientist is endowed with a certain conceptual apparatus, certain ways of formulating problems, a concept of intelligibility and explanation, and so on. Call this the science-forming capacity. As in other cases it may contain hidden resources that come to be recognized and used as the contingencies of life and experience permit, so access to this endowment may change over time. But we may assume it to be fixed, in the manner of the language faculty. The science-forming capacity is supplemented with certain background assumptions, determined by the state of current scientific understanding. So supplemented, the science-forming capacity addresses a query posed in terms accessible to it, or it formulates a query using its own resources, not at all a trivial task; the science-forming capacity then seeks to construct a theoretical explanation that will respond to this query. Its own internal criteria will determine whether the task has been successfully accomplished. If it is, the background assumptions may change, and the science-forming capacity is now prepared to face other queries, perhaps to formulate others that it will itself proceed to address. To approach the real situation of problem solving and theory construction, we must add much more, but let us keep to this schematic account.

In the case of language there is a special faculty that is a central element of the human mind. It operates quickly, in a deterministic fashion, unconsciously and beyond the limits of awareness and in a manner that is common to the species, yielding a rich and complex system of knowledge, a particular language. For problem solving and theory construction there is nothing so specific. The problems we face are too varied, and the differences among people who face them are far more striking, though it is worth emphasizing that those who share the same background assumptions can generally understand a proposed theory and evaluate it even if they did not construct it themselves and perhaps lacked whatever special abilities are involved in doing so.

In most cases, the science-forming capacity, presented with a query, provides no useful response at all. Most queries are just baffling. Sometimes a small number of intelligible theories are produced. The science-forming capacity, employing its resources, may then undertake a course of experiment to evaluate them. Sometimes the theories produced may be in the neighborhood of the truth, in which case we have potential knowledge, which can be refined by experiment, working at the margins. This partial congruence between the truth about the world and what the human science-forming capacity produces at a given moment yields science. Notice that it is just blind luck if the human science-forming capacity, a particular component of the human biological endowment, happens to yield a result that conforms more or less to the truth about the world.

Some have argued that this is not blind luck but rather a product of Darwinian evolution. The outstanding American philosopher Charles Sanders Peirce, who presented an account of science construction in terms similar to those just outlined, argued in this vein. His point was that through ordinary processes of natural selection our mental capacities evolved so as to be able to deal with the problems that arise in the world of experience. But this argument is not compelling. It is possible to imagine that chimpanzees have an innate fear of snakes because those who lacked this genetically determined property did not survive to reproduce, but one can hardly argue that humans have the capacity to discover quantum theory for similar reasons. The experience that shaped the course of evolution offers no hint of the problems to be faced in the sciences, and ability to solve these problems could hardly have been a factor in evolution. We cannot appeal to this *deus ex machina* to explain the convergence of our ideas and the truth about the world. Rather, it is largely a lucky accident that there is such a (partial) convergence, so it seems.

The human science-forming capacity, like other biological systems, has its scope and limits, as a matter of necessity. We can be confident that some problems will lie beyond the limits, however the science-forming capacity is supplemented by appropriate background information. Descartes's problem may be among them. At least, this would not be surprising, and there is little reason now to suspect otherwise.

One might imagine that, by investigating the history of science and by experimentation with human subjects, we might learn something about the nature of the human science-forming capacity. If so, we might also learn something about the kinds of problems that we can and cannot approach by the resources of the science-forming capacity, the methods of the sciences.

There is, incidentally, no reason to suppose that all the problems we face are best approached in these terms. Thus it is quite possible—overwhelmingly probable, one might guess—that we will always learn more about human life and human personality from novels than from scientific psychology. The science-forming capacity is only one facet of our mental endowment. We use it where we can but are not restricted to it, fortunately.

Can the study of language, conducted along the lines we have investigated, provide a useful model for other aspects of the study of human cognition? The general line of approach should be just as appropriate elsewhere, but it would be astonishing if we were to discover that the constituent elements of the language faculty enter crucially in other domains. The one other area of cognitive psychology, beyond language, that has made substantial progress in recent years is the study of vision. Here too, we can ask what are the properties of the human visual faculty. As I mentioned, in this case we can also learn something about the physical mechanisms involved, because of the possibility of experimentation with other organisms with similar capacities. Here too, we discover that the faculty has definite and specific properties and that some possibilities of variation are determined by visual experience—the density of horizontal and vertical receptors, for example. In this case experiment reveals that the growth of the faculty to its mature state observes *critical periods*; specific aspects of the faculty must develop within a certain time frame of general maturation or else they will not develop properly or at all. Certain kinds of visual experience are necessary to trigger development during these critical periods, patterned stimulation in early infancy, for example. The visual system is unlike the language faculty in many crucial ways; it does not yield a system of knowledge, for example, but is strictly a processing system. But there are some similarities in the way the problems can be addressed.

The human visual system observes certain principles, just as the language faculty does. One of these, recently discovered, is a certain "rigidity principle." Under a wide range of conditions the eye-brain interprets the phenomena presented to it as rigid objects in motion. Thus, if I were to have in my hands a plane figure, say in the shape of a circle, and were to present it to you perpendicular to the line of sight, you would see a circular figure. If I were to rotate it 90 degrees so that it finally disappeared, you would see a circular figure rotating. The visual information reaching your eye is consistent with the conclusion that what you saw was a plane figure shrinking and changing its shape until it becomes a line and disappears. But under a wide range of conditions, what you will "see" is a rigid plane figure rotating. The eye-brain imposes this interpretation on what it sees, because of the way it is constructed. In this case the physiology of the matter is understood to some degree as well.

To take another case, suppose that you look at a television screen with a large dot at one end. Suppose the dot disappears and another dot of the same size, shape, and color appears at the other end of the screen. If the timing and distance are properly chosen, what you will "see" is a dot moving from one position to the other, a phenomenon called apparent motion. The properties of apparent motion are quite remarkable. Thus, if a horizontal line is present in the middle of the screen and the experiment is repeated, what you will "see" under appropriate conditions is motion of the dot from one end of the screen to the other, not in a straight line but moving around the barrier. If the disappearing dot is red and the appearing one blue, you will see a red dot moving across the screen, becoming blue at a certain point and continuing to its final location. And so on, under a variety of other conditions. All these phenomena reflect the structure of the visual mechanisms.

The visual mechanisms of other organisms operate quite differently. Thus, in a series of classical experiments about twenty-five years ago, it was demonstrated that the eye of a frog is designed, in effect, to "see" a fly in motion. If there is a certain kind of motion, similar to that of a fly, the eye-brain will see it, but a dead fly placed in the line of sight will not trigger the visual mechanism and will not be seen. Here also the physiological mechanisms are known.

These principles might be regarded as in some sense comparable to the principles of the language faculty. They are, of course, entirely different principles. The language faculty does not include the rigidity principle or the principles that govern apparent motion, and the visual faculty does not include the principles of binding theory, case theory, structure dependence, and so on. The two systems operate in quite different ways, not surprisingly.

What is known about other cognitive domains suggests that the same is true elsewhere, though so little is known that one cannot be sure. It seems that the mind is *modular*, to use a technical term, consisting of separate systems with their own properties. Of course, the systems interact; we can describe what we see, hear, smell, taste, imagine, etc.—sometimes. There are thus central systems of some kind, but about these little is understood.

The evidence seems compelling, indeed overwhelming, that fundamental aspects of our mental and social life, including language, are determined as part of our biological endowment, not acquired by learning, still less by training, in the course of our experience. Many find this conclusion offensive. They would prefer to believe that humans are shaped by the environment, not that they develop in a manner that is predetermined in essential respects. I mentioned earlier the remarkable dominance of the behaviorist conception that language and other aspects of our beliefs and knowledge, and of our culture in general, are determined by experience. The Marxist tradition too has characteristically held that humans are products of history and society, not determined by their biological nature; of course this is not true of physical properties, such as the possession of arms rather than wings or the property of undergoing puberty at roughly a certain age, but it is held to be true of intellectual, social, and general cultural life. This standard view makes nonsense of the essentials of Marx's own thought, I believe, for reasons already briefly indicated, but let us put that aside; there is no doubt that it is proclaimed as a point of doctrine by many who call themselves Marxists. For several centuries now the dominant intellectual tradition in Anglo-American thought adopted similar conceptions. In this empiricist tradition, it was held that the constructions of the mind result from a few simple operations of association on the basis of contiguity, phenomenal similarity, and so on, perhaps extended by a capacity for induction from a limited class of cases to a larger class of the same type. These resources must then suffice for all intellectual achievements, including language learning and much else.

Within this array of doctrines there are some differences, but the similarities are much more striking. One striking feature is that, although they have been widely believed, indeed asserted as virtual doctrinal truths, they are supported by no compelling evidence. In fact, attention to the simplest facts suffices to undermine them, as I have indicated throughout these lectures. If there were any truth to these doctrines, human beings would be miserable creatures indeed, extremely limited in their capacities, unlike one another, mere reflections of some accidental experience. I made the point earlier in connection with physical growth, and the same is true in the domains of intellectual, social, and cultural life.

When some doctrine has such a powerful grip on the intellectual imagination over such a broad range and when it has little in the way of empirical support but is rather in conflict with the evidence at every point, it is fair to ask why the beliefs are so firmly maintained. Why should intellectuals be so wedded to the belief that humans are shaped by the environment, not determined by their nature?

In earlier years environmentalism was held to be a "progressive" doctrine. It undermined the belief that each person has a natural place fixed by nature: lord, servant, slave, and so on. It is true that if people have no endowments, then they are equal in endowments: equally miserable and unfortunate. Whatever appeal such a view may once have had, it is hard to take it seriously today. In fact, it was dubious even then; as noted, the traditional dualism to which it was opposed had deeper and far more persuasive reasons for assuming the essential unity of the human species and the lack of significant variation within it in any of these respects.

Such arguments for environmentalism are often heard today in connection with debates over race and IQ and the like. Again, it is true that if humans have no biologically determined intellectual endowments, then there will be no correlation between IQ (a socially determined property) and anything else: race, sex, or whatever. Again, though the motivation can be appreciated, it is difficult to take the argument seriously. Let us pretend for the moment that race and IQ are well-defined properties, and let us suppose that some correlation is found between them. Perhaps a person of a particular race, on the average, is likely to have a slightly higher IQ than a person of another race. Notice first that such a conclusion would have essentially null scientific interest. It is of no interest to discover a correlation between two traits selected at random, and if someone happens to be interested in this odd and pointless question, it would make far more sense to study properties that are much more clearly defined, say, length of fingernails and eye color. So the interest of the discovery must lie in the social domain. But here, it is clear that the discovery is of interest only to people who believe that each individual must be treated not as what he or she is but rather as an example of a certain category (racial, sexual, or whatever). To anyone not afflicted with these disorders, it is of zero interest whether the average value of IQ for some category of persons is such-and-such. Suppose we were to discover the height has a slight correlation with ability to do higher mathematics. Would that imply that no one under a certain height should be encouraged to study higher mathematics, or would it mean that each person should be considered as an individual, encouraged to study higher mathematics if their talents and interests so indicate? Obviously the latter, even though it would then turn out that a slightly higher percentage of taller people would end up pursuing this path. Since we do not suffer from the social disease of "heightism," the issue interests no one.

Surely people differ in their biologically determined qualities. The world would be too horrible to contemplate if they did not. But discovery of a correlation between some of these qualities is of no scientific interest and of no social significance, except to racists, sexists, and the like. Those who argue that there is a correlation between race and IQ and those who deny this claim are contributing to racism and other disorders, because what they are saying is based on the assumption that the answer to the question makes a difference; it does not, except to racists, sexists, and the like.

Case by case, it is difficult to take seriously the idea that environmentalism is somehow "progressive" and should therefore be adopted as doctrine. Furthermore, the issue is irrelevant, because the question is one of truth, not doctrine. Questions of fact cannot be resolved on the basis of ideological commitment. As I have observed throughout, we should be delighted that environmentalism is utterly misconceived, but the question of truth or falsity is not resolved by our preference for one or another outcome of inquiry.

Although factual questions are not resolved by doctrines of faith, it sometimes makes sense to inquire into the relation between ideological commitments and scientific beliefs. This is particularly appropriate in a case such as the one under discussion, a case in which beliefs about matters of fact are held by the intellectual community over such a broad range, over such a long period, and with such passion and intensity, in the face of rather obvious considerations of fact and logic. Why do these environmentalist ideas have such appeal to intellectuals?

One possible answer lies in the role that intellectuals characteristically play in contemporary—and not so contemporary—society. Since intellectuals are the ones who write history, we should be cautious about the alleged "lessons of history" in this regard; it would not be surprising to discover that the version of history presented is self-serving, and indeed it is. Thus the standard image is that the intellectuals are fiercely independent, honest, defenders of the highest values, opponents of arbitrary rule and authority, and so on. The actual record reveals a different story. Quite typically, intellectuals have been ideological and social managers, serving power or seeking to assume power themselves by taking control of popular movements of which they declare themselves to be the leaders. For people committed to control and manipulation it is quite useful to believe that human beings have no intrinsic moral and intellectual nature, that they are simply objects to be shaped by state and private managers and ideologues—who, of course, perceive what is good and right. Concern for intrinsic human nature poses moral barriers in the way of manipulation and control, particularly if this nature conforms to the libertarian conceptions that I have briefly reviewed. In accordance with these conceptions, human rights are rooted in human nature, and we violate fundamental human rights when people are forced to be slaves, wage slaves, servants of external power, subjected to systems of authority and domination, manipulated and controlled "for their own good."

I rather suspect that these speculations about the otherwise quite surprising appeal of environmentalist views has more than a little truth to it.

It is sometimes argued that even if we succeed in explaining properties of human language and other human capacities in terms of an innate biological endowment, nothing has really been achieved because it remains to explain how the biological endowment developed; the problem is simply displaced, not solved. This is a curious argument. By the same logic, we might argue that nothing is explained if we demonstrate that a bird does not learn to have wings but rather develops them because it is so constructed by virtue of its genetic endowment; the problem is only displaced, because it remains to explain how the genetic endowment evolved. It is perfectly correct that in each case new problems are raised. This is typically the case when we solve some problem, giving rise to others. But it would be absurd to argue that nothing has been achieved when we learn that birds grow wings by virtue of their genetic endowment, not by learning, or that humans undergo the processes of puberty because that is the way they are designed, not by observing others and deciding to do the same. True, it remains to account for the evolution of language, wings, etc. The problem is a serious one, but it belongs to a different domain of inquiry.

Can the problem be addressed today? In fact, little is known about these matters. Evolutionary theory is informative about many things, but it has little to say, as of now, about questions of this nature. The answers may well lie not so much in the theory of natural selection as in molecular biology, in the study of what kinds of physical systems can develop under the conditions of life on earth and why, ultimately because of physical principles. It surely cannot be assumed that every trait is specifically selected. In the case of such systems as language or wings it is not easy even to imagine a course of selection that might have given rise to them. A rudimentary wing, for example, is not "useful" for motion but is more of an impediment. Why then should the organ develop in the early stages of its evolution?

In some cases, it seems that organs develop to serve one purpose and, when they have reached a certain form in the evolutionary process, became available for different purposes, at which point the processes of natural selection may refine them further for these purposes. It has been suggested that the development of insect wings follows this pattern. Insects have the problem of heat exchange, and rudimentary wings can serve this function. When they reach a certain size, they become less useful for this purpose but begin to be useful for flight, at which point they evolve into wings. Possibly human mental capacities have in some cases evolved in a similar way.

Take the human number faculty. Children have the capacity to acquire the number system. They can learn to count and somehow know that it is possible to continue to add one indefinitely. They can also readily acquire the technique of arithmetical calculation. If a child did not already know that it is possible to add one indefinitely, it could never learn this fact. Rather, taught the numerals 1, 2, 3, etc., up to some number *n*, it would assume that that is the end of the story. It seems that this capacity, like the capacity for language, lies beyond the intellectual range of otherwise intelligent apes. It was, incidentally, thought for a time that certain birds could be taught to count. Thus it was shown that some birds could be taught that if they are presented with four dots, then they can find food in the fourth container in a linear array. The task could be performed up to about seven items, leading to the conclusion that birds can count. But the conclusion is incorrect. The most elementary property of the number system is that the series of numbers goes on indefinitely; you can always add one more. Birds may have certain limited capacities to match arrays of not too many items, but that has nothing to do with the faculty of number. The ability to count is not "more of the same" but something entirely different in character.

How did the number faculty develop? It is impossible to believe that it was specifically selected. Cultures still exist today that have not made use of this faculty; their language does not contain a method for constructing indefinitely many number words, and the people of these cultures are not aware of the possibility of counting. But they certainly have the capacity. Adults can quickly learn to count and to do arithmetic if placed in the appropriate environment, and a child from such a tribe, raised in a technological society, could become an engineer or a physicist as readily as anyone else. The capacity is present but latent.

In fact, the capacity was latent and unused throughout almost all of human history. It is only recently in evolutionary terms, at a time when human evolution had reached its current stage, that the number faculty was manifested. Plainly it is not the case that people who could count, or who could solve problems of arithmetic or number theory, were able to survive to produce more offspring, so that the capacity developed through natural selection. Rather, it developed as a by-product of something else, and was available for use when circumstances called it forth.

At this point one can only speculate, but it is possible that the number faculty developed as a by-product of the language faculty. The latter has features that are quite unusual, perhaps unique in the biological world. In technical terms it has the property of "discrete infinity." To put it simply, each sentence has a fixed number of words: one, two, three, forty-seven, ninety-three, etc. And there is no limit in principle to how many words the sentence may contain. Other systems known in the animal world are quite different. Thus the system of ape calls is finite; there are a fixed number, say, forty. The so-called bee language, on the other hand, is infinite, but it is not discrete. A bee signals the distance of a flower from the hive by some form of motion; the greater the distance, the more the motion. Between any two signals there is in principle another, signaling a distance in between the first two, and this continues down to the ability to discriminate. One might argue that this system is even "richer" than human language, because it contains "more signals" in a certain mathematically well-defined sense. But this is meaningless. It is simply a different system, with an entirely different basis. To call it a "language" is simply to use a misleading metaphor.

Human language has the extremely unusual, possibly unique, property of discrete infinity, and the same is true of the human number faculty. In fact, we might think of the human number faculty as essentially an "abstraction" from human language, preserving the mechanism of discrete infinity and eliminating the other special features of language. If so, that would explain the fact that the human number faculty is available though unused in the course of human evolution.

This still leaves the question of origin of human language. Here there are some speculations, nothing more, and they do not seem persuasive. It may be that at some remote period a mutation took place that gave rise to the property of discrete infinity, perhaps for reasons that have to do with the biology of cells, to be explained in terms of properties of physical mechanisms, now unknown. Without this capacity it might have been possible to "think thoughts" of a certain restricted character, but with the capacity in place, the same conceptual apparatus would be freed for the construction of new thoughts and operations such as inference involving them, and it would be possible to express and interchange these thoughts. At that point evolutionary pressures might have shaped the further development of the capacity, at least in part. Quite possibly other aspects of its evolutionary development again reflect the operation of physical laws applying to a brain of a certain degree of complexity. We simply do not know.

This seems to me roughly where things stand today. In particular areas, such as the study of language and vision, there has been substantial progress, and more is sure to come. But many questions lie beyond our intellectual grasp for the present, and perhaps forever.

16.

Containing the Enemy

In the first chapter [of *Necessary Illusions*], I mentioned three models of media organization: (1) corporate oligopoly, (2) state-controlled, and (3) a democratic communications policy as advanced by the Brazilian bishops. The first model reduces democratic participation in the media to zero, just as other corporations are, in principle, exempt from popular control by workforce or community. In the case of state-controlled media, democratic participation might vary, depending on how the political system functions; in practice, the state media are generally kept in line by the forces that have the power to dominate the state, and by an apparatus of cultural managers who cannot stray far from the bounds these forces set. The third model is largely untried in practice, just as a sociopolitical system with significant popular engagement remains a concern for the future: a hope or a fear, depending on one 's evaluation of the right of the public to shape its own affairs.

The model of media as corporate oligopoly is the natural system for capitalist democracy. It has, accordingly, reached its highest form in the most advanced of these societies, particularly the United States, where media concentration is high, public radio and television are limited in scope, and elements of the radical democratic model exist only at the margins, in such phenomena as listener-supported community radio and the alternative or local press, often with a noteworthy effect on the social and political culture and the sense of empowerment in the communities that benefit from these options.[1] In this respect, the United States represents the form toward which capitalist

---

This chapter first appeared in *Necessary Illusions: Thought Control in Democratic Societies* (Cambridge, MA: South End Press, 1989), 21–43.

democracy is tending; related tendencies include the progressive elimination of unions and other popular organizations that interfere with private power, an electoral system that is increasingly stage-managed as a public relations exercise, avoidance of welfare measures such as national health insurance that also impinge on the prerogatives of the privileged, and so on. From this perspective, it is reasonable for Cyrus Vance and Henry Kissinger to describe the United States as "a model democracy," democracy being understood as a system of business control of political as well as other major institutions.

Other Western democracies are generally a few steps behind in these respects. Most have not yet achieved the U.S. system of one political party, with two factions controlled by shifting segments of the business community. They still retain parties based on working people and the poor, which to some extent represent their interests. But these are declining, along with cultural institutions that sustain different values and concerns, and organizational forms that provide isolated individuals with the means to think and to act outside the framework imposed by private power.

This is the natural course of events under capitalist democracy, because of what Joshua Cohen and Joel Rogers call "the resource constraint" and "the demand constraint."[2] The former is straightforward: control over resources is narrowly concentrated, with predictable effects for every aspect of social and political life. The demand constraint is a more subtle means of control, one whose effects are rarely observed directly in a properly functioning capitalist democracy such as the United States, though they are evident, for example, in Latin America, where the political system sometimes permits a broader range of policy options, including programs of social reform. The consequences are well known: capital flight, loss of business and investor confidence, and general social decline as those who "own the country" lose the capacity to govern it—or simply a military coup, typically backed by the hemispheric guardian of order and good form. The more benign response to reform programs illustrates the demand constraint—the requirement that the interests of those with effective power be satisfied if the society is to function.

In brief, it is necessary to ensure that those who own the country are happy, or else all will suffer, for they control investment and determine what is produced and distributed and what benefits will trickle down to those who rent themselves to the owners when they can. For the homeless in the streets, then, the highest priority must be to ensure that the dwellers in the mansions are reasonably content. Given the options available within the system and the cultural values it reinforces, maximization of short-term individual gain appears to be the rational course, along with submissiveness, obedience, and abandonment of the public arena. The bounds on political action are correspondingly limited. Once the forms of capitalist democracy are in place, they remain very stable, whatever suffering ensues—a fact that has long been understood by U.S. planners.

One consequence of the distribution of resources and decision-making power in the society at large is that the political class and the cultural managers typically associate themselves with the sectors that dominate the private economy; they are either drawn directly from those sectors or expect to join them. The radical democrats of the seventeenth-century English revolution held that "it will never be a good world while knights and gentlemen make us laws, that are chosen for fear and do but oppress us, and do not know the people's sores. It will never be well with us till we have Parliaments of countrymen like ourselves, that know our wants." But Parliament and the preachers had a different vision: "when we mention the people, we do not mean the confused promiscuous body of the people," they held. With the resounding defeat of the democrats, the remaining question, in the words of a Leveller pamphlet, was "whose slaves the poor shall be," the king's or Parliament's.[3]

The same controversy arose in the early days of the American Revolution. "Framers of the state constitutions," Edward Countryman observes, "had insisted that the representative assemblies should closely reflect the people of the state itself"; they objected to a "separate caste" of political leaders insulated from the people. But the Federal Constitution guaranteed that "representatives, senators, and the president all would know that exceptional was just what they were." Under the Confederation, artisans, farmers, and others of the common people had demanded that they be represented by "men of their own kind," having learned from the revolutionary experience that they were "as capable as anyone of deciding what was wrong in their lives and of organizing themselves so they could do something about it." This was not to be. "The last gasp of the original spirit of the Revolution, with all its belief in community and cooperation, came from the Massachusetts farmers" during Shays's Rebellion in 1786. "The resolutions and addresses of their county committees in the year or two before the rebellion said exactly what all sorts of people had been saying in 1776." Their failure taught the painful lesson that "the old ways no longer worked," and "they found themselves forced to grovel and beg forgiveness from rulers who claimed to be the people's servants." So it has remained. With the rarest of exceptions, the representatives of the people do not come from or return to the workplace; rather, law offices catering to business interests, executive suites, and other places of privilege.[4]

As for the media, in England a lively labor-oriented press reaching a broad public existed into the 1960s, when it was finally eliminated through the workings of the market. At the time of its demise in 1964, the *Daily Herald* had over five times as many readers as the *Times* and "almost double the readership of the *Times*, the *Financial Times* and the *Guardian* combined," James Curran observes, citing survey research showing that its readers "were also exceptionally devoted to their paper." But this journal, partially owned by the unions and reaching a largely working-class audience, "appealed to the wrong people," Curran continues. The same was true of other elements of the social democratic press that died at the same time, in large part because they were "deprived of the same level of subsidy" through advertising and private capital as sustained "the quality press," which "not only reflects the values and interests of its middle-class readers" but also "gives them force, clarity and coherence" and "plays an important ideological role in amplifying and renewing the dominant political consensus."[5]

The consequences are significant. For the media, Curran concludes, there is "a remarkable growth in advertising-related editorial features" and a "growing convergence between editorial and advertising content" reflecting "the increasing accomodation of national newspaper managements to the selective needs of advertisers" and the business community generally; the same is likely true of news coverage and interpretation. For society at large, Curran continues, "the loss of the only social democratic papers with a large readership which devoted serious attention to current affairs," including sectors of the working class that had remained "remarkably radical in their attitudes to a wide range of economic and political issues," contributed to "the progressive erosion in post-war Britain of a popular radical tradition" and to the disintegration of "the cultural base that has sustained active participation within the Labour movement," which "has ceased to exist as a mass movement in most parts of the country." The effects are readily apparent. With the elimination of the "selection and treatment of news" and "relatively detailed political commentary and analysis [that] helped daily to sustain a social democratic sub-culture within the working class," there is no longer an articulate alternative to the picture of "a world where the subordination of working people [is] accepted as natural and inevitable," and no continuing expression of the view that working people are "morally entitled to a greater share of the wealth they created and a greater say in its allocation." The same tendencies are evident elsewhere in the industrial capitalist societies.

There are, then, natural processes at work to facilitate the control of "enemy territory" at home. Similarly, the global planning undertaken by U.S. elites during and after World War II assumed that principles of liberal internationalism would generally serve to satisfy what had been described as the "requirement of the United States in a world in which it proposes to hold unquestioned power."[6] The global policy goes under the name "containment." The manufacture of consent at home is its domestic counterpart. The two policies are, in fact, closely intertwined, since the domestic population must be mobilized to pay the costs of "containment," which may be severe—both material and moral costs.

The rhetoric of containment is designed to give a defensive cast to the project of global management, and it thus serves as part of the domestic system of thought control. It is remarkable that the terminology is so easily adopted, given the questions that it begs. Looking more closely, we find that the concept conceals a good deal.[7]

The underlying assumption is that there is a stable international order that the United States must defend. The general contours of this international order were developed by U.S. planners during and after World War II. Recognizing the extraordinary scale of U.S. power, they proposed to construct a global system that the United States would dominate and within which U.S. business interests would thrive. As much of the world as possible would constitute a Grand Area, as it was called, which would be subordinated to the needs of the U.S. economy. Within the Grand Area, other capitalist societies would be encouraged to develop, but without protective devices that would interfere with U.S. prerogatives.[8] In particular, only the United States would be permitted to dominate regional systems. The United States moved to take effective control of world energy production and to organize a world system in which its various components would fulfill their functions as industrial centers, as markets and sources of raw materials, or as dependent states pursuing their "regional interests" within the "overall framework of order" managed by the United States (as Henry Kissinger was later to explain).

The Soviet Union has been considered the major threat to the planned international order, for good reason. In part this follows from its very existence as a great power controlling an imperial system that could not be incorporated within the Grand Area; in part from its occasional efforts to expand the domains of its power, as in Afghanistan, and the alleged threat of invasion of Western Europe, if not world conquest, a prospect regularly discounted by more serious analysts in public and in internal documents. But it is necessary to understand how broadly the concept of "defense" is construed if we wish to evaluate the assessment of Soviet crimes. Thus the Soviet Union is a threat to world order if it supports people opposing U.S. designs, for example, the South Vietnamese engaging in "internal aggression" against their selfless American defenders (as explained by the Kennedy liberals), or Nicaraguans illegimately combating the depredations of the U.S.-run "democratic resistance." Such actions prove that Soviet leaders are not serious about détente and cannot be trusted, statesmen and commentators soberly observe. Thus, "Nicaragua will be a prime place to test the sanguine forecast that [Gorbachev] is now turning down the heat in the Third World," the *Washington*

Post editors explain, placing the onus for the U.S. attack against Nicaragua on the Russians while warning of the threat of this Soviet outpost to "overwhelm and terrorize" its neighbors.[9] The United States will have "won the Cold War," from this point of view, when it is free to exercise its will in the rest of the world without Soviet interference.

Though "containing the Soviet Union" has been the dominant theme of U.S. foreign policy only since the United States became a truly global power after World War II, the Soviet Union had been considered an intolerable threat to order since the Bolshevik revolution. Accordingly, it has been the main enemy of the independent media.

In 1920, Walter Lippmann and Charles Merz produced a critical study of *New York Times* coverage of the Bolshevik revolution, describing it as "nothing short of a disaster . . . from the point of view of professional journalism." Editorial policy, deeply hostile, "profoundly and crassly influenced their news columns." "For subjective reasons," the *Times* staff "accepted and believed most of what they were told" by the U.S. government and "the agents and adherents of the old regime." They dismissed Soviet peace offers as merely a tactic to enable the Bolsheviks to "concentrate their energies for a renewed drive toward world-wide revolution" and the imminent "Red invasion of Europe." The Bolsheviks, Lippmann and Merz wrote, were portrayed as "simultaneously . . . both cadaver and world-wide menace," and the Red Peril "appeared at every turn to obstruct the restoration of peace in Eastern Europe and Asia and to frustrate the resumption of economic life." When President Wilson called for intervention, the *New York Times* responded by urging that we drive "the Bolsheviki out of Petrograd and Moscow."[10]

Change a few names and dates, and we have a rather fair appraisal of the treatment of Indochina yesterday and Central America today by the national media. Similar assumptions about the Soviet Union are reiterated by contemporary diplomatic historians who regard the development of an alternative social model as in itself an intolerable form of intervention in the affairs of others, against which the West has been fully entitled to defend itself by forceful action in retaliation, including the defense of the West by military intervention in the Soviet Union after the Bolshevik revolution.[11] Under these assumptions, widely held and respected, aggression easily becomes self-defense.

Returning to post–World War II policy and ideology, it is, of course, unnecessary to *contrive* reasons to oppose the brutality of the Soviet leaders in dominating their internal empire and their dependencies while cheerfully assisting such contemporary monsters as the Ethiopian military junta or the neo-Nazi generals in Argentina. But an honest review will show that the primary enemies have been the indigenous populations within the Grand Area, who fall prey to the wrong ideas. It then becomes necessary to overcome these deviations by economic, ideological, or military warfare, or by terror and subversion. The domestic population must be rallied to the cause, in defense against "Communism."

These are the basic elements of containment in practice abroad, and of its domestic counterpart within. With regard to the Soviet Union, the concept has had two variants over the years. The doves were reconciled to a form of containment in which the Soviet Union would dominate roughly the areas occupied by the Red Army in the war against Hitler. The hawks had much broader aspirations, as expressed in the "rollback strategy" outlined in NSC 68 of April 1950, shortly before the Korean war. This crucial document, made public in 1975, interpreted containment as intended to "foster the seeds of destruction within the Soviet system" and make it possible to "negotiate a settlement with the Soviet Union (or a successor state or states)." In the early postwar years, the United States supported armies established by Hitler in the Ukraine and Eastern Europe, with the assistance of such figures as Reinhard Gehlen, who headed Nazi military intelligence on the Eastern front and was placed in charge of the espionage service of West Germany under close CIA supervision, assigned the task of developing a "secret army" of thousands of SS men to assist the forces fighting within the Soviet Union. So remote are these facts from conventional understanding that a highly knowledgeable foreign affairs specialist at the liberal *Boston Globe* could condemn tacit U.S. support for the Khmer Rouge by offering the following analogy, as the ultimate absurdity: "It is as if the United States had winked at the presence of a Nazi guerrilla movement to harass the Soviets in 1945"—exactly what the United States was doing into the early 1950s, and not just winking.[12]

It is also considered entirely natural that the Soviet Union should be surrounded by hostile powers, facing with equanimity major NATO bases with missiles on alert status as in Turkey, while if Nicaragua obtains jet planes to defend its airspace against regular U.S. penetration, this is considered by doves and hawks alike to warrant U.S. military action to protect ourselves from this grave threat to our security, in accordance with the doctrine of "containment."

Establishment of Grand Area principles abroad and necessary illusions at home does not simply await the hidden hand of the market. Liberal internationalism must be supplemented by the periodic resort to forceful intervention.[13] At home, the state has often employed force to curb dissent, and there have been regular and quite self-conscious campaigns by business to control "the public mind" and suppress challenges to private power when implicit controls do not suffice. The ideology of "anti-Communism" has served this purpose since World War I, with intermittent exceptions. In earlier years, the

United States was defending itself from other evil forces: the Huns, the British, the Spanish, the Mexicans, the Canadian Papists, and the "merciless Indian savages" of the Declaration of Independence. But since the Bolshevik revolution, and particularly in the era of bipolar world power that emerged from the ashes of World War II, a more credible enemy has been the "monolithic and ruthless conspiracy" that seeks to subvert our noble endeavors, in John F. Kennedy's phrase: Ronald Reagan's "Evil Empire."

In the early Cold War years, Dean Acheson and Paul Nitze planned to "bludgeon the mass mind of 'top government,' " as Acheson put it with reference to NSC 68. They presented "a frightening portrayal of the Communist threat, in order to overcome public, business, and congressional desires for peace, low taxes, and 'sound' fiscal policies" and to mobilize popular support for the full-scale rearmament that they felt was necessary "to overcome Communist ideology and Western economic vulnerability," William Borden observes in a study of postwar planning. The Korean War served these purposes admirably. The ambiguous and complex interactions that led to the war were ignored in favor of the more useful image of a Kremlin campaign of world conquest. Dean Acheson, meanwhile, remarked that in the Korean hostilities "an excellent opportunity is here offered to disrupt the Soviet peace offensive, which . . . is assuming serious proportions and having a certain effect on public opinion." The structure of much of the subsequent era was determined by these manipulations, which also provided a standard for later practice.[14]

In earlier years, Woodrow Wilson's Red Scare demolished unions and other dissident elements. A prominent feature was the suppression of independent politics and free speech, on the principle that the state is entitled to prevent improper thought and its expression. Wilson's Creel Commission, dedicated to creating war fever among the generally pacifist population, had demonstrated the efficacy of organized propaganda with the cooperation of the loyal media and the intellectuals, who devoted themselves to such tasks as "historical engineering," the term devised by historian Frederic Paxson, one of the founders of the National Board for Historical Service established by U.S. historians to serve the state by "explaining the issues of the war that we might the better win it." The lesson was learned by those in a position to employ it. Two lasting institutional consequences were the rise of the public relations industry, one of whose leading figures, Edward Bernays, had served on the wartime propaganda commission, and the establishment of the FBI as, in effect, a national political police. This is a primary function it has continued to serve as illustrated, for example, by its criminal acts to undermine the rising "crisis of democracy" in the 1960s and the surveillance and disruption of popular opposition to U.S. intervention in Central America twenty years later.[15]

The effectiveness of the state-corporate propaganda system is illustrated by the fate of May Day, a workers' holiday throughout the world that originated in response to the judicial murder of several anarchists after the Haymarket affair of May 1886, in a campaign of international solidarity with U.S. workers struggling for an eight-hour day. In the United States, all has been forgotten. May Day has become "Law Day," a jingoist celebration of our "200-year-old partnership between law and liberty" as Ronald Reagan declared while designating May 1 as Law Day 1984, adding that without law there can be only "chaos and disorder." The day before, he had announced that the United States would disregard the proceedings of the International Court of Justice that later condemned the U.S. government for its "unlawful use of force" and violation of treaties in its attack against Nicaragua. "Law Day" also served as the occasion for Reagan's declaration of May 1, 1985, announcing an embargo against Nicaragua "in response to the emergency situation created by the Nicaraguan Government's aggressive activities in Central America," actually declaring a "national emergency," since renewed annually, because "the policies and actions of the Government of Nicaragua constitute an unusual and extraordinary threat to the national security and foreign policy of the United States"—all with the approbation of Congress, the media, and the intellectual community generally; or, in some circles, embarrassed silence.

The submissiveness of the society to business dominance, secured by Wilson's Red Scare, began to erode during the Great Depression. In 1938, the board of directors of the National Association of Manufacturers, adopting the Marxist rhetoric that is common in the internal records of business and government documents, described the "hazard facing industrialists" in "the newly realized political power of the masses"; "[u]nless their thinking is directed," it warned, "we are definitely headed for adversity." No less threatening was the rise of labor organization, in part with the support of industrialists who perceived it as a means to regularize labor markets. But too much is too much, and business soon rallied to overcome the threat by the device of "employer mobilization of the public" to crush strikes, as an academic study of the 1937 Johnstown steel strike observed. This "formula," the business community exulted, was one that "business has hoped for, dreamed of, and prayed for." Combined with strongarm methods, propaganda campaigns were used effectively to subdue the labor movement in subsequent years. These campaigns spent millions of dollars "to tell the public that nothing was wrong and that grave dangers lurked in the proposed remedies" of the unions, the La Follette Committee of the Senate observed in its study of business propaganda.[16]

In the postwar period the public relations campaign intensified, employing the media and other devices to identify so-called free enterprise—meaning state-subsidized private profit with no infringement on managerial prerogatives—as "the American way," threatened by dangerous subversives. In 1954, Daniel Bell, then an editor of *Fortune* magazine, wrote that

> It has been industry's prime concern, in the post war years, to change the climate of opinion ushered in by . . . the depression. This "free enterprise" campaign has two essential aims: to rewin the loyalty of the worker which now goes to the union and to halt creeping socialism,

that is, the mildly reformist capitalism of the New Deal. The scale of business public relations campaigns, Bell continued, was "staggering," through advertising in press and radio and other means.[17] The effects were seen in legislation to constrain union activity, the attack on independent thought often mislabeled McCarthyism, and the elimination of any articulate challenge to business domination. The media and intellectual community cooperated with enthusiasm. The universities, in particular, were purged, and remained so until the "crisis of democracy" dawned and students and younger faculty began to ask the wrong kinds of questions. That elicited a renewed though less effective purge, while in a further resort to "necessary illusion," it was claimed, and still is, that the universities were virtually taken over by left-wing totalitarians—meaning that the grip of orthodoxy was somewhat relaxed.[18]

As early as 1947, a State Department public relations officer remarked that "smart public relations [has] paid off as it has before and will again." Public opinion "is not moving to the right, it has been moved—cleverly—to the right." "While the rest of the world has moved to the left, has admitted labor into government, has passed liberalized legislation, the United States has become anti-social change, anti-economic change, anti-labor."[19]

By that time, "the rest of the world" was being subjected to similar pressures, as the Truman administration, reflecting the concerns of the business community, acted vigorously to arrest such tendencies in Europe, Japan, and elsewhere, through means ranging from extreme violence to control of desperately needed food, diplomatic pressures, and a wide range of other devices.[20]

All of this is much too little understood, but I cannot pursue it properly here. Throughout the modern period, measures to control "the public mind" have been employed to enhance the natural pressures of the "free market," the domestic counterpart to intervention in the global system.

It is worthy of note that with all the talk of liberal free trade policies, the two major sectors of the U.S. economy that remain competitive in world trade—high-technology industry and capital-intensive agriculture—both rely heavily on state subsidy and a state-guaranteed market.[21] As in other industrial societies, the U.S. economy had developed in earlier years through protectionist measures. In the postwar period, the United States grandly proclaimed liberal principles on the assumption that U.S. investors would prevail in any competition, a plausible expectation in the light of the economic realities of the time, and one that was fulfilled for many years. For similar reasons, Great Britain had been a passionate advocate of free trade during the period of its hegemony, abandoning these doctrines and the lofty rhetoric that accompanied them in the interwar period, when it could not withstand competition from Japan. The United States is pursuing much the same course today in the face of similar challenges, which were quite unexpected forty years ago, indeed until the Vietnam War. Its unanticipated costs weakened the U.S. economy while strengthening its industrial rivals, who enriched themselves through their participation in the destruction of Indochina. South Korea owes its economic takeoff to these opportunities, which also provided an important stimulus to the Japanese economy, just as the Korean War launched Japan's economic recovery and made a major contribution to Europe's. Another example is Canada, which became the world's largest per capita exporter of war materiel during the Vietnam years, while deploring the immorality of the U.S. war to which it was enthusiastically contributing.

Operations of domestic thought control are commonly undertaken in the wake of wars and other crises. Such turmoil tends to encourage the "crisis of democracy" that is the persistent fear of privileged elites, requiring measures to reverse the thrust of popular democracy that threatens established power. Wilson's Red Scare served the purpose after World War I, and the pattern was re-enacted when World War II ended. It was necessary not only to overcome the popular mobilization that took place during the Great Depression but also "to bring people up to [the] realization that the war isn't over by any means," as presidential adviser Clark Clifford observed when the Truman Doctrine was announced in 1947, "the opening gun in [this] campaign."

The Vietnam War and the popular movements of the 1960s elicited similar concerns. The inhabitants of "enemy territory" at home had to be controlled and suppressed, so as to restore the ability of U.S. corporations to compete in the more diverse world market by reducing real wages and welfare benefits and weakening working-class organization. Young people in particular had to be convinced that they must be concerned only for themselves, in a "culture of narcissism"; every person may know, in private, that the assumptions are not true for them, but at a time of life when one is insecure about personal identity and social place, it is all too tempting to adapt to what the propaganda system asserts to be the norm. Other newly mobilized sectors of the "special interests" also had to be restrained or dissolved, tasks that sometimes required a degree of force, as in the programs of the FBI to undermine the ethnic movements and other elements of the rising dissident culture by instigating violence or its direct exercise, and by other means of intimidation and harassment. Another task was to overcome the dread "Vietnam syndrome," which impeded the resort to forceful means to control the dependencies; as explained by *Commentary* editor Norman Podhoretz, the task was to overcome "the sickly inhibitions against the use of military force" that developed in revulsion against the Indochina wars,[22] a problem that was resolved, he hoped, in the glorious conquest of Grenada, when 6,000 elite troops succeeded in overcoming the resistance of several dozen Cubans and some Grenadan militiamen, winning 8,000 medals of honor for their prowess.

To overcome the Vietnam syndrome, it was necessary to present the United States as the aggrieved party and the Vietnamese as the aggressors—a difficult task, it might be thought by those unfamiliar with the measures available for controlling the public mind, or at least those elements of it that count. By the late stages of the war, the general population was out of control, with a large majority regarding the war as "fundamentally wrong and immoral" and not "a mistake," as polls reveal up to the present. Educated elites, in contrast, posed no serious problem. Contrary to the retrospective necessary illusion fostered by those who now declare themselves "early opponents of the war," in reality there was only the most scattered opposition to the war among these circles, apart from concern over the prospects for success and the rising costs. Even the harshest critics of the war within the mainstream rarely went beyond agonizing over good intentions gone awry, reaching even that level of dissent well after corporate America had determined that the enterprise was proving too costly and should be liquidated, a fact that I have documented elsewhere.

The mechanisms by which a more satisfactory version of history was established have also been reviewed elsewhere,[23] but a few words are in order as to their remarkable success. By 1977, President Carter was able to explain in a news conference that Americans have no need "to apologize or to castigate ourselves or to assume the status of culpability" and do not "owe a debt," because our intentions were "to defend the freedom of the South Vietnamese" (by destroying their country and massacring the population), and because "the destruction was mutual"—a pronouncement that, to my knowledge, passed without comment, apparently being considered quite reasonable.[24] Such balanced judgments are, incidentally, not limited to soulful advocates of human rights. They are produced regularly, evoking no comment. To take a recent case, after the U.S. warship *Vincennes* shot down an Iranian civilian airliner over Iranian territorial waters, the *Boston Globe* ran a column by political scientist Jerry Hough of Duke University and the Brookings Institute in which he explained:

> If the disaster in the downing of the Iranian airliner leads this country to move away from its obsession with symbolic nuclear-arms control and to concentrate on the problems of war-fighting, command-and-control of the military and limitations on conventional weapons (certainly including the fleet), then 290 people will not have died in vain

—an assessment that differs slightly from the media barrage after the downing of KAL 007. A few months later, the *Vincennes* returned to its home port to "a boisterous flag-waving welcome . . . complete with balloons and a Navy band playing upbeat songs" while the ship's "loudspeaker blared the theme from the movie 'Chariots of Fire' and nearby Navy ships saluted with gunfire." Navy officials did not want the ship "to sneak into port," a public affairs officer said.[25] So much for the 290 Iranians.

A *New York Times* editorial obliquely took exception to President Carter's interesting moral judgment. Under the heading "The Indochina Debt that Lingers," the editors observed that "no debate over who owes whom how much can be allowed to obscure the worst horrors [of] . . . our involvement in Southeast Asia," referring to the "horrors experienced by many of those in flight" from the Communist monsters—at the time, a small fraction of the many hundreds of thousands fleeing their homes in Asia, including over 100,000 boat people from the Philippines in 1977 and thousands fleeing U.S.-backed terror in Timor, not to speak of tens of thousands more escaping the U.S.-backed terror states of Latin America, none of whom merited such concern or even more than cursory notice in the news columns, if that.[26] Other horrors in the wreckage of Indochina are unmentioned, and surely impose no lingering debt.

A few years later, concerns mounted that "The Debt to the Indochinese Is Becoming a Fiscal Drain," in the words of a *Times* headline, referring to the "moral debt" incurred through our "involvement on the losing side in Indochina"; by the same logic, had the Russians won the war in Afghanistan, they would owe no debt at all. But now our debt is fully "paid," a State Department official explained. We had settled the moral account by taking in Vietnamese refugees fleeing the lands we ravaged, "one of the largest, most dramatic humanitarian efforts in history," according to Roger Winter, director of the U.S. Committee for Refugees. But "despite the pride," *Times* diplomatic correspondent Bernard Gwertzman continues, "some voices in the Reagan Administration and in Congress are once again asking whether the war debt has now been paid."[27]

It is beyond imagining in responsible circles that we might have some culpability for mass slaughter and destruction, or owe some debt to the millions of maimed and orphaned, or to the peasants who still die from exploding ordnance left from the U.S. assault, while the Pentagon, when asked whether there is any way to remove the hundreds of thousands of anti-personnel bomblets that kill children today in such areas as the Plain of Jars in Laos, comments helpfully that "people should not live in those areas. They know the problem." The United States has refused even to give its mine maps of Indochina to civilian mine-deactivation teams. Ex-Marines who visited Vietnam in 1989 to help remove mines they had laid report that many remain in areas where people try to farm and plant trees, and were informed that many people are still being injured and killed as of January 1989.[28] None of this merits comment or concern.

The situation is of course quite different when we turn to Afghanistan—where, incidentally, the Soviet-installed regime *has* released its mine maps. In this case, headlines read: "Soviets Leave Deadly Legacy for Afghans," "Mines Put Afghans in Peril on Return," "U.S. Rebukes Soviets on Afghan Mine Clearing," "U.S. to Help Train Refugees To Destroy Afghan Mines," "Mines Left by Departing Soviets Are Maiming Afghans," and so on. The difference is that these are Soviet mines, so it is only natural for the United States to call for "an international effort to provide the refugees with training and equipment to destroy or dismantle" them and to denounce the Russians for their lack of cooperation in this worthy endeavor. "The Soviets will not acknowledge the problem they have created or help solve it," Assistant Secretary of State Richard Williamson observed sadly; "We are disappointed." The press responds with the usual selective humanitarian zeal.[29]

The media are not satisfied with "mutual destruction" that effaces all responsibility for major war crimes. Rather, the burden of guilt must be shifted to the victims. Under the heading "Vietnam, Trying to be Nicer, Still has a Long Way to Go," *Times* Asia correspondent Barbara Crossette quotes Charles Printz of Human Rights Advocates International, who said that "It's about time the Vietnamese demonstrated some good will." Printz was referring to negotiations about the Amerasian children who constitute a tiny fraction of the victims of U.S. aggression in Indochina. Crossette adds that the Vietnamese have also not been sufficiently forthcoming on the matter of remains of American soldiers, though their behavior may be improving: "There has been progress, albeit slow, on the missing Americans." But the Vietnamese have not yet paid their debt to us, so humanitarian concerns left by the war remain unresolved.[30]

Returning to the same matter, Crossette explains that the Vietnamese do not comprehend their "irrelevance" to Americans, apart from the moral issues that are still outstanding—specifically, Vietnamese recalcitrance "on the issue of American servicemen missing since the end of the war." Dismissing Vietnamese "laments" about U.S. unwillingness to improve relations, Crossette quotes an "Asian official" who said that "if Hanoi's leaders are serious about building their country, the Vietnamese will have to deal fairly with the United States." She also quotes a Pentagon statement expressing the hope that Hanoi will take action "to resolve this long-standing humanitarian issue" of the remains of U.S. servicemen shot down over North Vietnam by the evil Communists—the only humanitarian issue that comes to mind, apparently, when we consider the legacy of a war that left many millions of dead and wounded in Indochina and three countries in utter ruins. Another report deplores Vietnamese refusal to cooperate "in key humanitarian areas," quoting liberal congressmen on Hanoi's "horrible and cruel" behavior and Hanoi's responsibility for lack of progress on humanitarian issues, namely, the matter of U.S. servicemen "still missing from the Vietnam war." Hanoi's recalcitrance "brought back the bitter memories that Vietnam can still evoke" among the suffering Americans.[31]

The nature of the concern "to resolve this long-standing humanitarian issue" of the American servicemen missing in action (MIAs) is illuminated by some statistics cited by historian (and Vietnam veteran) Terry Anderson:

> The French still have 20,000 MIAs from their war in Indochina, and the Vietnamese list over 200,000. Furthermore, the United States still has 80,000 MIAs from World War II and 8,000 from the Korean War, figures that represent 20 and 15 percent, respectively, of the confirmed dead in those conflicts; the percentage is 4 percent for the Vietnam War.[32]

The French have established diplomatic relations with Vietnam, as the Americans did with Germany and Japan, Anderson observes, adding: "We won in 1945, of course, so it seems that MIAs only are important when the United States loses the war. The real 'noble cause' for [the Reagan] administration is not the former war but its emotional and impossible crusade to retrieve 'all recoverable remains.' " More precisely, the "noble cause" is to exploit personal tragedy for political ends: to overcome the Vietnam syndrome at home, and to "bleed Vietnam."

The influential House Democrat Lee Hamilton writes that "almost 15 years after the Vietnam war, Southeast Asia remains a region of major humanitarian, strategic, and economic concern to the United States." The humanitarian concern includes two cases: (1) "Nearly 2,400 American servicemen are unaccounted for in Indochina"; (2) "More than 1 million Cambodians died under Pol Pot's ruthless Khmer Rouge regime." The far greater numbers of Indochinese who died under Washington's ruthless attack, and who still do die, fall below the threshold. We should, Hamilton continues, "reassess our relations with Vietnam" and seek a "new relationship," though not abandoning our humanitarian concerns: "This may be an opportune time for policies that mix continued pressure with rewards for progress on missing US servicemen and diplomatic concessions in Cambodia." At the left-liberal end of the spectrum, in the journal of the Center for International Policy, a project of the Fund for Peace, a senior associate of the Carnegie Foundation for International Peace calls for reconciliation with Vietnam, urging that we put aside "the agony of the Vietnam experience" and "the injuries of the past," and overcome the "hatred, anger, and frustration" caused us by the Vietnamese, though we must not forget "the humanitarian issues left over from the war": the MIAs, those qualified to emigrate to the United States, and the remaining inmates of reeducation camps. So profound are the humanitarian impulses that guide this deeply moral society that even the right-wing Senator John McCain is now calling for diplomatic relations with Vietnam. He says that he holds "no hatred" for the Vietnamese even though he is "a former Navy pilot who spent 5½ years as an unwilling guest in the Hanoi Hilton," editor David Greenway of the *Boston Globe* comments, adding that "If McCain can put aside his bitterness, so can we all."[33] Greenway knows Vietnam well, having compiled an outstanding record as a war correspondent there. But in the prevailing moral climate, the educated community he addresses would not find it odd to urge that we overcome our natural bitterness against the Vietnamese for what they did to us.

"In history," Francis Jennings observes, "the man in the ruffled shirt and gold-laced waistcoat somehow levitates above the blood he has ordered to be spilled by dirty-handed underlings."[34]

These examples illustrate the power of the system that manufactures necessary illusions, at least among the educated elites who are the prime targets of propaganda, and its purveyors. It would be difficult to conjure up an achievement that might lie beyond the reach of mechanisms of indoctrination that can portray the United States as an innocent victim of Vietnam, while at the same time pondering the nation's excesses of self-flagellation.

Journalists not subject to the same influences and requirements see a somewhat different picture. In an Israeli mass-circulation daily, Amnon Kapeliouk published a series of thoughtful and sympathetic articles on a 1988 visit to Vietnam. One is headlined "Thousands of Vietnamese still die from the effects of American chemical warfare." He reports estimates of one-quarter of a million victims in South Vietnam in addition to the thousands killed by unexploded ordnance—3,700 since 1975 in the Danang area alone. Kapeliouk describes the "terrifying" scenes in hospitals in the south with children dying of cancer and hideous birth deformities; it was South Vietnam, of course, that was targeted for chemical warfare, not the North, where these consequences are not found, he reports. There is little hope for amelioration in the coming years, Vietnamese doctors fear, as the effects linger on in the devastated southern region of this "bereaved country," with its millions of dead and millions more widows and orphans, and where one hears "hair-raising stories that remind me of what we heard during the trials of Eichmann and Demjanjuk" from victims who, remarkably, "express no hatred against the American people." In this case, of course, the perpetrators are not tried, but are honored for their crimes in the civilized Western world.[35]

Here, too, some have been concerned over the effects of the chemical warfare that sprayed millions of gallons of Agent Orange and other poisonous chemicals over an area the size of Massachusetts in South Vietnam, more in Laos and Cambodia. Dr. Grace Ziem, a specialist on chemical exposure and disease who teaches at the University of Maryland Medical School, addressed the topic after a two-week visit to Vietnam, where she had worked as a doctor in the 1960s. She too described visits to hospitals in the south, where she inspected the sealed transparent containers with hideously malformed babies and the many patients from heavily sprayed areas, women with extremely rare malignant tumors, and children with deformities found far beyond the norm. But her account appeared far from the mainstream, where the story, when reported at all, has quite a different cast and focus. Thus, in an article on how the Japanese are attempting to conceal their World War II crimes, we read that one Japanese apologist referred to U.S. troops who scattered poisons by helicopter; "presumably," the reporter explains, he was referring to "Agent Orange, a defoliant suspected to have caused birth defects among Vietnamese and the children of American servicemen." No further reflections are suggested, in this context. And we can read about "the $180 million in chemical companies' compensation to Agent Orange victims"—U.S. soldiers, that is, not the Vietnamese civilians whose suffering is vastly greater. And somehow, these matters scarcely arose as indignation swelled in 1988 over alleged plans by Libya to develop chemical weapons.[36]

The right turn among elites took political shape during the latter years of the Carter administration and in the Reagan years, when the proposed policies were implemented and extended with a bipartisan consensus. But, as the Reaganite state managers discovered, the "Vietnam syndrome" proved to be a tough nut to crack; hence the vast increase in clandestine operations as the state was driven underground by the domestic enemy.

As it became necessary by the mid-1980s to face the costs of Reaganite military Keynesian policies, including the huge budget and trade deficits and foreign debt, it was predictable, and predicted, that the "Evil Empire" would become less threatening and the plague of international terrorism would subside, not so much because the world was all that different, but because of the new problems faced by the state management. Several years later, the results are apparent. Among the very ideologues who were ranting about the ineradicable evil of the Soviet barbarians and their minions, the statesmanlike approach is now mandatory, along with summitry and arms negotiations. But the basic long-term problems remain, and will have to be addressed.

Throughout this period of U.S. global hegemony, exalted rhetoric aside, there has been no hesitation to resort to force if the welfare of U.S. elites is threatened by what secret documents describe as the threat of "nationalistic regimes" that are responsive to popular demands for "improvement in the low living standards of the masses" and production for domestic needs, and that seek to control their own resources. To counter such threats, high-level planning documents explain, the United States must encourage "a political and economic climate conducive to private investment of both foreign and domestic capital," including the "opportunity to earn and in the case of foreign capital to repatriate a reasonable return."[37] The means, it is frankly explained, must ultimately be force, since such policies somehow fail to gain much popular support and are constantly threatened by the subversive elements called "Communist."

In the Third World, we must ensure "the protection of our raw materials" (as George Kennan put it) and encourage export-oriented production, maintaining a framework of liberal internationalism—at least insofar as it serves the needs of U.S. investors. Internationally, as at home, the free market is an ideal to be lauded if its outcome accords with the perceived needs of domestic power and privilege; if not, the market must be guided by efficient use of state power.

If the media, and the respectable intellectual community generally, are to serve their "societal purpose," such matters as these must be kept beyond the pale, remote from public awareness, and the massive evidence provided by the documentary record and evolving history must be consigned to dusty archives or marginal publications. We may speak in retrospect of blunders, misinterpretation, exaggeration of the Communist threat, faulty assessments of national security, personal failings, even corruption and deceit on the part of leaders gone astray; but the study of institutions and how they function must be scrupulously ignored, apart from fringe elements or a relatively obscure scholarly literature. These results have been quite satisfactorily achieved.

In capitalist democracies of the Third World, the situation is often much the same. Costa Rica, for example, is rightly regarded as the model democracy of Latin America. The press is firmly in the hands of the ultra-right, so there need be no concern over freedom of the press in Costa Rica, and none is expressed. In this case, the result was achieved not by force but rather by the free market assisted by legal measures to control "Communists," and, it appears, by an influx of North American capital in the 1960s.

Where such means have not sufficed to enforce the approved version of democracy and freedom of the press, others are readily available and are apparently considered right and proper, so long as they succeed. El Salvador in the past decade provides a dramatic illustration. In the 1970s, there was a proliferation of "popular organizations," many sponsored by the Church, including peasant associations, self-help groups, unions, and so on. The reaction was a violent outburst of state terror, organized by the United States with bipartisan backing and general media support as well. Any residual qualms dissolved after "demonstration elections" had been conducted for the benefit of the home front,[38] while the Reagan administration ordered a reduction in the more visible atrocities when the population was judged to be sufficiently traumatized and it was feared that reports of torture, murder, mutilation, and disappearance might endanger funding and support for the lower levels of state terror still deemed necessary.

There had been an independent press in El Salvador: two small newspapers, *La Crónica del Pueblo* and *El Independiente*. Both were destroyed in 1980–81 by the security forces. After a series of bombings, an editor of *La Crónica* and a photographer were taken from a San Salvador coffee shop and hacked to pieces with machetes; the offices were raided, bombed, and burned down by death squads, and the publisher fled to the United States. The publisher of *El Independiente*, Jorge Pinto, fled to Mexico when his paper's premises were attacked and equipment smashed by troops. Concern over these matters was so high in the United States that there was not one word in the *New York Times* news columns and not one editorial comment on the destruction of the journals, and no word in the years since, though Pinto was permitted a statement on the opinion page, in which he condemned the "Duarte junta" for having "succeeded in extinguishing the expression of any dissident opinion" and expressed his belief that the so-called death squads are "nothing more nor less than the military itself"—a conclusion endorsed by the Church and international human rights monitors.

In the year before the final destruction of *El Independiente*, the offices were bombed twice, an office boy was killed when the plant was machine-gunned, Pinto's car was sprayed with machine-gun fire, there were two other attempts on his life, and army troops in tanks and armored trucks arrived at his offices to search for him two days before the paper was finally destroyed. These events received no mention. Shortly before it was finally destroyed, there had been four bombings of *La Crónica* in six months; one of these, the last, received forty words in the *New York Times*.[39]

It is not that the U.S. media are unconcerned with freedom of the press in Central America. Contrasting sharply with the silence over the two Salvadoran newspapers is the case of the opposition journal *La Prensa* in Nicaragua.

Media critic Francisco Goldman counted 263 references to its tribulations in the *New York Times* in four years.[40] The distinguishing criterion is not obscure: the Salvadoran newspapers were independent voices stilled by the murderous violence of U.S. clients; *La Prensa* is an agency of the U.S. campaign to overthrow the government of Nicaragua, therefore a "worthy victim," whose harassment calls forth anguish and outrage. We return to further evidence that this is indeed the operative criterion.

Several months before his paper was destroyed, Dr. Jorge Napoleón Gonzales, the publisher of *La Crónica*, visited New York to plead for international pressure to "deter terrorists from destroying his paper." He cited right-wing threats and "what [his paper] calls Government repression," the *Times* noted judiciously. He reported that he had received threats from a death squad "that undoubtedly enjoys the support of the military," that two bombs had been found in his house, that the paper's offices were machine-gunned and set afire, and his home surrounded by soldiers. These problems began, he said, when his paper "began to demand reforms in landholdings," angering "the dominant classes." No international pressure developed, and the security forces completed their work.[41]

In the same years, the Church radio station in El Salvador was repeatedly bombed and troops occupied the Archdiocese building, destroying the radio station and ransacking the newspaper offices. Again, this elicited no media reaction.

These matters did not arise in the enthusiastic reporting of El Salvador's "free elections" in 1982 and 1984. Later, we were regularly informed by *Times* Central America correspondent James LeMoyne that the country enjoyed greater freedom than enemy Nicaragua, where nothing remotely comparable to the Salvadoran atrocities had taken place, and opposition leaders and media that are funded by the U.S. government and openly support its attack against Nicaragua complain of harassment, but not terror and assassination. Nor would the *Times* Central America correspondents report that leading Church figures who fled from El Salvador (including a close associate of the assassinated Archbishop Romero), well-known Salvadoran writers, and others who are by no stretch of the imagination political activists, and who are well-known to *Times* correspondents, cannot return to the death squad democracy they praise and protect, for fear of assassination. *Times* editors call upon the Reagan administration to use "its pressure on behalf of peace and pluralism in Nicaragua," where the government had a "dreadful record" of "harassing those who dare to exercise . . . free speech," and where there had never been "a free, contested election."[42] No such strictures apply to El Salvador.

In such ways, the Free Press labors to implant the illusions that are necessary to contain the domestic enemy.

17.

Introduction to *The Minimalist Program*

This work is motivated by two related questions: (1) what are the general conditions that the human language faculty should be expected to satisfy? and (2) to what extent is the language faculty determined by these conditions, without special structure that lies beyond them? The first question in turn has two aspects: what conditions are imposed on the language faculty by virtue of (A) its place within the array of cognitive systems of the mind/brain, and (B) general considerations of conceptual naturalness that have some independent plausibility, namely, simplicity, economy, symmetry, nonredundancy, and the like?

Question (B) is not precise, but not without content; attention to these matters can provide guidelines here, as in rational inquiry generally. Insofar as such considerations can be clarified and rendered plausible, we can ask whether a particular system satisfies them in one or another form. Question (A), in contrast, has an exact answer, though only parts of it can be surmised in the light of current understanding about language and related cognitive systems.

To the extent that the answer to question (2) is positive, language is something like a "perfect system," meeting external constraints as well as can be done, in one of the reasonable ways. The Minimalist Program for linguistic theory seeks to explore these possibilities.

This chapter first appeared in *The Minimalist Program* (Cambridge, MA: MIT Press, 1995), 1–11.

Any progress toward this goal will deepen a problem for the biological sciences that is already far from trivial: how can a system such as human language arise in the mind/brain, or for that matter, in the organic world, in which one seems not to find anything like the basic properties of human language? That problem has sometimes been posed as a crisis for the cognitive sciences. The concerns are appropriate, but their locus is misplaced; they are primarily a problem for biology and the brain sciences, which, as currently understood, do not provide any basis for what appear to be fairly well established conclusions about language.[1] Much of the broader interest of the detailed and technical study of language lies right here, in my opinion.

The Minimalist Program shares several underlying factual assumptions with its predecessors back to the early 1950s, though these have taken somewhat different forms as inquiry has proceeded. One is that there is a component of the human mind/brain dedicated to language—the language faculty—interacting with other systems. Though not obviously correct, this assumption seems reasonably well-established, and I will continue to take it for granted here, along with the further empirical thesis that the language faculty has at least two components: a cognitive system that stores information, and performance systems that access that information and use it in various ways. It is the cognitive system that primarily concerns us here.

Performance systems are presumably at least in part language-specific, hence components of the language faculty. But they are generally assumed not to be specific to particular languages: they do not vary in the manner of the cognitive system, as linguistic environments vary. This is the simplest assumption, and is not known to be false, though it may well be. Knowing of no better ideas, I will keep to it, assuming language variation to be restricted to the cognitive system.

I also borrow from earlier work the assumption that the cognitive system interacts with the performance systems by means of levels of linguistic representation, in the technical sense of this notion.[2] A more specific assumption is that the cognitive system interacts with just two such "external" systems: the articulatory-perceptual system A-P and the conceptual-intentional system C-I. Accordingly, there are two *interface levels*, Phonetic Form (PF) at the A-P interface and Logical Form (LF) at the C-I interface. This "double interface" property is one way to express the traditional description of language as sound with a meaning, traceable at least back to Aristotle.

Though commonly adopted, at least tacitly, these assumptions about the internal architecture of the language faculty and its place among other systems of the mind/brain are not at all obvious. Even within the general framework, the idea that articulation and perception involve the same interface representation is controversial, and arguably incorrect in some fundamental way.[3] Problems relating to the C-I interface are still more obscure and poorly understood. I will keep to these fairly conventional assumptions, only noting here that if they turn out to be correct, even in part, that would be a surprising and hence interesting discovery.

The leading questions that guide the Minimalist Program came into focus as the principles-and-parameters (P&P) model took shape about fifteen years ago. A look at recent history may be helpful in placing these questions in context. Needless to say, these remarks are schematic and selective, and benefit from hindsight.

Early generative grammar faced two immediate problems: to find a way to account for the phenomena of particular languages ("descriptive adequacy"), and to explain how knowledge of these facts arises in the mind of the speaker-hearer ("explanatory adequacy"). Though it was scarcely recognized at the time, this research program revived the concerns of a rich tradition, of which perhaps the last major representative was Otto Jespersen.[4] Jespersen recognized that the structures of language "come into existence in the mind of a speaker" by abstraction from experience with utterances, yielding a "notion of their structure" that is "definite enough to guide him in framing sentences of his own," crucially "free expressions" that are typically new to speaker and hearer.

We can take these properties of language to set the primary goals of linguistic theory: to spell out clearly this "notion of structure" and the procedure by which it yields "free expressions," and to explain how it arises in the mind of the speaker—the problems of descriptive and explanatory adequacy, respectively. To attain descriptive adequacy for a particular language L, the theory of L (its grammar) must characterize the state attained by the language faculty, or at least some of its aspects. To attain explanatory adequacy, a theory of language must characterize the initial state of the language faculty and show how it maps experience to the state attained. Jespersen held further that it is only "with regard to syntax" that we expect "that there must be something in common to all human speech"; there can be a "universal (or general) grammar," hence a perhaps far-reaching account of the initial state of the language faculty in this domain, though "no one ever dreamed of a universal morphology." That idea too has a certain resonance in recent work.

In the modern period these traditional concerns were displaced, in part by behaviorist currents, in part by various structuralist approaches, which radically narrowed the domain of inquiry while greatly expanding the database for some future inquiry that might return to the traditional—and surely valid—concerns. To address them required a better understanding of the fact that language involves "infinite use of finite means," in one classic formulation. Advances in the formal sciences provided that understanding, making it feasible to deal with the problems constructively. Generative grammar can be regarded as a kind of confluence of long-forgotten concerns of the study of language and mind, and new understanding provided by the formal sciences.

The first efforts to approach these problems quickly revealed that traditional grammatical and lexical studies do not begin to describe, let alone explain, the most elementary facts about even the best-studied languages. Rather, they provide hints that can be used by the reader who already has tacit knowledge of language, and of particular languages; the central topic of inquiry was, in substantial measure, simply ignored. Since the requisite tacit knowledge is so easily accessed without reflection, traditional grammars and dictionaries appear to have very broad coverage of linguistic data. That is an illusion, however, as we quickly discover when we try to spell out what is taken for granted: the nature of the language faculty, and its state in particular cases.

This is hardly a situation unique to the study of language. Typically, when questions are more sharply formulated, it is learned that even elementary phenomena had escaped notice, and that intuitive accounts that seemed simple and persuasive are entirely inadequate. If we are satisfied that an apple falls to the ground because that is its natural place, there will be no serious science of mechanics. The same is true if one is satisfied with traditional rules for forming questions, or with the lexical entries in the most elaborate dictionaries, none of which come close to describing simple properties of these linguistic objects.

Recognition of the unsuspected richness and complexity of the phenomena of language created a tension between the goals of descriptive and explanatory adequacy. It was clear that to achieve explanatory adequacy, a theory of the initial state must allow only limited variation: particular languages must be largely known in advance of experience. The options permitted in Universal Grammar (UG) must be highly restricted. Experience must suffice to fix them one way or another, yielding a state of the language faculty that determines the varied and complex array of expressions, their sound and meaning; and even the most superficial look reveals the chasm that separates the knowledge of the language user from the data of experience. But the goal of explanatory adequacy receded still further into the distance as generative systems were enriched in pursuit of descriptive adequacy, in radically different ways for different languages. The problem was exacerbated by the huge range of phenomena discovered when attempts were made to formulate actual rule systems for various languages.

This tension defined the research program of early generative grammar—at least, the tendency within it that concerns me here. From the early 1960s, its central objective was to abstract general principles from the complex rule systems devised for particular languages, leaving rules that are simple, constrained in their operation by these UG principles. Steps in this direction reduce the variety of language-specific properties, thus contributing to explanatory adequacy. They also tend to yield simpler and more natural theories, laying the groundwork for an eventual minimalist approach. There is no necessity that this be the case: it could turn out that an "uglier," richer, and more complex version of UG reduces permissible variety, thus contributing to the primary empirical goal of explanatory adequacy. In practice, however, the two enterprises have proven to be mutually reinforcing and have proceeded side by side. One illustration concerns redundant principles, with overlapping empirical coverage. Repeatedly, it has been found that these are wrongly formulated and must be replaced by nonredundant ones. The discovery has been so regular that the need to eliminate redundancy has become a working principle in inquiry. Again, this is a surprising property of a biological system.

These efforts culminated in the P&P model.[5] This constituted a radical break from the rich tradition of thousands of years of linguistic inquiry, far more so than early generative grammar, which could be seen as a revival of traditional concerns and approaches to them (perhaps the reason why it was often more congenial to traditional grammarians than to modern structural linguists). In contrast, the P&P approach maintains that the basic ideas of the tradition, incorporated without great change in early generative grammar, are misguided in principle—in particular, the idea that a language consists of rules for forming grammatical constructions (relative clauses, passives, etc.). The P&P approach held that languages have no rules in anything like the familiar sense, and no theoretically significant grammatical constructions except as taxonomic artifacts. There are universal principles and a finite array of options as to how they apply (parameters), but no language-particular rules and no grammatical constructions of the traditional sort within or across languages.

For each particular language, the cognitive system, we assume, consists of a computational system CS and a lexicon. The lexicon specifies the elements that CS selects and integrates to form linguistic expressions—(PF, LF) pairings, we assume. The lexicon should provide just the information that is required for CS, without redundancy and in some optimal form, excluding whatever is predictable by principles of UG or properties of the language in question. Virtually all items of the lexicon belong to the *substantive categories*, which we will take to be noun, verb, adjective, and particle, putting aside many serious questions about their nature and interrelations. The other categories we will call *functional* (tense, complementizer, etc.), a term that need not be made more precise at the outset, and that we will refine as we proceed.

Within the P&P approach the problems of typology and language variation arise in somewhat different form than before. Language differences and typology should be reducible to choice of values of parameters. A major research problem is to determine just what these options are, and in what components of language they are to be found. One proposal is that parameters are restricted to *formal features* with no interpretation at the interface.[6] A still stronger one is that they are restricted to formal features of functional categories.[7] Such theses could be regarded as a partial expression of Jespersen's intuition about the syntax-morphology divide. I will assume that something of the sort is correct, but without trying to be very clear about the matter, since too little is understood to venture any strong hypotheses, as far as I can see.

In this context, language acquisition is interpreted as the process of fixing the parameters of the initial state in one of the permissible ways. A specific choice of parameter settings determines a *language* in the technical sense that concerns us here: an I-language,[8] where I is understood to suggest "internal," "individual," and "intensional."

This way of formulating the issues, within the P&P model, brings out clearly a crucial inadequacy in the characterization of language as a state of the language faculty. The latter can hardly be expected to be an instantiation of the initial state with parameter values fixed. Rather, a state of the language faculty is some accidental product of varied experience, of no particular interest in itself, no more so than other collections of phenomena in the natural world (which is why scientists do experiments instead of recording what happens in natural circumstances). My personal feeling is that much more substantial idealization is required if we hope to understand the properties of the language faculty,[9] but misunderstandings and confusion engendered even by limited idealization are so pervasive that it may not be useful to pursue the matter today. *Idealization*, it should be noted, is a misleading term for the only reasonable way to approach a grasp of reality.

The P&P model is in part a bold speculation rather than a specific hypothesis. Nevertheless, its basic assumptions seem reasonable in the light of what is currently at all well understood, and they do suggest a natural way to resolve the tension between descriptive and explanatory adequacy. In fact, this departure from the tradition offered the first hope of addressing the crucial problem of explanatory adequacy, which had been put aside as too difficult. Earlier work in generative grammar sought only an evaluation measure that would select among alternative theories of a language (grammars) that fit the format prescribed by UG and are consistent with the relevant data. Beyond that, nothing seemed conceivable apart from some notion of "feasibility," left imprecise.[10] But if something like the P&P concept of I-language proves to be accurate—capturing the essential nature of the concept of language that is presupposed in the study of performance, acquisition, social interaction, and so on—then the question of explanatory adequacy can be seriously raised. It becomes the question of determining how values are set by experience for finitely many universal parameters, not a trivial problem by any means, but at least one that can be constructively pursued.

If these ideas prove to be on the right track, there is a single computational system C_{HL} for human language and only limited lexical variety. Variation of language is essentially morphological in character, including the critical question of which parts of a computation are overtly realized, a topic brought to the fore by Jean-Roger Vergnaud's theory of abstract case and James Huang's work on typologically varied interrogative and related constructions.

This account of the P&P approach overstates the case. Further variation among languages would be expected insofar as data are readily available to determine particular choices. There are several such domains. One is peripheral parts of the phonology. Another is "Saussurean arbitrariness," that is, the sound-meaning pairing for the substantive part of the lexicon. I put these matters aside, along with many others that appear to be of limited relevance to the computational properties of language that are the focus here, that is, that do not seem to enter into C_{HL}: among them, variability of semantic fields, selection from the lexical repertoire made available in UG, and nontrivial questions about the relation of lexical items to other cognitive systems.

Like the earliest proposals in generative grammar, formulation of the P&P model led to discovery and at least partial understanding of a vast range of new empirical materials, by now from a wide variety of typologically different languages. The questions that could be clearly posed and the empirical facts with which they deal are novel in depth and variety, a promising and encouraging development in itself.

With the tension between descriptive and explanatory adequacy reduced and the latter problem at least on the agenda, the tasks at hand become far harder and more interesting. The primary one is to show that the apparent richness and diversity of linguistic phenomena is illusory and epiphenomenal, the result of interaction of fixed principles under slightly varying conditions. The shift of perspective provided by the P&P approach also gives a different cast to the question of how simplicity considerations enter into the theory of grammar. As discussed in the earliest work in generative grammar, these considerations have two distinct forms: an imprecise but not vacuous notion of simplicity that enters into rational inquiry generally must be clearly distinguished from a theory-internal measure of simplicity that selects among I-languages.[11] The former notion of simplicity has nothing special to do with the study of language, but the theory-internal notion is a component of UG, part of the procedure for determining the relation between experience and I-language; its status is something like that of a physical constant. In early work, the internal notion took the form of an evaluation procedure to select among proposed grammars (in present terms, I-languages) consistent with the permitted format for rule systems. The P&P approach suggests a way to move beyond that limited though nontrivial goal and to address the problem of explanatory adequacy. With no evaluation procedure, there is no internal notion of simplicity in the earlier sense.

Nevertheless, rather similar ideas have resurfaced, this time in the form of economy considerations that select among derivations, barring those that are not optimal in a theory-internal sense. The external notion of simplicity remains unchanged: operative as always, even if only imprecisely.

At this point still further questions arise, namely, those of the Minimalist Program. How "perfect" is language? One expects "imperfections" in morphological-formal features of the lexicon and aspects of language induced by conditions at the A-P interface, at least. The essential question is whether, or to what extent, these components of the language faculty are the repository of departures from virtual conceptual necessity, so that the computational system C_{HL} is otherwise not only unique but in some interesting sense optimal. Looking at the same problem from a different perspective, we seek to determine just how far the evidence really carries us toward attributing specific structure to the language faculty, requiring that every departure from "perfection" be closely analyzed and well motivated.

Progress toward this further goal places a huge descriptive burden on the answers to the questions (A) and (B): the effect of the interface conditions, and the specific formulation of general considerations of internal coherence, conceptual naturalness, and the like—"simplicity," in the external sense. The empirical burden, already substantial in any P&P theory, now becomes far more severe.

The problems that arise are therefore extremely interesting. It is, I think, of considerable importance that we can at least formulate such questions today, and even approach them in some areas with a degree of success. If recent thinking along these lines is anywhere near accurate, a rich and exciting future lies ahead for the study of language and related disciplines. . . .

18.

New Horizons in the Study of Language and Mind

The study of language is one of the oldest branches of systematic inquiry, tracing back to classical India and Greece, with a rich and fruitful history of achievement. From a different point of view, it is quite young. The major research enterprises of today took shape only about forty years ago, when some of the leading ideas of the tradition were revived and reconstructed, opening the way to what has proven to be very productive inquiry.

That language should have exercised such fascination over the years is not surprising. The human faculty of language seems to be a true "species property," varying little among humans and without significant analogue elsewhere. Probably the closest analogues are found in insects, at an evolutionary distance of a billion years. There is no serious reason today to challenge the Cartesian view that the ability to use linguistic signs to express freely formed thoughts marks "the true distinction between man and animal" or machine, whether by "machine" we mean the automata that captured the imagination of the seventeenth and eighteenth century, or those that are providing a stimulus to thought and imagination today.

Furthermore, the faculty of language enters crucially into every aspect of human life, thought, and interaction. It is largely responsible for the fact that alone in the biological world, humans have a history, cultural evolution, and diversity of any complexity and richness, even biological success in the tech-

This chapter first appeared in *New Horizons in the Study of Language and Mind* (Cambridge: Cambridge University Press, 2000), 3–18.

nical sense that their numbers are huge. A Martian scientist observing the strange doings on Earth could hardly fail to be struck by the emergence and significance of this apparently unique form of intellectual organization. It is even more natural that the topic, with its many mysteries, should have stimulated the curiousity of those who seek to understand their own nature and their place within the wider world.

Human language is based on an elementary property that also seems to be biologically isolated: the property of discrete infinity, which is exhibited in its purest form by the natural numbers 1, 2, 3, . . . Children do not learn this property; unless the mind already possesses the basic principles, no amount of evidence could provide them. Similarly, no child has to learn that there are three and four word sentences, but no three-and-a half word sentences, and that they go on forever; it is always possible to construct a more complex one, with a definite form and meaning. Such knowledge must come to us from "the original hand of nature," in David Hume's phrase, as part of our biological endowment.[1]

This property intrigued Galileo, who regarded the discovery of a means to communicate our "most secret thoughts to any other person with 24 little characters" as the greatest of all human inventions.[2] The invention succeeds because it reflects the discrete infinity of the language that these characters are used to represent. Shortly after, the authors of the Port Royal Grammar were struck by the "marvellous invention" of a means to construct from a few dozen sounds an infinity of expressions that enable us to reveal to others what we think and imagine and feel—from a contemporary standpoint, not an "invention" but no less "marvellous" as a product of biological evolution, about which virtually nothing is known, in this case.

The faculty of language can reasonably be regarded as a "language organ" in the sense in which scientists speak of the visual system, or immune system, or circulatory system, as organs of the body. Understood in this way, an organ is not something that can be removed from the body, leaving the rest intact. It is a subsystem of a more complex structure. We hope to understand the full complexity by investigating parts that have distinctive characteristics, and their interactions. Study of the faculty of language proceeds in the same way.

We assume further that the language organ is like others in that its basic character is an expression of the genes. How that happens remains a distant prospect for inquiry, but we can investigate the genetically determined "initial state" of the language faculty in other ways. Evidently, each language is the result of the interplay of two factors: the initial state and the course of experience. We can think of the initial state as a "language acquisition device" that takes experience as "input" and gives the language as an "output"—an "output" that is internally represented in the mind/brain. The input and the output are both open to examination: we can study the course of experience and the properties of the languages that are acquired. What is learned in this way can tell us quite a lot about the initial state that mediates between them.

Furthermore, there is strong reason to believe that the initial state is common to the species: if my children had grown up in Tokyo, they would speak Japanese, like other children there. That means that evidence about Japanese bears directly on the assumptions concerning the initial state for English. In such ways, it is possible to establish strong empirical conditions that the theory of the initial state must satisfy, and also to pose several problems for the biology of language: How do the genes determine the initial state, and what are the brain mechanisms involved in the initial state and the later states it assumes? These are extremely hard problems, even for much simpler systems where direct experiment is possible, but some may be at the horizons of inquiry.

The approach I have been outlining is concerned with the faculty of language: its initial state, and the states it assumes. Suppose that Peter's language organ is in state L. We can think of L as Peter's "internalized language." When I speak of a language here, that is what I mean. So understood, a language is something like "the way we speak and understand," one traditional conception of language.

Adapting a traditional term to a new framework, we call the theory of Peter's language the "grammar" of his language. Peter's language determines an infinite array of expressions, each with its sound and meaning. In technical terms, Peter's language "generates" the expressions of his language. The theory of his language is therefore called a generative grammar. Each expression is a complex of properties, which provide "instructions" for Peter's performance systems: his articulatory apparatus, his modes of organizing his thoughts, and so on. With his language and the associated performance systems in place, Peter has a vast amount of knowledge about the sound and meaning of expressions, and a corresponding capacity to interpret what he hears, express his thoughts, and use his language in a variety of other ways.

Generative grammar arose in the context of what is often called "the cognitive revolution" of the 1950s, and was an important factor in its development. Whether or not the term "revolution" is appropriate, there was an important change of perspective: from the study of behavior and its products (such as texts), to the inner mechanisms that enter into thought and action. The cognitive perspective regards behavior and its products not as the object of inquiry, but as data that may provide evidence about the inner mechanisms of mind and the ways these mechanisms operate in executing actions and interpreting experience. The properties and patterns that were the focus of attention in structural linguistics find their place, but as phenomena to be explained along with innumerable others, in terms of the inner mechanisms that generate expressions. The approach is "mentalistic," but in what should be an uncontroversial sense. It is concerned with "mental aspects of the world," which stand alongside its mechanical, chemical, optical, and other aspects. It undertakes to study a real object in the natural world—the brain, its states, and its functions—and thus to move the study of the mind towards eventual integration with the biological sciences.

The "cognitive revolution" renewed and reshaped many of the insights, achievements, and quandaries of what we might call "the first cognitive revolution" of the seventeenth and eighteenth century, which was part of the scientific revolution that so radically modified our understanding of the world. It was recognized at the time that language involves "the infinite use of finite means," in Wilhelm von Humboldt's phrase; but the insight could be developed only in limited ways, because the basic ideas remained vague and obscure. By the middle of the twentieth century, advances in the formal sciences had provided appropriate concepts in a very sharp and clear form, making it possible to give a precise account of the computational principles that generate the expressions of a language, and thus to capture, at least partially, the idea of "infinite use of finite means." Other advances also opened the way to investigation of traditional questions with greater hope of success. The study of language change had registered major achievements. Anthropological linguistics provided a far richer understanding of the nature and variety of languages, also undermining many stereotypes. And certain topics, notably the study of sound systems, had been much advanced by the structural linguistics of the twentieth century.

The earliest attempts to carry out the program of generative grammar quickly revealed that even in the best studied languages, elementary properties had passed unrecognized, that the most comprehensive traditional grammars and dictionaries only skim the surface. The basic properties of languages are presupposed throughout, unrecognized and unexpressed. That is quite appropriate if the goal is to help people to learn a second language, to find the conventional meaning and pronunciation of words, or to have some general idea of how languages differ. But if our goal is to understand the language faculty and the states it can assume, we cannot tacitly presuppose "the intelligence of the reader." Rather, this is the object of inquiry.

The study of language acquisition leads to the same conclusion. A careful look at the interpretation of expressions reveals very quickly that from the earliest stages, the child knows vastly more than experience has provided. That is true even of simple words. At peak periods of language growth, a child is acquiring words at a rate of about one an hour, with extremely limited exposure under highly ambiguous conditions. The words are understood in delicate and intricate ways that are far beyond the reach of any dictionary, and are only beginning to be investigated. When we move beyond single words, the conclusion becomes even more dramatic. Language acquisition seems much like the growth of organs generally; it is something that happens to a child, not that the child does. And while the environment plainly matters, the general course of development and the basic features of what emerges are predetermined by the initial state. But the initial state is a common human possession. It must be, then, that in their essential properties and even down to fine detail, languages are cast to the same mold. The Martian scientist might reasonably conclude that there is a single human language, with differences only at the margins.

As languages were more carefully investigated from the point of view of generative grammar, it became clear that their diversity had been underestimated as radically as their complexity and the extent to which they are determined by the initial state of the faculty of language. At the same time, we know that the diversity and complexity can be no more than superficial appearance.

These were surprising conclusions, paradoxical but undeniable. They pose in a stark form what has become the central problem of the modern study of language: How can we show that all languages are variations on a single theme, while at the same time recording faithfully their intricate properties of sound and meaning, superficially diverse? A genuine theory of human language has to satisfy two conditions: "descriptive adequacy" and "explanatory adequacy." The grammar of a particular language satisfies the condition of descriptive adequacy insofar as it gives a full and accurate account of the properties of the language, of what the speaker of the language knows. To satisfy the condition of explanatory adequacy, a theory of language must show how each particular language can be derived from a uniform initial state under the "boundary conditions" set by experience. In this way, it provides an explanation of the properties of languages at a deeper level.

There is a serious tension between these two research tasks. The search for descriptive adequacy seems to lead to ever greater complexity and variety of rule systems, while the search for explanatory adequacy requires that language structure must be invariant, except at the margins. It is this tension that has largely set the guidelines for research. The natural way to resolve the tension is to challenge the traditional assumption, carried over to early generative grammar, that a language is a complex system of rules, each specific to particular languages and particular grammatical constructions: rules for forming relative clauses in Hindi, verb phrases in Swahili, passives in Japanese, and so on. Considerations of explanatory adequacy indicate that this cannot be correct.

The central problem was to find general properties of rule systems that can be attributed to the faculty of language itself, in the hope that the residue will prove to be more simple and uniform. About fifteen years ago, these efforts crystallized in an approach to language that was a much more radical departure from the tradition than earlier generative grammar had been. This "Principles and Parameters" approach, as it has been called, rejected the concept of rule and grammatical construction entirely: there are no rules for forming relative clauses in Hindi, verb phrases in Swahili, passives in Japanese, and so on. The familiar grammatical constructions are taken to be taxonomic artifacts, useful for informal description perhaps but with no theoretical standing. They have something like the status of "terrestrial mammal" or "household pet." And the rules are decomposed into general principles of the faculty of language, which interact to yield the properties of expressions.

We can think of the initial state of the faculty of language as a fixed network connected to a switch box; the network is constituted of the principles of language, while the switches are the options to be determined by experience. When the switches are set one way, we have Swahili; when they are set another way, we have Japanese. Each possible human language is identified as a particular setting of the switches—a setting of parameters, in technical terminology. If the research program succeeds, we should be able literally to deduce Swahili from one choice of settings, Japanese from another, and so on through the languages that humans can acquire. The empirical conditions of language acquisition require that the switches can be set on the basis of the very limited information that is available to the child. Notice that small changes in switch settings can lead to great apparent variety in output, as the effects proliferate through the system. These are the general properties of language that any genuine theory must capture somehow.

This is, of course, a program, and it is far from a finished product. The conclusions tentatively reached are unlikely to stand in their present form; and, needless to say, one can have no certainty that the whole approach is on the right track. As a research program, however, it has been highly successful, leading to a real explosion of empirical inquiry into languages of a very broad typological range, to new questions that could never even have been formulated before, and to many intriguing answers. Questions of acquisition, processing, pathology, and others also took new forms, which have proven very productive as well. Furthermore, whatever its fate, the program suggests how the theory of language might satisfy the conflicting conditions of descriptive and explanatory adequacy. It gives at least an outline of a genuine theory of language, really for the first time.

Within this research program, the main task is to discover and clarify the principles and parameters and the manner of their interaction, and to extend the framework to include other aspects of language and its use. While a great deal remains obscure, there has been enough progress to at least consider, perhaps to pursue, some new and more far-reaching questions about the design of language. In particular, we can ask how good the design is. How close does language come to what some super-engineer would construct, given the conditions that the language faculty must satisfy?

The questions have to be sharpened, and there are ways to proceed. The faculty of language is embedded within the broader architecture of the mind/brain. It interacts with other systems, which impose conditions that language must satisfy if it is to be usable at all. We might think of these as "legibility conditions," in the sense that other systems must be able to "read" the expressions of the language and use them as "instructions" for thought and action. The sensorimotor systems, for example, have to be able to read the instructions having to do with sound, that is the "phonetic representations" generated by the language. The articulatory and perceptual apparatus have specific design that enables them to interpret certain phonetic properties, not others. These systems thus impose legibility conditions on the generative processes of the faculty of language, which must provide expressions with the proper phonetic form. The same is true of conceptual and other systems that make use of the resources of the faculty of language: they have their intrinsic properties, which require that the expressions generated by the language have certain kinds of "semantic representations," not others. We may therefore ask to what extent language is a "good solution" to the legibility conditions imposed by the external systems with which it interacts. Until quite recently this question could not seriously be posed, even formulated sensibly. Now it seems that it can, and there are even indications that the language faculty may be close to "perfect" in this sense; if true, this is a surprising conclusion.

What has come to be called "the Minimalist Program" is an effort to explore these questions. It is too soon to offer a firm judgment about the project. My own judgment is that the questions can now profitably be placed on the agenda, and that early results are promising. I would like to say a few words about the ideas and the prospects, and then to return to some problems that remain at the horizons.

The Minimalist Program requires that we subject conventional assumptions to careful scrutiny. The most venerable of these is that language has sound and meaning. In current terms, that translates in a natural way to the thesis that the faculty of language engages other systems of the mind/brain at two "interface levels," one related to sound, and the other to meaning. A particular expression generated by the language contains a phonetic representation that is legible to the sensorimotor systems, and a semantic representation that is legible to conceptual and other systems of thought and action.

One question is whether there are levels other than the interface levels: Are there levels "internal" to the language, in particular, the levels of deep and surface structure that have been postulated in modern work?[3] The Minimalist Program seeks to show that everything that has been accounted for in terms of these levels has been misdescribed, and is as well or better understood in terms of legibility conditions at the interface: for those of you who know the technical literature, that means the projection principle, binding theory, case theory, the chain condition, and so on.

We also try to show that the only computational operations are those that are unavoidable on the weakest assumptions about interface properties. One such assumption is that there are wordlike units: the external systems have to be able to interpret such items as "Peter" and "tall." Another is that these items are organized into larger expressions, such as "Peter is tall." A third is that the items have properties of sound and meaning: the word "Peter" begins with closure of the lips and is used to refer to persons. The language therefore involves three kinds of elements:

- the properties of sound and meaning, called "features";
- the items that are assembled from these properties, called "lexical items"; and
- the complex expressions constructed from these "atomic" units.

It follows that the computational system that generates expressions has two basic operations: one assembles features into lexical items, the second forms larger syntactic objects out of those already constructed, beginning with lexical items.

We can think of the first operation as essentially a list of lexical items. In traditional terms, this list—called the lexicon—is the list of "exceptions," arbitrary associations of sound and meaning and particular choices among the inflectional properties made available by the faculty of language that determine how we indicate that nouns and verbs are plural or singular, that nouns have nominative or accusative case, and so on. These inflectional features turn out to play a central role in computation.

Optimal design would introduce no new features in the course of computation. There should be no indices or phrasal units and no bar levels (hence no phrase-structure rules or X-bar theory).[4] We also try to show that no structural relations are invoked other than those forced by legibility conditions or induced in some natural way by the computation itself. In the first category, we have such properties as adjacency at the phonetic level, and argument-structure and quantifier-variable relations at the semantic level. In the second category, we have very local relations between features, and elementary relations between two syntactic objects joined together in the course of computation: the relation holding between one of these and the parts of the other is the relation of c-command; as Samuel Epstein[5] has pointed out, this is a notion that plays a central role throughout language design and has been regarded as highly unnatural, though it falls into place in a natural way from this perspective. But we exclude government, binding relations internal to the derivation of expressions, and a variety of other relations and interactions.

As anyone familiar with recent work will be aware, there is ample empirical evidence to support the opposite conclusion throughout. Worse yet, a core assumption of the work within the Principles-and-Parameters framework, and its fairly impressive achievements, is that everything I have just proposed is false—that language is highly "imperfect" in these respects, as might well be expected. So it is no small task to show that such apparatus is eliminable as unwanted descriptive technology; or even better, that descriptive and explanatory force are extended if such "excess baggage" is shed. Nevertheless, I think that work of the past few years suggests that these conclusions, which seemed out of the question before that, are at least plausible, and quite possibly correct.

Languages plainly differ, and we want to know how. One respect is in choice of sounds, which vary within a certain range. Another is in the association of sound and meaning, which is essentially arbitrary. These are straightforward and need not detain us. More interesting is the fact that languages differ in inflectional systems: case systems, for example. We find that these are fairly rich in Latin, even more so in Sanskrit or Finnish, but minimal in English and invisible in Chinese. Or so it appears; considerations of explanatory adequacy suggest that here too appearance may be misleading, and in fact, recent work[6] indicates that these systems vary much less than appears to be the case from the surface forms. Chinese and English, for example, may have the same case system as Latin, but the phonetic realization is different. Furthermore, it seems that much of the variety of language can be reduced to properties of inflectional systems. If this is correct, then language variation is located in a narrow part of the lexicon.

Legibility conditions impose a three-way division among the features assembled into lexical items:

1. semantic features, interpreted at the semantic interface;
2. phonetic features, interpreted at the phonetic interface; and
3. features that are not interpreted at either interface.

In a perfectly designed language, each feature would be semantic or phonetic, not merely a device to create a position or to facilitate computation. If so, there are no uninterpretable formal features. That is too strong a requirement, it seems. Such prototypical formal features as structural case—Latin nominative and accusative, for example—have no interpretation at the semantic interface, and need not be expressed at the phonetic level. And there are other examples as well within inflectional systems.

In the syntactic computation, there seems to be a second and more dramatic imperfection in language design, at least an apparent one: the "displacement property" that is a pervasive aspect of language: phrases are interpreted as if they were in a different position in the expression, where similar items sometimes do appear and are interpreted in terms of natural local relations. Take the sentence "Clinton seems to have been elected." We understand the relation of "elect" and "Clinton" as we do when they are locally related in the sentence "It seems that they elected Clinton": "Clinton" is the direct object of "elect," in traditional terms, though "displaced" to the position of subject of "seems"; the subject and verb agree in inflectional features in this case, but have no semantic relation; the semantic relation of the subject is to the remote verb "elect."

We now have two "imperfections": uninterpretable features, and the displacement property. On the assumption of optimal design, we would expect them to be related, and that seems to be the case: uninterpretable features are the mechanism that implements the displacement property.

The displacement property is never built into the symbolic systems that are designed for special purposes, called "languages" or "formal languages" in a metaphoric usage: "the language of arithmetic," or "computer languages," or "the languages of science." These systems also have no inflectional systems, hence no uninterpreted features. Displacement and inflection are special properties of human language, among the many that are ignored when symbolic systems are designed for other purposes, which may disregard the legibility conditions imposed on human language by the architecture of the mind/brain.

The displacement property of human language is expressed in terms of grammatical transformations or by some other device, but it is always expressed somehow. Why language should have this property is an interesting question, which has been discussed since the 1960s without resolution. My suspicion is that part of the reason has to do with phenomena that have been described in terms of surface structure interpretation; many of these are familiar from traditional grammar: topic-comment, specificity, new and old information, the agentive force that we find even in displaced position, and so on. If that is correct, then the displacement property is, indeed, forced by legibility conditions: it is motivated by interpretive requirements that are externally imposed by our systems of thought, which have these special properties (so the study of language use indicates). These questions are currently being investigated in interesting ways, which I cannot go into here.

From the origins of generative grammar, the computational operations were assumed to be of two kinds:

- phrase-structure rules that form larger syntactic objects from lexical items, and
- transformational rules that express the displacement property.

Both have traditional roots, but it was quickly found that they differ substantially from what had been supposed, with unsuspected variety and complexity. The research program sought to show that the complexity and variety are only apparent, and that the two kinds of rules can be reduced to simpler form. A "perfect" solution to the problem of variety of phrase-structure rules would be to eliminate them entirely in favor of the irreducible operation that takes two objects already formed and attaches one to the other, forming a larger object with just the properties of the target of attachment: the operation we can call Merge. Recent work indicates that this goal may well be attainable.

The optimal computational procedure consists, then, of the operation Merge and operations to construct the displacement property: transformational operations or some counterpart. The second of the two parallel endeavors sought to reduce the transformational component to the simplest form; though unlike phrase-structure rules, it seems to be ineliminable. The end result was the thesis that for a core set of phenomena, there is just a single operation Move—basically, move anything anywhere, with no properties specific to languages or particular constructions. How it applies is determined by general principles interacting with the specific parameter choices—switch settings—that determine a particular language. The operation Merge takes two distinct objects X and Y and attaches Y to X. The operation Move takes a single object X and an object Y that is part of X, and merges Y to X.

The next problem is to show that it is, indeed, the case that uninterpretable features are the mechanism that implements the displacement property, so that the two basic imperfections of the computational system reduce to one. If it turns out that the displacement property is motivated by legibility conditions imposed by external systems of thought, as I just suggested, then the imperfections are eliminated completely and language design turns out to be optimal after all: uninterpreted features are required as a mechanism to satisfy a legibility condition imposed by the general architecture of the mind/brain.

The way this unification proceeds is quite simple, but to explain it coherently would go beyond the scope of these remarks. The basic intuitive idea is that uninterpretable features have to be erased to satisfy the interface condition, and erasure requires a local relation between the offending feature and a matching feature that can erase it. Typically these two features are remote from one another for reasons having to do with the way semantic interpretation proceeds. For example, in the sentence "Clinton seems to have been elected," semantic interpretation requires that "elect" and "Clinton" be locally related in the phrase "elect Clinton" for the construction to be properly interpreted, as if the sentence were actually "seems to have been elected Clinton." The main verb of the sentence, "seems," has inflectional features that are uninterpretable: it is singular/third person/masculine, properties that add nothing independent to the meaning of the sentence, since they are already expressed in the noun phrase that agrees with it, and are ineliminable there. These offending features of "seems" therefore have to be erased in a local relation, an explicit version of the traditional descriptive category of "agreement." To achieve this result, the matching features of the agreeing phrase "Clinton" are attracted by the offending features of the main verb "seems," which are then erased under local matching. But now the phrase "Clinton" is displaced.

Note that only the *features* of "Clinton" are attracted; the full phrase moves for reasons having to do with the sensorimotor system, which is unable to "pronounce" or "hear" isolated features separated from the phrase in which they belong. However, if for some reason the sensorimotor system is inactivated, then the features alone raise, and alongside of such sentences as "an unpopular candidate seems to have been elected," with overt displacement, we have sentences of the form "seems to have been elected an unpopular candidate"; here the remote phrase "an unpopular candidate" agrees with the verb "seems," which means that its features have been attracted to a local relation with "seem" while leaving the rest of the phrase behind. The fact that the sensorimotor system has been inactivated is called "covert movement," a phenomenon with quite interesting properties. In many languages—Spanish for example—there are such sentences. English has them too, though it is necessary for other reasons to introduce the semantically empty element "there," giving the sentence "there seems to have been elected an unpopular candidate"; and also, for quite interesting reasons, to carry out an inversion of order, so it comes out "there seems to have been an unpopular candidate elected." These properties follow from specific choices of parameters, which have effects through the languages generally and interact to give a complex array of phenomena which are only superficially distinct. In the case we are looking at, all reduce to the simple fact that uninterpretable formal features must be erased in a local relation with a matching feature, yielding the displacement property required for semantic interpretation at the interface.

There is a fair amount of hand-waving in this brief description. Filling in the blanks yields a rather interesting picture, with many ramifications in typologically different languages. But to go on would take us well beyond the scope of these remarks.

I'd like to finish with at least brief reference to other issues, having to do with the ways the internalist study of language relates to the external world. For simplicity, let's keep to simple words. Suppose that "book" is a word in Peter's lexicon. The word is a complex of properties, phonetic and semantic. The sensorimotor systems use the phonetic properties for articulation and perception, relating them to external events: motions of molecules, for example. Other systems of mind use the semantic properties of the word when Peter talks about the world and interprets what others say about it.

There is no far-reaching controversy about how to proceed on the sound side, but on the meaning side there are profound disagreements. Empirically oriented studies seem to me to approach problems of meaning rather in the way they study sound, as in phonology and phonetics. They try to find the semantic properties of the word "book": that it is nominal not verbal, used to refer to an artifact not a substance like water or an abstraction like health, and so on. One might ask whether these properties are part of the meaning of the word "book" or of the concept associated with the word; on current understanding, there is no good way to distinguish these proposals, but perhaps some day an empirical issue will be unearthed. Either way, some features of the lexical item "book" that are internal to it determine modes of interpretation of the kind just mentioned.

Investigating language use, we find that words are interpreted in terms of such factors as material constitution, design, intended and characteristic use, institutional role, and so on. Things are identified and assigned to categories in terms of such properties—which I am taking to be semantic features—on a par with phonetic features that determine its sound. The use of language can attend in various ways to these semantic features. Suppose the library has two copies of Tolstoy's *War and Peace*, Peter takes out one, and John the other. Did Peter and John take out the same book, or different books? If we attend to the material factor of the lexical item, they took out different books; if we focus on its abstract component, they took out the same book. We can attend to both material and abstract factors simultaneously, as when we say that "the book that he is planning will weigh at least five pounds if he ever writes it," or "his book is in every store in the country." Similarly, we can paint the door white and walk through it, using the pronoun "it" to refer ambiguously to figure and ground. We can report that the bank was blown up after it raised the interest rate, or that it raised the rate to keep from being blown up. Here the pronoun "it," and the "empty category" that is the subject of "being blown up," simultaneously adopt both the material and institutional factors.

The facts about such matters are often clear, but not trivial. Thus referentially dependent elements, even the most narrowly constrained, observe some distinctions but ignore others, in ways that vary for different types of words in curious ways. Such properties can be investigated in many ways: language acquisition, generality among languages, invented forms, etc. What we discover is surprisingly intricate; and, not surprisingly, known in advance of any evidence, hence shared among languages. There is no *a priori* reason to expect that human language will have such properties; Martian could be different. The symbolic systems of science and mathematics surely are. No one knows to what extent the specific properties of human language are a consequence of general biochemical laws applying to objects with general features of the brain, another important problem at a still distant horizon.

An approach to semantic interpretation in similar terms was developed in interesting ways in seventeenth- and eighteenth-century philosophy, often adopting Hume's principle that the "identity which we ascribe" to things is "only a fictitious one," established by the human understanding.[7] Hume's conclusion is very plausible. The book on my desk does not have these strange properties by virtue of its internal constitution; rather, by virtue of the way people think, and the meanings of the terms in which these thoughts are expressed. The semantic properties of words are used to think and talk about the world in terms of the perspectives made available by the resources of the mind, rather in the way phonetic interpretation seems to proceed.

Contemporary philosophy of language follows a different course. It asks to what a word refers, giving various answers. But the question has no clear meaning. The example of "book" is typical. It makes little sense to ask to what *thing* the expression "Tolstoy's *War and Peace*" refers, when Peter and John take identical copies out of the library. The answer depends on how the semantic features are used when we think and talk, one way or another. In general, a word, even of the simplest kind, does not pick out an entity of the world, or of our "belief space." Conventional assumptions about these matters seem to me very dubious.

I mentioned that modern generative grammar has sought to address concerns that animated the tradition; in particular, the Cartesian idea that "the true distinction"[8] between humans and other creatures or machines is the ability to act in the manner they took to be most clearly illustrated in the ordinary use of language: without any finite limits, influenced but not determined by internal state, appropriate to situations but not caused by them, coherent and evoking thoughts that the hearer might have expressed, and so on. The goal of the work I have been discussing is to unearth some of the factors that enter into such normal practice. Only *some* of these, however.

Generative grammar seeks to discover the mechanisms that are used, thus contributing to the study of *how* they are used in the creative fashion of normal life. How they are used is the problem that intrigued the Cartesians, and it remains as mysterious to us as it was to them, even though far more is understood today about the mechanisms that are involved.

In this respect, the study of language is again much like that of other organs. Study of the visual and motor systems has uncovered mechanisms by which the brain interprets scattered stimuli as a cube and the arm reaches for a book on the table. But these branches of science do not raise the question of how people decide to look at a book on the table or to pick it up, and speculations about the use of the visual or motor systems, or others, amount to very little. It is these capacities, manifested most strikingly in language use, that are at the heart of traditional concerns: for Descartes in the early seventeenth century, they are "the noblest thing we can have" and all that "truly belongs" to us. Half a century before Descartes, the Spanish philosopher-physician Juan Huarte observed that this "generative faculty" of ordinary human understanding and action is foreign to "beasts and plants"[9] though it is a lower form of understanding that falls short of true exercise of the creative imagination. Even the lower form lies beyond our theoretical reach, apart from the study of mechanisms that enter into it.

In a number of areas, language included, a lot has been learned in recent years about these mechanisms. The problems that can now be faced are hard and challenging, but many mysteries still lie beyond the reach of the form of human inquiry we call "science," a conclusion that we should not find surprising if we consider humans to be part of the organic world, and perhaps one we should not find distressing either.

19.

Intentional Ignorance and Its Uses

The twentieth century ended with terrible crimes, and reactions by the great powers that were widely heralded as opening a remarkable "new era" in human affairs, marked by dedication to human rights and high principle with no historical precedent. The torrent of self-adulation, which may well have been unprecedented in scale and quality, was not merely a display of millenarian rhetorical flourishes. Western leaders and intellectuals assured their audiences emphatically that the new era was very real, and of unusual significance.

The new phase in human history opened with NATO's bombing of Serbia on March 24, 1999. "The new generation draws the line," Tony Blair proclaimed, fighting "for values," for "a new internationalism where the brutal repression of whole ethnic groups will no longer be tolerated" and "those responsible for such crimes have nowhere to hide." NATO has unleashed the first war in history fought "in the name of principles and values," Vaclav Havel declared, signalling "the end of the nation-state," which will no longer be "the culmination of every national community's history and its highest earthly value." The "enlightened efforts of generations of democrats, the terrible experience of two world wars, . . . and the evolution of civilization have finally brought humanity to the recognition that human beings are more important than the state." [1]

The new generation is to carry out its good works under the guiding hand of an "idealistic New World bent on ending inhumanity," joined by its British partner. In the lead article in *Foreign Affairs*, a legal scholar with a distin-

---

This chapter first appeared in *A New Generation Draws the Line: Kosovo, East Timor and the Standards of the West* (London: Verso, 2000), 1–47.

guished record in defending human rights explained that the "enlightened states," freed at last from the shackles of "restrictive old rules" and archaic concepts of world order, may now use force when they "believe it to be just," obeying "modern notions of justice" that they fashion as they discipline "the defiant, the indolent, and the miscreant," the "disorderly" elements of the world, with a nobility of purpose so "evident" that it requires no evidence.[2] The grounds for membership in the club of enlightened states—"the international community," as they conventionally describe themselves—are also self-evident. Past and current practice are boring old tales that may be dismissed under the doctrine of "change of course," which has been regularly invoked when needed in recent years.

Praising NATO troops in Macedonia for their achievement in opening the new era, President Clinton "propounded a Clinton Doctrine of military intervention," Bob Davis reported in the *Wall Street Journal*. The Doctrine "amounts to the following: Tyrants Beware." In the president's own words: "If somebody comes after innocent civilians and tries to kill them en masse because of their race, their ethnic background or their religion, and it's within our power to stop it, we will stop it"; "where we can make a difference, we must try, and that is clearly the case in Kosovo." "There are times when looking away simply is not an option," the president explained to the nation; "we can't respond to every tragedy in every corner of the world," but that doesn't mean that "we should do nothing for no one."[3]

Well before the dawn of the new era, Clinton's "neo-Wilsonianism" had convinced observers that American foreign policy had entered a "noble phase" with a "saintly glow," though some saw dangers from the outset, warning that by "granting idealism a near exclusive hold on our foreign policy" we might neglect our own interests in the service of others. Clinton's "open-ended embrace of humanitarian intervention" in 1999 also "has worried foreign-policy experts inside the administration and out," Davis reported. Senator John McCain derided it as "foreign policy as social work"; others agreed. To alleviate such concerns, Clinton's National Security Adviser Sandy Berger underscored the fact that ethnic cleansing, which "happens in dozens of countries around the world," cannot be the occasion for intervention. In Kosovo, U.S. national interest was at stake: intervention "involved bolstering the credibility of NATO and making sure Kosovar refugees didn't overwhelm neighboring countries"—as they did shortly after the NATO bombing commenced, eliciting the massive ethnic cleansing that was an anticipated consequence. We are left, then, with "bolstering the credibility of NATO" as the surviving justification.[4]

Washington's official version, which has remained fairly constant throughout, was reiterated in January 2000 by Secretary of Defense William

Cohen and Chairman of the Joint Chiefs of Staff Henry Shelton, in a lengthy summary of the war provided to Congress. The United States and NATO had three primary interests: "Ensuring the stability of Eastern Europe," "Thwarting ethnic cleansing," and "Ensuring NATO's credibility." Prime Minister Blair adopted the same stance[5]:

> The bottom line was we couldn't lose. If we lost, it's not just that we would have failed in our strategic objective; failed in terms of the moral purpose—we would have dealt a devastating blow to the credibility of NATO and the world would have been less safe as a result of that.

Let us put aside until later a closer look at the official positions, and ask how the world outside the "international community" understands NATO's efforts to assure its safety. Some insight into the matter was provided in April 2000 at the South Summit of G-77, accounting for 80 percent of the world's population. The meeting, in Havana, was of unusual significance, the first meeting ever of G-77 (now 133 nations) at the level of heads of state, prepared shortly before by a summit of foreign ministers in Cartagena, Colombia. They issued the Declaration of the South Summit, declaring that "We reject the so-called 'right' of humanitarian intervention," along with other forms of coercion that the Summit also sees as traditional imperialism in a new guise, including the specific forms of corporate-led international integration called "globalization" in Western ideology.[6]

The most respected voices of the South joined in condemnation of NATO's operative principles. Visiting England in April 2000, Nelson Mandela "accused the [British] government of encouraging international chaos, together with America, by ignoring other nations and playing 'policeman of the world,' " saying that "he resented the behaviour of both Britain and America in riding roughshod over the United Nations and launching military actions against Iraq and Kosovo." "Such disregard for international conventions was more dangerous to world peace than anything that was currently happening in Africa, Mr. Mandela said." In his own words, "What they are doing is far more serious than what is happening in Africa—especially the US and Britain. It is proper for me to say that."[7]

While in progress a year earlier, NATO's bombing of Yugoslavia had been bitterly condemned in the world's largest democracy, and even in Washington's most loyal and dependent client state, highly regarded strategic analysts regarded the operation with considerable skepticism. Amos Gilboa described NATO's reversion to the "colonial era" in the familiar "cloak of moralistic righteousness" as "a danger to the world," warning that it would lead to proliferation of weapons of mass destruction for deterrence. Others simply took it to be a precedent for resort to force when deemed appropriate. If the need arises, military historian Ze'ev Schiff commented, "Israel will do to Lebanon what NATO did to Kosovo"; Israeli forces are being restructured for quick and destructive air war, relying particularly on the Kosovo precedent. Similar attitudes were expressed in the semi-official press of the second leading recipient of U.S. aid, and elsewhere.[8]

Among East European dissidents, the one most prominently featured in the West was Vaclav Havel, with his welcome appreciation for the high moral purpose of Western leaders. Long before, he had achieved top rank among the West's favorites, particularly in 1990, when he addressed a joint session of Congress, receiving a standing ovation and rapturous acclaim from commentators who were deeply moved by his praise for his audience as "the defender of freedom" who "understood the responsibility that flowed" from power. A few weeks before, the responsibility had been demonstrated once again when U.S.-armed state terrorists fresh from renewed U.S. training blew out the brains of six leading Latin American dissident intellectuals in the course of yet another paroxysm of terror supervised by "the defender of freedom." One can imagine the reaction to a similar performance in the Duma by a Latin American dissident, had the situation been reversed. The reaction in the West in this case is instructive, and not without import.[9]

There once was a dissident intellectual named Alexander Solzhenitsyn, who was also highly respected when he had the right things to say. But not in 1999. He saw the new era rather in the manner of the South Summit, Mandela, and others outside of the circles of enlightenment:

> The aggressors have kicked aside the UN, opening a new era where might is right. There should be no illusions that NATO was aiming to defend the Kosovars. If the protection of the oppressed was their real concern, they could have been defending for example the miserable Kurds

—"for example," because that is only one case, though a rather striking one.[10]

Solzhenitsyn remains a man "whom many see as the country's voice of conscience," admired for his "elegant and reasoned style" when he condemns government corruption in Russia.[11] But not when he provides the wrong interpretation of the new era. In this case, he received the same treatment as the South Summit, and others who do not see the light.

Though unwanted world opinion has scarcely been reported, it has been watched with concern by more perceptive analysts. University of Chicago political scientist John Mearsheimer observed that the Gulf War of 1991 and the Kosovo war of 1999 "hardened India's determination to possess nuclear weapons" as a deterrent to U.S. violence. Harvard government professor

Samuel Huntington warned that "in the eyes of many countries"—most, he indicates—the United States "is becoming the rogue superpower," perceived as "the single greatest external threat to their societies." He quotes a British diplomat who says, "One reads about the world's desire for American leadership only in the United States," while "[e]verywhere else one reads about American arrogance and unilateralism," which will lead to consolidation of counterforces, Huntington suggests. Five years earlier, shortly after publicity about a possible North Korean nuclear arsenal, "the Japanese named the United States as 'the biggest threat to world peace,' followed by Russia and only then by North Korea," Chalmers Johnson recalls. During the Kosovo war, strategic analyst and former NATO planner Michael MccGwire writes,

> the world at large saw a political-military alliance that took unto itself the role of judge, jury and executioner, . . . [which] claimed to be acting on behalf of the international community and was ready to slight the UN and skirt international law in order to enforce its collective judgement. The world saw an organization given to moralistic rhetoric, one no less economical with the truth than others of its kind; a grouping of Western states with an unmatched technical capacity to kill, maim, and destroy, that was limited only by their unwillingness to put their "warriors" at risk.

That seems a fair assessment, judging by the information available.[12]

The world at large does not seem to be overly impressed by the exploits and moral purpose of the new generation, or reassured by its commitment to make the world safe by establishing the credibility of NATO. If evidence is deemed relevant, we may ask which evaluation of the new era is more credible: the flattering self-image with its visionary promise, or the skepticism of those outside who see "more of the same."

The matter should be examined carefully, at least by those who are concerned about the likely future, and who feel bound by moral truisms. Among these, several might be mentioned as particularly pertinent:

1. People are responsible for the anticipated consequences of their choice of action (or inaction), a responsibility that extends to the policy choices of one's own state to the extent that the political community allows a degree of influence over policy formation.
2. Responsibility is enhanced by privilege, by the opportunity to act with relative impunity and a degree of effectiveness.
3. For profession of high principles to be taken seriously, the principles must first and foremost be applied to oneself, not only to official enemies or others designated as unworthy in the prevailing political culture.

Let us assume the truisms to be true. It is, however, hard to miss the fact that throughout history, and in virtually all societies, they are commonly honored in the breach. A fair question, then, is whether the familiar pattern was exhibited once again in the terminal year of the twentieth century, as most of the world seems to believe, or whether a new era has really dawned, as the new generation and its admirers declare.

One question that instantly comes to mind is how often, and how carefully, the inquiry is undertaken. Rarely, to my knowledge: the conclusions are taken to be self-evident. No inquiry is needed, and even to undertake it is considered dishonorable.

It is clear how such an inquiry should proceed. To determine who has the stronger case, those who hail the new era or the skeptics, we should examine how the new generation responds to circumstances in the world "where we can make a difference" and therefore "must try," as Clinton phrased the matter in propounding the Clinton Doctrine.

We therefore consider various measures of U.S. involvement in the world. One criterion is foreign aid: the world's richest and most privileged state would surely be able to "make a difference" by helping those in need. The political leadership has taken up this challenge by compiling the most miserly record in the industrial world, even if we include the major component, aid to a rich country (Israel) and to Egypt because of its association with Israel. As the new era dawns, the record is becoming still worse. The Foreign Aid Bill passed by the Senate in June 2000 "provided only $75 million for the world's poorest countries, a reduction from the administration's $252 million request," a shameful pittance.[13] In comparison, the bill provides $1.3 billion for the Colombian army, a matter to which we return. Without proceeding, by this criterion the evaluation of the skeptics is confirmed, with no contest.

Perhaps this criterion is irrelevant for some (unclear) reason. Let us put it aside, then, and turn to the next natural criteria: military aid and response to atrocities. The top-ranking recipient of U.S. military aid through the Clinton years has been Turkey,[14] the home of 15 million of Solzhenitsyn's "miserable Kurds." That seems an appropriate place to begin.

At the peak of enthusiasm over our dedication to principles and values, in April 1999, NATO commemorated its fiftieth anniversary. It was not a celebration; rather, a somber occasion, under the shadow of vicious atrocities and ethnic cleansing in Kosovo. It was agreed that the "modern notions of justice" crafted by the enlightened states do not permit such horrors so close to the borders of NATO. Only *within* the borders of NATO: here large-scale atrocities and ethnic cleansing are not only tolerable, but it is furthermore our duty to expedite them. We must not merely "stand by and watch the systematic state-directed murder of other people," but must go on to make an essential contribution to ensuring that it reaches proper heights of terror and destruction, while directing our gaze with laserlike intensity to the evil work of official enemies.

It took considerable discipline at the NATO anniversary for participants and commentators "not to notice" that some of the worst ethnic cleansing of the 1990s was taking place within NATO itself, in south-eastern Turkey; and furthermore, that these massive atrocities relied on a huge flow of arms from the West, overwhelmingly from the United States, which provided about 80 percent of Turkey's arms as the atrocities peaked by the mid-1990s. As a strategic ally and military outpost, Turkey had received a substantial flow of U.S. arms throughout the post-World War II era. Arms transfers increased sharply in 1984, as Turkey initiated a military campaign against its miserably-oppressed Kurdish population. Military, police, and paramilitary operations increased in intensity and violence in the 1990s, along with atrocities and US arms and military training. Turkey set two records in 1994, correspondent Jonathan Randal observed: 1994 was "the year of the worst repression in the Kurdish provinces," and the year when Turkey became "the biggest single importer of American military hardware and thus the world's largest arms purchaser," including advanced armaments, "all of which were eventually used against the Kurds," along with extensive co-production and other co-operation with Turkey's military and its military industry. In the year 1997 alone, arms from the Clinton Administration surpassed the entire period from 1950 to 1983.[15]

Thanks to the steady supply of heavy armaments, military training, and diplomatic support, Turkey was able to crush Kurdish resistance, leaving tens of thousands killed, 2–3 million refugees, and 3,500 villages destroyed (seven times Kosovo under NATO bombing).

In this case, responsibility is easy to determine. Oppression of Kurds, and Turks who called for justice, has been outrageous since the founding of the modern Turkish state. The brutality of the counter-insurgency war has been amply recorded by highly credible sources. There is not the slightest question about the contribution of "the idealistic New World bent on ending inhumanity." Presumably, it is the impossibility of conjuring up a pretext of even minimal plausibility that accounts for the virtual suppression of these atrocities and Washington's role in implementing them.[16]

On the rare occasions when the matter breaks through the silence, the typical reaction is that the "American failure to protect Kurds in Turkey is inconsistent with its self-declared intention to protect Kosovars," in the words of Thomas Cushman. Or, according to Aryeh Neier, that the United States "tolerated" the abuses suffered by the Kurds.[17] These regrettable lapses show that we are sometimes "inconsistent" and "look away"—because of the limits of our capacity to stop injustice, according to a common theme, articulated by the leader of the enlightened states in the manner quoted above.

Such reactions constitute a particularly sharp rejection of the moral truisms mentioned earlier: they are cynical apologetics for major atrocities for which one shares direct responsibility. There was no "looking away" in the case of Turkey and the Kurds: Washington "looked right there," as did its allies, saw what was happening, and acted decisively to intensify the atrocities, particularly during the Clinton years. The United States did not "fail to protect the Kurds" or "tolerate" the abuses they suffered, any more than Russia "fails to protect" the people of Grozny or "tolerates" their suffering. The new generation drew the line by consciously putting as many guns as possible into the hands of the killers and torturers—not just guns, but jet planes, tanks, helicopter gunships, all the most advanced instruments of terror—sometimes in secret, because arms were sent in violation of congressional legislation.

At no point was there any defensive purpose, nor any relation to the Cold War. That should come as no surprise: much the same has been true elsewhere as well through the Cold War years. This we learn from close attention to the historical events and internal planning record, though great power confrontations were always in the background and provided useful pretexts for the resort to force, terror, and economic warfare. Furthermore, the charge of "inconsistency" requires proof, not mere assertion: it is necessary to demonstrate, not merely proclaim, that other actions are humanitarian in intent, a posture that accompanies virtually every resort to force throughout history.

A more realistic interpretation is given by Tim Judah in his account of the conflict in Kosovo: "Western countries may well sympathize with the plight of the Kurds or Tibetans," or the victims of Russian bombing in Chechnya, "but *realpolitik* means that there is little they are willing, or able, to do to help them."[18] In the case of Tibetans and Chechens, helping them might lead to a major war. In the case of the Kurds, helping them would interfere with U.S. power interests. Accordingly, we cannot help them but must rather join in perpetrating atrocities against them; and responsible intellectuals must keep the truth hidden under a veil of silence, apologetics, and deceit while hailing their leaders, and themselves, for their unique devotion to "principles and values."

One of the regions most devastated by the U.S.-Turkish assault was Tunceli, north of the Kurdish capital of Dyirbakir, where one-third of the villages were destroyed and vast tracts were set aflame by U.S.-supplied helicopters and jets. "The terror in Tunceli is state terror," a Turkish minister conceded in 1994, reporting that village burning and terror had already driven 2 million people from their homes, left without even a tent to protect them. On April 1, 2000, 10,000 Turkish troops began a new sweep of the area, while 5–7,000 troops with helicopter gunships crossed into Iraq to attack Kurds there once again—in a "no-fly zone," where Kurds are protected by the U.S. Air Force from the (temporarily) wrong oppressor.[19]

Recall that in Serbia, NATO was "fighting because no decent person can stand by and watch the systematic state-directed murder of other people," as Vaclav Havel puts it. While, according to Tony Blair, the "new generation" of leaders was enforcing "a new internationalism where the brutal repression of whole ethnic groups will no longer be tolerated" and "those responsible for such crimes have nowhere to hide." And, in the words of President Clinton, "If somebody comes after innocent civilians and tries to kill them en masse because of their race, their ethnic background or their religion, and it's within our power to stop it, we will stop it." But it is not within our power to stop our own enthusiastic participation in "systematic state-directed murder" and "brutal repression of whole ethnic groups," and those responsible for such crimes have no need to hide; rather, they enjoy the accolades of the educated classes, who marvel at the "saintly glow" of their deeds and the high ideals that inspire them.

Furthermore, "decent people" are expected to understand that NATO powers are not only entitled to oppress and terrorize their own populations, with our lavish assistance, but also to invade other countries at will. The same prerogative extends to non-NATO client states, notably Israel, which occupied South Lebanon for twenty-two years in violation of Security Council orders, but with U.S. authorization and assistance, and during those years killed tens of thousands of people, repeatedly driving hundreds of thousands from their homes and destroying civilian infrastructure, again in early 2000—always with U.S. support and arms. Virtually none of this had to do with self-defense, as is well recognized within Israel and by human rights organizations, though different stories are preferred in the U.S. information system.[20]

In June 2000, Israel did at last withdraw from Lebanon, or more accurately, was driven out by Lebanese resistance. The UN General Assembly voted to provide almost $150 million for UN (UNIFIL) monitors to ensure security in southern Lebanon and facilitate reconstruction of the devastated region. The resolution passed 110–2. The United States and Israel voted against it because it also called upon Israel to pay the United Nation some $1.28 million in compensation for its attack on a UN compound, killing over 100 civilians who had taken refuge there, during its 1996 invasion of Lebanon.[21]

The achievements of Western terror are highly regarded. Just as Turkey was launching new military campaigns in its southeast region and across the border on April 1, 2000, Secretary of Defense William Cohen addressed the American–Turkish Council Conference in a festive event with much laughter and applause. He praised Turkey for taking part in the humanitarian bombing of Serbia and announced that Turkey would participate in developing the

Pentagon's advanced Joint Strike fighter, just as it was co-producing the F-16s that it has been using to such good effect in approved forms of ethnic cleansing and other atrocities—within NATO, not near its borders. "This is an exciting time to really not only be alive, but to be in positions of public service," Cohen continued, as "we have entered, with the turn of the century, a brave new world" with "so much creative opportunity out there that all of us can take advantage of," symbolized by the U.S.-Turkey jet fighter project that will "put Turkey in the forefront and leadership of building a secure and stable Middle East" along with its close Israeli ally.

Shortly after, the State Department released its "latest annual report describing the administration's efforts to combat terrorism," Judith Miller reported. The report singled out Turkey for praise for its "positive experiences" in showing how "tough counter-terrorism measures plus political dialogue with non-terrorist opposition groups" can overcome the plague of violence and atrocities, reported without a trace of embarrassment.[22]

The first case study strongly confirms the evaluation of the new era by the skeptics. Perhaps it even gives some insight into the "moral purpose" that inspires us: "A gross injustice had been done to people, right on the doorstep of the European Union, which we were in a position to prevent and reverse, and we had to do that," in the words of Tony Blair.[23] Blair is not referring to righteous terror and ethnic cleansing that his government and its allies help to implement within NATO, but rather the atrocities that were being carried out by an official enemy, under NATO's bombs.

In 1999, Turkey relinquished its position as the leading recipient of U.S. military aid, replaced by Colombia.[24] We therefore have a second natural case study for the inquiry into the alternative evaluations of the new era.

Colombia has had the worst human rights record in the Western hemisphere through the 1990s and has also been the hemisphere's leading beneficiary of U.S. military aid and training, a longstanding correlation.[25] Colombia receives more than the rest of Latin America and the Caribbean combined, with a threefold increase from 1998 to 1999. The total is scheduled to increase sharply with the U.S. contribution to the $7.5 billion "Plan Colombia," attributed to Bogota though "with heavy coaching from the Americans," as the *Wall Street Journal* puts it; according to non-U.S. diplomats, the plan was written in English. Plan Colombia calls for the U.S. to provide over $1 billion in military aid, while others are to fund social, economic, and human rights programs. The military component was put in place during 1999, extending earlier programs; the rest is in abeyance.[26]

The shift in rank reflects the fact that Turkey's ethnic cleansing operations and other atrocities through the 1990s largely succeeded, at severe human cost; while state terror in Washington's client state of Colombia is still far from having achieved its goals, despite some 3,000 political murders and 300,000 refugees a year, the total by now perhaps approaching 2 million, the third largest population of displaced people in the world after Sudan and Angola. A political party outside the traditional elite power-sharing arrangement was permitted to function in 1985. It was soon "annihilated," with over 3,500 members "murdered or disappeared,"[27] including presidential candidates, mayors, and others, a feat accomplished without tarnishing Colombia's democratic credentials in Washington.

The overwhelming mass of atrocities are attributed to paramilitaries, who are closely linked to the military that receives US aid and training, all heavily involved in narco-trafficking. According to the Colombian government and leading human rights groups (the Colombian Commission of Jurists and others), the rate of killings increased by almost 20 percent in 1999 and the proportion attributed to the paramilitaries rose from 46 percent in 1995 to almost 80 percent in 1998, continuing through 1999. The State Department confirms the general picture in its annual human rights reports. Its report covering 1999 concludes that "security forces actively collaborated with members of paramilitary groups" while "Government forces continued to commit numerous, serious abuses, including extrajudicial killings, at a level that was roughly similar to that of 1998," when the department attributed to the military and paramilitaries about 80 percent of atrocities with an identifiable source.

Massacres reached over one a day in early 1999, as Colombia displaced Turkey as the leading recipient of U.S. arms. In June–August 1999, 200,000 more people were driven from their homes, according to Colombian and international human rights organizations.

The escalating U.S. military aid is under the pretext of a drug war that is taken seriously by few competent observers, for substantial reasons. Quite apart from the matter of plausibility, it is noteworthy that the pretext is based on the remarkable presupposition, virtually unquestioned, that the United States has the right to carry out military actions and chemical and biological warfare in other countries to eradicate a crop it does not like, though presumably "modern notions of justice" do not entitle Colombia—or Thailand, or China, or many others—to do the same in North Carolina, to eliminate a far more lethal drug, which they have been compelled to accept (along with advertising) under threat of trade sanctions, at a cost of millions of lives.

The second case study leads to the same conclusion as the first: the new era is much like earlier ones, including the familiar "cloak of moralistic righteousness."

Let us turn to a third example, perhaps the most obvious test case for evaluating the conflicting interpretations of the new era.

While Colombia replaced Turkey as leading recipient of U.S. military aid, and the United States and Britain were preparing to bomb Serbia in pursuit of their moral purpose, important events were under way in another part of the world, the scene of one of the worst human rights catastrophes of the late twentieth century: East Timor, which in 1999 was subjected to new atrocities, so extreme that they came to rank alongside of Kosovo in the concerns of the new era for human rights, humanitarian intervention, and limits of sovereignty.

The modern tragedy of East Timor has unfolded since December 1975, when Indonesia invaded and occupied the former Portuguese colony after it had declared independence, later annexing it. The invasion led to the slaughter of some 200,000 people, almost one-third of the population, and vast destruction, torture, and terror, renewed once again in 1999. To determine how the second major example of 1999 bears on the conflicting interpretations of the new era, we want to determine what has taken place, and how it is depicted.

The events of 1999 are reviewed in the January 2000 issue of the *American Journal of International Law*, offering the standard Western version: that the atrocities in East Timor took place six months after Kosovo—that is, after the August 30, 1999, referendum on independence—but that:

> Unlike the case of Kosovo, which preceded the events in East Timor by six months, no state (including the United States) advocated a forcible military intervention in East Timor. The apparent reasons for this reluctance were that Indonesia possessed a strong military, that such an intervention was likely to be strongly opposed by nearby China, and that concerned states believed that Indonesia's consent to a multinational force would, in any case, soon be forthcoming.[28]

The account is indeed standard. To select another example virtually at random, consider William Shawcross's recent study of the interaction of the three "benign forces" in the world—the UN, the NGOs, and the liberal democracies—and the "malign force" of "warlords who have dominated the 1990s." Saddam Hussein and Slobodan Milosevic being "the two who stand out."[29] Some places were "bathed by the light of the West's concern—Bosnia and Kosovo, for example," though "others were obscured by our lack of interest." The book ends with a chapter entitled "From Kosovo to East Timor," reflecting the perceived order of events in these two major crises of 1999: "in both cases the international community was forced to confront a humanitarian disaster which was in part the product of its own neglect, and had to decide what price it was prepared to pay to right it."

Many commentators have described the intervention in Kosovo as a precedent for the dispatch of peacekeeping forces to East Timor. Hence, even critics of the NATO bombing agree that it had benign effects. Others point out that "the United States does not want to be a 'globocop' now any more than it did in the past, sacrificing American resources and lives to the East Timors of the world," as when a UN peacekeeping force entered "Indonesian territory . . . to stop the killing" at U.S. initiative.[30]

Virtually none of this is tenable. The truth of the matter, readily established, tells us a good deal about the norms of conduct that are likely to prevail if self-serving doctrine remains immune to critical reflection, and moral truisms are kept at the margins of consciousness.

The humanitarian catastrophe in East Timor was not "the product of [the] neglect" of the liberal democracies. It was substantially their creation, as in the previous cases discussed. When invading East Timor in 1975, Indonesia relied almost entirely on U.S. arms and diplomatic support, renewed as atrocities reached near-genocidal levels in 1978 and persisting as violent oppression took its toll at the hands of a criminal who ranks high among the elite of Shawcross's "malign force," and was routinely praised as a "moderate" who is "at heart benign"—"our kind of guy," in the words of the Clinton administration—until he lost control in 1997 and had to be discarded. In 1978, as Suharto's slaughter in East Timor peaked in fury, the United States was joined by Britain, along with France and other powers. U.S.-British support and participation continued through the escalating humanitarian catastrophe of 1999 and its consummation after the August 30 referendum on independence. East Timor was "Indonesian territory" only in that leaders of the liberal democracies effectively authorized the conquest in violation of Security Council directives and a World Court ruling.

The order of events in the standard version is crucially reversed. The latest wave of atrocities in East Timor was underway from November 1998. Well before the referendum on independence, atrocities in 1999 alone had reached levels beyond Kosovo prior to the NATO bombing, the relevant standard of comparison. Furthermore, ample public information was available indicating that much worse was to come unless the population submitted to Indonesian terror, and far more was known to Australian and surely U.S. intelligence. Nonetheless, the new generation continued to provide military aid, even to conduct joint military exercises just prior to the referendum, while opposing any move to deter the further atrocities they had every reason to expect. Even after the August 30 referendum, the United States insisted that Indonesia must remain in control of the illegally occupied territory while its forces virtually destroyed the country and drove 750,000 people—85 percent of the population—out of their homes.

Whatever one thinks of Kosovo, it could not have served as a precedent for humanitarian intervention in East Timor because of the timing alone; and more fundamentally, because humanitarian intervention never took place. There was, in fact, no "intervention" at all in any serious sense of the term, nor could there have been, if only because there was no question of sovereignty. Even Australia, the one Western country to have granted explicit *de jure* recognition to the Indonesian annexation (in large measure because of its interest in joint exploitation of Timorese oil), had renounced that stand in January 1999. Indonesia's sovereign rights were comparable to those of Nazi Germany in occupied Europe. They rested solely on great power ratification of aggression and massacre in this Portuguese-administered territory, a UN responsibility. The Russian drive to the West during World War II and the Normandy landing were not interventions; *a fortiori*, the entry of Australian-led UN peacekeeping forces after the Indonesian army withdrew does not qualify as intervention. The issue of humanitarian intervention does not even arise, though this is one of the rare cases when it is possible to speak seriously of humanitarian intent, at least on the part of Australia, or, more accurate, its population, who were bitterly critical of their government's failure to act as the toll of victims mounted from early 1999.

One element of the standard version is correct: no state advocated military intervention—reasonably enough, since there is little reason to suppose that any form of "intervention" would have been needed to terminate the atrocities, either those of 1999 or of the preceding decades of horror. There was no need to impose sanctions or to bomb Jakarta. Even the hint of withdrawal of participation in mid-September 1999 sufficed to make it clear to the Indonesian generals that the game was over. The result could very likely have been achieved in similar ways long before, had there been any willingness to interfere with the exploits of the "malign force" who was so ably serving the interests of Western power and privilege.

The standard reasons put forth to distinguish Kosovo from East Timor, just quoted, are not very convincing. Serbia "possessed a strong military," the main reason why invasion was never contemplated and bombers kept to a safe distance. More important, Indonesia's army, unlike that of Serbia, is heavily dependent on the United States, as was revealed in mid-September 1999, when Clinton finally gave the signal to desist. Russia strongly opposed the NATO bombing, but that did not deter the United States and its allies. Prior to mid-September, there was no expectation that Indonesia would "consent to a multinational force," if only because the "concerned states" had evinced no serious interest in this outcome (and Indonesia firmly rejected it). The main opponent of even unarmed "intervention" in the earlier months of rising terror had been Washington, and its opposition persisted at the height of the post-referendum atrocities.

Washington's principles were outlined succinctly by the highly regarded

Australian diplomat Richard Butler, who transmitted to his fellow countrymen what he had learned from "senior American analysts": the United States will act in its own perceived interest; others are to shoulder the burdens and face the costs, unless some power interest is served.[31] That seems a fair rendition of the reality of the new era of enlightenment and high principle, as the case of East Timor dramatically illustrates, adding another informative case study to the list.

One of the leading principles of the new era is that sovereignty may now be disregarded in the interest of defending human rights; disregarded by the "enlightened states," that is, not by others. Thus, the United States and Britain accord themselves the right to carry out military and economic warfare with the alleged intent of containing Saddam Hussein, but there is no thought of endorsing an Iranian invasion of Iraq to overthrow the tyrant, though Iran suffered grievously from the Iraqi invasion of Iran, backed by the United States and Britain, among others. The proclaimed principle has merit, or would, if it were upheld in a way that honest people could take seriously. The restriction of agents already undercuts that possibility. The two prime examples brought forth in 1999 suffice to eliminate any further illusions.

Indonesia's nonexistent claim to sovereignty in East Timor was accorded the most delicate respect under the operative principles of the enlightened states. They insisted that its military forces must be assigned responsibility for security while they were conducting yet another reign of terror. As for Kosovo, the United States and its allies require that it must remain under Serbian sovereignty, probably out of fear of a "greater Albania." But the sovereignty that NATO insists upon in Serbia is "trumped" by its claim that it is defending human rights, unlike East Timor, where nonsovereignty "trumps" any concern for the human rights that the leaders of NATO are brutally violating.

The new era is a dazzling one indeed.

The realities that Richard Butler described were well illustrated in East Timor in April 1999, the peak moment of exuberance about the new era. By then massacres organized by the troops armed and trained by the United States and Britain were a regular occurrence, some extraordinary, extensively reported in Australia particularly. On August 6—by coincidence the day of the report on the new Clinton Doctrine with its commitment "to stop" the killing of "innocent civilians" if "it's within our power" to do so—the Church in East Timor reported that 3–5,000 people had been killed so far in 1999, about twice the number killed on all sides in Kosovo in the year before the NATO bombing, according to NATO. And under very different circumstances. The East Timorese victims of Western-supported Indonesian aggression were defenseless civilians. There was no active fighting, no takeover of substantial territory by foreign-based guerrillas, no attacks on police and civilians with the avowed goal of eliciting violent retaliation that would lead to Western military intervention. The small resistance forces were confined to isolated mountain areas with virtually no international contact, and the atrocities were almost entirely attributable to the occupying army and its paramilitary associates, and of course to their foreign backers, primarily the United States and Britain, as had been true for twenty-four years. The situation in Kosovo was different in all of these respects.

In East Timor in 1999, the principles and values of the enlightened states dictated the same conclusion as in Turkey and in Colombia, where massacres had reached over one a day: support the killers. There was also one reported massacre in Kosovo, at Racak on January 15 (forty-five killed). That event allegedly inspired such horror among Western humanitarians that it was necessary to bomb Yugoslavia ten weeks later with the expectation, quickly fulfilled, that the consequence might be a sharp escalation of atrocities.[32]

These examples constitute only a partial sample of the circumstances that evoked the remarkable chorus of self-congratulation about the new era in which Western leaders devote themselves to their "moral purpose" in the name of "the international community"—which objects, strenuously and irrelevantly. Putting aside the actual facts about Kosovo, the performance was greatly facilitated by silence or deceit about what would have been highlighted at the same time, if the moral truisms mentioned at the outset could be entertained.

The test cases most directly relevant to the conflicting evaluations of the new era are those just briefly reviewed: major atrocities of the current period that could have easily been mitigated or terminated merely by withdrawal of direct and decisive participation—or in the terminology favored by apologists for state violence, atrocities that the United States "tolerated" while "failing to protect" the victims. The preferred test cases, however, are Chechnya, Tibet, and others that have the advantage that the current phase of the crimes can be attributed to others. The only questions that arise have to do with our reaction to the other fellow's crimes, a far more comfortable stance.

The most extreme examples of this category are the African wars. Putting aside highly relevant history, the atrocities are not directly sponsored by the new generation, as in the examples reviewed. Here Washington's attitude is very much as outlined by National Security Adviser Sandy Berger and diplomat Richard Butler: there is no perceived gain in assisting the victims of terror, so there is no need to respond (except by sending arms to fuel the conflicts). As plans to bomb Serbia were reaching their final stages in February 1999, Western diplomats described Clinton's policies in Africa as "leaving Africa to solve its own crises." European and UN diplomats reported that "the United States has actively thwarted efforts by the United Nations to take on peacekeeping operations that might have prevented some of Africa's wars." In the Congo, Clinton's refusal to provide trivial sums for UN peacekeepers "torpedoed" the UN proposal, according to the UN's senior Africa envoy. Sierra Leone is a striking example. In 1997, "Washington dragged out discussions on a British proposal to deploy peacekeepers," then did nothing in the face of mounting horrors. In May 2000, UN Secretary-General Kofi Annan called for military support for the UN peacekeeping forces that were unable to contain the atrocities. But U.S. officials reported that "the Clinton administration would not budge from offering only logistical and technical support," which turned out to be a fraud. Clinton offered U.S. planes, but only for an exorbitant fee. "When Washington offers support equipment, like planes to fly in other countries' troops, 'the US offers are usually three times the commercial rate;' " Annan said, and "Washington will not put an American officer on the ground." It is difficult for the UN to afford even commercial rates because of the United States' refusal to pay its debt.[33]

Again the same conclusions. With a degree of clarity rare in international affairs, the evaluation of the new era by the skeptics wins hands down. Though without any possible effect, because of the impenetrable cocoon spun by responsible intellectuals: at worst, we "tolerate" the crimes of others, and we may then proceed to castigate ourselves for failing to react properly to them, thereby revealing our commitment to high moral principles and willingness to acknowledge even our most serious flaws.

While elementary considerations suffice to put to rest the triumphalism that accompanied the bombing of Serbia, nonetheless the question of why the decision was made to go to war remains open, as does the question of its legitimacy. It remains possible that there really is an "inconsistency," though not of the kind discussed in the apologetic literature: it is possible that in the special case of Kosovo, the new generation was violating standard operating procedure and acting with a "moral purpose," as claimed—with considerable passion, but little detectable argument.

As noted, the official justifications, which remained fairly constant throughout, were reiterated by Secretary of Defense William Cohen and Chairman of the Joint Chiefs Henry Shelton in January 2000: the primary motivating factors were:

1. "ensuring the stability of Eastern Europe"
2. "thwarting ethnic cleansing"
3. "ensuring NATO's credibility"

though the second alone would not have sufficed, National Security Adviser Sandy Berger elaborated. "National interest" must be at stake, the first and third reasons.

The third reason is the one that has been most insistently advanced, and it has merit, when properly understood: "credibility of NATO" means "credibility of US power"; the "disorderly" elements of the world must understand the price they will pay if they do not heed the orders of the master in Washington.[34] The first reason—"ensuring stability"—also has plausibility, though again terms must be understood properly: not in their literal but in their doctrinal sense. Correctly understood, a region is "stable" if it is incorporated within the U.S.-dominated global system with approved interests served and the right power centers in charge.

In the literal but not the doctrinal sense, Eastern Europe was mostly stable under Kremlin rule. In the doctrinal sense, the regions dominated by Jakarta became stable in 1965 when a military dictatorship was imposed after a Rwanda-style slaughter that destroyed the mass-based party of poor peasants, the PKI, which "had won widespread support not as a revolutionary party but as an organization defending the interests of the poor within the existing system," developing a "mass base among the peasantry" through its "vigor in defending the interests of the . . . poor." Concern that the PKI could not be blocked by "ordinary democratic means" was a primary reason for Washington's clandestine war aiming to dismantle Indonesia in 1958, and when that failed, support for the military, whose goal was "to exterminate the PKI."[35] For this reason, along with its pro-China stance, the PKI was a source of "instability." U.S.-UK participation in subsequent atrocities of the perpetrators of the 1965 slaughter is understandable, given that Indonesia is "so central to the stability of the region," as explained once again in September 1999 as Indonesia's assaults mounted in ferocity.

Similarly, Washington had to impose a murderous military dictatorship in Guatemala because its first democratic government "has become an increasing threat to the stability of Honduras and El Salvador," State Department officials warned. Stability in the doctrinal sense was threatened because Guatemala's "agrarian reform is a powerful propaganda weapon; its broad social program of aiding the workers and peasants in a victorious struggle against the upper classes and large foreign enterprises has a strong appeal to the populations of Central American neighbors where similar conditions prevail." After forty years of terror, there are no such programs, so Guatemala is not a threat to stability. In the doctrinal sense, it is even possible, without contradiction, to "destabilize" in order to bring "stability." Thus Nixon-Kissinger "efforts to destabilize a freely elected Marxist government in

Chile" were undertaken because "we were determined to seek stability," a leading foreign affairs analyst observed.[36]

Understanding terms in their doctrinal sense, it is reasonable to suppose that "ensuring the stability of Eastern Europe" was a goal of the bombing, along with "ensuring NATO's credibility."

The second justification—"thwarting ethnic cleansing"—had little credibility during the war, and that little has diminished considerably in the light of extensive evidence that has since been provided by the United States and other Western sources. Elaborating this second justification, Cohen and Shelton assert that prior to the bombing, "the Belgrade regime's cruel repression in Kosovo [had] created a humanitarian crisis of staggering proportions," and "Milosevic's campaign, which he dubbed 'Operation Horseshoe,' would have led to even more homelessness, starvation, and loss of life had his ruthlessness gone unchecked." Before the March 24, 1999, bombing, Milosevic was "finalizing this barbaric plan," and on March 21, the day after the withdrawal of the Kosovo Verification Mission (KVM) monitors, Serb forces "launched a major offensive," "dubbed 'Operation Horseshoe.' " Testifying before Congress a few months earlier, Cohen said that "now we know, in retrospect, that he had an Operation Horseshoe whereby he was determined he was going to carry out his objectives, and he believed that he could carry them out in a very short period of time, in a week or so," had the bombing not thwarted his plans.[37]

"Operation Horseshoe" has been adduced by many knowledgeable commentators as a justification for the bombing. To mention only one example, Brookings Institution senior fellows Ivo Daalder and Michael O'Hanlon, with experience in and out of government on Balkans-related issues, write that in late 1998, "Milosevic approved Operation Horseshoe—a plan of truly evil proportions designed to reengineer Kosovo by pushing much of its civilian population permanently out of the province." Therefore current "problems in Kosovo are nothing compared with what would have happened if NATO had not intervened."[38]

One fact is unquestioned: the NATO bombing was followed by a rapid escalation of atrocities and ethnic cleansing. But that, in itself, is a condemnation of the bombing, not a justification for it. As for the rest, the picture has several problems.

One problem is that the massive documentation provided by Washington, NATO, and other Western sources provides no meaningful evidence of a Serb offensive after the withdrawal of the monitors, though it provides rich evidence of Serb ethnic cleansing operations immediately after the bombing began. We return to this matter, noting, however, that even if a Serb offensive was launched after the withdrawal of the monitors in clear preparation for a military assault, that would hardly serve to justify their withdrawal over official Serbian objection (a fact not yet reported in the mainstream, though it was public knowledge the day before the bombing),[39] and the military attack that it effectively announced.

Another problem has to do with the distinction between plans and implementation. The contingency plans of the great powers and their clients, insofar as they are known, are horrendous; those that are unknown are doubtless worse.[40] That Milosevic had plans "of truly evil proportions" for Kosovo has scarcely been in doubt, even without access to internal records, just as it is a near certainty that Israel has plans to expel much of the Palestinian population, and if under serious threat of bombing and invasion by Iran or Syria, would be preparing to carry them out. It is also hardly in doubt that in March 1999, under constant and highly credible threats of bombing and invasion by the reigning superpower and the military alliance it dominates, Serbian military forces were preparing to carry out such plans in Kosovo. But it is a long step from the existence of plans and preparation to the conclusion that the plans will be implemented unless the planner is subjected to military attack—eliciting the implementation of the plans, which retrospectively justifies the attack by an impressive feat of logic.

It is appropriate to be "in no doubt that the ethnic cleansing was systematically planned before the NATO bombing"; it would be astonishing if that were not true, under the circumstances. But evidence is required to support the statement that "Western intelligence confirms [ethnic cleansing] was already underway before the first NATO airstrikes"—and before the withdrawal of the monitors, if the evidence is to have any force.[41] It is also necessary to account for Washington's inability to make the evidence public in the extensive documentation it has released, to which we return.

Further questions arise with regard to "Operation Horseshoe," allegedly discovered by German authorities two weeks after the bombing began and known only "in retrospect," according to Secretary of Defense Cohen, hence not a motive for the bombing. Curiously, the plan was kept secret from NATO Commanding General Wesley Clark, who, when asked about Operation Horseshoe a month after the bombing began, informed the press that plans for it "have never been shared with me."[42] Retired German general Heinz Loquai, who works for the Organisation for Security and Co-operation in Europe (OSCE), alleges in a new book that "the plan was fabricated from run-of-the-mill Bulgarian intelligence reports," and has "come to the conclusion that no such operation ever existed." According to the German news weekly *Die Woche*, the alleged plan was "a general analysis by a Bulgarian intelligence agency of Serbian behaviour in the war." The journal reports further that "maps broadcast around the world as proof of NATO's information were drawn up at the German defence headquarters," and that the Bulgarian report "concluded that the goal of the Serbian military was to destroy the Kosovo Liberation Army, and not to expel the entire Albanian population, as was later argued by [German Defence Minister Rudolf] Scharping and the Nato leadership." Loquai claims further that the German defense ministry "even coined the name 'Horseshoe.' " He also notes "a fundamental flaw in the German account: it named the operation 'Potkova,' which is the Croatian word for horseshoe," instead of using the Serbian word "Potkovica." Loquai's book was favorably received in the German press, which also criticized Scharping's "propaganda lies" (e.g. doubling the alleged number of Serbian troops prior to the bombing from 20,000 to 40,000) and his evasion of the charges.[43]

Yet another problem is that General Clark also had no knowledge of any plan to "thwart ethnic cleansing." When the bombing began on March 24, he informed the press—repeatedly, insistently, forcefully—that brutal Serb atrocities would be an "entirely predictable" consequence of the bombing, later elaborating that NATO military operations were not designed to block "Serb ethnic cleansing" or even to wage war against Serbian forces in Kosovo. U.S. government and other sources available at the time lent considerable plausibility to Clark's judgment. Substantial documentation has been released since by the State Department, NATO, the KVM, the OSCE, and other Western and independent sources, much of it produced in an effort to justify NATO's war. This strongly confirms General Clark's analysis, to an extent I found surprising. Even more surprising, the documentation lends little support to the belief that atrocities mounted significantly after withdrawal of the KVM monitors on March 20, contrary to what seemed to me a natural expectation at the time.

The conclusions about the anticipated effects of NATO's policy choices do not comport well with the stance of nobility. Accordingly, the preferred account during the bombing, repeated endlessly since, is that its objective was "to stem Belgrade's expulsion of ethnic Albanians from Kosovo" under Operation Horseshoe—the expulsion apparently precipitated by the bombing (or its virtual announcement, according to the Secretary of Defense, contrary to Washington's official record to which we return), and an objective unknown to the military commander and forcefully denied by him, just as he was unaware of Operation Horseshoe. Similarly, critics of the air war as ineffectual conclude "that air power failed to prevent the very ethnic cleansing that prompted Western leaders to act in the first place," a reversal of the chronological of events; at least that much seems reasonably clear, whatever one's judgment about the actions undertaken. In a widely praised book on the war, historian David Fromkin asserts without argument that the United States and its allies acted out of "altruism" and "moral fervor" alone, forging "a new kind of approach to the use of power in world politics," as they "reacted to the deportation of more than a million Kosovars from their homeland" by bombing so as to save them "from horrors of suffering, or from death." He is referring to those expelled as the anticipated consequence of the bombing. International affairs and security specialist Alan Kuperman writes that in East Timor and Kosovo, "the threat of economic sanctions or bombing has provoked a tragic backlash," and "Western intervention arrived too late to prevent the widespread atrocities." In Kosovo, the threat of bombing did not arrive "too late to prevent the widespread atrocities," but preceded them, as did the bombing itself if official documents are to be believed. In East Timor, no Western action "provoked a tragic backlash." The use of force was not proposed, and even the threat of sanctions was delayed until after the consummation of the atrocities; and there was no "Western intervention" in any significant sense of the term.[44]

We are left with two plausible justifications for the bombing: ensuring "stability" and "the credibility of NATO," both understood in the doctrinal sense.

The surviving official reasons will plainly not do as support for the thesis that the new generation was pursuing a "moral purpose" in the case of Kosovo, let alone the more visionary theses about the new era. Therefore other arguments have been sought. One, noted earlier, is that the war served as a precedent for "humanitarian intervention" in East Timor six months later. Even if correct, that would not justify the bombing, plainly, but since the conclusion has no basis, the question is academic.

A common current version of Western motives for the 1999 bombing of Serbia is that the West was shamed by its failure to act in Bosnia. NATO chose to bomb, Fouad Ajami asserts.

> against the advice of the pollsters and realists and believers in the primacy of "geoeconomics," to prosecute a just war, pulled into Kosovo as they had earlier been into Bosnia by the shame of what they had witnessed, by the image of themselves they had seen in that Balkan mirror.

According to Aryeh Neier, what "inspired the advocates of humanitarian intervention" in Kosovo was that "many persons in and out of government were determined not to allow a repetition in Kosovo" of what had happened in Bosnia.[45]

These claims are presented without argument as self-evident truths, following the norm for justification for state violence. The claims reject the official reasons offered at the time or since. That aside, though offered in justification of "the advocates of humanitarian intervention" in Kosovo, these claims are, in fact, a severe indictment of them, and of Western political and moral culture generally. According to this account, in radical violation of moral truisms the West is shamed by its image in the "Balkan mirror," where it is guilty only of inadequate response to the crimes of others, but not by its image in other mirrors, where the crimes trace right back home: those discussed earlier for example, where the West did not "tolerate" atrocities as Neier and others prefer to see it, but participated actively in escalating them. Furthermore, on this interpretation, while the guiding principles and values call for determination not to allow a repetition of crimes committed by an official enemy, they say nothing about repetition of our own comparable or worse crimes, and thus free the agents of "humanitarian intervention" and the "many persons" who support them from any concern over these, even recollection of them.

Because of the pairing of Kosovo and East Timor in public discourse in 1999, the latter offers a particularly striking illustration of these conclusions. It should therefore be stressed that the huge slaughter of earlier years in East Timor is (at least) comparable to the terrible atrocities that can plausibly be attributed to Milosevic in the earlier wars in Yugoslavia, and responsibility is far easier to assign, with no complicating factors. If proponents of the "repetition of Bosnia" thesis intend it seriously, they should certainly have been calling for bombing of Jakarta—indeed Washington and London—in early 1999, so as "not to allow a repetition in East Timor" of the crimes that Indonesia, the United States, and United Kingdom had perpetrated there for a quarter-century. And when the new generation of leaders refused to pursue this honorable course, they should have been leading honest citizens to do so themselves, perhaps joining the Bin Laden network. These conclusions follow straightforwardly, if we assume that the thesis is intended as something more than apologetics for state violence.

Quite apart from the startling self-indictment, and the lack of even a pretense of evidence, the argument must be one of the most remarkable justifications for state violence on record. According to this doctrine, military force is legitimate if failure to apply it might induce the target of the attack to carry out autrocities (as it did, as anticipated, after the attack and presumably in response to it). By that standard, violent states are free to act as they like, with the acclaim of the educated classes.

Another device for evading the consequences of "advocacy of humanitarian intervention" in Kosovo is to hold that NATO should have invaded outright, not bombed. That is easy to say, and could be taken seriously if accompanied by a reasoned proposal, at the time or since, taking account of the likely consequences of invasion (particularly in the light of US military doctrine), quite aside from nontrivial logistic and other problems.[46] One will search in vain for that, clearly the minimum that is required to meet the heavy burden of proof that must be borne, always, by advocates of the use of force, whatever the alleged intent.

Another useful mode of justification is to invent and refute absurd arguments against the bombing, while ignoring those actually presented. A favorite target is the argument, attributed to unnamed "leftists" or "revisionists," that the United States has no right to intervene because of its disgraceful record. That the record of a state should be taken into account in considering the right of intervention is another truism, accepted by everyone who even pretends to be serious. But the argument that a disgraceful record automatically rescinds that right would be wholly irrational, hence easy to refute. This exercise can only be understood, once again, as a form of tacit recognition of inability to bear the burden of justification for the resort to violence—always heavy though not insuperable in principle, apart from dedicated pacifists.

The conclusion becomes even more clear when we inspect the occasional efforts to cite an actual source. This is rare, but there are a few examples. Thus, correspondent Ian Williams, who has compiled a distinguished record on other issues, writes that Edward Said and I "looked at the record of inaction by the West, in Palestine, East Timor, Kurdistan and so on, and therefore deduced that any action over Kosovo could not be for good motives and should therefore be opposed." To support the charge, and his ridicule of this "excessively theological attitude" and "moralizing element" that was "common to leftists across the spectrum," he cites nothing by Said and one statement of mine that says nothing even remotely relevant.[47] Even the most cursory reading of what I wrote makes it obvious, without the slightest doubt, that my position was exactly the opposite, even to the extent of reviewing the few examples of military intervention with benign consequences, hence arguably legitimate despite the ugly records of the agents. More striking is the way Williams falls so easily into the common mode of apologetics for state violence. Said and I did not look at the "record of inaction" of the West in the cases he mentions, but at the record of quite decisive *action*, a fact that evidently cannot be assimilated by many Western intellectuals. Again, the only reasonable conclusion is that the burden of justification cannot be met.

It takes considerable effort not to recognize the accuracy of the report to the UN Commission on Human Rights in March 2000 by former Czech dissident Jiri Dienstbier, now UN Special Investigator for the former Yugoslavia: "The bombing hasn't solved any problems," he reported: "It only multiplied the existing problems and created new ones." Or the corroborating assessment of Michael MccGwire that "while Serb forces were clearly the instrument of the unfolding 'humanitarian disaster,' NATO's long-trailered urge to war was undoubtedly a primary cause," and reference to the "bombing as 'humanitarian intervention' " is "really grotesque":

> No one questions the underlying good intentions, but one suspects that much of the moralistic rhetoric, the demonizing, the claim to be pioneering a foreign policy based on values as well as interests, was a form of denial. It served to conceal from all of us the unpalatable fact that leaders and their people have to accept their share of the blame for unintended consequences—in this case the humanitarian disaster and the civilian casualties in Serbia,

which are, in fact, only part of the disaster.[48]

MccGwire's comments seem realistic, with qualifications about the matter of "intentions." The phrase "unintended consequences" obscures the fact that they were anticipated, even if they were not as "entirely predictable" as the NATO commander felt at the outset, in words that MccGwire quotes. Furthermore, it is far from true that "no one questions the underlying good intentions." They are most definitely questioned by those MccGwire calls "the world at large," as he emphasizes (see p. 304). The conviction about unquestionable good intentions is particularly dubious against the background of the record of past and present practice, including the crucial test cases just reviewed in an effort to evaluate the conflicting interpretations of the new era.

Quite generally, it is hard to find significant inconsistency in the practices of the great powers, or in the principles and values that actually guide policy. None of that should be in the least surprising to those who do not prefer what has sometimes been called "intentional ignorance."[49]

20.

A World Without War

I hope you won't mind if I set the stage with a few truisms. It is hardly exciting news that we live in a world of conflict and confrontation. There are lots of dimensions and complexities, but in recent years, lines have been drawn fairly sharply. To oversimplify, but not too much, one of the participants in the conflict is concentrated power centers, state and private, closely interlinked. The other is the general population, worldwide. In old-fashioned terms, it would have been called "class war."

Concentrated power pursues the war relentlessly, and very self-consciously. Government documents and publications of the business world reveal that they are mostly vulgar Marxists, with values reversed, of course. They are also frightened—back to seventeenth-century England in fact. They realize that the system of domination is fragile, that it relies on disciplining the population by one or another means. There is a desperate search for such means: in recent years, Communism, crime, drugs, terrorism, and others. Pretexts change, policies remain rather stable. Sometimes the shift of pretext along with continuity of policy is dramatic and takes real effort to miss: immediately after the collapse of the USSR, for example. They naturally grasp every opportunity to press their agenda forward: 9-11 is a typical case. Crises make it possible to exploit fear and concern to demand that the adversary be submissive, obedient, silent, distracted, while the powerful use the window of oppor-

---

This chapter is the written version of the opening address of the World Social Forum on January 31, 2002, in Porto Alegre, Brazil, and appeared on ZNet on May 29, 2002; reprinted in C. P. Otero, ed., *Radical Priorities*, 3rd ed. (Oakland: AK Press, 2003), 319–32.

tunity to pursue their own favored programs with even greater intensity. These programs vary, depending on the society: in the more brutal states, escalation of repression and terror; in societies where the population has won more freedom, measures to impose discipline while shifting wealth and power even more to their own hands. It is easy to list examples around the world in the past few months.

Their victims should certainly resist the predictable exploitation of crisis, and should focus their own efforts, no less relentlessly, on the primary issues that remain much as they were before: among them, increasing militarism, destruction of the environment, and a far-reaching assault against democracy and freedom, the core of "neoliberal" programs.

The ongoing conflict is symbolized right now by the World Social Forum (WSF) here and the World Economic Forum (WEF) in New York. The WEF—to quote the national U.S. press—is a gathering of "movers and shakers," the "rich and famous," "wizards from around the world," "government leaders and corporate executives, ministers of state and of God, politicians and pundits" who are going to "think deep thoughts" and address "the big problems confronting humankind." A few examples are given, for example, "how do you inject moral values into what we do?" Or a panel entitled "Tell Me What You Eat," led by the "reigning prince of the New York gastronomic scene," whose elegant restaurants will be "mobbed by forum participants." There is also mention of an "anti-forum" in Brazil where fifty thousand people are expected. These are "the freaks who assemble to protest the meetings of the World Trade Organization." One can learn more about the freaks from a photo of a scruffy-looking guy, with face concealed, writing "world killers" on a wall.

At their "carnival," as it is described, the freaks are throwing stones, writing graffiti, dancing and singing about a variety of boring topics that are unmentionable, at least in the U.S.: investment, trade, financial architecture, human rights, democracy, sustainable development, Brazilian-African relations, GATS, and other marginal issues. They are not "thinking deep thoughts" about "big problems"; that is left to the wizards of Davos in New York.

The infantile rhetoric, I presume, is a sign of well-deserved insecurity.

The freaks at the "anti-forum" here are defined as being "opposed to globalization," a propaganda weapon we should reject with scorn. "Globalization" just means international integration. No sane person is "anti-globalization." That should be particularly obvious for the labor movement and the left; the term "international" is not exactly unknown in their history. In fact, the WSF is the most exciting and promising realization of the hopes of the left and popular movements from their modern origins for a true International, which will pursue a program of globalization concerned with the needs and interests of people, rather than of illegitimate concentrations of power. These, of course, want to appropriate the term "globalization," to restrict it to *their* peculiar version of international integration, concerned with their own interests, those of people being incidental. With this ridiculous terminology in place, those who seek a sane and just form of globalization can be labelled "anti-globalization," derided as primitivists who want to return to the stone age, to harm the poor, and other terms of abuse with which we are familiar.

The wizards of Davos modestly call themselves the "international community," but I personally prefer the term used by the world's leading business journal, the *Financial Times*: "the masters of the universe." Since the masters profess to be admirers of Adam Smith, we might expect them to abide by his account of their behavior, though he only called them "the masters of mankind"—that was before the space age.

Smith was referring to the "principal architects of policy" of his day, the merchants and manufacturers of England, who made sure that their own interests are "most peculiarly attended to" however "grievous" the impact on others, including the people of England. At home and abroad, they pursue "the vile maxim of the masters of mankind": "all for ourselves and nothing for other people." It should hardly surprise us that today's masters honor the same "vile maxim." At least they try, though they are sometimes impeded by the freaks—the "great beast," to borrow a term used by the Founding Fathers of American democracy to refer to the unruly population that did not comprehend that the primary goal of government is "to protect the minority of the opulent from the majority," as the leading Framer of the Constitution explained in the debates of the Constitutional Convention.

I'll return to these matters, but first a few words about the immediate topic of this session, which is closely related: "A World Without War." We cannot say much about human affairs with any confidence, but sometimes it is possible. We can, for example, be fairly confident that either there will be a world without war or there won't be a world—at least, a world inhabited by creatures other than bacteria and beetles, with some scattering of others. The reason is familiar: humans have developed means of destroying themselves, and much else, and have come dangerously close to using them for half a century. Furthermore, the leaders of the civilized world are now dedicated to enhancing these dangers to survival, in full awareness of what they are doing, at least if they read the reports of their own intelligence agencies and respected strategic analysts, including many who strongly favor the race to destruction. Still more ominous, the plans are developed and implemented on grounds that are rational within the dominant framework of ideology and values, which ranks survival well below "hegemony," the goal pursued by advocates of these programs, as they frankly insist.

Wars over water, energy, and other resources are not unlikely in the future, with consequences that could be devastating. For the most part, however, wars have had to do with the imposition of the system of nation-states, an unnatural social formation that typically has to be instituted by violence. That's a primary reason why Europe was the most savage and brutal part of the world for many centuries, meanwhile conquering most of the world. European efforts to impose state systems in conquered territories are the source of most conflicts underway right now, after the collapse of the formal colonial system. Europe's own favorite sport of mutual slaughter had to be called off in 1945, when it was realized that the next time the game was played would be the last. Another prediction that we can make with fair confidence is that there won't be a war among great powers; the reason is that if the prediction turns out to be wrong, there will be no one around to care to tell us.

Furthermore, popular activism within the rich and powerful societies has had a civilizing effect. The "movers and shakers" can no longer undertake the kinds of long-term aggression that were options before, as when the U.S. attacked South Vietnam forty years ago, smashing much of it to pieces before significant popular protest developed. Among the many civilizing effects of the ferment of the 1960s was broad opposition to large-scale aggression and massacre, reframed in the ideological system as unwillingness to accept casualties among the armed forces ("the Vietnam syndrome"). That is why the Reaganites had to resort to international terrorism instead of invading Central America directly, on the Kennedy-Johnson model, in their war to defeat liberation theology, as the School of the Americas describes the achievement with pride. The same changes explain the intelligence review of the incoming Bush-I administration in 1989, warning that in conflicts against "much weaker enemies"—the only kind it makes sense to confront—the United States must "defeat them decisively and rapidly," or the campaign will lose "political support," understood to be thin. Wars since have kept to that pattern, and the scale of protest and dissent have steadily increased. So there are changes, of a mixed nature.

When pretexts vanish, new ones have to be concocted to control the great beast while traditional policies are continued, adapted to new circumstances. That was already becoming clear twenty years ago. It was hard not to recognize that the Soviet enemy was facing internal problems and might not be a credible threat much longer. That is part of the reason why the Reagan administration, twenty years ago, declared that the "war on terror" would be the focus of U.S. foreign policy, particularly in Central America and the Middle East, the main source of the plague spread by "depraved opponents of civilization itself" in a "return to barbarism in the modern age," as administration moderate George Shultz explained, also warning that the solution is violence, avoiding "utopian, legalistic means like outside mediation, the World Court, and the United Nations." We need not tarry on how the war was waged in those two regions, and elsewhere, by the extraordinary network of proxy states and mercenaries—an "axis of evil," to borrow a more up-to-date term.

It is of some interest that in the months since the war was re-declared, with much the same rhetoric, after 9-11, all of this has been entirely effaced, even the fact that the U.S. was condemned for international terrorism by the World Court and Security Council (vetoed) and responded by sharply escalating the terrorist attack it was ordered to terminate; or the fact that the very people who are directing the military and diplomatic components of the re-declared war on terror were leading figures in implementing terrorist atrocities in Central America and the Middle East during the first phase of the war. Silence about these matters is a real tribute to the discipline and obedience of the educated classes in the free and democratic societies.

It's a fair guess that the "war on terror" will again serve as a pretext for intervention and atrocities in coming years, not just by the U.S.; Chechnya is only one of a number of examples. In Latin America, there is no need to linger on what that portends; certainly not in Brazil, the first target of the wave of repression that swept Latin America after the Kennedy administration, in a decision of historic importance, shifted the mission of the Latin American military from "hemispheric defense" to "internal security"—a euphemism for state terror directed against the domestic population. That still continues, on a huge scale, particularly in Colombia, well in the lead for human rights violations in the hemisphere in the 1990s and by far the leading recipient of U.S. arms and military training, in accord with a consistent pattern documented even in mainstream scholarship.

The "war on terror" has, of course, been the focus of a huge literature, during the first phase in the 1980s and since it was re-declared in the past few months. One interesting feature of the flood of commentary, then and now, is that we are not told what "terror" is. What we hear, rather, is that this is a vexing and complex question. That is curious: there are straightforward definitions in official U.S. documents. A simple one takes terror to be the "calculated use of violence or threat of violence to attain goals that are political, religious, or ideological in nature . . ." That seems appropriate enough, but it cannot be used, for two good reasons. One is that it also defines official policy, called "counterinsurgency" or "low-intensity conflict." Another is that it yields all the wrong answers, facts too obvious to review though suppressed with remarkable efficiency.

The problem of finding a definition of "terror" that will exclude the most prominent cases is indeed vexing and complex. But fortunately, there is an easy solution: define "terror" as terror that *they* carry out against *us*. A review of the scholarly literature on terror, the media, and intellectual journals will show that this usage is close to exceptionless, and that any departure from it elicits impressive tantrums. Furthermore, the practice is probably universal: the generals in South America were protecting the population from "terror directed from outside," just as the Japanese were in Manchuria and the Nazis in occupied Europe. If there is an exception, I haven't found it.

Let's return to "globalization," and the linkage between it and the threat of war, perhaps terminal war.

The version of "globalization" designed by the masters of the universe has very broad elite support, not surprisingly, as do the so-called "free trade agreements"—what the *Wall Street Journal*, more honestly, has called "free investment agreements." Very little is reported about these issues, and crucial information is simply suppressed; for example, after a decade, the position of the U.S. labor movement on NAFTA, and the conforming conclusions of Congress's own Research Bureau (the Office of Technology Assessment, OTA), have yet to be reported outside of dissident sources. And the issues are off the agenda in electoral politics. There are good reasons. The masters know well that the public will be opposed if information becomes available. They are fairly open when addressing one another, however. Thus a few years ago, under enormous public pressure, Congress rejected the "fast track" legislation that grants the President authority to enact international economic arrangements with Congress permitted to vote "Yes" (or, theoretically, "No) with no discussion, and the public uninformed. Like other sectors of elite opinion, the *Wall Street Journal* was distraught over the failure to undermine democracy. But it explained the problem: opponents of these Stalinist-style measures have an "ultimate weapon," the general population, which must therefore be kept in the dark. That is very important, particularly in the more democratic society, where dissidents can't simply be jailed or assassinated, as in the leading recipients of U.S. military aid, such as El Salvador, Turkey, and Colombia, to list the recent and current world champions (Israel-Egypt aside).

One might ask why public opposition to "globalization" has been so high for many years. That seems strange, in an era when it has led to unprecedented prosperity, so we are constantly informed, particularly in the U.S., with its "fairy tale economy." Through the 1990s, the U.S. has enjoyed "the greatest economic boom in America's history—and the world's," Anthony Lewis wrote in the *New York Times* a year ago, repeating the standard refrain from the left end of the admissible spectrum. It is conceded that there are flaws: some have been left behind in the economic miracle, and we good-hearted folk must do something about that. The flaws reflect a profound and troubling dilemma: the rapid growth and prosperity brought by "globalization" has as a concomitant growing inequality, as some lack the skills to enjoy the wondrous gifts and opportunities.

The picture is so conventional that it may be hard to realize how little resemblance it has to reality, facts that have been well-known right through the miracle. Until the brief late 1990s boomlet (which scarcely compensated for earlier stagnation or decline for most people), per capita growth in the "roaring 1990s" was about the same as the rest of the industrial world, much lower than in the first twenty-five postwar years before so-called "globalization," and vastly lower than the war years, the greatest economic boom in American history, under a semi-command economy. How then can the conventional picture be so radically different from uncontroversial facts? The answer is simplicity itself. For a small sector of the society, the 1990s really were a grand economic boom. That sector happens to include those who tell others the joyous news. And they cannot be accused of dishonesty. They have no reason to doubt what they are saying. They read it all the time in the journals for which they write, and it accords with their personal experience: it is true of the people they meet in editorial offices, faculty clubs, elite conferences like the one the wizards are now attending, and the elegant restaurants where they dine. It's only the world that is different.

Let's have a quick look at the record over a longer stretch. International economic integration—one facet of "globalization," in a neutral sense of the term—increased rapidly before World War I, stagnated or declined during the interwar years, and resumed after World War II, now reaching levels of a century ago by gross measures; the fine structure is more complex. By some measures, globalization was greater before World War I: one illustration is "free circulation of labor," the foundation of free trade for Adam Smith, though not his contemporary admirers. By other measures, globalization is far greater now: one dramatic example—not the only one—is the flow of short-term speculative capital, far beyond any precedent. The distinction reflects some central features of the version of globalization preferred by the masters of the universe: to an extent even beyond the norm, capital has priority, people are incidental.

The Mexican border is an interesting example. It is artificial, the result of conquest, like most borders, and has been porous in both directions for a variety of socioeconomic reasons. It was militarized after NAFTA by Clinton in order to block the "free circulation of labor." That was necessary because of the anticipated effects of NAFTA in Mexico: an "economic miracle," which would be a disaster for much of the population, who would seek to escape. In the same years, the flow of capital, already very free, was expedited further, along with what is called "trade," about two thirds of which is now centrally managed within private tyrannies, up from half before NAFTA. That is "trade" only by doctrinal decision. The effects of NAFTA on actual trade have not been examined, to my knowledge.

A more technical measure of globalization is convergence to a global market, with a single price and wage. That plainly has not happened. With respect to incomes at least, the opposite is more likely true. Though much depends on exactly how it is measured, there is good reason to believe that inequality has increased within and across countries. That is expected to continue. U.S. intelligence agencies, with the participation of specialists from the academic professions and the private sector, recently released a report on expectations for 2015. They expect "globalization" to proceed on course: "Its evolution will be rocky, marked by chronic financial volatility and a widening economic divide." That means less convergence, less globalization in the technical sense, but more globalization in the doctrinally preferred sense. Financial volatility implies still slower growth and more crises and poverty.

It is at this point that a clear connection is established between "globalization" in the sense of the masters of the universe and the increasing likelihood of war. Military planners adopt the same projections, and have explained, forthrightly, that these expectations lie behind the vast expansion of military power. Even pre-September 11, U.S. military expenditures surpassed those of allies and adversaries combined. The terror attacks have been exploited to increase the funding sharply, delighting key elements of the private economy. The most ominous program is militarization of space, also being expanded under the pretext of "fighting terror."

The reasoning behind these programs is explained publicly in Clinton-era documents. A prime reason is the growing gap between the "haves" and the "have-nots," which is expected to continue, contrary to economic theory but consistent with reality. The "have-nots"—the "great beast" of the world—may become disruptive, and must be controlled, in the interests of what is called "stability" in technical jargon, meaning subordination to the dictates of the masters. That requires means of violence, and having "assumed, out of self-interest, responsibility for the welfare of the world capitalist system," the United States must be far in the lead; I'm quoting diplomatic historian Gerald Haines, also the senior historian of the CIA, describing U.S. planning in the 1940s in a scholarly study. Overwhelming dominance in conventional forces and weapons of mass destruction is not sufficient. It is necessary to move on to the new frontier: militarization of space, undermining the Outer Space Treaty of 1967, so far observed. Recognizing the intent, the UN General Assembly has reaffirmed the treaty several times; the United States has refused to join, in virtual isolation. And Washington has blocked negotiations at the

UN Conference on Disarmament for the past year over this issue—all scarcely reported, for the usual reasons. It is not wise to allow citizens to know of plans that may bring to an end biology's only experiment with "higher intelligence."

As widely observed, these programs benefit military industry, but we should bear in mind that the term is misleading. Throughout modern history, but with a dramatic increase after World War II, the military system has been used as a device to socialize cost and risk while privatizing profit. The "new economy" is to a substantial extent an outgrowth of the dynamic and innovative state sector of the U.S. economy. The main reason why public spending in biological sciences has been rapidly increasing is that intelligent right-wingers understand that the cutting edge of the economy relies on these public initiatives. A huge increase is scheduled under the pretext of "bioterror," just as the public was deluded into paying for the new economy under the pretext that the Russians are coming—or after they collapsed, by the threat of the "technological sophistication" of Third World countries as the Party Line shifted in 1990, instantly, without missing a beat and with scarcely a word of comment. That's also a reason why national security exemptions have to be part of international economic agreements: it doesn't help Haiti, but it allows the U.S. economy to grow under the traditional principle of harsh market discipline for the poor and a nanny state for the rich—what's called "neoliberalism," though it is not a very good term: the doctrine is centuries old, and would scandalize classical liberals.

One might argue that these public expenditures were often worthwhile. Perhaps, perhaps not. But it is clear that the masters were afraid to allow democratic choice. All of this is concealed from the general public, though the participants understand it very well.

Plans to cross the last frontier of violence by militarization of space are disguised as "missile defense," but anyone who pays attention to history knows that when we hear the word "defense," we should think "offense." The present case is no exception. The goal is quite frankly stated: to ensure "global dominance," "hegemony." Official documents stress prominently that the goal is "to protect U.S. interests and investments," and control the "have-nots." Today that requires domination of space, just as in earlier times the most powerful states created armies and navies "to protect and enhance their commercial interests." It is recognized that these new initiatives, in which the U.S. is far in the lead, pose a serious threat to survival. And it is also understood that they could be prevented by international treaties. But as I've already mentioned, hegemony is a higher value than survival, a moral calculus that has prevailed among the powerful throughout history. What has changed is that the stakes are much higher, awesomely so.

The relevant point here is that the expected success of "globalization" in the doctrinal sense is a primary reason given for the programs of using space for offensive weapons of instant mass destruction.

Let us return to "globalization," and "the greatest economic boom in America's history—and the world's" in the 1990s.

Since World War II, the international economy has passed through two phases: the Bretton Woods phase to the early 1970s, and the period since, with the dismantling of the Bretton Woods system of regulated exchange rates and controls on capital movement. It is the second phase that is called "globalization," associated with the neoliberal policies of the "Washington consensus." The two phases are quite different. The first is often called the "golden age" of (state) capitalism. The second phase has been accompanied by marked deterioration in standard macroeconomic measures: rate of growth of the economy, productivity, capital investment, even world trade; much higher interest rates (harming economies); vast accumulation of unproductive reserves to protect currencies; increased financial volatility; and other harmful consequences. There were exceptions, notably the East Asian countries that did not follow the rules: they did not worship the "religion" that "markets know best," as Joseph Stiglitz wrote in a World Bank research publication shortly before he was appointed chief economist, later removed (and winning the Nobel prize). In contrast, the worst results were found where the rules were rigorously applied, as in Latin America, facts widely acknowledged, among others, by José Antonio Ocampo, director of the Economic Commission for Latin America and the Caribbean (ECLAC), in an address before the American Economic Association a year ago. The "promised land is a mirage," he observed; growth in the 1990s was far below that of the three decades of "state-led development" in Phase I. He too noted that the correlation between following the rules and economic outcomes holds worldwide.

Let us return, then, to the profound and troubling dilemma: the rapid growth and great prosperity brought by globalization has brought inequality because some lack skills. There is no dilemma, because the rapid growth and prosperity are a myth.

Many international economists regard liberalization of capital as a substantial factor in the poorer outcomes of Phase II. But the economy is a complex affair, so poorly understood that one has to be cautious about causal connections. But one consequence of liberalization of capital is rather clear: it undercuts democracy. That was understood by the framers of Bretton Woods: one reason why the agreements were founded on regulation of capital was to allow governments to carry out social democratic policies, which had enormous popular support. Free capital movement creates what has been called a "virtual Senate" with "veto power" over government decisions, sharply restricting policy options. Governments face a "dual constituency:" voters, and speculators, who "conduct moment-by-moment referendums" on government policies (quoting technical studies of the financial system). Even in the rich countries, the private constituency prevails.

Other components of investor-rights "globalization" have similar consequences. Socioeconomic decisions are increasingly shifted to unaccountable concentrations of power, an essential feature of neoliberal "reforms" (a term of propaganda, not description). Extension of the attack on democracy is presumably being planned, without public discussion, in the negotiations for a General Agreement on Trade in Services (GATS). The term "services," as you know, refers to just about anything that might fall within the arena of democratic choice: health, education, welfare, postal and other communications, water and other resources, etc. There is no meaningful sense in which transferring such services to private hands is "trade," but the term has been so deprived of meaning that it might as well be extended to this travesty as well.

The huge public protests in Quebec last April at the Summit of the Americas, set in motion by the freaks in Porto Alegre a year ago, were in part directed against the attempt to impose the GATS principles in secret within the planned Free Trade Area of the Americas (FTAA). Those protests brought together a very broad constituency, North and South, all strongly opposed to what is apparently being planned by trade ministers and corporate executives behind closed doors.

The protests did receive coverage, of the usual kind: the freaks are throwing rocks and disrupting the wizards thinking about the big problems. The invisibility of their actual concerns is quite remarkable. For example, *New York Times* economics correspondent Anthony DePalma writes that the GATS agreement "has generated none of the public controversy that has swirled about [WTO] attempts to promote merchandise trade," even after Seattle. In fact, it has been a prime concern for years. As in other cases, this is not deceit. DePalma's knowledge about the freaks is surely limited to what passes through the media filter, and it is an iron law of journalism that the serious concerns of activists must be rigidly barred, in favor of someone throwing a rock, perhaps a police provocateur.

The importance of protecting the public from information was revealed dramatically at the April Summit. Every editorial office in the United States had on its desk two important studies, timed for release just before the Summit. One was from Human Rights Watch, the second from the Economic Policy Institute in Washington; neither organization is exactly obscure. Both studies investigated in depth the effects of NAFTA, which was hailed at the Summit as a grand triumph and a model for the FTAA, with headlines trumpeting its praises by George Bush and other leaders, all accepted as Gospel

Truth. Both studies were suppressed with near-total unanimity. It's easy to see why. HRW analyzed the effects of NAFTA on labor rights, which, it found, were harmed in all three participating countries. The EPI report was more comprehensive: it consisted of detailed analyses of the effects of NAFTA on working people, written by specialists on the three countries. The conclusion is that this is one of the rare agreements that has harmed the majority of the population in all of the participating countries.

The effects on Mexico were particularly severe, and particularly significant for the South. Wages had declined sharply with the imposition of neoliberal programs in the 1980s. That continued after NAFTA, with a 24 percent decline in incomes for salaried workers, and 40 percent for the self-employed, an effect magnified by the rapid increase in unsalaried workers. Though foreign investment grew, total investment declined, as the economy was transferred to the hands of foreign multinationals. The minimum wage lost 50 percent of its purchasing power. Manufacturing declined, and development stagnated or may have reversed. A small sector became extremely wealthy, and foreign investors prospered.

These studies confirm what had been reported in the business press and academic studies. The *Wall Street Journal* reported that although the Mexican economy was growing rapidly in the late 1990s after a sharp post-NAFTA decline, consumers suffered a 40 percent drop in purchasing power, the number of people living in extreme poverty grew twice as fast as the population, and even those working in foreign-owned assembly plants lost purchasing power. Similar conclusions were drawn in a study of the Latin American section of the Woodrow Wilson Center, which also found that economic power had greatly concentrated as small Mexican companies cannot obtain financing, traditional farming sheds workers, and labor-intensive sectors (agriculture, light industry) cannot compete internationally with what is called "free enterprise" in the doctrinal system. Agriculture suffered for the usual reasons: peasant farmers cannot compete with highly subsidized U.S. agribusiness, with effects familiar throughout the world.

Most of this was predicted by critics of NAFTA, including the suppressed OTA and labor movement studies. Critics were wrong in one respect, however Most anticipated a sharp increase in the urban-rural ratio, as hundreds of thousands of peasants were driven off the land. That didn't happen. The reason, it seems, is that conditions deteriorated so badly in the cities that there was a huge flight from them as well to the United States. Those who survive the crossing—many do not—work for very low wages, with no benefits, under awful conditions. The effect is to destroy lives and communities in Mexico and to improve the U.S. economy, where "consumption of the urban middle class continues to be subsidized by the impoverishment of farm laborers both in the United States and Mexico," the Woodrow Wilson Center study points out.

These are among the costs of NAFTA, and neoliberal globalization generally, that economists generally choose not to measure. But even by the highly ideological standard measures, the costs have been severe.

None of this was allowed to sully the celebration of NAFTA and the FTAA at the Summit. Unless they are connected to activist organizations, most people know about these matters only from their own lives. And carefully protected from reality by the Free Press, many regard themselves as somehow failures, unable to take part in the celebration of the greatest economic boom in history.

Data from the richest country in the world are enlightening, but I'll skip the details. The picture generalizes, with some variation of course, and exceptions of the kind already noted. The picture is much worse when we depart from standard economic measures. One cost is the threat to survival implicit in the reasoning of military planners, already described. There are many others. To take one, the ILO reported a rising "worldwide epidemic" of serious mental health disorders, often linked to stress in the workplace, with very substantial fiscal costs in the industrial countries. A large factor, they conclude, is "globalization," which brings "evaporation of job security," pressure on workers, and a higher workload, particularly in the United States. Is this a cost of "globalization?" From one point of view, it is one of its most attractive features. When he lauded U.S. economic performance as "extraordinary," Alan Greenspan stressed particularly the heightened sense of job insecurity, which leads to subdued costs for employers. The World Bank agrees. It recognizes that "labor market flexibility" has acquired "a bad name . . . as a euphemism for pushing wages down and workers out," but nevertheless, "it is essential in all the regions of the world . . . The most important reforms involve lifting constraints on labor mobility and wage flexibility, as well as breaking the ties between social services and labor contracts."

In brief, pushing workers out, pushing wages down, undermining benefits are all crucial contributions to economic health, according to prevailing ideology.

Unregulated trade has further benefits for corporations. Much, probably most, "trade" is centrally managed through a variety of devices: intrafirm transfers, strategic alliances, outsourcing, and others. Broad trading areas benefit corporations by making them less answerable to local and national communities. This enhances the effects of neoliberal programs, which regularly have reduced labor share of income. In the United States, the 1990s were the first postwar period when division of income shifted strongly to owners of capital, away from labor.

Trade has a wide range of unmeasured costs: subsidizing energy, resource depletion, and other externalities not counted. It also brings advantages, though here too some caution is necessary. The most widely hailed is that trade increases specialization—which reduces choices, including the choice to modify comparative advantage, otherwise known as "development." Choice and development are values in themselves: undermining them is a substantial cost. If the American colonies had been compelled to accept the WTO regime two hundred years ago, New England would be pursuing its comparative advantage in exporting fish, surely not producing textiles, which survived only by exorbitant tariffs to bar British products (mirroring Britain's treatment of India). The same was true of steel and other industries, right to the present, particularly in the highly protectionist Reagan years—even putting aside the state sector of the economy. There is a great deal to say about all of this. Much of the story is masked in selective modes of economic measurement, though it is well-known to economic historians and historians of technology.

As everyone here is aware, the rules of the game are likely to enhance deleterious effects for the poor. The rules of the WTO bar the mechanisms used by every rich country to reach its current state of development, while also providing unprecedented levels of protectionism for the rich, including a patent regime that bars innovation and growth in novel ways, and allows corporate entities to amass huge profits by monopolistic pricing of products often developed with substantial public contribution.

Under contemporary versions of traditional mechanisms, half the people in the world are effectively in receivership, their economic policies managed by experts in Washington. But even in the rich countries democracy is under attack by virtue of the shift of decision-making power from governments, which may be partially responsive to the public, to private tyrannies, which have no such defects. Cynical slogans such as "trust the people" or "minimize the state" do not, under current circumstances, call for increasing popular control. They shift decisions from governments to other hands, but not "the people:" rather, the management of collectivist legal entities, largely unaccountable to the public, and effectively totalitarian in internal structure, much as conservatives charged a century ago when opposing "the corporatization of America."

Latin American specialists and polling organizations have observed for some years that extension of formal democracy in Latin America has been accompanied by increasing disillusionment about democracy, "alarming trends," which continue, analysts have observed, noting the link between "declining economic fortunes" and "lack of faith" in democratic institutions (*Financial Times*). As Atilio Borón pointed out some years ago, the new wave of democratization in Latin America coincided with neoliberal economic "reforms," which undermine effective democracy, a phenomenon that extends worldwide, in various forms.

To the United States as well. There has been much public clamor about the "stolen election" of November 2000, and surprise that the public does not seem to care. Likely reasons are suggested by public opinion studies, which reveal that on the eve of the election, three-quarters of the population regarded the process as largely a farce: a game played by financial contributors, party leaders, and the public relations industry, which crafted candidates to say "almost anything to get themselves elected" so that one could believe little they said even when it was intelligible. On most issues, citizens could not identify the stands of the candidates, not because they are stupid or not trying, but because of the conscious efforts of the PR industry. A Harvard University project that monitors political attitudes found that the "feeling of powerlessness has reached an alarming high," with more than half saying that people like them have little or no influence on what government does, a sharp rise through the neoliberal period.

Issues on which the public differs from elites (economic, political, intellectual) are pretty much off the agenda, notably questions of economic policy. The business world, not surprisingly, is overwhelmingly in favor of corporate-led "globalization," the "free investment agreements" called "free trade agreements," NAFTA and the FTAA, GATS, and other devices that concentrate wealth and power in hands unaccountable to the public. Also not surprisingly, the great beast is generally opposed, almost instinctively, even without knowing crucial facts from which they are carefully shielded. It follows that such issues are not appropriate for political campaigns, and did not arise in the mainstream for the November 2000 elections. One would have been hard-pressed, for example, to find discussion of the upcoming Summit of the Americas and the FTAA, and other topics that involve issues of prime concern for the public. Voters were directed to what the PR industry calls "personal qualities," not "issues." Among the half the population that votes, heavily skewed toward the wealthy, those who recognize their class interests to be at stake vote for those interests: overwhelmingly, for the more reactionary of the two business parties. But the general public splits its vote in other ways, leading to a statistical tie. Among working people, noneconomic issues such as gun ownership and "religiosity" were primary factors, so that people often voted against their own primary interests—apparently assuming that they had little choice.

What remains of democracy is to be construed as the right to choose among commodities. Business leaders have long explained the need to impose on the population a "philosophy of futility" and "lack of purpose in life," to "concentrate human attention on the more superficial things that comprise much of fashionable consumption." Deluged by such propaganda from infancy, people may then accept their meaningless and subordinate lives and forget ridiculous ideas about managing their own affairs. They may abandon their fate to the wizards, and in the political realm, to the self-described "intelligent minorities" who serve and administer power.

From this perspective, conventional in elite opinion particularly through the last century, the November 2000 elections do not reveal a flaw of U.S. democracy, but rather its triumph. And generalizing, it is fair to hail the triumph of democracy throughout the hemisphere, and elsewhere, even though the populations somehow do not see it that way.

The struggle to impose that regime takes many forms, but never ends, and never will as long as high concentrations of effective decision-making power remain in place. It is only reasonable to expect the masters to exploit any opportunity that comes along—at the moment, the fear and anguish of the population in the face of terrorist attacks, a serious matter for the West now that, with new technologies available, it has lost its virtual monopoly of violence, retaining only a huge preponderance.

But there is no need to accept these rules, and those who are concerned with the fate of the world and its people will surely follow a very different course. The popular struggles against investor-rights "globalization," mostly in the South, have influenced the rhetoric, and to some extent the practices, of the masters of the universe, who are concerned and defensive. These popular movements are unprecedented in scale, in range of constituency, and in international solidarity; the meetings here are a critically important illustration. The future to a large extent lies in their hands. It is hard to overestimate what is at stake.

21.

Reflections on 9-11

It is widely argued that the September 11 terrorist attacks have changed the world dramatically, that nothing will be the same as the world enters into an "age of terror"—the title of a collection of academic essays by Yale University scholars and others, which regards the anthrax attack as even more ominous.

There is no doubt that the 9-11 atrocities were an event of historic importance, not—regrettably—because of their scale, but because of the choice of innocent victims. It had been recognized for some time that with new technology, the industrial powers would probably lose their virtual monopoly of violence, retaining only an enormous preponderance. No one could have anticipated the specific way in which the expectations were fulfilled, but they were. For the first time in modern history, Europe and its offshoots were subjected, on home soil, to the kind of atrocity that they routinely have carried out elsewhere. The history should be too familiar to review, and though the West may choose to disregard it, the victims do not. The sharp break in the traditional pattern surely qualifies 9-11 as a historic event, and the repercussions are sure to be significant.

Several crucial questions arose at once:

1. who is responsible?
2. what are the reasons?
3. what is the proper reaction?
4. what are the longer-term consequences?

This chapter first appeared in *Aftonbladet* in Sweden, August 2002, reprinted in *9-11*, 2nd ed., (New York: Seven Stories Press, 2002), 119–28.

As for (1), it was assumed, plausibly, that the guilty parties were Bin Laden and his Al-Qaeda network. No one knows more about them than the CIA, which, together with its counterparts among U.S. allies, recruited radical Islamists from many countries and organized them into a military and terrorist force, not to help Afghans resist Russian aggression, which would have been a legitimate objective, but for normal reasons of state, with grim consequences for Afghans after the Mujahidin took control. U.S. intelligence has surely been following the other exploits of these networks closely ever since they assassinated President Sadat of Egypt twenty years ago, and more intensively since the attempt to blow up the World Trade Center and many other targets in a highly ambitious terrorist operation in 1993. Nevertheless, despite what must be the most intensive international intelligence investigation in history, evidence about the perpetrators of 9-11 has been hard to find. Eight months after the bombing, FBI director Robert Mueller, testifying to Congress, could say only that U.S. intelligence now "believes" the plot was hatched in Afghanistan, though planned and implemented elsewhere. And long after the source of the anthrax attack was localized to U.S. government weapons laboratories, it has still not been identified. These are indications of how hard it may be to counter acts of terror targeting the rich and powerful in the future. Nevertheless, despite the thin evidence, the initial conclusion about 9-11 is presumably correct.

Turning to (2), scholarship is virtually unanimous in taking the terrorists at their word, which matches their deeds for the past twenty years: their goal, in their terms, is to drive the infidels from Muslim lands, to overthrow the corrupt governments they impose and sustain, and to institute an extremist version of Islam.

More significant, at least for those who hope to reduce the likelihood of further crimes of a similar nature, are the background conditions from which the terrorist organizations arose, and that provide a mass reservoir of sympathetic understanding for at least parts of their message, even among those who despise and fear them. In George Bush's plaintive words, "Why do they hate us?" The question is not new, and answers are not hard to find. Forty-five years ago President Eisenhower and his staff discussed what he called the "campaign of hatred against us" in the Arab world, "not by the governments but by the people." The basic reason, the National Security Council advised, is the recognition that the U.S. supports corrupt and brutal governments that block democracy and development, and does so because of its concern "to protect its interest in Near East oil." The *Wall Street Journal* found much the same when it investigated attitudes of wealthy westernized Muslims after 9-11, feelings now exacerbated by specific U.S. policies with regard to Israel/Palestine and Iraq.

Commentators generally prefer a more comforting answer: their anger is rooted in resentment of our freedom and love of democracy, their cultural failings tracing back many centuries, their inability to take part in the form of "globalization" (in which they happily participate), and other such deficiencies. More comforting, perhaps, but not wise.

What about proper reaction, question (3)? The answers are doubtless contentious, but at least the reaction should meet the most elementary moral standards: specifically, if an action is right for us, it is right for others; and if wrong for others, it is wrong for us. Those who reject that standard simply declare that acts are justified by power; they can therefore be ignored in any discussion of appropriateness of action, of right or wrong. One might ask what remains of the flood of commentary on question (3) (debates about "just war," etc.) if this simple criterion is adopted.

To illustrate with a few uncontroversial cases, forty years have passed since President Kennedy ordered that "the terrors of the earth" must be visited upon Cuba until their leadership is eliminated, having violated good form by successful resistance to U.S.-run invasion. The terrors were extremely serious, continuing into the 1990s. Twenty years have passed since President Reagan launched a terrorist war against Nicaragua, conducted with barbaric atrocities and vast destruction, leaving tens of thousands dead and the country ruined perhaps beyond recovery—and also leading to condemnation of the U.S. for international terrorism by the World Court and the UN Security Council (in a resolution the U.S. vetoed). But no one believes that Cuba or Nicaragua had the right to set off bombs in Washington or New York, or to assassinate U.S. political leaders. And it is all too easy to add many far more severe cases, up to the present.

Accordingly, those who accept elementary moral standards have some work to do to show that the U.S. and Britain were justified in bombing Afghans in order to compel them to turn over people who the U.S. suspected of criminal atrocities, the official war aim, announced by the president as the bombing began; or to overthrow their rulers, the war aim announced several weeks later.

The same moral standard holds of more nuanced proposals about an appropriate response to terrorist atrocities. The respected Anglo-American military historian Michael Howard proposed "a police operation conducted under the auspices of the United Nations . . . against a criminal conspiracy whose members should be hunted down and brought before an international court, where they would receive a fair trial and, if found guilty, be awarded an appropriate sentence" (*Guardian*, *Foreign Affairs*). That seems reasonable, though we may ask what the reaction would be to the suggestion that the proposal should be applied universally. That is unthinkable, and if the suggestion were to be made, it would arouse outrage and horror.

Similar questions arise with regard to the "Bush doctrine" of "preemptive strike" against suspected threats. It should be noted that the doctrine is not new. High-level planners are mostly holdovers from the Reagan administration, which argued that the bombing of Libya was justified under the UN Charter as "self-defense against future attack." Clinton planners advised "preemptive response" (including nuclear first strike). And the doctrine has earlier precedents. Nevertheless, the bold assertion of such a right is novel, and there is no secret as to whom the threat is addressed. The government and commentators are stressing loud and clear that they intend to apply the doctrine to Iraq. The elementary standard of universality, therefore, would appear to justify Iraqi preemptive terror against the United States. Of course, no one accepts this conclusion. Again, if we are willing to adopt elementary moral principles, obvious questions arise, and must be faced by those who advocate or tolerate the selective version of the doctrine of "preemptive response" that grants the right to those powerful enough to exercise it with little concern for what the world may think. And the burden of proof is not light, as is always true when the threat or use of violence is advocated or tolerated.

There is, of course, an easy counter to such simple arguments: *we* are good, and *they* are evil. That useful principle trumps virtually any argument. Analysis of commentary and much of scholarship reveals that its roots commonly lie in that crucial principle, which is not argued but asserted. Occasionally, but rarely, some irritating creatures attempt to confront the core principle with the record of recent and contemporary history. We learn more about prevailing cultural norms by observing the reaction, and the interesting array of barriers erected to deter any lapse into this heresy. None of this, of course, is an invention of contemporary power centers and the dominant intellectual culture. Nonetheless, it merits attention, at least among those who have some interest in understanding where we stand and what may lie ahead.

Let us turn briefly to these last considerations: question (4).

In the longer term, I suspect that the crimes of 9-11 will accelerate tendencies that were already under way: the Bush doctrine, just mentioned, is an illustration. As was predicted at once, governments throughout the world seized upon 9-11 as a window of opportunity to institute or escalate harsh and repressive programs. Russia eagerly joined the "coalition against terror" expecting to receive authorization for its terrible atrocities in Chechnya, and was not disappointed. China happily joined for similar reasons. Turkey was the first country to offer troops for the new phase of the United States' "war on terror," in gratitude, as the Prime Minister explained, for the U.S. contribution to Turkey's campaign against its miserably repressed Kurdish population, waged with extreme savagery and relying crucially on a huge flow of U.S. arms. Turkey is highly praised for its achievements in these campaigns of state terror, including some of the worst atrocities of the grisly 1990s, and was rewarded by grant of authority to protect Kabul from terror, funded by the same superpower that provided the military means, and the diplomatic and ideological support, for its recent atrocities. Israel recognized that it would be able to crush Palestinians even more brutally, with even firmer U.S. support. And so on throughout much of the world.

More democratic societies, including the United States, instituted measures to impose discipline on the domestic population and to institute unpopular measures under the guise of "combating terror," exploiting the atmosphere of fear and the demand for "patriotism"—which in practice means: "You shut up and I'll pursue my own agenda relentlessly." The Bush administration used the opportunity to advance its assault against most of the population, and future generations, in service to the narrow corporate interests that dominate the administration to an extent even beyond the norm.

In brief, initial predictions were amply confirmed.

One major outcome is that the United States, for the first time, has major military bases in Central Asia. These are important to position U.S. multinationals favorably in the current "great game" to control the considerable resources of the region, but also to complete the encirclement of the world's major energy resources, in the Gulf region. The U.S. base system targeting the Gulf extends from the Pacific to the Azores, but the closest reliable base before the Afghan war was Diego Garcia. Now that situation is much improved, and forceful intervention, if deemed appropriate, will be greatly facilitated.

The Bush administration perceives the new phase of the "war on terror" (which in many ways replicates the "war on terror" declared by the Reagan administration twenty years earlier) as an opportunity to expand its already overwhelming military advantages over the rest of the world, and to move on to other methods to ensure global dominance. Government thinking was articulated clearly by high officials when Prince Abdullah of Saudi Arabia visited the U.S. in April to urge the administration to pay more attention to the reaction in the Arab world to its strong support for Israeli terror and repression. He was told, in effect, that the U.S. did not care what he or other Arabs think. As the *New York Times* reported, a high official explained that "if he thought we were strong in Desert Storm, we're 10 times as strong today. This was to give him some idea what Afghanistan demonstrated about our capabilities." A senior defense analyst gave a simple gloss: others will "respect us for our toughness and won't mess with us." That stand too has many historical precedents, but in the post–September 11 world it gains new force.

We do not have internal documents, but it is reasonable to speculate that such consequences were one primary goal of the bombing of Afghanistan: to warn the world of what the United States can do if someone steps out of line. The bombing of Serbia was undertaken for similar reasons. Its primary goal was to "ensure NATO's credibility," as Blair and Clinton explained—not referring to the credibility of Norway or Italy, but of the United States and its prime military client. That is a common theme of statecraft and the literature of international relations; and with some reason, as history amply reveals.

Without continuing, the basic issues of international society seem to me to remain much as they were, but 9-11 surely has induced changes, in some cases, with significant and not very attractive implications.

22.

Language and the Brain

The right way to address the announced topic would be to review the fundamental principles of language and the brain and to show how they can be unified, perhaps on the model of chemistry and physics sixty-five years ago, or the integration of parts of biology within the complex a few years later. But that course I am not going to try to attempt. One of the few things I can say about this topic with any confidence is that I do not begin to know enough to approach it in the right way. With less confidence I suspect it may be fair to say that current understanding falls well short of laying the basis for the unification of the sciences of the brain and higher mental faculties, language among them, and that many surprises may lie along the way to what seems a distant goal—which would itself come as no surprise if the classical examples I mentioned are indeed a realistic model.

This somewhat skeptical assessment of current prospects differs from two prevalent but opposing views. The first holds that the skepticism is unwarranted, or more accurately, profoundly in error, because the question of unification does not even arise. It does not arise for psychology as the study of mind, because the topic does not fall within biology, a position taken to define the "computer model of mind";[1] nor for language, because language is an extra-human object, the standard view within major currents of philosophy of mind and language, and also put forth recently by prominent figures in neuroscience and ethology. At least that is what the words seem to imply; the intentions may be different. I will return to some prominent current examples.

This chapter first appeared in *On Nature and Language* (Cambridge: Cambridge University Press, 2002), 61–91.

A contrasting view holds that the problem of unification does arise, but that the skepticism is unwarranted. Unification of the brain and cognitive sciences is an imminent prospect, overcoming Cartesian dualism. This optimistic assessment is expressed forthrightly by evolutionary biologist E. O. Wilson in a recent publication of the American Academy of Arts and Sciences devoted to the brain, summarizing the state of the art, and seems to be shared rather broadly: "Researchers now speak confidently of a coming solution to the brain-mind problem."[2] Similar confidence has been expressed for half a century, including announcements by eminent figures that the brain-mind problem has been solved.

We can, then, identify several points of view with regard to the general problem of unification:

1. There is no issue: language and higher mental faculties generally are not part of biology.
2. They belong to biology in principle, and any constructive approach to the study of human thought and its expression, or of human action and interaction, relies on this assumption, at least tacitly.

Category (2), in turn, has two variants: (A) unification is close at hand; (B) we do not currently see how these parts of biology relate to one another, and suspect that fundamental insights may be missing altogether.

The last point of view, (2B), seems to me the most plausible. I will try to indicate why, and to sketch some of the terrain that should be covered in a careful and comprehensive overview of these topics.

As a framework for the discussion, I would like to select three theses that seem to me generally reasonable, and have for a long time. I will quote current formulations by leading scientists, however, not my own versions from past years.

The first thesis is articulated by neuroscientist Vernon Mountcastle, introducing the American Academy study I mentioned. A guiding theme of the contributions, and the field generally, he observes, is that "Things mental, indeed minds, are emergent properties of brains," though "these emergences are not regarded as irreducible but are produced by principles that control the interactions between lower level events—principles we do not yet understand."

The second thesis is methodological. It is presented clearly by ethologist Mark Hauser in his comprehensive study *Evolution of Communication*.[3] Following Tinbergen, he argues, we should adopt four perspectives in studying "communication in the animal kingdom, including human language." To understand some trait, we should:

1. Seek the mechanisms that implement it, psychological and physiological; the mechanistic perspective.
2. Sort out genetic and evironmental factors, which can also be approached at psychological or physiological levels; the ontogenetic perspective.
3. Find the "fitness consequences" of the trait, its effects on survival and reproduction; the functional perspective.
4. Unravel "the evolutionary history of the species so that the structure of the trait can be evaluated in light of ancestral features"; the phylogenetic perspective.

The third thesis is presented by cognitive neuroscientist C. R. Gallistel:[4] the "modular view of learning," which he takes to be "the norm these days in neuroscience." According to this view, the brain incorporates "specialized organs," computationally specialized to solve particular kinds of problems, as they do with great facility, apart from "extremely hostile environments." The growth and development of these specialized organs, sometimes called "learning," is the result of internally directed processes and environmental effects that trigger and shape development. The language organ is one such component of the human brain.

In conventional terminology, adapted from earlier usage, the language organ is the faculty of language (FL); the theory of the initial state of FL, an expression of the genes, is universal grammar (UG); theories of states attained are particular grammars; the states themselves are internal languages, "languages" for short. The initial state is, of course, not manifested at birth, as in the case of other organs, say the visual system.

Let us now look more closely at the three theses—reasonable I think, but with qualifications—beginning with the first: "Things mental, indeed minds, are emergent properties of brains."

The thesis is widely accepted, and is often considered a distinctive and exciting contribution of the current era, if still highly controversial. In the past few years it has been put forth as an "astonishing hypothesis," "the bold assertion that mental phenomena are entirely natural and caused by the neurophysiological activities of the brain" and "that capacities of the human mind are in fact capacities of the human brain"; or as a "radical new idea" in the philosophy of mind that may at last put an end to Cartesian dualism, though some continue to believe that the chasm between body and mind cannot be bridged.

The picture is misleading, and it is useful to understand why. The thesis is not new, and it should not be controversial, for reasons understood centuries ago. The thesis was articulated clearly in the eighteenth century, and for compelling reasons—though controversially then, because of affront to religious doctrines. By 1750, David Hume casually described thought as a "little agitation of the brain."[5] A few years later the thesis was elaborated by the eminent chemist Joseph Priestley: "the powers of sensation or perception and thought" are properties of "a certain organized system of matter"; properties "termed mental" are "the result [of the] organical structure" of the brain and "the human nervous system" generally. Equivalently: "Things mental, indeed minds, are emergent properties of brains" (Mountcastle). Priestley of course could not say how this emergence takes place, nor can we do much better after two hundred years.

I think the brain and cognitive sciences can learn some useful lessons from the rise of the emergence thesis in early modern science, and the ways the natural sciences have developed since right up to the mid-twentieth century, with the unification of physics–chemistry–biology. Current controversies about mind and brain are strikingly similar to debates about atoms, molecules, chemical structures and reactions, and related matters, which were very much alive well into the twentieth century. Similar, and in ways that I think are instructive.

The reasons for the eighteenth-century emergence thesis, recently revived, were indeed compelling. The modern scientific revolution, from Galileo, was based on the thesis that the world is a great machine, which could in principle be constructed by a master artisan, a complex version of the clocks and other intricate automata that fascinated the seventeenth and eighteenth centuries, much as computers have provided a stimulus to thought and imagination in recent years; the change of artifacts has limited consequences for the basic issues, as Alan Turing demonstrated sixty years ago. The thesis—called "the mechanical philosophy"—has two aspects: empirical and methodological. The factual thesis has to do with the nature of the world: it is a machine constructed of interacting parts. The methodological thesis has to do with intelligibility: true understanding requires a mechanical model, a device that an artisan could construct.

This Galilean model of intelligibility has a corollary: when mechanism fails, understanding fails. For this reason, when Galileo came to be disheartened by apparent inadequacies of mechanical explanation, he finally concluded that humans will never completely understand even "a single effect in nature." Descartes, in contrast, was much more optimistic. He thought he could demonstrate that most of the phenomena of nature could be explained in mechanical terms: the inorganic and organic world apart from humans, but also human physiology, sensation, perception, and action to a large extent. The limits of mechanical explanation were reached when these human functions are mediated by thought, a unique human possession based on a principle that escapes mechanical explanation: a "creative" principle that underlies acts of will and choice, which are "the noblest thing we can have" and all that "truly belongs" to us (in Cartesian terms). Humans are only "incited and inclined" to act in certain ways, not "compelled" (or random), and in this respect are unlike machines—that is, the rest of the world. The most striking example for the Cartesians was the normal use of language: humans can express their thoughts in novel and limitless ways that are constrained by bodily state but not determined by it, appropriate to situations but not caused by them, and that evoke in others thoughts that they could have expressed in similar ways—what we may call "the creative aspect of language use."

It is worth bearing in mind that these conclusions are correct, as far as we know.

In these terms, Cartesian scientists developed experimental procedures to determine whether some other creature has a mind like ours—elaborate versions of what has been revived as the Turing test in the past half century, though without some crucial fallacies that have attended this revival, disregarding Turing's explicit warnings, an interesting topic that I will put aside.[6] In the same terms, Descartes could formulate a relatively clear mind-body problem: having established two principles of nature, the mechanical and mental principles, we can ask how they interact, a major problem for seventeenth-century science. But the problem did not survive very long. As is well-known, the entire picture collapsed when Newton established, to his great dismay, that not only does mind escape the reach of the mechanical philosophy, but so does everything else in nature, even the simplest terrestrial and planetary motion. As pointed out by Alexander Koyré, one of the founders of the modern history of science, Newton showed that "a purely materialistic or mechanistic physics is impossible."[7] Accordingly, the natural world fails to meet the standard of intelligibility that animated the modern scientific revolution. We must accept the "admission into the body of science of incomprehensible and inexplicable 'facts' imposed upon us by empiricism," as Koyré puts the matter.

Newton regarded his refutation of mechanism as an "absurdity," but could find no way around it despite much effort. Nor could the greatest scientists of his day, or since. Later discoveries introduced still greater "absurdities." Nothing has lessened the force of David Hume's judgment that by refuting the self-evident mechanical philosophy, Newton "restored Nature's ultimate secrets to that obscurity in which they ever did and ever will remain."

A century later, in his classic history of materialism, Friedrich Lange pointed out that Newton effectively destroyed the materialist doctrine as well as the standards of intelligibility and the expectations that were based on it: scientists have since "accustomed ourselves to the abstract notion of forces, or rather to a notion hovering in a mystic obscurity between abstraction and concrete comprehension," a "turning-point" in the history of materialism that removes the surviving remnants of the doctrine far from those of the "genuine Materialists" of the seventeenth century, and deprives them of much significance.

Both the methodological and the empirical theses collapsed, never to be reconstituted.

On the methodological side, standards of intelligibility were considerably weakened. The standard that inspired the modern scientific revolution was abandoned: the goal is intelligibility of theories, not of the world—a considerable difference, which may well bring into operation different faculties of mind, a topic some day for cognitive science, perhaps. As the preeminent Newton scholar I. Bernard Cohen put the matter, these changes "set forth a new view of science" in which the goal is "not to seek ultimate explanations," rooted in principles that appear to us self-evident, but to find the best theoretical account we can of the phenomena of experience and experiment. In general, conformity to commonsense understanding is not a criterion for rational inquiry.

On the factual side, there is no longer any concept of body, or matter, or "the physical." There is just the world, with its various aspects: mechanical, electromagnetic, chemical, optical, organic, mental—categories that are not defined or delimited in an a priori way, but are at most conveniences: no one asks whether life falls within chemistry or biology, except for temporary convenience. In each of the shifting domains of constructive inquiry, one can try to develop intelligible explanatory theories, and to unify them, but no more than that.

The new limits of inquiry were understood by working scientists. The eighteenth-century chemist Joseph Black observed that "chemical affinity must be accepted as a first principle, which we cannot explain any more than Newton could explain gravitation, and let us defer accounting for the laws of affinity until we have established such a body of doctrine as Newton has established concerning the laws of gravitation." That is pretty much what happened. Chemistry proceeded to establish a rich body of doctrine; "its triumphs [were] built on no reductionist foundation but rather achieved in isolation from the newly emerging science of physics," a leading historian of chemistry observes.[8] In fact, no reductionist foundation was discovered. What was finally achieved by Linus Pauling sixty-five years ago was unification, not reduction. Physics had to undergo fundamental changes in order to be unified with basic chemistry, departing even more radically from commonsense notions of "the physical": physics had to "free itself" from "intuitive pictures" and give up the hope of "visualizing the world," as Heisenberg put it,[9] yet another long leap away from intelligibility in the sense of the scientific revolution of the seventeenth century.

The early modern scientific revolution also brought about what we should properly call "the first cognitive revolution"—maybe the only phase of the cognitive sciences to deserve the name "revolution." Cartesian mechanism laid the groundwork for what became neurophysiology. Seventeenth- and eighteenth-century thinkers also developed rich and illuminating ideas about perception, language, and thought that have been rediscovered since, sometimes only in part. Lacking any conception of body, psychology could then—and can today—only follow the path of chemistry. Apart from its theological framework, there has really been no alternative to John Locke's cautious speculation, later known as "Locke's suggestion": God might have chosen to "superadd to matter a faculty of thinking" just as he "annexed effects to motion which we can in no way conceive motion able to produce"—notably the property of attraction at a distance, a revival of occult properties, many leading scientists argued (with Newton's partial agreement).

In this context the emergence thesis was virtually inescapable, in various forms:

> For the eighteenth century: "the powers of sensation or perception and thought" are properties of "a certain organized system of matter"; properties "termed mental" are "the result [of the] organical structure" of the brain and "the human nervous system" generally.
>
> A century later, Darwin asked rhetorically why "thought, being a secretion of the brain," should be considered "more wonderful than gravity, a property of matter."[10]
>
> Today, the study of the brain is based on the thesis that "Things mental, indeed minds, are emergent properties of brains."

Throughout, the thesis is essentially the same, and should not be contentious: it is hard to imagine an alternative in the post-Newtonian world.

The working scientist can do no better than to try to construct "bodies of doctrine" for various aspects of the world, and seek to unify them, recognizing that the world is not intelligible to us in anything like the way the pioneers of modern science hoped, and that the goal is unification, not necessarily reduction. As the history of the sciences clearly reveals, one can never guess what surprises lie ahead.

It is important to recognize that Cartesian dualism was a reasonable scientific thesis, but one that disappeared three centuries ago. There has been no mind-body problem to debate since. The thesis did not disappear because of inadequacies of the Cartesian concept of mind, but because the concept of body collapsed with Newton's demolition of the mechanical philosophy. It is common today to ridicule "Descartes's error" in postulating mind, his "ghost in the machine." But that mistakes what happened: Newton exorcized the machine; the ghost remained intact. Two contemporary physicists, Paul Davies and John Gribbin, close their recent book *The Matter Myth* by making that point once again, though they misattribute the elimination of the machine: to the new quantum physics. True, that adds another blow, but the "matter myth" had been demolished 250 years earlier, a fact that was understood by working scientists at the time, and has become part of the standard history of the sciences since. These are issues that merit some thought, I believe.

For the rejuvenated cognitive science of the twentieth century, it is also useful, I think, to pay close attention to what followed the unification of a virtually unchanged chemistry with a radically revised physics in the 1930s, and what preceded the unification. The most dramatic event that followed was the unification of biology and chemistry. This was a case of genuine reduction, but to a newly created physical chemistry; some of the same people were involved, notably Pauling. This genuine reduction has sometimes led to the confident expectation that mental aspects of the world will be reduced to something like the contemporary brain sciences. Maybe so, maybe not. In any event, the history of science provides little reason for confident expectations. True reduction is not so common in the history of science, and need not be assumed automatically to be a model for what will happen in the future.

Still more instructive is what was taking place just before the unification of chemistry and physics. Prior to unification, it was commonly argued by leading scientists that chemistry is just a calculating device, a way to organize results about chemical reactions, sometimes to predict them. In the early years of the last century, molecules were regarded the same way. Poincaré ridiculed the belief that the molecular theory of gases is more than a mode of calculation; people fall into that error because they are familiar with the game of billiards, he said. Chemistry is not about anything real, it was argued: the reason is that no one knew how to reduce it to physics. In 1929, Bertrand Russell—who knew the sciences well—pointed out that chemical laws "cannot at present be reduced to physical laws";[11] not false, but misleading in an important way. It turned out that the phrase "at present" was out of place. Reduction was impossible, as was soon discovered, until the conception of physical nature and law was (radically) revised.

It should now be clear that the debates about the reality of chemistry were based on fundamental misunderstanding. Chemistry was "real" and "about the world" in the only sense of these concepts that we have: it was part of the best conception of how the world works that human intelligence had been able to contrive. It is impossible to do better than that.

The debates about chemistry a few years ago are in many ways echoed in philosophy of mind and cognitive science today—and theoretical chemistry, of course, is hard science, merging indistinguishably with core physics: it is not at the periphery of scientific understanding, like the brain and cognitive sciences, which are trying to study systems that are vastly more complex, and poorly understood. These very recent debates about chemistry, and their unexpected outcome, should be instructive for the brain and cognitive sciences. They suggest that it is a mistake to think of computer models of the mind that are divorced from biology—that is, in principle unaffected by anything that might be discovered in the biological sciences—or Platonistic or other nonbiological conceptions of language, also insulated from important evidence, to their detriment, or to hold that the relation of the mental to the physical is not reducibility but the weaker notion of *supervenience*: any change in mental events or states entails a "physical change," though not conversely, and there is nothing more specific to say. The preunification debates over chemistry could be rephrased in these terms: those denying the reality of chemistry could have held that chemical properties supervene on physical properties, but are not reducible to them. That would have been an error: the right physical properties had not yet been discovered. Once they were, talk of supervenience became superfluous and we move towards unification. The same stance seems to me reasonable in the study of mental aspects of the world.

In general, it seems sensible to follow the good advice of post-Newtonian scientists, and Newton himself for that matter, and seek to construct "bodies of doctrine" in whatever terms we can, unshackled by commonsense intuitions about how the world must be—we know that it is not that way—and untroubled by the fact that we may have to "defer accounting for the principles" in terms of general scientific understanding, which may turn out to be inadequate to the task of unification, as has regularly been the case for three hundred years. A good deal of discussion of these topics seems to me misguided, perhaps seriously so, for reasons such as these.

There are other similarities worth remembering between preunification chemistry and current cognitive science. The "triumphs of chemistry" provided valuable guidelines for the eventual reconstruction of physics: they provided conditions that core physics would have to meet. In a similar way, discoveries about bee communication provide conditions that have to be met by some future account in terms of cells. In both cases, it is a two-way street: the discoveries of physics constrain possible chemical models, as those of basic biology should constrain models of insect behavior.

There are familiar analogues in the brain and cognitive sciences: the issue of computational, algorithmic, and implementation theories emphasized by David Marr, for example. Or Eric Kandel's work on learning in marine snails, seeking "to translate into neuronal terms ideas that have been proposed at an abstract level by experimental psychologists," and thus to show how cognitive psychology and neurobiology "may begin to converge to yield a new perspective in the study of learning." [12] Very reasonable, though the actual course of the sciences should alert us to the possibility that the convergence may not take place because something is missing—where, we cannot know until we find out.

I have been talking so far about the first of the three theses I mentioned at the outset: the guiding principle that "Things mental, indeed minds, are emergent properties of brains." That seems correct, but close to truism, for reasons understood by Darwin and by eminent scientists a century earlier, and that followed from Newton's discovery of "absurdities" that were nonetheless true.

Let us turn to the second: the methodological thesis, quoted from Mark Hauser's Evolution of Communication: to account for some trait we must adopt the ethological approach of Tinbergen, with its four basic perspectives: (1) mechanisms, (2) ontogenesis, (3) fitness consequences, (4) evolutionary history.

For Hauser, as for others, the "Holy Grail" is human language: the goal is to show how it can be understood if we investigate it from these four perspectives, and only that way. The same should be true of vastly simpler systems: the "dance language" of the honeybee, to select the sole example in the animal world that, according to standard (though not uncontroversial) accounts, seems to have at least some superficial similarity to human language: infinite scope, and the property of "displaced reference"—the ability to communicate information about something not in the sensory field. Bees have brains the size of a grass seed, with less than a million neurons; there are related species that differ in mode of communication; there are no restrictions on invasive experiment. But basic questions remain unanswered: questions about physiology and evolution, in particular.

In his review of this topic, Hauser does not discuss mechanisms, and the few suggestions that have been made seem rather exotic; for example, mathematician/biologist Barbara Shipman's theory that the bee's performance is based on an ability to map a certain six-dimensional topological space into three dimensions, perhaps by means of some kind of "quark detector." [13] On evolution, Hauser has only a few sentences, which essentially formulate the problem. The same is true of other cases he reviews. For example, songbirds, which are "the success story in developmental research," although there is no "convincing scenario" about selection—or even an unconvincing one, it seems.

It should hardly surprise us, then, that questions about physiological mechanisms and phylogenesis remain so mysterious in the incomparably more difficult case of human language.

A closer look at Hauser's study gives some indication of the remoteness of the goal that he and others set—a worthy goal, but we should be realistic about where we stand in relation to it. First, the title of the book is misleading: it is not about the evolution of communication, a topic that receives only passing mention. Rather, it is a comparative study of communication in many species. That is made explicit in the comments in Derek Bickerton's review in *Nature* that are quoted on the jacket cover; and in the final chapter, which speculates about "future directions." The chapter is entitled "Comparative communication," realistically; there is little speculation about evolution, a quite different matter. Rather generally, what Hauser and others describe as the record of natural selection turns out to be an account of the beautiful fit of an organism to its ecological niche. The facts are often fascinating and suggestive, but they do not constitute evolutionary history: rather, they formulate the problem to be solved by the student of evolution.

Second, Hauser points out that this comprehensive study of comparative communication is "irrelevant to the formal study of language" (an overstatement, I think). That is no small point: what he calls the "formal study of language" includes the psychological aspects of the first two perspectives of the ethological approach: (1) the mechanisms of language, and (2) their ontogenesis. And what is irrelevant to psychological aspects is irrelevant to physiological aspects as well, since anything that has bearing on physiological aspects imposes conditions on psychological aspects. Accordingly, the first two perspectives of the recommended approach of Tinbergen are effectively abandoned, for human language. For similar reasons, the comparative study may be "irrelevant," in the same sense, to contemporary inquiry into bee communication, largely a richly detailed variety of "descriptive linguistics." That seems a plausible conclusion: a great deal has been learned about particular species at a descriptive level—insects, birds, monkeys, and others. But little emerges of any generality.

The "irrelevance" to human language is, however, far deeper. The reason is that—as Hauser also observes—language is not properly regarded as a system of communication. It is a system for expressing thought, something quite different. It can of course be used for communication, as can anything people do—manner of walking or style of clothes or hair, for example. But in any useful sense of the term, communication is not *the* function of language, and may even be of no unique significance for understanding the functions and nature of language. Hauser quotes Somerset Maugham's quip that "if nobody spoke unless he had something to say, . . . the human race would very soon lose the use of speech." His point seems accurate enough, even apart from the fact that language use is largely to oneself: "inner speech" for adults, monologue for children. Furthermore, whatever merit there may be to guesses about selectional processes that might, or might not, have shaped human language, they do not crucially depend on the belief that the system is an outgrowth of some mode of communication. One can devise equally meritorious (that is, equally pointless) tales of the advantage conferred by a series of small mutations that facilitated planning and clarification of thought; perhaps even less fanciful, since it is unnecessary to suppose that the mutations took place in parallel in the group—not that I am proposing this or any other story. There is a rich record of the unhappy fate of highly plausible stories about what might have happened, once something was learned about what did happen—and in cases where far more is understood.

In the same connection, it is noteworthy that human language does not even appear in Hauser's "taxonomy of communicative information" (mating, survival, identity of caller). Language can surely be used for alarm calls, identification of speaker, and so on, but to study the functioning of language in these terms would be hopelessly misleading.

A related difficulty is that Hauser restricts the functional perspective to "adaptive solutions." That sharply limits the study of evolution, a point that Darwin forcefully emphasized and is now much better understood. In fact, Hauser cites case after case of traits that have no adaptive function, so he argues—appearing only in contrived situations with no counterpart in nature.

These matters are barely discussed; what I have cited are scattered remarks, a sentence here and there. But they indicate the immensity of the gaps that we must contemplate if we take the ethological perspective seriously—as of course we should, so I believe, and have been arguing for forty years.[14] Hauser's speculations about some future inquiry into the evolution of human language highlight the mystery. He refers to the two familiar basic problems: it is necessary to account for (1) the massive explosion of the lexicon, and (2) the recursive system for generating an infinite variety of meaningful utterances. For the latter, no speculation is offered. As for (1), Hauser reports that there is nothing analogous in the animal kingdom, including his own specialty (nonhuman primates). He observes that a precondition for the explosion of the lexicon is an innate human capacity to imitate, which he finds to be fundamentally different from anything in the animal world, perhaps unique. He was able to find only one possible exception: apes subjected to training. His conclusion is that "certain features of the human environment are required for engaging the capacity to imitate in apes," which, if true, would seem to imply that the capacity is not the result of the adaptive selection to which he and others insist we must restrict ourselves in studying evolution. As for the origins of the human capacity to imitate, he points out that we know nothing and may never be able to find out when—or for that matter how—it appeared in hominid evolution.

Furthermore, like many others, Hauser seriously underestimates the ways in which the human use of words to refer differs in its essential structural and functional properties from the rare examples of "referential signals" in other species, including some monkeys (possibly some apes, though the evidence, he says, is uncertain), a matter that goes well beyond the issues of displaced and situation-free reference. And he also seriously overstates what has been shown. Thus, citing some of Darwin's cautious speculations, he writes that "we thus learn two important lessons" about "human language evolution": that "the structure and function of human language can be accounted for by natural selection," and that "the most impressive link between human and nonhuman-animal forms of communication lies in the ability to express emotional state." Similarly, Steven Pinker "*shows* how a Darwinian account of language evolution is the only possible account, . . . because natural selection is the only mechanism that can account for the complex design features of a trait such as language" (my emphasis). It would be remarkable if something had been "shown" about the evolution of human language, let alone the vastly more ambitious claim cited; or if we could "learn" anything significant from speculations about the topic. Surely, nothing so amazing has taken place. Cautious speculation and confident pronouncement do not show anything, and the most that we learn is that there might be a useful path to follow. Perhaps.

That aside, the conclusions that have supposedly been demonstrated make little sense, apart from a charitable reading; uncontroversially, natural selection operates within a space of options determined by natural law (and historical/ecological contingencies), and it would be the sheerest dogmatism to issue a priori proclamations on the role of these factors in what comes to pass. That is true whether we are considering the appearance of the Fibonacci series in nature, or human language, or anything else in the biological world. What has been "shown" or "persuasively argued" is that natural selection is plausibly taken to be a primary factor in evolution, as Darwin argued, and as no one (within the circles that Hauser considers) even questions; why he has decided that I (or anyone) have insisted that "natural selection theory cannot account for the design features of human language," he does not say (and it is manifestly untrue, under the charitable reading required to grant the statement some meaning). Beyond the generally shared assumptions about natural selection and other mechanisms in evolution, one tries to find out what took place, whether studying the eye, the giraffe's neck, the bones of the middle ear, mammalian visual systems, human language, or anything else. Confident pronouncement is not to be confused with demonstration or even persuasive argument.

Though I suppose Hauser would deny this, it seems to me that on a close look, his actual conclusions do not differ much from the extreme skepticism of his Harvard colleague, evolutionary biologist Richard Lewontin, who concludes—forcefully—that the evolution of cognition is simply beyond the reach of contemporary science.[15]

The remoteness of the proclaimed goals leads to what seem to me some strange proposals: for example, that "the human brain, vocal tract, and language appear to have co-evolved" for the purposes of linguistic communication. Hauser is borrowing the notion of co-evolution of language and the brain from neuroscientist Terrence Deacon.[16] Deacon argues that students of language and its ontogenesis—the first two perspectives of the ethological approach—are making a serious error when they adopt the standard approach of the neurosciences: seeking to discover a genetically determined component of the mind-brain and the state changes it undergoes through experience and maturation. They have overlooked a more promising alternative: "that the extra support for language learning," beyond the data of experience, "is vested neither in the brain of the child nor in the brains of parents or teachers, but outside brains, in language itself." Language and languages are extra-human entities with a remarkable "capacity . . . to evolve and adapt with respect to human hosts." These creatures are not only extra-human, but apparently outside the biological world altogether.

What are these strange entities, and where did they come from? What they are is left unstated, except that they have evolved to incorporate the properties of language that have been mistakenly attributed to the brain. Their origin is no less mysterious, though once they somehow appeared, "the world's languages evolved spontaneously," through natural selection, in a "flurry of adaptation" that has "been going on outside the human brain." They have thereby "become better and better adapted to people"—like parasites and hosts, or perhaps prey and predator in the familiar cycle of co-evolution; or perhaps viruses provide the best analogy, he suggests. We also derive an account of language universals: they have "emerged spontaneously and independently in each evolving language . . . They are convergent features of language evolution," like the dorsal fins of sharks and dolphins. Having evolved spontaneously and acquired the universal properties of language by rapid natural selection, one of these extra-human creatures attaches itself to my granddaughter in New England, and a different one to my granddaughter in Nicaragua—actually she is infected by two of these mysterious viruses. It is a mistake to seek an explanation of the outcome in these and all other cases by investigating the interplay of experience and innate structure of the brain; rather, the right parasites attach themselves to hosts in a particular community in some mystical fashion—by a "magician's trick," to borrow Deacon's term for the ordinary assumptions of naturalistic science—yielding their knowledge of specific languages.

Deacon agrees, of course, that infants are "predisposed to learn human languages" and "are strongly biased in their choices" of "the rules underlying language," acquiring within a few years "an immensely complex rule system and a rich vocabulary" at a time when they cannot even learn elementary arithmetic. So there is "something special about human brains that enables us to do with ease what no other species can do even minimally without intense effort and remarkably insightful training." But it is a mistake to approach these predispositions and special structures of the brain the way we do other aspects of nature—the visual system, for example; no one would propose that insect and mammalian visual organs evolved spontaneously by rapid natural selection and now attach themselves to hosts, yielding the visual capacities of bees and monkeys; or that the waggle dance of bees or the calls of vervets are organism-external parasites that have co-evolved to provide the capacities of the host. But in the special case of human language, we are not to pursue the normal course of the natural sciences, seeking to determine the nature of the "predispositions" and "special structures" and the ways they are realized in brain mechanisms (in which case the extra-organic entities that have co-evolved with language vanish from the scene).

Since in this unique case extra-organic "viruses" have evolved that attach themselves to hosts in just the right way, we need not attribute to the child more than a "general theory of learning." So we discover once we overcome the surprising failure of linguists and psychologists to recognize that the languages of the world—in fact, the possible languages that are as yet unspoken—may have evolved spontaneously, outside of brains, coming to "embody the predispositions of children's minds" by natural selection.

There is, I think, a sense in which Deacon's proposals are on the right track. The idea that a child needs no more than a "general theory of learning" to attain language and other cognitive states can be sustained only with quite heroic moves. That is a basic thrust of the third of the framework theses introduced at the outset, to which we return directly. Much the same conclusion is illustrated by the extraordinarily rich innatist and modular assumptions embedded within attempts to implement what are often misleadingly presented as unstructured general learning theories, and the no less extraordinary assumptions about innate structure built into approaches based on speculative evolutionary scenarios that explicitly assume extreme modularity.[17]

The only real problem, Deacon argues, is "symbolic reference." The rest will somehow fall into place if we account for this in evolutionary terms. How the rest falls into place is not discussed. But perhaps that does not matter, because "symbolic reference" is also left as a complete mystery, in part because of failure to attend to its most elementary properties in human language.

I have been giving quotes, because I have no idea what this means. And understanding is not facilitated by an account of "linguistics" (including views attributed to me) that is unrecognizable, with allusions so vague that it is often hard even to guess what might have been the source of the misunderstanding (sometimes it is easy; e.g., misunderstanding of terminology used in a technical sense, such as "competence"). Whatever the meaning may be, the conclusion seems to be that it is an error to investigate the brain to discover the nature of human language; rather, studies of language must be about the extra-biological entities that co-evolved with humans and somehow "latch on" to them. These proposals have been highly acclaimed by prominent evolutionary psychologists and biologists, but I do not see why. Taken at all seriously, they seem only to reshape standard problems of science as utter mysteries, placing them beyond any hope of understanding, while barring the procedures of rational inquiry that have been taken for granted for hundreds of years.

Returning to the methodological thesis that we should adopt an ethological approach, it is reasonable enough in principle, but the ways it is pursued raise many questions. As far as I can see, the renewed call to pursue this approach, as advocated forty years ago in the critical literature on "behavioral science," leaves us about where we were. We can study the genetically determined component of the brain—and maybe more than the brain—that is dedicated to the structure and use of language, and the states it attains (the various languages), and we can investigate the process by which the state changes take place (language acquisition). We can try to discover the psychological and physiological mechanisms and principles, and to unify them, standard problems of science. These inquiries constitute the first two perspectives of the ethological approach: the study of mechanisms and ontogenesis. Turning to the third perspective, the functional perspective, we can investigate the use of language by the person who has attained a particular state, though the restriction to effects on survival and reproduction is far too narrow, if we hope to understand much about language. The fourth perspective—phylogenesis—seems a remote prospect at best, and does not seem much advanced by the comparative study of communication, a wholly different matter.

Let us turn finally to the third thesis I mentioned, quoting Gallistel: the substantive thesis that in all animals, learning is based on specialized mechanisms, "instincts to learn" in specific ways; what Tinbergen called "innate dispositions to learn." [18] These "learning mechanisms" can be regarded as "organs within the brain [that] are neural circuits whose structure enables them to perform one particular kind of computation," as they do more or less reflexively apart from "extremely hostile environments." Human language acquisition is instinctive in this sense, based on a specialized "language organ." This "modular view of learning" Gallistel takes to be "the norm these days in neuroscience." He argues that this framework includes whatever is fairly well understood, including conditioning, insofar as it is a real phenomenon. "To imagine that there exists a general purpose learning mechanism in addition to all these problem-specific learning mechanisms . . . is like trying to imagine the structure of a general purpose organ, the organ that takes care of problems not taken care of by adaptively specialized organs like the liver, the kidney, the heart and the lungs," or a "general purpose sensory organ, which solves the problem of sensing" for the cases not handled by the eye, the ear, and other specialized sensory organs. Nothing like that is known in biology: "Adaptive specialization of mechanism is so ubiquitous and so obvious in biology, at every level of analysis, and for every kind of function, that no one thinks it necessary to call attention to it as a general principle about biological mechanisms." Accordingly, "it is odd but true that most past and contemporary theorizing about learning" departs so radically from what is taken for granted in the study of organisms—a mistake, he argues.

As far as I know, the approach Gallistel recommends is sound; in the special case of language, it seems to me to be adopted by all substantive inquiry, at least tacitly, even when that is heatedly denied. It is hard to avoid the conclusion that a part of the human biological endowment is a specialized "language organ," the faculty of language (FL). Its initial state is an expression of the genes, comparable to the initial state of the human visual system, and it appears to be a common human possession to close approximation. Accordingly, a typical child will acquire any language under appropriate conditions, even under severe deficit and in "hostile environments." The initial state changes under the triggering and shaping effect of experience, and internally determined processes of maturation, yielding later states that seem to stabilize at several stages, finally at about puberty. We can think of the initial state of FL as a device that maps experience into state L attained: a "language acquisition device" (LAD). The existence of such a LAD is sometimes regarded as controversial, but it is no more so than the (equivalent) assumption that there is a dedicated "language module" that accounts for the linguistic development of an infant as distinct from that of her pet kitten (or chimpanzee, or whatever), given essentially the same experience. Even the most extreme "radical behaviorist" speculations presuppose (at least tacitly) that a child can somehow distinguish linguistic materials from the rest of the confusion around it, hence postulating the existence of FL (= LAD);[19] and as discussion of language acquisition becomes more substantive, it moves to assumptions about the language organ that are more rich and domain specific, without exception to my knowledge. That includes the acquisition of lexical items, which turn out to have rich and complex semantic structure, even the simplest of them. Knowledge of these properties becomes available on very limited evidence and, accordingly, would be expected to be essentially uniform among languages; and is, as far as is known.

Here we move to substantive questions within the first three perspectives of the ethological approach, though again without restricting inquiry into language use to fitness consequences: survival and reproduction. We can inquire into the fundamental properties of linguistic expressions, and their use to express thought, sometimes to communicate, and sometimes to think or talk about the world. In this connection, comparative animal research surely merits attention. There has been important work on the problem of *representation* in a variety of species. Gallistel introduced a compendium of review articles on the topic a few years ago by arguing that representations play a key role in animal behavior and cognition; here "representation" is understood as isomorphism, a one-to-one relation between mind-brain processes and "an aspect of the environment to which these processes adapt the animal's behavior"—e.g., when an ant represents the corpse of a conspecific by its odor.[20] It is a fair question whether, or how, the results relate to the mental world of humans; in the case of language, to what is called "phonetic" or "semantic representation."

As noted, from the biolinguistic point of view that seems to me appropriate—and tacitly adopted in substantive work—we can think of a particular language L as a state of FL. L is a recursive procedure that generates an infinity of expressions. Each expression can be regarded as a collection of information for other systems of the mind-brain. The traditional assumption, back to Aristotle, is that the information falls into two categories, phonetic and semantic; information used, respectively, by sensorimotor systems and conceptual-intentional systems—the latter "systems of thought," to give a name to something poorly understood. That could well be a serious oversimplification, but let us keep to the convention. Each expression, then, is an internal object consisting of two collections of information: phonetic and semantic. These collections are called "representations," phonetic and semantic representations, but there is no isomorphism holding between the representations and aspects of the environment. There is no pairing of internal symbol and thing represented, in any useful sense.

On the sound side, this is taken for granted. It would not be false to say that an element of phonetic representation—say the internal element/ba/in my language—picks out a thing in the world, namely the sound BA. But that would not be a helpful move, and it is never made. Rather, acoustic and articulatory phonetics seek to understand how the sensorimotor system uses the information in the phonetic representation to produce and interpret sounds, no trivial task. One can think of the phonetic representation as an array of instructions for the sensorimotor systems, but a particular element of the internal representation is not paired with some category of events in the outside world, perhaps a construction based on motions of molecules. Similar conclusions seem to me appropriate on the meaning side. It has been understood at least since Aristotle that even the simplest words incorporate information of many different kinds: about material constitution, design and intended use, origin, gestalt and causal properties, and much more. These topics were explored in some depth during the cognitive revolution of the seventeenth and eighteenth centuries, though much of the work, even including the well-studied British empiricist tradition from Hobbes to Hume, remains little known outside of historical scholarship. The conclusions hold for simple nouns, count and mass—"river," "house," "tree," "water," personal and place names—the "purest referential terms" (pronouns, empty categories), and so on; and the properties become more intricate as we turn to elements with relational structure (verbs, tense and aspect, . . .), and of course far more so as we move on to more complex expressions. As to how early in ontogenesis these complex systems of knowledge are functioning, little is known, but there is every reason to suppose that the essentials are as much a part of the innate biological endowment as the capacity for stereoscopic vision or specific kinds of motor planning, elicited in considerable richness and specificity on the occasion of sense, in the terminology of the early modern scientific revolution.

There seems nothing analogous in the rest of the animal world, even at the simplest level. It is doubtless true that the massive explosion of lexicon, and symbolic representation, are crucial components of human language, but invoking imitation or symbol-thing correspondence does not carry us very far, and even those few steps could well be on the wrong track. When we turn to the organization and generation of representations, analogies break down very quickly beyond the most superficial level.

These properties of language are almost immediately obvious on inspection—which is not to say that they are deeply investigated or well understood; they are not. Moving beyond, we find other properties that are puzzling. The components of expressions—their *features*, in standard terminology—must be interpretable by the systems that access them; the representations at the interface with sensorimotor and thought systems consist of interpretable features. One would therefore expect that the features that enter computation should be interpretable, as in well-designed artificial symbolic systems: formal systems for metamathematics, computer languages, etc. But it is not true for natural language; on the sound side, perhaps never true. One crucial case has to do with inflectional features that receive no semantic interpretation: structural case (nominative, accusative), or agreement features such as plurality (interpretable on nouns, but not on verbs or adjectives). The facts are not obvious in surface forms, but are reasonably well substantiated. Work of the past twenty years has provided considerable reason to suspect that these systems of uninterpretable features are quite similar among languages, though the external manifestation of the features differs in fairly systematic ways; and that a good deal of the typological variety of language reduces to this extremely narrow subcomponent of language. It could be, then, that the recursive computational system of the language organ is fixed and determinate, an expression of the genes, along with the basic structure of possible lexical items. A particular state of FL—a particular internal language—is determined by selecting among the highly structured possible lexical items and fixing parameters that are restricted to uninterpretable inflectional features and their manifestation. It could be that that is not a bad first approximation, maybe more than that.

It seems that the same uninterpretable features may be implicated in the ubiquitous dislocation property of natural language. The term refers to the fact that phrases are commonly articulated in one position but interpreted as if they were somewhere else, where they can be in similar expressions: the dislocated subject of a passive construction, for example, interpreted as if it were in the object position, in a local relation to the verb that assigns it a semantic role. Dislocation has interesting semantic properties. It may be that the "external" systems of thought (external to FL, internal to the mind-brain) require that FL generate expressions with these properties, to be properly interpreted. There is also reason to believe that the uninterpretable features may be the mechanism for implementing the dislocation property, perhaps even an optimal mechanism for satisfying this externally imposed condition on the language faculty. If so, then neither the dislocation property nor uninterpretable features are "imperfections" of FL, "design flaws" (here using the term "design" metaphorically, of course). These and other considerations raise more general questions of optimal design: could it be that FL is an optimal solution to interface conditions imposed by the systems of the mind-brain in which it is embedded, the sensorimotor and thought systems?

Such questions have been seriously posed only quite recently. They could not be raised before there was a fairly good grasp of the fixed principles of the faculty of language and the restricted options that yield the rich typological variety that we know must be rather superficial, despite appearances, given the empirical conditions on language acquisition. Though naturally partial and tentative, such understanding has increased markedly in the past twenty years. Now it seems that questions of optimal design can be seriously raised, sometimes answered. Furthermore, the idea that language may be an optimal solution to interface conditions, in nontrivial respects, seems a good deal more plausible than it did a few years ago. Insofar as it is true, interesting questions arise about the theory of mind, the design of the brain, and the role of natural law in the evolution of even very complex organs such as the language faculty, questions that are very much alive in the theory of evolution at elementary levels, in work of the kind pioneered by D'Arcy Thompson and Alan Turing that has been somewhat at the margins until recently. It is conceivable that the comprehensive ethological approach discussed earlier might be enriched in these terms, though that remains a distant prospect.

Still more remote are the fundamental questions that motivated the classical theory of mind—the creative aspect of language use, the distinction between action appropriate to situations and action caused by situations, between being "compelled" to act in certain ways or only "incited and inclined" to do so; and in general, the question of how "members of animal bodies move at the command of the will," Newton's phrase in his review of mysteries that remain unresolved, including the causes of interaction of bodies, electrical attraction and repulsion, and other basic issues that remained unintelligible, by the standards of the scientific revolution.

In some domains, inquiry into components of the mind-brain has made dramatic progress. There is justified enthusiasm about the promise of new technologies, and a wealth of exciting work waiting to be undertaken in exploring mental aspects of the world and their emergence. It is not a bad idea, however, to keep in some corner of our minds the judgment of great figures of early modern science—Galileo, Newton, Hume, and others—concerning the "obscurity" in which "nature's ultimate secrets ever will remain," perhaps for reasons rooted in the biological endowment of the curious creature that alone is able even to contemplate these questions.

23.

United States—Israel—Palestine

In 2001, Hebrew University sociologist Baruch Kimmerling observed that "what we feared has come true." Jews and Palestinians are "in a process of regression to superstitious tribalism. . . . War appears an unavoidable fate," an "evil colonial" war.[1] After Israel's invasion of Palestinian refugee camps in spring 2002, Kimmerling's colleague Ze'ev Sternhell wrote that "in colonial Israel . . . human life is cheap." The leadership is "no longer ashamed to speak of war when what they are really engaged in is colonial policing, which recalls the takeover by the white police of the poor neighborhoods of the blacks in South Africa during the apartheid era."[2] Both stress the obvious: there is no symmetry between the "ethnonational groups" regressing to tribalism. The conflict is centered in territories that have been under harsh military occupation for thirty-five years. The conqueror is a major military power, acting with massive military, economic, and diplomatic support from the global superpower. Its subjects are alone and defenseless, many barely surviving in miserable camps, currently suffering even more brutal terror of a kind familiar in "evil colonial" wars and now carrying out terrible atrocities of their own in revenge.

The Oslo "peace process" changed the modalities of the occupation but not the basic concept. Shortly before joining the Ehud Barak government, historian Shlomo Ben-Ami wrote that "the Oslo agreements were founded on a neo-colonialist basis, on a life of dependence of one on the other forever."[3] He soon became an architect of the U.S.-Israel proposals at Camp David in

---

This chapter first appeared in *Middle East Illusions* (Lanham, MD: Rowman & Littlefield Publishers, 2003), 227–32.

summer 2000, which kept to this condition of dependence. These proposals were highly praised in U.S. commentary. The Palestinians and their evil leader were blamed for the failure of the talks and the subsequent violence. But that is outright "fraud," as Kimmerling reported, along with all other serious commentators.[4]

True, the Clinton-Barak proposal advanced a few steps toward a Bantustan-style settlement. Just prior to Camp David, West Bank Palestinians were confined to more than two hundred scattered areas, and Clinton-Barak did propose an improvement: consolidation to three cantons, under Israeli control, virtually separated from one another and from the fourth enclave, a small area of East Jerusalem, the center of Palestinian life and of communications in the region. In the fifth canton, Gaza, the outcome was left unclear except that the population was also to remain virtually imprisoned. It is understandable that no maps or details of the proposals are to be found in the U.S. mainstream.

No one can seriously doubt that the U.S. role will continue to be decisive. It is therefore of crucial importance to understand what that role has been and how it is internally perceived. The version of the doves is presented by the editors of the *New York Times*, who praised the president's "path-breaking speech" and the "emerging vision" he articulated. Its first element is "ending Palestinian terrorism," immediately. Sometime later comes "freezing, then rolling back, Jewish settlements and negotiating new borders" to end the occupation and allow the establishment of a Palestinian state. If Palestinian terror ends, Israelis will be encouraged to "take the Arab League's historic offer of full peace and recognition in exchange for an Israeli withdrawal more seriously." But first, Palestinian leaders must demonstrate that they are "legitimate diplomatic partners."[5]

The real world has little resemblance to this self-serving portrayal—virtually copied from the 1980s, when the United States and Israel were desperately seeking to evade the Palestine Liberation Organization's (PLO) offers of negotiation and political settlement while keeping to the demand that there will be no negotiations with the PLO, no "additional Palestinian state" (Jordan already being a Palestinian state), and "no change in the status of Judea, Samaria and Gaza other than in accordance with the basic guidelines of the [Israeli] Government."[6] All of this remained unpublished in the U.S. mainstream, as was regularly the case before, while commentary denounced the Palestinians for their single-minded commitment to terror, undermining the humanistic endeavors of the United States and its allies.

In the real world, the primary barrier to the "emerging vision" has been, and remains, unilateral U.S. rejectionism. There is little new in the "historic offer" of March 2002. It repeats the basic terms of a Security Council resolution of January 1976 backed by virtually the entire world, including the leading Arab states, the PLO, Europe, the Soviet bloc—in fact, everyone who mattered. It was opposed by Israel and vetoed by the United States, thereby vetoing it from history. The resolution called for a political settlement on the internationally recognized borders "with appropriate arrangements . . . to guarantee . . . the sovereignty, territorial integrity, and political independence of all states in the area and their right to live in peace within secure and recognized borders"—in effect, a modification of UN Resolution 242 (as officially interpreted by the United States as well), amplified to include a Palestinian state. Similar initiatives from the Arab states, the PLO, and Europe have since been blocked by the United States and mostly suppressed or denied in public commentary.

Not surprisingly, the guiding principle of the occupation has been incessant and degrading humiliation, along with torture, terror, destruction of property, displacement and settlement, and takeover of basic resources, crucially water. That has, of course, required decisive U.S. support, extending through the Clinton-Barak years. "The Barak government is leaving Sharon's government a surprising legacy," the Israeli press reported as the transition took place, "the highest number of housing starts in the territories since the time when Ariel Sharon was Minister of Construction and Settlement in 1992 before the Oslo agreements." The funding for these settlements is provided by the American taxpayer, deceived by fanciful tales of the "visions" and "magnanimity" of U.S. leaders, foiled by terrorists like Arafat who have forfeited "our trust," and perhaps also by some Israeli extremists who are overreacting to their crimes.

How Arafat must act to regain our trust is explained succinctly by Edward Walker, the State Department official responsible for the region under Clinton. The devious Arafat must announce without ambiguity that "we put our future and fate in the hands of the U.S.," which has led the campaign to undermine Palestinian rights for thirty years.[7]

More serious commentary recognized that the "historic offer" largely reiterated the Saudi Fahd Plan of 1981—undermined, it was regularly claimed, by Arab refusal to accept the existence of Israel. The facts are again quite different. The 1981 plan was undermined by an Israeli reaction that even its mainstream press condemned as "hysterical." Shimon Peres warned that the Fahd plan "threatened Israel's very existence." President Haim Herzog charged that the "real author" of the Fahd plan was the PLO, and that it was even more extreme than the January 1976 Security Council resolution that was "prepared by" the PLO when he was Israel's UN ambassador.[8] These claims can hardly be true (though the PLO publicly backed both plans), but they are an indication of the desperate fear of a political settlement on the part of Israeli doves, with the unremitting and decisive support of the United States.

The basic problem then, as now, traces back to Washington, which has persistently backed Israel's rejection of a political settlement in terms of the broad international consensus, reiterated in essentials in "the Arab League's historic offer."

Current modifications of U.S. rejectionism are tactical and so far minor. With plans for an attack on Iraq endangered, the United States permitted a UN resolution calling for Israeli withdrawal from the newly invaded territories "without delay"—meaning "as soon as possible," Secretary of State Colin Powell explained at once. Palestinian terror is to end "immediately," but far more extreme Israeli terror, going back thirty-five years, can take its time. Israel at once escalated its attack, leading Powell to say, "I'm pleased to hear that the prime minister says he is expediting his operations."[9] There is much suspicion that Powell's arrival in Israel was delayed so that the operations could be "expedited" further.

The United States also allowed a UN resolution calling for a "vision" of a Palestinian state.[10] This forthcoming gesture, which received much acclaim, does not rise to the level of South Africa forty years ago when the apartheid regime actually implemented its "vision" of black-run states that were at least as viable and legitimate as the neocolonial dependency that the United States and Israel have been planning for the occupied territories.

Meanwhile the United States continues to "enhance terror," to borrow President George W. Bush's words, by providing Israel with the means for terror and destruction, including a new shipment of the most advanced helicopters in the U.S. arsenal.[11]

Washington's commitment to enhancing terror was illustrated again in December 2001, when it vetoed a Security Council resolution calling for implementation of the Mitchell Plan and dispatch of international monitors to oversee reduction of violence, the most effective means as generally recognized but opposed by Israel and regularly blocked by Washington.[12] The veto took place during a twenty-one-day period of "calm"—a period in which only one Israeli soldier was killed, along with twenty-one Palestinians including eleven children, and in which there were sixteen Israeli incursions into areas under Palestinian control.[13] Ten days before the veto, the United States boycotted—and thus undermined—an international conference in Geneva that once again concluded that the Fourth Geneva Convention applies to the occupied territories, so that virtually everything the United States and Israel do there is a "grave breach"—a "war crime" in simple terms. The conference specifically declared the U.S.-funded Israeli settlements to be illegal and condemned the practice of "willful killing, torture, unlawful deportation, willful depriving of the rights of fair and regular trial, extensive destruction and appropriation of property . . . carried out unlawfully and wantonly."[14] As a High Contracting Party, the United States is obligated by solemn treaty to prosecute those responsible for such crimes, including its own leadership. Accordingly, all of this passes in silence.

The United States has not officially withdrawn its recognition of the applicability of the Geneva Conventions to the occupied territories or its censure of Israeli violations as the "occupying power" (affirmed, for example, by George Bush I when he was UN ambassador). In October 2000, the Security Council reaffirmed the consensus on this matter, "call[ing] on Israel, the occupying power, to abide scrupulously by its legal obligations and responsibilities under the Fourth Geneva Convention."[15] The vote was 14–0. Clinton abstained, presumably not wanting to veto one of the core principles of international humanitarian law, particularly in light of the circumstances in which it was enacted: to criminalize formally the atrocities of the Nazis. All of this too was consigned quickly to the memory hole, another contribution to "enhancing terror."

Until such matters are permitted to enter discussion and their implications are understood, it is meaningless to call for "U.S. engagement in the peace process," and prospects for constructive action will remain grim.

24.

Imperial Grand Strategy

High on the global agenda by fall 2002 was the declared intention of the most powerful state in history to maintain its hegemony through the threat or use of military force, the dimension of power in which it reigns supreme. In the official rhetoric of the National Security Strategy, "Our forces will be strong enough to dissuade potential adversaries from pursuing a military build-up in hopes of surpassing, or equaling, the power of the United States."[1]

One well-known international affairs specialist, John Ikenberry, describes the declaration as a "grand strategy [that] begins with a fundamental commitment to maintaining a unipolar world in which the United States has no peer competitor," a condition that is to be "permanent [so] that no state or coalition could ever challenge [the US] as global leader, protector, and enforcer." The declared "approach renders international norms of self-defense—enshrined by Article 51 of the UN Charter—almost meaningless." More generally, the doctrine dismisses international law and institutions as of "little value." Ikenberry continues: "The new imperial grand strategy presents the United States [as] a revisionist state seeking to parlay its momentary advantages into a world order in which it runs the show," prompting others to find ways to "work around, undermine, contain and retaliate against U.S. power." The strategy threatens to "leave the world more dangerous and divided—and the United States less secure,"[2] a view widely shared within the foreign policy elite.

This chapter first appeared in *Hegemony or Survival: America's Quest for Global Dominance* (New York: Metropolitan Books, 2003; New York: Owl Books, 2004), 11–49.

ENFORCING HEGEMONY

The imperial grand strategy asserts the right of the United States to undertake "preventive war" at will: *Preventive*, not preemptive.[3] Preemptive war might fall within the framework of international law. Thus if Russian bombers had been detected approaching the United States from the military base in Grenada conjured up by the Reagan administration in 1983, with the clear intent to bomb, then, under a reasonable interpretation of the UN Charter, a preemptive attack destroying the planes and perhaps even the Grenadan base would have been justifiable. Cuba, Nicaragua, and many others could have exercised the same right for many years while under attack from the United States, though of course the weak would have to be insane to implement their rights. But the justifications for preemptive war, whatever they might be, do not hold for preventive war, particularly as that concept is interpreted by its current enthusiasts: the use of military force to eliminate an imagined or invented threat, so that even the term *preventive* is too charitable.

Preventive war falls within the category of war crimes. If indeed it is an idea "whose time has come,"[4] then the world is in deep trouble.

As the invasion of Iraq began, the prominent historian and Kennedy adviser Arthur Schlesinger wrote that

> The president has adopted a policy of "anticipatory self-defense" that is alarmingly similar to the policy that imperial Japan employed at Pearl Harbor, on a date which, as an earlier American president said it would, lives in infamy. Franklin D. Roosevelt was right, but today it is we Americans who live in infamy.[5]

He added that "the global wave of sympathy that engulfed the United States after 9-11 has given way to a global wave of hatred of American arrogance and militarism," and even in friendly countries the public regards Bush "as a greater threat to peace than Saddam Hussein." International law specialist Richard Falk finds it "inescapable" that the Iraq war was a "Crime against Peace of the sort for which surviving German leaders were indicted, prosecuted, and punished at the Nuremberg trials."[6]

Some defenders of the strategy recognize that it runs roughshod over international law but see no problem in that. The whole framework of international law is just "hot air," legal scholar Michael Glennon writes: "The grand attempt to subject the rule of force to the rule of law" should be deposited in the ashcan of history—a convenient stance for the one state able to adopt the new non-rules for its purposes, since it spends almost as much as the rest of the world combined on means of violence and is forging new and dangerous paths in developing means of destruction, over near-unanimous world opposition. The proof that the system is all "hot air" is straightforward: Washington "made it clear that it intends to do all it can to maintain its preeminence," then "announced that it would ignore" the UN Security Council over Iraq and declared more broadly that "it would no longer be bound by the [UN] Charter's rules governing the use of force." QED. Accordingly, the rules have "collapsed" and "the entire edifice came crashing down." This, Glennon concludes, is a good thing, since the US is the leader of the "enlightened states" and therefore "must resist [any effort] to curb its use of force."[7]

The enlightened leader is also free to change the rules at will. When the military forces occupying Iraq failed to discover the weapons of mass destruction that allegedly justified the invasion, the administration's stance shifted from "absolute certainty" that Iraq possessed WMD on a scale that required immediate military action to the assertion that American accusations had been "justified by the discovery of equipment that potentially could be used to produce weapons." Senior officials suggested a "refinement in the controversial concept of a 'preventive war' " that entitles Washington to take military action "against a country that has deadly weapons in mass quantities." The revision "suggests instead that the administration will act against a hostile regime that has nothing more than the intent and ability to develop [WMD]."[8]

Virtually any country has the potential and ability to produce WMD, and intent is in the eye of the beholder. Hence the refined version of the grand strategy effectively grants Washington the right of arbitrary aggression. Lowering the bar for the resort to force is the most significant consequence of the collapse of the proclaimed argument for the invasion.

The goal of the imperial grand strategy is to prevent any challenge to the "power, position, and prestige of the United States." The quoted words are not those of Dick Cheney or Donald Rumsfeld, or any of the other statist reactionaries who formulated the National Security Strategy of September 2002. Rather, they were spoken by the respected liberal elder statesman Dean Acheson in 1963. He was justifying U.S. actions against Cuba in full knowledge that Washington's international terrorist campaign aimed at "regime change" had been a significant factor in bringing the world close to nuclear war only a few months earlier, and that it was resumed immediately after the Cuban missile crisis was resolved. Nevertheless, he instructed the American Society of International Law that no "legal issue" arises when the United States responds to a challenge to its "power, position, and prestige."

Acheson's doctrine was subsequently invoked by the Reagan administration, at the other end of the political spectrum, when it rejected World Court jurisdiction over its attack on Nicaragua, dismissed the court order to terminate its crimes, and then vetoed two Security Council resolutions affirming the court judgment and calling on all states to observe international law. State Department legal adviser Abraham Sofaer explained that most of the world cannot "be counted on to share our view" and that "this same majority often opposes the United States on important international questions." Accordingly, we must "reserve to ourselves the power to determine" which matters fall "essentially within the domestic jurisdiction of the United States"—in this case, the actions that the court condemned as the "unlawful use of force" against Nicaragua; in lay terms, international terrorism.[9]

Contempt for international law and institutions was particularly flagrant in the Reagan-Bush years—the first reign of Washington's current incumbents—and their successors continued to make it clear that the US reserved the right to act "unilaterally when necessary," including the "unilateral use of military power" to defend such vital interests as "ensuring uninhibited access to key markets, energy supplies, and strategic resources."[10] But the posture was not exactly new.

The basic principles of the imperial grand strategy of September 2002 go back to the early days of World War II. Even before the United States entered the war, high-level planners and analysts concluded that in the postwar world the United States would seek "to hold unquestioned power," acting to ensure the "limitation of any exercise of sovereignty" by states that might interfere with its global designs. They recognized further that "the foremost requirement" to secure these ends was "the rapid fulfillment of a program of complete rearmament"—then, as now, a central component of "an integrated policy to achieve military and economic supremacy for the United States." At the time, these ambitions were limited to "the non-German world," which was to be organized under the U.S. aegis as a "Grand Area," including the Western Hemisphere, the former British Empire, and the Far East. After it became fairly clear that Germany would be defeated, the plans were extended to include as much of Eurasia as possible.[11]

The precedents, barely sampled here, reveal the narrow range of the planning spectrum. Policy flows from an institutional framework of domestic power, which remains fairly stable. Economic decision-making power is highly centralized, and John Dewey scarcely exaggerated when he described politics as "the shadow cast on society by big business." It is only natural that state policy should seek to construct a world system open to U.S. economic penetration and political control, tolerating no rivals or threats.[12] A crucial corollary is vigilance to block any moves toward independent development that might become a "virus infecting others," in the terminology of planners. That is a leading theme of postwar history, often disguised under thin Cold War pretexts that were also exploited by the superpower rival in its narrower domains.

The basic missions of global management have endured from the early postwar period, among them: containing other centers of global power within the "overall framework of order" managed by the United States; maintaining control of the world's energy supplies; barring unacceptable forms of independent nationalism; and overcoming "crises of democracy" within domestic enemy territory. The missions assume different forms, notably in periods of fairly sharp transition: the changes in the international economic order from about 1970; the restoration of the superpower enemy to something like its traditional quasi-colonial status twenty years later; the threat of international terrorism aimed at the United States itself from the early 1990s, shockingly consummated on 9-11. Over the years, tactics have been refined and modified to deal with these shifts, progressively ratcheting up the means of violence and driving our endangered species closer to the edge of catastrophe.

Nevertheless, the September 2002 unveiling of the imperial grand strategy justifiably sounded alarm bells. Acheson and Sofaer were *describing* policy guidelines, and within elite circles. Their stands are known only to specialists or readers of dissident literature. Other cases may be regarded as worldly wise reiterations of the maxim of Thucydides that "large nations do what they wish, while small nations accept what they must." In contrast, Cheney-Rumsfeld-Powell and their associates are officially *declaring* an even more extreme policy, one aimed at permanent global hegemony by reliance on force where necessary. They intend to be heard, and took action at once to put the world on notice that they mean what they say. That is a significant difference.

NEW NORMS OF INTERNATIONAL LAW

The declaration of the grand strategy was rightly understood to be an ominous step in world affairs. It is not enough, however, for a great power to declare an official policy. It must go on to establish the policy as a new norm of international law by carrying out exemplary actions. Distinguished specialists and public intellectuals may then soberly explain that law is a flexible living instrument so that the new norm is now available as a guide to action. Accordingly, as the new imperial strategy was announced, the war drums began to beat to rouse public enthusiasm for an attack on Iraq. At the same time, the midterm election campaign opened. The conjunction, already noted, should be kept in mind.

The target of preventive war must have several characteristics:

1. It must be virtually defenseless.
2. It must be important enough to be worth the trouble.
3. There must be a way to portray it as the ultimate evil and an imminent threat to our survival.

Iraq qualified on all counts. The first two conditions are obvious. The third is easy to establish. It is only necessary to repeat the impassioned orations of Bush, Blair, and their colleagues: the dictator "is assembling the world's most dangerous weapons [in order to] dominate, intimidate, or attack"; and he "has already used them on whole villages—leaving thousands of his own citizens dead, blind, or transfigured. . . . If this is not evil, then evil has no meaning."[13]

The president's eloquent denunciation in his January 2003 State of the Union address surely rings true. And certainly those who contribute to enhancing evil should not enjoy impunity—among them, the speaker of those lofty words and his current associates, who long supported the man of ultimate evil in full awareness of his crimes. It is impressive to see how easy it is, while recounting the monster's worst offenses, to suppress the crucial words "with our help, which continued because we didn't care." Praise and support shifted to denunciation as soon as the monster committed his first authentic crime: disobeying (or perhaps misunderstanding) orders by invading Kuwait in 1990. Punishment was severe—for his subjects. The tyrant, however, escaped unscathed and was further strengthened by the sanctions regime then imposed by his former friends.

As the time approached to demonstrate the new norm of preventive war in September 2002, National Security Adviser Condoleezza Rice warned that the next evidence of Saddam Hussein's intentions might be a mushroom cloud—presumably in New York; Hussein's neighbors, including Israeli intelligence, dismissed the allegations, which were later undermined by the UN inspectors, though Washington continued to claim otherwise. From the first moments of the propaganda offensive, it was apparent that the pronouncements lacked credibility. " 'This administration is capable of any lie . . . in order to advance its war goal in Iraq,' says a US government source in Washington with some two decades of experience in intelligence." Washington opposed inspections, he suggested, because it feared that nothing much would be found. The president's claims about Iraqi threats "should be viewed as transparent attempts to scare Americans into supporting a war," two leading international-relations scholars added. That is standard operating procedure. Washington still refuses to provide evidence to support its 1990 claims of a huge Iraqi military buildup on the Saudi border, the primary justification offered for the 1991 war, claims instantly undermined by the one journal that investigated them, but to no effect.[14]

Evidence or not, the president and his associates issued grim warnings about the dire threat Saddam posed to the United States and to his neighbors, and his links to international terrorists, hinting broadly that he was involved in the 9-11 attacks. The government-media propaganda assault had its effects. Within weeks, some 60 percent of Americans came to regard Saddam Hussein as "an immediate threat to the US" who must be removed quickly in self-defense. By March, almost half believed that Saddam Hussein was personally involved in the 9-11 attacks and that the hijackers included Iraqis. Support for the war was strongly correlated with these beliefs.[15]

Abroad, "public diplomacy . . . failed badly," the international press reported, but "at home it has succeeded brilliantly in linking the war on Iraq with the trauma of September 11. . . . [N]early 90 percent believe [Saddam's] regime is aiding and abetting terrorists who are planning future strikes against the US." Political analyst Anatol Lieven commented that most Americans had been "duped . . . by a propaganda programme which for systematic mendacity has few parallels in peacetime democracies."[16] The September 2002 propaganda campaign also proved sufficient to give the administration a bare majority in the midterm elections, as voters put aside their immediate concerns and huddled under the umbrella of power in fear of the demonic enemy.

Public diplomacy worked its magic with Congress instantaneously. In October, Congress granted the president authority to go to war "to defend the national security of the United States against the continuing threat posed by Iraq." This particular script is familiar. In 1985, President Reagan declared a national emergency, renewed annually, because "the policies and the actions of the government of Nicaragua constitute an unusual and extraordinary threat to the national security and foreign policy of the United States." In 2002, Americans again had to tremble in fear, this time before Iraq.

The brilliant success of public diplomacy at home was revealed once again when the president "provided a powerful Reaganesque finale to a six-week war" on the deck of the aircraft carrier *Abraham Lincoln* on May 1, 2003. He was free to declare—without concern for skeptical domestic comment—that he had won a "victory in a war on terror" by having "removed an ally of Al-Qaeda."[17] It is immaterial that the alleged link between Saddam Hussein and Osama bin Laden, in fact, his bitter enemy, was based on no credible evidence and largely dismissed by competent observers. Also immaterial is the only known connection between the Iraq invasion and the threat of terror: that the invasion enhanced the threat, as had been widely predicted; it appears to have been a "huge setback in the 'war on terror' " by sharply increasing Al-Qaeda recruitment.[18]

The propaganda impact persisted past the end of the war. After the failure of intense efforts to discover WMD, a third of the population believed that U.S. forces had found WMD and more than 20 percent believed Iraq had used them during the war.[19] These may simply be the reactions of people who are subject to fear of just about anything after many years of intense propaganda designed to tame the "great beast" by inducing panic.

The phrase "powerful Reaganesque finale" is presumably a reference to Reagan's proud announcement that the United States was "standing tall" after having overcome the terrible threat posed by Grenada. Astute commentators added that Bush's carefully staged USS *Abraham Lincoln* extravaganza marked "the beginning of his 2004 reelection campaign," which the White House hopes "will be built as much as possible around national-security themes, a staple of the campaign being the removal of Iraqi leader Saddam Hussein." To further drive home the message, the official campaign opening was delayed until mid-September 2004 so that the Republican Convention, meeting in New York, would be able to celebrate the wartime leader who alone can save Americans from a reenactment of 9-11, as he did in Iraq. The electoral campaign will focus on "the *battle* of Iraq, not the war," chief Republican political strategist Karl Rove explained. This is part of a "far larger and longer war against terrorism that [Rove] sees clearly, perchance fortuitously, stretching well toward Election Day 2004."[20] And surely beyond.

By September 2002, then, all three necessary factors for establishing the new norm of international law were in place: Iraq was defenseless, extremely important, and an imminent threat to our very existence. There was always the possibility that things might go wrong. But it was unlikely, at least for the invaders. The disparity of force was so phenomenal that overwhelming victory was assured, and any humanitarian consequences could be blamed on Saddam Hussein. If unpleasant, they would not be investigated, and traces would disappear from view, at least if the past is any guide. Victors do not investigate their own crimes, so that little is known about them, a principle that brooks few exceptions: the death toll of the U.S. wars in Indochina, for example, is not known within a range of millions. The same principle underlay the war crimes trials after World War II. The operational definition of *crimes of war* and *crimes against humanity* was straightforward: crimes qualified as crimes if they were carried out by the enemy, not by the Allies. Destruction of urban civilian concentrations, for example, was excluded. The principle has been applied in subsequent tribunals, but only to defeated enemies or others who can be safely despised.

After the invasion of Iraq was declared a success, it was publicly recognized that one motive for the war had been to establish the imperial grand strategy as a new norm: "Publication of the [National Security Strategy] was the signal that Iraq would be the first test, not the last," the *New York Times* reported. "Iraq became the petri dish in which this experiment in pre-emptive policy grew." A high official added that "we will not hesitate to act alone, if necessary, to exercise our right of self-defense by acting pre-emptively," now that the norm has been established. "The exemplary nature of the whole exercise [in Iraq] is well recognized by the rest of the world," Harvard Middle East historian Roger Owen observed. Peoples and regimes will have to change the way they see the world "from a view based on the United Nations and international law to one based on an identification" with Washington's agenda. They are being instructed by the display of force to put aside "any serious considerations of national interest" in favor of reflecting "American goals."[21]

The need for a demonstration of strength to "maintain credibility" in the eyes of the world may have tipped the balance on the war with Iraq. In a review of planning, the *Financial Times* traced the decision to go to war to mid-December 2002, after Iraq's submission of its declaration on armaments to the UN. " 'There was a feeling that the White House was being mocked,' says one person who worked closely with the National Security Council during those days after the declaration was delivered on December 8. 'A tinpot dictator was mocking the president. It provoked a sense of anger inside the White House. After that point, there was no prospect of a diplomatic solution.' "[22] What followed was just diplomatic theater for obfuscation while military forces were put in place.

With the grand strategy not only officially declared but also implemented, the new norm of preventive war takes its place in the canon. The United States may now find it possible to turn to harder cases. There are many tempting possibilities: Iran, Syria, the Andean region, and a number of others. The prospects depend in large part on whether the "second superpower" can be intimidated and contained.

The modalities for establishing norms merit further reflection. Most important, only those with the guns and the faith have the authority to impose their demands on the world. A revealing example of the prerogatives of power is the widely hailed "normative revolution" that ended the millennium. After a few false starts, the 1990s became "the decade of humanitarian intervention." The new right to intervene on "humanitarian" grounds was established by the courage and altruism of the United States and its allies, particularly in Kosovo and East Timor, the two jewels in the diadem. The Kosovo bombing in particular is understood by distinguished authorities to have established the norm of resort to force without Security Council authorization.

A simple question arises: Why were the 1990s considered "the decade of humanitarian intervention" but not the 1970s? Since World War II, there have been two major examples of resort to force that really did put an end to terrible crimes, in both cases arguably in self-defense: India's invasion of East Pakistan in 1971, ending a mass slaughter and other horrors, and Vietnam's invasion of Cambodia in December 1978, terminating Pol Pot's atrocities as they were picking up through 1978. Nothing remotely comparable took place under the Western aegis in the 1990s. Accordingly, someone who does not understand the conventions might be pardoned for asking why "the new norm" was not recognized as such in the 1970s.

The idea is unthinkable, and the reasons seem clear. The real examples of intervention that terminated huge atrocities were carried out by the wrong people. Still worse, in both cases the United States was adamantly opposed to intervention and moved instantly to punish the offender, particularly Vietnam, by subjecting it to a U.S.-backed Chinese invasion, then even harsher sanctions than before, while the United States and United Kingdom offered direct support for the ousted Khmer Rouge. It follows that the 1970s cannot have been the decade of humanitarian intervention, and no new norms could have been established then.

The essential insight was formulated by a unanimous vote of the International Court of Justice in one of its earliest rulings, in 1949:

> The Court can only regard the alleged right of intervention as the manifestation of a policy of force, such as has, in the past, given rise to most serious abuses and such as cannot, whatever be the defects in international organization, find a place in international law . . . ; from the nature of things, [intervention] would be reserved for the most powerful states, and might easily lead to perverting the administration of justice itself.[23]

While Western powers and intellectuals were admiring themselves for having established the new norm of humanitarian intervention in the late 1990s, the rest of the world also had some thoughts on the matter. It is illuminating to see how they reacted, say, to Tony Blair's repetition of the official reasons for the bombing of Serbia in 1999: failure to bomb "would have dealt a devastating blow to the credibility of NATO" and "the world would have been less safe as a result of that." The objects of NATO's solicitude did not seem overly impressed by the need to safeguard the credibility of those who had been crushing them for centuries. Nelson Mandela, for example, condemned Blair for "encouraging international chaos, together with America, by ignoring other nations and playing 'policeman of the world' " in their attacks on Iraq in 1998 and Serbia the next year. In the world's largest democracy—which, after independence, began to recover from the grim effects of centuries of British rule—the Clinton-Blair efforts to shore up NATO's credibility and make the world safe were also not appreciated, but official and press condemnations in India remained unheard. Even in Israel, the client state par excellence, the pretensions of Clinton-Blair and a host of domestic admirers were ridiculed by leading military and political analysts as a return to old-fashioned "gunboat diplomacy" under the familiar "cloak of moralistic righteousness," and as a "danger to the world." [24]

Another source of information might have been the nonaligned movement, the governments of about 80 percent of the world's population at the time of their South Summit in April 2000. The meeting was the most important in their history, the first ever at the level of heads of state, who, in addition to issuing a detailed and sophisticated critical analysis of the neoliberal socioeconomic programs called "globalization" by Western ideologues, also firmly rejected "the so-called 'right' of humanitarian intervention." That stand was reiterated in the summit of nonaligned countries in Malaysia in February 2003, in the same words.[25] Perhaps they had learned too much history, the hard way, to be comforted by exalted rhetoric and had heard enough about "humanitarian intervention" over the centuries.

It is an exaggeration to say that only the most powerful are granted the authority to establish norms of appropriate behavior—for themselves. The authority is sometimes delegated to reliable clients. Thus, Israel's crimes are permitted to establish norms: for example, its regular resort to "targeted killings" of suspects—called "terrorist atrocities" when carried out by the wrong hands. In May 2003, two leading Israeli civil rights attorneys provided "a detailed list of all of the liquidations and all of the attempted assassinations that Israel's security forces carried out" during the al-Aqsa Intifada, from November 2000 through April 2003. Using official and semiofficial records, they found that "Israel carried out no less than 175 liquidation attempts"—one attempt every five days—killing 235 people, of whom 156 were suspected of crimes. "It greatly pains us to say the following," the lawyers wrote, but "the consistent, widespread policy of targeted liquidations bounds on a crime against humanity." [26]

Their judgment is not quite accurate. Liquidation is a crime in the wrong hands, but it is a justified, if regrettable, act of self-defense when carried out by a client, and even establishes norms for the "the boss-man called 'partner,' " [27] who provides authorization. The "boss-man" himself made use of Israel's precedent with the assassination by missile of a suspect in Yemen, along with five other people who happened to be nearby, to much acclaim. The hit was "conveniently timed [as an] October surprise . . . to show the incumbent in his finest hour, on the eve of the midterm elections," and offer "a taste of what is to come."[28]

A more far-reaching example of establishing norms was Israel's bombing of the Osirak reactor in Iraq in June 1981. At first the attack was criticized as a violation of international law. Later, after Saddam Hussein was transformed from favored friend to unspeakable fiend in August 1990, the reaction to the Osirak bombing also shifted. Once a (minor) crime, it was now considered an honored norm, and was greatly praised for having impeded Saddam Hussein's nuclear weapons program.

The norm, however, required the evasion of a few inconvenient facts. Shortly after the 1981 bombing, the Osirak site was inspected by a prominent nuclear physicist, Richard Wilson, then chair of the physics department at Harvard University. He concluded that the installation bombed was not suited for plutonium production, as Israel had charged, unlike Israel's own Dimona reactor, which had reportedly produced several hundred nuclear weapons. His conclusions were supported by the Iraqi nuclear physicist Imad Khadduri, who was in charge of experimental work at the reactor before the bombing and later fled the country. He too reported that the Osirak reactor was unsuitable for the production of plutonium, though after the Israeli bombing in 1981, Iraq took the "solid decision to go full speed ahead with weaponization." Khadduri estimated that it would have taken Iraq decades to obtain the required amount of weapons-grade material, had the program not been sharply accelerated as a result of the bombing. "Israel's action increased the determination of Arabs to produce nuclear weapons," Kenneth Waltz concluded. "Israel's strike, far from foreclosing Iraq's nuclear career, gained Iraq support from some other Arab states to pursue it."[29]

Whatever the facts, thanks to Iraq's invasion of Kuwait a decade later, the norm that Israel established in 1981 is now firmly in place. And if indeed the 1981 bombing accelerated the proliferation of WMD, that in no way tarnishes the deed, and teaches no lessons about the consequences of resort to force in violation of old-fashioned conceptions of international law—conceptions that must be discarded now that they have been demonstrated to be "hot air" by the boss-man's contempt for them. In the future, the United States and its Israeli client and perhaps some highly favored others can resort to the norm as they see fit.

THE RULE OF LAW

The grand strategy extends to domestic U.S. law. As in many other countries, the government used the occasion of the terrorist atrocities of 9-11 to discipline its own population. After 9-11, often with questionable relation to terror, the Bush administration claimed, and exercised, the right to declare people—including U.S. citizens—to be "enemy combatants" or "suspected terrorists" and to imprison them without charge or access to lawyers or family until the White House determines that its "war on terror" has been successfully concluded: that is, indefinitely. The Ashcroft Justice Department takes it to be "fundamental [that] if you hold someone as an enemy combatant, obviously you hold them without access to family members and without access to counsel." These claims of executive authority have been partially upheld by the courts, which have ruled "that a wartime president can indefinitely detain a United States citizen captured as an enemy combatant on the battlefield and deny that person access to a lawyer."[30]

The treatment of "enemy combatants" in Washington's Guantánamo prison camp in a still-occupied part of Cuba elicited substantial protest from human rights organizations and others, even the Justice Department's own inspector general, in a scathing report that the department disregarded. After the conquest of Iraq, evidence soon surfaced that Iraqi prisoners were being subjected to similar treatment: gagged, bound, hooded, beaten "in the manner of the Afghans and other captives held at Guantánamo Bay in Cuba—treatment in itself questionable under international law," to put it mildly. The Red Cross strongly protested the refusal of the U.S. command to allow it access to prisoners of war, in violation of the Geneva Conventions, and to captured civilians.[31] Moreover, the designations are capricious. An enemy combatant can be anyone that the United States chooses to attack, with no credible evidence, as Washington concedes.[32]

Justice Department thinking is illuminated by a confidential plan leaked to the Center for Public Integrity, entitled "Domestic Security Enhancement Act of 2003." This "new assault on our civil liberties" vastly expands state power, Yale Law professor Jack Balkin writes. It undermines constitutional rights by granting the state the authority to rescind citizenship on the charge of providing "material support" to an organization on the attorney general's blacklist even if the accused has no idea that the organization has been blacklisted. "Give a few dollars to a Muslim charity Ashcroft thinks is a terrorist organization," Balkin writes, "and you could be on the next plane out of this country." The plan states that "an intent to relinquish nationality need not be manifested in words, but can be inferred from conduct"; inferred by the attorney general, whose judgment we must honor, on faith. Analogies have been drawn to the darkest days of McCarthyism, but these new proposals are more extreme. The plan also extends powers of surveillance without court authorization, permits secret arrests, and further protects the state from the scrutiny of citizens, a matter of great significance to the reactionary statists of the Bush II regime. "There is no civil right—not even the precious right of citizenship—that this Administration will not abuse to secure ever greater control over American life," Balkin concludes.[33]

President Bush is said to have on his desk a bust of Winston Churchill, a gift from his friend Tony Blair. Churchill had a few things to say on these topics:

> The power of the executive to cast a man into prison without formulating any charge known to the law, and particularly to deny him the judgment of his peers, is in the highest degree odious, and the foundation of all totalitarian government whether Nazi or Communist.[34]

The powers the Bush administration is demanding go well beyond even these odious practices. Churchill's warning against such abuse of executive power for intelligence and preventive purposes was issued in 1943, when Britain was facing possible destruction at the hands of the most vicious mass murder machine in human history. Perhaps someone in the Justice Department might want to contemplate the thoughts of the man whose image faces their leader every day.

INTERNATIONAL LAW AND INSTITUTIONS

The imperial grand strategy effectively dispenses with "the international rule of law as an overarching goal of policy," a critical review by the American Academy of Arts and Sciences points out, noting that neither international law nor the UN Charter is even mentioned in the National Security Strategy. "The primacy of law over force [that] has been a major thread in American foreign policy since the end of World War II" disappears from the new strategy. Also "all but disappeared" are the international institutions "that extend the reach of law, and seek to constrain the powerful as well as to grant the weak a voice." From now on, force reigns, and the United States will exercise that force as it sees fit. The analysts conclude that the strategy will increase "the motivation of U.S. enemies to act [in reaction to their growing] resentment of perceived intimidation." They will seek "cheap and easy ways of exploiting U.S. vulnerabilities," which abound. Lack of concern with this on the part of Bush planners is also illustrated by the fact that the National Security Strategy contains just a single sentence on enhancing arms control efforts, for which the administration has only contempt.[35] Writing in the academy's journal, two international affairs specialists describe the plans for "extended confrontation, not political accommodation," as "inherently provocative." They warn that "the apparent commitment of the United States to active military confrontation for decisive national advantage" carries immense risks.[36] Many concur, even on narrow grounds of self-interest.

The academy's assessment of the primacy of law over force in American policy requires serious qualifications. Since World War II, the U.S. government has adopted the standard practice of powerful states, regularly choosing force over law when that was considered expedient for "the national interest," a technical term referring to the special interests of domestic sectors that are in a position to determine policy. For the Anglo-American world, that truism is as old as Adam Smith. He bitterly condemned the "merchants and manufacturers" in England who were "by far the principal architects" of policy and made sure their own interests were "most peculiarly attended to," no matter how "grievous" the effect on others, including the victims of their "savage injustice" abroad and the people of England as well.[37] Truisms have a way of remaining true.

The dominant elite view with regard to the UN was well expressed in 1992 by Francis Fukuyama, who had served in the Reagan-Bush State Department: the UN is "perfectly serviceable as an instrument of American unilateralism and indeed may be the primary mechanism through which that unilateralism will be exercised in the future." His prediction proved accurate, presumably because it was based on consistent practice going back to the early days of the UN. At that time, the state of the world guaranteed that the UN would be virtually an instrument of U.S. power. The institution was greatly admired, though elite distaste for it increased notably in subsequent years. The shift of attitude roughly traced the course of decolonization, which opened a small window for "the tyranny of the majority": that is, for concerns emanating from outside the centers of concentrated power that the business press calls the "de facto world government" of "the masters of the universe."[38]

When the UN fails to serve as "an instrument of American unilateralism" on issues of elite concern, it is dismissed. One of many illustrations is the record of vetoes. Since the 1960s, the United States has been far in the lead in vetoing Security Council resolutions on a wide range of issues, even those calling on states to observe international law. Britain is second, France and Russia far behind. Even that record is skewed by the fact that Washington's enormous power often compels the weakening of resolutions to which it objects, or keeps crucial matters off the agenda entirely—Washington's wars in Indochina, to cite one example that was of more than a little concern to the world.

Saddam Hussein was rightly condemned for his failure to comply fully with numerous Security Council resolutions, though less was said about the fact that the United States rejected the same resolutions. The most important of them, Resolution 687, called for ending sanctions when Iraqi compliance was determined by the Security Council, and moving on to eliminate WMD and delivery systems from the Middle East (Article 14, a coded reference to Israel). There was never a possibility that the United States would accept Article 14, and it was removed from discussion.

President Bush I and his secretary of state, James Baker, announced at once that the United States would reject the primary condition of 687 as well, barring even "relaxation of sanctions as long as Saddam Hussein is in power." Clinton concurred. His secretary of state, Warren Christopher, wrote in 1994 that Iraqi compliance is not "enough to justify lifting the embargo," thus "changing the rules unilaterally," Dilip Hiro points out.[39] Washington's use of UN inspectors (UNSCOM) to spy on Iraq also undermined inspections, which were terminated by Iraq after Clinton and Blair bombed the country in December 1998, in defiance of the UN. The likely outcome of these inspections is known with confidence only to ideologues on all sides. It was clear enough throughout, however, that disarmament through international inspectors was not the U.S.-UK objective and that the two warrior states would not comply with the relevant UN resolutions.

Some commentators have pointed out that Israel has the lead in violating resolutions. U.S.-backed Turkey and Morocco have also violated more Security Council resolutions than Iraq. These resolutions have to do with highly significant matters: aggression, harsh, and brutal practices during decades-long military occupations, grave breaches of the Geneva Conventions (war crimes, in terms of U.S. law), and other matters that rank higher than incomplete disarmament. The resolutions concerning Iraq also refer to internal repression, and in this respect Saddam Hussein's record was horrendous, but that was (regrettably) only a side issue, as revealed by the support for him by the current incumbents in Washington well past his worst crimes and the war with Iran. Resolutions concerning Israel do not come under Chapter VII, which would carry the threat of force, but any such proposal would instantly be vetoed by the United States.

The veto brings up another important matter missing from the discussions of Iraq's incomplete compliance with Security Council resolutions. Plainly, if Iraq had had the right of veto, it would have been in defiance of no UN resolutions. No less plainly, any serious discussion of defiance of the Security Council must take into account vetoes, the most extreme form of noncompliance. That exercise is excluded, however, because of the conclusions that would follow at once.

The issue of the veto was not entirely ignored during the preparation for the Iraq invasion. France's threat to veto a UN declaration of war was bitterly condemned. "They said they are going to veto anything that held Saddam to account," Bush declared, with his familiar concern for truth, as he delivered his ultimatum to the Security Council on March 16, 2003. There was much fury about France's iniquity, and talk of actions to punish the country that did not follow orders from Crawford, Texas. In general, threat of veto by others is a scandal, revealing the "failure of diplomacy" and the miserable behavior of the United Nations. To select virtually at random, "If lesser powers contrive to turn the council into a forum for counter-balancing American power with votes, words, and public appeals, they will further erode its legitimacy and credibility," according to Edward Luck, director of the Center on International Organization at Columbia University.[40] Routine resort to the veto by the world champion is generally ignored or downplayed, occasionally hailed as demonstrating the principled stand of embattled Washington. But there is no concern that this erodes the legitimacy and credibility of the United Nations.

There should have been little reason for surprise, therefore, when a senior Bush administration official explained in October 2002 that "we don't need the Security Council," so if it "wants to stay relevant, then it has to give us similar authority" to that just granted by Congress—authority to use force at will. The stand was endorsed by the president and by Secretary of State Colin Powell, who added that "obviously, the Council can always go off and have other discussions," but "we have the authority to do what we believe is necessary." Washington agreed to submit a resolution to the Security Council (UN 1441), leaving no doubt, however, that the exercise was meaningless. "Whatever the diplomatic niceties, Mr. Bush made it clear that he regarded the resolution to be all the authority he needed to act against Iraq should Mr. Hussein balk," diplomatic correspondents observed. "Though Washington would consult other members of the Security Council, it would not feel it necessary to win their approval." Echoing Powell, White House chief of staff Andrew Card explained that "the UN can meet and discuss, but we don't need their permission."[41]

The administration's "decent respect for the opinion of mankind [in declaring] the causes which impel" it to action was reemphasized when Powell addressed the Security Council a few months later, announcing Washington's intention to go to war. "US officials were adamant that his briefing should not be interpreted as part of a protracted effort to garner support for a resolution authorizing the use of force," the international press reported. A U.S. official said, "We're not going to negotiate on a second resolution because we don't need to. . . . If the rest of the Council wants to catch up to us we might stop briefly to sign on the dotted line," but nothing more.[42] The world was placed on notice that Washington will use force as it chooses; the debating society can "catch up" and join the enterprise or suffer the consequences that befall those who are not "with us" and are therefore "with the terrorists," as the president laid out the options.

Bush and Blair underscored their contempt for international law and institutions at their subsequent summit meeting at a U.S. military base in the Azores, where they were joined by Spain's prime minister, José Maria Aznar. The U.S.-UK leaders "issued an ultimatum" to the United Nations Security Council: capitulate in twenty-four hours or we will invade Iraq and impose the regime of our choice without your meaningless seal of approval, and we will do so—crucially—whether or not Saddam Hussein and his family leave the country. Our invasion is legitimate, Bush declared, because "the United States of America has the sovereign authority to use force in assuring its own national security," threatened by Iraq with or without Saddam. The UN is irrelevant because it "has not lived up to its responsibilities"—that is, to follow Washington's orders. The United States will "enforce the just demands of the world" even if the world overwhelmingly objects.[43]

Washington also took pains to ensure that the essential hollowness of official declarations was in plain view, for all the world to see. At a news conference on March 6, the president stated that there is only "a single question: Has the Iraqi regime fully and unconditionally disarmed as required by 1441, or has it not?" He then immediately went on to make it clear that the answer to the single question did not matter, announcing that "when it comes to our security we really don't need anyone's permission." UN inspections and Security Council deliberations were therefore a farce, and even completely verified compliance was irrelevant. A few days earlier Bush had declared the answer to the "single question" immaterial: the United States will institute the regime of its choice even if Saddam disarms completely, and even if he and his cohorts disappear, as underscored at the Azores summit.[44]

The president's disregard of the single question was in fact already on the record. A few months earlier, White House spokesman Ari Fleischer had informed the press that "the policy of the United States is regime change, with or without inspectors"; "regime change" does not mean a regime that Iraqis might prefer, but one that the conqueror will impose, calling it "democratic," which is standard practice; even Russia installed "people's democracies." Later, with the war winding down, Fleischer restored the "single question" to its primary status: Iraq's possession of WMD "is what this war was about and is about." As Bush was presenting his self-contradictory stance at his news conference, British Foreign Minister Jack Straw announced that if Saddam Hussein disarmed, "we accept that the government of Iraq stays in place," so that the "single question" is disarmament: talk about "liberation" and "democracy" is mere fluff, and Britain will not support Bush's resort to war on his grounds—except that Britain made it clear that it would do as it was told.[45]

Meanwhile, Colin Powell contradicted the president's declaration that the United States will take control of Iraq no matter what: "The question simply is: has Saddam Hussein made a strategic, political decision to comply with the United Nations Security Council resolutions [and] to get rid of his weapons of mass destruction? That's it in a nutshell. . . . That's the question. There is no other question." Back to the "single question," rejected by the president five days earlier and again the following day. As the invasion began, Powell returned to the "single question." Iraq "was being attacked because it had violated its 'international obligations' under its 1991 surrender agreement, which required the disclosure and disarmament of its dangerous weapons."[46] Everything else that has been claimed is therefore irrelevant: the United States will unilaterally decide that the inspectors should not be permitted to do their work, and the 1991 agreement entitles the United States to resort to violence, contrary to its explicit wording.

Pick some other day and audience and the goal is "liberation" and "democracy" not only for Iraq but for the region, a "noble dream." The message is clear: We will do what we choose, giving whatever pretext happens to be on hand. You will "catch up," or else.

Unexplained is why the threat of WMD became so severe after September 2002, while before National Security Adviser Rice had accepted the consensus that "if they do acquire WMD, their weapons will be unusable because any attempt to use them will bring national obliteration."[47]

Punishment for being "against us" can be severe, and the benefits of catching up and remaining "relevant" are substantial. Senior U.S. officials were dispatched to Security Council members to "urge leaders to vote with the United States on Iraq or risk 'paying a heavy price,'" not an insignificant concern for fragile countries "whose concerns drew little attention before they landed seats on the council." Mexican diplomats tried to explain to Washington's emissaries that the people "are overwhelmingly opposed to a war," but that plea was dismissed as ridiculous.[48]

A special problem arose for "countries that have succumbed to popular pressure to embrace democracy [and] now have a public to answer to." For them, repercussions for taking democratic forms seriously may include economic strangulation. In contrast, "Mr. Powell made clear that US political and military allies will benefit from handouts." Ari Fleischer meanwhile "hotly denied" that Bush was offering quid pro quos in exchange for votes, "evoking peals of laughter from the press corps," the *Wall Street Journal* reported.[49]

Rewards for following orders include not only financial handouts but also authorization to escalate terrorist atrocities. Russian president Vladimir Putin, whose relations with Bush are reported to be particularly soulful, was awarded "a diplomatic nod for Russia's crackdown on Chechen separatists—a move that some analysts here and in the Middle East contend could damage long-term US interests." One might imagine some other reasons to be concerned about Washington's support for state terrorism. To make it clear that such reactions are "irrelevant," the head of a Muslim charity was sentenced in federal court on the charge of having diverted funds to Chechens resisting the vicious Russian military occupation, just as Putin was receiving his green light. The head of the same charity was also charged with funding ambulances for Bosnia; in that case, the crime was apparently committed at about the same time that Clinton was flying Al-Qaeda and Hezbollah operatives to Bosnia to support the U.S. side in the ongoing wars.[50]

Turkey was offered similar inducements: a huge financial package and the right to invade Kurdish northern Iraq. Remarkably, Turkey did not fully submit, teaching a lesson in democracy to the West that aroused great ire and, as Secretary of State Powell sternly announced at once, instant punishment for the misdeed.[51]

The "diplomatic niceties" are for those who prefer to be deluded, as is the apparent support of Security Council members for the U.S.-initiated Resolution 1441. The support is in fact submission; signers understood what the alternative would be. In systems of law that are intended to be taken seriously, coerced acquiescence is invalid. In international affairs, however, it is honored as diplomacy.

After the Iraq war, the United Nation again proved "irrelevant," because its "complicated trade system for Iraq" caused problems for U.S. companies granted contracts under U.S. military rule. The complicated trade system was in fact imposed by the United States as part of its sanctions regime, for which there was virtually no support outside the UK. But now it was in the way. Hence, in the words of a "coalition diplomat," the United States wanted "the message to be, 'We're coming here [to the Security Council] because we want to, not because we have to.' " The background issue, diplomats on all sides agree, is "how much of a free hand the U.S. should be given to manage Iraqi oil and establish a successor government." Washington demands a free hand. Other countries, a large majority of the U.S. population, and (to the extent that we have information) the people of Iraq prefer "to extend U.N. oversight there" and "to normalize Iraq's diplomatic and economic relations," as well as its internal affairs, within that framework.[52]

Through all the shifts of justifications and pretexts, one principle remains invariant: the United States must end up in effective control of Iraq, under some façade of democracy if that proves feasible.

That "America's imperial ambition" should extend to the whole world after the collapse of its sole major rival should hardly elicit surprise—and there are, needless to say, numerous predecessors, with consequences not too pleasant to recall. The current situation, however, is different. There has never in history been anything remotely like the near-monopoly of means of large-scale violence in the hands of one state—all the more reason for subjecting its practices and operative doctrines to extra-careful scrutiny.

ELITE CONCERNS

Within establishment circles, there has been considerable concern that "America's imperial ambition" is a serious threat even to its own population. Their alarm reached new heights as the Bush administration declared itself to be a "revisionist state" that intends to rule the world permanently, becoming, some felt, "a menace to itself and to mankind" under the leadership of "radical nationalists" aiming for "unilateral world domination through absolute military superiority."[53] Many others within the mainstream spectrum have been appalled by the adventurism and arrogance of the radical nationalists who have regained the power they wielded through the 1980s, but now operate with fewer external constraints.

The concerns are not entirely new. During the Clinton years, the prominent political analyst Samuel Huntington observed that for much of the world the United States is "becoming the rogue superpower, [considered] the single greatest external threat to their societies." Robert Jervis, then president of the American Political Science Association, warned that "in the eyes of much of the world, in fact, the prime rogue state today is the United States." Like others, they anticipated that coalitions might arise to counterbalance the rogue superpower, with threatening implications.[54]

Several leading figures of the foreign policy elite have pointed out that the potential targets of America's imperial ambition are not likely simply to await destruction. They "know that the United States can be held at bay only by deterrence," Kenneth Waltz has written, and that "weapons of mass destruction are the only means to deter the United States." Washington's policies are therefore leading to proliferation of WMD, Waltz concludes, tendencies accelerated by its commitment to dismantle international mechanisms to control the resort to violence. These warnings were reiterated as Bush prepared to attack Iraq: one consequence, according to Steven Miller, is that others "are likely to draw the conclusion that weapons of mass destruction are necessary to deter American intervention." Another well-known specialist warned that the "general strategy of preventive war" is likely to provide others with "overwhelming incentives to wield weapons of terror and mass destruction" as a deterrent to "the unbridled use of American power." Many have noted the likely impetus to Iranian nuclear weapons programs. And "there is no question that the lesson that the North Koreans have learned from Iraq is that it needs a nuclear deterrent," Selig Harrison commented.[55]

As the year 2002 drew to a close, Washington was teaching an ugly lesson to the world: if you want to defend yourself from us, you had better mimic North Korea and pose a credible military threat, in this case, conventional: artillery aimed at Seoul and at U.S. troops near the DMZ. We will enthusiastically march on to attack Iraq, because we know that it is devastated and defenseless; but North Korea, though an even worse tyranny and vastly more dangerous, is not an appropriate target as long as it can cause plenty of harm. The lesson could hardly be more vivid.

Still another concern is the "second superpower," public opinion. Not only was the "revisionism" of the political leadership without precedent; so too was the opposition to it. Comparisons are often drawn to Vietnam. The common query "What happened to the tradition of protest and dissent?" makes clear how effectively the historical record has been cleansed and how little sense there is, in many circles, of the changes in public consciousness over the past four decades. An accurate comparison is revealing: In 1962, public protest was nonexistent, despite the announcement that year that the Kennedy administration was sending the U.S. Air Force to bomb South Vietnam, as well as initiating plans to drive millions of people into what amounted to concentration camps and launching chemical warfare programs to destroy food crops and ground cover. Protest did not reach any meaningful level until years later, after hundreds of thousands of U.S. troops had been dispatched, densely populated areas had been demolished by saturation bombing, and the aggression had spread to the rest of Indochina. By the time protest became significant, the bitterly anticommunist military historian and Indochina specialist Bernard Fall had warned that "Vietnam as a cultural and historic entity . . . is threatened with extinction" as "the countryside literally dies under the blows of the largest military machine ever unleashed on an area of this size."[56]

In 2002, forty years later, in striking contrast, there was large-scale, committed, and principled popular protest before the war had been officially launched. Absent the fear and illusion about Iraq that were unique to the United States prewar opposition would probably have reached much the same levels as elsewhere. That reflects a steady increase over these years in unwillingness to tolerate aggression and atrocities, one of many such changes.

The leadership is well aware of these developments. By 1968, fear of the public was so serious that the Joint Chiefs of Staff had to consider whether "sufficient forces would still be available for civil disorder control" if more troops were sent to Vietnam. The Department of Defense feared that further troop deployments ran the risk of "provoking a domestic crisis of unprecedented proportions."[57] The Reagan administration at first tried to follow Kennedy's South Vietnam model in Central America but backed down in the face of an unanticipated public reaction that threatened to undermine more important components of the policy agenda, turning instead to clandestine terror—clandestine in the sense that it could be more or less concealed from the general public. When Bush I took office in 1989, public reaction was again very much on the agenda. Incoming administrations typically commission a review of the world situation from the intelligence agencies. These reviews are secret, but in 1989 a passage was leaked concerning "cases where the U.S. confronts much weaker enemies." The analysts advised that the United States must "defeat them decisively and rapidly." Any other outcome would be "embarrassing" and might "undercut political support," understood to be thin.[58]

We are no longer in the 1960s, when the population would tolerate a murderous and destructive war for years without visible protest. The activist movements of the past forty years have had a significant civilizing effect in many domains. By now, the only way to attack a much weaker enemy is to construct a propaganda offensive depicting it as an imminent threat or perhaps engaged in genocide, with confidence that the military campaign will scarcely resemble an actual war.

Elite concerns extend to the impact of Bush administration radical nationalists on world public opinion, which was overwhelmingly opposed to their war plans and militant posturing. These have surely been factors in the general decline of trust in leadership revealed by a World Economic Forum poll released in January 2003. According to the poll, only NGO leaders had the trust of a clear majority, followed by UN and spiritual/religious leaders, then leaders of Western Europe and economic managers, and right below them, corporate executives. Far below, at the very bottom, were the leaders of the United States.[59]

A week after the poll was released, the annual World Economic Forum opened in Davos, Switzerland, but without the exuberance of earlier years. "The mood has darkened," the press noted: for the "movers and shakers," it was not "global party time" anymore. The founder of the WEF, Klaus Schwab, identified the most pressing reason: "Iraq will be the overwhelming theme of all the discussions." Powell's aides warned him before his presentation that the mood was "ugly" at Davos, the *Wall Street Journal* reported. "A chorus of international complaints about the American march toward war with Iraq was reaching a crescendo at this gathering of some 2,000 corporate executives, politicians and academics." They were not overwhelmed by Powell's "sharp new message": in his own words, "when we feel strongly about something we will lead," even if no one is following us. "We will act even if others are not prepared to join us."[60]

The theme of the WEF was "Building Trust," for good reasons.

In his speech, Powell stressed that the United States reserves the "sovereign right to take military action" when and how it chooses. He said further that no one "trusts Saddam and his regime," which was certainly true, though his comment left out some other leaders who are not trusted. Powell also assured his audience that Saddam Hussein's weapons were "meant to intimidate Iraq's neighbors," failing to explain why those neighbors did not seem to perceive the threat.[61] Much as they despised the murderous tyrant, Iraq's neighbors joined the "many outside the United States mystified at why Washington is so obsessed and fearful of what is, in the end, a minor power whose wealth and power have been truncated by internationally imposed constraints." Aware of the dire effects of the sanctions on the general population, they also knew that Iraq was one of the weakest states in the region: its economy and military expenditures were a fraction of Kuwait's, which has 10 percent of Iraq's population, and much farther below those of others nearby.[62] For these and other reasons, the neighboring countries had been mending fences with Iraq for some years over strong U.S. opposition. Like the U.S. Department of Defense and the CIA, they knew "perfectly well that today's Iraq poses no threat to anyone in the region, let alone in the United States," and that "To argue otherwise is dishonest."[63]

By the time they met, the "movers and shakers" at Davos had heard even more unpleasant news about "building trust." An opinion poll in Canada found that more than "36 percent of Canadians viewed the US as the biggest threat to world peace, against just 21 percent naming Al-Qaeda, 17 percent choosing Iraq and 14 percent North Korea." That despite the fact that the general image of the United States had improved to 72 percent in Canada, in contrast to dropping sharply in Western Europe. An informal poll run by *Time* magazine found that more than 80 percent of respondents in Europe regarded the United States as the greatest threat to world peace. Even if these numbers were wrong by some substantial factor, they are dramatic. Their significance is magnified by contemporaneous international polls on the U.S.-UK drive for war with Iraq.[64]

"The messages from U.S. embassies around the globe have become urgent and disturbing," the *Washington Post* noted in a lead story. "Many people in the world increasingly think President Bush is a greater threat to world peace than Iraqi President Saddam Hussein." "The debate has not been about Iraq," a State Department official was quoted as saying. "There is real angst in the world about our power, and what they perceive as the rawness, the arrogance, the unipolarity" of the administration's actions. The headline read, "Danger Ahead? The World Sees President Bush as a Threat." A cover story in *Newsweek* three weeks later, by its senior foreign affairs editor, also warned that the global debate was not about Saddam: "It is about America and its role in the new world. . . . A war with Iraq, even if successful, might solve the Iraq problem. It doesn't solve the America problem. What worries people around the world above all else is living in a world shaped and dominated by one country—the United States. And they have come to be deeply suspicious and fearful of us."[65]

After 9-11, at a time of enormous global sympathy and solidarity with the United States, George Bush asked, "Why do they hate us?" The question was wrongly put, and the right question was scarcely addressed. But within a year, the administration succeeded in providing an answer: "Because of you and your associates, Mr. Bush, and what you have done. And if you continue, the fear and hatred you have inspired may extend to the country you have shamed as well." On that, the evidence is hard to ignore. For Osama bin Laden, it is a victory probably beyond his wildest dreams.

INTENTIONAL IGNORANCE

The fundamental assumption that lies behind the imperial grand strategy, often considered unnecessary to formulate because its truth is taken to be so obvious, is the guiding principle of Wilsonian idealism: We—at least the circles who provide the leadership and advise them—are good, even noble. Hence our interventions are necessarily righteous in intent, if occasionally clumsy in execution. In Wilson's own words, we have "elevated ideals" and are dedicated to "stability and righteousness," and it is only natural, then, as Wilson wrote in justifying the conquest of the Philippines, that "our interest must march forward, altruists though we are; other nations must see to it that they stand off, and do not seek to stay us."[66]

In the contemporary version, there is a guiding principle that "defines the parameters within which the policy debate occurs," a consensus so broad as to exclude only "tattered remnants" on the right and left and "so authoritative as to be virtually immune to challenge." The principle is "*America as historical vanguard*": "History has a discernible direction and destination. Uniquely among all the nations of the world, the United States comprehends and manifests history's purpose." Accordingly, U.S. hegemony is the realization of history's purpose, and what it achieves is for the common good, the merest truism, so that empirical evaluation is unnecessary, if not faintly ridiculous. The primary principle of foreign policy, rooted in Wilsonian idealism and carried over from Clinton to Bush II, is "*the imperative of America's mission as the vanguard of history, transforming the global order and, in doing so, perpetuating its own dominance*," guided by "*the imperative of military supremacy, maintained in perpetuity and projected globally*."[67]

By virtue of its unique comprehension and manifestation of history's purpose, America is entitled, indeed obligated, to act as its leaders determine to be best, for the good of all, whether others understand or not. And like its noble predecessor and current junior partner, Great Britain, America should not be deterred in realizing history's transcendent purpose even if it is "held up to obloquy" by the foolish and resentful, as was its predecessor in global rule, according to its most prestigious advocates.[68]

To still any qualms that might arise, it suffices to refresh our understanding that "Providence summons Americans" to the task of reforming global order: the "Wilsonian tradition . . . to which all recent occupants of the Oval Office, regardless of party, have adhered"—as have, commonly, their predecessors, their counterparts elsewhere, and their most reviled enemies, with required change of names.[69] But to reassure ourselves that the powerful are motivated by "elevated ideals" and "altruism" in the quest of "stability and righteousness," we have to adopt the stance called "intentional ignorance" by a critic of the terrible atrocities in Central America in the 1980s backed by the political leadership that is again at the helm in Washington.[70] Adopting that stance, not only can we tidy up the past, conceding the inevitable flaws that accompany even the best of intentions, but more recently, since the advent of the new norm of humanitarian intervention, we can even go on to portray U.S. foreign policy as having entered a "noble phase" with a "saintly glow." Washington's "post-Cold War interventions were, on the whole, noble but half-hearted; they were half-hearted *because* they were noble," historian Michael Mandelbaum assures us. Perhaps we are even too saintly: we must beware of "granting idealism a near exclusive hold on our foreign policy," more sober voices warn, thus neglecting our own legitimate interests in our dedicated service to others.[71]

Somehow, Europeans have failed to understand the unique idealism of American leaders. How can this be, since it is the merest truism? Max Boot suggests an answer. Europe has "often been driven by avarice," and the "cynical Europeans" cannot comprehend the "strain of idealism" that animates U.S. foreign policy: "After 200 years, Europe still hasn't figured out what makes America tick." Their ineradicable cynicism leads Europeans to attribute base motives to Washington and to fail to join its noble ventures with sufficient enthusiasm. Another respected historian and political commentator,

Robert Kagan, offers a different explanation. Europe's problem is that it is consumed with "paranoid, conspiratorial anti-Americanism," which has "reached a fevered intensity," though fortunately a few figures, like Berlusconi and Aznar, brave the storm.[72]

Unwittingly, no doubt, Boot and Kagan are plagiarizing John Stuart Mill's classic essay on humanitarian intervention, in which he urged Britain to undertake the enterprise vigorously—specifically, to conquer more of India. Britain must pursue this high-minded mission, Mill explained, even though it will be "held up to obloquy" on the continent. Unmentioned was that by doing so, Britain was striking still further devastating blows at India and extending the near-monopoly of opium production that it needed both to force open Chinese markets by violence and to sustain the imperial system more broadly by means of its immense narcotrafficking enterprises, all well known in England at the time. But such matters could not be the source of the "obloquy." Rather, Europeans are "exciting odium against us," Mill wrote, because they are unable to comprehend that England is truly "a novelty in the world," a remarkable nation that acts only "in the service of others." It is dedicated to peace, though if "the aggressions of barbarians force it to a successful war," it selflessly bears the cost while "the fruits it shares in fraternal equality with the whole human race," including the barbarians it conquers and destroys for their own benefit. England is not only peerless but near perfect, in Mill's view, with no "aggressive designs," desiring "no benefit to itself at the expense of others." Its policies are "blameless and laudable." England was the nineteenth-century counterpart of the "idealistic new world bent on ending inhumanity," motivated by pure altruism and uniquely dedicated to the highest "principles and values," though also sadly misunderstood by the cynical or perhaps paranoid Europeans.[73] Mill's essay was written as Britain engaged in some of the worst crimes of its imperial reign. It is hard to think of a more distinguished and truly honorable intellectual—or a more disgraceful example of apologetics for terrible crimes. Such facts might inspire some reflection as Boot and Kagan illustrate Marx's dictum about tragedy replayed as farce. It is also worth recalling that the record of continental imperialism is even worse, and the rhetoric that accompanied it no less glorious, as when France gained Mill's approval by carrying out its civilizing mission in Algeria—while "exterminating the indigenous population," the French minister of war declared.[74]

Kagan's concept of "anti-Americanism," while conventional, also merits reflection. In such pronouncements, the term *anti-American* and its variants ("hating America," and the like) are regularly employed to defame critics of state policy who may admire and respect the country, its culture, and its achievements, indeed think it is the greatest place on earth. Nevertheless, they "hate America" and are "anti-American" on the tacit assumption that the society and its people are to be identified with state power. This usage is drawn directly from the lexicon of totalitarianism. In the former Russian empire, dissidents were guilty of "anti-Sovietism." Perhaps critics of Brazil's military dictatorship were labeled "anti-Brazilian." Among people with some commitment to freedom and democracy, such attitudes are inconceivable. It would only arouse ridicule in Rome or Milan if a critic of Berlusconi's policies were condemned as "anti-Italian," though perhaps it would have passed in Mussolini's day.

It is useful to remember that no matter where we turn, there is rarely any shortage of elevated ideals to accompany the resort to violence. The words accompanying the "Wilsonian tradition" may be stirring in their nobility, but should also be examined in practice, not just rhetoric: for example, Wilson's call for conquest of the Philippines, already mentioned; or as president, his interventions in Haiti and the Dominican Republic that left both countries in ruins; or what Walter LaFeber calls the "Wilson corollary" to the Monroe Doctrine, which dictated "that only American oil interests receive concessions" within the reach of its power.[75]

The same is true of the worst tyrants. In 1990, Saddam Hussein warned Kuwait of possible retribution for actions that were undermining Iraq's battered economy after Iraq had protected Kuwait during the war with Iran. But he assured the world that he wanted not "permanent fighting, but permanent peace . . . and a dignified life."[76] In 1938, President Roosevelt's close confidant Sumner Welles praised the Munich agreement with the Nazis and felt that it might lead to a "new world order based upon justice and upon law." Shortly after, they carried the project forward by occupying parts of Czechoslovakia, while Hitler explained that they were "filled with earnest desire to serve the true interests of the peoples dwelling in this area, to safeguard the national individuality of the German and Czech peoples, and to further the peace and social welfare of all." Mussolini's concerns for the "liberated populations" of Ethiopia were no less exalted. The same was true of Japan's aims in Manchuria and North China and its sacrifices to create an "earthly paradise" for the suffering people and to defend their legitimate governments from Communist "bandits." What could be more moving than Japan's "exalted responsibility" to establish a "New Order" in 1938 to "insure the permanent stability of East Asia" based on "mutual aid" of Japan, Manchuria, and China "in political, economic, and cultural fields," their "joint defence against Communism," and their cultural, economic, and social progress?[77]

After the war, interventions were routinely declared to be "humanitarian" or in self-defense and therefore in accord with the UN Charter: for example, Russia's murderous invasion of Hungary in 1956, justified by Soviet lawyers on the grounds that it was undertaken at the invitation of the government of Hungary as a "defensive response to foreign funding of subversive activities and armed bands within Hungary for purposes of overthrowing the democratically elected government"; or, with comparable plausibility, the U.S. attack against South Vietnam a few years later, undertaken in "collective self-defense" against "internal aggression" by the South Vietnamese and their "assault from the inside" (Adlai Stevenson and John F. Kennedy, respectively).[78]

We need not assume that these protestations are disingenuous, no matter how grotesque they may be. Often one finds the same rhetoric in internal documents, where there is no obvious reason to dissemble: for example, the argument by Stalin's diplomats that "to create real democracies, some outside pressure would be necessary. . . . We should not hesitate to use this kind of 'interference into the domestic affairs' of other nations . . . since democratic government is one of the main guarantees of durable peace."[79]

Others agree, doubtless with no less sincerity, urging that

> we should not hesitate before police repression by the local government. This is not shameful since the Communists are essentially traitors. . . . It is better to have a strong regime in power than a liberal government if it is indulgent and relaxed and penetrated by Communists.

George Kennan, in this case, briefing U.S. ambassadors in Latin America on the need to be guided by a pragmatic concern for "the protection of our raw materials"—ours, wherever they happen to be located, to which we must preserve our inherent "right of access," by conquest if necessary, in accord with the ancient law of nations.[80] It requires a heavy dose of intentional ignorance and loyalty to power to delete from memory the human consequences of instituting and sustaining "strong regimes." The same talents are needed to sustain faith in the appeal to national security invoked to justify the use of force, a pretext that can rarely be upheld for any state, on inspection of the historical and documentary record.

As these few examples illustrate, even the harshest and most shameful measures are regularly accompanied by profession of noble intent. An honest look would only generalize Thomas Jefferson's observation on the world situation of his day:

> We believe no more in Bonaparte's fighting merely for the liberties of the seas, than in Great Britain's fighting for the liberties of mankind. The object is the same, to draw to themselves the power, the wealth, and the resources of other nations.[81]

A century later, Woodrow Wilson's secretary of state, Robert Lansing (who also appears to have had few illusions about Wilsonian idealism), commented scornfully on "how willing the British, French or Italians are to accept a mandate" from the League of Nations, as long as "there are mines, oil fields, rich grain fields or railroads" that will "make it a profitable undertaking." These "unselfish governments" declare that mandates must be accepted "for the good of mankind": "they will do their share by administering the rich regions of Mesopotamia, Syria, &c." The proper assessment of these pretensions is "so manifest that it is almost an insult to state it."[82]

And manifest indeed it is, when declarations of noble intent are proferred by others. For oneself, different standards apply.

One may choose to have selective faith in the domestic political leadership, adopting the stance that Hans Morgenthau, one of the founders of modern international relations theory, condemned as "our conformist subservience to those in power," the regular stance of most intellectuals throughout history.[83] But it is important to recognize that profession of noble intent is predictable, and therefore carries no information, even in the technical sense of the term. Those who are seriously interested in understanding the world will adopt the same standards whether they are evaluating their own political and intellectual elites or those of official enemies. One might fairly ask how much would survive this elementary exercise of rationality and honesty.

It should be added that there are occasional departures from the common stance of subordination to power on the part of the educated classes. Some of the most important current illustrations are to be found in two countries whose harsh and repressive regimes have been sustained by U.S. military aid: Turkey and Colombia. In Turkey, prominent writers, journalists, academics, publishers, and others not only protest atrocities and draconian laws but also carry out regular civil disobedience, facing and sometimes enduring severe and prolonged punishment. In Colombia, courageous priests, academics, human rights and union activists, and others face the constant threat of assassination in one of the world's most violent states.[84] Their actions should elicit humility and shame among their Western counterparts, and would if the truth were not veiled by the intentional ignorance that makes a crucial contribution to ongoing crimes.

25.

Afterword to *Failed States*

No one familiar with history should be surprised that the growing democratic deficit in the United States is accompanied by declaration of messianic missions to bring democracy to a suffering world. Declarations of noble intent by systems of power are rarely complete fabrication, and the same is true in this case. Under some conditions, forms of democracy are indeed acceptable. Abroad, as the leading scholar-advocate of "democracy promotion" concludes, we find a "strong line of continuity": democracy is acceptable *if and only if* it is consistent with strategic and economic interests (Thomas Carothers). In modified form, the doctrine holds at home as well.

The basic dilemma facing policy makers is sometimes candidly recognized at the dovish liberal extreme of the spectrum, for example, by Robert Pastor, President Carter's national security advisor for Latin America. He explained why the administration had to support the murderous and corrupt Somoza regime in Nicaragua, and, when that proved impossible, to try at least to maintain the U.S.-trained National Guard even as it was massacring the population "with a brutality a nation usually reserves for its enemy," killing some forty thousand people. The reason was the familiar one: "The United States did not want to control Nicaragua or the other nations of the region, but it also did not want developments to get out of control. It wanted Nicaraguans to act independently, *except* when doing so would affect U.S. interests adversely."[1]

This chapter first appeared in *Failed States: The Abuse of Power and the Assault on Democracy* (New York: Metropolitan Books, 2006; New York: Owl Books, 2007), 251–63.

Similar dilemmas faced Bush administration planners after their invasion of Iraq. They want Iraqis "to act independently, *except* when doing so would affect U.S. interests adversely." Iraq must therefore be sovereign and democratic, but within limits. It must somehow be constructed as an obedient client state, much in the manner of the traditional order in Central America. At a general level, the pattern is familiar, reaching to the opposite extreme of institutional structures. The Kremlin was able to maintain satellites that were run by domestic political and military forces, with the iron fist poised. Germany was able to do much the same in occupied Europe even while it was at war, as did fascist Japan in Manchuria (its Manchukuo). Fascist Italy achieved similar results in North Africa while carrying out virtual genocide that in no way harmed its favorable image in the West and possibly inspired Hitler. Traditional imperial and neocolonial systems illustrate many variations on similar themes.[2]

To achieve the traditional goals in Iraq has proven to be surprisingly difficult, despite unusually favorable circumstances, as already reviewed. The dilemma of combining a measure of independence with firm control arose in a stark form not long after the invasion, as mass nonviolent resistance compelled the invaders to accept far more Iraqi initiative than they had anticipated. The outcome even evoked the nightmarish prospect of a more or less democratic and sovereign Iraq taking its place in a loose Shiite alliance comprising Iran, Shiite Iraq, and possibly the nearby Shiite-dominated regions of Saudi Arabia, controlling most of the world's oil and independent of Washington.

The situation could get worse. Iran might give up on hopes that Europe could become independent of the United States, and turn eastward. Highly relevant background is discussed by Selig Harrison, a leading specialist on these topics. "The nuclear negotiations between Iran and the European Union were based on a bargain that the EU, held back by the US, has failed to honour," Harrison observes. The bargain was that Iran would suspend uranium enrichment, and the EU would undertake security guarantees. The language of the joint declaration was "unambiguous. 'A mutually acceptable agreement,' it said, would not only provide 'objective guarantees' that Iran's nuclear programme is 'exclusively for peaceful purposes' but would 'equally provide firm commitments on security issues.' "[3]

The phrase "security issues" is a thinly veiled reference to the threats by the United States and Israel to bomb Iran, and preparations to do so. The model regularly adduced is Israel's bombing of Iraq's Osirak reactor in 1981, which appears to have initiated Saddam's nuclear weapons programs, another demonstration that violence tends to elicit violence. Any attempt to execute similar plans against Iran could lead to immediate violence, as is surely understood in Washington. During a visit to Teheran, the influential Shiite cleric Muqtada al-Sadr warned that his militia would defend Iran in the case of any attack, "one of the strongest signs yet," the *Washington Post* reported, "that Iraq could become a battleground in any Western conflict with Iran, raising the specter of Iraqi Shiite militias—or perhaps even the U.S.-trained Shiite-dominated military—taking on American troops here in sympathy with Iran." The Sadrist bloc, which registered substantial gains in the December 2005 elections, may soon become the most powerful single political force in Iraq. It is consciously pursuing the model of other successful Islamist groups, such as Hamas in Palestine, combining strong resistance to military occupation with grassroots social organizing and service to the poor.[4]

Washington's unwillingness to allow regional security issues to be considered is nothing new. It has also arisen repeatedly in the confrontation with Iraq. In the background is the matter of Israeli nuclear weapons, a topic that Washington bars from international consideration. Beyond that lurks what Harrison rightly describes as "the central problem facing the global non-proliferation regime": the failure of the nuclear states to live up to their NPT obligation "to phase out their own nuclear weapons"—and, in Washington's case, formal rejection of the obligation.[5]

Unlike Europe, China refuses to be intimidated by Washington, a primary reason for the growing fear of China on the part of U.S. planners. Much of Iran's oil already goes to China, and China is providing Iran with weapons, presumably considered a deterrent to U.S. threats. Still more uncomfortable for Washington is the fact that "the Sino-Saudi relationship has developed dramatically," including Chinese military aid to Saudi Arabia and gas exploration rights for China. By 2005, Saudi Arabia provided about 17 percent of China's oil imports. Chinese and Saudi oil companies have signed deals for drilling and construction of a huge refinery (with Exxon Mobil as a partner). A January 2006 visit by Saudi King Abdullah to Beijing was expected to lead to a Sino-Saudi memorandum of understanding calling for "increased cooperation and investment between the two countries in oil, natural gas, and minerals."[6]

Indian analyst Aijaz Ahmad observes that Iran could "emerge as the virtual lynchpin in the making, over the next decade or so, of what China and Russia have come to regard as an absolutely indispensable Asian Energy Security Grid, for breaking Western control of the world's energy supplies and securing the great industrial revolution of Asia." South Korea and southeast Asian countries are likely to join, possibly Japan as well. A crucial question is how India will react. It rejected U.S. pressures to withdraw from an oil pipeline deal with Iran. On the other hand, India joined the United States and the EU in voting for an anti-Iranian resolution at the IAEA, joining also in their hypocrisy, since India rejects the NPT regime to which Iran, so far, appears to be largely conforming. Ahmad reports that India may have secretly reversed its stand under Iranian threats to terminate a $20 billion gas deal. Washington later warned India that its "nuclear deal with the US could be ditched" if India did not go along with U.S. demands, eliciting a sharp rejoinder from the Indian foreign ministry and an evasive tempering of the warning by the U.S. embassy.[7]

India too has options. It may choose to be a U.S. client, or it may prefer to join a more independent Asian bloc that is taking shape, with growing ties to Middle East oil producers. In a series of informative commentaries, the deputy editor of the *Hindu* observes that "if the 21st century is to be an 'Asian century,' Asia's passivity in the energy sector has to end." Though it "hosts the world's largest producers and fastest growing consumers of energy," Asia still relies "on institutions, trading frameworks and armed forces from outside the region in order to trade with itself," a debilitating heritage from the imperial era. The key is India-China cooperation. In 2005, he points out, India and China "managed to confound analysts around the world by turning their much-vaunted rivalry for the acquisition of oil and gas assets in third countries into a nascent partnership that could alter the basic dynamics of the global energy market." A January 2006 agreement signed in Beijing "cleared the way for India and China to collaborate not only in technology but also in hydrocarbon exploration and production, a partnership that eventually could alter fundamental equations in the world's oil and natural gas sector." At a meeting in New Delhi of Asian energy producers and consumers a few months earlier, India had "unveiled an ambitious $22.4 billion pan-Asian gas grid and oil security pipeline system" extending throughout all of Asia, from Siberian fields through central Asia and to the Middle East energy giants, also integrating the consumer states. Furthermore, Asian countries "hold more than two trillion dollars worth of foreign reserves," overwhelmingly denominated in dollars, though prudence suggests diversification. A first step, already being contemplated, is an Asian oil market trading in euros. The impact on the international financial system and the balance of global power could be significant. The United States "sees India as the weakest link in the emerging Asian chain," he continues, and is "trying actively to divert New Delhi away from the task of creating new regional architecture by dangling the nuclear carrot and the promise of world power status in alliance with itself." If the Asian project is to succeed, he warns, "India will have to resist these allurements." Similar questions arise with regard to the Shanghai Cooperation Organization formed in 2001 as a Russia-China-based counterweight to the expansion of U.S. power into former Soviet central Asia, now evolving "rapidly toward a regional security bloc [that] could soon induct new members such as India, Pakistan, and Iran," longtime Moscow correspondent Fred Weir reports, perhaps becoming a "Eurasian military confederacy to rival NATO."[8]

The prospect that Europe and Asia might move toward greater independence has seriously troubled U.S. planners since World War II, and concerns have significantly increased as the tripolar order has continued to evolve, along with new south-south interactions and rapidly growing EU engagement with China.[9]

U.S. intelligence has projected that the United States, while controlling Middle East oil for the traditional reasons, will itself rely mainly on more stable Atlantic Basin resources (West Africa, Western Hemisphere). Control of Middle East oil is now far from a sure thing, and these expectations are also threatened by developments in the Western Hemisphere, accelerated by Bush administration policies that have left the United States remarkably isolated in the global arena. The Bush administration has even succeeded in alienating Canada, an impressive feat. Canada's relations with the United States are more "strained and combative" than ever before as a result of Washington's rejection of NAFTA decisions favoring Canada, Joel Brinkley reports. "Partly as a result, Canada is working hard to build up its relationship with China [and] some officials are saying Canada may shift a significant portion of its trade, particularly oil, from the United States to China." Canada's minister of natural resources said that within a few years one-quarter of the oil that Canada now sends to the United States may go to China instead. In a further blow to Washington's energy policies, the leading oil exporter in the hemisphere, Venezuela, has forged probably the closest relations with China of any Latin American country, and is planning to sell increasing amounts of oil to China as part of its effort to reduce dependence on the openly hostile U.S. government. Latin America as a whole is increasing trade and other relations with China, with some setbacks, but likely expansion, in particular for raw materials exporters like Brazil and Chile.[10]

Meanwhile, Cuba-Venezuela relations are becoming very close, each relying on its comparative advantage. Venezuela is providing low-cost oil while in return Cuba organizes literacy and health programs, sending thousands of highly skilled professionals, teachers, and doctors, who work in the poorest and most neglected areas, as they do elsewhere in the Third World. Cuba-Venezuela projects are extending to the Caribbean countries, where Cuban doctors are providing health care to thousands of people with Venezuelan funding. Operation Miracle, as it is called, is described by Jamaica's ambassador to Cuba as "an example of integration and south-south cooperation," and is generating great enthusiasm among the poor majority. Cuban medical assistance is also being welcomed elsewhere. One of the most horrendous tragedies of recent years was the October 2005 earthquake in Pakistan. In addition to the huge toll, unknown numbers of survivors have to face brutal winter weather with little shelter, food, or medical assistance. One has to turn to the South Asian press to read that "Cuba has provided the largest contingent of doctors and paramedics to Pakistan," paying all the costs (perhaps with Venezuelan funding), and that President Musharraf expressed his "deep gratitude" for the "spirit and compassion" of the Cuban medical teams. These are reported to comprise more than one thousand trained personnel, 44 percent of them women, who remained to work in remote mountain villages, "living in tents in freezing weather and in an alien culture" after the Western aid teams had been withdrawn, setting up nineteen field hospitals and working twelve-hour shifts.[11]

Some analysts have suggested that Cuba and Venezuela might even unite, a step towards further integration of Latin America in a bloc that is more independent from the United States. Venezuela has joined Mercosur, the South American customs union, a move described by Argentine president Néstor Kirchner as "a milestone" in the development of this trading bloc, and welcomed as opening "a new chapter in our integration" by Brazilian president Luiz Inácio Lula da Silva. Independent experts say that "adding Venezuela to the bloc furthers its geopolitical vision of eventually spreading Mercosur to the rest of the region." At a meeting to mark Venezuela's entry into Mercosur, Venezuelan president Chávez said, "We cannot allow this to be purely an economic project, one for the elites and for the transnational companies," a not very oblique reference to the U.S.-sponsored "Free Trade Agreement for the Americas," which has aroused strong public opposition. Venezuela also supplied Argentina with fuel oil to help stave off an energy crisis, and bought almost a third of Argentine debt issued in 2005, one element of a region-wide effort to free the countries from the control of the U.S.-dominated IMF after two decades of disastrous effects of conformity to its rules. The IMF has "acted towards our country as a promoter and a vehicle of policies that caused poverty and pain among the Argentine people," President Kirchner said in announcing his decision to pay almost $1 trillion to rid itself of the IMF forever. Radically violating IMF rules, Argentina enjoyed a substantial recovery from the disaster left by IMF policies.[12]

Steps toward independent regional integration advanced further with the election of Evo Morales in Bolivia in December 2005, the first president from the indigenous majority. Morales moved quickly to reach energy accords with Venezuela. The *Financial Times* reported that these "are expected to underpin forthcoming radical reforms to Bolivia's economy and energy sector" with its huge gas reserves, second only to Venezuela's in South America. Morales too committed himself to reverse the neoliberal policies that Bolivia had pursued rigorously for twenty-five years, leaving the country with lower per capita income than at the outset. Adherence to the neoliberal programs was interrupted during this period only when popular discontent compelled the government to abandon them, as when it followed World Bank advice to privatize water supply and "get prices right"—incidentally, to deprive the poor of access to water.[13]

Venezuelan "subversion," as it is described in Washington, is extending to the United States as well. Perhaps that calls for expansion of the policies of "containment" of Venezuela ordered by Bush in March 2005. In November 2005, the *Washington Post* reported, a group of senators sent a letter "to nine big oil companies: With huge increases in winter heating bills expected, the letter read, we want you to donate some of your record profits to help low-income people cover those costs." They received one response: from CITGO, the Venezuelan-controlled company. CITGO offered to provide low-cost oil to low-income residents of Boston, later elsewhere. Chávez is only doing it "for political gain," the State Department responded; it is "somewhat akin to the government of Cuba offering scholarships to medical school in Cuba to disadvantaged American youth." Quite unlike aid from the United States and other countries, which is pure-hearted altruism. It is not clear that these subtleties will be appreciated by the recipients of the "12 million gallons of discounted home-heating oil [provided by CITGO] to local charities and 45,000 low-income families in Massachusetts." The oil is distributed to poor people facing a 30–50 percent rise in oil prices, with fuel assistance "woefully underfunded, so this is a major shot in the arm for people who otherwise wouldn't get through the winter," according to the director of the nonprofit organization that distributes low-cost oil to "homeless shelters, food banks, and low-income housing groups." He also "said he hoped the deal would present 'a friendly challenge' to US oil companies—which recently reported record quarterly profits—to use their windfall to help poor families survive the winter," apparently in vain.[14]

Though Central America was largely disciplined by Reaganite violence and terror, the rest of the hemisphere is falling out of control, particularly from Venezuela to Argentina, which was the poster child of the IMF and the Treasury Department until its economy collapsed under the policies they imposed. Much of the region has left-center governments. The indigenous populations have become much more active and influential, particularly in Bolivia and Ecuador, both major energy producers, where they either want oil and gas to be domestically controlled or, in some cases, oppose production altogether. Many indigenous people apparently do not see any reason why their lives, societies, and cultures should be disrupted or destroyed so that New Yorkers can sit in SUVs in traffic gridlock. Some are even calling for an

"Indian nation" in South America. Meanwhile the economic integration that is under way is reversing patterns that trace back to the Spanish conquests, with Latin American elites and economies linked to the imperial powers but not to one another. Along with growing south-south interaction on a broader scale, these developments are strongly influenced by popular organizations that are coming together in the unprecedented international global justice movements, ludicrously called "anti-globalization" because they favor globalization that privileges the interests of people, not investors and financial institutions. For many reasons, the system of U.S. global dominance is fragile, even apart from the damage inflicted by Bush planners.

One consequence is that the Bush administration's pursuit of the traditional policies of deterring democracy faces new obstacles. It is no longer as easy as before to resort to military coups and international terrorism to overthrow democratically elected governments, as Bush planners learned ruefully in 2002 in Venezuela. The "strong line of continuity" must be pursued in other ways, for the most part. In Iraq, as we have seen, mass nonviolent resistance compelled Washington and London to permit the elections they had sought to evade. The subsequent effort to subvert the elections by providing substantial advantages to the administration's favorite candidate, and expelling the independent media, also failed. Washington faces further problems. The Iraqi labor movement is making considerable progress despite the opposition of the occupation authorities. The situation is rather like Europe and Japan after World War II, when a primary goal of the United States and United Kingdom was to undermine independent labor movements—as at home, for similar reasons: organized labor contributes in essential ways to functioning democracy with popular engagement. Many of the measures adopted at that time—withholding food, supporting fascist police—are no longer available. Nor is it possible today to rely on the labor bureaucracy of AIFLD to help undermine unions. Today, some American unions are supporting Iraqi workers, just as they do in Colombia, where more union activists are murdered than anywhere in the world. At least the unions now receive support from the United Steelworkers of America and others, while Washington continues to provide enormous funding for the government, which bears a large part of the responsibility.[15]

The problem of elections arose in Palestine much in the way it did in Iraq. As already discussed, the Bush administration refused to permit elections until the death of Yasser Arafat, aware that the wrong man would win. After his death, the administration agreed to permit elections, expecting the victory of its favored Palestinian Authority candidates. To promote this outcome, Washington resorted to much the same modes of subversion as in Iraq, and often before. Washington used USAID as an "invisible conduit" in an effort to "increase the popularity of the Palestinian Authority on the eve of crucial elections in which the governing party faces a serious challenge from the radical Islamic group Hamas," spending almost $2 million "on dozens of quick projects before elections this week to bolster the governing Fattah faction's image with voters." In the United States, or any Western country, even a hint of such foreign interference would destroy a candidate, but deeply rooted imperial mentality legitimates such routine measures elsewhere. However, the attempt to subvert the elections again resoundingly failed.[16]

The U.S. and Israeli governments now have to adjust to dealing somehow with a radical Islamic party that approaches their traditional rejectionist stance, though not entirely, at least if Hamas really does mean to agree to an indefinite truce on the international border as its leaders state. The United States and Israel, in contrast, insist that Israel must take over substantial parts of the West Bank (and the forgotten Golan Heights). Hamas's refusal to accept Israel's "right to exist" mirrors the refusal of Washington and Jerusalem to accept Palestine's "right to exist"—a concept unknown in international affairs; Mexico accepts the existence of the United States but not its abstract "right to exist" on almost half of Mexico, acquired by conquest. Hamas's formal commitment to "destroy Israel" places it on a par with the United States and Israel, which vowed formally that there could be no "additional Palestinian state" (in addition to Jordan) until they relaxed their extreme rejectionist stand partially in the past few years, in the manner already reviewed. Although Hamas has not said so, it would come as no great surprise if Hamas were to agree that Jews may remain in scattered areas in the present Israel, while Palestine constructs huge settlement and infrastructure projects to take over the valuable land and resources, effectively breaking Israel up into unviable cantons, virtually separated from one another and from some small part of Jerusalem where Jews would also be allowed to remain. And they might agree to call the fragments "a state." If such proposals were made, we would—rightly—regard them as virtually a reversion to Nazism, a fact that might elicit some thoughts. If such proposals were made, Hamas's position would be essentially like that of the United States and Israel for the past five years, after they came to tolerate some impoverished form of "statehood." It is fair to describe Hamas as radical, extremist, and violent, and as a serious threat to peace and a just political settlement. But the organization is hardly alone in this stance.

Elsewhere traditional means of undermining democracy have succeeded. In Haiti, the Bush administration's favorite "democracy-building group, the International Republican Institute," worked assiduously to promote the opposition to President Aristide, helped by the withholding of desperately needed aid on grounds that were dubious at best. When it seemed that Aristide would probably win any genuine election, Washington and the opposition chose to withdraw, a standard device to discredit elections that are going to come out the wrong way: Nicaragua in 1984 and Venezuela in December 2005 are examples that should be familiar. Then followed a military coup, expulsion of the president, and a reign of terror and violence vastly exceeding anything under the elected government.[17]

The persistence of the strong line of continuity to the present again reveals that the United States is very much like other powerful states. It pursues the strategic and economic interests of dominant sectors of the domestic population, to the accompaniment of rhetorical flourishes about its dedication to the highest values. That is practically a historical universal, and the reason why sensible people pay scant attention to declarations of noble intent by leaders, or accolades by their followers.

One commonly hears that carping critics complain about what is wrong, but do not present solutions. There is an accurate translation for that charge: "They present solutions, but I don't like them." In addition to the proposals that should be familiar about dealing with the crises that reach to the level of survival, a few simple suggestions for the United States have already been mentioned: (1) accept the jurisdiction of the International Criminal Court and the World Court; (2) sign and carry forward the Kyoto protocols; (3) let the UN take the lead in international crises; (4) rely on diplomatic and economic measures rather than military ones in confronting terror; (5) keep to the traditional interpretation of the UN Charter; (6) give up the Security Council veto and have "a decent respect for the opinion of mankind," as the Declaration of Independence advises, even if power centers disagree; (7) cut back sharply on military spending and sharply increase social spending. For people who believe in democracy, these are very conservative suggestions: they appear to be the opinions of the majority of the U.S. population, in most cases the overwhelming majority. They are in radical opposition to public policy. To be sure, we cannot be very confident about the state of public opinion on such matters because of another feature of the democratic deficit: the topics scarcely enter into public discussion and the basic facts are little known. In a highly atomized society, the public is therefore largely deprived of the opportunity to form considered opinions.

Another conservative suggestion is that facts, logic, and elementary moral principles should matter. Those who take the trouble to adhere to that suggestion will soon be led to abandon a good part of familiar doctrine, though it is surely much easier to repeat self-serving mantras. Such simple truths carry us some distance toward developing more specific and detailed answers. More important, they open the way to implement them, opportunities that are readily within our grasp if we can free ourselves from the shackles of doctrine and imposed illusion.

Though it is natural for doctrinal systems to seek to induce pessimism, hopelessness, and despair, reality is different. There has been substantial progress in the unending quest for justice and freedom in recent years, leaving a legacy that can be carried forward from a higher plane than before. Opportunities for education and organizing abound. As in the past, rights are not likely to be granted by benevolent authorities, or won by intermittent actions—attending a few demonstrations or pushing a lever in the personalized quadrennial extravaganzas that are depicted as "democratic politics." As always in the past, the tasks require dedicated day-by-day engagement to create—in part re-create—the basis for a functioning democratic culture in which the public plays some role in determining policies, not only in the political arena, from which it is largely excluded, but also in the crucial economic arena, from which it is excluded in principle. There are many ways to promote democracy at home, carrying it to new dimensions. Opportunities are ample, and failure to grasp them is likely to have ominous repercussions: for the country, for the world, and for future generations.

Acknowledgments

Thanks to André Schiffrin, Ellen Adler, Colin Robinson, Marc Favreau, Sarah Fan, The New Press, Dao Tran, Sean Petty, Brenda Coughlin, James Peck, dix!, and Sara Bershtel. Thanks also to the many people who originally worked to edit and publish and those who granted permission to include the materials included in this collection.

Permissions

Chapter 1 first appeared in the journal *Language* 35:1 (January–March 1959), 26–58. Copyright 1959. Permission courtesy of the Linguistic Society of America.

Chapter 2 first appeared in *Aspects of the Theory of Syntax* (Cambridge, MA: MIT Press, 1965), v–vii. Copyright 1965 The Massachusetts Institute of Technology. Permission courtesy of The MIT Press.

Chapter 3 first appeared as part 1 of "Methodological Preliminaries," in *Aspects of the Theory of Syntax* (Cambridge, MA: MIT Press, 1965), 3–9. Copyright 1965 The Massachusetts Institute of Technology. Permission courtesy of The MIT Press.

Chapter 4 is a revised version of a talk given at Harvard and published in *Mosaic*, June 1966. It appeared in substantially this form in the *New York Review of Books*, February 23, 1967. The present version is reprinted from Theodore Roszak, ed., *The Dissenting Academy* (New York: Pantheon Books, 1968), reprinted in *American Power and the New Mandarins* (New York: Pantheon Books, 1969; New York: The New Press, 2002), 323–66. Copyright 1969 and 2002 Noam Chomsky. Permission courtesy of The New Press.

Chapter 5 first appeared in the *New York Review of Books*, December 7, 1967. This chapter is reprinted from *American Power and the New Mandarins* (New York: Pantheon Books, 1969; New York: The New Press, 2002), 367–85. Copyright 1969 and 2002 Noam Chomsky. Permission courtesy of The New Press.

Chapter 6 was presented as a lecture at the University Freedom and Human Sciences Symposium, Loyola University, Chicago, January 8–9, 1970. It appeared in the Proceedings of the Symposium, edited by Thomas R. Gorman. It also was published in *Abraxas*, vol. 1, no. 1 (1970), and in *TriQuarterly*, nos. 23–24 (1972). This chapter reprinted in *For Reasons of State* (New York: Pantheon Books, 1973; New York: The New Press, 2003), 387–408. Copyright 1973 and 2003 Noam Chomsky. Permission courtesy of The New Press.

Chapter 7 is a revised version of the introduction to Daniel Guérin's *Anarchism: From Theory to Practice* (New York: Monthly Review Press, 1970). In a slightly different version, it appeared in the *New York Review of Books*, May 21, 1970, reprinted in *For Reasons of State* (New York: Pantheon Books, 1973; New York: The New Press, 2003), 370–86. Copyright 1973 and 2003 Noam Chomsky. Permission courtesy of The New Press.

Chapter 8 is a revised version of a contribution to a symposium on war crimes, based on Telford Taylor, *Nuremberg and Vietnam: An American Tragedy*. The original version was published in the *Yale Law Journal*, vol. 80, no. 7 (June 1971), reprinted in *For Reasons of State* (New York: Pantheon Books, 1973; New York: The New Press, 2003), 212–58. Copyright 1973 and 2003 Noam Chomsky. Permission courtesy of The New Press.

Chapter 9 first appeared in the *New York Review of Books* 20:14 (September 20, 1973), 3–8. Copyright 1973 New York Review of Books. Permission courtesy of *New York Review of Books*.

Chapter 10 first appeared in *Towards a New Cold War: U.S. Foreign Policy from Vietnam to Reagan* (New York: Pantheon Books, 1982; New York: The New Press, 2003), 144–64. Copyright 1982 Noam Chomsky and 2003 Aviva Chomsky, Diane Chomsky, and Harry Chomsky. Permission courtesy of The New Press.

Chapter 11 first appeared in *"Human Rights" and American Foreign Policy* (Nottingham: Spokesman, 1978) and reprinted in *Towards a New Cold War* (New York: Pantheon Books, 1982; New York: The New Press, 2003), 86–114. Copyright 1982 Noam Chomsky and 2003 Aviva Chomsky, Diane Chomsky, and Harry Chomsky. Permission courtesy of The New Press.

Chapter 12 first appeared in *Towards a New Cold War: U.S. Foreign Policy from Vietnam to Reagan* (New York: Pantheon Books, 1982; New York: The New Press, 2003), 358–69. Copyright 1982 Noam Chomsky and 2003 Aviva Chomsky, Diane Chomsky, and Harry Chomsky. Permission courtesy of The New Press.

Chapter 13 first appeared in *Fateful Triangle: The United States, Israel, and the Palestinians* (Cambridge, MA: South End Press, 1983; expanded edition Cambridge, MA: South End Press, 1999), 9–37. Copyright 1983 and 1999 Noam Chomsky. Permission courtesy of South End Press and Pluto Press.

Chapter 14 first appeared in *Turning the Tide: U.S. Intervention in Central America and the Struggle for Peace* (Cambridge, MA: South End Press, 1985), 62–73. Copyright 1985 and 1987 Noam Chomsky. Permission courtesy of South End Press and Pluto Press.

Chapter 15 first appeared in *Language and Problems of Knowledge: The Managua Lectures* (Cambridge, MA: MIT Press, 1988), 133–70. Copyright

1988 Massachusetts Institute of Technology. Permission courtesy of The MIT Press.

Chapter 16 first appeared in *Necessary Illusions: Thought Control in Democratic Societies* (Cambridge, MA: South End Press, 1989), 21–43. Copyright 1989 Noam Chomsky. Permission courtesy of House of Anansi, South End Press, and Pluto Press.

Chapter 17 first appeared in *The Minimalist Program* (Cambridge, MA: MIT Press, 1995), 1–11. Copyright 1995 Massachusetts Institute of Technology. Permission courtesy of The MIT Press.

Chapter 18 appeared in *New Horizons in the Study of Language and Mind* (Cambridge: Cambridge University Press, 2000), 3–18. Copyright 2000 Diane Chomsky Irrevocable Trust. Permission courtesy of Cambridge University Press.

Chapter 19 first appeared in *A New Generation Draws the Line: Kosovo, East Timor and the Standards of the West* (London: Verso, 2000), 1–47. Copyright 2000 Noam Chomsky. Permission courtesy of the author.

Chapter 20 is the written version of the opening address of the World Social Forum on January 31, 2002, in Porto Alegre, Brazil, and appeared on ZNet on May 29, 2002; reprinted in C. P. Otero, ed., *Radical Priorities*, 3rd ed. (Oakland: AK Press, 2003), 319–32. Copyright 2003 Noam Chomsky. Permission courtesy of AK Press.

Chapter 21 first appeared in *Aftonbladet* in Sweden, August 2002, reprinted in *9–11* (New York: Seven Stories Press, 2002), 119–28. Copyright 2002 Noam Chomsky. Permission courtesy of Seven Stories Press.

Chapter 22 first appeared in *On Nature and Language*, ed. Adriana Belletti and Luigi Rizzi (Cambridge: Cambridge University Press, 2002), 61–91. Copyright 2002 Noam Chomsky, Adriana Belletti, and Luigi Rizzi. Permission courtesy of Cambridge University Press.

Chapter 23 first appeared in *Middle East Illusions* (Lanham, MD: Rowman & Littlefield Publishers, 2003), 227–32. Copyright 2003 Noam Chomsky. Permission courtesy of Rowman & Littlefield Publishers.

Chapter 24 first appeared in *Hegemony or Survival: America's Quest for Global Dominance* (New York: Metropolitan Books, 2003; New York: Owl Books, 2004), 11–49. Copyright 2003 Aviva Chomsky, Diane Chomsky, and Harry Chomsky. Permission courtesy of Henry Holt, Inc.

Chapter 25 first appeared in *Failed States: The Abuse of Power and the Assault on Democracy* (New York: Metropolitan Books, 2006; New York: Owl Books, 2007), 251–63. Copyright 2006 Chomsky Grandchildren Nominee Trust. Permission courtesy of Henry Holt, Inc.

Notes

In some chapters, the numbering and format of the endnotes has been altered from the original for consistency of style.

FOREWORD

1. Noam Chomsky's essays in the *New York Review of Books* are all available online at the magazine's website (www.nybooks.com), though some are available only to subscribers. See also Noam Chomsky, *Hegemony or Survival: America's Quest for Global Dominance*, expanded edition (New York: Owl Books, 2004), *Failed States: The Abuse of Power and the Assault on Democracy* (New York: Owl Books, 2007), and *Interventions* (San Francisco: City Lights Books/Open Media Series, 2007).

2. Noam Chomsky, "The Responsibility of Intellectuals," *American Power and the New Mandarins* (New York: Pantheon Books, 1969; New York: The New Press, 2002), 313. See also Noam Chomsky, *At War with Asia* (New York: Pantheon Books, 1970; Oakland: AK Press, 2003).

3. Noam Chomsky, interview by James Peck in *The Chomsky Reader* (New York: Pantheon Books, 1987), 13.

4. Quoted in Milan Rai, *Chomsky's Politics* (London: Verso, 1995), 8.

5. Noam Chomsky, quoted in Robert F. Barsky, *Noam Chomsky: A Life of Dissent* (Cambridge, MA: MIT Press, 1997), 80.

6. See, for example, Noam Chomsky, *The Minimalist Program* (Cambridge, MA: MIT Press, 1995).

1. A REVIEW OF B. F. SKINNER'S *VERBAL BEHAVIOR*

1. Skinner's confidence in recent achievements in the study of animal behavior and their applicability to complex human behavior does not appear to be widely shared. In many recent publications of confirmed behaviorists there is a prevailing note of skepticism with regard to the scope of these achievements. For representative comments, see the contributions to *Modern Learning Theory* by W. Estes et al. (New York: Appleton-Century-Crofts, 1954); B. R. Bugelski, *Psychology of Learning* (New York: Holt, 1956); S. Koch, in *Nebraska Symposium on Motivation*, vol. 58 (Lincoln, 1956); W. S. Verplanck, "Learned and Innate Behavior," *Psychological Review* 52 (1955): 139. Perhaps the strongest view is that of H. Harlow who has asserted ("Mice, Monkeys, Men, and Motives," *Psychological Review* 60 [1953]: 26–32) that "strong case

can be made for the proposition that the importance of the psychological problems studied during the last 15 years has decreased as a negatively accelerated function approaching an asymptote of complete indifference." N. Tinbergen, a leading representative of a different approach to animal behavior studies (comparative ethology), concludes a discussion of "functional analysis" with the comment that "we may now draw the conclusion that the causation of behavior is immensely more complex than was assumed in the generalisations of the past. A number of internal and external factors act upon complex central nervous structures. Second, it will be obvious that the facts at our disposal are very fragmentary indeed"—*The Study of Instinct* (Oxford: Clarendon Press, 1951), 74.

2. In *Behavior of Organisms* (New York: D. Appleton-Century Company, 1938), Skinner remarks that "although a conditioned operant is the result of the correlation of the response with a particular reinforcement, a relation between it and a discriminative stimulus acting prior to the response is the almost universal rule" (178–79). Even emitted behavior is held to be produced by some sort of "originating force" (51) which, in the case of operant behavior is not under experimental control. The distinction between eliciting stimuli, discriminated stimuli, and "originating forces" has never been adequately clarified, and becomes even more confusing when private internal events are considered to be discriminated stimuli (see below).

3. In a famous experiment, chimpanzees were taught to perform complex tasks to receive tokens which had become secondary reinforcers because of association with food. The idea that money, approval, prestige, etc., actually acquire their motivating effects on human behavior according to this paradigm is unproved, and not particularly plausible. Many psychologists within the behaviorist movement are quite skeptical about this (cf. fn. 23). As in the case of most aspects of human behavior, the evidence about secondary reinforcement is so fragmentary, conflicting, and complex that almost any view can find some support.

4. Skinner's remark quoted above about the generality of his basic results must be understood in the light of the experimental limitations he has imposed. If it were true in any deep sense that the basic processes in language are well understood and free of species restrictions, it would be extremely odd that language is limited to man. With the exception of a few scattered observations (cf. his article, "A Case History in Scientific Method, *American Psychologist* 11 [1956]: 221–33), Skinner is apparently basing this claim on the fact that qualitatively similar results are obtained with bar-pressing of rats and pecking of pigeons under special conditions of deprivation and various schedules of reinforcement. One immediately questions how much can be based on these facts, which are in part at least an artifact traceable to experimental design and the definition of "stimulus" and "response" in terms of "smooth dynamic curves" (see below). The dangers inherent in any attempt to "extrapolate" to complex behavior from the study of such simple responses as bar-pressing should be obvious, and have often been commented on (cf. e.g., Harlow, op. cit.). The generality of even the simplest results is open to serious question. Cf. in this connection M. E. Bitterman, J. Wodinsky, and D. K. Candland, "Some Comparative Psychology," *The American Journal of Psychiatry* 71 (1958): 94–110, where it is shown that there are important qualitative differences in solution of comparable elementary problems by rats and fish.

5. An analogous argument, in connection with a different aspect of Skinner's thinking, is given by M. Scriven in "A Study of Radical Behaviorism," in H. Fiegl and M. Scriven, eds., *Minnesota Studies in the Philosophy of Science*, vol. 1, *Foundations of Science & the Concepts of Psychology and Psychoanalysis* (Minneapolis: University of Minnesota Press, 1956). Cf. W. S. Verplanck's contribution to *Modern Learning Theory* (283–88) for more general discussion of the difficulties in formulating an adequate definition of 'stimulus' and "response.' He concludes, quite correctly, that in Skinner's sense of the word, stimuli are not objectively identifi-

able independently of the resulting behavior, nor are they manipulable. Verplanck presents a clear discussion of many other aspects of Skinner's system, commenting on the untestability of many of the so-called "laws of behavior" and the limited scope of many of the others, and the arbitrary and obscure character of Skinner's notion of "lawful relation"; and, at the same time, noting the importance of the experimental data that Skinner has accumulated.

6. In *Behavior of Organisms,* Skinner apparently was willing to accept this consequence. He insists (41–42) that the terms of casual description in the popular vocabulary are not validly descriptive until the defining properties of stimulus and response are specified, the correlation is demonstrated experimentally, and the dynamic changes in it are shown to be lawful. Thus, in describing a child as hiding from a dog, "It will not be enough to dignify the popular vocabulary by appealing to essential properties of 'dogness' or 'hidingness' and to suppose them intuitively known." But this is exactly what Skinner does in the book under review, as we will see directly.

7. 253f. and elsewhere, repeatedly. As an example of how well we can control behavior using the notions developed in this book, Skinner shows here how he would go about evoking the response *pencil.* The most effective way, he suggests, is to say to the subject "Please say *pencil* "(our chances would, presumably, be even further improved by use of "aversive stimulation," e.g., holding a gun to his head). We can also "make sure that no pencil or writing instrument is available, then hand our subject a pad of paper appropriate to pencil sketching, and offer him a handsome reward for a recognizable picture of a cat." It would also be useful to have voices saying *pencil* or *pen and* . . . in the background; signs reading *pencil* or *pen and* . . . ; or to place a "large and unusual pencil in an unusual place clearly in sight." Under such circumstances, it is highly probable that our subject will say *pencil.*" "The available techniques are all illustrated in this sample." These, contributions of behavior theory to the practical control of human behavior are amply illustrated elsewhere in the book, as when Skinner shows (113–14) how we can evoke the response *red* (the device suggested is to hold a red object before the subject and say "Tell me what color this is.").

In fairness, it must be mentioned that there are certain nontrivial applications of "operant conditioning" to the control of human behavior. A wide variety of experiments have shown that the number of plural nouns (for example) produced by a subject will increase if the experimenter says "right" or "good" when one is produced (similarly, positive attitudes on a certain issue, stories with particular content, etc.; cf. L. Krasner, "Studies of the Conditioning of Verbal Behavior," *Psychological Bulletin* 55 [1958], for a survey of several dozen experiments of this kind, mostly with positive results). It is of some interest that the subject is usually unaware of the process. Just what insight this gives into normal verbal behavior is not obvious. Nevertheless, it is an example of positive and not totally expected results using the Skinnerian paradigm.

8. "Are Theories of Learning Necessary?" *Psychological Review* 57 (1950): 193–216.

9. And elsewhere. In his paper "Are Theories of Learning Necessary?," Skinner considers the problem how to extend his analysis of behavior to experimental situations in which it is impossible to observe frequencies, rate of response being the only valid datum. His answer is that "the notion of probability is usually extrapolated to cases in which a frequency analysis cannot be carried out. In the field of behavior we arrange a situation in which frequencies are available as data, but we use the notion of probability in analyzing or formulating instances of even types of behavior which are not susceptible to this analysis" (199). There are, of course, conceptions of probability not based directly on frequency, but I do not see how any of these apply to the cases that Skinner has in mind. I see no way of interpreting the quoted passage other than as signifying an intention to use the word "probability" in describing behavior quite independently of whether the notion of probability is at all relevant.

10. Fortunately, "In English this presents no great difficulty" since, for example, "relative pitch levels . . . are not . . . important" (25). No reference is made to the numerous studies of the function of relative pitch levels and other intonational features in English.

11. The vagueness of the word "tendency," as opposed to "frequency," saves the latter quotation from the obvious incorrectness of the former. Nevertheless, a good deal of stretching is necessary. If "tendency" has anything like its ordinary meaning, the remark is clearly false. One may believe strongly the assertion that Jupiter has four moons, that many of Sophocles' plays have been irretrievably lost, that the earth will burn to a crisp in ten million years, etc., without experiencing the slightest tendency to set upon these verbal stimuli. We may, of course, turn Skinner's assertion into a very unilluminating truth by defining "tendency to act" to include tendencies to answer questions in certain ways, under motivation to say what one believes is true.

12. One should add, however, that it is in general not the stimulus as such that is reinforcing, but the stimulus in a particular situational context. Depending on experimental arrangement, a particular physical event or object may be reinforcing, punishing, or unnoticed. Because Skinner limits himself to a particular, very simple experimental arrangement, it is not necessary for him to add this qualification, which would not be at all easy to formulate precisely. But it is of course necessary if he expects to extend his descriptive system to behavior in general.

13. This has been frequently noted.

14. See, for example, "Are Theories of Learning Necessary?," 199. Elsewhere, he suggests that the term "learning" be restricted to complex situations, but these are not characterized.

15. "A child acquires verbal behavior when relatively unpatterned vocalisations, selectively reinforced, gradually assume forms which produce appropriate consequences in a given verbal community" (31). "Differential reinforcement shapes up all verbal forms and when a prior stimulus enters into the contingency, reinforcement is responsible for its resulting control . . . The availability of behavior, its probability or strength, depends on whether reinforcements *continue* in effect and according to what schedules" (203–4). Elsewhere, frequently.

16. Talk of schedules of reinforcement here is entirely pointless. How are we to decide, for example, according to what schedules covert reinforcement is "arranged," as in thinking or verbal fantasy, or what the scheduling is of such factors as silence, speech, and appropriate future reactions to communicated information?

17. See, for example, N. Miller and J. Dollard, *Social Learning and Imitation* (New Haven: Institute of Human Relations, 1941), 82–83, for a discussion of the "meticulous training" that they seem to consider necessary for a child to learn the meanings of words and syntactic patterns. The same notion is implicit in O. H. Mowrer's speculative account of how language might be acquired, in *Learning Theory and Personality Dynamics* (New York: Ronald Press, 1950), chap. 23. Actually, the view appears to be quite general.

18. For a general review and analysis of this literature, see D. Thistlethwaite, "A Critical Review of Latent Learning and Related Experiments," *Psychological Bulletin* 48 (1951): 97–129. K. MacCorquodale and P. E. Meehl, in their contribution to *Modern Learning Theory*, carry out a serious and considered attempt to handle the latent learning material from the standpoint of drive reduction theory, with (as they point out) not entirely satisfactory results. W. H. Thorpe reviews the literature from the standpoint of the ethologist, adding also material on homing and topographical orientation *(Learning and Instinct in Animals* [Cambridge: Methuen, 1956]).

19. E. R. Hilgard, *Theories of Learning* (New York: Appleton-Century-Crofts, 1956), 214.

20. D. E. Berlyne, "Novelty and Curiosity as Determinants of Exploratory Behavior," *British Journal of Psychiatry* 41 (1950): 68–80; id., "Perceptual Curiosity in the Rat," *Journal of*

Comparative Physiology and Psychiatry 48 (1955): 238–46; W. R. Thompson and L. M. Solomon, "Spontaneous Pattern Discrimination in the Rat," *Journal of Comparative Physiology and Psychiatry* 47 (1954): 104–7.

21. K. C. Montgomery, "The Role of the Exploratory Drive in Learning," *Journal of Comparative Physiology and Psychiatry* 47 (1954): 60–63. Many other papers in the same journal are designed to show that exploratory behavior is a relatively independent primary "drive" aroused by novel external stimulation.

22. R. A. Butler, "Discrimination Learning by Rhesus Monkeys to Visual-Exploration Motivation," *Journal of Comparative Physiology and Psychiatry* (1953): 95–98. Later experiments showed that this "drive" is highly persistent, as opposed to derived drives which rapidly extinguish.

23. H. F. Harlow, M. K. Harlow, and D. R. Meyer, "Learning Motivated by a Manipulation Drive," *Journal of Experimental Psychology* 40 (1950): 228–34, and later investigations initiated by Harlow. Harlow has been particularly insistent on maintaining the inadequacy of physiologically based drives and homeostatic need states for explaining the persistence of motivation and rapidity of learning in primates. He points out, in many papers, that curiosity, play, exploration, and manipulation are, for primates, often more potent drives than hunger and the like, and that they show none of the characteristics of acquired drives. D. O. Hebb also presents behavioral and supporting neurological evidence in support of the view that in higher animals there is a positive attraction in work, risk, puzzle, intellectual activity, mild fear and frustration, etc. ("Drives and the CNS," *Psychological Review* 62 [1955]: 243–54). He concludes that "we need not work out tortuous and improbable ways to explain why men work for money, why children learn without pain, why people dislike doing nothing."

In a brief note ("Early Recognition of the Manipulative Drive in Monkeys," *British Journal of Animal Behaviour* 3 [1955]: 71–72), W. Dennis calls attention to the fact that early investigators (Romanes, 1882; Thorndike, 1901), whose "perception was relatively unaffected by learning theory, did note the intrinsically motivated behavior of monkeys," although, he asserts, no similar observations on monkeys have been made until Harlow's experiments. He quotes G. J. Romanes *(Animal Intelligence* [1882]) as saying that "much the most striking feature in the psychology of this animal, and the one which is least like anything met with in other animals, was the tireless spirit of investigation." Analogous developments, in which genuine discoveries have blinded systematic investigators to the important insights of earlier work, are easily found within recent structural linguistics as well.

24. Thus J. S. Brown, in commenting on a paper of Harlow's in *Current Theory and Research in Motivation* (Lincoln: University of Nebraska Press, 1953), argues that "in probably every instance [of the experiments cited by Harlow] an ingenious drive-reduction theorist could find some fragment of fear, insecurity, frustration, or whatever, that he could insist was reduced and hence was reinforcing (53). The same sort of thing could be said for the ingenious phlogiston or ether theorist.

25. Cf. H. G. Birch and M. E. Bitterman, "Reinforcement and Learning: The Process of Sensory Integration," *Psychological Review* 56 (1949): 292–308.

26. See, for example, his paper "A Physiological Study of Reward" in D. C. McClelland, ed., *Studies in Motivation*, 134–43 (New York: Appleton Century-Crofts, 1955).

27. See Thorpe, op. cit., particularly 115–18 and 337–76, for an excellent discussion of this phenomenon, which has been brought to prominence particularly by the work of K. Lorenz (cf. *Der Kumpan in der Umwelt des Vogels*, parts of which are reprinted in C. H. Schiller, ed., English translation in *Instinctive Behavior*, 83–128 (New York: International Universities Press, 1967).

28. Op. cit. 372.

29. See e.g., J. Jaynes, "Imprinting: Interaction of Learned and Innate Behavior," *Journal of Comparative Physiology and Psychiatry* 49 (1956): 201–6, where the conclusion is reached that "the experiments prove that without any observable reward young birds of this species follow a moving stimulus object and very rapidly come to prefer that object to others."

30. Of course it is perfectly possible to incorporate this fact within the Skinnerian framework. If, for example, a child watches an adult using a comb and then, with no instruction tries to comb his own hair, we can explain this act by saying that he performs it because he finds it reinforcing to do so, or because of the reinforcement provided by behaving like a person who is "reinforcing" (cf. 164). Similarly, an automatic explanation is available for any other behavior. It seems strange at first that Skinner pays so little attention to the literature on latent learning and related topics, considering the tremendous reliance that he places on the notion of reinforcement; I have seen no reference to it in his writings. Similarly, F. S. Keller and W. N. Schoenfeld, in what appears to be the only text written under predominantly Skinnerian influence, *Principles of Psychology* (New York: Appleton-Century-Crofts, 1956), dismiss the latent-learning literature in one sentence as "beside the point," serving only "to obscure, rather than clarify, a fundamental principle" (the law of effect, 41). However, this neglect is perfectly appropriate in Skinner's case. To the drive-reductionist, or anyone else for whom the notion "reinforcement" has some substantive meaning, these experiments and observations are important (and often embarrassing). But in the Skinnerian sense of the word, neither these results nor any conceivable others can cast any doubt on the claim that reinforcement is essential for the acquisition and maintenance of behavior. Behavior certainly has some concomitant circumstances, and whatever they are, we can call them "reinforcement."

31. Tinbergen (op. cit., chap. VI) reviews some aspects of this problem, discussing the primary role of maturation in the development of many complex motor patterns (e.g., flying, swimming) in lower organisms, and the effect of an "innate disposition to learn" in certain specific ways and at certain specific times. Cf. also Schiller, *Instinctive Behavior*, 285–88, for a discussion of the role of maturing motor patterns in apparently insightful behavior in the chimpanzee.

E. H. Lenneberg (*Language, Evolution, and Purposive Behavior*, unpublished) presents a very interesting discussion of the part that biological structure may play in the acquisition of language, and the dangers in neglecting this possibility.

32. From among many cited by Tinbergen op. cit. (this on page 85).

33. Cf. K. S. Lashley, "In Search of the Engram," *Symposium of the Society for Experimental Biology* 4 (1950): 454–82. R. Sperry, "On the Neural Basis of the Conditioned Response," *British Journal of Animal Behavior* 3 (1955): 41–44, argues that to account for the experimental results of Lashley and others, and for other facts that he cites, it is necessary to assume that high-level cerebral activity of the type of insight, expectancy, etc., is involved even in simple conditioning. He states that "we still lack today a satisfactory picture of the underlying neural mechanism" of the conditioned response.

34. Furthermore, the motivation on the speaker does not, except in the simplest cases, correspond in intensity to the duration of deprivation. An obvious counter-example is what D. O. Hebb has called the "salted-nut phenomenon" (*Organization of Behavior* [New York: Wiley, 1949], 199). The difficulty is of course even more serious when we consider "deprivations" not related to physiological drives.

35. Just as he may have the appropriate reaction, both emotional and behavioral, to such utterances as *The volcano is erupting* or *There's a homicidal maniac in the next room* without any

previous pairing of the verbal and the physical stimulus. Skinner's discussion of Pavlovian conditioning in language (154) is similarly unconvincing.

36. J. S. Mill, *A System of Logic* (1843). R. Carnap gives a recent reformulation in "Meaning and Synonymy in Natural Languages," *Philosophical Studies* 6 (1955): 33–47, defining the meaning (intension) of a predicate "Q" for a speaker X as "the general condition which an object y must fulfill in order for X to be willing to ascribe the predicate 'Q' to y. The connotation of an expression is often said to constitute its "cognitive meaning" as opposed to its "emotive meaning," which is, essentially, the emotional reaction to the expression.

Whether or not this is the best way to approach meaning, it is clear that denotation, cognitive meaning, and emotive meaning are quite different things. The differences are often obscured in empirical studies of meaning, with much consequent confusion. Thus C. E. Osgood has set himself the task of accounting for the fact that a stimulus comes to be a sign for another stimulus (a) busser becomes a sign for food, a word for a thing, etc.). This is clearly (for linguistic signs) a problem of denotation. The method that he actually develops for quantifying and measuring meaning (cf. Osgood, G. J. Suci, and P. H. Tannenbaum, *The Measurement of Meaning* [Urbana: University of Illinois Press, 1957]) applies, however, only to emotive meaning. Suppose, for example, that A hates both Hitler and science intensely, and considers both highly potent and "active," while B, agreeing with A about Hitler, likes science very much, although he considers it rather ineffective and not too important. Then A may assign to "Hitler" and "science" the same position on the semantic differential, while B will assign "Hitler" the same position as A did, but 'science' a totally different position. Yet A does not think that "Hitler" and "science" are synonymous or that they have the same reference, and A and B may agree precisely on the cognitive meaning of "science." Clearly it is the attitude toward the things (the emotive meaning of the words) that is being measured here. There is a gradual shift in Osgood's account from denotation to cognitive meaning to emotive meaning. The confusion is caused, no doubt, by the fact that the term "meaning" is used in all three senses (and others). (See J. B. Carroll's review of the book by Osgood, Suci, and Tannenbaum in *Language* 35:1 [January-March 1959]).

37. Most clearly by W. V. Quine. See *From a Logical Point of View* (Cambridge: Harvard University Press, 1953),

38. A method for characterizing synonymy in terms of reference is suggested by N. Goodman, "On Likeness of Meaning," *Analysis* 10 (1949): 1–7. Difficulties are discussed by Goodman, "On Some Differences About Meaning," *Analysis* 13 (1953): 90–96. Carnap (op. cit.) presents a very similar idea (§6), but somewhat misleadingly phrased, since he does not bring out the fact that only extensional (referential) notions are being used.

39. In general, the examples discussed here are badly handled, and the success of the proposed analyses is overstated. In each case, it is easy to see that the proposed analysis, which usually has an air of objectivity, is not equivalent to the analyzed expression. To take just one example, the response *I am looking for my glasses* is certainly not equivalent to the proposed paraphrases: "When I have behaved in this way in the past, I have found my glasses and have then stopped behaving in this way," or "Circumstances have arisen in which I am inclined to emit any behavior which in the past has led to the discovery of my glasses; such behavior includes the behavior of looking in which I am now engaged." One may look for one's glasses for the first time; or one may emit the same behavior in looking for one's glasses as in looking for one's watch, in which case *I am looking for my glasses* and *I am looking for my watch* are equivalent, under the Skinnerian paraphrase. The difficult questions of purposiveness cannot be handled in this superficial manner.

40. Skinner takes great pains, however, to deny the existence in human beings (or parrots) of any innate faculty or tendency to imitate. His only argument is that no one would suggest an innate tendency to read, yet reading and echoic behavior have similar "dynamic properties." This similarity, however, simply indicates the grossness of his descriptive categories.

In the case of parrots, Skinner claims that they have no instinctive capacity to imitate, but only to be reinforced by successful imitation (59). Given Skinner's use of the word "reinforcement," it is difficult to perceive any distinction here, since exactly the same thing could be said of any other instinctive behavior. For example, where another scientist would say that a certain bird instinctively builds a nest in a certain way, we could say in Skinner's terminology (equivalently) that the bird is instinctively reinforced by building the nest in this way. One is therefore inclined to dismiss this claim as another ritual introduction of the word "reinforce." Though there may, under some suitable clarification, be some truth in it, it is difficult to see how many of the cases reported by competent observers can be handled if "reinforcement" is given some substantive meaning. Cf. Thorpe, op. cit. 353f.; K. Lorenz, *King Solomon's Ring* (New York: Crowell, 1952), 85–88; even Mowrer, who tries to show how imitation might develop through secondary reinforcement, cites a case, op. cit. 694, which he apparently believes, but where this could hardly be true. In young children, it seems most implausible to explain imitation in terms of secondary reinforcement.

41. Though even this possibility is limited. If we were to take these paradigm instances seriously, it should follow that a child who knows how to count from one to 100 could learn an arbitrary 10 x 10 matrix with these numbers as entries as readily as the multiplication table.

42. Similarly, "the universality of a literary work refers to the number of potential readers inclined to say the same thing" (275; i.e., the most "universal" work is a dictionary of clichés and greetings); a speaker is "stimulating" if he says what we are about to say ourselves (272); etc.

43. Similarly, consider Skinner's contention (362–65) that communication of knowledge or facts is just the process of making a new response available to the speaker. Here the analogy to animal experiments is particularly weak. When we train a rat to carry out some peculiar act, it makes sense to consider this a matter of adding a response to his repertoire. In the case of human communication, however, it is very difficult to attach any meaning to this terminology. If A imparts to B the information (new to B) that the railroads face collapse, in what sense can the response *The railroads face collapse* be said to be now, but not previously, available to B? Surely B could have said it before (not knowing whether it was true), and known that it was a sentence (as opposed to *Collapse face railroads the)*. Nor is there any reason to assume that the response has increased in strength, whatever this means exactly (e.g., B may have no interest in the fact, or he may want it suppressed). It is not clear how we can characterize this notion of "making a response available" without reducing Skinner's account of "imparting knowledge" to a triviality.

44. 332. On the next page, however, the *s* in the same example indicates that "the object described as *the boy* possesses the property of running." The difficulty of even maintaining consistency with a conceptual scheme like this is easy to appreciate.

45. One might just as well argue that exactly the opposite is true. The study of hesitation pauses has shown that these tend to occur before the large categories—noun, verb, adjective; this finding is usually described by the statement that the pauses occur where there is maximum uncertainty or information. Insofar as hesitation indicates on going composition (if it does at all), it would appear that the "key responses" are chosen only after the "grammatical frame." Cf. C. E. Osgood, unpublished paper; F. Goldman-Eisler, "Speech Analysis and Mental Processes," *Language and Speech* 1 (1958), 67.

46. E.g., what are in fact the actual units of verbal behavior? Under what conditions will a physical event capture the attention (be a stimulus) or be a reinforcer? How do we decide what stimuli are in "control" in a specific case? When are stimuli "similar"? And so on. (It is not interesting to be told e.g., that we say *Stop* to an automobile or billiard ball because they are sufficiently similar to reinforcing people [46].)

The use of unanalyzed notions like "similar" and "generalization" is particularly disturbing, since it indicates an apparent lack of interest in every significant aspect of the learning or the use of language in new situations. No one has ever doubted that in some sense, language is learned by generalization, or that novel utterances and situations are in some way similar to familiar ones. The only matter of serious interest is the specific "similarity." Skinner has, apparently, no interest in this. Keller and Schoenfeld (op. cit.) proceed to incorporate these notions (which they identify) into their Skinnerian "modern objective psychology" by defining two stimuli to be similar when "we make the same sort of response to them" (124; but when are responses of the "same sort"?). They do not seem to notice that this definition converts their "principle of generalization" (116), under any reasonable interpretation of this, into a tautology. It is obvious that such a definition will not be of much help in the study of language learning or construction of new responses in appropriate situations.

47. "The Problem of Serial Order in Behavior," in L. A. Jeffress, ed., *Hixon Symposium on Cerebral Mechanisms in Behavior* (New York: Wiley, 1961).

48. There is nothing essentially mysterious about this. Complex innate behavior patterns and innate "tendencies to learn in specific ways" have been carefully studied in lower organisms. Many psychologists have been inclined to believe that such biological structure will not have an important effect on acquisition of complex behavior in higher organisms, but I have not been able to find any serious justification for this attitude. Some recent studies have stressed the necessity for carefully analyzing the strategies available to the organism, regarded as a complex "information-processing system" (cf. J. S. Bruner, J. J. Goodnow, and G. A. Austin, *A Study of Thinking* [New York: Wiley, 1956]; A. Newell, J. C. Shaw, and H. A. Simon, "Elements of a Theory of Human Problem Solving," *Psychological Review* 65 [1958]: 151–66); if anything significant is to be said about the character of human learning. These may be largely innate, or developed by early learning processes about which very little is yet known. (But see H. F. Harlow, "The Formation of Learning Sets," *Psychological Review* 58 (1949): 51–65, and many later papers, where striking shifts in the character of learning are shown as a result of early training; also Hebb, *Organization of Behavior*, 109ff.) They are undoubtedly quite complex. Cf. Lenneberg, op. cit., and R. B. Lees, review of Chomsky's *Syntactic Structures* in *Language* 33 (1957): 406f., for discussion of the topics mentioned in this section.

3. METHODOLOGICAL PRELIMINARIES

1. To accept traditional mentalism, in this way, is not to accept Bloomfield's dichotomy of "mentalism" versus "mechanism." Mentalistic linguistics is simply theoretical linguistics that uses performance as data (along with other data, for example, the data provided by introspection) for the determination of competence, the latter being taken as the primary object of its investigation. The mentalist, in this traditional sense, need make no assumptions about the possible physiological basis for the mental reality that he studies. In particular, he need not deny that there is such a basis. One would guess, rather, that it is the mentalistic studies that will ultimately be of the greatest value for the investigation of neurophysiological mechanisms, since they alone are concerned with determining abstractly the properties that such mechanisms must exhibit and the functions they must perform.

In fact, the issue of mentalism versus antimentalism in linguistics apparently has to do only with goals and interests, and not with questions of truth or falsity, sense or nonsense. At least three issues are involved in this rather idle controversy: (1) dualism—are the rules that underlie performance represented in a nonmaterial medium? (2) behaviorism—do the data of performance exhaust the domain of interest to the linguist, or is he also concerned with other facts, in particular those pertaining to the deeper systems that underlie behavior? and (3) introspectionism—should one make use of introspective data in the attempt to ascertain the properties of these underlying systems? It is the dualistic position against which Bloomfield irrelevantly inveighed. The behaviorist position is not an arguable matter. It is simply an expression of lack of interest in theory and explanation. This is clear, for example, in W. F. Twaddell's critique (*On Defining the Phoneme. Language Monograph No. 16*, 1935, reprinted in part in M. Joos, ed., *Reading in Linguistics* [Washington: 1957]) of Sapir's mentalistic phonology, which used informant responses and comments as evidence bearing on the psychological reality of some abstract system of phonological elements. For Twaddell, the enterprise has no point because all that interests him is the behavior itself, "which is already available for the student of language, though in less concentrated form." Characteristically, this lack of interest in linguistic theory expresses itself in the proposal to limit the term "theory" to "summary of data" (as in Twaddell's paper, or, to take a more recent example, in R. W. Dixon, *Linguistic Science and Logic* [The Hague: Mouton & Co., 1963], although the discussion of "theories" in the latter is sufficiently vague as to allow other interpretations of what he may have in mind). Perhaps this loss of interest in theory, in the usual sense, was fostered by certain ideas (e.g., strict operationalism or strong verificationism) that were considered briefly in positivist philosophy of science, but rejected forthwith, in the early 1930s. In any event, question (2) poses no substantive issue. Question (3) arises only if one rejects the behaviorist limitations of (2). To maintain, on grounds of methodological purity, that introspective judgments of the informant (often, the linguist himself) should be disregarded is, for the present, to condemn the study of language to utter sterility. It is difficult to imagine what possible reason might be given for this. We return to this matter later. For further discussion, see J. J. Katz, "Mentalism in Linguistics," *Language* 40 (1964), 124–37.

2. For discussion, see N. Chomsky, *Current Issues in Linguistic Theory* (The Hague: Mouton & Co., 1964). A slightly earlier version appears in J. A. Fodor and J. J. Katz, eds., *The Structure of Language: Readings in the Philosophy of Language* (Englewood Cliffs, NJ: Prentice-Hall, 1964). This is a revised and expanded version of a paper presented to the session "The Logical Basis of Linguistic Theory," at the Ninth International Congress of Linguists, Cambridge, MA, 1962. It appears under the title of the session in H. Lunt, ed., *Proceedings of the Ninth Congress of Linguists* (The Hague: Mouton & Co., 1964).

3. This has been denied recently by several European linguists (e.g., Dixon, *Linguistic Science and Logic*; E. M. Uhlenbeck, "An Appraisal of Transformation Theory," *Lingua* 12 (1963), 1–18; E. M. Uhlenbeck, discussion in the session "The Logical Basis of Linguistic Theory," in Lunt, *Proceedings*, 981–83). They offer no reasons for their skepticism concerning traditional grammar, however. Whatever evidence is available today seems to me to show that by and large the traditional views are basically correct, so far as they go, and that the suggested innovations are totally unjustifiable. For example, consider Uhlenbeck's proposal that the constituent analysis of "the man saw the boy" is [*the man saw*] [*the boy*], a proposal which presumably also implies that in the sentences [*the man put*] [*it into the box*], [*the man aimed*] [*it at John*], [*the man persuaded*] [*Bill that it was unlikely*], etc., the constituents are as indicated. There are many considerations relevant to the determination of constituent structure (cf. note 7); to my knowledge, they support the traditional analysis without exception against this proposal, for

which the only argument offered is that it is the result of a "pure linguistic analysis." Cf. Uhlenbeck, discussion in the session "The Logical Basis of Linguistic Theory," and the discussion there. As to Dixon's objections to traditional grammars, since he offers neither any alternative nor any argument (beyond the correct but irrelevant observation that they have been "long condemned by professional linguists"), there is nothing further to discuss, in this case.

4. J. Beattie, *Theory of Language* (London: A. Stahan, 1788).

5. C. Ch. Du Marsais, *Les véritables principes de la grammaire* (1729); on the dating of this manuscript, see G. Sahlin, *César Chesneau du Marsais et son rôle dans l'évolution de la grammaire générale* (Paris: Presses Universitaires, 1928). Quoted in Sahlin, 29–30.

6. For references, see N. Chomsky, *Cartesian Linguistics: A Chapter in the History of Rationalist Thought* (New York: Harper & Row, 1966).

7. C. Lancelot, A. Arnaud, et al., *Grammaire générale et raisonnée* (1660).

8. D. Diderot, *Lettre sur les Sourds et Muets* (1751); page references are to J. Assézat, ed., *Oeuvres Complètes de Diderot*, vol. 1 (Paris: Garnier Frères, 1875).

9. Ibid., 390.

10. Ibid., 371.

11. Ibid., 372.

12. Ibid., 371–72.

13. For example, G. Ryle, "Ordinary Language," *Philosophical Review* 62 (1953), 167–86.

14. For various attempts to clarify this point, see N. Chomsky, *Syntactic Structures* (The Hague: Mouton & Co., 1957); H. A. Gleason, *Introduction to Descriptive Linguistics*, 2d ed. (New York: Holt, Rinehart & Winston, 1961); G. A. Miller and N. Chomsky, "Finitary Models of Language Users," in R. D. Luce, R. Bush, and E. Galanter, eds., *Handbook of Mathematical Psychology*, vol. 2 (New York: Wiley, 1963), ch. 13, 419–92; and many other publications.

4. THE RESPONSIBILITY OF INTELLECTUALS

1. Such a research project has now been undertaken and published as a "Citizens' White Paper": F. Schurmann, P. D. Scott, and R. Zelnik, *The Politics of Escalation in Vietnam* (New York: Fawcett World Library; Boston: Beacon, 1966). For further evidence of American rejection of UN initiatives for diplomatic settlement, just prior to the major escalation of February 1965, see Mario Rossi, "The US Rebuff to U Thant," *New York Review of Books*, November 17, 1966. See also Theodore Draper, "How Not to Negotiate," *New York Review of Books*, May 4, 1967. There is further documentary evidence of NLF attempts to establish a coalition government and to neutralize the area, all rejected by the United States and its Saigon ally, in Douglas Pike, *Viet Cong* (Cambridge, MA: MIT Press, 1966). In reading material of this latter sort one must be especially careful to distinguish between the evidence presented and the "conclusions" that are asserted, for reasons noted briefly below (see note 33).

It is interesting to see the first, somewhat oblique published reactions to *The Politics of Escalation* by those who defend our right to conquer South Vietnam and institute a government of our choice. For example, Robert Scalapino (*New York Times Magazine*, December 11, 1966) argues that the thesis of the book implies that our leaders are "diabolical." Since no right-thinking person can believe this, the thesis is refuted. To assume otherwise would betray "irresponsibility," in a unique sense of this term—a sense that gives an ironic twist to the title of this chapter. He goes on to point out the alleged central weakness in the argument of the book, namely, the failure to perceive that a serious attempt on our part to pursue the possibilities for a diplomatic settlement would have been interpreted by our adversaries as a sign of weakness.

2. *New York Times*, October 14, 1965.

3. Ibid., February 6, 1966.

4. *Boston Globe*, November 19, 1965.

5. At other times, Schlesinger does indeed display admirable scholarly caution. For example, in his introduction to *The Politics of Escalation* he admits that there may have been "flickers of interest in negotiations" on the part of Hanoi. As to the administration's lies about negotiations and its repeated actions undercutting tentative initiatives towards negotiations, he comments only that the authors may have underestimated military necessity and that future historians may prove them wrong. This caution and detachment must be compared with Schlesinger's attitude toward renewed study of the origins of the Cold War: in a letter to the *New York Review of Books*, October 20, 1966, he remarks that it is time to "blow the whistle" on revisionist attempts to show that the Cold War may have been the consequence of something more than mere Communist belligerence. We are to believe, then, that the relatively straightforward matter of the origins of the Cold War is settled beyond discussion, whereas the much more complex issue of why the United States shies away from a negotiated settlement in Vietnam must be left to future historians to ponder.

It is useful to bear in mind that the U.S. government itself is on occasion much less diffident in explaining why it refuses to contemplate a meaningful negotiated settlement. As is freely admitted, this solution would leave it without power to control the situation. See, for example, note 37.

6. Arthur M. Schlesinger, Jr., *A Thousand Days: John F. Kennedy in the White House* (Boston: Houghton Mifflin Company, 1965), 121.

7. Walt W. Rostow, *The View from the Seventh Floor* (New York: Harper & Row, 1964), 149. See also his *United States in the World Arena* (New York: Harper & Row, 1960), 144: "Stalin, exploiting the disruption and weakness of the postwar world, pressed out from the expanded base he had won during the Second World War in an effort to gain the balance of power in Eurasia . . . turning to the East, to back Mao and to enflame the North Korean and Indochinese Communists . . ."

8. For example, the article by CIA analyst George Carver, "The Faceless Viet Cong," in *Foreign Affairs* 44 (April 1966): 317–72. See also note 33.

9. Cf. Jean Lacouture, *Vietnam: Between Two Truces* (New York: Random House, 1966), 21. Diem's analysis of the situation was shared by Western observers at the time. See, for example, the comments of William Henderson, Far Eastern specialist and executive, Council on Foreign Relations, in Richard W. Lindholm, ed., *Vietnam: The First Five Years* (East Lansing: Michigan State University Press, 1959). He notes "the growing alienation of the intelligentsia," "the renewal of armed dissidence in the South," the fact that "security has noticeably deteriorated in the last two years," all as a result of Diem's "grim dictatorship," and predicts "a steady worsening of the political climate in free Vietnam, culminating in unforeseen disasters."

10. See Bernard Fall, "Vietnam in the Balance," *Foreign Affairs* 45 (October 1966): 1–18.

11. Stalin was pleased neither by the Titoist tendencies inside the Greek Communist party nor by the possibility that a Balkan federation might develop under Titoist leadership. It is nevertheless conceivable that Stalin supported the Greek guerrillas at some stage of the rebellion, in spite of the difficulty in obtaining firm documentary evidence. Needless to say, no elaborate study is necessary to document the British or American role in this civil conflict, from late 1944. See D. G. Kousoulas, *The Price of Freedom* (Syracuse, NY: Syracuse University Press, 1953), and *Revolution and Defeat* (New York: Oxford University Press, 1965), for serious study of these events from a strongly anti-Communist point of view.

12. For a detailed account, see James Warburg, *Germany: Key to Peace* (Cambridge, MA: Harvard University Press, 1953), 189, for Warburg concludes that apparently "the Kremlin was now prepared to accept the creation of an All-German democracy in the Western sense of the word," whereas the Western powers, in their response, "frankly admitted their plan 'to secure the participation of Germany in a purely defensive European community' " (i.e., NATO).

13. *The United States in the World Arena*, 344–45. Incidentally those who quite rightly deplore the brutal suppression of the East German and Hungarian revolutions would do well to remember that these scandalous events might have been avoided had the United States been willing to consider proposals for neutralization of Central Europe. Some of George Kennan's recent statements provide interesting commentary on this matter, for example, his comments on the falsity, from the outset, of the assumption that the USSR intended to attack or intimidate by force the Western half of the continent and that it was deterred by American force, and his remarks on the sterility and general absurdity of the demand for unilateral Soviet withdrawal from East Germany together with "the inclusion of a united Germany as a major component in a Western defense system based primarily on nuclear weaponry" (Edward Reed, ed., *Peace on Earth* [New York: Pocket Books, 1965]).

It is worth noting that historical fantasy of the sort illustrated in Rostow's remarks has become a regular State Department specialty. Thus, we have Thomas Mann justifying our Dominican intervention as a response to actions of the "Sino-Soviet military bloc." Or, to take a more considered statement, we have William Bundy's analysis of stages of development of Communist ideology in his Pomona College address, February 12, 1966, in which he characterizes the Soviet Union in the 1920s and early 1930s as "in a highly militant and aggressive phase." What is frightening about fantasy, as distinct from outright falsification, is the possibility that it may be sincere and may actually serve as the basis for formation of policy.

14. *New York Times*, February 6, 1966.

15. *United States Policy Toward Asia*, Hearings before the Subcommittee on the Far East and the Pacific of the Committee on Foreign Affairs, House of Representatives (Washington: Government Printing Office, 1966), 89.

16. *New York Times Book Review*, November 20, 1966. Such comments call to mind the remarkable spectacle of President Kennedy counseling Cheddi Jagan on the dangers of entering into a trading relationship "which brought a country into a condition of economic dependence." The reference, of course, is to the dangers in commercial relations with the Soviet Union. See Schlesinger, *A Thousand Days*, 776.

17. *A Thousand Days*, 252.

18. Ibid., 769.

19. Though this too is imprecise. One must recall the real character of the Trujillo regime to appreciate the full cynicism of Kennedy's "realistic" analysis.

20. Walt W. Rostow and R. W. Hatch, *An American Policy in Asia* (New York: Technology Press and John Wiley & Sons, Inc., 1955).

21. "End of Either/Or," *Foreign Affairs* 45 (January 1967): 189–201.

22. *Christian Science Monitor*, November 26, 1966.

23. Ibid., December 5, 1966.

24. Although, to maintain perspective, we should recall that in his wildest moments, Alfred Rosenberg spoke of the elimination of thirty million Slavs, not the imposition of mass starvation on a quarter of the human race. Incidentally, the analogy drawn here is highly "irresponsible," in the technical sense of this neologism discussed earlier. That is, it is based on the assumption that statements and actions of Americans are subject to the same standards and open to the same interpretations as those of anyone else.

25. *New York Times,* February 6, 1966. What is more, Goldberg continues, the United States is not certain that all of these are voluntary adherents. This is not the first such demonstration of Communist duplicity. Another example was seen in the year 1962, when according to United States government sources 15,000 guerrillas suffered 30,000 casualties. See Schlesinger, *A Thousand Days,* 982.

26. Reprinted in a collection of essays entitled *The End of Ideology: On the Exhaustion of Political Ideas in the Fifties* (New York: The Free Press, 1960), 369–75. I have no intention here of entering into the full range of issues that have been raised in the discussion of the "end of ideology" for the past dozen years. It is difficult to see how a rational person could quarrel with many of the theses that have been put forth, e.g., that at a certain historical moment the "politics of civility" is appropriate, and perhaps efficacious; that one who advocates action (or inaction—a matter less frequently noted) has a responsibility to assess its social cost; that dogmatic fanaticism and "secular religions" should be combated (or if possible ignored); that technical solutions to problems should be implemented, where possible; that *"le dogmatisme idéologique devait disparaître pour que les idées reprissent vie"* (Aron); and so on. Since this is sometimes taken to be an expression of an "anti-Marxist" position, it is worth keeping in mind that such sentiments as these have no bearing on non-Bolshevik Marxism, as represented, for example, by such figures as Luxemburg, Pannekoek, Korsch, Arthur Rosenberg, and many others.

27. Rostow and Hatch, *An American Policy in Asia,* p. 10.

28. The extent to which this "technology" is value-free is hardly very important, given the clear commitments of those who apply it. The problems with which research is concerned are those posed by the Pentagon or the great corporations, not, say, by the revolutionaries of northeast Brazil or by SNCC. Nor am I aware of a research project devoted to the problem of how poorly armed guerrillas might more effectively resist a brutal and devastating military technology—surely the kind of problem that would have interested the free-floating intellectual who is now hopelessly out of date.

29. In view of the unremitting propaganda barrage on "Chinese expansionism," perhaps a word of comment is in order. Typical of American propaganda on this subject is Adlai Stevenson's assessment, shortly before his death (cf. *New York Times Magazine,* March 13, 1966): "So far, the new Communist 'dynasty' has been very aggressive. Tibet was swallowed, India attacked, the Malays had to fight 12 years to resist a 'national liberation' they could receive from the British by a more peaceful route. Today, the apparatus of infiltration and aggression is already at work in North Thailand."

As to Malaya, Stevenson is probably confusing ethnic Chinese with the government of China. Those concerned with the actual events would agree with Harry Miller, in *Communist Menace in Malaya* (New York: Frederick A. Praeger, Inc., 1954), 230, that "Communist China continues to show little interest in the Malayan affair beyond its usual fulminations via Peking Radio." There are various harsh things that one might say about Chinese behavior in what the Sino-Indian Treaty of 1954 refers to as "the Tibet region of China," but it is no more proof of a tendency towards expansionism than is the behavior of the Indian government with regard to the Naga and Mizo tribesmen. As to North Thailand, "the apparatus of infiltration" may well be at work, though there is little reason to suppose it to be Chinese—and it is surely not unrelated to the American use of Thailand as a base for its attack on Vietnam. This reference is the sheerest hypocrisy.

The "attack on India" grew out of a border dispute that began several years after the Chinese had completed a road from Tibet to Sinkiang in an area so remote from Indian control that the Indians learned about this operation only from the Chinese press. According to American Air Force maps, the disputed area is in Chinese territory. Cf. Alastair Lamb, *China Quarterly*, No. 23 (July–September 1965), 202–7. To this distinguished authority, "it seems unlikely that the Chinese have been working out some master plan . . . to take over the Indian subcontinent lock, stock and overpopulated barrel." Rather, he thinks it likely that the Chinese were probably unaware that India even claimed the territory through which the road passed. After the Chinese military victory, Chinese troops were, in most areas, withdrawn beyond the McMahon Line, a border which the British had attempted to impose on China in 1914 but which has never been recognized by China (Nationalist or Communist), the United States, or any other government.

It is remarkable that a person in a responsible position could describe all of this as Chinese expansionism. In fact, it is absurd to debate the hypothetical aggressiveness of a China surrounded by American missiles and a still expanding network of military bases backed by an enormous American expeditionary force in Southeast Asia. It is conceivable that at some future time a powerful China may be expansionist. We may speculate about such possibilities if we wish, but it is American aggressiveness that is the central fact of current politics.

30. W. S. Churchill, *The Second World War*, vol. 5, *Closing the Ring* (Boston: Houghton Mifflin Company, 1951), 382.

31. *United States Policy Toward Asia*, 104. See note 15.

32. Ibid., 105.

33. Pike, *Viet Cong*, 110. This book, written by a foreign service officer working at the Center for International Studies, MIT, poses a contrast between our side, which sympathizes with "the usual revolutionary stirrings . . . around the world because they reflect inadequate living standards or oppressive and corrupt governments," and the backers of "revolutionary guerrilla warfare," which "opposes the aspirations of people while apparently furthering them, manipulates the individual by persuading him to manipulate himself." Revolutionary guerrilla warfare is "an imported product, revolution from the outside" (other examples besides the Vietcong are "Stalin's exportation of armed revolution," the Haganah in Palestine, and the Irish Republican Army—see 32–33). The Vietcong could not be an indigenous movement since it has "a social construction program of such scope and ambition that of necessity it must have been created in Hanoi" (76—but on 77–79 we read that "organizational activity had gone on intensively and systematically for several years" before the Lao Dong party in Hanoi had made its decision "to begin building an organization"). On 80 we find that "such an effort had to be the child of the North," even though elsewhere we read of the prominent role of the Cao Dai (74), "the first major social group to begin actively opposing the Diem government" (222), and of the Hoa Hao sect, "another early and major participant in the NLF" (69). Pike takes it as proof of Communist duplicity that in the South the party insisted it was "Marxist-Leninist," thus "indicating philosophic but not political allegiance," whereas in the North it described itself as a "Marxist-Leninist organization," thus "indicating that it was in the mainstream of the world-wide Communist movement" (150). And so on. Also revealing is the contempt for "Cinderella and all the other fools [who] could still believe there was magic in the mature world if one mumbled the secret incantation: solidarity, union, concord"; for the "gullible, misled people" who were "turning the countryside into a bedlam, toppling one Saigon government after another, confounding the Americans"; for the "mighty force of people" who in their mindless innocence thought that "the meek, at last, were to inherit the earth," that "riches would be theirs and all in the name of justice and virtue." One can appreciate the chagrin with which a sophisticated Western political scientist must view this "sad and awesome spectacle."

34. Lacouture, op. cit., 188. The same military spokesman goes on, ominously, to say that

this is the problem confronting us throughout Asia, Africa, and Latin America, and that we must find the "proper response."

35. Charles Mohr, *New York Times,* February 11, 1966. Italics mine.

36. *New York Times,* February 18, 1966.

37. William Bundy, "The United States and Asia," in Alastair Buchan, ed., *China and the Peace of Asia* (New York: Frederick A. Praeger, Inc., 1965), 29–30.

38. Op. cit., 80.

39. *United States Policy Toward Asia,* 191–201, passim.

40. Rostow and Hatch, *An American Policy in Asia,* 10.

41. *United States Policy Toward Asia,* 128.

42. Lindholm, op. cit., 322.

6. LANGUAGE AND FREEDOM

1. F. W. J. Schelling, *Philosophical Inquiries into the Nature of Human Freedom.*

2. See, for example, the remarks of Paul Ricoeur cited in Noam Chomsky, *For Reasons of State* (New York: Pantheon Books, 1970), chap. 6, 308–9.

3. R. D. Masters, introduction to his edition of *First and Second Discourses,* by Jean-Jacques Rousseau (New York: St. Martin's Press, 1964).

4. Compare Proudhon, a century later: "No long discussion is necessary to demonstrate that the power of denying a man his thought, his will, his personality, is a power of life and death, and that to make a man a slave is to assassinate him."

5. Cited in Lehning, ed., Bakunin, *Etatisme et anarchie,* editor's note 50, from P. Schrecker, "Kant et la révolution française," *Revue philosophique de la France, et de l'Etranger,* September–December 1939.

6. Chomsky has discussed this matter in *Cartesian Linguistics* (New York: Harper & Row, 1966) and *Language and Mind* (New York: Harcourt, Brace & World, 1968).

7. See the references of note 5, and also Noam Chomsky, *Aspects of the Theory of Syntax* (Cambridge, MA: MIT Press, 1965), chap. 1, sec. 8.

8. For discussion, see E. H. Lenneberg, *Biological Foundations of Language* (New York: Wiley, 1967); Chomsky, *Language and Mind;* E. A. Drewe, G. Ettlinger, A. D. Milner, and R. E. Passingham, "A Comparative Review of the Results of Behavioral Research on Man and Monkey," Institute of Psychiatry, London, unpublished draft, 1969; P. H. Lieberman, D. H. Klatt, and W. H. Wilson, "Vocal Tract Limitations on the Vowel Repertoires of Rhesus Monkey and other Nonhuman Primates," *Science,* June 6, 1969; and P. H. Lieberman, "Primate Vocalizations and Human Linguistic Ability," *Journal of the Acoustical Society of America* 44, no. 6 (1968).

9. In the books cited above, and in Noam Chomsky, *Current Issues in Linguistic Theory* (The Hague: Mouton, 1969).

10. J. W. Burrow, introduction to his edition of *The Limits of State Action,* by Wilhelm von Humboldt (London: Cambridge University Press, 1969), from which most of the following quotes are taken.

11. Compare the remarks of Kant, quoted above. Kant's essay appeared in 1793; Humboldt's was written in 1791–1792. Parts appeared but it did not appear in full during his lifetime. See Burrow, introduction to Humboldt, *Limits of State Action.*

12. Thomas G. Sanders, "The Church in Latin America," *Foreign Affairs* 48, no. 2 (1970).

13. Ibid. The source is said to be the ideas of Paulo Freire. Similar criticism is widespread

in the student movement in the West. See, for example, Mitchell Cohen and Dennis Hale, eds., *The New Student Left* (Boston: Beacon, 1967), chap. 3.

14. Namely, that a man "only attains the most matured and graceful consummation of his activity, when his way of life is harmoniously in keeping with his character"—that is, when his actions flow from inner impulse.

15. The latter quote is from Humboldt's comments on the French Constitution, 1791—parts translated in Marianne Cowan, ed., *Humanist Without Portfolio* (Detroit: Wayne State University Press, 1963).

16. Rudolf Rocker, "Anarchism and Anarcho-syndicalism," in Paul Eltzbacher, *Anarchism* (New York: Libertarian Book Club, 1960). In his book *Nationalism and Culture* (1947), Rocker describes Humboldt as "the most prominent representative in Germany" of the doctrine of natural rights and of the opposition to the authoritarian state. Rousseau he regards as a precursor of authoritarian doctrine, but he considers only the *Social Contract*, not the far more libertarian *Discourse on Inequality*. Burrow observes that Humboldt's essay anticipates "much nineteenth century political theory of a populist, anarchist and syndicalist kind" and notes the hints of the early Marx. See also Chomsky, *Cartesian Linguistics*, n. 51, for some comments.

17. Karl Polanyi, *The Great Transformation* (New York: Octagon Books, 1975).

18. Cited by Paul Mattick, "Workers' Control," in Priscilla Long, ed., *The New Left* (Boston: Porter Sargent, 1969), 377. See also chap. 7, 96.

19. Cited in Martin Buber, *Paths in Utopia* (Boston: Beacon, 1985), 19.

20. Yet Rousseau dedicates himself, as a man who has lost his "original simplicity" and can no longer "do without laws and chiefs," to "respect the sacred bonds" of his society and "scrupulously obey the laws, and the men who are their authors and ministers," while scorning "a constitution that can be maintained only with the help of so many respectable people . . . and from which, despite all their care, always arise more real calamities than apparent advantages."

21. See chap. 7.

22. See chap. 7 in *For Reasons of State* for a discussion of the fraudulent claims in this regard of certain varieties of behavioral science.

7. NOTES ON ANARCHISM

1. Octave Mirbeau, quoted in James Joll, *The Anarchists* (Boston: Little, Brown, 1964), 145–6.

2. Rudolf Rocker, "Anarchism and Anarcho-syndicalism," in Paul Eltzbacher, *Anarchism* (New York: Libertarian Book Club, 1960).

3. Cited by Rocker, ibid., 77. This quotation and that in the next sentence are from Michael Bakunin, "The Program of the Alliance," in Sam Dolgoff, ed. and trans., *Bakunin on Anarchy* (Montreal: Black Rose Books, 1980), 255.

4. Diego Abad de Santillán, *After the Revolution* (New York: Greenberg, 1937), 86. In the last chapter, written several months after the revolution had begun, he expresses his dissatisfaction with what had so far been achieved along these lines. On the accomplishments of the social revolution in Spain, see my *American Power and the New Mandarins* (New York: Pantheon Books, 1969), chap. 1, and references cited there; the important study by Broué and Témime has since been translated into English. Several other important studies have appeared since, in particular: Frank Mintz, *L'Autogestion dans l'Espagne révolutionnaire* (Paris: Editions Bélibaste, 1971); César M. Lorenzo, *Les Anarchistes espagnols et le pouvoir, 1868–1969* (Paris:

Editions du Seuil, 1969); Gaston Leval, *Espagne libertaire, 1936–1939: L'Oeuvre constructive de la Révolution espagnole* (Paris: Editions du Cercle, 1971). See also Vernon Richards, *Lessons of the Spanish Revolution* (London: Freedom Press, 1972), enlarged 1972 edition.

5. Cited by Robert C. Tucker, *The Marxian Revolutionary Idea*, in his discussion of Marxism and anarchism.

6. Bakunin, in a letter to Herzen and Ogareff, 1866. Cited by Daniel Guérin, *Jeunesse du socialisme libertaire* (Paris: M. Rivière, 1959), 119.

7. Fernand Pelloutier, cited in Joll, *Anarchists*. The source is "L'Anarchisme et les syndicats ouvriers," *Les Temps nouveaux*, 1895. The full text appears in Daniel Guérin, ed., *Ni Dieu, ni maître* (Lausanne: La Cité Éditeur, 1969), an excellent historical anthology of anarchism.

8. Martin Buber, *Paths in Utopia* (New York: Collier Books, 1986), 127.

9. "No state, however democratic," Bakunin wrote, "not even the reddest republic—can ever give the people what they really want, i.e., the free self-organization and administration of their own affairs from the bottom upward, without any interference or violence from above, because every state, even the pseudo-People's State concocted by Mr. Marx, is in essence only a machine ruling the masses from above, through a privileged minority of conceited intellectuals, who imagine that they know what the people need and want better than do the people themselves. . . ." "But the people will feel no better if the stick with which they are being beaten is labeled 'the people's stick' " (*Statism and Anarchy* [1873], in Dolgoff, *Bakunin on Anarchy*, 338)—"the people's stick" being the democratic Republic.

Marx, of course, saw the matter differently.

For discussion of the impact of the Paris Commune on this dispute, see Daniel Guérin's comments in *Ni Dieu, ni maître*; these also appear, slightly extended, in his *Pour un marxisme libertaire* (Paris: R. Laffont, 1969). See also note 24.

10. On Lenin's "intellectual deviation" to the left during 1917, see Robert Vincent Daniels, "The State and Revolution: A Case Study in the Genesis and Transformation of Communist Ideology," *American Slavic and East European Review* 12, no. 1 (1953).

11. Paul Mattick, *Marx and Keynes* (Boston: Porter Sargent, 1969), 295.

12. Michael Bakunin, "La Commune de Paris et la notion de l'état," reprinted in Guérin, *Ni Dieu, ni maître*. Bakunin's final remark on the laws of individual nature as the condition of freedom can be compared with the approach to creative thought developed in the rationalist and romantic traditions, discussed in chap. 9. See N. Chomsky, *Cartesian Linguistics* and *Language and Mind*.

13. Shlomo Avineri, *The Social and Political Thought of Karl Marx* (London: Cambridge University Press, 1968), 142, referring to comments in *The Holy Family*. Avineri states that within the socialist movement only the Israeli *kibbutzim* "have perceived that the modes and forms of present social organization will determine the structure of future society." This, however, was a characteristic position of anarchosyndicalism, as noted earlier.

14. Rocker, *Anarchosyndicalism*, 28.

15. See Guérin's works cited earlier.

16. Karl Marx, *Critique of the Gotha Program* (Moscow: Foreign Languages Publishing House, 1947).

17. Karl Marx, *Grundrisse der Kritik der Politischen Ökonomie*, cited by Mattick, *Marx and Keynes*, 306. In this connection, see also Mattick's essay "Workers' Control," in Priscilla Long, ed., *The New Left* (Boston: Porter Sargent, 1969); and Avineri, *Social and Political Thought of Marx*.

18. Karl Marx, *Capital*, quoted by Robert Tucker, who rightly emphasizes that Marx sees

the revolutionary more as a "frustrated producer" than a "dissatisfied consumer" (*The Marxian Revolutionary Idea*). This more radical critique of capitalist relations of production is a direct outgrowth of the libertarian thought of the Enlightenment.

19. Marx, *Capital*, cited by Avineri, *Social and Political Thought of Marx*, 233.

20. Pelloutier, "L'anarchisme."

21. "Qu'est-ce que la propriété?" The phrase "property is theft" displeased Marx, who saw in its use a logical problem, theft presupposing the legitimate existence of property. See Avineri, *Social and Political Thought of Marx*.

22. Cited in Buber's *Paths in Utopia*, 19.

23. Cited in J. Hampden Jackson, *Marx, Proudhon and European Socialism* (London: English Universities Press, 1957), 60.

24. Karl Marx, *The Civil War in France* (New York: International Publishers, 1968), 24. Avineri observes that this and other comments of Marx about the Commune refer pointedly to intentions and plans. As Marx made plain elsewhere, his considered assessment was more critical than in this address.

25. For some background, see Walter Kendall, *The Revolutionary Movement in Britain, 1900–1921: The Origins of British Communism* (London: Weidenfeld & Nicolson, 1969).

26. *Collectivisations: L'Oeuvre constructive de la Révolution espagnole*, 8.

27. For discussion, see Mattick, *Marx and Keynes*, and Michael Kidron, *Western Capitalism Since the War* (Harmondsworth: Penguin, 1970). See also discussion and references cited in Noam Chomsky, *At War with Asia* (New York: Pantheon Books, 1970), chap. 1, 23–26.

28. See Hugh Scanlon, *The Way Forward for Workers' Control* (Nottingham: Institute for Workers' Control, 1968). Scanlon is president of the AEF, one of Britain's largest trade unions.

The institute was established as a result of the sixth Conference on Workers' Control, March 1968, and serves as a center for disseminating information and encouraging research.

29. Guérin, *Ni Dieu, ni maître*, introduction.

30. Ibid.

31. Arthur Rosenberg, *A History of Bolshevism* (New York: Russell & Russell, 1965), 88.

32. Marx, *Civil War in France*, 62–63.

8. THE RULE OF FORCE IN INTERNATIONAL AFFAIRS

1. Telford Taylor, *Nuremberg and Vietnam: An American Tragedy*, 29.

2. Whether Taylor is aware of the extent of American bombing in North Vietnam is unclear. Other commentators are not. For example, Neil Sheehan wrote: "Although the North Vietnamese may not believe it, in the North a conscious effort was made to bomb only military, and what limited industrial targets were available, and to weigh probable civilian casualties against the military advantages to be gained . . ." ("Should We Have War Crimes Trials?" *New York Times*, March 28, 1971). The thirty-three books which Sheehan reviews in this piece contain much evidence to the contrary, and Sheehan does not explain why he discounts that evidence. From my own limited observations in the neighborhood of Hanoi, I join the North Vietnamese in "not believing it." Nor do I think that Sheehan would "believe it" if he were to walk through the ruins of Phu Ly or Thanh Hoa, let alone the much more heavily bombed areas farther from Hanoi. Nevertheless, the bombing of North Vietnam, despite its enormous scale, has been well below that of South Vietnam and Laos in intensity and destructiveness.

3. Justice Radhabinod Pal, dissenting at Tokyo, argued that the dropping of the atom bomb was a criminal act exceeding any charged against those accused at the Tokyo trials. *International Military Tribunal for the Far East* (Calcutta: Sanyal & Co., 1953), 621. The relevant passages are cited in *American Power and the New Mandarins* (New York: Pantheon Books, 1969), 168–69. Pal did not, however, suggest prosecution for the decision to use the atom bombs. Taylor believes that the Nagasaki bombing, at least, can be considered a war crime (143).

4. Taylor, *Nuremberg and Vietnam*, 79; United Nations, General Assembly, *Report of the International Law Commission*, Suppl. 12 (A/1316), 1950, 11, reprinted in Herbert W. Briggs, ed., *The Law of Nations: Cases, Documents and Notes*, 2nd ed. (New York: Appleton-Century-Crofts, 1952).

5. One might raise the question whether the Nuremberg and United Nations charters are equivalent in status. I will not pursue the question here. But it does seem to me, as argued below, that there is a powerful case that the United States has grossly violated both in Indochina.

The recent release of the Pentagon Papers would appear to go a long way towards overcoming the difficulty regarding "evidentiary problems" that Taylor cites and, in my opinion, greatly overestimates. One of the interesting features of these documents is how well they corroborate the interpretations of American policy in Indochina that appear, for example, in Franz Schurmann et al., *The Politics of Escalation in Vietnam* (Boston: Beacon, 1966). The documentary record shows that the publicly available evidence was sufficient to determine the main lines of American policy. These documents would appear to provide direct evidence of a conspiracy to wage an expanding war of aggression and to violate the provisions of the United Nations Charter regarding pacific settlement of disputes. See *For Reasons of State* (New York: Pantheon Books, 1973), chap. 1.

6. Whether Taylor still accepts this assessment is not entirely clear.

7. The United States formally submitted the Vietnam question to the Security Council only in January 1966 (United Nations, Security Council, *Official Records*, vol. 21, suppl. January–March [S/7105], 1966, 105). Prior to that, the United States asked the council to consider the (alleged) Tonkin Gulf incident in August 1964 (*Official Records*, vol. 19, suppl. July–September [S/5849], 1964, 135), and submitted reports in February 1965 (*Official Records*, vol. 20, suppl. January-March [S/6174], 1965, 43) after the sharp escalation of American bombing in South and North Vietnam. See "The Legality of U.S. Participation in the Defense of Viet-Nam," *U.S. Department of State Bulletin*, vol. 54 (1966), reprinted in Richard A. Falk, ed., *The Vietnam War and International Law*, 583, 590 (henceforth cited as *Falk—Vietnam*). Direct United States military engagement began in 1961–1962.

8. Richard A. Falk, "International Law and the United States Role in Viet Nam: A Response to Professor Moore," *Yale Law Journal* 76 (1967): 1051, 1130 n. 80, reprinted in *Falk—Vietnam*, 445, 480 n. 80.

9. Thomas J. Farer, "Intervention in Civil Wars: A Modest Proposal," *Columbia Law Review* 67 (1967): 266, 271, reprinted in *Falk—Vietnam*, 509, 514.

10. Robert Scigliano, *South Vietnams* (Westport, CT: Greenwood Press, 1964), 145. Scigliano was a member of the Michigan State University Vietnam Advisory Group.

11. See, for example, George McT. Kahin and John W. Lewis, *The United States in Vietnam* (New York: Dial Press, 1967), 137.

12. Bernard Fall, *Street Without Joy* (Harrisburg, PA: Stackpole, 1961), 346.

13. *New York Times*, March 10, 1962; October 17, 1962. The 30 percent figure excludes hel-

icopter flights. By the beginning of 1964, the United States had 248 helicopters in Vietnam; by the end of the year, there were 327. See V. S. G. Sharp and W. C. Westmoreland, *Report on the War in Vietnam* (*As of 30 June 1968*), 85 (1968). By comparison, the French never had more than ten operational helicopters in Indochina until April 1954 (Fall, *Street Without Joy*, 242).

14. Robert Shaplen, *The Lost Revolution*, 170ff. No North Vietnamese were discovered in the delta until 1968. American bombing of civilians in the Camau Peninsula in the early 1960s has been confirmed by Colonel Fletcher Prouty (retired), who served at the time in liaison between the CIA and the air force ("Review of the War," WNET-TV, Channel 13, New York, February 15, 1971). American airstrikes on villages in the early 1960s have been confirmed by reporters. Malcolm Browne (AP correspondent in Vietnam from 1961) described visits to hamlets that had been hit by napalm and heavy bombs in American airstrikes; "there is no question that the results are revolting. Unfortunately, the Viet Cong builds bunkers so skillfully it is rarely touched by aerial bombs or napalm, except in cases of direct hits. But huts are flattened, and civilian loss of life is generally high. In some, the charred bodies of children and babies have made pathetic piles in the middle of the remains of market places" (*The New Face of War* [Indianapolis: Bobbs-Merrill, 1965], 118). Obviously, this was known to the American command and civilian leadership. To cite only the most obvious evidence, the introduction to Browne's book is written by Henry Cabot Lodge, then between two terms as United States Ambassador to Vietnam. It should be noted that the Tokyo Tribunal judged cabinet members responsible for war crimes in connection with the treatment of prisoners if, having knowledge of them, they did not resign. See Erwin Knoll and Judith N. McFadden, eds., *War Crimes and the American Conscience* (New York: Holt, Rinehart and Winston, 1970), 195, for relevant excerpts from the tribunal.

15. Richard Tregaskis, *Vietnam Diary* (New York: Holt, Rinehart and Winston, 1963), 108.

16. Donald Robinson, "America's Air Guerrillas—Will They Stop Future Vietnams?" *Parade*, supplement to *Boston Sunday Globe*, January 31, 1971. It was the SOF, according to this account, that conducted the raid against an abandoned prisoner-of-war camp near Son Tay in North Vietnam, in November 1970.

17. Even Douglas Pike, who is often hardly more than a propagandist for the American government, admits that the NLF constituted the only "mass-based political party in South Vietnam" and that in late 1964, it was impossible for the American-supported government to consider a coalition with the NLF, for fear that "the whale would swallow the minnow" (*Viet Cong* [Cambridge, MA: MIT Press, 1966], 110, 361–62). Elsewhere, Pike has estimated that in 1963, "perhaps half the population of South Vietnam at least tacitly supported the NLF" (*War, Peace, and the Viet Cong* [Cambridge, MA: MIT Press, 1969], 6). See also 216 above. It is, of course, not very difficult for a great power to establish a government that will applaud its intervention. For example, the 14th Congress of the Czechoslovak Communist Party, the first "officially recognized" Congress since 1966, opened with "applause and cheers" for the Russian invasion of 1968 (*Boston Globe*, Reuters, May 26, 1971).

18. I refer, in this instance, to the United States-supported refusal of the regime it had instituted in South Vietnam to adhere to the election provision of the Geneva Agreements of 1954. Similarly, in Laos, when the Pathet Lao won an unexpected victory in the election of 1958 (after substantial American efforts to buy the election for the right), the United States played a major role in the overthrow of the coalition government. See Len Ackland, "No Place for Neutralism: The Eisenhower Administration and Laos," in Nina S. Adams and Alfred W. McCoy, eds., *Laos: War and Revolution* (New York: Harper & Row, 1970); Jonathan

Mirsky and Stephen Stonefield, "The United States in Laos," in Edward Friedman and Mark Selden, eds., *America's Asia* (New York: Pantheon Books, 1971), 253–323. See also chap. 2, sec. I.

19. Whether it is "certainly the law" is open to question.

20. Cited by Leo Goodstadt, "Might and Right," *Far Eastern Economic Review*, April 10, 1971, 22. Goodstadt observes that "physical force was always a second-best choice for Mao."

21. Pike, *Viet Cong*, 91–92. Pike later observed that "armed combat was a GVN imposed requirement; the NLF was obliged to use counterforce to survive" (101).

22. Truong Chinh, *La résistance vaincra*, cited in Fall, *Street Without Joy*, 372–3 (excerpt translated by Fall).

23. Fall, *Street Without Joy*, 372–73.

24. On Japan's professedly defensive and idealistic motivations in the 1930s, see the references in chap. 2 of *American Power and the New Mandarins*, 176–77, 179–84, 189–90, 193–202.

25. American innocence in this regard is if anything surpassed by that of our British allies. For example, the anonymous weekly columnist (presumably the editor) of the *Far Eastern Economic Review*, generally a sober journal, writes that "it must be evident to any openminded person that, whatever the effects of America's intervention in Vietnam, the action was taken with the most idealistic of motives and with the best of intentions. . . . [To] claim that the United States is in Vietnam for imperialist reasons . . . is manifest nonsense" (column "Traveller's Tales," *Far Eastern Economic Review*, February 20, 1971). Conceivably one might argue that despite ample evidence to the contrary, the United States is thus unique in world history, but to insist on the certainty of this most dubious judgment is merely a form of hysteria. The columnist also demonstrates the neutrality of the *Review*, as contrasted with "committed" scholars: thus the *Review*, he writes, does not hesitate to "criticize what it regards as mistakes in [American] strategy or policy," or to publish "bitter attacks on Vietcong atrocities." True objectivity. The columnist also prides himself on his "sophistication" for "printing one of the few editorials which attempted to establish a sympathetic understanding for the troops who took part in the massacre at My Lai," failing to note that the American peace movement, which he denounces, had almost universally taken the same position, but without glorying in its sophistication for its ability to distinguish the acts of soldiers in the field from the calculated decisions of planners who are remote from any threat.

26. Fall, *Street Without Joy*, 373. Note that this was written in the early 1960s, at a time when Taylor "supported American intervention in Vietnam as an aggression-checking undertaking in the spirit of the United Nations Charter" (206). Three years after this work appeared, Secretary of Defense McNamara testified before Congress that the Vietcong and the North Vietnamese were "operating . . . without, for all practical purposes, a single wheeled vehicle in all of South Vietnam." See the statement by Senator Proxmire, *Congressional Record*, vol. 177 (April 5, 1971), S4585.

27. Fall, *Street Without Joy*, 378.

28. Interview in the *Ottawa Citizen*, January 12, 1970. An American working in Quang Ngai hospital estimated in 1967, a year before My Lai, that about 70 percent of the civilian war casualties there were caused by American and allied bombardment—that is, in an area more or less under American control, where victims could reach the town hospital. For quotations and references, see Chomsky, *American Power and the New Mandarins*, 284, and *At War with Asia* (New York: Pantheon Books, 1970), 270–71.

29. *New York Times*, May 25, 1971. The reference is to Ronald L. Ridenhour, the Vietnam veteran who disclosed the incident to the secretary of defense a year after it occurred. The incident has been noted at once by the NLF, along with many other incidents that are still not ac-

knowledged or discussed. Details were disclosed in Paris on June 15, 1968, but were neglected by the Western media. For a justifiably bitter account, see Erich Wulff, "Le Crime de Song My: Avec les félicitations du commandant en chef," *Africasia* [Paris], April 26–May 9, 1971. Wulff is a West German physician who spent six years in Vietnam and who testified concerning the "new 'Ouradours and Lidices' " before the Russell Tribunal in 1967. His testimony is recorded in "A Doctor Reports from South Vietnam—Testimony by Erich Wulff," in John Duffett, ed., *Against the Crime of Silence* (New York: Simon & Schuster, 1970).

30. *New York Times*, April 29, 1971; *Boston Globe*, May 10, 1971. The Dellums Committee Hearings have since been published (1972) by Vintage Books (Citizens' Commission of Inquiry, *The Dellums Committee Hearings on War Crimes in Vietnam*).

31. *Congressional Record*, vol. 177 (1971), E2826–2900. Published by Beacon in 1972 (Vietnam Veterans Against the War, eds., *The Winter Soldier Investigation*).

32. *New York Times*, April 26, 1972.

33. Statement of E. Opton, in Knoll and McFadden, *War Crimes*, 114.

34. R. W. Apple, "Calley: The Real Guilt," *New Statesman*, April 2, 1971, 449. The coercive character of earlier population removal was also well understood by the American command. Sharp and Westmoreland wrote that the first Strategic Hamlet Program in March 1962 "involved forced relocation of rural peasants, notwithstanding their strong attachment to their ancestral plots of land" (*Report on the War in Vietnam*, 79). This report consists largely of apologetics and is not, in my opinion, to be taken seriously, unless independently confirmed, except with regard to the details of the American military engagement.

35. Apple, "Calley: The Real Guilt," 34.

36. This occasionally heard explanation is plainly absurd, even if we believe its original formulation by Samuel P. Huntington, "The Bases of Accommodation," *Foreign Affairs* 46, no. 4 (1968). The Huntington article appeared prior to the massive escalation of the American bombing in the countryside of Indochina. But if the effects of millions of tons of bombs and thousands of square miles of defoliation could not have been predicted beforehand, which is difficult enough to believe, it was surely known by mid-1968. The same cynical pretense is maintained by Lieutenant Colonel John Paul Vann (retired), senior United States adviser for "pacification" in South Vietnam (see below, 232–33). He is quoted in *Newsweek* (January 20, 1969) as stating that "we inadvertently stumbled on the solution to guerrilla warfare—urbanization" (cited by L. A. G. Moss and Z. M. Shalizi, "War and Urbanization in Indochina," in Jonathan S. Grant et al., eds., *Cambodia: The Widening War in Indochina* [New York: Washington Square Press, 1971], 192).

37. Sheehan, "Should We Have War Crimes Trials?"

38. Cf. note 36 above.

39. Sheehan, "Should We Have War Crimes Trials?"

40. *New York Times*, April 6, 1971. The quotations and most of the cited material comes from this report. The rest is taken from an earlier report by Henry Kamm in the *New York Times*, November 15, 1969, and from a White Paper of the American Friends Service Committee (May 5, 1969), which gives the reports of Vietnamese-speaking field workers on the scene.

41. Fall, *Street Without Joy*.

42. It might be argued that domestic political considerations made it impossible for the president to saturate Vietnam with enough American troops to obviate the need for destructive firepower. Recall, however, that the French never sent conscripts to Vietnam and probably deployed no more than about 70,000 native French troops in all of Indochina. For references on French military strength, see Chomsky, *For Reasons of State*, chap. 1, note 4. The American war in Vietnam is unusual, if not unique, in that the public was willing to tolerate,

for a time, the deployment of an enormous conscript army to fight what was in essence a colonial war.

43. See note 46 below.

44. Arthur Westing, "Poisoning Plants for Peace," *Friends Journal* 16 (1970). Figures cited in text come from this article and that cited in note 45 below.

45. Arthur Westing, "Ecocide in Indochina," *Natural History*, March 1971.

46. Ngo Vinh Long, "Leaf Abscission," in Barry Weisberg, ed., *Ecocide in Indochina* (San Francisco: Canfield Press, 1970), 54. Long mentions that crop destruction was used at that time to force the population into strategic hamlets.

In *Thoi-Bao Ga* (a Vietnamese student journal published in Cambridge, MA) Long writes that according to the Saigon newspaper *Tin Sang*, November 12, 1970, the chairman of the Committee on Agriculture of the GVN declared that American chemical defoliants had destroyed approximately 60 percent of all crops in South Vietnam. The March 9, 1971, issue of the Saigon daily *Duoc Nha Nam* reports that South Vietnam imported one-half million metric tons of rice from the United States in 1970, enough, in Long's estimate, to feed five million persons. Nevertheless, journalists and others report widespread hunger, even starvation (*Thoi-Bao Ga*, March–April 1971, 6).

Bryce Nelson, a *Los Angeles Times* reporter who was formerly a reporter for *Science*, writes that an unreleased report of the AAAS Herbicide Assessment Commission notes the death of ninety people within a four-month period (September to December 1970) from exposure to spraying and drinking water contaminated with herbicides (*Village Voice*, January 28, 1971). A former IVS worker with four years experience in South Vietnam reports "numerous encounters" with farmers in Can Tho and Tay Ninh provinces whose crops were destroyed. He also reports seeing patients in Tay Ninh hospital "with limbs and faces burned mercilessly by phosphorus" and "child after child scarred or disfigured in some hideous way" in hospitals in the Mekong Delta (Letter to the editor from Roger Montgomery, *New York Times*, January 22, 1971). See Chomsky, *For Reasons of State*, chap. 1, note 10.

47. Richard Dudman, *Forty Days with the Enemy*, 69.

48. See *New York Times*, April 22, 1971; *Boston Globe*, April 16, 1971; *Boston Globe*, April 23, 1971. See also *Congressional Record*, vol. 117 (February 18, 1971), formal testimony of Representative McCloskey, H794–800. See also Chomsky, *For Reasons of State*, chap. 2, section 1.

49. *Congressional Record*, vol. 117 (1971), H796. Similar reports on Quang Ngai and Quang Tin provinces were given in 1967 before the massive escalation of the air war in 1968 (Jonathan Schell, *The Military Half*).

50. *The Law of Land Warfare*, Department of the Army Field Manual FM 27-10 (1956), 18, par. 37.

51. Statement by George Bunn, professor of law at the University of Wisconsin and formerly General Counsel, U.S. Arms Control and Disarmament Agency, "The Broad Implications of the Continued Use of Herbicides in Southeast Asia," AAAS Annual Meeting, December 29, 1970. Mimeographed.

52. William A. Nighswonger, *Rural Pacification in Vietnam*.

53. For discussion, see Jeffrey Race, "How They Won," *Asian Survey*, August 1970; Robert L. Sansom, *The Economics of Insurgency in the Mekong Delta of Vietnam* (Cambridge, MA: MIT Press, 1970). Race was an adviser to a district chief in Long An Province, south of Saigon, while in the United States Army. Sansom is an air force captain and a member of the staff of the National Security Council. Noncommunist reporters who have visited NLF-controlled areas give substantiating evidence. See the report by Jacques Doyon cited in Com-

mittee of Concerned Asian Scholars, *The Indochina Story* (New York: Pantheon Books, 1970), 36. See also Katsuichi Honda, *The National Liberation Front* and *Vietnam: A Voice from the Villages* (collections of articles by Honda, privately translated and reprinted from the Japanese journal *Asahi Shimbun* in 1967). See also Chomsky, *For Reasons of State,* chap. 1, references of note 215. Regarding Pathet Lao programs as seen by refugees, see the verbatim interview in Adams and McCoy, *Laos,* 451–59, and Chomsky, *At War with Asia,* 239. See also Mark Selden, "People's War and the Transformation of Peasant Society," in Selden and Friedman, *America's Asia;* chap. 2, sec. I, above.

54. Robert Shaplen, "The Challenge Ahead," *Columbia Journalism Review* 9, no. 4 (1970–71).

55. For some discussion and further references, see Edward S. Herman, *Atrocities in Vietnam* (Philadelphia: Pilgrim Press, 1970), chap. 2. All of this was well understood at the time. See, for example, R. W. Lindholm, ed., *Vietnam: The First Five Years* (East Lansing: Michigan State University Press, 1959).

56. See, for example, the remarks on Chinese nationalist terrorism against collaborators with the Japanese cited in Noam Chomsky, *Problems of Knowledge and Freedom* (New York: Pantheon Books, 1971), 95.

57. On the resort to violence by the NLF see the comments by Douglas Pike, 219 above, and the far more detailed analysis by Jeffrey Race, *War Comes to Long An* (Berkeley: University of California Press, 1972).

58. See Herman, *Atrocities in Vietnam,* for an effort to estimate relative scale.

59. Don Oberdorfer, *Tet!* (Garden City, NY: Doubleday, 1971), 201.

60. Len Ackland, "Hue," unpublished, one of the sources used by Oberdorfer. Predictably, others play the numbers game quite fast and loose. Donald Kirk, a very well informed correspondent, reports that "about 4000 citizens were massacred then before U.S. forces drove the North Vietnamese from the citadel . . . after 28 days of house-to-house fighting," implying that the 4,000 were massacred by the North Vietnamese (*Chicago Tribune*, May 4, 1972). Sir Robert Thompson claims that the Communists executed 5,700 people and that "in captured documents they gloated over those figures and only complained that they had not killed enough" (*New York Times*, June 15, 1972). No such document has ever been produced, even including the "captured documents" that were mysteriously discovered immediately after the publicity over the My Lai incidents in November 1969, allegedly "mislaid" for a year and a half. Senator William Saxbe will settle for no less than 7,000 murdered by the "North Vietnamese," considerably more than the total number killed from all causes during the fighting (*Congressional Record*, May 3, 1972).

61. Oberdorfer, incidently, reports "something over a hundred civilians" killed at My Lai, referring as a source to Seymour Hersh, *My Lai 4* (New York: Random House, 1970), where the number is estimated at about 400 to 500.

62. Oriana Fallaci, "Working Up to Killing," *Washington Monthly*, February 1972.

63. Richard West, *New Statesman,* January 28, 1972.

64. Philip Jones Griffiths, *Vietnam Inc.* (New York: Macmillan, 1971), 137. Griffiths's book contains pictures of the ongoing fighting in Hue. See my *At War with Asia,* 295–96, and Herman, *Atrocities in Vietnam,* for some discussion and references concerning both massacres, including references not identified above.

65. See note 53 above.

66. This report, untitled in Chomsky's copy, was given personally by Vann in 1971 to the Australian social psychologist Alex Carey, who has studied in particular the Australian role in Vietnam. See Carey's carefully documented pamphlet, *Australian Atrocities in Vietnam* 1–19

(undated pamphlet), which describes what he refers to as "our drift towards the standards of Hitler and the Gestapo."

67. See note 55 above.

68. Robert W. Komer, "Impact of Pacification on Insurgency in South Vietnam," *Journal of International Affairs* 25, no. 1 (1971). He is referring to the outright American invasion and bombing escalation in the South in February 1965.

69. Ibid. Recall the remarks by Richard Falk, 216 above, on capacity to govern as an element in claiming political legitimacy.

70. Komer, "Impact of Pacification." These benevolent imperialists, it should be noted, did not dissociate themselves from United States policies despite their reservations even after the grim effects were obvious. See note 14 above.

71. The Phoenix program is "aimed at neutralizing the clandestine Vietcong politico-administrative apparatus, which many regard as the key to their insurgent capabilities" (Komer, "Impact of Pacification"). "Neutralization" is Bureaucratese for "assassination or capture." Estimates as to the numbers "neutralized" vary. Deputy United States Ambassador William E. Colby, principal United States official in charge of pacification, testified before the Senate Foreign Relations Committee that close to 20,000 were "neutralized" in 1969, of whom 6,187 were killed. For comparison, the Saigon government claims that 4,619 civilians were killed by "the enemy" in 1969. The Phoenix program of course accounts for only a small fraction of the civilians killed by combined American-GVN forces. Len Ackland, a former IVS worker in South Vietnam and then a team leader and analyst for RAND, points out that the Phoenix program is designed to capture or murder civilians: "people who serve the political party, the National Liberation Front, as tax collectors, clerks, postmen, etc." For references and further documentation, see Chomsky, *At War with Asia*, 301–2; Herman, *Atrocities in Vietnam*, 46–47. See also 91–93, 161, above.

72. See note 66 above.

73. The latter phrase is a code term in American political terminology, for rule of South Vietnam by a noncommunist government. The NLF political program of 1962, largely ignored—even suppressed—in the United States, called for the neutralization of South Vietnam, Laos, and Cambodia. One might argue that this was a deception, but it is unclear that the United States has unilateral authority to use military force in acting on its skepticism.

74. This is another formulation of the inexpressible statement that South Vietnam must be ruled by the American-imposed noncommunist government. Goodwin was well aware, and explains in this book, that the insurgency even at that time was overwhelmingly domestic.

75. Richard Goodwin, *Triumph or Tragedy* (New York: Random House, 1966), 38. For many other expressions of related views, see the citations and references in Chomsky, *American Power and the New Mandarins*, particularly chap. 3, "The Logic of Withdrawal," 221–94.

76. *New York Times*, May 24, 1971.

77. Ibid. See note 71 above (identifying William Colby).

78. In October 1937 President Manuel Quezon pointed out that while "the rich can live in extravagant luxury . . . the men and women who till the soil or work in the factories are hardly better off now than they were during the Spanish regime. . . . thirty-five years of American regime has brought him only disappointments and sometimes despair . . ." (G. E. Taylor, *The Philippines and the United States* [New York: Council on Foreign Relations, 1964], 22). Taylor adds much information to confirm this judgment and concludes that by the late 1930s, "the mass of the people may have been worse off than before" the American occupation (85). The Bell report of 1950 revealed that inequalities of income had become even more marked while the average standard of living had not reached prewar levels (137).

The director of the USAID Mission in the Philippines, Wesley D. Haraldson, testified before a House subcommittee on April 25, 1967, that the condition of the average farmer "has not changed in the last fifty years. . . . In the past ten years the rich have become richer and the poor have become poorer" (Haraldson cited in Hernando J. Abaya, *The Untold Philippine Story* [Quezon City: Malaya Books, 1967], 360).

79. Phi-Van, "The Peasants (Dan Que)," appendix to Ngo Vinh Long, *Before the August Revolution.*

80. See, for example, Lawyers Committee on American Policy Towards Vietnam, *Vietnam and International Law* (Flanders, NJ: O'Hare, 1967). See also several papers in *Falk—Vietnam.* The most recent study, which appeared after Taylor's book, is William L. Standard, *Aggression: Our Asian Disaster* (New York: Random House, 1971). See also chap. 1, sec. III, VI (subsections 5, 6).

81. Chester Cooper, *The Lost Crusade* (New York: Dodd, Mead, 1970), 276–77. Emphasis added.

82. For details see Theodore Draper, *Abuse of Power* (New York: Viking Press, 1967), 73–82. There has been no attempt to respond to Draper's devastating critique of administration claims regarding the North Vietnamese troop involvement in the South. The astonishing internal contradictions suffice in themselves to make the government case unbelievable. See also the references in note 80 above. Recall that this North Vietnamese battalion was allegedly detected in the South two and a half months after the regular bombing of North Vietnam had been initiated, eight and a half months after the first bombing of strategic targets in North Vietnam in a "reprisal" for an incident which probably never occurred. The government claims regarding North Vietnamese aggression in Laos and Cambodia are no more compelling. See Chomsky, *For Reasons of State,* chap. 2.

83. Cooper, *Lost Crusade,* 264–65.

84. I. F. Stone, "A Reply to the White Paper," *I. F. Stone's Weekly*, March 8, 1965.

85. "It appears from the International Control Commission's reports that through February 28, 1961, about 154 violations had been registered against the South and only one violation against the North" (Scigliano, *South Vietnam,* 154). Scigliano argues that the North has the advantage of being "more acute, or devious" and that the "inability of ICC teams to perform their duties . . . is much greater in North than South Vietnam" (155). However, one ICC report states: "As has been revealed in the preceding paragraphs, the degree of co-operation given to the Commission by the two parties has not been the same. While the Commission has experienced difficulties in North Vietnam, the major part of its difficulties has arisen in South Vietnam" (International Control Commission, *Sixth Interim Report of the International Commission for Supervision and Control in Vietnam,* Cmnd. No. 31, 26–31, reprinted in Marvin E. Gettleman, ed., *Viet Nam: History, Documents and Opinions* (Greenwich, CT: Fawcett Publications, 1965), 170–72. On the matter of the obligations of North and South Vietnam with regard to the Geneva Agreements, see Daniel G. Partan, "Legal Aspects of the Vietnam Conflict," in *Falk—Vietnam,* 201, 209–16.

86. Bernard Fall, "Vietnam: The Agonizing Reappraisal," *Current History,* February 1965. For further references see Chomsky, *American Power and the New Mandarins,* 242–43, 281–82. For further confirmation, see Joseph Zasloff, *Political Motivation of the Viet Cong* RAND Memorandum RM-4703–2-ISA/ARPA (May 1968), 124. From the Pentagon Papers, we now know that these actions began in 1954.

87. See note 80 above.

88. Taylor's only reference to the issue is the following, in a different context: "When we sent hundreds of thousands of troops to South Vietnam, bombed North Vietnam, and moved

into Cambodia, were our national leaders as guilty of launching a war of aggression as were Hitler and his generals. . . ?" (13). The question is not taken up again.

89. Thomas M. Franck, "Who Killed Article 2(4)? or: Changing Norms Governing the Use of Force by States," *American Journal of International Law* 64, no. 4 (1970).

90. Bernard Fall, *Last Reflections on a War* (Garden City, NY: Doubleday, 1967), 276.

91. Franck, "Who Killed Article 2(4)?"

92. For recent discussion of this possibility, see Walter Goldstein, "The American Political System and the Next Vietnam," *Journal of International Affairs* 25, no. 1 (1971).

93. George W. Grayson, Jr., *Washington Post*, January 10, 1971. Grayson is associate professor of government at William and Mary College, a specialist in Latin American politics and the theory of revolution.

94. Hearings on Defense Department Appropriations Before a Subcommittee of the House Committee on Appropriations, 1963, cited in M. Klare, "The Pentagon's Counterinsurgency Research Infrastructure," *NACLA Newsletter* 4, no. 9 (1971).

95. Exactly the same point was made by Malcolm Browne as early as 1964 (*The New Face of War*, xi).

96. Gall, "Guerrilla Movements in Latin America," *New York Times*, March 28, 1971. The leader of the campaign, he points out, is now the elected president of Guatemala; his regime is the most brutal in the country's history, with large numbers killed in early 1971, including members of the legal noncommunist opposition.

97. Ibid. See also note 16 above. These operations, incidentally, are worldwide. According to the same report, Colonel Fletcher Prouty states that air force—CIA units that preceded the formation of SOF flew Tibetan tribesmen to Colorado for combat training and then returned them to Tibet; a resistance force of up to 42,000 was organized, he claims. Robinson also reports that they form part of the American counterinsurgency operations in Thailand and that they have conducted missions in Saudi Arabia and even North Korea.

98. Marcel Neidergang, "Violence et terreur," *Le Monde*, January 19, 1968.

99. See particularly Henry Kissinger, *Nuclear Weapons and Foreign Policy* (New York: Council on Foreign Relations, 1957), 132–233; *The Necessity for Choice* (New York: Harper, 1961), 57–98. Kissinger discusses "limited war strategy" within the framework of great-power conflict. If we ask ourselves where these "limited wars" will be fought, however, a different interpretation suggests itself. In fact, each of the superpowers regularly interprets its efforts to maintain its hegemony within its own empire as a defense of some principle (freedom, socialism) from the encroachments of its rival. In this respect, the cold war has served the leadership of the superpowers as an admirable propaganda device for mobilizing their respective populations behind expensive and dangerous efforts to maintain imperial dominions. See, for example, Franck, "Who Killed Article 2(4)?"; and chap. 1, sec. V.

9. WATERGATE: A SKEPTICAL VIEW

1. John Kifner, " 'Best Friend' of Gainesville 8 Defendant Testifies to Being FBI Informer," *New York Times*, August 18, 1973.

2. Those whose memories are short might turn to James Aronson's review of the record in *The Press and the Cold War* (Indianapolis: Bobbs-Merrill, 1970).

3. To be sure, this is not the official version. With the complicity of television and the press, the government has succeeded once again in imposing on events an interpretation that is wholly at variance with the facts. For some details on government and press deception with re-

gard to the Paris Agreements and the events that led to them, see Chomsky, "Indochina and the Fourth Estate," *Social Policy* (September 1973).

4. See John W. Finney, *New York Times*, April 12, 1973.

5. May 28, 1971, Department of the Treasury News, cited by David P. Calleo and Benjamin M. Rowland in *America and the World Political Economy* (Bloomington: Indiana University Press, 1973), 99. The editors of the *Monthly Review* have been particularly effective in explaining the contribution of imperial policy to the economic crisis. One might also recall Seymour Melman's efforts to arouse awareness of the debilitating effects of the policies of the militarized state capitalist institutions long before the topic became fashionable.

6. See Jack Foisie, "US still financing Thai forays into Cambodia," *Los Angeles Times-Boston Globe*, August 19, 1973. He reports from Bangkok that "Cambodia still is a clandestine target for U.S. financed and directed activities from bases inside Thailand," noting that the Thai retain their "long-range hope—to regain Battambang Province." The attempted August 19 coup in Laos was also launched from Thailand, suggesting that the Thai may still intend to incorporate parts of Laos in their mini-empire, in accordance with policies outlined by such doves as George Ball in 1965. Cf. *Pentagon Papers*, Senator Gravel edition (Boston: Beacon, 1971), vol. 4, 618.

7. American Foreign Policy (New York: Norton, 1969), 97. This is properly the concern of the United States, in his view, rather than "the management of every regional enterprise," to be left to subordinates.

8. Generally called the "Brezhnev Doctrine," though it was explicit in virtually the same terms in the earlier doctrines of Eisenhower, Khrushchev, Kennedy, and Johnson, as Thomas M. Franck and Edward Weisband have shown in their important study *Word Politics: Verbal Strategy Among the Superpowers* (New York: Oxford University Press, 1971).

9. For some congressional reactions to earlier exposures, see Noam Chomsky, *For Reasons of State* (New York: Pantheon Books, 1973), 13f.

10. Much was known before, at least to those who wished to know. See *For Reasons of State*, chap. 2, and references cited there. For some recent revelations, see Tad Szulc, "Mum's the War," *New Republic*, August 18–25, 1973; Walter V. Robinson, "Cambodian Raids—the Real Story," *Boston Globe*, August 12, 1973.

11. See Marcel Barang, "Le Laos, ou le mirage de la neutralité," *Le monde diplomatique*, June 1973.

12. See note 6 for a rare exception.

13. As early as January 1962, Roger Hilsman observed the bombing of a Cambodian village by American planes, who then attacked the Vietnamese village that was the intended target. Cf. *To Move a Nation* (New York: Delta, 1967). For a partial record, see my *At War with Asia* (New York: Pantheon Books, 1970), chap. 3.

10. THE REMAKING OF HISTORY

1. See *At War with Asia* (New York: Pantheon Books, 1970), chap. 1; *For Reasons of State* (New York: Pantheon Books, 1973), chap. 1, sec. 5. On the dangers posed by Communist successes in South Vietnam, see Douglas Pike, *Viet Cong* (Cambridge, MA: MIT Press, 1966). See also the important study by Jeffrey Race, *War Comes to Long An* (Berkeley: University of California Press, 1971). Also William A. Nighswonger, *Rural Pacification in Vietnam* (New York: Praeger, 1967); Robert L. Sansom, *The Economics of Insurgency in the Mekong Delta of Vietnam* (Cambridge, MA: MIT Press, 1970).

It is this concern over the dangers of Communist successes in organizing the rural population that explains the savagery of the U.S. attack on the rural societies of South Vietnam and Laos, compounded in the case of South Vietnam by the fear that the NLF might realize its efforts to neutralize South Vietnam, along with Laos and Cambodia. It is important to recognize that in terms of its basic objectives, the United States won the war in Indochina, despite the major defeat it suffered. The National Liberation Front of South Vietnam was destroyed, particularly in the post-Tet accelerated pacification campaigns, along with the rural society in which it was embedded. All of Indochina was reduced to a level of bare survival from which it may never recover. Postwar U.S. policy has been designed to ensure that the prospects for recovery are slight. For further discussion of the substantial, though not complete U.S. victory in Indochina, and the ways in which the facts are presented to the public in the free press, see Noam Chomsky and Edward S. Herman, *The Political Economy of Human Rights*, vol. 2 (Cambridge, MA: South End Press, 1979).

2. Robert W. Tucker, *The Radical Left and American Foreign Policy* (Baltimore: Johns Hopkins University Press, 1971); "Vietnam: The Final Reckoning," *Commentary* (May 1975).

3. Equally faulty is Tucker's argument that since "the costs of imperialism may prove harmful to the greater economy, thus creating dissension among the corporate rulers" (as happened in Vietnam, by early 1968), there must be a fallacy in the "radical critique" that attributes the main thrust of U.S. imperial intervention to "benefits . . . calculated primarily in terms of the interests of America's 'corporate rulers.' " In fact, as the "radical critique" he is discussing consistently observed, it was just this reassessment of costs that led to a shift toward less "costly" tactics, including greater reliance on surrogate forces and a more capital-intensive war, and finally toward liquidation of the enterprise. By Tucker's logic, one could prove that corporate managers do not pursue the maximization of profit, since sometimes they shut down an inefficient plant. For further discussion of errors of fact and logic in Tucker's critique, see Chomsky, *For Reasons of State*. This is, nevertheless, the best and most serious effort in mainstream scholarship to come to terms with the so-called radical critique, to which the term "radical" hardly applies, in my view.

4. Arthur M. Schlesinger, *The Bitter Heritage* (Boston: Houghton-Mifflin, 1967).

5. There is an enlightening account of the early days, and the lost opportunities, in Archimedes L. A. Patti, *Why Viet Nam? Prelude to America's Albatross* (Berkeley: University of California Press, 1980). Many important documents bearing on this and later periods are assembled in Gareth Porter, *Vietnam: The Definitive Documentation*, 2 vols. (New York: Coleman, Stanfordville, 1979). See Chomsky, *For Reasons of State*, chap. 1, for discussion of the record in the Pentagon Papers. See also Richard B. Duboff, "Business Ideology and Foreign Policy: The National Security Council and Vietnam," in N. Chomsky and Howard Zinn, eds., *Critical Essays*, vol. 5 of *The Pentagon Papers* (Gravel ed.) (Boston: Beacon, 1972). On the post-Geneva period, see particularly Race, op. cit.

6. Roger Hilsman, *To Move a Nation* (Garden City, NY: Doubleday, 1967).

7. On this period, see George McT. Kahin, "Political Polarization in South Vietnam: U.S. Policy in the Post-Diem Period," *Pacific Affairs* (Winter 1979–80). As Kahin observes, the group of South Vietnamese generals and civilians who ousted the Diem regime "had a set of priorities that differed markedly from those of the administration in Washington and hinged on a political rather than a military solution. . . . They looked towards a negotiated agreement among the Vietnamese parties themselves without American intervention." But this view was intolerable to the United States because, as Under-Secretary of State George Ball explained, "Nothing is further from USG mind than 'neutral solution for Vietnam.' We intend to win." Ball is widely regarded as a "dove," since he was later opposed to a full-scale invasion be-

yond the level of about 75,000 men. The post-Diem Vietnamese leadership regarded the NLF as "overwhelmingly non-communist, with the PRP [People's Revolutionary Party—its avowedly Communist component] still having no dominance and indeed only a minor position within the organization," and "sufficiently free of Hanoi's control to have made [a peaceful settlement in South Vietnam] quite possible," with a pro-Western neutralist government: "Unfortunately there were leaks of our plans [for a negotiated settlement among South Vietnamese] and it is apparent that the American government got wind of them" (Nguyen Ngoc Tho, the civilian prime minister, in 1969). The South Vietnamese generals were also opposed to the American plan to bomb North Vietnam, put into operation a year later. For these reasons, the post-Diem government was overthrown in a U.S.-organized coup placing General Khanh in power, to be overthrown a year later in another U.S.-backed coup. At each stage, the United States imposed a regime that could then "invite" the United States to "defend it" against aggression (sometimes, the United States failed even to notify its client of these steps, so that the "request" was subsequent to them). The great fear of the United States that there might be neutralization of South Vietnam in 1964, in accordance with the official program of the NLF, is well documented in the Pentagon Papers; cf. *For Reasons of State*.

8. Maxwell D. Taylor, *Swords and Plowshares* (New York: Norton, 1972).

9. See chap. 3 in Chomsky, *Towards a New Cold War: U.S. Foreign Policy from Vietnam to Reagan* (New York: The New Press, 2003).

10. Taylor, *Swords and Plowshares*, see chap. 3.

11. Ibid., see the references cited in chap. 3, note 35.

12. *New York Times*, April 21, 24, May 1, 1975. Subsequently, Lewis has repeatedly made clear his evaluation of the U.S. war in Indochina, with such references to it as the following: Regarding Rhodesia, America should do nothing, because "if we remember Vietnam, we know that intervention, *however well-intended*, may do terrible harm if it is uninformed" (*New York Times*, February 1, 1979); in Cambodia, the United States dropped three times the tonnage of bombs that fell on Japan in World War II, with the result that "thousands of square miles of what had been fertile land, dotted with villages, were devastated," meanwhile "creat[ing] the Khmer Rouge" (citing Sihanouk)—"in short, the policy, *however sincerely intended*, had disastrous results" (September 24, 1979); the argument against the war "was that the United States had misunderstood the cultural and political forces at work in Indochina—that it was in a position where it could not impose a solution *except at a price too costly to itself*" (December 27, 1979); the Christmas bombing of Hanoi "was the symbol of a much larger failure: the continuation of the war for four years after every informed person knew *it could not be won*. The price of that failure was and still is enormous. From 1969 through 1972 the United States spent $50 billion on the Indochina war, dropped 4 million tons of bombs, lost 20,492 American lives. But *the highest cost* was not measurable in figures. *It was the further polarization of this country, the political embitterment*" (December 22, 1980); "what we learned in Vietnam, and have to keep recalling, is that there are limits to what the greatest power can do" (December 27, 1979); etc. (my emphases).

Recall that I am quoting from one of the most outspoken critics of the war in the mainstream American press, a person who in some cases was almost alone in refusing to join the chauvinist consensus (see below). It would be a sad enough commentary on the United States and its ideological institutions if such sentiments as these had been quoted from the jingoist extreme of the spectrum of mainstream opinion.

With tedious predictability, Lewis unquestioningly repeats the government propaganda line on the Christmas bombings: Thieu and his Saigon colleagues "blocked" the October agreements after "Kissinger declared that peace was 'at hand,' " and thus "forced the last bloody chapter," namely, the bombing of Hanoi. On the facts, see chaps. 3 and 6 of *Towards a New Cold War.*

13. Bernard Fall, "Vietcong—the Unseen Enemy in Vietnam," *New Society*, April 25, 1965, reprinted in Fall and M. G. Raskin, eds., *The Vietnam Reader* (New York: Vintage, 1965).

14. Cited from the Nuremberg Documents by Karl Dietrich Bracher, *The German Dictatorship* (New York: Praeger, 1970), 423.

15. For discussion, based on research by Kevin Buckley and Alex Shimkin, see *The Political Economy of Human Rights*, vol. 1, chap. 5, section 1.3. See also chap. 5 of *Towards a New Cold War.*

16. Charles E. Bohlen, *The Transformation of American Foreign Policy* (New York: Norton, 1969).

17. Charles Kadushin, *The American Intellectual Elite* (Boston: Little, Brown, 1974); see chap. 1, above. On the polls, see Andre Modigliani, *American Political Science Review*, September 1972.

18. Evelyn Keene, *Boston Globe*, May 18; commencement address at Bentley College.

19. James McCartney, *Boston Globe*, May 29, 1975.

20. See chap. 8 of *Towards a New Cold War.*

21. Editorial, *New Republic*, February 1, 1975. The editors warn against the kind of "arbitrarily consistent policy" that would have us eschew the use or threat of force (as required by law). They reassure the Pentagon that it is "wrong to assume that those who opposed the Vietnam horror are blindly bound to permanent opposition to military action"—rather, "they will be receptive to arguments about national interest and for that matter about ethical obligations to democratic allies threatened by terror and aggression" (read: "Israel, threatened with loss of control over the occupied territories"). They stress, of course, the benevolent purposes of our military intervention in the Middle East, if we are driven to such steps.

The reader may check to see when U.S. actions in Indochina were described as "aggression" by these editors, or when they have soberly discussed invading Canada, England, Venezuela, Iran (during the period when it was a client regime), countries that also committed "aggression" by supporting the rise of oil prices.

22. Cf. Jonathan Power, *New York Times*, March 15, 1975; several articles in *Middle East International* (April 1975); the analysis by the Pakistani director of policy planning and program review at the World Bank, reported by David Francis, *Christian Science Monitor*, May 5, 1975; and many other sources.

11. FOREIGN POLICY AND THE INTELLIGENTSIA

1. For references and further comment, see Chomsky, *For Reasons of State* (New York: Pantheon Books, 1973). Cf. also the description of refugees in South Vietnam by Leo Cherne, chairman of the executive committee of Freedom House and chairman of the board of directors of the International Rescue Committee: "There are more than 700,000 additional refugees who have recently fled the countryside dominated by the Vietcong and with their act of flight have chosen the meager sanctuary provided by the government of South Vietnam" ("Why We Can't Withdraw," *Saturday Review*, December 18, 1965). On U.S. programs of forced generation of refugees at that time and later (and indeed, since 1962), see *For Reasons of State*, see also chap. 5 of *"Human Rights" and American Foreign Policy* (Nottingham: Spokesman, 1978). To cite one example, as Cherne wrote about the refugees fleeing the Vietcong, a government-sponsored study explained that U.S. air and artillery bombardment impel the vil-

lagers "to move where they will be safe from such attacks . . . regardless of their attitude to the GVN [the U.S. client government]." No doubt some Soviet Cherne is now writing about how refugees are fleeing to the meager sanctuary of Kabul, trying to escape the murderous terrorists who dominate the countryside, agents of Western imperialism.

To show that there are no limits to cynicism, Cherne adds that "the South Vietnamese ask only to be left in peace to overcome" the defects of the GVN, "its instability, the imperfections of its democratic institutions, and the inadequacy of its economic and social programs." With as much justice, his Soviet counterpart could now explain how the people of Afghanistan ask only to be left in peace to overcome the similar problems of their struggling nation, defended from aggression by Soviet benevolence. The extent to which such remarkable assertions pass without arousing horror and indignation, even comment, is a fair measure of the extent to which Bakunin was correct in describing "worship of the state" as the malady of the intellectuals.

2. *New York Times*, February 6, 1966.

3. *New York Times*, September 28, 1974. See chap. 1 of *"Human Rights" and American Foreign Policy*, note 33, for a similar example from liberal scholarship. Examples are legion.

4. Peter L. Berger, "When Two Elites Meet," *Washington Post*, April 18, 1976, reprinted from *Commentary*, March 1976.

5. Samuel P. Huntington, in M. J. Crozier, S. P. Huntington, and J. Watanuki, *The Crisis of Democracy: Report on the Governability of Democracies to the Trilateral Commission* (New York: New York University Press, 1975). See also chap. 1 of *"Human Rights" and American Foreign Policy*, note 34.

6. See chaps. 3 and 4 of *"Human Rights" and American Foreign Policy* for some specific examples, and N. Chomsky and E. S. Herman, *The Political Economy of Human Rights*, 2 vols. (Cambridge, MA: South End Press, 1979), for extensive documentation and discussion.

7. See Chomsky articles "Watergate: A Skeptical View," *New York Review of Books*, September 20, 1973; editorial, *More*, December 1975; and introduction to N. Blackstock, ed., *COINTELPRO* (New York: Vintage Books, 1976).

8. On the limited nature of opposition to the Vietnam War among the intelligentsia, see chap. 1 of *"Human Rights" and American Foreign Policy*. For some acute commentary on critique of the student movement and the refusal to join popular opposition to the war, see Julius Jacobson, "In Defense of the Young," *New Politics*, June 1970.

9. *Boston Globe*, October 18, 1976. Variants of this argument are common. Recall the observation by Martin Peretz, editor of the *New Republic*, cited in chap. 1 of *"Human Rights" and American Foreign Policy*: "The American collapse [in Indochina] will read in history as among the ugliest of national crimes" (June 11, 1977). Peretz makes an interesting contribution to the new version of history now being created. He states that the book he is reviewing "stakes out significant independent ground—implicitly against the peace movement" by arguing "that a political settlement was possible," thus implying that "the peace movement" was against a political settlement. Of course, everyone on every side was in favor of a political settlement, but they differed on the terms: Crucially, should the National Liberation Front, which the United States government always knew to be the only mass-based political force in South Vietnam, be permitted to share in (hence presumably to dominate) the governance of the South? The "peace movement," to the extent that such an entity can be identified, argued for a political settlement on these terms, which the United States government rejected on the grounds that if the group it supported were to enter a coalition with the NLF, "the whale would swallow the minnow," in the picturesque phrase of government expert Douglas Pike. Until it committed the ugly crime of failing, the United States government was committed to blocking any such po-

litical settlement. Placed against the background of the actual history, which he knows well enough, Peretz's argument that it was criminal for the United States to desist can be understood in its full significance.

10. See chaps. 3 and 6 of *"Human Rights" and American Foreign Policy*.

11. Bruce Andrews, *Public Constraint and American Policy in Vietnam*, SAGE Publications, International Studies Series, vol. 4 (1976). Note that the facts are somewhat ambiguous, as Andrews explains, in that much of this opposition was of the "win or get out" variety.

12. *Crisis of Democracy* (above, note 5). See chap. 1, above.

13. For particularly inane musings along these lines, see Sandy Vogelsang, *The Long Dark Night of the Soul* (New York: Harper & Row, 1974).

14. Nathan Glazer, "American Jews and Israel: The Last Support," *Interchange*, November 1976.

15. Gordon Connell-Smith, *The Inter-American System* (Oxford: Royal Institute of International Affairs, 1966), 343.

16. Consider Henry Kissinger's characterization of the "statesman": "He judges ideas on their utility and not on their 'truth.' " The word "truth" is placed in quotes, reflecting the contempt that Kissinger has always felt for this concept. In the same essay he complains of the difficulty of dealing with the "ideological leadership" of the Communist states: "The essence of Marxism-Leninism . . . is the view that 'objective' factors such as the social structure, the economic process, and, above all, the class struggle are more important than the personal convictions of statesmen . . . Nothing in the personal experience of Soviet leaders would lead them to accept protestations of good will at face value," as we do all the time. "Domestic structure and foreign policy," in *American Foreign Policy* (New York: Norton, 1969).

A few pages later Kissinger identifies "the deepest problem of the contemporary international order": It is nothing like starvation, war, oppression, or other trivia that occupy superficial minds, but rather the fact that current debates are peripheral to the "basic division" between two styles of policy and a "difference of philosophical perspective" that separates the West, which "is deeply committed to the notion that the real world is external to the observer," from "cultures which escaped the early impact of Newtonian thinking," and still believe "that the real world is almost completely *internal* to the observer." The French Revolution, Lenin, Mao, and others failed to cross this philosophical barrier (though Russia, he concedes, has partly come to recognize that there is a real world outside of our heads). Just how this squares with the idea that the Communists are difficult because of their absurd concern for objective reality is not easy to determine, but perhaps this all-too-typical nonsense should simply be dismissed as a parody of the academic intellectual, which was in fact quite effective with the media and, remarkably, with the academic world as well. See chap. 6 of *"Human Rights" and American Foreign Policy*.

17. The term is used by Isaiah Berlin, "The Bent Twig," *Foreign Affairs*, October 1972. The context suggests that he has in mind primarily the subservient intelligentsia of the state socialist societies, an apt but insufficiently general usage.

18. It is worth noting Kissinger's uncritical acceptance of the legitimacy of this concept of "the expert" as someone who grovels before authority, whatever may be the truth—or as he would say, the "truth" (see note 16).

19. In the essay cited in note 16, Kissinger observes that "law and business . . . furnish the core of the leadership groups in America." So far, he is correct. But which lawyers? Those who defend civil rights of blacks? Obviously not. Rather, overwhelmingly, those linked to corporate power. And which businessmen? The corner grocer? Evidently it is the "business élite," whose special talent, Kissinger adds, is their "ability to manipulate the known"—an

ability that they share with carpenters and the peasants who have yet to learn about the existence of the external world. Putting aside the typical obfuscation, the fact that Kissinger carefully skirts is that foreign policy is largely in the hands of those with private power. Some ideologists are more straightforward, e.g., Huntington, who writes (in *The Crisis of Democracy*) that "Truman had been able to govern the country with the cooperation of a relatively small number of Wall Street lawyers and bankers," though he fears that these happy days are gone, since other groups have been "mobilized and organized" to advance their own interests, leading to a "crisis of democracy." See chap. 1 of *"Human Rights" and American Foreign Policy*.

20. See chap. 1 of *"Human Rights" and American Foreign Policy*, 82.

21. *Trialogue*, Fall 1976.

22. For example, Leon Wieseltier explains that my political writings "are a monument to left-wing paranoia, devoted as they are to demonstrating that the press in this country is 'a system of state-supported propaganda'; nothing that Chomsky wrote about the slaughter in Cambodia was quite as angry as his attack on Jean Lacouture for misquoting the number of its victims" (*New Republic*, September 23, 1981). Turning to the facts, the alleged quote is simply a fabrication. Secondly, the nature of my "attack" on Lacouture is accurately illustrated in this summary passage: "In what passes for intellectual discourse in the West, political discussion included, correction of errors is rare indeed, as a glance at review journals will indicate. Lacouture deserves credit for departing from the general norm. We think that his corrections are inadequate and disagree with some of the conclusions expressed in them, but we want to stress that it is no crime to misread—it is a rare review that avoids error—and it is only proper to issue corrections when errors are discovered" (*Political Economy of Human Rights*, vol. 2, 377). In contrast, we described "the record of atrocities" of the Khmer Rouge as "substantial and often gruesome," etc.

Wieseltier does believe that some criticism of the press is not paranoid: "There *is* a scandal, and it is the moral and political prestige of the PLO [in media] coverage of the Middle East," something that will be apparent to every reader of the American press.

Since my "attack on Lacouture" has taken on a mythical life of its own, perhaps a word about the facts is in order (ibid., for details). Lacouture's review of François Ponchaud's *Cambodge année zéro* appeared in the *Nouvel Observateur* and the *New York Review* in early 1977, and was widely quoted in the press here as an authoritative account of Ponchaud's work. I read the book and found that there was scarcely a reference to it in the review that was even near accurate. In the case to which Wieseltier alludes, Lacouture claimed that the Khmer Rouge had "boasted" of having murdered some 2 million people, apparently basing himself on Ponchaud's estimate that 800,000 had been killed during the war and that some 1.2 million had died from all causes since. I wrote Lacouture a personal letter, pointing out a series of such errors and suggesting that he issue corrections. In publishing partial corrections in the *New York Review* (never in France), Lacouture posed to me the question whether it is an important matter "whether the regime has murdered thousands or hundreds of thousands of wretched people" (the original claim was a "boast" of 2 million murdered). In a review-article in the *Nation* in which we recommended Ponchaud's book as "serious and worth reading," noting his "grisly account of what refugees have reported to him about the barbarity of their treatment at the hands of the Khmer Rouge," E. S. Herman and I responded to Lacouture's rhetorical question, stating that we felt that facts do matter, and that a factor of 100 or 1000 in estimates of killings is not insignificant. We also noted that there was wide disparity in estimates of killings, ranging from the *Far Eastern Economic Review* ("possibly thousands" killed) to Lacouture's original 2 million figure, adding that we were in no position to determine which estimates were correct; Lacouture himself oscillated from a boast of 2 million murdered to possibly thousands killed, within a few months. This was followed by a remarkable campaign of deceit and outright prevarication in the international press, alleging that I was denying Pol Pot crimes; some of the press (including the *New Republic*, repeatedly) refused the normal right of reply. To mention only one example, in the author's preface to the American edition of his book, Ponchaud cites my praise for it and in turn praises me for "the responsible attitude and precision of thought" shown in what I had written about Cambodia (which in fact includes everything that appeared during the Pol Pot period). In the author's preface to the world edition, dated the very same day, these passages are eliminated and replaced by the allegation that I "sharply criticized" his book, claim that there were "no massacres," and insist that one rely on "deliberately chosen official statements" of the regime while excluding the testimony of refugees—all falsehoods, as Ponchaud knew very well; compare the simultaneous American edition, which is not available elsewhere while the world edition is unavailable in the U.S. His allegations in the world edition were widely repeated and in fact seeped back to the United States, while his comments here were ignored, as was the exposure of this deception. This is not the place to review the record, which provides an intriguing insight into the attitude of much of the intelligentsia toward the curious idea that one should try to keep to the truth, even when joining in the chorus of condemnation of an official enemy.

23. The following remarks on the War-Peace Studies Project relies on Laurence H. Shoup, "Shaping the Postwar World," *Insurgent Sociologist* 5, no. 3 (Spring 1975), where there are explicit references for the quotes that appear below. See now also the important study by Laurence Shoup and William Minter, *Imperial Brain Trust* (New York: Monthly Review Press, 1977), to my knowledge the first serious study of this project, issued in early 1977 to a resounding silence, apart from ritual denunciation in the journal of the CFR by William Bundy (*Foreign Affairs*, October 1977).

24. Cf. Gabriel Kolko, *The Politics of War* (New York: Random House, 1968), and David P. Calleo and Benjamin M. Rowland, *America and the World Political Economy* (Bloomington: Indiana University Press, 1973). Kolko is, to my knowledge, the first historian to have seriously investigated this question. Calleo and Rowland conclude that "the war had exhausted British economic power. To a considerable extent, the United States was responsible. Throughout the War, Hull, determined to break up the British bloc, had used the leverage of Lend-Lease skillfully and systematically to reduce Britain to a financial satellite." The British, of course, were aware of what was going on; Calleo and Rowland quote an "outraged" communication from Churchill to Roosevelt on the subject. See also Introduction, note 16 of *"Human Rights" and American Foreign Policy.*

25. There has been much debate over the question of how or whether Western policy deliberately contributed to this outcome. Albert Speer recalls "one single case" of direct cooperation between Hitler and the West—namely, an arrangement for the transfer of German troops cut off by the British fleet on a Greek island to the Russian front, to allow the British, rather than the Russians, to take Salonika. Albert Speer, *Inside the Third Reich* (New York: Macmillan, 1970; Avon Books, 1971), 509.

26. Cf. chap. 11 of *"Human Rights" and American Foreign Policy*, note 4.

27. Cf. Kolko, op. cit. 302f.

28. The Western Hemisphere was then and for many years after the major producing area. Until 1968 North America surpassed the Middle East in oil production. Cf. John Blair, *The Control of Oil* (New York: Pantheon Books, 1976).

29. For discussion of how this principle was applied or abrogated to extend the power of the American oil companies, see *Multinational Oil Corporations and U.S. Foreign Policy* (hence-

forth, *MNOC)*, Report to the Committee on Foreign Relations, U.S. Senate, January 2, 1975 (Washington, DC: Government Printing Office, 1975).

30. Cf. Michael Tanzer, *The Energy Crisis* (New York: Monthly Review Press, 1974), in particular, his discussion of the devices used to shift other countries to an oil-based economy. Cf. also Joyce and Gabriel Kolko, *The Limits of Power* (New York: Harper & Row, 1972).

31. This plan was actually imposed on the oil companies by the government, naturally over the strong objections of the British. This is one of several instances that reveal how the government may disregard the parochial short-term interests of even major segments of the corporate system in order to safeguard the more general interests of American capitalism. For discussion, see chap. 11 of *"Human Rights" and American Foreign Policy.*

The 40 percent American share was distributed among the five major American companies, who were persuaded to relinquish 1 percent each to American independent companies for "window dressing," according to the Middle East coordinator for Exxon (*MNOC*, 71). It should be remembered that this was shortly after President Truman had killed a grand jury investigation of the oil cartel on grounds of "national security," on recommendation of the Departments of State, Defense, and Interior, who advised that the "American oil operations are, for all practical purposes, instruments of our foreign policy"—and who might have added, reciprocally, that our foreign policy is to a significant extent guided by long-term oil company interests.

32. Yoshio Tsurumi, "Japan," in "The Oil Crisis: In Perspective," *Daedalus*, Fall 1975. Discussing the prewar period, the same author has commented on "the American myth that the government and business circles of the United States operate at arms-length, if not in outright adversary relationships"—Reviews, *Journal of International Affairs*, Spring/Summer 1976. It should be noted that under the conditions cited in the preceding note, local conflict may occasionally arise, since, insofar as it functions as a generalized agency of American capitalism, the government may have concerns different from those of some particular segment.

33. For a review of the contents of these memoranda, see Richard B. Du Boff, "Business Ideology and Foreign Policy," in N. Chomsky and H. Zinn, eds., *Critical Essays*, published as volume 5 of the Gravel edition of the Pentagon Papers (Boston: Beacon, 1972). For further analysis of the contribution of the Pentagon Papers to the understanding of United States imperial planning, see John Dower, "The Superdomino in Postwar Asia," in the same volume, and my *For Reasons of State*, particularly 31–66.

34. *Annals of the American Academy of Political and Social Science*, March 1976.

35. Robert L. Gallucci, *Neither Peace nor Honor: the Politics of American Military Policy in Vietnam* (Baltimore: Johns Hopkins University Press, 1975). The limitation to "military policy" is crucial; basic decision-making with regard to the American involvement in Vietnam is nowhere discussed.

36. Largely as a result of the impact of the student movement, it became difficult to ignore completely the so-called radical critique—though, as noted, it is not obvious why the assumption that the United States behaves much as all other great powers do should be considered particularly "radical." There are, in fact, several publications attempting to deal with it. The most serious, to my knowledge, is Robert W. Tucker, *The Radical Left and American Foreign Policy* (Baltimore: Johns Hopkins University Press, 1971). For a discussion of gross errors of fact and logic that entirely undermine his analysis (and others), see *For Reasons of State*. For a very penetrating discussion of critical literature on the "radical critique," see Stephen Shalom, "Economic Interests and United States Foreign Policy," unpublished, adapted from the author's Boston University Ph.D. dissertation: "US-Philippine Relations: A Study of Neo-Colonialism" (1976).

An interesting example of the evasion and misrepresentation of the "radical critique" appears in the study by Leslie H. Gelb, who was director of the Pentagon Papers project (*The Irony of Vietnam: The System Worked*, with Richard K. Betts [Washington, DC: Brookings Institution, 1979]). He begins by outlining nine "wide-ranging explanations of U.S. involvement given in the Vietnam War literature." The first two of these are "idealistic imperialism" and "economic imperialism" (the latter explanation is allegedly mine; for comment, see *For Reasons of State*, 63–65). Gelb then explains why these "stereotypes fail," including the first two, and crucially the second, which, when presented without his distortion, is the thesis that is documented in the Pentagon Papers and elsewhere, a fact that Gelb systematically ignores. Curiously, his analysis of defects covers all of the theories presented with the exception of the first two theses, which are ignored in this analysis of defects and subsequently. The only comment that has even marginal bearing on the alleged failure of this "stereotype" is this: "But however these explanations are combined, they are better as answers to the question of why the United States originally became involved and committed in Vietnam than as analyses of the process of involvement, the strategy for fighting the war, and the strategy for ending it." Even that statement is false: In fact, the "radical" thesis documented in Gelb's Pentagon Papers study and ignored in his book provides quite a convincing explanation for the evolution of U.S. strategy throughout Indochina and also for the Nixon-Kissinger effort to salvage victory from defeat (cf. chap. 3 of *"Human Rights" and American Foreign Policy*), and furthermore for the postwar policy of exploiting and maintaining the quite substantial, even if only partial, U.S. victory—namely, the destruction of Indochina, which succeeds in deflecting the dread "domino effect" of successful development that might be emulated elsewhere (cf. chap. 4, note 1 of *"Human Rights" and American Foreign Policy*). But even assuming Gelb's comment to be accurate, note the implications. A study of the sources of U.S. policy is dismissed as irrelevant and beside the point; we must restrict attention to the execution of this policy. When Gelb refers to "doves," he restricts attention to "pessimists," who thought that the United States would fail, and who "were not ignored," Gelb observes, which shows that "the system worked." The only analyses of U.S. policy that can be seriously considered are those that sought to explain why "the United States failed in Vietnam," not those that reject the assumption that the United States had a right to succeed.

Gelb is one of those who regard concern for French sensibilities and the French role in Europe as being of paramount importance in guiding U.S. policy in the early years. While this may have been a minor factor, the documentary record shows clearly that imperial strategy concerning the Far East was a far more predominant one. Gelb is not unaware of the latter factor, but misrepresents it, without providing any evidence, as "an inversion of Marxist theory," in which "economic interest was used as a cloak for political interest." The popularity of the former thesis (which is widely regarded as the "sophisticated" theory) can easily be explained by the fact that it is far less threatening to the state religion than the actual record of planning revealed in considerable detail in the Pentagon Papers.

Even on the narrow issue of strategy for realizing the objectives that Gelb misstates, his use of documentary evidence is worth careful investigation. For example, in discussing the aftermath of the Geneva Accords in 1954, he does not so much as mention the National Security Council response (NSC 5429/2, August 20, 1954); for good reason, as we see when we consider the contents of this document, which laid plans for U.S. subversion and aggression throughout East Asia in response to the dangerous threat that peace might be brought to Indochina. Cf. *For Reasons of State*, 100f. (Also 140, below.) Interestingly, this document is even severely misrepresented in the Pentagon Papers study itself, as noted in *For Reasons of State*.

37. See chap. 1 of *"Human Rights" and American Foreign Policy*, note 23 for one of many examples.

38. Lawrence B. Krause, "The International Economic System and the Multinational Corporation," in *The Multinational Corporation, Annals of the American Academy of Political and Social Science,* September 1972.

39. Ray, "Corporations and American Foreign Relations."

40. Gaddis Smith, "The United States as Villain," *New York Times Book Review*, October 10, 1976.

41. Cited in Charles B. Maurer, *Call to Revolution* (Detroit: Wayne State University Press, 1971), 174.

42. A fact of which the business press is not unaware, though businessmen constantly whine of their difficulties in reaching public opinion with their "message." See chap. 1 of *"Human Rights" and American Foreign Policy.*

43. See chap. 11 of *"Human Rights" and American Foreign Policy.*

44. "International Economics," *Business Week*, March 29, 1976.

45. *Winning the Cold War: The U.S. Ideological Offensive*, Hearings before the Subcommittee on International Organizations and Movements of the Committee on Foreign Affairs, House of Representatives, 88th Congress, second session, Part VIII, U.S. Government Agencies and Programs, January 15 and 16, 1964 (Washington, DC: U.S. Government Printing Office), 953f.

46. In much of Latin America and Asia, the AID-trained police have proven to be among the most vicious torturers and murderers. El Salvador is a recent example. See Introduction of *"Human Rights" and American Foreign Policy*. The U.S.-trained military have been no less adept at repression and slaughter. On this topic, see *The Political Economy of Human Rights*, vol. I, and references cited there.

To cite only one example, consider Somoza's Nicaragua. A National Guard offensive resulted "in thousands of deaths in the countryside, where whole villages suspected of harboring guerillas were destroyed," and villagers describe "aerial bombings, summary executions and gruesome tortures . . . it is also believed by many that an ongoing American-backed 'peasant welfare ' program [heavily financed by AID] is actually a cover for anti-guerilla activities" in the north, where these military exercises were being conducted. Furthermore, "about 85 percent of the National Guard leadership is directly trained in anti-guerilla warfare by the United States" in Nicaragua, which is "the only country which sends the entire annual graduating class of its military academy for a full year of training" at the United States Army school in the Panama Canal Zone. Stephen Kinzer, "Nicaragua, a Wholly Owned Subsidiary," *New Republic,* April 9, 1977. In a pastoral letter the seven principal Catholic prelates of Nicaragua denounced the "atrocious climate of terror" that reigned in the country. Jean-Claude Buhrer, "Les droits de l'homme en Amérique centrale," *Le Monde diplomatique,* May 1977. Even the generally ludicrous State Department *Human Rights Reports* concede that there may have been a few problems in Nicaragua (primarily, as a result of Cuban-supported guerrilla activities), while naturally ignoring entirely the United States role. Cf. *Human Rights Reports,* submitted to the Subcommittee on Foreign Assistance of the Committee on Foreign Relations, of the U.S. Senate, March 1977 (Washington, DC: U.S. Government Printing Office, 1977). For discussion of these reports, see *Political Economy of Human Rights,* vol. I.

47. Otto H. Kahn, *The Myth of American Imperialism*, publication of the Committee of American Business Men, an address given December 30, 1924, at a meeting on the subject of American imperialism organized by the League for Industrial Democracy, 4, section entitled "The Allegation of Political or Military Imperialism."

48. For references, see chap. 4 of *"Human Rights" and American Foreign Policy*.

49. James Chace, "American Intervention," *New York Times*, September 13, 1976.

50. Chace, "How 'Moral' Can We Get?" *New York Times Magazine*, May 22, 1977.

51. To be sure, the contradiction can easily be resolved. We can take these statements as an indication of what is really meant by the term "stability" in the rhetoric of American political analysis.

52. Norman A. Graebner, *Cold War Diplomacy: 1945–60* (New York: D. Van Nostrand, 1962).

53. Sixto Lopez, "The Philippine Problem: A Proposition for a Solution," *The Outlook*, April 13, 1901.

54. "How 'Moral' Can We Get?" The word "often" is a bit of an understatement.

55. News conference, March 24, 1977; reprinted in the *New York Times*, March 25.

56. Commencement address at Bentley College. *Boston Globe*, May 18, 1975. See chap. 4.

57. William Beecher, "US show of force impressed N. Korea," *Boston Globe*, September 3, 1976.

58. Quarterly Review Staff Study, "The Attack on the Irrigation Dams in North Korea," *Air Universities Quarterly Review* 6, no. 4 (Winter 1953–54). Cf. also Robert Frank Futrell, *The United States Air Force in Korea, 1950–1953* (New York: Duell, Sloan and Pearce, 1961), 623f.

59. John Osborne, *New Republic*, June 7, 1975. See chap. 4 of *"Human Rights" and American Foreign Policy* for the further thoughts of this courageous defender of the nation's honor.

12. THE UNITED STATES AND EAST TIMOR

1. For documentation bearing on the period through 1978 and much further detail, see Chomsky and E. S. Herman, *The Political Economy of Human Rights*, vol. 1 (Cambridge, MA: South End Press, 1979), chap. 3, section 4.4, and references cited there. Also Arnold Kohen and John Taylor, *An Act of Genocide*, TAPOL, U.K. (1979); available from the East Timor Human Rights Committee, Box 363, Clinton Station, Syracuse, NY 13201.

2. Jack Anderson, *Washington Post*, November 9, 1979. Air Force General Brent Scowcroft, President Ford's National Security Adviser, stated: "I guess it was fundamentally a matter of recognizing reality. We really had no reasonable options. . . . It made no sense to antagonize the Indonesians. . . . East Timor was not a viable entity"; Daniel Southerland, "U.S. role in plight of Timor: an issue that won't go away," *Christian Science Monitor*, March 6, 1980.

U.S. officials have repeatedly claimed that the United States was unaware of what was happening in Timor, but it has always been obvious that this was mere pretense; cf. Chomsky and Herman, op. cit. and the Afterword which follows. Anderson notes a classified U.S. intelligence report of September 19, 1975, describing an Indonesian attack that met "stiff resistance from Fretilin fighters." Another report states that Indonesian generals were "losing patience with President Suharto's go-slow approach to the Portuguese Timor problem and . . . pressing him to authorize direct military intervention." A December 3 intelligence report states that "ranking Indonesian civilian government leaders have decided that the only solution in the Portuguese Timor situation is for Indonesia to launch an open offensive against Fretilin," and another report alerted Ford and Kissinger that Suharto would bring up the Timor issue on their visit to Jakarta and would "try and elicit a sympathetic attitude" from Ford, who informed Anderson that the U.S. national interest "had to be on the side of Indonesia," while giving what Anderson calls his "tacit approval" to the invasion. In fact, there is no doubt that the United States was keeping close watch on the situation.

3. Fully aware of what they were doing, the Ford and then the Carter Administration not only provided the material support for the massacre, but placed no constraints on how U.S. equipment should be used, in clear violation of the 1958 U.S.-Indonesian bilateral arms agreement which requires that U.S. arms be used only for defensive purposes. Administration witness David Kenney stated in congressional hearings that "as long as we are giving military assistance of any sort to Indonesia we are not telling where they will or will not use it. We have not done so so far" (Hearings before the Subcommittees on Asian and Pacific Affairs and on International Organizations of the Committee on Foreign Affairs, House of Representatives, 96th Congress, and session, February 1980, 193). Kenney was at the time Legislative Management Officer for Human Rights *(sic)* in the Congressional Relations Office at the State Department and is a specialist on Indonesia. From 1975 through 1979, the United States furnished over $250 million in military assistance to Indonesia, most of it after the Carter Administration accelerated the arms flow. See Scott Sidel, "The United States and Genocide in East Timor," *Journal of Contemporary Asia* 11, no. 1 (1981).

4. Daniel P. Moynihan with Suzanne Weaver, *A Dangerous Place* (Boston: Little, Brown, 1978).

5. Not for lack of effort. On December 8, 1980, the *New York Times* published a report of an address by now-Senator Moynihan (whose gall knows no limits) to the Committee for United Nations Integrity. The *Times* reports: "The conference addressed by Senator Moynihan, which was called to assess the direction of the United Nations, issued a statement signed by more than 100 scholars, scientists and artists that denounced the world body as 'no longer the guardian of social justice, human rights and equality among nations.' It said the organization is 'perverted by irrelevant political machinations' and 'is in danger of becoming a force against peace itself.' " On the same day, the *Times* carried an editorial on the Indonesian invasion of East Timor, which led to the death of "a tenth to a third" of the population in a country which "like Cambodia . . . has become synonymous with starvation and refugees." "Americans have given some emergency aid," the editorial notes, "but Washington's role has not been glorious." The actual role of Washington is not further detailed; the editorial is entitled "The Shaming of Indonesia." A letter of mine, commenting on the oversight and on the interesting conjunction of the editorial and the report of the address by the man who takes pride in rendering the United Nations ineffective in preventing the massacre while condemning it as a danger against peace because it is "perverted by irrelevant political machinations," was not published.

The Committee for United Nations Integrity was, of course, concerned not with Timor but with U.N. support for Palestinian rights, a major crime of the U.N. in American eyes. Those who might appreciate some comic relief may turn to an advertisement in the *New York Times* on October 16, 1980, where an Israeli lobbying group that operates part-time as a human rights organization denounces the U.N. for its "silence concerning human rights violations of the Kurds, Berbers and millions of beleaguered people in Cambodia, Vietnam and Timor." The United Nations has been far from silent concerning Timor, our specific concern here, though the U.S. press has effectively silenced U.N. protests as well as U.S. efforts to block them. Moynihan, incidentally, is one of the great heroes of the organization that placed this advertisement in the *Times* (the Anti-Defamation League of B'nai B'rith, which is described in the Israeli press as "one of the main pillars" of Israeli propaganda in the U.S.; Beni Landau, *Ha'aretz*, July 28, 1981). Nineteen eighty-four approaches.

The reference to U.N. silence with regard to Cambodia and Vietnam presumably does not allude to the period when the United States was ravaging these lands. No doubt with Moynihan in mind, a State Department official conceded that our policy in Timor "has not been a policy of benign neglect. It's been a policy of malign neglect" (Southerland, op. cit.—though a quarter billion dollars' worth of arms and active efforts to pervert the United Nations by irrelevant political machinations may not qualify exactly as "neglect" of any sort).

6. For extensive detail, see Chomsky and Herman, op. cit. U.S. efforts to "pervert" the United Nations were apparently not limited to "political machinations" of the Moynihan variety. The United Nations sent a fact-finding mission to East Timor a few weeks after the Indonesian invasion, but Indonesia prevented it from reaching the territory by such tactics as bombing areas where the mission was scheduled to land. A U.S. contribution is reported by Jack Anderson (*Washington Post*, November 8, 1979) on the basis of U.S. intelligence documents. At one point Indonesian authorities considered sinking the frigate with the U.N. observers on board. "U.S. intelligence agencies learned of the bizarre plot but buried the information deep in their files without alerting the U.N. representatives that their ship might be torpedoed."

7. Congressional Research Service, *Human Rights and U.S. Foreign Assistance*, Report for the Senate Committee on Foreign Relations (November 1979), 144.

8. Kathleen Teltsch, "Timor Priest, Charging Genocide, Seeks U.S. Help," *New York Times*, December 14, 1979.

9. Robert Levey, "Power play cripples E. Timor," *Boston Globe*, January 20, 1980, to date, the most accurate and comprehensive account by a professional U.S. journalist. Father Leoneto's testimony is also reported by Daniel Southerland, "East Timor's agony rivals that of Cambodia," *Christian Science Monitor*, international edition, December 17, 1979, citing his description of how "the Indonesians attacked relentlessly with infantry and with US-supplied, armed reconnaissance planes known as the OV-10 (Bronco). They concentrated people around the villages and resettlement centers. They stole at least part of the relief food and sold it."

Southerland notes that "Fr. Leoneto would have been glad to testify before the U.S. congressmen. He was not invited to do so. It might have offended the Indonesians, and it would, of course, have revived disputes about what happened in the past." He is discussing a December 4 congressional hearing. The reference to "reviving" disputes is a bit misleading, in that the disputes, far from the mainstream, were rarely noted in the U.S. media. See also Daniel Southerland, "East Timor: plight worse than Cambodia?," *Christian Science Monitor*, December 6, 1979.

10. Teltsch, op. cit. However, Father Leoneto's testimony did lead to a strong *New York Times* editorial ("An Unjust War in East Timor," December 24, 1979), its first condemnation of the war since 1975, noting that "although most of the weapons of suppression are American-made, Washington has muted its concern for the familiar pragmatic reasons. . . . American silence about East Timor contrasts oddly with the indignation over Cambodia; the suffering is great in both places." There is nothing odd about the contrast, however; in Cambodia, the suffering could be attributed to an official enemy, while in Timor it is the responsibility of the United States, so that the contrast is quite predictable. The editorial also notes correctly that "Americans have only gradually become aware of the unjust war Indonesia has been waging in remote East Timor," without, however, explaining the reasons for the lack of awareness while the U.S.-backed massacre was proceeding for four years.

11. Jimmy Burns, "Indonesian troops 'taking supplies for the starving,' " *Observer*, January 20, 1980.

12. David Watts, "Relief is reaching East Timor but thousands have already died from Indonesian starvation policy," *The Times* (London), December 14, 1979.

13. For specific references and further discussion, see Chomsky and Herman, op. cit.

14. Henry Kamm, "War-Ravaged Timor Struggles Back from Abyss," *New York Times*, January 28, 1980. Kamm remarks that "Maj. Benny Mandalika of Indonesian military intelligence from Jakarta was always present, took notes during interviews not only with ordinary people but also with Indonesian officials of Timorese origin and often peered openly at the notes the reporter was taking. Explaining his actions when challenged, he said: 'I must stay with you so you get the right information. My boss told me to go with you wherever you go. If you interview the man in the street you may get the wrong information.' "

Kamm observes that the process of Indonesian annexation and pacification "remains enshrouded in partisan propaganda by both sides," but fails to explain on what basis he identifies "the least partisan sources," who believe "that both sides brought pressure on the population and that the savagery with which they conducted the war incited many to flee." Why, for example, is Father Leoneto not one of the "least partisan sources"? Or the many other anti-Fretilin refugees, Catholic priests, and letter-writers who smuggled out their pleas to put pressure on Indonesia to terminate the massacre, and whom the *Times* Southeast Asia correspondent studiously ignored for many years, and still does? These sources do not allege that the savagery of the war was equally divided—hardly plausible in any event, given the scale of force available and the very nature of the Indonesian attack on the civilian population. Kamm's show of evenhandedness is hardly more convincing than his parroting of the allegations of Indonesian generals in earlier years. His reference to "partisan propaganda by both sides" also fails to convey the fact that the partisan propaganda of one side, the U.S. government, completely dominated media coverage, typically presented as objective fact by the free press. See Chomsky and Herman, op. cit., for extensive detail.

Alongside of Kamm's article, there is a page-long advertisement of the International Rescue Committee signed by its chairman, Leo Cherne, calling for action to compel the Vietnamese and their Russian backers to permit aid to be sent to Cambodia: "What is needed now, in addition to the expansion of humanitarian aid, is an outcry of indignation so loud that it will be heard in Vietnam and the Soviet Union. It is not true that the men in Moscow and Hanoi are impervious to world opinion. They can be shamed into action. And if they cannot, at least we will have tried. By keeping silent, we are letting them get away with murder." In Cambodia, that is; where, incidentally, international relief officials at the same time were insisting that the Vietnamese and the regime they had installed in Cambodia were successfully doing what could be done to alleviate the famine in that ravaged land.

On Cherne's solicitude for refugees, see chap. 2, note 1 of *Towards a New Cold War*.

15. James M. Markham, "Refugees from East Timor Report Famine Situation," *New York Times*, January 29, 1980. Markham reports the testimony of refugees from late 1979, ethnic Chinese who had succeeded in bribing their way out of East Timor, which one describes in these terms: "Everyone wants to leave. It is the land of the devil." They were reluctant to speak "for fear of Indonesian reprisals against family members whose freedom they hoped to purchase." They describe beatings, executions, massive deaths from starvation, diversion of humanitarian relief by Indonesian officers, torture and disappearances, efforts to impose Indonesian nationality, regular bombing by what "appeared to be small American-made Bronco observation planes," and many Indonesian casualties "ferried to the military hospital in Dili by helicopter." One described Dili as "a world of terror." Like the other refugees in Lisbon, most seemed apolitical. One "tough-looking man" said that he had been "taken into the mountains by the guerrillas because they suspected him of being a member" of UDT: "His sentiments seemed to lie more with his one-time Fretilin captors than with the Indonesians."

Previously, American journalists had scrupulously avoided the refugees in Lisbon—or at least their testimony concerning Timor (cf. Chomsky and Herman, op. cit.). Refugees with tales of Communist atrocities receive a rather different treatment. In an effort to overcome this press failure to report refugee testimony, Timorese refugees were brought to the United States by private parties concerned with the issue; for example, four refugees (including three who were Markham's informants) were brought to the United States in mid-January 1980 and taken to see editors of several major newspapers, but not a word of their testimony appeared in the U.S. press, to my knowledge, and these efforts led to no notable efforts to seek out or attend to refugee testimony. One might argue that the press should be skeptical of "pre-selected" refugees, possibly a valid argument, had the press not been so careful to avoid selecting them itself.

In avoiding Timorese refugees with their unacceptable and unwanted information, the press was mimicking the behavior of the State Department. See 372, *Towards a New Cold War.*

16. See the articles cited above; and many important reports and comments by Alexander Cockburn in the *Village Voice;* also "Another Cambodia, with Uncle Sam in a supporting role," *New Republic*, November 3, 1979, a generally accurate article signed by editor Morton Kondracke; and a *Christian Science Monitor* editorial, "East Timor—the other famine," December 18, 1979, which calls for an "outpouring of compassion" while completely ignoring the U.S. role in bringing about the horrors it describes.

17. On the Western reaction to this massacre, see 372–73, *Towards a New Cold War.*

18. Cf. Chomsky and Herman, op. cit., chap. 4, section 1, for discussion and references.

19. Arnold Kohen, "The Cruel Case of Indonesia," *Nation*, November 26, 1977.

20. A. J. Langguth, review of Chomsky and Herman, op. cit., *Nation*, February 16, 1980.

21. "The New Foreign Correspondence," *Washington Journalism Review,* March 1980.

22. See, *inter alia*, the statement submitted by Father Francisco Maria Fernandes and Father Apolinario Guterres, Catholic priests "who represent the East Timor Refugee Committee in Portugal," and who state that they "were forced to leave Timor by the Indonesians because we had issued an appeal to the Royal Netherlands Ambassador in Jakarta on behalf of East Timorese in West Timor, requesting his assistance in evacuating these people to Portugal." They give an extensive account of Indonesian atrocities in East Timor, execution of many refugees in West Timor, expulsion of seven thousand refugees from West to East Timor in May 1976 to prevent them from going to Portugal in accordance with arrangements by the Netherlands ambassador, etc. "We are talking about genocide," they say, alleging that "Indonesia's war of saturation bombing and indiscriminate killing continues unabated" while thousands of Timorese are barred from emigration and "most of the people of our country have not received any aid due to the inaccessibility of their camps and, in particular, because of widespread Indonesian official corruption." Half of the budget for the International Red Cross program is spent on helicopters to transport aid around East Timor, they observe: "This is money that will go directly to the Indonesian government. Indonesia has planes and helicopters [thanks to the United States] to kill our people, but helicopters to help them must be leased for profit."

See also the testimony of Father Fernandes at the June 10, 1980, session of the hearings before a subcommittee of the Committee on Appropriations, House of Representatives, 96th Congress, 2nd session, Subcommittee on Foreign Operations and Related Agencies, Part 6 (Washington, DC: U.S. Government Printing Office, 1980), also unreported in the U.S. press. Father Fernandes states here that as many as 300,000 Timorese may have died in the course of the invasion. See "Accounts of Repression in East Timor Contradict U.S. View in House Inquiry," Reuters, *International Herald Tribune*, June 13, 1980.

23. Bernard D. Nossiter, *New York Times*, October 26, November 12, 1979.

24. "Cambodia and Timor," editorial, *Wall Street Journal*, February 6, 1980.

13. THE ORIGINS OF THE "SPECIAL RELATIONSHIP"

1. Bernard D. Nossiter, *New York Times*, June 27, 1982.

2. *Boston Globe*, June 27; June 9, 1982.

3. Nadav Safran, *Israel: The Embattled Ally* (Cambridge, MA: Harvard University Press, 1978), 576, 110, a study that bends over backwards to provide an interpretation sympathetic to Israel; see Noam Chomsky, *Towards a New Cold War* (New York: Pantheon Books, 1982) [hereinafter *TNCW*], chap. 13, for discussion.

4. G. Neal Lendenmann, "The Struggle in Congress over Aid Levels to Israel," *American-Arab Affairs*, Winter 1982–3 (see chap. 4, note 60, *The Fateful Triangle*); *Boston Globe*, September 26, 1982.

5. For an attempt to assess the actual level of U.S. aid, see Thomas Stauffer, *Christian Science Monitor*, December 29, 1981. For the specific details of the official record, see Yosef Priel, *Davar*, December 10, 1982; Ignacio Klich, *South*, February 1983.

6. Bernard Weinraub, *New York Times*, May 26, 1982.

7. "Senate OK's foreign aid plan with $2.6b for Israel," *Washington Post—Boston Globe*, December 18, 1982.

8. Ian S. Lustick, "Israeli Politics and American Foreign Policy," *Foreign Affairs*, Winter 1982/83; Amanda Mitchison, "Gift horses," *New Statesman*, February 4, 1983.

9. "Israel: Foreign Intelligence and Security Services," reprinted in *Counterspy*, May-June 1982; one of the documents brought by American journalists from Iran, where they were released after the takeover of the American Embassy. Given the circumstances, one cannot be certain of the authenticity of the document, though this tends to be confirmed both by its character and the subsequent discussion concerning it. A former chief of the Israeli Mossad (essentially, the Israeli CIA), Isser Harel, accepted the authenticity of the document but condemned it as "anti-Semitic," "one-sided and malicious," "dilletantish," reflecting a tendency in the CIA to "rewrite history" at the time the report was written in 1979; Yuval Elizur, *Boston Globe*, February 5, 1982, citing an interview in *Ma'ariv*.

10. General (Res.) Mattityahu Peled, *New Outlook* (Tel Aviv), May/June 1975, reporting on a visit to the United States.

11. *New Outlook* editor Simha Flapan, speaking at an October 1979 conference in Washington; cited by Merle Thorpe, Jr., President, Foundation for Middle East Peace, Hearing before the Subcommittee on Europe and the Middle East of the Committee on Foreign Affairs, House of Representatives, 97th Congress, First Session, December 16, 1981 (Washington, DC: U.S. Government Printing Office, 1982), 143.

12. See chap. 5, sections 5–8, *The Fateful Triangle*.

13. See chap. 4, below.

14. Jessie Lurie, *Jewish Post & Opinion*, May 28, 1982.

15. On the political influence of what he calls "the Israeli lobby," see Seth Tillman, *The United States in the Middle East* (Bloomington: Indiana University Press, 1982). Tillman was on the staff of the Senate Foreign Relations Committee with special concern for the Middle East.

16. Leon Hadar, "Labour of Love," *Jerusalem Post*, March 2, 1982.

17. See Stephen Zunes, "Strange Bedfellows," *Progressive*, November 1981. He notes that passionate support for Israel combines readily with fervent anti-Semitism. See also Richard Bernstein, "Evangelicals Strengthening Bonds With Jews," *New York Times*, February 6, 1983, and J. A. James, "Friends in need," *Jerusalem Post*, January 20, 1983, discussing the "potential importance of Evangelical support" in American politics and the "immense infra-

structure" of media at their command, and also the vast wealth that can be tapped. *Davar* reports that the Temple Mount Fund, "established in Israel and the U.S. and financed by Christian extremists," intends to donate tens of millions of dollars to Jewish settlements in the West Bank; January 23, 1983 *(Israleft News Service)*. It is a reasonable surmise—now sometimes voiced in Israel—that an Israeli-Evangelical Protestant alliance may become more prominent in Latin America, following the model of Guatemala, where the Rios Montt regime (which has succeeded even in surpassing its predecessors in its murderous barbarity) is supported by Evangelical Protestant movements and advised and supplied by Israel. See note 42.

18. Cited by Amnon Kapeliouk, *Israel: la fin des mythes* (Paris: Albin Michel, 1975, 219). This book by an outstanding Israeli journalist is the best account of Israeli government (Labor Party) policies from 1967–1973. Many U.S. publishers were approached for an English edition, but none was willing to undertake it.

19. Cited by Zunes, "Strange Bedfellows."

20. See, for example, *Pro-Arab Propaganda in America: Vehicles and Voices: a Handbook* (Anti-Defamation League of B'nai Brith, 1983); Thomas Mountain, "Campus anti-Zionism," *Focus* (Brandeis University), February 1983 (thanking the League for what passes as "fact"); and many handouts and pamphlets circulated in colleges around the country, typically without identification, which students distributing them often attribute to the League.

21. See *The Fateful Triangle*, 284f.

22. Benny Landau, *Ha'aretz*, July 28, 1981; Tillman, *The United States in the Middle East*, 65; Jolanta Benal, Interview with Meir Pail, *Win*, March 1, 1983.

23. Nathan and Ruth Ann Perlmutter, *The Real Anti-Semitism in America* (New York: Arbor House, 1982, 72, 111, 116, 136, 133f., 159, 125, 231). The book also contains the kinds of defamation of critics of Israeli policies and distortion of their views that one has come to expect in such circles and that merit no more comment than similar exercises in Communist Party literature.

24. Jon Kimche, *There Could Have Been Peace* (New York: Dial Press, 1973, 310–11).

25. Abba Eban, *Congress Bi-Weekly*, March 30, 1973; speech delivered July 31, 1972; Irving Howe, "Thinking the Unthinkable About Israel: A Personal Statement," *New York*, December 24, 1973.

26. Christopher Sykes, *Crossroads to Israel: 1917–1948* (Bloomington: Indiana University Press, 1965), 247.

27. Interview, *Jewish Post & Opinion*, November 19, 1982. The interviewer, Dale V. Miller, interprets him, quite accurately and it seems approvingly, as holding that the "province" of criticism is "the sole right of the Israelis themselves." On Wiesel's attitudes concerning the September Beirut massacre, see 386–7.

28. Safran, *Israel*, 571.

29. Cited by Joyce and Gabriel Kolko, *The Limits of Power* (New York: Harper & Row, 1972), 242.

30. For some discussion of this point, see my chapter "What directions for the disarmament movement?," in Michael Albert and David Dellinger, eds., *Beyond Survival: New Directions for the Disarmament Movement* (Cambridge, MA: South End Press, 1983).

31. Cited in Gabriel Kolko, *The Politics of War* (New York: Random House, 1968) 188; from Winston Churchill, *Triumph and Tragedy* (Boston: Houghton-Mifflin, 1953), 249. For more recent discussion, see Lawrence S. Wittner, *American Intervention in Greece* (New York: Columbia University Press, 1982). The two volumes of the Kolkos' (see note 29) remain invaluable for understanding the general wartime and postwar period, though much useful work has appeared since, including much documentation that basically supports their analyses, in

my view, though the fact is rarely acknowledged; since they do not adhere to approved orthodoxies, it is considered a violation of scholarly ethics to refer to their contributions.

32. Wittner, *American Intervention in Greece*, 119, 88.

33. Ibid., 1, 149, 154, 296; see the same source for an extensive review and documentation.

34. Ibid., 80, 232.

35. For discussion, see *TNCW*, chaps. 2, 11, and references cited there.

36. *New York Times*, August 6, 1954; see *TNCW*, 99, for further quotes and comment.

37. Cited in *TNCW*, 457, from *MERIP Reports*, May 1981; also, *J. of Palestine Studies*, Spring 1981. The source is a memorandum obtained under the Freedom of Information Act.

38. The man in direct charge of these operations, Avri el-Ad, describes them in his *Decline of Honor* (Chicago: Regnery, 1976). See Livia Rokach, *Israel's Sacred Terrorism* (Belmont: AAUG, 1981), for excerpts from the diaries of Prime Minister Moshe Sharett concerning these events and how they were viewed at the time, at the highest level. On the ensuing political-military crisis (the "Lavon affair"), see Yoram Peri, *Between Battles and Ballots: Israeli Military in Politics* (New York: Cambridge University Press, 1983), an important study that undermines many illusions.

39. "Issues Arising Out of the Situation in the Near East," declassified 12/10/81, commenting on NSC 5801 / 1, January 24, 1958.

40. Michael Bar-Zohar, *Ben-Gurion: A Biography* (New York: Delacorte, 1978), 261f.

41. Ibid., 315–6; Peri, *Between Battles and Ballots*, 80. It has been suggested that the Israeli attack on the U.S. spy ship *Liberty* was motivated by concern that the U.S. might detect the plans for this attack. See James Ennes, *Assault on the Liberty* (New York: Random House, 1979). See also Richard K. Smith, *U.S. Naval Institute Proceedings*, June 1978, who describes how "with the greatest ease . . . the Israeli pilots [and later torpedo boats] butchered the large, slow-moving, and defenseless *Liberty*," which was clearly and unmistakeably identified, in accordance with "a vital part of Israel's war plan," namely, "to keep foreign powers in the dark" so as to avoid "superpower pressures for a cease-fire before they could seize the territory which they considered necessary for Israel's future security"—a rather charitable interpretation, given the facts about the cease-fire and some questions that might be raised about "security."

42. See *TNCW*, 315 and references cited. See also the CIA study cited in note 9, which states that "The Israelis also have undertaken widescale covert political, economic and paramilitary action programs—particularly in Africa." In his report on U.S. labor leaders, Leon Hadar notes that they have been particularly "impressed with Israel's success in establishing links with the Third World, especially in Africa, to resist Soviet influence"—the latter phrase being the usual code word for resistance to unwanted forms of nationalism. That American labor bureaucrats should be pleased by support for Mobutu and the like no longer comes as any surprise. See note 16.

43. Yoav Karni, "Dr. Shekel and Mr. Apartheid," *Yediot Ahronot*, March 13, 1983. On the extensive Israeli relations, military and other, with South Africa, see *TNCW*, 293f. and references cited; Israel Shahak, *Israel's Global Role* (Belmont: AAUG, 1982); Benjamin Beit-Hallahmi, "South Africa and Israel's Strategy of Survival," *New Outlook* (Tel Aviv), April/May 1977; Beit-Hallahmi, "Israel and South Africa 1977–1982: Business As Usual—And More," *New Outlook*, March 1983, with further details on the enthusiasm shown by both Labor and Likud for South Africa though Labor prefers to keep the matter hidden, on the arrangements to use Israel for transshipment of South African goods to Europe and the U.S. to evade boycotts, etc.; Uri Dan, "The Angolan Battlefield," *Monitin*, January 1982; Carole Collins, *National Catholic Reporter*, January 22, 1982; and many other sources.

44. See *TNCW*, 290f. and references cited; Shahak, *Israel's Global Role;* Ignacio Klich, *Le Monde diplomatique*, October 1982, February 1983; *Washington Report on the Hemisphere* (Council on Hemispheric Affairs), June 29, 1982; *Latin America Weekly Report*, August 6, September 24, December 17, 24, 1982; *El Pais* (Spain), March 8–10, 1983; Steve Goldfield, Jane Hunter, and Paul Glickman, *In These Times*, April 13, 1983; and many other sources. It was reported recently that Kibbutz Beit Alpha (Mapam) has been providing equipment to the Chilean army (*Ha'aretz*, January 7, 1983). In particular, Israel is now Guatemala's biggest arms supplier (*Economist*, April 3, 1982), helping the U.S. government evade the congressional ban on arms, and Israeli military advisers are active. The new regime in Guatemala, which has been responsible for horrible massacres, credits its success in obtaining power to its many Israeli advisers; its predecessor, the murderous Lucas Garcia regime, openly expressed its admiration for Israel as a "model" (see 290). On the new levels of barbarism achieved by the Rios Montt regime, see Allan Nairn, "The Guns of Guatemala," *New Republic*, April 11, 1983 (ignoring the Israeli connection, which could hardly be discussed in this journal). See references cited, and an unpublished paper by Benjamin Beit-Hallahmi, "Israel's support for Guatemala's military regimes," with information from the Israeli press. We return to further details. On Israel's arms sales as a "U.S. proxy supplier of arms to various 'hot spots' in the Third World," see *SOUTH*, April 1982. Arms sales now constitute a third of Israel's industrial exports (*Dvar Hashavua*, August 27, 1982).

45. See Michael Klare, in Leila Meo, ed., *U.S. Strategy in the Gulf* (Belmont, MA: AAUG, 1981).

46. Michael Klare, *Beyond the "Vietnam Syndrome"* (Washington, DC: Institute for Policy Studies, 1981).

47. Advertisement, *New York Times*, October 13, 1982; Joseph Churba, letter, *New York Times*, November 21, 1982. See also Steven J. Rosen, *The Strategic Value of Israel*, AIPAC Papers on U.S.-Israel Relations, 1982; AIPAC is the officially-registered pro-Israel lobbying organization in Washington.

48. Thomas L. Friedman, "After Lebanon: The Arab World in Crisis," *New York Times*, November 22, 1982.

49. Tamar Golan, *Ma'ariv*, December 1, 1982; Reuters, *Boston Globe*, January 20, 1983; UPI, *New York Times*, January 22, 1983.

50. *New York Times*, December 6, 1982.

51. Susan Morgan, *Christian Science Monitor*, December 14, 1982; "Guatemala: Rightists on the warpath," *Latin America Weekly Report*, March 4, 1983.

52. For one of many recent examples, see Marlise Simons, *New York Times*, December 14, 1982, citing American Roman Catholic missionaries who report that "the raiders had lately been torturing and mutilating captured peasants or Sandinist sympathizers, creating the same terror as in the past," giving examples. The Somozist National Guard was trained in the U.S. Army School of the Americas in the Panama Canal Zone.

53. Charles Maechling Jr., "The Murderous Mind of the Latin Military," *Los Angeles Times,* March 18, 1982.

54. See *TNCW*, 429 and chap. 13, and references cited.

55. Yoav Karni, "The secret alliance of the 'Fifth World'," *Yediot Ahronot*, November 22, 1981. See *TNCW*, 292–3.

56. Leslie H. Gelb, "Israel Said to Step Up Latin Role, Offering Arms Seized in Lebanon," *New York Times*, December 17, 1982.

57. See Chomsky, *For Reasons of State* (New York: Pantheon Books, 1973, 51), for citation and discussion.

58. Adam Clymer, *New York Times*, June 27, 1982. *Le Monde*, June 11, for the full text; *Christian Science Monitor*, June 11, 1982.

59. For references, see John Cooley, *Green March, Black September* (London: Frank Cass, 1973), 161–62; Chomsky, *Peace in the Middle East?* (New York: Pantheon Books, 1974), 140.

60. The U.S. press appears to have ignored this important discussion among Israeli military commanders, apart from a report by John Cooley, *Christian Science Monitor*, July 17, 1972. For some discussion of what he refers to as "the 'David and Goliath' legend surrounding the birth of Israel," see Simha Flapan, *Zionism and the Palestinians* (New York: Barnes & Noble, 1979), 317f.

61. *Yediot Ahronot*, July 26, 1973; see *Peace in the Middle East?*, 142.

62. See Chomsky, "Israel and the New Left," in Mordecai S. Chertoff, ed., *The New Left and the Jews* (New York: Pitman, 1971); and *Peace in the Middle East?*, chap. 5, including a discussion of some of the remarkable contributions of Irving Howe, Seymour Martin Lipset, and others. See chap. 5, below, for further discussion.

63. See the references of the preceding note on this and other examples, all presented without a pretense of evidence or rational argument, a stance always available when the targets are outside the approved consensus.

64. *Jewish Post & Opinion*, November 5, 1982.

65. Jerusalem Domestic Television Service, September 24, 1982. Reprinted in *The Beirut Massacre* (New York: Claremont Research and Publications, 1982), from the U.S. government Foreign Broadcast Information Service (FBIS).

66. Amos Oz, "Has Israel Altered Its Visions?" *New York Times Magazine*, July 11, 1982. On misrepresentation of these events in scholarship, referring to Safran, *Israel*, see *TNCW*, 331.

67. For a rare recording of the facts in the press, see the article by staff correspondents of the *Christian Science Monitor*, June 4, 1982; also Cecilia Blalock, ibid., June 22, 1982 and Philip Geyelin, *Washington Post (Manchester Guardian Weekly*, June 20, 1982). On the events and the cover-up, see references of note 41; also Anthony Pearson, *Conspiracy of Silence* (New York: Quartet, 1978) and James Bamford, *The Puzzle Palace* (Boston: Houghton Mifflin, 1982).

68. See *The Fateful Triangle*, 5, citing *Time*, a journal regarded as *critical* of Israel.

14. PLANNING FOR GLOBAL HEGEMONY

1. Gabriel Kolko, *The Politics of War* (New York: Random House, 1968), 471.

2. William Roger Louis, *Imperialism at Bay* (Oxford: Clarendon Press, 1977), 481.

3. This and what follows is drawn from an illuminating study by Melvyn Leffler, "The American Conception of National Security and the Beginnings of the Cold War, 1945–48," *AHR Forum*, *American Historical Review*, April 1984.

4. Kolko, *Politics of War*.

5. Samuel Huntington, in M. J. Crozier, S. P. Huntington, and J. Watanuki, *The Crisis of Democracy* (New York: New York University Press, 1975), report of the Trilateral Commission. On this commission, see Holly Sklar, ed., *Trilateralism* (Cambridge, MA: South End Press, 1980) and Noam Chomsky, *Towards a New Cold War* (New York: Pantheon Books, 1982) [hereinafter *TNCW*].

6. Laurence Shoup and William Minter, *Imperial Brain Trusty* (New York: Monthly Review Press, 1977); see *TNCW* for a brief review. See Robert Schulzinger, *The Wise Men of Foreign Affairs* (New York: Columbia University Press, 1984), a much more superficial conventional history that omits the crucial material Shoup and Minter discuss while citing the "of-

ficial rebuttal" by William Bundy, which condemned them for "selectivity" *(Foreign Affairs*, October 1977). Both Bundy and Schulzinger dismiss the Shoup and Minter study without analysis as a paranoid vision comparable to that of the Far Right. Their important study was otherwise ignored. Standard histories also ignore Kennan's positions cited here, as do his memoirs. On the wartime and early postwar period, see especially Kolko, *Politics of War;* Gabriel and Joyce Kolko, *The Limits of Power* (New York: Harper & Row, 1972), two seminal contributions to a large literature.

7. See Noam Chomsky, *For Reasons of State* (New York: Pantheon Books, 1970), chap. 1, V, for references and discussion.

8. James Chace, "How 'Moral' Can We Get," *New York Times Magazine*, May 22, 1977.

9. See *TNCW*, chap. 2.

10. President Lyndon B. Johnson, speeches on November 1, November 2, 1966; *Public Papers of the Presidents of the United States*, 1966, Book II (Washington, 1967), 563, 568; *Congressional Record*, March 15, 1948, House, 2883.

11. Dean Acheson, *Present at the Creation* (New York: Norton, 1969), 219; see *TNCW*, 195f., for more extensive discussion.

12. Seymour Hersh, *The Price of Power* (New York: Summit, 1983), 270, quoting Roger Morris; Morton Halperin et al., *The Lawless State* (New York: Penguin, 1976), 17, citing Hersh, *New York Times*, September 11, 1974.

13. LaFeber, *Inevitable Revolutions* (New York: Norton, 1983), 157.

14. Walter Laqueur, *Wall Street Journal*, April 9, 1981; *Economist*, September 19, 1981. On the terrorist war against Cuba conducted from US bases under US government auspices, see Herman, *Real Terror Network, TNCW*, and sources cited. Sterling's much-admired fables may be based in part on a document fabricated by the CIA to test the veracity of a defector, then circulated through the sleazy network of peddlars of planted "intelligence leaks." See Alexander Cockburn, *Nation*, August 17, 1985.

15. *For Reasons of State*, 31–37, citing documents in the *Pentagon Papers.*

16. Minutes summarizing PPS 51, April 1949, cited by Michael Schaller, "Securing the Great Crescent: Occupied Japan and the Origins of Containment in Southeast Asia," *Journal of American History*, September 1982; the study also suggested that "some diversification of their economies" should be permitted. For fuller development of this topic, see Schaller; essays by John Dower and Richard Du Boff in Chomsky and Howard Zinn, eds., *Critical Essays*, vol. 5 of the *Pentagon Papers* (Boston: Beacon, 1972); *For Reasons of State*, chap. 1, V.

17. Perkins, I, 131, 167, 176f. The last phrase is Perkins's summary of "a widespread, nay, almost general, viewpoint" among European statesmen.

18. See *For Reasons of State*, 37; *PEHR*, II; *TNCW*; Joel Charny and John Spragens, *Obstacles to Recovery in Vietnam and Kampuchea: U.S. Embargo of Humanitarian Aid* (Boston: Oxfam America, 1984).

19. Noam Chomsky, *At War with Asia* (New York: Pantheon Books, 1970), 286.

20. On this matter, see *PEHR*, II, 2.2.

21. *At War with Asia; For Reasons of State; PEHR*, II; and sources cited.

16. CONTAINING THE ENEMY

1. Distaste for democracy sometimes reaches such extremes that state control is taken to be the only imaginable alternative to domination by concentrated private wealth. It must be this tacit assumption that impels Nicholas Lemann *(New Republic*, January 9, 1989) to assert that in our book *Manufacturing Consent* (New York: Pantheon Books, 1988), Herman and I advocate

"more state control" over the media, basing this claim on our statement that "In the long run, a democratic political order requires far wider control of and access to the media" on the part of the general public (307). This quoted statement follows a review of some of the possible modalities, including the proliferation of public-access TV channels that "have weakened the power of the network oligopoly"and have "a potential for enhanced local-group access," "local nonprofit radio and television stations," ownership of radio stations by "community institutions" (a small cooperative in France is mentioned as an example), listener-supported radio in local communities, and so on. Such options indeed challenge corporate oligopoly and the rule of the wealthy generally. Therefore, they can only be interpreted as "state control" by someone who regards it as unthinkable that the general public might, or should, gain access to the media as a step towards shaping their own affairs. There are various complexities and qualifications, of course, when we turn from very general features of the system to fine details and minor effects. It should be understood that these are features of the analysis of any complex system.

2. See their *On Democracy*, where more wide-ranging consequences are elaborated.

3. Christopher Hill, *The World Turned Upside Down* (New York: Penguin, 1984, 60, 71), quoting contemporary authors.

4. Edward Countryman, *The American Revolution* (New York: Hill and Wang, 1985, 200, 224ff.)

5. James Curran, "Advertising and the Press," in Curran, ed., *The British Press: A Manifesto* (London: MacMillan, 1978).

6. Lawrence Shoup and William Minter, *Imperial Brain Trust* (New York: Monthly Review Press, 1977, 130), a study of the War and Peace Studies Project of the Council on Foreign Relations and the State Department from 1939 to 1945.

7. See my *Necessary Illusions* (Cambridge, MA: South End Press,1989), appendix II, sec. 1, for further discussion.

8. Exceptions were tolerated in the early years because of the special need for recovery of the centers of industrial capitalism by exploiting their former colonies, but this was understood to be a temporary expedient. For details, see William S. Borden, *The Pacific Alliance: United States Foreign Economic Policy and Japanese Trade Recovery, 1947–1955* (Madison, WI: University of Wisconsin Press, 1984); Andrew J. Rotter, *The Path to Vietnam: Origins of the American Commitment to Southeast Asia* (Ithaca, NY: Cornell University Press, 1987).

9. *WP Weekly*, December 28, 1987.

10. Lippmann and Merz, "A Test of the News," Supplement, *New Republic*, August 4, 1920. Quotes here from citations in James Aronson, *The Press and the Cold War* (Boston: Beacon, 1973), 25f.

11. See *Necessary Illusions*, appendix II, section 1.

12. H. D. S. Greenway, *Boston Globe*, July 8, 1988. On the backgrounds, see *Turning the Tide*, 194f., and sources cited; Christopher Simpson, *Blowback* (New York: Weidenfeld & Nicolson, 1988).

13. By the late 1960s, it was already clear that these were the basic factors behind the U.S. intervention in Southeast Asia, which, in U.S. global planning, was to be reconstituted as a "coprosperity sphere" for Japan, within the U.S.-dominated Grand Area, while also serving as a market and source of raw materials and recycled dollars for the reconstruction of Western European capitalism. See my *At War with Asia* (New York: Pantheon Books, 1970), introduction) *For Reasons of State* (New York: Pantheon Books, 1973); Chomsky and Howard Zinn, eds., *Critical Essays*, vol. 5 of the *Pentagon Papers* (Boston: Beacon, 1972); and other work of the period. See also, among others, Borden, *Pacific Alliance;* Michael Schaller, *The American*

Occupation of Japan (New York: Oxford University Press, 1985); Andrew Rotter, *Path to Vietnam* (Ithaca, NY: Cornell University Press, 1987).

14. Acheson, *Present at the Creation* (Norton, 1969, 374, 489); Borden, op. cit., 44, 144.

15. See *Necessary Illusions*, appendix II, section 2.

16. Carey, "Managing Public Opinion."

17. Ibid., citing Bell, "Industrial Conflict and Public Opinion," in A. R. Dubin and A. Ross, eds., *Industrial Conflict* (New York: McGraw-Hill, 1954).

18. See *Necessary Illusions*, appendix V, section 5.

19. Carey, "Managing Public Opinion." On the purge of the universities in the 1950s, see Ellen Schrecker, *No Ivory Tower* (New York: Oxford University Press, 1986). For a small sample of the later purge, see several essays in Philip J. Meranto, Oneida J. Meranto, and Matthew R. Lippman, *Guarding the Ivory Tower* (Denver: Lucha Publications, 1985).

20. For some discussion, see my article "Democracy in the Industrial Societies" in *Z Magazine*, January 1989.

21. The Food for Peace program (PL 480) is a notable example. Described by Ronald Reagan as "one of the greatest humanitarian acts ever performed by one nation for the needy of other nations," PL 480 has effectively served the purposes for which it was designed: subsidizing U.S. agribusiness; inducing people to "become dependent on us for food" (Senator Hubert Humphrey, one of its architects in the interest of his Minnesota farming constituency); contributing to counterinsurgency operations; and financing "the creation of a global military network to prop up Western and Third World capitalist governments" by requiring that local currency counterpart funds be used for rearmament (William Borden), thus also providing an indirect subsidy to U.S. military producers. The U.S. employs such "export subsidies (universally considered an 'unfair' trading practice) to preserve its huge Japanese market," among other cases (Borden). The effect on Third World agriculture and survival has often been devastating. See Tom Barry and Deb Preusch, *The Soft War* (New York: Grove Press, 1988, 67f.); Borden, *Pacific Alliance*, 182f.; and other sources.

22. *New York Times*, October 30, 1985.

23. See *Political Economy of Human Rights* and *Manufacturing Consent*.

24. *New York Times*, March 25, 1977; transcript of news conference.

25. *Los Angeles Times*, October 25, 1988; Robert Reinhold, *New York Times*, same day.

26. For comparative estimates at the time, see *Political Economy of Human Rights*, II, chap. 3.

27. *New York Times*, March 3, 1985.

28. T. Hunter Wilson, *Indochina Newsletter* (Asia Resource Center), November–December 1987. Mary Williams Walsh, *Wall Street Journal*, January 3; George Esper, Associated Press, January 18; *Boston Globe*, picture caption, January 20, 1989.

29. Mary Williams Walsh, *Wall Street Journal*, January 3, 1989; Robert Pear, *New York Times*, August 14; Elaine Sciolino, *New York Times*, August 17; Paul Lewis, *New York Times*, October 8; Walsh, *Wall Street Journal*, September 1, 1988. In her January 3, 1989, article, Walsh notes, a touch ruefully, that "the release of the Afghan maps could even count as a small propaganda victory for the Kabul regime, since its enemies in Washington" have yet to do as much as fourteen years after their departure. The propaganda victory will be extremely small, since there is no recognition that the U.S. has failed to provide this information, or has any responsibility to do so.

30. Barbara Crossette, *New York Times*, November 10, 1985.

31. Crossette, *New York Times*, February 28; E. W. Wayne, *Christian Science Monitor*, August 24, 1988.

32. Anderson, "The Light at the End of the Tunnel," *Diplomatic History*, Fall 1988.

33. Lee H. Hamilton, "Time for a new American relationship with Vietnam," *Christian Science Monitor*, December 12, 1988; Frederick Z. Brown, *Indochina Issues* 85, November 1988; *Boston Globe*, July 8, 1988.

34. Francis Jennings, *Empire of Fortune* (New York: Norton, 1988), 215.

35. Kapeliouk, *Yediot Ahronot*, April 7, 1988; also April 1, 15.

36. Ziem, *Indochina Newsletter* (Asia Resource Center), July-August 1988; Susan Chira, *New York Times,* October 5, 1988; *Wall Street Journal,* April 4, 1985. See *Manufacturing Consent* on how the tenth anniversary retrospectives (1985) evaded the effects of the war on the South Vietnamese, the main victims of the U.S. attack.

37. NSC 144/1, 1953; NSC 5432, 1954; and many others. For more detailed discussion, see *On Power and Ideology*. The basic principles are reiterated constantly, often in the same words.

38. On this propaganda device, aimed at the home front, see Herman and Brodhead, *Demonstration Elections*.

39. Jorge Pinto, *New York Times,* op-ed, May 6, 1981; Ricardo Castañeda, senior partner of a Salvadoran law firm, Edward Mason Fellow, Kennedy School, Harvard University, p.c.; "Salvador Groups Attack Paper and U.S. Plant," World News Briefs, *New York Times,* April 19, 1980. The information on *Times* coverage is based on a search of the *Times* index by Chris Burke of FAIR.

40. "Sad Tales of La Libertad de Prensa," *Harper's*, August 1988. See *Necessary Illusions*, appendix IV, section 6, for further discussion.

41. Deirdre Carmody, *New York Times*, February 14, 1980. Perhaps we might regard the brief notice of April 19, cited above, as a response to his plea.

42. *New York Times,* editorial, March 25, 1988.

17. INTRODUCTION FROM *THE MINIMALIST PROGRAM*

1. For some discussion of this issue, see N. Chomsky, "Bare Phrase Structure," *MIT Occasional Papers in Linguistics* 5 (1994), Department of Linguistics and Philosophy, MIT, to appear in H. Campos and P. Kempchinsky, eds., *Evolution and Revolution in Linguistic Theory: Essays in Honor of Carlos Otero* (Washington, DC: Georgetown University Press, 1995), also published in G. Webelhuth, ed., *Government and Binding and the Minimalist Program* (Oxford: Blackwell, 1995); N. Chomsky, "Naturalism and Dualism in the Study of Language and Mind," *International Journal of Philosophical Studies* 2 (1994): 181–209, referring to Edelman, *Bright Air, Brilliant Fire: On the Matter of the Mind* (New York: Basic Books, 1992). Edelman takes the crisis to be serious if not lethal for cognitive science generally, whether computational, connectionist, or whatever.

2. Adapted, essentially, from N. Chomsky, *The Logical Structure of Linguistic Theory* (New York: Plenum, 1975), excerpted from 1956 revision of 1955 ms., Harvard University and MIT (Chicago: University of Chicago Press, 1985).

3. The term *articulatory* is too narrow in that it suggests that the language faculty is modality-specific, with a special relation to vocal organs. Work of the past years in sign language undermines this traditional assumption. I will continue to use the term, but without any implications about specificity of output system, while keeping to the case of spoken language.

4. For some discussion, see N. Chomsky, *Essays on Form and Interpretations* (Amsterdam: Elsevier North-Holland, 1977), chap. 1.

5. See N. Chomsky, *Lectures on Government and Binding* (Dordrecht: Foris, 1981), for one formulation.

6. *Interpret* here is of course to be understood in a theory-internal sense. In a looser informal sense, interpretations are assigned by the language faculty (in a particular state) to all sorts of objects, including fragments, nonsense expressions, expressions of other languages, and possibly nonlinguistic noises as well.

7. See H. Borer, *Parametric Syntax* (Dordrecht: Foris, 1984); N. Fukui, "A Theory of Category Projection and Its Applications" (PhdD diss., MIT, 1986), revised version published as *Theory of Projection in Syntax* (Stanford, CA: CSLI Publications, 1995), distributed by University of Chicago Press; N. Fukui, "Deriving the Differences Between English and Japanese: A Case Study in Parametric Syntax," *English Linguistics* 5 (1988), 249–70.

8. See N. Chomsky, *Knowledge of Language* (New York: Praeger, 1986).

9. Thus, what we call "English," "French," "Spanish," and so on, even under idealizations to idiolects in homogenous speech communities, reflect the Norman Conquest, proximity to Germanic areas, a Basque substratum, and other factors that cannot seriously be regarded as properties of the language faculty. Pursuing the obvious reasoning, it is hard to imagine that the properties of the language faculty—a real object of the natural world—are instantiated in any observed system. Similar assumptions are taken for granted in the study of organisms generally.

10. See N. Chomsky, *Aspects of the Theory of Syntax* (Cambridge, MA: MIT Press, 1965).

11. See Chomsky, *Logical Structure of Linguistic Theory*, chap. 4.

18. NEW HORIZONS IN THE STUDY OF LANGUAGE AND MIND

1. David Hume, *An Enquiry Concerning Human Understanding*, ed., L. A. Selby-Bigge, 3d ed., rev. by P. H. Nidditch (Oxford: Clarendon Press, 1748, 1975), 108, sec. 85.

2. Galileo Galilei, *Dialogues on the Great World Systems*, trans. Thomas Salusbury (1632, 1661), end of first day.

3. See, for example, Noam Chomsky, *Aspects of the Theory of Syntax* (Cambridge, MA: MIT Press, 1965); Chomsky, *Lectures on Government and Binding* (Dordrecht: Foris, 1981); Chomsky, *Knowledge of Language* (New York: Praeger, 1986).

4. See Noam Chomsky, *The Minimalist Program* (Cambridge, MA: MIT Press, 1995).

5. Samuel Epstein, "UN-principled Syntax and the Derivation of Syntactic Relations," in Samuel Epstein and Norbert Hornstein, eds., *Working Minimalism* (Cambridge, MA: MIT Press, 1999).

6. Noam Chomsky, *Minimalist Program*; Chomsky, "Minimalist Inquiries: The Framework," ms., MIT, 1998.

7. David Hume, *A Treatise of Human Nature*, ed., L. A. Selby-Bigge, 2d ed., rev. by P. H. Nidditch (Oxford: Clarendon Press, 1740, 1748), sec. 27.

8. René Descartes, letter (to Morus), in R. M. Eaton, ed., *Descartes Selections* (1649, 1927).

9. Juan Huarte, *Examen de Ingenios*, trans. Bellamy (1575, 1698), 3; see also Noam Chomsky, *Cartesian Linguistics* (New York: Harper & Row, 1966).

19. INTENTIONAL IGNORANCE AND ITS USES

1. Tony Blair, in "A New Generation Draws the Line," *Newsweek,* April 19, 1999; Vaclav Havel, "Kosovo and the End of the Nation-State," *New York Review of Books,* June 10, 1999.

2. Michael Wines, "Two Views of Inhumanity Split the World, Even in Victory," *New York Times,* "Week in Review" lead article, June 13, 1999; Michael Glennon, "The New Interventionism," *Foreign Affairs,* May/June 1999.

3. Bob Davis, "Cop of the World? Clinton Pledges U.S. Power Against Ethnic Cleansing,

but His Aides Hedge," *Wall Street Journal*, August 6, 1999. William Jefferson Clinton, "A Just and Necessary War," *New York Times*, May 23; April 1, speech at Norfolk Air Station, *New York Times*, April 2, 1999.

4. Sebastian Mallaby, "Uneasy Partners," *New York Times Book Review*, September 21, 1997. Senior Administration policymaker cited by Thomas Friedman, *New York Times*, January 12, 1992. Davis, op. cit., paraphrasing Sandy Berger in an interview.

5. Department of Defense Report to Congress, *Kosovo/Operation Allied Force After-Action Report*, January 31, 2000. Tony Blair, Alan Little, "Moral Combat: NATO At War," BBC2 Special, March 12, 2000.

6. Declaration of Group of 77 South Summit, April 10–14, 2000. For background, see *Third World Resurgence* (Penang), no. 117, 2000.

7. Anthony Sampson, "Mandela accuses 'policeman' Britain," *Guardian*, April 5, 2000.

8. Schiff, Amnon Barzilai, *Ha'aretz*, April 5, 2000. On Indian, Israeli, and Egyptian reactions, see Noam Chomsky, *The New Military Humanism: Lessons of Kosovo* (Monroe, ME: Common Courage Press, 1999), chap. 6.

9. On these events, see Noam Chomsky, *Deterring Democracy* (London, New York: Verso, 1991), and *The New Military Humanism: Lessons of Kosovo.*

10. Ibid. On Turkey and the Kurds, see *The New Military Humanism: Lessons of Kosovo*, and some comments below.

11. Andrew Kramer, "Putin following Yeltsin's misguided policies, Solzhenitsyn says," AP, *Boston Globe*, May 17, 2000.

12. John Mearsheimer, "India Needs The Bomb," *New York Times* op-ed, March 24, 2000; Samuel Huntington, "The Lonely Superpower," *Foreign Affairs*, March/April 1999. Chalmers Johnson, *Blowback* (New York: Henry Holt, 2000), 59. Michael MccGwire, "Why did we bomb Belgrade?" *International Affairs* (Royal Academy of International Affairs, London), 76.1, January 2000.

13. Christopher Marquis, "Bankrolling Colombia's War on Drugs," *New York Times*, June 23, 2000, last paragraph.

14. Tamar Gabelnick, William Hartung, and Jennifer Washburn, *Arming Repression: U.S. Arms Sales to Turkey During the Clinton Administration* (New York and Washington: World Policy Institute and Federation of Atomic Scientists, October 1999). For further sources, see NMH. On Latin America and the Caribbean, see Adam Isacson and Joy Olson, *Just the Facts: 1999 Edition* (Washington: Latin America Working Group and Center for International Policy, 1999). Here and below, the perennial front-runners Israel and Egypt, which belong to a separate category, are excluded. Rankings are for fiscal years, and are qualitative, depending on exactly which aspects are counted (grants, sales, training, co-production, joint exercises, etc.).

15. See preceding note. Jonathan Randal, *After Such Knowledge, What Forgiveness: My Encounters with Kurdistan* (Boulder, CO: Westview Press, 1999).

16. On the events and their refraction through doctrinal prisms, see *The New Military Humanism: Lessons of Kosovo.* For an update, *Rogue States* (Cambridge, MA: South End Press, 2000), chap. 5.

17. Thomas Cushman, editor, "Human Rights and the Responsibility of Intellectuals," *Human Rights Review*, January–March 2000; Aryeh Neier, "Inconvenient Facts," *Dissent*, spring 2000; in both cases, reaction to the review of U.S.-backed Turkish atrocities in *The New Military Humanism: Lessons of Kosovo.*

18. Tim Judah, *Kosovo: War and Revenge* (New Haven: Yale University Press, 2000), 308.

19. Ferit Demer, Reuters, datelined Tunceli, Turkey, April 1; Chris Morris, *Guardian* (London), April 3, 2000. AP, *Los Angeles Times*, April 2, 2000.

20. See *Fateful Triangle: US., Israel, and the Palestinians* (Cambridge, MA: South End Press, 1999, updated from 1983 edition). The Lebanese government and international relief agencies report 25,000 killed since 1982; the toll of the 1982 invasion is estimated at about 20,000.

21. "Israel, US vote against funding for UN force in Lebanon," AP Worldstream, June 15; Marilyn Henry, "Israel, US angered by Kana clause in UN peacekeeping package," *Jerusalem Post*, June 18, 2000. On the circumstances of the invasion, see *Fateful Triangle*. For detailed documentation, including the Amnesty International and UN inquiries that concluded that the shelling of the compound was intentional, see Shifra Stern, *Israel's Operation "Grapes of Wrath" and the Qana Massacre*, ms., April–May 1996.

22. Federal News Service, Department of Defense Briefing, Secretary William Cohen, "Turkey's Importance to 21st Century International Security," Grand Hyatt Hotel, Washington DC, March 31; Charles Aldinger, "U.S. praises key NATO ally Turkey," Reuters, March 31, 2000. Judith Miller, "South Asia Called Major Terror Hub in a Survey by U.S.," *New York Times*, April 30, 2000, lead story.

23. Little, op. cit.

24. See note 14.

25. See Lars Schoultz, *Comparative Politics*, January 1981; Schoultz is the author of the leading scholarly study of human rights and U.S. policy in Latin America. For broader confirmation and inquiry, which helps explain the reasons, see the studies by economist Edward Herman reported in Chomsky and Herman, *Political Economy of Human Rights* (Cambridge, MA: South End Press, 1979), vol. I. chap. 2.1.1, and Herman, *The Real Terror Network* (Cambridge, MA: South End Press, 1982), 126ff. Note that these reviews precede the Reagan years, when inquiry would have been superfluous.

26. Carla Anne Robbins, "How Bogota Wooed Washington to Open New War on Cocaine," *Wall Street Journal*, June 23, 2000. For sources on what follows, and further information and discussion, see *Rogue States*, chap. 5.

27. Rafael Pardo, "Colombia's Two-Front War," *Foreign Affairs*, July/August 2000; Pardo was special government adviser on peace negotiations and Minister of Defense while the guerrilla-backed party was destroyed by assassination.

28. Sean Murphy, "Contemporary Practice of the United States Relating to International Law," *American Journal of International Law* (henceforth *AJIL)* 94, no. 1 (January 2000).

29. William Shawcross, *Deliver Us from Evil: Peacekeepers, Warlords and a World of Endless Conflict* (New York: Simon & Schuster, 2000), 26ff. Shawcross attributes this picture to US Deputy Secretary of State Strobe Talbott, but then adopts it with little qualification. In a critical review, *Wall Street Journal* editor Max Boot praises Shawcross for his "progress" in having come to understand that the United States is a "benign force," after having sunk so low as to criticize "U.S. attacks on North Vietnamese bases in Cambodia" (the approved term for Cambodian civilians), *Foreign Affairs*, March/April 2000.

30. *Newsweek* diplomatic correspondent Michael Hirsh, "The Fall Guy," *Foreign Affairs*, November/December 1999.

31. Richard Butler, "East Timor: Principle v. Reality," *The Eye* (Australia), 7–20, 1999.

32. On the reporting of the Racak massacre, and the available evidence, see Edward Herman and David Peterson, "CNN: Selling Nato's War Globally," in Philip Hammond and Edward Herman, eds., *Degraded Capability: The Media and the Kosovo Crisis* (London: Pluto, 2000).

33. Colum Lynch, "US seen leaving Africa to solve its own crisis," *Boston Globe* (henceforth *BG*), February 19, 1999. John Donnelly and Joe Lauria, "UN peace efforts on trial in

Africa; Annan angry as U.S. holds to limits on military role," *BG*, May 11; Barbara Crossette, "U.N. Chief Faults Reluctance of U.S. To Help in Africa," *New York Times*, May 13, 2000.

34. On the notion of "credibility," and its nature and scope as understood by top planners and policy intellectuals, see *The New Military Humanism: Lessons of Kosovo*, chap. 6.

35. PKI success, Harold Crouch, *Army and Politics in Indonesia* (Ithaca, NY: Cornell University Press, 1978), 351, 155, a standard source. See chap. 2, "Green Light for War Crimes," and sources cited in *A New Generation Draws the Line*.

36. Piero Gleijeses, *Shattered Hope: The Guatemalan Revolution and the United States, 1944–1954* (Princeton, NJ: Princeton University Press, 1991), 365. *Foreign Affairs* editor James Chace, *New York Times Magazine*, May 22, 1977.

37. Note 5, above; William Cohen's testimony at the Hearing of the Senate Armed Services Committee on Kosovo operations, October 14, 1999, Federal News Service.

38. Ivo Daalder and Michael O'Hanlon, "Without the air war, things could have been worse," *Washington Post National Weekly*, April 3, 2000.

39. See *The New Military Humanism: Lessons of Kosovo*, 22, and chap. 3 below.

40. See *The New Military Humanism: Lessons of Kosovo*, chap. 6; and chap. 3 below.

41. Michael Ignatieff, "What is war for? And should we have done it?" *National Post* (Canada), April 18, 2000; lengthy excerpts from his correspondence with Robert Skidelsky, taken from his book *Virtual War*.

42. "Panorama: War Room," BBC, April 19, 1999.

43. John Goetz and Tom Walker, "Serbian ethnic cleansing scare was a fake, says general," *Sunday Times*, April 2, 2000. Franziska Augstein, "Im Kosovo war es anders," *Frankfurter Allgemeine Zeitung*, March 25; also *Die Woche*, March 24; *Der Spiegel*, March 17; *Sueddeutsche Zeitung*, April 4; *Le Monde*, April 11, 2000. Heinz Loquai, *Der Kosovo-Konflict: Wege in einen vermeidbaren Krieg* (Baden-Baden: Nomos Verlag, 2000).

44. Ruth Wedgwood, "NATO's Campaign in Yugoslavia," *AJIL* 93, no. 4 (October 1999), a legal defense of the bombing; Donald Byman and Matthew Waxman of Rand Corporation, "Kosovo and the Great Air Power Debate," *International Security* 24, no. 4 (Spring 2000); David Fromkin, *Kosovo Crossing* (New York: The Free Press, 1999); Alan Kuperman, "Rwanda in Retrospect," *Foreign Affairs,* January/February 2000. For many other examples, see *NMH* and chap. 3, below.

45. Fouad Ajami, "Wars and Rumors of War," *New York Times Book Review*, June 11 2000; Aryeh Neier, op. cit., and many others. Neier's point is that it is "dishonest" for me (in *The New Military Humanism: Lessons of Kosovo*) to ignore this self-evident truth while keeping to the justifications that were actually put forth, and continue to be, as noted.

46. Testifying before the Defence Select Committee, Britain's second most senior defence minister during the war, Lord Gilbert, defence minister of state formally responsible for intelligence, ridiculed the suggestion that NATO could have invaded even by September 1999, informing the Committee that "a land invasion of Kosovo would have been possible by September, but by September this year [2000], not by September last year." Patrick Wintour, "War strategy ridiculed," *Guardian*, July 21, 2000.

47. Ian Williams, "Left Behind: American Socialists, Human Rights, and Kosovo," *Human Rights Review* 1–2 (January-March 2000).

48. Jiri Dienstbier, BBC Summary of World Broadcasts, March 25; Naomi Koppel, "Ground Troops Urged for Yugoslavia." AP Online, March 29, 2000; Elizabeth Sullivan, "A Threatening Thaw in the Balkans," *Cleveland Plain Dealer*, April 3; Laura Coffey, *Prague Post*, March 29, 2000. MccGwire, op. cit. Dienstbier was a leading Czech dissident, imprisoned in the late 1970s and early 1980s, later the first post-Communist foreign minister.

49. Donald Fox and Michael Glennon, "Report to the International Human Rights Law Group and the Washington Office on Latin America," Washington, DC, April 1985, referring to State Department evasion of U.S.-backed state terror in El Salvador.

22. LANGUAGE AND THE BRAIN

1. Ned Block, "The Computer Model of the Mind," in D. N. Osherson and E. E. Smith, eds., *An Invitation to Cognitive Science*, vol. 3, *Thinking* (Cambridge, MA: MIT Press, 1990).

2. "The Brain," *Daedalus*, Spring 1998.

3. Mark Hauser, *The Evolution of Communication* (Cambridge, MA: MIT Press, 1996).

4. C. R. Gallistel, "Neurons and Memory," in M. S. Gazzaniga, ed., *Conversations in the Cognitive Neurosciences* (Cambridge, MA: MIT Press, 1997); "The Replacement of General-Purpose Learning Models with Adaptively Specialized Learning Modules," in M. S. Gazzaniga, ed., *The Cognitive Neurosciences*, 2d ed. (Cambridge, MA: MIT Press, 1999).

5. David Hume, *Dialogues Concerning Natural Religion*, ed. Martin Bell (New York: Penguin, 1990).

6. Noam Chomsky, "Language and Cognition," welcoming address for the Conference of the Cognitive Science Society, MIT, July 1990, in D. Johnson and C. Emeling, eds., *The Future of the Cognitive Revolution* (New York: Oxford University Press, 1997). Chomsky, "Language and Nature," *Mind* 104, no. 413 (January 1995): 1–61, reprinted in Chomsky, *New Horizons in the Study of Language and Mind* (Cambridge: Cambridge University Press, 2000). See the latter collection for many sources not cited here.

7. Alexandre Koyré, *From the Closed World to the Infinite Universe* (Baltimore: Johns Hopkins University Press, 1957).

8. Arnold Thackray, *Atoms and Powers* (Cambridge, MA: Harvard University Press, 1970).

9. Cited by Gerald Holton, "On the Art of Scientific Imagination," *Daedalus*, Spring 1996,183–208.

10. Cited by V. S. Ramachandran and Sandra Blakeslee, *Phantoms in the Brain* (London: Fourth Estate, 1998).

11. Bertrand Russell, *The Analysis of Matter* (Leipzig: B. G. Teubner, 1929).

12. R. D. Hawkins and E. R. Kandel, "Is There a Cell-Biological Alphabet for Simple Forms of Learning?," *Psychological Review* 91 (1984): 376–91.

13. Adam Frank, "Quantum Honeybees," *Discover* 80 (November 1997).

14. Noam Chomsky, review of B. F. Skinner, *Verbal Behavior*, *Language* 35, no. 1 (1959): 26–57.

15. R. C. Lewontin, "The Evolution of Cognition," *Thinking: An Invitation to Cognitive Science*, vol. 3, ed. Daniel N. Osherson and Edward E. Smith (Cambridge, MA: MIT Press, 1990), 229–46.

16. Terrence Deacon, *The Symbolic Species: The Co-evolution of Language and the Brain* (New York: Norton, 1998).

17. For current discussion of these topics, see, *inter alia*, Jerry Fodor, *The Mind Doesn't Work That Way: Scope and Limits of Computational Psychology* (Cambridge, MA: MIT Press, 2000); Gary Marcus, "Can Connectionism Save Constructivism?," *Cognition* 66 (1998): 153–82.

18. See Chomsky, review of B. F. Skinner, *Verbal Behavior*, and for more general discussion, focusing on language, Chomsky, *Reflections on Language* (New York: Pantheon Books, 1975).

19. On the non-triviality of this rarely recognized assumption, see Fodor, *Mind Doesn't Work That Way.*

20. C. R. Gallistel, ed., *Animal Cognition, Cognition,* special issue, 37, no. 1–2 (1990).

23. UNITED STATES—ISRAEL—PALESTINE

1. Baruch Kimmerling, "Preparing for the War of His Choosing," *Ha'aretz*, July 12, 2001. Available online at www.palestinemonitor.org/israelipoli/preparing_for_the_war_of_his_cho.htm.

2. Ze'ev Sternhell, "Balata Has Fallen," *Ha'aretz*, March 7, 2002.

3. Shlomo Ben-Ami, *Makom Lekulam* [A Place for All] (Jerusalem: Hakibbutz Hameuchad, 1987). Cited in Efraim Davidi, "Globalization and Economy in the Middle East—A Peace of Markets or a Peace of Flags?" *Palestine-Israel Journal*, vol. 7, nos. 1–2 (2002).

4. Kimmerling, op. cit.

5. "Moving Past War in the Middle East," *New York Times*, April 7, 2002.

6. Text of a peace initiative authorized by the government of Israel on May 15, 1989 (the Peres-Shamir coalition plan, endorsed by the first President Bush in the Baker plan of December 1989). See my *World Orders Old and New* (New York: Columbia University Press, 1999, 231–2 for an informal translation of this peace initiative; see also http://domino.un.org/UNISPAL.NSF/bdd57d15a29f428d85256c3800701fc4/2fa32a5884d90dc985256282007942fa!OpenDocument.

7. John Donnelly and Charles A. Radin, "Powell's Trip Is Called a Way to Buy Time for Sharon Sweep," *Boston Globe*, April 9, 2002, A1.

8. See *Fateful Triangle: The United States, Israel, and the Palestinians*, updated ed. (Cambridge, MA: South End Press, 1999), 75.

9. Patrick E. Tyler, "Arab Ministers Announce Support for Arafat," *New York Times*, April 7, 2002, section 1, 17; Agence France-Presse, "Israeli Troops Keep Up Offensive as Powell Starts Regional Tour," April 8, 2002; Toby Harnden, "It Is When, Not If, the Withdrawal Will Start," *Daily Telegraph* (London), April 8, 2002; Robert Fisk, "Mr. Powell Must See for Himself What Israel Inflicted on Jenin," *The Independent* (London), April 14, 2002, 25.

10. Melissa Radler, "UN Security Council Endorses Vision of Palestinian State," *Jerusalem Post*, March 14, 2002.

11. See chap. 8 in *Middle East Illusions* and, for more details, my introduction to Roane Carey, ed., *The New Intifada* (New York: Verso, 2001). Reprinted in Chomsky, *Pirates and Emperors, Old and New: International Terrorism in the Real World* (Cambridge, MA: South End Press, 2002).

12. Fiona Fleck, "114 States Condemn Israelis," *Daily Telegraph* (London), December 6, 2001; Herb Keinon, "Geneva Parley Delegates Blast Israel," *Jerusalem Post*, December 6, 2001.

13. Graham Usher, "Ending the Phony Cease-Fire," *Middle East International*, January 25, 2002, 4.

14. Geoffrey Aronson, ed., "Report on Israeli Settlements in the Occupied Territories," *Foundation for Middle East Peace* 12, no. 1 (January-February 2002); Ian Williams, *Middle East International*, December 21, 2001; Judy Dempsey and Frances Williams, "EU Seeks to Reassert Mideast Influence," *Financial Times* (London), December 6, 2001, 7.

15. Francis A. Boyle, "Law and Disorder in the Middle East," *The Link* (Americans for Middle East Understanding) 35, no. 1 (January-March 2002): 1–13. (Full text available online at www.ameu.org/uploads/vol35_issue1_2002.pdf.)

24. IMPERIAL GRAND STRATEGY

1. White House, *The National Security Strategy of the United States of America*, released September 17, 2002.

2. John Ikenberry, *Foreign Affairs*, September–October 2002.

3. On this crucial distinction, see Carl Kaysen, Steven Miller, Martin Malin, William Nordhaus, and John Steinbruner, *War with Iraq* (Cambridge, MA: American Academy of Arts and Sciences, 2002).

4. Steven Weisman, *New York Times*, March 23, 2003.

5. Arthur Schlesinger, *Los Angeles Times*, March 23, 2003.

6. Richard Falk, *Frontline* (India) 20, no. 8 (April 12–25, 2003).

7. Michael Glennon, *Foreign Affairs*, May–June 2003 and May–June 1999.

8. Dana Milbank, *Washington Post*, June 1, 2003. Guy Dinmore, James Harding, and Cathy Newman, *Financial Times*, May 3–4, 2003.

9. Dean Acheson, *Proceedings of the American Society of International Law*, no. 13/14 (1963). Abraham Sofaer, U.S. Department of State, *Current Policy*, no. 769 (December 1985). Acheson was referring specifically to U.S. economic war, but he surely knew about the international terrorism.

10. President Clinton, address to the UN, September 27, 1993; William Cohen, *Annual Report to the President and Congress* (Washington, DC: U.S. Government Printing Office, 1999).

11. Memorandum of the War and Peace Studies Project; Laurence Shoup and William Minter, *Imperial Brain Trust* (New York: Monthly Review Press, 1977), 130ff.

12. See Bacevich, *American Empire: The Realities and Consequences of U.S. Diplomacy* (Cambridge, MA: Harvard University Press, 2002), for unusually strong claims in this regard.

13. George W. Bush, State of the Union address, transcribed in *New York Times*, January 29, 2003.

14. Condoleezza Rice, interview with Wolf Blitzer, CNN, September 8, 2002. Scott Peterson, *Christian Science Monitor*, September 6, 2002. John Mearsheimer and Stephen Walt, *Foreign Policy*, January–February 2003. The 1990 claims, based on alleged satellite images, were investigated by the *St. Petersburg Times*. Experts who analyzed photos from commercial satellites found nothing. Inquiries were rebuffed, and still are. See Peterson, *Christian Science Monitor*, for a review of how "some facts [are] less factual." For independent confirmation, see Peter Zimmerman, *Washington Post*, August 14, 2003.

15. *Christian Science Monitor*—TIPP poll, *Christian Science Monitor*, January 14, 2003. Linda Feldmann, *Christian Science Monitor*, March 14, 2003. Jim Rutenberg and Robin Toner, *New York Times*, March 22, 2003.

16. Edward Alden, *Financial Times*, March 21, 2003; Anatol Lieven, *London Review of Books*, May 8, 2003.

17. Elisabeth Bumiller, *New York Times*, May 2, 2003; transcript of George W. Bush's comments, *New York Times*, May 2, 2003.

18. Jason Burke, *Sunday Observer*, May 18, 2003. See 211.

19. Program on International Policy Attitudes (PIPA), news release, June 4, 2003.

20. Jeanne Cummings and Greg Hite, *Wall Street Journal*, May 2, 2003; Francis Clines, *New York Times*, May 10, 2003. Rove's emphasis.

21. David Sanger and Steven Weisman, *New York Times*, April 10, 2003; Roger Owen, *Al-Ahram Weekly*, April 3, 2003.

22. Comment and Analysis, *Financial Times*, May 27, 2003.

23. International Court of Justice, Corfu Channel Case (Merits), Judgment of April 9, 1949.

24. See my *New Military Humanism* (Monroe, ME: Common Courage Press, 1999).

25. See my *A New Generation Draws the Line* (New York: Verso, 2000), 4ff. Statement by Nonaligned Movement, Kuala Lumpur, February 25, 2003.

26. Aryeh Dayan, *Ha'aretz*, May 21, 2003.

27. Amir Oren, *Ha'aretz*, November 29, 2002.

28. Suzanne Nossel, *Fletcher Forum*, Winter-Spring 2003.

29. Richard Wilson, *Nature* 302, no. 31 (March 1983). Michael Jansen, *Middle East International*, January 10, 2003. Imad Khadduri, *Uncritical Mass*, memoirs (manuscript), 2003. Scott Sagan and Kenneth Waltz, *The Spread of Nuclear Weapons* (New York: Norton, 1995), 18–19.

30. Neely Tucker, *Washington Post*, December 3, 2002; Neil Lewis, *New York Times*, January 9, 2003.

31. Ed Vulliamy, *Sunday Observer*, May 25, 2003.

32. See Chomsky, *Hegemony or Survival* (New York: Metropolitan Books, 2003), 200.

33. Jack Balkin, *Los Angeles Times*, February 13, 2003, and *Newsday*, February 17, 2003. Nat Hentoff, *Progressive*, April 2003.

34. Winston Churchill cited by A. W. B. Simpson, *Human Rights and the End of Empire: Britain and the Genesis of the European Convention* (New York: Oxford University Press, 2001), 55.

35. Kaysen et al., *War with Iraq*. Michael Krepon, *Bulletin of the Atomic Scientists*, January–February 2003.

36. John Steinbruner and Jeffrey Lewis, *Daedalus*, fall 2002.

37. See Chomsky, *Year 501* (Cambridge, MA: South End Press, 1993), chap. 1.

38. James Morgan, *Financial Times*, April 25–26, 1992, referring to G-7, the IMF, GATT, and other institutions of "the new imperial age." Guy de Jonquières, *Financial Times*, January 24, 2001. Fukuyama cited by Mark Curtis, *The Ambiguities of Power* (London: Zed, 1995), 183.

39. Bush and Baker cited by Sam Husseini, *Counterpunch*, March 8, 2003. Dilip Hiro, *Iraq: In the Eye of the Storm* (New York: Thunder's Mouth Press/Nation Books, 2002), 102f.

40. Edward Luck, *New York Times*, March 22, 2003.

41. Elisabeth Bumiller and Carl Hulse, *New York Times*, October 12, 2002. Colin Powell cited by Julia Preston, *New York Times*, October 18, 2002. David Sanger and Julia Preston, *New York Times*, November 8, 2002. Andrew Card cited by Doug Sanders, *Toronto Globe and Mail*, November 11, 2002.

42. Mark Turner and Roula Khalaf, *Financial Times*, February 5, 2003.

43. David Sanger and Warren Hoge, *New York Times*, March 17, 2003. Michael Gordon, *New York Times*, March 18, 2003.

44. Excerpts from George W. Bush's news conference, *New York Times*, March 7, 2003. Felicity Barringer and David Sanger, *New York Times*, March 1, 2003.

45. Alison Mitchell and David Sanger, *New York Times*, September 4, 2002. Ari Fleischer cited by Christopher Adams and Mark Huband, *Financial Times*, April 12–13, 2003. Jack Straw cited by David Sanger and Felicity Barringer, *New York Times*, March 7, 2003.

46. "In Powell's Words: Saddam Hussein Remains Guilty," *New York Times*, March 6, 2003. Weisman, *New York Times*, March 23, 2003.

47. Condoleezza Rice, *Foreign Affairs*, January February 2000. Cited by John Mearsheimer and Stephen Walt, *Foreign Policy*, January–February 2003. Note that 9-11 had no effect on these risk assessments.

48. Dafna Linzer, AP, *Boston Globe*, February 24, 2003.

49. Guy Dinmore and Mark Turner, *Financial Times*, February 12, 2003. Jeanne Cummings and Robert Block, *Wall Street Journal*, February 26, 2003.

50. Geneive Abdo, "US Offers Incentives for Backing on Iraq," *Boston Globe,* February 13, 2003. Eric Lichtblau, "Charity Leader Accepts a Deal in a Terror Case," *New York Times,* February 11, 2003. See Chomsky, *Hegemony or Survival,* 208.

51. Richard Boudreaux and John Hendren, *Los Angeles Times,* March 15, 2003.

52. Neil King and Jess Bravin, *Wall Street Journal,* May 5, 2003. For U.S. attitudes quoted here, see April 18–22, 2003 poll by the Program on International Policy Attitudes (PIPA). On Iraqi attitudes, see Susannah Sirkin, deputy director, Physicians for Human Rights, reporting PHR poll finding that over 85 percent wanted the UN to "play the lead role" (Letters, *New York Times,* August 21, 2003).

53. John Ikenberry, *Foreign Affairs,* September–October 2002. Anatol Lieven, *London Review of Books,* October 3, 2002.

54. Samuel Huntington, *Foreign Affairs,* March–April 1999. Robert Jervis, *Foreign Affairs,* July–August 2001.

55. Kenneth Waltz in Kim Booth and Tim Dunne, eds., *Worlds in Collision: Terror and the Future of the Global Order* (New York: Palgrave Macmillan, 2002). Steven Miller in Kaysen et al., *War with Iraq.* Jack Snyder, *National Interest,* spring 2003. Selig Harrison, *New York Times,* June 7, 2003.

56. Bernard Fall, *Last Reflections on a War* (Garden City, NY: Doubleday, 1967).

57. See Chomsky, *For Reasons of State,* 25, for a review of the final material in the *Pentagon Papers,* which ends at this point.

58. Maureen Dowd, *New York Times,* February 23, 1991.

59. World Economic Forum press release, January 14, 2003. Guy de Jonquières, *Financial Times,* January 15, 2003.

60. Alan Cowell, *New York Times,* January 23, 2003; Mark Landler, *New York Times,* January 24, 2003. Marc Champion, David Cloud, and Carla Anne Robbins, *Wall Street Journal,* January 27, 2003.

61. Foreign Desk, "Powell on Iraq: 'We Reserve Our Sovereign Right to Take Military Action,' " *New York Times,* January 27, 2003.

62. Kaysen et al., *War with Iraq.*

63. Hans von Sponeck, *Guardian,* July 22, 2002.

64. Ken Warn, *Financial Times,* January 21, 2003. On international polls, see Chomsky, *Hegemony or Survival,* chap. 5.

65. Glenn Kessler and Mike Allen, *Washington Post Weekly,* March 3, 2003. Fareed Zakaria, *Newsweek,* March 24, 2003.

66. See Chomsky, *Hegemony or Survival,* chap. 1, note 6. *Atlantic Monthly,* 1901, cited by Ido Oren, *Our Enemies and Us* (Ithaca, NY: Cornell University Press, 2002), 42.

67. Andrew Bacevich, *American Empire,* 215ff. His emphasis.

68. *The Collected Works of John Stuart Mill,* vol. 21, ed. John M. Robson (Toronto: University of Toronto Press; London: Routledge and Kegan Paul, 1984). See *Hegemony or Survival,* 44–45. Britain's attitude toward the nobility of its successor was a bit different; see *Hegemony or Survival,* 149.

69. Andrew Bacevich, *World Policy Journal,* fall 2002.

70. Michael Glennon, *Christian Science Monitor,* March 20, 1986.

71. Sebastian Mallaby, *New York Times Book Review,* September 21, 1997. Michael Mandelbaum, *The Ideas That Conquered the World* (New York: PublicAffairs, 2002), 195. Senior administration policymaker cited by Thomas Friedman, *New York Times,* January 12, 1992.

72. Boot, *New York Times,* February 13, 2003. Robert Kagan, *Washington Post Weekly,* February 10, 2003.

73. On Mill's essay and the circumstances in which it was written, see my *Peering into the Abyss of the Future*. Britain's crimes in India and China shocked many Englishmen, including classical liberals like Richard Cobden. See Chomsky, *Hegemony or Survival*, chap. 7, note 52.

74. Henri Alleg, *La Guerre d'Algérie*, cited in Yousef Bedjauoi, Abbas Aroua, and Méziane Ait-Larbi, eds., *An Inquiry into the Algerian Massacres* (Plan-les-Ouates [Genève]: Hoggar, 1999).

75. Walter LaFeber, *Inevitable Revolutions* (New York: Norton, 1983), 50ff., 75ff.

76. Mohammad-Mahmoud Mohamedou, *Iraq and the Second Gulf War* (San Francisco: Austin & Winfield, 1998), 123.

77. David Schmitz, *Thank God They're on Our Side* (Chapel Hill: North Carolina Press, 1999). "Japan Envisions a 'New Order' in Asia, 1938," reprinted in Dennis Merrill and Thomas Paterson, eds., *Major Problems in American Foreign Relations, Volume II: Since 1914* (New York: Houghton Mifflin, 2000).

78. Soviet lawyers, see Sean Murphy, *Humanitarian Intervention* (Philadelphia: University of Pennsylvania Press, 1996). Kennedy administration, see Chomsky, *Rethinking Camelot*.

79. Ivan Maisky, January 1944, cited in Vladimir Pechatnov, *The Big Three After World War II* (Woodrow Wilson International Center, Working Paper no. 13, July 1995).

80. Cited by LaFeber, *Inevitable Revolutions*. Robert Tucker, *Commentary*, January 1975.

81. Cited by Mexican historian José Fuentes Mares in Cecil Robinson, ed. and trans., *The View from Chapultepec: Mexican Writers on the Mexican-American War* (Tucson: University of Arizona Press, 1989), 160.

82. Cited by William Stivers, *Supremacy and Oil* (Ithaca, NY: Cornell Unversity Press, 1982).

83. Morgenthau, *New York Review of Books*, September 24, 1970.

84. See regular Human Rights Watch and Amnesty International reports and, among many publications, Javier Giraldo, *Colombia: The Genocidal Democracy* (Monroe, ME: Common Courage Press, 1996), and Garry Leech, *Killing Peace: Colombia's Conflict and the Failure of U.S. Intervention* (New York: Information Network of the Americas, 2002).

25. AFTERWORD TO *FAILED STATES*

1. Robert Pastor, *Condemned to Repetition: The United States and Nicaragua* (Princeton: Princeton University Press, 1987), his emphasis.

2. Ali Abdullatif Ahmida, *Forgotten Voice: Power and Agency in Colonial and Postcolonial Libya* (London: Routledge, 2005).

3. Selig Harrison, *Financial Times*, January 18, 2006.

4. Ellen Knickmeyer and Omar Fekeiki, *Washington Post*, January 24, 2006. Charles Levinson, *Christian Science Monitor*, January 30, 2006. For Osirak, see *Hegemony or Survival*, 25.

5. See Chomsky, *Failed States* (New York: Metropolitan Books, 2006), 77; and *Hegemony or Survival* (New York: Metropolitan Books, 2003), 157–58.

6. Anthony Bubalo, *Financial Times*, October 6, 2005. Shai Oster, *Wall Street Journal*, January 23, 2006.

7. Aijaz Ahmad, *Frontline* (India), October 8, 2005. Katrin Bennhold, *International Herald Tribune*, October 5, 2004. Also Victor Mallet and Guy Dinmore, *Financial Times*, March 17, 2005. Daniel Dombey et al., *Financial Times*, January 26, 2006. David Sanger and Elaine Sciolino, *New York Times*, January 27, 2006.

8. Siddharth Varadarajan, *Hindu*, January 24, 2006; *Hindu*, January 25, 2006; *International Herald Tribune*, January 25, 2006. Fred Weir, *Christian Science Monitor*, October 26, 2005. See

"Declaration of Heads of Member-States of Shanghai Cooperation Organisation" (China, Russian Federation, Kazakhstan, Kyrgyz Republic, Tajikistan, Uzbekistan), July 5, 2005, Astana, Kazakhstan; *World Affairs* (New Delhi), Autumn 2005.

9. For background see *Hegemony or Survival*, chap. 6.

10. NIC, *Global Trends*. Joel Brinkley, *New York Times*, October 25, 2005. Dan Molinski, AP, October 24, 2005. Bush policies have even alienated Australians, traditionally supportive of the United States. A 2005 survey found that a majority regarded "the external threat posed by both US foreign policy and Islamic extremism" as primary and equivalent concerns, compared with one-third concerned about China. Only 58 percent "viewed the US positively, compared with 94 per cent for New Zealand, 86 per cent for Britain, 84 per cent for Japan, and 69 per cent for China." Half favored a free trade agreement with China, only a third with the United States. Tom Allard and Louise Williams, *Sydney Morning Herald*, March 29, 2005.

11. Marc Frank, *Financial Times*, October 21, 2005. John Cherian, *Frontline* (India), December 30, 2005, citing Pakistan's leading daily *Dawn*.

12. Gwynne Dyer, *Guardian*, October 25, 2005. Adam Thomson, *Financial Times*, December 11, 2005. Economist Mark Weisbrot, codirector of the Center for Economic and Policy Research (Washington), CEPR release, January 28, 2006.

13. Andy Webb-Vidal, *Financial Times*, January 3, 2005. Diego Cevallos, IPS, December 19, 2005. Weisbrot, CEPR release, January 28, 2006. For more on the water issue, see William Blum, *Rogue State* (Monroe, ME: Common Courage Press, 2000), 77–78.

14. Andy Webb-Vidal, *Financial Times*, March 13, 2005. Justin Blum, *Washington Post*, November 22, 2005. Michael Levenson and Susan Milligan, *Boston Globe*, November 20, 2005.

15. David Bacon, *Z Magazine*, January 2006; *Multinational Monitor*, September–October 2005.

16. Scott Wilson and Glenn Kessler, *Washington Post*, January 22, 2006. Steven Erlanger, *New York Times*, January 23, 2006.

17. Walt Bogdanich and Jenny Nordberg, *New York Times*, January 29, 2006. See references of chap. 4, note 14, and 154 in *Failed States*. Gregory Wilpert, Znet commentary, December 2005.

Select Bibliography of Works by Noam Chomsky

1951. "Morphophonemics of Modern Hebrew." Master's thesis, University of Pennsylvania.

1953. "Systems of Syntactic Analysis." *Journal of Symbolic Logic* 18, no. 3 (September).

1954. Review of *Modern Hebrew* by E. Reiger. *Language* 30, no. 1 (January–March).

1955. "Logical Syntax and Semantics: Their Linguistic Relevance." *Language* 31, nos. 1–2 (January–March).

1955. *Logical Structure of Linguistic Theory*. Manuscript (microfilm). Reprints, New York: Plenum Press, 1975; Chicago: University of Chicago Press, 1985.

1955. "Transformational Analysis." Ph.D. dissertation. Philadelphia: University of Pennsylvania.

1955. "Semantic Considerations in Grammar." Monograph no. 8. Georgetown: Georgetown University Institute of Languages and Linguistics.

1957. *Syntactic Structures*. The Hague: Mouton. Reprints, Berlin and New York, 1985; Berlin and New York: Mouton de Gruyter, 2002.

1958. "Linguistics, Logic, Psychology, and Computers." *Computer Programming and Artificial Intelligence* (March).

1959. Review of *Verbal Behavior* by B. F. Skinner. *Language* 35, no. 1 (January–March).

1961. "Some Methodological Remarks on Generative Grammar." *Word* 17, no. 2 (August).

1965. *Aspects of the Theory of Syntax*. Cambridge, MA: MIT Press.

1965. *Cartesian Linguistics*. New York: Harper & Row. Reprints, Lanham, MD: University Press of America, 1986; Christchurch, New Zealand: Cybereditions Corporation, 2002; Cambridge: Cambridge University Press, 2008.

1968. With Morris Halle. *Sound Pattern of English*. New York: Harper & Row. Reprint, Cambridge, MA: MIT Press, 1991.

1968. "Vietnam: A Symptom of the Crisis in America." *Folio* 6, no. 2 (Spring–Summer).

1969. Review of *No More Vietnams*, edited by R. M. Pfeiffer. *New York Review of Books*, January 2.

1969. *American Power and the New Mandarins*. New York: Pantheon Books; London: Chatto and Windus. Reprint, New York: The New Press, 2002.

1969. "Some Tasks for the Left." *Liberation* 14, nos. 5–6 (August–September).

1969. "Knowledge and Power: Intellectuals and the Welfare-Warfare State." In *The New Left: A Collection of Essays*, ed. Patricia Long. Boston: Porter Sargent.

1970. *At War with Asia*. New York: Pantheon Books. Reprint, Oakland, CA: AK Press, 2005.

1970. "A Visit to Laos." *New York Review of Books* 15, no. 2 (July 23).

1970. "In North Vietnam." *New York Review of Books* 15, no. 3 (August 13).

1970. *For Reasons of State*. New York: Pantheon Books. Reprint, New York: The New Press, 2003.

1970. *Current Issues in Linguistic Theory*. Berlin and New York: Mouton de Gruyter.

1971. *Chomsky: Selected Readings*, ed. J. P. B. Allen and Paul Van Buren. London: Oxford University Press.

1971. *Problems of Knowledge and Freedom*. New York: Pantheon Books. Reprint, New York: The New Press, 2003.

1968. *Language and Mind*. New York: Harcourt Brace and World. Expanded ed., New York: Harcourt Brace Jovanovich, 1972.

1972. *Studies on Semantics in Generative Grammar*. The Hague: Mouton.

1972. "The Pentagon Papers as Propaganda and as History." In *The Pentagon Papers*, vol. 5, eds. Noam Chomsky and Howard Zinn. Boston: Beacon.

1973. "Endgame: The Tactics of Peace in Vietnam." *Ramparts* 11, no. 10 (April): 25–28, 5–60.

1973. With Edward S. Herman. *Counter-Revolutionary Violence: Bloodbaths in Fact and Propaganda*, Module no. 57. Andover, MA: Warner Modular Publications.

1973. "Watergate: A Skeptical View." *New York Review of Books* 20, no. 4 (September 20).

1974. *Peace in the Middle East?* New York: Pantheon Books. (See *Middle East Illusions* below.)

1975. *Reflections on Language*. New York: Pantheon Books. (See *On Language* below.)

1976. "Conditions on Rules of Grammar." *Linguistic Analysis* 2, no. 4.

1977. "Human Rights: A New Excuse for U.S. Interventions." *Seven Days* 1, no. 8 (May 23).

1977. "Workers Councils: Not Just a Slice of the Pie, But a Hand in Making It." *Seven Days* 1, no. 10 (June 20).

1977. "Why American Business Supports Third World Fascism." *Business and Society Review* (Fall).

1977. *Essays on Form and Interpretation*. New York: Elsevier North-Holland.

1978. *"Human Rights" and American Foreign Policy*. Nottingham: Spokesman Books.

1978. "Against Apologetics for Israeli Expansionism." *New Politics* 12, no. 1 (Winter): 15–46.

1978. *Language and Responsibility*. New York: Pantheon Books. (See *On Language* below.)

1978. "An Exception to the Rules." Review of *Just and Unjust Wars* by Michael Walzer. *Inquiry* (April 17).

1979. "The Hidden War in East Timor." *Resist*, January–February.

1979. With Edward S. Herman. *The Political Economy of Human Rights. The Washington Connection and Third World Fascism*, vol. 1. *After the Cataclysm: Postwar Indochina and the Reconstruction of Imperial Ideology*, vol. 2. Cambridge, MA: South End Press.

1980. *Rules and Representations*. New York: Columbia University Press; Oxford: Basil Blackwell Publisher. Reprint, New York: Columbia University Press, 2005.

1981. *Lectures on Government and Binding: The Pisa Lectures*. Holland: Foris Publications. Reprint, Berlin and New York: Mouton de Gruyter, 1993.

1981. "Resurgent America: On Reagan's Foreign Policy." *Our Generation* 14, no. 4 (Summer).

1981. "On the Representation of Form and Function." *The Linguistic Review* 1.

1981. *Radical Priorities*, ed. Carlos P. Otero. Montréal: Black Rose Books. Expanded ed., Oakland, CA: AK Press, 2003.

1982. *Towards a New Cold War: Essays on the Current Crisis and How We Got There*. New York: Pantheon Books. Reprinted as *Towards a New Cold War: U.S. Foreign Policy from Vietnam to Reagan*. New York: The New Press, 2003.

1982. *Some Concepts and Consequences of the Theory of Government and Binding*. Cambridge, MA: MIT Press.

1983. *The Fateful Triangle: Israel, the United States, and the Palestinians*. Cambridge, MA: South End Press. Expanded ed., Cambridge, MA: South End Press, 1999.

1984. *Modular Approaches to the Study of the Mind*. San Diego: San Diego State University Press.

1985. "Crimes by victims are called terrorism." *In These Times*, July 24–August 6.

1985. "Dominoes." *Granta* 15 (Spring).

1985. *Turning the Tide: U.S. Intervention in Central America and the Struggle for Peace*. Cambridge, MA: South End Press. Expanded ed., Montréal: Black Rose Books, 1988; Cambridge, MA: South End Press, 2000.

1986. *Knowledge of Language: Its Nature, Origin, and Use*. New York: Praeger Publishers.

1986. "The Soviet Union vs. Socialism." *Our Generation* 7, no. 2 (Spring/Summer).

1986. *Barriers*. Cambridge, MA: MIT Press.

1986. "Visions of Righteousness." *Cultural Critique*, no. 3 (Spring).

1986. "Middle East Terrorism and the US Ideological System." *Race and Class* 28, no. 1.

1986. *Pirates and Emperors: International Terrorism in the Real World*. New York: Claremont Research and Publications; Brattleboro, VT: Amana Books; Montréal: Black Rose Books, 1987. (See *Pirates and Emperors, Old and New* below.)

1987. *On Power and Ideology: The Managua Lectures*. Cambridge, MA: South End Press.

1987. *Language and Problems of Knowledge: The Managua Lectures*. Cambridge, MA: MIT Press.

1987. *The Chomsky Reader*, ed. James Peck. New York: Pantheon Books.

1988. *The Culture of Terrorism*. Cambridge, MA: South End Press.

1988. *Language and Politics*, ed. Carlos P. Otero. Montréal: Black Rose Books. Expanded ed., Oakland, CA: AK Press, 2004.

1988. "Scenes from the Uprising." *Z Magazine*, July/August.

1988. "The Palestinian Uprising: A Turning Point?" *Z Magazine*, May.

1988. With Edward S. Herman. *Manufacturing Consent: The Political Economy of the Mass Media*. New York: Pantheon Books. Expanded ed., New York: Pantheon Books, 2002.

1989. *Necessary Illusions: Thought Control in Democratic Societies*. Cambridge, MA: South End Press.

1990. "The Dawn, So Far, Is in the East." *Nation* 250, no. 4 (January 29).

1991. *On U.S. Gulf Policy*. Open Magazine Pamphlet Series, no 1. Westfield, NJ: Open Media.

1991. "International Terrorism: Image and Reality." In *Western State Terrorism*, ed. Alexander George, 12–38. Oxford: Polity Press.

1991. "Some Notes on Economy of Derivation and Representation." In *Principles and Parameters in Comparative Grammar*, ed. Robert Freidin. Cambridge, MA: MIT Press.

1991. *The New World Order*. Open Magazine Pamphlet Series, no. 6. Westfield, NJ: Open Media.

1991. *Deterring Democracy*. New York: Verso. Expanded ed., London: Vintage, 1992; New York: Hill and Wang, 1992.

1991. *Media Control: The Spectacular Achievements of Propaganda*. Open Magazine Pamphlet Series, no. 10. Westfield, NJ: Open Media. Expanded ed., New York: Seven Stories Press/Open Media, 2002.

1992. " 'What We Say Goes': The Middle East in the New World Order." In *Collateral Damage: The "New World Order" at Home and Abroad*, ed. Cynthia Peters. Cambridge, MA: South End Press.

1992. "Language and Mind: Challenges and Prospects." Talk given at the Commemorative

Lecture Meeting, 1988 Kyoto Prizes, Kyoto, November 11, 1988. In *Kyoto Prizes and Inamori Grants, 1988*. Kyoto: Inamori Foundation.

1992. "A Minimalist Program for Linguistic Theory." *MIT Occasional Papers in Linguistics* 1. Cambridge, MA: MIT Working Papers in Linguistics. Reprinted in *The View from Building 20*, eds. Kenneth Hale and Samuel Jay Keyser. Cambridge, MA: MIT Press, 1993.

1992. *What Uncle Sam Really Wants*. Berkeley: Odonian Press.

1992. With David Barsamian. *Chronicles of Dissent*. Monroe, ME: Common Courage Press.

1993. "The Masters of Mankind." *Nation*. March 29.

1993. *Enter a World That Is Truly Surreal: President Clinton's Sudden Use of International Violence*. Westfield, NJ: Open Media.

1993. "On US Gulf Policy." In *Open Fire: The Open Magazine Pamphlet Series Anthology*, eds. Greg Ruggiero and Stuart Sahulka. New York: The New Press.

1993. *Letters from Lexington: Reflections on Propaganda*. Monroe, ME: Common Courage Press; Toronto, ON: Between the Lines. Expanded ed., Boulder: Paradigm Publishers, 2004.

1993. *Year 501: The Conquest Continues*. Cambridge, MA: South End Press.

1993. *Rethinking Camelot: JFK, the Vietnam War, and U.S. Political Culture*. Cambridge, MA: South End Press.

1993. *Language and Thought*. Wakefield, RI: Moyer Bell.

1993. With David Barsamian. *The Prosperous Few and the Restless Many*. Berkeley, CA: Odonian Press.

1994. "Humanitarian Intervention." *Boston Review* 18, no. 6 (December 1993–January 1994).

1994. *World Orders Old and New*. Cairo: The American University in Cairo Press; New York: Columbia University Press. Expanded ed., New York: Columbia University Press, 1996.

1994. With David Barsamian. *Keeping the Rabble in Line*. Monroe, ME: Common Courage Press.

1994. With David Barsamian. *Secrets, Lies and Democracy*. Berkeley, CA: Odonian Press.

1995. "Rollback." In *The New American Crisis: Radical Analyses of the Problems Facing America Today*, eds. Greg Ruggiero and Stuart Sahulka. New York: The New Press.

1995. "Memories." *Z Magazine*, July/August.

1995. *The Minimalist Program*. Cambridge, MA: MIT Press.

1996. With David Barsamian. *Class Warfare: Interviews with David Barsamian*. Monroe, ME: Common Courage Press.

1996. " 'Consent without Consent': Reflections on the Theory and Practice of Democracy." *Cleveland State Law Review* 44, no. 4.

1996. *Powers and Prospects: Reflections on Human Nature and the Social Order*. St. Leonards, Australia: Allen and Unwin; Cambridge, MA: South End Press.

1996. "Hamlet without the Prince of Denmark." Review of *In Retrospect* by Robert McNamara. In *Diplomatic History* 20, no. 3 (Summer).

1997. "The Cold War and the University." In *The Cold War and the University: Toward an Intellectual History of the Postwar Years*. New York: The New Press.

1998. *On Language: Chomsky's Classic Works* Language and Responsibility *and* Reflections on Language *in One Volume*. New York: The New Press.

1998. With David Barsamian. *The Common Good*. Monroe, ME: Odonian Press.

1998. "Power in the Global Arena." *New Left Review* 230 (July/August).

1999. *The Umbrella of U.S. Power: The Universal Declaration of Human Rights and the Contradictions of U.S. Policy*. New York: Seven Stories Press/Open Media.

1999. *Profit Over People: Neoliberalism and Global Order*. New York: Seven Stories Press.

1999. *The New Military Humanism: Lessons from Kosovo.* Monroe, ME: Common Courage Press.

1999. With Heinz Dieterich. *Latin America: From Colonization to Globalization.* Melbourne: Ocean Press.

1999. "The United States and the University of Human Rights." *International Journal of Health Services* 29, no. 3.

1999. "Domestic Terrorism: Notes on the State System of Oppression." *New Political Science* 21, no. 3.

2000. "US Iraq Policy: Motives and Consequences." In *Iraq Under Siege: The Deadly Impact of Sanctions and War*, ed. Anthony Arnove. Cambridge, MA: South End Press.

2000. *New Horizons in the Study of Language and Mind.* Cambridge: Cambridge University Press.

2000. *Rogue States: The Rule of Force in World Affairs.* Cambridge, MA: South End Press.

2000. *A New Generation Draws the Line: Kosovo, East Timor and the Standards of the West.* London and New York: Verso.

2000. *Chomsky on MisEducation*, edited by Donaldo Macedo. Lanham, MD: Rowman and Littlefield Publishers.

2000. *The Architecture of Language*, ed. Nirmalangshu Mukherji, Bibudhendra Narayan Patnaik, and Rama Kant Agnihotri. New Delhi: Oxford University Press.

2001. With David Barsamian. *Propaganda and the Public Mind: Conversations with Noam Chomsky.* Cambridge, MA: South End Press.

2001. "Elections 2000." *Z Magazine*, January.

2001. "Update: Elections." *Z Magazine*, February.

2001. *9-11*, ed. Greg Ruggiero. New York: Seven Stories Press. Expanded ed., New York: Seven Stories Press, 2002.

2002. *Understanding Power: The Indispensable Chomsky*, eds. Peter R. Mitchell and John Schoeffel. New York: The New Press.

2002. *On Nature and Language*, eds. Adriana Belletti and Luigi Rizzi. Cambridge: Cambridge University Press.

2002. With W. Tecumseh Fitch and Marc D. Hauser. "The Faculty of Language: What Is It, Who Has It, and How Did It Evolve?" *Science* 298 (November 22).

2002. *Pirates and Emperors, Old and New: International Terrorism in the Real World.* Cambridge, MA: South End Press.

2003. *Power and Terror: Post-9/11 Talks and Interviews*, eds. John Junkerman and Takei Masakazu. New York: Seven Stories Press.

2003. *Chomsky on Democracy and Education*, ed. Carlos P. Otero. New York: RoutledgeFalmer.

2003. *Middle East Illusions.* Lanham, MD: Rowman and Littlefield.

2003. *Hegemony or Survival: America's Quest for Global Dominance.* New York: Metropolitan Books. Expanded ed., New York: Owl Books, 2004.

2003. *Objectivity and Liberal Scholarship.* New York: The New Press.

2004. *The Generative Enterprise Revisited: Discussions with Riny Huybregts, Henk van Riemsdijk, Naoki Fukui and Mihoko Zushi.* Berlin and New York: Mouton de Gruyter.

2004. "Turing on the 'Imitation Game.' " In *The Turing Test*, ed. Stuart Shieber. Cambridge, MA: MIT Press.

2005. "Three Factors in Language Design." *Linguistics Inquiry* 36, no. 1 (Winter).

2005. "What We Know: On the Universals of Language and Rights." *Boston Review* 30, nos. 3–4 (Summer).

2005. With W. Tecumseh Fitch and Marc D. Hauser. "The Evolution of the Language Faculty: Clarifications and Implications." *Cognition* 97, no. 2 (September).

2005. *Government in the Future*. New York: Seven Stories Press/Open Media.

2005. *Chomsky on Anarchism*. Oakland: AK Press.

2005. *Imperial Ambitions: Conversations of the Post-9/11 World*. New York: Metropolitan Books.

2006. *Failed States: The Abuse of Power and the Assault on Democracy*. New York: Metropolitan Books. Paperback ed., New York: Owl Books, 2007.

2006. "Latin America at the Tipping Point." *International Socialist Review*, no. 46 (March/April).

2006. "On Phases." In *Foundational Issues in Linguistic Theory*, eds. Robert Freidin, Carlos P. Otero, and Maria-Luisa Zubizaretta. Cambridge, MA: MIT Press.

2007. With Gilbert Achcar. *Perilous Power: The Middle East and U.S. Foreign Policy: Dialogues on Terror, Democracy, War and Justice*, ed. Stephen R. Shalom. Boulder: Paradigm Publishers.

2007. *Interventions*. San Francisco: City Lights Books/Open Media Series.

2007. With Ervand Abrahamian, David Barsamian, and Nahid Mozaffari. *Targeting Iran*. San Francisco: City Lights Books/Open Media Series.

2007. *Inside Lebanon: Journey to a Shattered Land with Noam and Carol Chomsky*, ed. Assaf Kfoury. New York: Monthly Review Press.

2007. With David Barsamian. *What We Say Goes: Conversations on U.S. Power in a Changing World*. New York: Metropolitan Books.

Index

Abdullah, king of Saudi Arabia, 345, 405
Abrams, Creighton W., Jr., 115, 153
Acheson, Dean, 147, 227, 264, 375, 377
Ackland, Ken, 120
aesthetic theory, 88, 244–45
Afghanistan:
  Soviet invasion of, 167, 208, 261, 269, 270, 342, 452n1
  and "war on terror," 343, 345–46
Africa:
  and Cold War, 227
  and Israel, 210, 211, 213–14
  U.S. policies in, 183, 211, 315–16
Agency for International Development (USAID), 132, 179–80, 410–11
Agent Orange, 273
aggressive war, Taylor on, 107–9, 129
agriculture:
  capital-intensive, 266
  and NAFTA, 336
Ahmad, Aijaz, 405
AIFLD, 410
Air Force, U.S., report on Korea (1953), 185–86
Ajami, Fouad, 321
Albania, 314, 320
Algeria, 399
alienation, problems of, 53
Allende, Salvador, 181, 227
Al-Qaeda, 342, 379–80, 392
Alsop, Joseph, 146
Amalgamated Engineering and Foundryworkers' Union, 102
American Academy of Arts and Sciences, 386, 387
American Journal of International Law, 311
American Professors for Peace in the Middle East (APPME), 220–21
American Revolution, 131, 229, 259
American Society of International Law, 375
"American way," 231, 266
Amin, Idi, 211
anarchism, viii, 92–104
  as anti-capitalist, 97–99
  and Bolsheviks, 95–96, 262
  destruction of state power in, 93, 95, 101
  Guérin on, 92, 97, 103
  of nineteenth vs. twentieth century, 103
  and "red bureaucracy," 95
  rehabilitation of, 103
  and revolution, 94–96, 100–102
  and socialism, 97, 100, 103
  worker control in, 101
anarchosyndicalists, 98, 101
Andean region, 381
Anderson, Benedict, 188
Anderson, Jack, 188
Anderson, Terry, 271
Andrews, Bruce, 163
animal behavior:
  applicability to humans, 2, 3, 5, 234–35, 422n4, 423n9
  effects of intermittent reinforcement on, 5
  external factors isolated in, 3
  imprinting of, 14
  latent learning in, 13
  mechanical principle of, 83, 237
  and mind-body considerations, 237
  operant, 4
  scope and limitations of, 241–42
Annan, Kofi, 316
Anti-Defamation League, 203, 205, 212
appeasement, danger of, 58
Apple, R.W., 115
APPME (American Professors for Peace in the Middle East), 220–21
Arab League, 369, 371
Arafat, Yasir, 370, 410
Aramco, in Saudi Arabia, 172

Argentina:
and IMF, 409
neo-Nazis in, 215, 262
and trading blocs, 408
Aristide, Jean-Betrand, 411–12
Aristotle, 278
articularity, use of term, 473n3
articulatory-perceptual system, 278
Ashcroft, John, 385
Asia:
domino theory in, 43, 45, 69, 70, 142–43, 226–29, 231, 457n36
economic growth in, 228, 405
Grand Area principles in, 174, 228
and Israel, 216
nationalist revolutions in, 55–56, 64
"new order" in, 143
rice famines in, 185–86
and "rotten apple theory," 227, 228–29, 231
security of, 58, 406–7
USAID in, 180
U.S. military bases in, 345
U.S. policies in, 44–45, 158–59, 170, 183, 184, 223, 225
see also specific nations
Asian Energy Security Grid, 405–7
Atlantic Basin resources, 407
Atlantic Charter, 173
attention, and behavior, 5
Australia, 313, 314
autoclitics, 25–26
automatic self-reinforcement, 11–12
"aversive control," Skinner's use of phrase, 19
Azerbaijan:
and access to Iranian oil, 42–43
guerrilla warfare in, 42
Aznar, José Maria, 390, 399

Baker, James A. 3rd, 388
Bakunin, Michael, 95–96, 97, 100, 101, 103, 246, 452n1
Balkin, Jack, 385–86
Ball, George, 448n6, 450n7
Barak, Ehud, 368, 369, 370
Barnea, Nahum, 210n
Batista, Fulgencio, 132
Bavaria, 178
Bay of Pigs, 40, 44
Beattie, James, 35
Beecher, William, 185
Begin, Menachem, 201
behavior:
and attention, 5
characteristics of, 2
cognitive perspective of, 287–88
contribution of the organism to, 2–3
controlling variables of, 8–9
definitions in study of, 5, 6–10
factors involved in, 5
identifying the unit of, 8
mind-body aspects of, 235–37
observation of, 2–3
operant, 4
patterns of, 29
prediction of, 3
reinforcement of, 3, 5, 15
shaping of, 82, 89
Skinner's framework for description of, 4–6
stimulation of, 3
textual, 24
untestable laws of, 422–23n5
verbal, *see* verbal behavior
behaviorist psychology:
definitions of terms in, 5
and human mental faculties, 3
and language, 1–4, 27
Behavior of Organisms (Skinner), 4–5, 6, 10
Bell, Daniel, 52–53, 266
Ben-Ami, Shlomo, 368
Ben-Elissar, Eliahu, 221
Ben-Gurion, David, 210
Berger, Sandy, 301, 315, 317
Berle, A. A., 43
Berlusconi, Silvio, 399, 400
Bernays, Edward, 264
Bickerton, Derek, 357
bin Laden, Osama, 379–80, 397
bin Laden network, 322, 342
bioterrorism, 333
birds, songs of, 14
Black, Joseph, 352
Blair, Tony:
and G. W. Bush, 386
and Iraq, 378, 383, 388
and NATO's bombing of Serbia, 300, 302, 308, 309, 346, 382–83
and NATO's credibility, 302, 346, 382–83
Blodgett, A. L., 13
Bloomfield, Leonard, 23
B'nai Brith, 203
body:
concept of, 239–40, 241
and contact mechanics, 236, 238, 239, 240, 241
mind-body problem, 235–41, 246, 351
physical world of, 239, 240
Bohlen, Charles, 153
Bokassa, Jean-Bédel, 211
Bolivia, 408–9
Bolsheviks, 95–96, 262, 264

Bonaparte, Napoleon, 401
Boot, Max, 398, 399
Borden, William, 264, 471–72n21
Borón, Atilio, 338
Bosnia, 311, 321–22, 392
Boston Globe, 268–69
Bracken, Harry, 237
brain:
  and cognitive sciences, 353, 354, 355–56
  and communication, 348–49, 356–60; *see also* language
  and creativity, 350–51
  emergent properties of, 348, 349–56
  and evolution, 359–60
  functional perspective of, 362
  and intelligibility, 350, 351, 352
  and language, 347–67
  learning mechanisms of, 349, 362–67
  mechanical explanation of, 350, 351
  methodological thesis of, 356–62
  and mind-body problem, 351
  neurophysiological activities of, 349
  in phylogenetic perspective, 349, 357, 362
  thought as product of, 353
Brazil:
  and China, 407
  U.S. policies in, 181
Bretton Woods economic phase, 334
Brezhnev doctrine, 129, 448–49n8
Brinkley, Joel, 407
Britain:
  and Afghanistan, 343
  council communism in, 102
  and East Timor, 312, 315, 322
  and empire, 60–61, 74, 112, 170, 223, 224, 225
  English revolution (17th century), 259
  freedom of inquiry in, 166
  and free trade, 267
  and Greece, 130, 207–9
  and India, 399
  and Iraq, 314, 378, 383, 388, 391
  and Khmer Rouge, 382
  and Lend-Lease aid, 170, 171–72
  and Middle East oil, 171, 209, 225
  and Suez, 209
  and World War II, 170
British Communist Party, 101
Brookings Institution, 318
Browne, Malcolm, 47, 440n13
Buber, Martin, 95
Bullitt, William, 171
Bundy, McGeorge, 47, 119, 134
Bundy, William, 57–58, 469n6
Burnham, Walter Dean, 166
Burrow, J. W., 83
Bush, George H. W.:
  administration of, 328, 376, 388
  and public opinion, 395
  as UN ambassador, 372
Bush, George W.:
  aim to rule the world, 393, 398
  and Blair, 386
  civil rights stomped on by, 385–86
  decline of trust in, 395
  and Iran, 404–6
  and Iraq, 389–92, 404–5
  narrow corporate interests of, 345
  and National Security Strategy, 387
  propaganda output of, 378–80, 395
  and September 11 attacks, 342, 344, 345, 374, 379, 385, 397
  State of the Union message (2003), 378
  and terrorism, 371, 377, 378–80
  as threat to world peace, 374, 396–97
  and U.S. isolation, 407, 410
Business Week, 179
Butler, Richard, 314, 315
Byrnes, James F., 224

Calley, William L., 114, 153
Cambodia:
  and Khmer Rouge, 155, 263, 271, 382, 451n12, 455n22
  and *Mayagüez* incident, 154–56, 184, 186
  MIAs in, 272
  public indignation over, 462n10
  refugees in, 117–18
  Soviet aid to, 196–97, 463n14
  Thai mercenaries in, 140, 155, 448n6
  and UN, 461n5
  U.S. bombing of, 111, 118, 137, 139, 140, 156
  U.S. chemical warfare in, 273
  U.S. military aggression in, 125, 136–37, 138, 152, 154–55, 168, 196, 226, 230, 231
  U.S. subversive activities in, 154–55
  Vietnamese invasion of, 382
  White Book of, 140
Camp David proposals, 200, 368–69
Canada:
  and NAFTA, 407
  U.S. distrusted by, 396, 407
  and Vietnam War, 267
capitalism:
  anarchism vs., 97–99
  and competition, 97
  corporate, 86
  free market, 247, 266, 274
  industrial, 96, 97
  investor rights in, 335

capitalism (*cont.*)
limitations of, 89
macroeconomic measures, 334
and militarized state, 89, 165
predatory, 88–89
and production, 97, 98–99
state, 98, 102, 165, 334
and technology, 89
unrestrained, 87
and wage labor, 97–99, 258
capitalist democracy, 257–59
labor in, 258, 410
resource constraint and demand constraint in, 258
stability of, 259
Card, Andrew, 389
Carmichael, Stokely, 220
Carothers, Thomas, 403
Carter, Jimmy, 268, 269
Carter administration:
and East Timor, 460n3
human rights as focus in, 165, 184
Cartesian model, *see* Descartes, René
Castro, Fidel, 44, 227
Center for International Policy, 272
Center for International Security, 212
Center for Public Integrity, 385
Central America:
solidarity movement in, ix
see also Latin America
CFR (Council on Foreign Relations), War and Peace Studies Project, 169–74, 175, 224–25
Chace, James, 181–82, 184, 226
Chávez, Hugo, 408, 409
Chechnya, 307, 315, 329, 344, 392
Cherne, Leo, 452n1, 463n14
Chile:
and China, 407
and Israel, 467n44
U.S. policies in, 181, 182, 226, 227, 318
China:
and Chile, 407
and Cold War, 69, 70, 183
Communism in, 49
economic development in, 60, 228
and EU, 407
expansionism of, 435n29
and India, 406
and Iran, 405
Japanese aggression in, 61, 69, 118, 330, 400, 404
massive capital gifts to, 54
missionaries in, 43
and oil, 405, 407
opium wars in, 43, 399
possibility of nuclear war in, 46, 61
and Saudi Arabia, 405
starvation in, 48
and Tibet, 307
and Vietnam War, 69, 70, 72, 130–31, 382
and "war on terror," 344
"China incident," 39
Chomsky, Avram Noam:
activism of, viii, ix, 63–74
basic themes in work of, viii–ix
birth and background of, vii–viii
influence of, ix
Chomsky, William (father), vii
Christopher, Warren M., 388
Chungking, bombing of, 61
Churba, Joseph, 212
Churchill, Winston, 55, 207, 223, 386
CIA:
in Cambodia, 155
in Iran, 171, 172–73, 182, 209
in Laos, 231
and radical Islam, 342
and Tibet, 447–48n97
CITGO, 409
Citizens' Commission of Inquiry on United States War Crimes, 114
Citizens Committee for Peace with Freedom, 68, 69, 70
civil disobedience, 66, 67, 68–69, 71, 74, 156, 402; *see also* resistance
civil rights movement, 68, 135
civil society, Rousseau on, 77
Civil War, U.S., postwar power concentrations, 166
Clark, Wesley, 319, 320
classical liberalism, viii
Clifford, Clark, 267
Clinton, Bill:
and Bosnia, 392
and former Yugoslavia, 301, 346
and Middle East, 369, 370, 372, 388
and NAFTA, 331
and NATO, 383
Clinton administration:
African policies of, 316
aid to Turkey from, 306
and East Timor, 312, 313, 314
intentional ignorance of, 307, 308
and preemptive response, 344
and UN, 316
Clinton Doctrine, 301, 305, 314
Clio (goddess of history), 144–45
Clymer, Adam, 217–18
Coffin, Frank M., 179–80

Coffin, William Sloane, 63n
cognition, evolution of, 360
cognitive meaning, 426n36
cognitive revolution, 287–88, 353, 354
Cohen, I. Bernard, 352
Cohen, Joshua, 258
Cohen, William, 301–2, 308–9, 316, 318, 319, 320
Colby, William, 125
Cold War:
  in Asia, 43, 45, 69, 70, 183
  in Central Europe, 42
  communication blocked in, 174
  containment in, 262–63
  domino theory in, 43, 45, 69, 70, 142–43, 226–29, 231, 457n36
  and Greece, 207–9, 227
  issue of Communism in, 53–54, 135, 136, 183, 263–66
  in Latin America, 261–62
  negotiations avoided in, 42
  and postwar international order, 261–62, 377
  propaganda in, 48–49, 217, 263–67
  "rollback strategy" in, 263
  "rotten apple theory" in, 227, 228, 231
Colombia:
  civil disobedience in, 402
  labor in, 410
  narco-trafficking in, 310
  refugees in, 310
  U.S. military aid to, 305–6, 309–10, 315, 329, 330, 402
commands, as mands, 20
Committee for United Nations Integrity, 461n5
Committee to Re-elect the President (CREEP), 135
communication:
  and brain, 348–49, 356–60
  comparative, 357
  evolution of, 348, 356–60
  human, *see* language
  in other species, 358–59
Communist Party:
  and Haymarket riots (1886), 265
  and May Day, 265
  and McCarthyism, 266, 386
  postwar attacks on, 135, 136, 263–66
  Red Scare, 264, 265, 267
composition, grammatical, 26
conceptual-intentional system, 278
conditioning:
  law of, 10
  operant, 12, 423n7
  Pavlovian, 12, 426n35
  sensory-sensory, 14
  Skinner's use of term, 12–13
Congo:
  UN peacekeepers in, 316
  U.S. intervention in, 181
Congressional Research Service, 190
Connally, John B., 137
Constitution, U.S., 135, 259, 327
contact mechanics, 236, 238, 239, 240, 241
containment, global policy of, 260–63
control:
  aversive, 19
  uses of term, 10
Cooper, Chester, 127, 128, 153
Cordemoy, Géraud de, 80
Costa Rica:
  and Israel, 215
  as model democracy, 274
Council on Foreign Relations (CFR), War and Peace Studies Project, 169–74, 175, 224–25
counterinsurgency, official policy of, 329
Countryman, Edward, 259
Cranston, Alan, 199
creative principle, 350–51
creativity:
  and brain, 350–51
  and choices, 244–45
  and language, 37, 83, 87–88, 234, 235–36, 351, 367
Creel Commission, 264
CREEP (Committee to Re-elect the President), 135
critical periods of growth, 249
Crossette, Barbara, 270–71
Cuba:
  Bay of Pigs, 40, 44
  in Cold War, 47, 227, 375
  Guantánamo prison camp in, 385
  massive capital gifts to, 54
  state socialism in, 227–28
  U.S. intervention in, 182, 343, 374, 375
  and Venezuela, 407–8
Cuban missile crisis, 375
Curran, James, 259–60
Cushman, John H., 125
Cushman, Thomas, 306
Czechoslovakia, 105, 218, 400

Daalder, Ivo, 318
Darwin, Charles, 353, 356, 358, 359
Darwinian evolution, 248
Davies, Paul, 354
Davis, Bob, 301
Dayan, Moshe, 210, 218

Deacon, Terrence, 360, 361
Declaration of Independence, 264, 412
Declaration of the South Summit, 302, 383
Decornoy, Jacques, 140
definition, uses of term, 7, 22
de Cordemoy, *see* Cordemoy, Géraud de
de Gaulle, Charles, 45
Dellinger, Dave, 66, 67, 68
Dellums, Ronald, 114
Demjanjuk, John, 273
democracy:
  acceptable forms of, 403
  capitalist, 257–59
  choice among commodities in, 339–40
  "crisis" of, 267, 454n19
  distaste for, 470n1
  formation of social policy in, 234, 259
  as free mutual agreements, 94, 97
  guarantee of individual rights in, 87
  limitations of, 101
  as open society, 165–66
  people's control in, 87, 102, 267, 391
  political liberty in, 40
  role of labor in, 258, 410
DePalma, Anthony, 335
deprivation, Skinner's use of term, 18–19
Descartes, René:
  and contact mechanics, 236, 238, 239, 240
  and free choice, 241–43, 351
  and language production (Descartes's problem), 234, 235–37, 241–43, 244, 249, 285, 299, 348, 351
  mechanical theory of the universe, 235–37, 238, 239, 240, 350, 353, 354
  and mind-body considerations (dualism), 235–39, 246, 298, 348, 349, 351, 353–54
  on nature of man, 80–83
  on rationalism, viii, 88
  and second substance *(res cogitans)*, 238, 239, 240, 241
Desert Storm, 345
Devillers, Philippe, 72
Dewey, John, 84, 376
Diderot, Denis, 36
Diego Garcia, 345
Dienstbier, Jiri, 323
differential reinforcement, 15, 16
Discourse on Inequality (Rousseau), 77–83, 96
discrete infinity, 255–56, 286
"discriminated operant," Skinner's use of phrase, 4
divine intervention, 240
Domestic Security Enhancement Act (2003), 385
Dominican Republic, U.S. intervention in, 43, 181, 230, 400
domino theory, 43, 45, 69, 142–43, 226–29, 231, 457n36
Dower, John, 228
draft resistance, 74, 79
drive reduction, 13, 14
Dudman, Richard, 118
Dulles, John Foster, 210
Du Marsais, C. Ch., 35–36
Dunn, James, 188
dynamic laws, 6

East Pakistan, India's invasion of, 382
East Timor:
  crop destruction in, 188, 191, 192
  and Indonesia, 187–97, 216, 311–15, 321, 322
  media silence and slant on, 190–91, 193–94, 195–97
  oil in, 313
  political parties in, 188, 192–94
  as Portuguese colony, 187, 188, 193, 313
  refugees from, 168, 188, 189, 192, 194, 196, 269
  self-determination sought by, 188, 195, 311, 312
  and sovereignty, 313, 314
  and UN, 189–90, 196, 312, 313
  and U.S. military aid, 190–97
Eban, Abba, 205
echoic operant, use of term, 23–24
echoic repertoire, 21, 24
Economic Commission for Latin America and the Caribbean (ECLAC), 334
Economic Policy Institute, 335, 336
Ecuador, 154, 409
education, self-fulfillment via, 84–85
Egypt:
  British interests in, 61
  and Cold War, 227
  and Israel, 210, 222, 305
  Lavon affair in, 221, 222
  U.S. aid to, 200, 305
Ehrlichman, John, 137
Eichmann, Karl Adolf, 273
Eisenhower, Dwight D., 41, 226
Eisenhower administration:
  and Arab hatred of U.S., 342
  in Cold War, 42
Ellsberg, Daniel, 137–38
El Salvador:
  elections in, 276
  and Israel, 204, 212, 214
  newspapers in, 275–76
  U.S. policies in, 215, 228, 275, 330
emergence thesis, 348, 349–56
emotive meaning, 426n36

empirical thesis, 350, 351, 352
Engels, Friedrich, 95
England, *see* Britain
Enlightenment, viii, 84, 96, 97
environmentalism, 251–53
Epstein, Samuel, 293
Eritrea, 197
Ethiopia:
  and Eritrea, 197
  and Israel, 210
  and Italy, 400
  war in, 39, 262
ethological approach to language, 362
European Union (EU):
  and China, 407
  and Iran, 404
evolution, 248, 254, 255, 349, 356–62, 367
experience, boundary conditions set by, 289
expert, cult of, 51, 53, 165
Exxon Mobil, 405

factual thesis, 350
Fahd Plan (1981), 370
Falk, Richard, 108, 374
Falklands war, 215
Fall, Bernard:
  on UN Charter, article 2(4), 131
  on Vietnam, 72, 109, 111, 113, 116, 128, 152, 159, 394
Farer, Thomas J., 108
Farrell, William, 217
fascism, state-worship of, 206
FBI:
  activities during Vietnam War, 268
  establishment of, 264–65
  and September 11 attacks, 342
feedback, 17
Ferber, Michael, 63n
Fernandes, Father Francisco Maria, 464n22
Fibonacci series, 359
Fifth Freedom, 225, 227, 230, 231
Fifth World, 216
Fischer, Adolph, 97
Flapan, Simha, 201
Fleischer, Ari, 390, 391–92
Food for Peace, 471n21
Ford, Gerald R., 151, 155, 184, 188
Ford administration, and East Timor, 460n3
Foreign Affairs, 186, 226, 300–301
Foreign Aid Bill (2000), 305
foreign policy, 160–86
  in Africa, 183, 211, 315–16
  centralization of power in, 176
  concern for democracy in, 164
  and conspiracy theory, 167–68
  corporate influence on, 166, 168, 176–77, 179, 181
  crimes of the state vs. crimes of official enemies, 168–69
  and domestic social structure, 160, 168, 178
  empirical inquiry into, 167, 168, 175–78
  executive decision making, 176
  and Grand Area planning, *see* Grand Area
  and intelligentsia, 160, 162–65, 174–78, 183–86
  in Latin America, *see* Latin America
  and militarized state sector, 165
  and national purpose, 165–66, 178
  and oil, *see* oil
  post–World War II, 169–74, 176
  and propaganda, 161–62, 163, 165, 178–79, 183
  and state censorship, 178–79
  in underdeveloped countries, 172–73, 183, 186
  in Vietnam, *see* Vietnam; Vietnam War
  Wilsonian principles of, 182–83, 301, 397, 398, 400, 402
Fortas, Abe, 223
Fourier, Charles, 87
France:
  and Algeria, 399
  council communism in, 102, 227
  and East Timor, 312
  and empire, 74, 112, 147
  and Indochina, 226, 231, 443n42
  and Middle East oil, 225
  Reign of Terror in, 80, 99–100
  and Saudi Arabia, 171
  Second Empire of, 104
  and Suez, 209
  support in American Revolution, 131
  and UN vetoes, 389
France, Anatole, 77
Franck, Thomas M., 129–31
Franco, Francisco, 102
Frankel, Max, 57
Frederika, Queen (Greece), 207
freedom:
  consciousness of, 81
  contradiction of necessity and, 88
  and language, 81–82, 84, 87–89, 90–91
  maturity of, 96
  and philosophy, 76
  problems of, 77
  and property, 77, 79
  Rousseau on, 77–82
  of the spirit, 76
  of thought, 81, 84
  value of, 79–80

Freedom of Information Act, 166
free trade agreements, 330, 331–32, 335–38, 339, 407
Free Trade Area of the Americas (FTAA), 335, 337, 339
French Revolution, 80, 96, 97, 99–100, 103–4
Fretilin party, East Timor, 188, 192–94
Friedman, Thomas, 213
Fromkin, David, 320
Fukuyama, Francis, 387
Fulbright, J. William, 46
Fund for Peace, 272

G-77, 302
Galileo Galilei, 237, 286, 350, 367
Gallistel, C. R., 349, 362–64
Galluci, Robert, 175
Garcia, Lucas, 467n44
GATS (General Agreement on Trade in Services), 335, 339
Gelb, Leslie, 216–17, 457–58n36
generalization, 30, 428n46
Geneva Accords, 65, 110, 127, 128, 147, 371–72, 385, 388, 458n36
Germany:
  council communism in, 102
  "good Germans," 64
  Munich analogy, 58, 400
  Nazi, 48, 58, 152, 159, 330, 372, 400, 411
  post–World War I, 101
  rearmament of, 42, 169
  unification of, 42
  and World War II, 170, 404
gestalt psychology, 238
Giannou, Chris, 220
Gilboa, Amos, 302
Glennon, Michael, 374–75
globalization:
  before World War I, 331
  and free trade agreements, 330, 331–32, 335–38, 339, 407
  international economic integration, 331
  and job insecurity, 337
  and liberalization of capital, 334–35
  and likelihood of war, 332–34
  "masters of the universe" and, 327
  and militarism of space, 332–34
  and national security exemptions, 333
  neoliberal, 337
  public opposition to, 326–27, 330–31, 383, 410
  short-term speculative capital in, 331
  and stability, 332
  true program of, 327
  and U.S. commercial interests, 333–34, 377
  and wealth gap, 331, 332, 334, 338, 339, 340
Goering, Hermann, 118
Goldberg, Arthur, 49
Goldman, Francisco, 276
Gonzales, Jorge Napoleón, 276
Goodman, Mitchell, 63n
Goodwin, Richard, 125
governments:
  anarchist dismantling of, 93, 95, 101
  arbitrary power of, 77–78, 93
  political legitimacy of, 108–9
  repressive, 89, 93
Graebner, Norman, 182–83
grammar:
  and cognitive revolution, 287–88
  and competence, 34
  construction of, 28–29, 232
  functional categories of, 281
  generative, 31, 33–38, 75, 88, 89–90, 279, 280–81, 282, 283, 287, 289, 295–96, 298–99
  inadequacies of, 37
  limitations of, 35
  particular, 35–36, 349
  rules of, 17, 28, 31, 37, 75, 87–88, 295–96
  scientific, 238
  structuralist, 35
  substantive categories of, 281–82
  systems of, 27–29
  transformational rules of, 295–96
  typologically varied constructions, 283
  universal, 35–36, 75–76, 232–33, 238, 279, 280–81, 282, 283, 349
Grand Area:
  in Asia, 174, 228
  CFR planning for, 169–74, 175, 224–25
  erosion of, 227
  instilling U.S. moral principles in an ungrateful world, 186, 262–63
  military force for preservation of, 181, 184, 186, 263
  other nations competing in, 170, 171–72
  reconstitution of, 179
  U.S. access to resources of, 170–72
  and U.S. economy, 170–72, 225, 261
  and world control, 225, 261
gravitational force, 239
Great Britain, *see* Britain
Great Depression, vii, 265, 267
Greece:
  British and U.S. interventions in, 130, 132, 207–9, 224

Cold War in, 207–9, 227
guerrilla warfare in, 42
Truman Doctrine in, 207–8, 227
U.S. corporations in, 208
Greenspan, Alan, 337
Greenway, David, 272
Grenada, U.S. invasion of, 230–31, 268, 374, 380
Gribbin, John, 354
Griffiths, Philip Jones, 121
Guantánamo prison camp, 385
Guatemala:
agrarian reform in, 317
invasion of (1954), 41, 129, 133, 182
and Israel, 204, 214, 215, 216, 467n44
and U.S. foreign policy, 162, 164, 215, 228, 317–18
Guérin, Daniel:
Anarchism, 92, 97, 103
on Spanish revolution, 101–2
Gulf War (1991), 303, 345
Guterres, Father Apolinario, 464n22
Gwertzman, Bernard, 269

Ha'aretz, 201
Hadar, Leon, 213n
Hague Convention (1907), 106
Haile Selassie, 211
Haines, Gerald, 332
Haiti, 230, 400, 411–12
Hamilton, Lee, 271
Hanoi, *see* North Vietnam
Harkin, Tom, 194
Harris, Zellig, viii
Harrison, Selig, 394, 404, 405
Hauser, Mark, 348, 356–60
Havel, Vaclav, 300, 308
Haymarket riots (1886), 265
Heidegger, Martin, 40
Heisenberg, Werner, 352
Henderson, Oran, 113–14
Herman, E. S., 455n22
Herzog, Haim, 370
hesitation pauses, 428n45
Hezbollah, 392
Hilgard, E. R., 13
Hilsman, Roger, 148
Himmler, Heinrich, 152, 215
Hiro, Dilip, 388
Hiroshima, 39
Hitler, Adolf, 152, 400, 404
Ho Chi Minh, 147, 225
Holocaust, 39, 152
Holst, Willem, 58–59
Honduras, 214, 215, 216
Hook, Sidney, 161
Hoopes, Townsend, 120
Hough, Jerry, 268–69
Howard, Michael, 343
Howe, Irving, 205, 219
Huang, James, 283
Huarte, Juan, 299
Hughes, Stuart, 50
Hull, Cordell, 61, 456n24
human rights, 246
Human Rights Watch, 335–36
humans:
creative choices of, 244–45
critical periods of growth, 249
and environmentalism, 251–53
limitations of, 242–43
mental development of, 244, 247, 249
moral judgment of, 245–46
number faculty of, 254–56
as part of natural world, 242–43
physical growth of, 243–44
visual faculty of, 249–50
Humboldt, Wilhelm von, viii
on *Bildung* (development of human potential), 83–88, 98
on human nature, 83–84, 87, 246
on language generation *(erzeugen)*, 38, 87–88, 89–90
language "makes infinite use of finite means," 31, 37, 90, 279, 288
Limits of State Action, 96–98
on private power, 85–86
on the role of the state, 85, 87
Hume, David, 286, 298, 350, 351, 367
Humphrey, Hubert H., 471n21
Hungary, 111, 400–401
Huntington, Samuel, 304, 393, 443n36
Hussaini, Hatem, 220
Hussein, Saddam, 311
G.W. Bush compared with, 374, 396
and Iran, 314, 388, 400
and Kuwait, 400
and Osirak nuclear reactor, 384, 404
and September 11 attacks, 378
and UN, 388, 391
and U.S. propaganda, 378, 379–80, 384, 388, 396
and "war on terror," 379–80, 389–91, 396, 397
Huynh Tan Phat, 149

Ibn Saud, 171
idealism, viii
idealization, 282

ideology:
end of, 52
Marxist analysis of, 52
use of term, 52
ignorance, 300–324
and African wars, 315–16
and Colombian aid, 309–10, 315
and East Timor genocide, 311–14, 315, 322
and Latin America, 317–18
of moral truisms, 304–5, 307, 315, 316, 320, 321–22, 402
and NATO bombing, 300–309, 311, 314, 315–17, 318–24
new era in, 305, 314, 315, 316, 320–21
and Turkey's ethnic cleansing, 305–8, 309–10, 315
in U.S. imperial grand strategy, 397–402
Ikenberry, John, 373
IMF (International Monetary Fund), 408, 409
imitation:
learning by, 15, 16–17, 23
mimicry vs., 16
and reinforcement, 427n40
imperial grand strategy, *see* National Security Strategy
imprinting, 14
India:
and Asian Energy Security Grid, 405–7
British conquest of, 399
and China, 406
economic development in, 47–48, 59–60, 228
invasion of East Pakistan, 382
nuclear weapons of, 303
Indochina:
French war in, 226, 231, 443n42
guerrilla warfare in, 41–42
and "rotten apple theory," 228
U.S. intervention in, 181, 229, 380, 449n1, 458n36
see also Cambodia; Laos; Vietnam; Vietnam War
Indonesia:
and East Timor, 187–97, 216, 311–15, 321, 322
human rights record of, 190
and Israel, 216
military coup in, 229, 317
as U.S. client, 190–91, 194–95, 196, 312, 313, 460n3
industrial revolution, 54, 88, 96
input-output relations, study of, 2
inquisitiveness, natural, 16
intelligibility, 350, 351, 352
International Bank for Reconstruction and Development, 60
International Conference on Alternative Perspectives in Vietnam (1965), 51
International Control Commission, 446n85
International Court of Justice, 265, 382
International Criminal Court, 412
International Days of Protest (1965), 65
international law:
coerced acquiescence in, 392
and crimes against peace, 107, 126–33, 142, 374
disregarded by the enemy, 110, 111, 112
and Geneva Conventions, 110
and great-power intervention, 105–33, 374–76
as "hot air," 374–76, 384
inconsistent application of, 153, 376
and justice, 105–11
and *Mayagüez* incident, 155
and military necessity, 107, 121–26
new norms of, 377–84
and Nuremberg Tribunal, 105, 106–7, 108, 109, 111, 126, 133
as ratification of imperialist practice, 112, 374–75
and U.S. imperial grand strategy, 386–93
validity of, 106, 111
and war crimes in Vietnam, 113–21, 159
and wars of aggression, 107–8
as without moral force, 109, 111–12
International Monetary Fund (IMF), 408, 409
International Red Cross:
and East Timor, 188, 189, 192
and Guantánamo prison camp, 385–86
and Israel, 217, 221
International Republican Institute, 411–12
International Rescue Committee, 463n14
IQ, 252
Iran:
and China, 405
CIA-backed coup in, 171, 172–73, 182, 209
Cold War in, 227
and Iraq, 314, 400
and Israel, 210, 211, 319, 404
nuclear capability of, 394, 404
oil in, 42–43, 171, 172, 209, 211, 405
and preventive war, 381, 394
and regional security, 407
U.S. attacks on, 268–69
U.S. security issues in, 404–6
Iraq:
as experiment, 381, 404–5
and Iran, 314, 400
Kurds attacked in, 307–8

Kuwait invaded by, 378, 384, 400
labor movement in, 410
military action against, ix, 302, 314, 371, 374, 375, 377–82, 383, 388–91, 394, 397
Osirak nuclear reactor in, 384, 404
and preventive war, 344
and public opinion, 394, 395–96
and September 11 attacks, 342, 379
and WEF meeting, Davos, 395–96
and WMD, 375, 378, 380, 390
Islam, 342
Israel:
and Africa, 210, 211, 213–14
Arab-Israeli conflict(s), 200, 210–11, 370
and Asia, 216
censorship in, 201, 206
and crimes against humanity, 383–84
"David and Goliath" legend of, 218, 219
Dimona nuclear reactor, 384, 405
and "Fifth World" weapons development, 216
foreign aid to, 198–99, 206
invasion of Lebanon, 198, 199–200, 212–13, 217–18, 219, 221, 303, 308
and Iran, 210, 211, 319, 404
kibbutzim of, 87, 438n13, 467n44
and Latin America, 204, 211, 212, 213, 214–16
media coverage of, 199, 200, 201–2, 216, 217–18, 222
and Middle East oil, 207–10, 211
occupied territories, 201, 205, 206, 210, 219, 369
and Palestine, 198, 201, 204, 319, 342, 345, 368–72, 411
and PLO, 198, 204, 206, 219–20
radical nationalism in, 210–13
and "right to exist," 370, 411
subsidiary services of, 213–17
and Suez, 209
terrorist attacks on U.S. facilities by, 221–22
and UN, 198, 217, 308, 369–72, 388
U.S. aid to, 305
and U.S. "Israeli lobby," 201, 202–6, 212, 214, 217–22
U.S. special relationship with, 198–222
U.S. strategic interests in, 206–7
and Zionists, 200n, 203
Italy:
and Cold War, 227
and North Africa, 400, 404
post-World War I, 101

Jackson, Robert H., 106
Jaegher, R. J. de, 48
Japan:
and China, 61, 69, 118, 330, 400, 404
competition from, 267
economic growth in, 228–29, 267
and empire, 74, 112
energy resources in, 171
and Grand Area, 174, 228
and Middle East, 209
New Order as goal of, 400
and Pacific war, 61
and Pearl Harbor, 374
as stabilizing power, 61
Jefferson, Thomas, 401
Jennings, Francis, 272
Jervis, Robert, 393
Jespersen, Otto, 279, 282
Johnson, Chalmers, 304
Johnson, Lyndon B.:
and Latin America, 328
and Vietnam War, 41, 47, 72, 115, 119, 127, 226–27
Johnstown steel strike (1937), 265
Jordan, and Palestine, 211, 369, 411
Judah, Tim, 307

Kagan, Robert, 399–400
Kahn, Herman, *On Thermonuclear War*, 50
KAL 007, 269
Kalish, Donald, 66
Kalmar (Polish trawler), 154, 155
Kamm, Henry, 194
Kandel, Eric, 355–56
Kant, Immanuel, 80, 84, 96, 238
Kapeliouk, Amnon, 272–73
Karni, Yoav, 211n
Karnow, Stanley, 195
Kendall, Walter, 102
Kennan, George, 182, 183, 224, 225, 226, 274, 401
Kennedy, Edward "Ted," 155, 184
Kennedy, John F., 264
Kennedy administration:
and Bay of Pigs, 40, 44
counterinsurgency activities of, 215
intellectuals in, 40–42, 44, 215n
Latin American policies of, 215n, 328, 329, 343
New Frontier of, 41, 44
and Vietnam War, 41–42, 117–18, 119, 133, 147, 261, 394, 395, 401
Kenney, David, 460n3
Keynesian economic policies, 273
Khadduri, Imad, 384
Khanh, General, 148–49, 450n7

Khmer Rouge, 155, 263, 271, 382, 451n12, 455n22
Khomeini, Ayatollah Ruhollah, 209
Kimche, Jon, 205n
Kimmerling, Baruch, 368, 369
Kirchner, Néstor, 408
Kirk, Donald, 445n60
Kissinger, Henry A.:
on the "age of the expert," 164
on democracy, 258
and East Timor, 188
on foreign policy and private power, 454n19
on international order, 261
and Latin America, 227, 317–18
and *Mayagüez* incident, 154, 155, 156, 184
and Middle East oil, 209
Realpolitik of, 182, 226
on statesmanship, 453–54n16
on use of force, 157, 182, 229
and Vietnam War, 43–44, 133, 136–37, 140, 149, 151, 162–63, 184
Klare, Michael, 212
Kleindienst, Richard, 137
Kolko, Gabriel, 178
Komer, Robert W., 124–25
Korea:
demilitarized zone (DMZ) in, 184–86, 394
economic growth of, 267
nuclear capability of, 304, 394
USAF report on (1953), 185–86
U.S. intervention in (1945), 126, 181
and U.S. national interest, 228
Korean War, 264
Kosovo:
Albanian population in, 314, 320
ethnic cleansing in, 302, 305, 318, 320
media attention to, 311
NATO bombing of, 301–3, 306, 311–12, 313, 314, 316, 318–19, 321, 381–82
Operation Horseshoe in, 318, 319, 320
as precedent, 311–12, 315, 321
refugees from, 301, 321
and Serbia, 314, 319
Kosovo Liberation Army, 320
Kosovo Verification Mission (KVM), 318, 320
Koyré, Alexander, 351
Kraft, Joseph, 162–63
Kristol, Irving, 46–47, 48–49, 52
Kuperman, Alan, 321
Kuwait, 378, 384, 396, 400
Kyoto protocols, 412

labor:
and AIFLD, 410
and anarchism, 97–98, 101
in capitalist democracy, 258, 410
as commodity, 53, 86–87
and exploitation, 85–87
free circulation of, 331
freely undertaken, 98–99
and job insecurity, 337
and media, 259–60
and postwar anti-Communism, 264–66, 410
and propaganda, 266
reduced share of income for, 337
and socialism, 266
and solidarity, ix, 100, 265
specialization of, 98
strikes, 265
workers' control movement, 101, 102, 246
and workplace stress, 337
Lacouture, Jean, 454–55n22
La Crónica, El Salvador, 275, 276
LaFeber, Walter, 400
La Follette Committee, 265
Landauer, Carl, 178
Lange, Friedrich, 351
Langguth, A. J., 195
language:
abstract case theory, 283
acquisition of, 13, 15–17, 21, 24, 27–30, 84, 90, 233–35, 243, 244, 247, 282, 286–87, 288–89, 290, 298, 363–64
and analogy, 235
articulatory-perceptual system, 278
basic properties of, 288
and behaviorist psychology, 1–4, 27
biological endowment of, 253–54
c-command in, 293
and cognitive revolution, 287–88
and communication, 286, 357, 428n43
competence in, 34
conceptual-intentional system, 278
conceptual naturalness in, 277
creative processes of, 37, 83, 87–88, 234, 235–36, 351, 367
Descartes's problem of, 234, 235–37, 241–43, 244, 249, 299, 348, 351
descriptive adequacy of, 279, 280, 283, 289
discrete infinity of, 255–56, 286
dislocation property of, 366
displacement property of, 294–97
elements of, 292
ethological approach to, 362
evolution of, 254, 359–62
explanatory adequacy of, 279, 280, 281, 283, 289

external world related to, 297
figurative use of, 36
and freedom, 81–82, 84, 87–89, 90–91
free expression of, 279
functional perspective of, 362
general conditions satisfied by, 277
genetic aspects of, 250–51, 286, 287
grammar of, 34; *see also* grammar
and human brain, 347–67
and human cognition, 249, 250, 277–78, 281
human possession of, 83, 233, 243, 285, 298, 351, 365
Humboldt on, 31, 37, 38, 87–88, 89–90, 279, 288
and ideas, 82–83
I-language, 282–83
inflection as property of, 294
inner speech, 358
interface levels of, 278–79, 295
internalized, 287, 349
legibility conditions of, 293–94, 295
lexicon of, 281, 292
mechanisms of, 357, 362
and mind-body considerations, 235–41, 277
Minimalist Program of, 277–84, 291–93
as mirror of the mind, 238
ontogenesis of, 357, 362
origin of, 82–83, 256
as output, 286–87
parameter setting in, 233, 247
perfectibility of, 284
performance of, 33–34, 37, 278
philosophy of, 298
phonology and phonetics of, 283, 297, 364–65
phylogenetic perspective of, 349, 357, 362
principles-and-parameters (P&P) model, 279, 281–84, 290–91, 293
production of, 234, 235–37, 241–43, 244, 249, 285, 299, 351
properties of, 365–66
redundant principles of, 281
semantic properties of, 28, 297, 364
study of, 28, 75–76, 83, 90, 232, 248, 249, 285–99
and supervenience, 355
symbolic reference in, 361–62
and syntax, 31–32, 33, 279
syntax-morphology divide in, 282
as system for expressing thought, 357
theory construction of, 248, 279, 289
theory-internal measure of simplicity, 283–84
unification of, 295, 347–48
"unlearnable," 243
uses of, 235, 297, 298–99, 351
variations in, 282, 283, 289, 293
language acquisition device (LAD), 363
language faculty:
architecture of, 278–79, 280, 282, 284, 366
imperfections of, 366
initial state of, 287, 290, 349
interface levels of, 291
as language organ, 286, 363
Lansing, Robert, 402
Laos:
Communists in, 130–31
military aggression in, 111, 118, 125, 139, 140, 168, 230, 231, 270, 273, 449n1
Plain of Jars in, 117, 270
Thai mercenaries in, 139, 140
Laotian model, 148
La Prensa, Nicaragua, 275–76
Laqueur, Walter, 228
Lashley, K. S., 27, 28, 29
latent learning, 13, 426n30
Latin America:
Andean region, 381
and China, 407
Cold War in, 261–62
Communism in, 44, 227
democracy in, 338–39
and Israel, 204, 211, 212, 213, 214–16
and Monroe Doctrine, 166, 223–24, 400
and NAFTA, 331–32, 336, 338
Operation Miracle in, 407–8
radical Catholics of, 84–85
regional agreements in, 407–10
rule of law in, 43
social reform in, 258
USAID in, 180
and U.S. foreign policy, 161, 162, 166, 170, 180–82, 215, 216, 223–24, 225, 262, 265, 269, 275–76, 309, 317–18, 329, 343, 375–76, 379, 401, 404
U.S. interventions in, 132, 181–82, 230, 264, 268, 303, 328, 374, 380, 398, 400
see also specific nations
Lavon, Pinhas, 210n, 221, 222
law of conditioning, 10
law of effect, 10
League of Nations, 402
learning:
contribution of the organism to, 2–3
drive reduction in, 13, 14

learning (*cont.*)
by experience, 17
general theory of, 361
and imitation, 15, 16–17, 23
information processing in, 16
innate dispositions toward, 362–67
latent, 13, 426n30
modular view of, 363
motivation for, 14
by observation, 15, 16
reinforcement in, 15
Skinner's use of term, 10
Lebanon:
Israeli invasion of, 198, 199–200, 212–13, 217–18, 219, 221, 303, 308
and UN, 308
U.S. intervention in, 181
Leffler, Melvyn, 224
Lelyveld, Joseph, 114
LeMay, Curtis, 65–66
LeMoyne, James, 276
Lend-Lease, 170, 171–72
Lenin, V. I., 101
Leninism, 96
Lens, Sidney, 66
Lewis, Anthony, 151, 155, 330
Lewontin, Richard, 360
liberation theology, 328
libertarian socialism, 87, 95, 96, 97, 101, 102–4, 246
Libya, bombing of, 344
Lieven, Anatol, 379
Lifschultz, Lawrence, 167
Limits of State Action (Humboldt), 96–98
Lindholm, Richard, 61
Linguet, Simon, 86
linguistics:
creative processes of, 37
descriptive, 34
and universal grammar, 35
linguistic theory, 33–38
Lin Piao, 70
Lippmann, Walter, 46, 69, 72, 262
Locke, John, 353
Lodge, Henry Cabot, 148, 208, 441n14
logic, 242, 243
London Naval Treaty (1930), 107
Lopez Fuentes, Mario, 214
Loquai, Heinz, 319–20
Lowell, Robert, 66
Luck, Edward, 389
Lula da Silva, Luiz Inácio, 408
Lustick, Ian, 200
MacArthur, Douglas, 171
Macdonald, Dwight, 39, 40, 62, 66
Macedonia, NATO troops in, 301
machines:
intelligent behavior of, 237, 350
use of term, 285
MacVeagh, Lincoln, 208
Madrid Congress (1931), 101
Maechling, Charles, 215
"magical mands," Skinner's use of phrase, 19
Mailer, Norman, 68
Mandalika, Benny, 462n14
Mandela, Nelson, 302, 303, 382–83
Mandelbaum, Michael, 398
mands:
forms of, 20
pseudo, 19
Skinner's use of term, 18–20
Mansfield, Mike, 65, 155
Mao Tse-tung, 70
Marcos, Imelda, 213n
marine snails, learning in, 355–56
Markham, James, 194
Marr, David, 355
Marroquin Rojas, Clemente, 133
Marshall Plan, 179
Marx, Karl, 95, 97, 98, 101
humans as products of history and society, 251
on Paris Commune, 99–100, 103–4
theory of alienated labor, 246
on tragedy as farce, 399
Marxism, 100, 103, 226, 251, 265, 317, 325
mass media:
constraints on, 258
corporate oligopoly in, 257
and cult of expertise, 165
democratic models of, 257
and East Timor, 190–91, 193–94, 195–97
foreign, U.S. intervention in, 275–76
and Israel, 199, 200, 201–2, 216, 217–18, 222
labor-oriented, 259–60
propaganda in, 144, 163, 193–94, 264, 265–66, 276, 337
and public relations industry, 264, 265–66
state-controlled, 257, 274, 275–76
stories concealed by, 231
stories ignored by, 185, 275
thought control in, 261
viciousness of, 44
and Vietnam War, 272–73
materialism, 351–52

maturation, and performance, 16
Maugham, Somerset, 357
Mavromichalis, Petros, 207
Mayagüez incident, 154–56, 184, 186
May Day, 265
McCain, John, 272, 301
McCarthy, Joseph, 136, 139
McCarthyism, 266, 386
McGwire, Michael, 304, 323–24
McCloskey, Paul, 118
McDermott, John, 72
McGrory, Mary, 138
McKinley, William, 112, 126
McNamara, Robert S., 70, 119
McNaughton, John, 124
Meagher, Robert, 58–59
meaning:
  cognitive vs. emotive, 426n36
  Skinner's use of term, 22
Mearsheimer, John, 303
mechanical theory of the universe, 235–37, 238, 239, 240, 350, 351, 353, 354
mechanism vs. mentalism, 429–30n1
media, *see* mass media; *specific media*
Meir, Golda, 203
mentalism, 429–30n1
mentalistic description, 10
Mercosur, 408
Merz, Charles, 262
methodological thesis, 350, 352, 356–62
Metternich, Klemens von, 229
Mexico:
  NAFTA and, 331–32, 336–37
  U.S. border with, 331, 411
Middle East:
  Arab-Israeli conflict, 200, 210–11, 370
  Arab nationalism in, 210
  Desert Storm in, 345
  oil in, 42–43, 157–58, 171–72, 205, 207–10, 211–12, 224, 225, 404, 405
  peace negotiations for, 204–5, 220–21, 368, 370
  U.S. Rapid Deployment Force in, 211
  and "war on terror," 328–29, 345
  see also specific nations
Mikoyan, Anastas Ivanovich, 47
Mill, John Stuart, 96
  on humanitarian intervention, 399
  On Liberty, 83
Miller, Judith, 309
Miller, Steven, 393
Milosevic, Slobodan, 311, 318, 319, 322
Milson, Menachem, 201, 219
mimicry vs. imitation, 16
mind:
  classical theory of, 367
  empiricist tradition of, 251
  modularity of, 250
mind-body considerations, 235–41, 246, 277, 351, 353–54
mind-brain considerations, 347–67
missile defense, 333
Mitchell Plan (2001), 371
Mobutu Sese Seko, 211, 213–14
Mohr, Charles, 57
Monge, Luis Alberto, 215
Monroe Doctrine, 45, 223–24, 229
  Roosevelt corollary to, 166
  Wilson corollary to, 224, 400
Moorer, Thomas H., 222
Morales, Evo, 408–9
Moral Majority, 203
Morgenthau, Hans, 60, 72, 166, 402
Morocco, 228, 388
motivation:
  novelty and variety of stimulus as, 13–14
  reinforcement as, 4
Mountcastle, Vernon, 348, 350
Moynihan, Daniel Patrick, 189–90
Mueller, Robert, 342
Munich, analogy of, 58, 400
Musharraf, Pervez, 408
Muskie, Edmund, 134, 140
Mussolini, Benito, 400
Muste, A. J., 74

NAFTA, 330, 331–32, 335–38, 339, 407
Nagasaki, 39, 439n3
Nanking, rape of, 61
Nasser, Gamal Abdel, 210
Nation, 195
National Association of Manufacturers (NAM), 265
National Council of Churches, 204
National Guardian, 136
National Security Council:
  NSC 48/1, 225–26
  NSC 68, 263, 264
  NSC 5429/2, 458n36
National Security Strategy, 373–402
  concerns of foreign policy elite, 393–97
  domestic civil liberties disregarded in, 385–86
  as experiment in preventive war, 381
  intentional ignorance in, 397–402
  new norms of international law in, 377–84

National Security Strategy (*cont.*)
official rhetoric of, 373
permanent global rule as aim of, 393
and UN, 386–93
U.S. hegemony enforced in, 374–77
nation-state, 300
NATO:
credibility of, 301, 302, 304, 316, 318, 321, 346, 382–83
and Eastern Europe stability, 302, 316, 317, 318, 321
fiftieth anniversary of, 305, 306
Serbia bombed by, 300–309, 311–12, 313, 314, 315–17, 318–24, 346, 381–83
in Turkey, 263
natural selection, 248, 254, 359
Nazis:
atrocities of, 39, 372
comparisons with, 48, 58, 152, 159, 330, 400, 411
Neier, Aryeh, 306, 321
Nelson, Bryce, 444n46
neoliberalism, 326, 333, 337, 338–39
Neoplatonists, 238
neurophysiology, 349, 353
neutralization:
of South Vietnam, 450n7
use of term, 445n71
New Deal, 266
new era, 305, 314, 315, 316, 320–21
New Frontier, 41, 44
New Left, 53, 76, 219
New Republic, 155, 212
Newsweek, 193
Newton, Isaac, 239, 240, 241, 351, 353, 354, 355, 356, 367
New York Times:
on Bolsheviks, 262
on East Timor, 191, 193–94, 195–96
and Israel, 212, 216, 217–18, 222
on Latin America, 161, 275–76
and McCarthy, 136
on Middle East oil, 173, 209
on Vietnam War, 46, 144–45, 151, 269
on Watergate, 135
Ngo Dinh Diem, 119, 149
Nguyen Van Thieu, 150–51
Nicaragua:
elections in, 412
and Israel, 214, 216
and U.S. policy, 162, 215, 216, 228, 230, 261–62, 263, 265, 275–76, 343, 374, 375–76, 379, 403, 459n46
Niebuhr, Reinhold, 162
Nighswonger, William, 118
Nimitz, Chester W., 107
Nitze, Paul, 264
Nixon, Richard M.:
"enemies list" of, viii, 134, 139
and foreign policy, 182, 226, 317–18
and impeachment, 138, 139
and presidential powers, 137–38
Realpolitik of, 182, 226
and Vietnam War, 114, 115, 136–37, 139, 149, 184
and Watergate, 134–40
North Vietnam:
collective self-defense against, 127–29
guerrilla warfare of, 41–42, 110, 132, 435n33
national interest of, 217
negotiations sought by, 42
U.S. bombing of, 47, 48, 64, 65, 68, 106, 109, 118, 450n7, 451n12
see also Vietnam War
Nossiter, Bernard, 196, 217
number faculty, 254–56
Nuremberg Tribunal:
and crimes against humanity, 380
and crimes against peace, 107, 126, 132, 374
and international law, 105, 106–7, 108, 109, 111, 126, 133
as judgment of victors, 107
and military necessity, 107
secret files of, 107–8
silence of, on aerial bombardment, 109–11
and Vietnam War, 105, 109–10, 113, 126–27, 132
and war crimes, 105–13, 118, 119, 123, 215, 273, 380
and wars of aggression, 107–8, 129

Oberdorfer, Don, 120
obligatory rules, 28
observables, use of term, 2
observation, learning by, 15, 16
Ocampo, José Antonio, 334
"occasion," Skinner's use of term, 4
Office of Technology Assessment (OTA), 330, 336
Official Secrets Act, 166
O'Hanlon, Michael, 318
oil:
Asian Energy Security Grid, 405–7
in East Timor, 313
in Iran, 42–43, 171, 172, 209, 211, 405
in Middle East, 42–43, 157–58, 171–72, 205, 207–10, 211–12, 224, 225, 404, 405

"Petroleum Policy of the United States" (1944), 171
price of, 452n21
Red Line agreement (1928), 171
in Saudi Arabia, 171–72, 207, 404
U.S. quest for control of, 42–43, 157–58, 171–73, 179–80, 207–10, 211–12, 224, 225, 342, 345, 392, 400, 405, 407, 409–10
in Venezuela, 407, 408, 409
O'Neill, Thomas P. "Tip," 155
On Liberty (Mill), 83
On Thermonuclear War (Kahn), 50
Open Door principle, 171
operant behavior, 4
operant conditioning, 12, 423n7
operants:
autoclitics, 25–26
discriminated, 4
echoic, 23–24
intraverbal, 24
Skinner's use of term, 4, 8
verbal, 8, 18–23
Operation Desert Storm, 345
Operation Horseshoe, 318, 319, 320
Operation Junction City, 115
Operation Miracle, 407–8
Operation Speedy Express, 153
optional rules, 28
Orwell, George, 230
Osborne, John, 155–56
OSCE (Organisation for Security and Co-operation in Europe), 319
Oslo peace agreements, 368, 370
OTA (Office of Technology Assessment), 330, 336
Outer Space Treaty (1967), 332
Owen, Roger, 381
Oz, Amos, 222

Pahlavi, Reza Shah, 171, 172, 209, 211
Pail, Meir, 203
Pakistan, 407, 408
Pal, Radhabinod, 439n3
Palestine:
elections in, 410–11
Hamas in, 405, 411
and Israel, 198, 201, 204, 319, 342, 345, 368–72, 411
and Jordan, 211, 369, 411
rights of, 461n5
and UN votes, 198
Palestine Liberation Organization (PLO), 198, 204, 206, 217, 219–20, 369–70
Panini, 31
Pannekoek, Anton, 100, 102
parameter setting, 233, 247
Paris Agreements (1973), 137, 150, 151, 163
Paris Commune, 96, 99–100, 103–4
Pastor, Robert, 403
Pat, Gidon, 211n
Patterson, Robert P., 223
Paul, king of Greece, 207
Paul, William, 101, 102
Pauling, Linus, 352, 354
Pavlovian conditioning, 12, 426n35
Paxson, Frederic, 264
peace movement, 71, 453n9
Pearl Harbor, 374
Peck, Jim, 68
Peirce, Charles, 248
Peled, Mattityahu, 201, 211, 217
Pelloutier, Fernand, 95
Pentagon Papers, 124, 137, 147, 149, 174, 175–76, 217, 440n5, 450n7
Percy, Charles, 199
Peres, Shimon, 370
performance:
contribution of the organism to, 2–3
inborn structure in, 16
of language, 33–34, 37, 278
and maturation, 16
Perlmutter, Nathan and Ruth, 203–4
"Petroleum Policy of the United States" (1944), 171
Phanomyong, Pridi, 126
Philippines:
boat people from, 269
U.S. intervention in, 126, 184, 230, 397, 400
phonemic systems, 21
phonetic representation, 297, 364–65
phonology, 283, 297
phylogenesis, 349, 357, 362
Pike, Douglas, 70, 110, 120, 148, 453n9
Pinker, Steven, 359
Pinto, Jorge, 275
Plato, 233
Podhoretz, Norman, 268
Poincaré, Jules-Henri, 354
Poland, *Kalmar* trawler incident, 154, 155
Polanyi, Karl, 86
Pol Pot, 271, 382, 455n22
Port Royal Grammar, viii, 286
Post, E. L., 38
Potsdam agreements, 42
Powell, Colin, 371, 377, 389, 391, 392, 395–96
prayer, as mand, 20

presidency, U.S.:
as beyond the reach of the law, 137, 138
centralization of power in, 138, 176, 386
and impeachment, 138, 139
Pressberg, Gail, 220
Priestley, Joseph, 239, 350
principles-and-parameters (P&P) model of language, 279, 281–84, 290–91, 293
Printz, Charles, 270
"probability," Skinner's use of term, 8, 9
problem solving, mental faculty for, 248
property:
abolishing, 94, 99
anarchism vs., 94, 97, 99
right of, 99
Skinner's use of term, 22
Proudhon, Pierre-Joseph, 98
Prouty, Fletcher, 440n13, 447–48n97
public opinion, as "second superpower," 394–97
Putin, Vladimir, 392

quantum physics, 354
questions, as mands, 20
Quezon, Manuel, 446n78

Rabin, Yitzhak, 202–3, 211n
racism, 252
radical critique, 457n36
Rahman, Hassan, 220
Rahv, Philip, 160
Randal, Jonathan, 306
Rankin, Karl, 208
rationalism, viii, 88
rats, limitations of, 241–42
Ray, Dennis M., 176–77
Reagan, Ronald:
on Evil Empire, 264, 273–74
on Law Day, 265
Reagan administration:
contempt for international law in, 376
and the economy, 273, 338
and Israel, 199, 214
and Latin America, 215, 216, 265, 275, 276, 328, 343, 374, 375–76, 379, 380, 395, 409
and Middle East, 328–29, 344
and Vietnam War costs, 269
and "war on terror," 328–29, 345, 395
Red Line agreement (1928), 171
Red Scare, 264, 265, 267
reinforcement:
automatic self-reinforcement, 11–12
contingencies of, 13
differential, 15, 16
drive reduction in, 13, 14
and imitation, 427n40
importance of, 3
and intention, 20
intermittent, 5
in language acquisition, 16
strength in, 12
theories of, 15
uses of term, 5, 10–13, 17, 19
reinforcer:
primary, 4
secondary, 4
Skinner's use of term, 4
reinforcing event, Skinner's use of term, 4
reinforcing stimulus, Skinner's use of term, 10
religious fundamentalism, and Israel, 202, 203
requests, as mands, 20
resistance, 63–74, 218
as civil disobedience, 66, 67, 68–69, 71, 74, 156, 402
forms of, 71, 74
International Days of Protest (1965), 65
as moral responsibility, 74, 402
to official government statements, 65–66, 68, 69–70, 71–72
peace demonstrations (1967), 63n, 64–65, 66–68
purposes of, 70–74, 88
transition from dissent to, 63, 68–69
transition to violence, 67–68, 80
widening circle of, 64, 103
"respondents," Skinner's use of term, 4
response:
autoclitic, 25–26
frequency of, 8–9
and stimulus, 7
uses of term, 5, 6, 7–10, 17
"response differentiation," Skinner's use of phrase, 4
"response strength," Skinner's use of phrase, 8–10
responsibility of intellectuals, 39–62
in academic circles, 49–50
in Asia, 44–45, 55–56, 61, 158–59
in Cold War, 41–42, 43, 44–45, 61
in creation and analysis of ideology, 52–53, 178, 183, 273
in democracy building, 54–55, 58–60
and "expert knowledge" in world affairs, 46–47, 51–52, 53, 55
to expose lies, 40–41
in foreign policy, 160, 162–65, 174–78, 183–86

Iran and, 42–43
Israel and, 220–22
in Kennedy administration, 40–42, 44, 215n
mass media vs., 44
"policy-oriented" vs. "value-oriented," 163–65
in protest movements, 46, 49, 51
to speak the truth, 40
and subordination to power, 402
to uncover propaganda, 177–79
in underdeveloped world, 43, 44, 47, 54
and use of force, 158, 186
U.S. expansionism and, 45–46, 47, 142
and U.S. "will to power," 45–47, 48, 55, 59–60, 74
Vietnam War and, 40–44, 45–52, 61–62, 74, 142, 153–54, 159, 162–63, 174–76
in wealth gap, 53
to write history, 253
Reston, James, 134, 150–51
revolution:
and anarchism, 94–96, 100–102
and censorship, 178–79
contagion of, 229
democratic elements in, 54–55
and freedom, 76
in industrial society, 101
and inequality, 77, 80
nationalist, 55–56, 64
normative, 381–82
people's wars, 110, 262–63
Rousseau on, 77–82
social, 100–101
spontaneous action of, 101
in Third World, 76, 85
uses of term, 76
wars of national liberation, 131
see also specific nations
Rhodesia, 211
Rice, Condoleezza, 378, 391
Rice, Monsignor, 66
Ridenhour, Ronald L., 114
rigidity principle, 249–50
Rios Montt, José Efraín, 214
Roberts, Chalmers, 41
Robertson, Walter, 49
Robinson, Donald, 133
Rocker, Rudolf, 92–94, 97
Rogers, Joel, 258
Romanticism, 246
Romero, Archbishop Oscar, 276
Roosevelt, Franklin D., 171, 374, 400
Roosevelt, Theodore, 166
Roosevelt administration, 171–72
Roosevelt Corollary to Monroe Doctrine, 166
Rosenberg, Arthur, 103
Rosenberg, Ethel and Julius, 136
Rostow, Eugene, 69
Rostow, Walt:
on development of Third World, 54
on guerrilla warfare, 42
on Iran, 42–43
on U.S. Asian policies, 44–45, 60
on Vietnam War, 41–42, 74, 119
"rotten apple theory," 227, 228–29, 230, 231
Rousseau, Jean-Jacques, 96
Discourse on Inequality, 77–83, 96
libertarian ideas of, 238–39, 246
on the nature of man, 78–79, 81–82, 84, 87
on origin of language, 82–83
on rational social order, 81
on reason, 78
on self-perfection, 81–82, 84
Rove, Karl, 380
Rowe, David N., 48
Rusk, Dean, 57, 69, 70, 74, 119
Russell, Bertrand, 21, 354
Russia:
Bolsheviks in, 95–96, 262, 264
and Central Europe, 42
and Chechnya, 307, 315, 329, 344, 392
and empire, 112
guerrilla warfare supported by, 42
and NATO, 313
purges in, 39
"red bureaucracy" of, 95
and "war on terror," 344
and World War II, 170, 313
see also Soviet Union
Russian Revolution, 95–96

Sadat, Anwar, 342
Sadr, Muqtada al-, 405
Safran, Nadav, 199
Said, Edward, 220, 323
Saigon, *see* South Vietnam
"salted-nut phenomenon," 426n34
Santillan, Diego Abad de, 94–95, 101
Saragossa Congress (1936), 101
Saudi Arabia:
British interest in, 171–72
and China, 405
Fahd Plan of, 370
French interest in, 171
and Iraq, 379, 404
and Japan, 209n

Saudi Arabia (*cont.*)
oil in, 171–72, 207, 404
U.S. influence in, 170, 171–72
Saussure, Ferdinand de, 37
Saussurean arbitrariness, 283
Scharping, Rudolf, 320
Schedules of Reinforcement (Ferster and Skinner), 5
Schelling, Thomas, 43, 56, 76, 77, 88
Schiff, Ze'ev, 303
Schlesinger, Arthur:
on Bay of Pigs, 40, 44
on human rights, 165
on U.S. invasion of Iraq, 374
on Vietnam War, 41, 43, 146, 161
Schwab, Klaus, 395
science-forming capacity, 247–49
sciences, unification of, 350, 352, 354–55
scientific beliefs vs. ideological commitments, 253
scientific revolution, 353
Scowcroft, Brent, 460n2
"secondary reinforcer," Skinner's use of phrase, 4
second substance, 238, 239, 240, 241
selective service, 71
self-fulfillment, 84–85, 96
self-perfection, faculty of, 81–82, 83–84, 89
self-reinforcement, automatic, 11–12
sentence structure:
and rules of grammar, 37
Skinner's view of, 26
September 11 attacks:
and anthrax attacks, 341, 342
and civil rights of U.S. citizens, 385–86
innocent victims of, 341
longer-term consequences of, 344–46
proper reactions to, 343–44
questions arising from, 341
reasons for, 342–43, 397
responsibility for, 342
and U.S. militarism, 374, 377
and "war on terror," 329, 345, 379
and window of opportunity, 325–26
Serbia:
ethnic cleansing in, 318
and Kosovo, 314, 319
NATO bombing of, 300–309, 311, 313, 314, 315–17, 318–24, 346, 382–83
set, and attention, 5
sexism, 245–46, 252
Shah of Iran. *See* Pahlavi, Reza Shah
Shahak, Israel, 220
Shamir, Yitzhak, 213–14
Shannon, William V., 161
Shaplen, Robert, 119
Sharett, Moshe, 466n38
Sharon, Ariel, 201, 214, 216, 217, 221, 370
Shawcross, William, 311
Shays's Rebellion (1786), 259
Sheehan, Neil, 115
Shelton, Henry, 302, 316, 318
Shipman, Barbara, 356
Shultz, George, 329
Sierra Leone, 316
sign stimuli, responses to, 16
similarity, 428n46
Simonofsky, Elsie, vii
Skinner, B. F.:
Behavior of Organisms, 4–5, 6, 10
experimental limitations of, 422n4
extrapolation by, 8
inconsistency of results, 5–6
inconsistent use of terms by, 6–10
latitude of interpretation by, 9–10, 26–30
on law of conditioning, 10
on learning, 10, 15
Verbal Behavior, 1–30
slavery, 245, 246
Smith, Adam, 247, 327, 331, 387
Smith, Gaddis, 178
Smith, Richard, 222n
socialism:
and anarchism, 97, 100, 103
council communism in, 101
Engels's vision of, 95
and labor, 266
libertarian, 87, 95, 96, 97, 101, 102–4, 246
revolutionary, 100–101
Rocker's vision of, 93–94, 97
state, 102
Socialist Labor Party, 101
Socialist Workers Party, 135
social order:
and anarchism, 92–104
vision of, 88–89, 90–91, 93
Sofaer, Abraham, 376, 377
Solzhenitsyn, Alexander, 303, 305
Somoza Debayle, Anastasio, 204, 214, 215, 216, 230, 403, 459n46
Souchy, Augustin, 102
soul:
immortality of, 238
inner life of, 84
South Africa:
aid to, 211
apartheid era in, 368, 371
and weapons development, 216
South America, *see* Latin America

South Summit (2000), 302, 383
South Vietnam:
- Diem regime in, 119, 149, 152
- "free bombing zones" in, 47, 110
- GVN in, 110, 129
- inability to compete, 57
- National Liberation Front (NLF) in, 56–57, 109, 110, 112, 121, 147, 449n1, 450n7
- People's Revolutionary Party (PRP) in, 450n7
- Thieu regime in, 150–51
- U.S. intervention in domestic affairs of, 149–52, 163, 261, 441n18, 453n9
- U.S. military action in, 109–11, 112, 120, 122, 124–25, 149, 158, 159, 161, 272–73, 328, 401, 449n1
- as U.S. military base, 58
- U.S. support of, 42, 127–28, 268
- *see also* Vietnam War

Soviet Union:
- Afghanistan invaded by, 167, 208, 261, 269, 270, 342, 452n1
- in Cold War, 42, 64, 174, 183, 207–9, 210, 224, 227, 262–63
- collapse of, 328
- in Eastern Europe, 224, 317, 400–401, 404
- as "Evil Empire," 264, 273–74
- and international order, 261–62

space, militarization of, 332–34
Spanish-American War, 112
Spanish Civil War, 39
Spanish Revolution, 94, 101–2
Speer, Albert, 456n25
Spock, Benjamin, 63n, 66, 67
"stability," use of term, 226
Stalin, Joseph, 41–42, 55, 95, 203, 208, 401
Stalinism, 204, 206
The State, Its Origins and Function (Paul), 101, 102
State and Revolution (Lenin), 101
Sterling, Claire, 228
Sternhell, Ze'ev, 368
Stevenson, Adlai E., 58, 401, 434n29
Stiglitz, Joseph E., 334
Stilwell, Joseph, 70
Stimson, Henry L., 223, 224
stimulation:
- aversive, 19
- importance of, 3

stimulus:
- novelty and variety in, 13–14
- reinforcing, 10
- and response, 7
- uses of term, 5, 6–7, 10, 17

stimulus control, 6–7
- prior, 23–24
- and tacts, 21, 22

stimulus discrimination, Skinner's use of term, 4
stimulus generalization, 15
Stone, I. F., 128, 205
Straw, Jack, 391
strength:
- in reinforcement, 12
- Skinner's use of term, 9, 10

Strout, Richard, 152
student movement, 103, 457n36
Suez invasion (1956), 209
Suharto, 312, 460n2
Summit of the Americas, 335, 339
supervenience, 355
symbolic reference, 361–62
Symington, Stuart, 73, 140
"synonymy," Skinner's use of term, 22–23
syntax, theory of, 31–32, 33, 279
syntax-morphology divide, 282
Syria, 211, 319, 381

"tacts," Skinner's use of term, 20–23
Taiwan, 216
Taylor, Maxwell, 132, 148–49
Taylor, Telford, 115
- on aggressive war, 107–9, 129
- and applicability of Nuremberg standards to Vietnam War, 105, 109–10, 113, 126–27, 132
- on causation of Vietnam War, 122–24, 125, 126–27, 128–29
- on legitimacy of Vietnam War, 122–24, 127, 132
- and Nuremberg Tribunal, 105, 106, 108
- on responsibility of the intelligentsia, 119
- and "silence of Nuremberg" on aerial warfare, 109–10, 111
- on war crimes, 105, 106–13

technology:
- government subsidy of, 266
- value-free, 55

television, 250
terrorism, 227–28, 329–30
textual behavior, 24
Thailand, military coup in, 126
theory construction, 247–48, 279, 289
thinking substance, 238, 239, 240
Third World:
- capital accumulation in, 54
- democracy building in, 43, 55, 58, 87
- ideologists of, 53–54

Third World (*cont.*)
nationalism in, 172, 174, 219
and nonaligned movement, 383
revolutionary guerrilla warfare in, 435n33
revolution in, 76, 85
technology in, 333
and UN, 196
U.S. access to, 58, 59, 274
and U.S. sincerity, 44, 47
U.S. will imposed by force on, 58, 161, 226, 274–76
Thompson, D'Arcy, 367
Thorpe, Benjamin, 14
thought control, 261, 264–67
Thucydides, 377
Tibet, 307, 315
Tillman, Seth, 202, 203
Timorese Liberation Movement, 192
Tinbergen, Nikolaas, 348, 356, 357, 362
Tocqueville, Alexis de, 99
Torczyner, Jacques, 203
totalitarianism, 98, 178
trade:
costs and benefits of, 338
tariff protection of, 338
TRB (Richard Strout), 152
Tregaskis, Richard, 109
Trilateral Commission, 163–64, 166, 175
Trujillo Molina, Rafael Leónidas, 44, 45
Truman administration:
and business, 266, 454n19
in Cold War, 42, 147
Truman Doctrine, 207–8, 227, 267
Truong Chinh, 111
truth:
disregard for, 43, 164, 168–69
doctrine vs., 253
in historical perspective, 58
and lies, 40–41, 168
and propaganda, 41, 47
search for, 49
Turing, Alan, 237, 350, 367
Turing test, 237, 351
Turkey:
Cold War in, 227
and Israel, 210
Kurds decimated in, 305–8, 309–10, 315, 344–45, 392
NATO bases in, 263
and NATO bombing of Serbia, 308–9
and UN, 388
and U.S. foreign policy, 224, 392
U.S. military aid to, 305, 306, 309–10, 330, 344, 402
and "war on terror," 344
Turki, Fawaz, 220
Turley, William S., 175

unification:
of language, 295, 347–48
of sciences, 350, 352, 354–55
United Nations:
and Africa, 316
Charter of, 412
Conference on Disarmament, 333
and East Timor, 189–90, 196, 312, 313
and former Yugoslavia, 323
and human rights, 323
and Iraq, 381, 388–91
and Israel, 198, 217, 308, 369–72, 388
and Lebanon, 308
and *Mayagüez* incident, 154, 155
and Outer Space Treaty, 332
and Palestinian rights, 461n5
and PLO, 217, 369–70
public trust in, 395
and Third World, 196
U.S. condemned for terrorism by, 329, 343
U.S. debt unpaid to, 316
U.S. disregard of, 302–3, 316, 329, 373, 375, 382, 386, 387–92
veto record in, 387–89, 412
and Vietnam War, 65, 107–8, 121, 127, 128, 129–32
and "war on terror," 343
United States:
and anti-Americanism, 399–400
civil liberties disregarded in, 385–86
condemned for terrorism, 329, 343
expansionism of, 45–46, 47, 60, 142, 223–24
foreign aid, 305
foreign investment, 47
and global competition, 267
Human Rights Administration, 189, 190, 191, 195, 216
interventionist tradition of, 112, 125–26, 132, 143, 157, 181–86, 189, 274, 300–324, 329, 394
military aid from, 305
military expenditures of, 332, 373
"national interest" of, 157, 173–74, 225, 301, 314, 317, 387, 403
National Security Strategy of, 373, 381, 386–93
and Outer Space Treaty, 332
presidential election (2000), 339–40
as rogue superpower, 304, 373, 374–77, 381–84, 386–93, 395–97

suggestions for future action, 412–13
world control as aim of, 170–71, 223–31, 393, 398
United States Army Field Manual, 118
United Steelworkers of America, 410
unity of consciousness, 238
universe, mechanical theory of, 235–37
USAID (Agency for International Development), 132, 179–80, 410–11
U.S. Committee for Refugees, 269
USS *Abraham Lincoln,* 379–80
USS *Liberty,* 221–22
USSR, *see* Soviet Union
USS *Vincennes,* 268–69
U Thant, 131

Valeriani, Richard, 195
Vance, Cyrus, 258
Vann, John Paul, 121–22, 124–25, 126
variables, controlling, 8–9
Venezuela:
and Cuba, 407–8
elections in, 412
and Mercosur, 408
oil in, 407, 408, 409
and regional agreements, 408–9
U.S. failure to overthrow government in, 410
Vennema, Alje, 113
verbal behavior:
complexity of, 15, 27
controlling variables of, 1, 15
functional analysis of, 1–2, 3–4, 6, 9, 23, 27
prediction of, 3
Skinner's system for description of, 17–18, 26–30
unit of, 8, 428n46
Verbal Behavior (Skinner), 1–30
verbal operant:
tact as, 20–23
use of term, 8, 18–20
Vergnaud, Jean-Roger, 283
Vieira do Rego, Father Leoneto, 191, 194
Vietcong:
military attacks on, 109, 147
numbers of, 49, 127, 152
pacification program for, 57
political structure of, 57
popular support of, 118–19, 121–22, 147, 158
U.S. refusal to recognize, 57
Vietnam:
Cambodia invaded by, 382
coalition government of, 57–58
crop destruction in, 117, 118
government of, 66, 72, 112, 124
nationalist movement of, 225
and UN, 461n5
unification of, 127
U.S. aid to, 61
and U.S. national interest, 125, 228–30
"Vietnam syndrome," 215, 268, 273, 328
Vietnam War:
alternative endings in, 71–73
antiwar protests, ix, 46, 49, 51, 63–74, 135, 153–54, 156, 204, 267, 268, 328, 394–95, 457n36
atrocities in, 62, 272–73
and China, 69, 70, 72, 130–31, 382
Christmas bombing (1972), 136–37
costs of, 218, 267, 269
and credibility gap, 142
and crimes against peace, 126–33, 142
death toll unknown in, 380
and domino theory, 226–27, 457n36
government propaganda about, 41, 69–70, 156–59, 174, 181, 261, 268, 271–73
history of rewritten, 268
Hue massacre, 120–21
and international law, 105–21
Kien Hoa massacre, 153
lack of popular support for, 113, 153, 157, 163
lessons of, 151–52, 156
Mayagüez incident, 154–56, 184, 186
"mere gook rule" in, 115
MIAs in, 270, 271, 272
and military necessity, 121–26
My Lai massacre, 113–16, 119, 152–53, 442n25
National Liberation Front (NLF) in, 56–57
Nuremberg standards applied to, 105, 109–10, 113, 126–27, 132
Operation Junction City, 115
Operation Speedy Express, 153
peace negotiations in, 73, 149
and Pentagon Papers, 124, 147, 149, 174, 175–76, 217, 440n5, 450n7
Phuqui massacre, 116
"quagmire hypothesis" about, 175
refugees of, 65, 115, 117–18
responsibility of intellectuals in, 40–44, 45–52, 61–62, 74, 142, 153–54, 159, 162–63, 174–76
as revolutionary people's war, 110–11, 124, 129, 137
secret files of, 107–8
Son My massacre, 112
Tet offensive, 120, 123, 137
and UN, 65, 107–8, 121, 127, 128, 129–32

Vietnam War (*cont.*)
U.S. bombing in, 41, 47, 48, 64, 65, 68, 106, 109, 111, 115–18, 120–21, 136–37, 149
and U.S. economy, 267
U.S. escalation of, 41, 124–25, 127, 140
U.S. failure in, 141–56, 163, 175, 218, 450n5
and U.S. foreign policy, 161–63, 174–75, 179, 184
U.S. goals in, 126, 229–30, 449n1
as U.S. "laboratory," 132
and U.S. politics, 73, 74, 148, 175
U.S. refusal to permit political settlement of, 56–57
U.S. withdrawal from, 74, 125
war crimes in, 106, 112, 113–21, 122–23, 125, 152, 159
White Paper on, 127
Winter Soldier Investigation, 114
vision, study of, 249–50
volition, and behavior, 5

Walker, Edward, 370
Wall Street Journal, 196–97
Waltz, Kenneth, 384, 393
war:
against much weaker enemies, 328
aggressive, 107–9, 129
and bioterror, 333
capability of global destruction, 327–28
class, 325
concentrated power and, 325–26, 328
European, 328
likelihood of, 332–34
between nation-states, 328
preventive, 374–77, 378–82, 394
proxy, 329, 449n3
public opposition to, 328
war crimes:
and military necessity, 121–26
and Nuremberg, 105–13, 118, 119, 123, 215, 273, 380
operational definitions of, 380
preventive war as, 374
in Vietnam, 106, 112, 113–21, 122–23, 125, 152, 159
war guilt, 39
"war on terror," 328–30
and bioterror, 333
and domestic elections, 380
domestic freedoms curtailed in, 345, 385–86
and militarization of space, 332–34
preventive war in, 344
and September 11 attacks, 329, 345, 379
Washington, George, 131
Washington consensus, 334
Washington Post, 146–47, 149, 155, 156
Watergate, 134–40, 162
Watson, John B., 21
Watson, Thomas, 134
Watts, David, 192, 193
wealth gap, 53, 331, 332, 334, 338, 339, 340
weapons of mass destruction (WMD):
absence of, 375, 380
as deterrent against U.S. powers, 393–94
inspections for, 378, 390
intention to develop, 375
proliferation of, 302, 303, 384, 393
propaganda about, 378, 390–91, 396
Weir, Fred, 407
welfare state:
pluralistic society of, 52
scholar-experts on, 53
Welles, Sumner, 400
West, Richard, 121
West Africa, 407
Westing, Arthur, 117
Westmoreland, William, 71, 115, 148, 149
Wiesel, Elie, 206
Wieseltier, Leon, 454–55n22
Williams, Ian, 323
Williams, William Appleman, 178
Williamson, Richard, 270
Wilson, Dagmar, 66
Wilson, E. O., 348
Wilson, Richard, 384
Wilson, Woodrow, 43, 262, 264, 265, 267, 397
Wilson corollary to Monroe Doctrine, 224, 400
Wilsonian peace principle, 182–83, 301, 397, 398, 400, 402
Winter, Roger, 269
Winter Soldier Investigation, 114
Wolf, Charles, 55–56, 58
Woodrow Wilson Center, 337
workers' control movement, 101, 102, 246
World Bank:
and Bolivia, 409
and East Asia, 334
and India, 59–60
and labor market, 337
World Court, 312, 329, 343, 376, 412
World Economic Forum (WEF), 326
Davos meeting of, 395–97
public poll of, 395
World Social Forum (WSF), opening address (2002), 325–40

World Trade Center, attack on (1993), 342
World Trade Organization (WTO), 326, 335, 338
World War I:
  Creel Commission, 264
  postwar anti-Communism, 263, 267
  postwar Bavaria, 178
World War II:
  aerial bombing in, 106–7, 109
  comparisons with, 119–20, 152, 404
  documentary evidence in, 107–8
  and Holocaust, 39, 152
  leadership quality in, 124
  "national interest" in, 173
  and Nuremberg, *see* Nuremberg Tribunal
  ordnance expended in, 65
  and Pearl Harbor, 374
  postwar international order, 260–61, 264
  postwar U.S. foreign policy, 169–74, 376
World Zionist Organization, 203

Yaakovi, Gad, 211n
Yamashita, General, 153
Yugoslavia, former:
  NATO bombing of, *see* NATO
  UN Special Investigator for, 323
  workers' councils in, 87

Zaire, 211, 213–14
Ziem, Grace, 273
Zinn, Howard, 64
Zionism, 200n, 203
Zionist Organization of America, 203
Zogby, James, 220